Holt Saunders

Individual Rights and the State in Foreign Affairs

edited by
Elihu Lauterpacht
John G. Collier
introduction by
Krzysztof Skubiszewski

The Praeger Special Studies program—utilizing the most modern and efficient book production techniques and a selective worldwide distribution network—makes available to the academic, government, and business communities significant, timely research in U.S. and international economic, social, and political development.

Individual Rights and the State in Foreign Affairs

An International Compendium

PRAEGER SPECIAL STUDIES IN INTERNATIONAL POLITICS AND GOVERNMENT

Praeger Publishers New York London

Library of Congress Cataloging in Publication Data

Main entry under title:

Individual rights and the State in foreign affairs.

(Praeger special studies in international politics and government)

Includes index.

1. Persons (International law)--Congresses.
I. Lauterpacht, Elihu. II. Collier, John Greenwood.

JX4000.I5 341.48 77-8010

ISBN 0-275-24350-8

Published under the auspices of the American Society of International Law with the cosponsorship of the Carnegie Endowment for International Peace

PRAEGER SPECIAL STUDIES
200 Park Avenue, New York, N.Y., 10017, U.S.A.

Published in the United States of America in 1977
by Praeger Publishers,
A Division of Holt, Rinehart and Winston, CBS, Inc.

789 038 987654321

Printed in the United States of America

LIST OF PARTICIPANTS IN THE CONFERENCE ON INDIVIDUAL RIGHTS AND THE STATE IN FOREIGN AFFAIRS, BELLAGIO, ITALY June 1972

C. F. Amerasinghe, International Bank for Reconstruction and Development

Gaetano Arangio-Ruiz, University of Bologna

Joseph-Marie Bipoun-Woum, Federal University of Cameroon

Yehuda Blum, Hebrew University of Jerusalem

Lucius Caflisch, Graduate Institute of International Studies

John Collier, Cambridge University

Isi Foighel, University of Copenhagen

Elihu Lauterpacht, Cambridge University, currently with Department of Foreign Affairs, Australia

Monroe Leigh, District of Columbia Bar, currently with U.S. Department of State

Jacques Yvan Morin, University of Montreal

P. J. Mugerwa, Attorney General of Uganda (1972)

Stephen M. Schwebel, American Society of International Law, currently with U.S. Department of State

Ignaz Seidl-Hohenveldern, University of Cologne

Cesar Sepúlveda, Mexican Bar

Ibrahim Shihata, University of Cairo, currently with Kuwait Fund for Arab Economic Development

Krzysztof Skubiszewski, University of Poznan

Sompong Sucharitkul, Embassy of Thailand to The Netherlands, currently with Embassy of Thailand to Japan

Francisco Orrego Vicuña, Organization of American States, currently with University of Chile

Michel Waelbroeck, Free University of Brussels

Prosper Weil, University of Paris

Ralph Zacklin, Carnegie Endowment for International Peace, currently with United Nations Secretariat

FOREWORD

The genesis of the papers collected here was a suggestion by Elihu Lauterpacht of a comparative study of aspects of state activities in foreign affairs that touch importantly on the lives and activities of individuals. That suggestion led to a conference of 21 international lawyers at the Rockefeller Foundation's Villa Serbelloni in Bellagio, Italy, in 1972, where drafts of the 19 country-by-country studies were presented and discussed.

By design the studies did not purport to treat the whole array of state activities directly affecting the affairs of individuals in relating to other countries, but rather excluded certain questions that are already subjects of extensive and often technical literature (namely nationality, extradition, asylum, and the disabilities of aliens). Consequently the studies were concerned mainly with questions of individual rights respecting movement among countries and location within a country, diplomatic and other forms of protection, freedom of activity abroad, and the consequences of legal injuries incurred abroad, and with the various forms of national implementation of international rights and duties affecting the position of individuals. Taken together, this large and variegated cluster of individual rights and duties, the corresponding rights and duties of states, and the bodies of national law and practice in which they are reflected provide important insights into the evolving role of the individual as an actor in the global community.

Precisely because of the scarcity of the literature on the subjects discussed, the American Society of International Law (ASIL) and the Carnegie Endowment for International Peace (CEIP), the co-sponsors of the project, felt that the studies prepared for it should be made a part of the public record. Accordingly they were again placed in the hands of the authors for revision in light of the conference discussion and updating where possible, and in due course the manuscript as a whole was edited by John Collier and Elihu Lauterpacht.* Finally, Krzysztof Skubiszewski, who authored the study on Poland and who participated in the Conference, has prepared an introductory chapter that provides an overview and synthesis of the subsequent chapters.

---

*Intervening events in Uganda rendered impracticable any revision of P. J. Nkambo Mugerwa's paper on that country, and it is accordingly presented without substantial alteration.

The society and the endowment are grateful to Lauterpacht for his initiative in suggesting the conference and guiding the direction it took; to him and to John Collier for having edited this book and to Krzysztof Skubiszewski for having pulled the whole together in his introductory essay. The individual studies, of course, represent the personal views of the participants, whose affiliations are listed for purposes of identification only. The ASIL and the CEIP provided the forum for the Conference and take no positions on the views expressed in the papers.

The sponsors are grateful to the Rockefeller Foundation for making Villa Serbelloni available for the 1972 Conference. They also gratefully acknowledge the help of Vera Gowlland, who prepared the summary discussion of the Conference, and of Rozanne Oliver and Elizabeth Scheetz of the society staff for their editorial assistance with the manuscript. Special appreciation is due to Helen Philos, the patient and persistent librarian of the American Society of International Law.

John Lawrence Hargrove
Director of Studies
American Society of International Law

CONTENTS

Chapter | Page

Chapter | Page

CHAPTER

1

INTRODUCTION

Krzysztof Skubiszewski

The papers collected as chapters of the present volume investigate some aspects of the activities of the state in the field of foreign affairs that touch on the individual and his interests. The topic itself is wide, and a selection of problems was necessary. The directing idea of the choice was the desire to break at least some new ground and to avoid the discussion of problems that are already the subjects of extensive literature, such as nationality or extradition.

The chapters each describe and analyze the various national standards of a particular country. Once gathered around the conference table in Bellagio the authors attempted to discover the analogies and discrepancies among these standards and to define the relationship between national conduct and the rights and duties that states have under international law. The research covers three main areas: the substance of certain rights of the individual and the attitude of the state; national implementation of international rights and duties and how it affects the individual; and treaties and the individual.

1. In exploring certain rights of the human person, the papers deal with the individual as a national and describe the individual's freedom of movement and its limitations, concentrating on passports, departure, return, and expulsion. The question of the extent to which the state controls the activities of its nationals abroad is

---

This introduction was written in 1975 and slightly revised in 1976.

followed by the problem of diplomatic protection, in particular the possible right of the individual to require that his state intervene on his behalf. There is also some inquiry into the methods of special protection. However, whenever there is injury to the individual by a foreign state, there is the parallel danger of a waiver: can the individual's own state waive his claim for reparation? Compensation also comes within the purview of these chapters. They discuss the distribution of compensation, payment of additional sums if the amount received from the foreign state is not adequate, and in general the responsibility of the state for injury induced by its own conduct. Although the chapters devote more attention to nationals than to aliens, the latter have not been neglected. They explore the alien's right of entry, if any, and departure, both voluntary and involuntary; they also discuss, rather briefly, the right of the alien to protection.

2. Discussion of the individual and national implementation of international rights and duties might have involved the authors of the chapters in a general comparison of the relationship of international law and municipal law within the various national systems. There was not much point in undertaking a study of this kind, but it would have been impossible for the authors to avoid this theme. They focus on some selected subjects, which are the Act of State doctrine; implementation of decisions of international organizations, particularly when such decisions affect individual rights and obligations; and procedures relating to the issue of certificates or suggestions of the executive in connection with litigation in national courts.

3. The problem of treaties and the individual was not easy to define, which is probably why it has not been fully explored or, rather, why several authors preferred to deal with the subject not only or not necessarily in a separate part but in connection with the questions that fit into the framework of other topics. Nonetheless an effort has been made to locate the areas in which treaties are more evidently related to the advancement or protection of individual interests. The reader, it is hoped, can then identify the practices that may stand as examples for future development.

It was not possible to discuss all these questions in equal depth during the five-day conference in Bellagio. The papers were written and distributed before the meeting started, enabling the gathering to try to arrive at a synthesis and to draw some conclusions. While the subjects of aliens and of treaties and the individual were not discussed in separate sessions, all the other problems were introduced by rapporteurs and then debated. The rapporteurs, in order of discussion, were this writer for freedom of movement, Lucius Caflisch for the granting of passports and the right of departure, Ignaz Seidl-Hohenveldern for diplomatic protection, Isi Foighel for compensation, Ibrahim Shihata for the Act of State doctrine, C. F. Amerasinghe for certificates of the executive, Elihu Lauterpacht for recognition, and Jacques Yvan Morin for implementation of decisions of international organizations.

The purpose of this introduction is to bring the reader into the framework of these problems while tracing some of the discussions that took place in Bellagio. Though opinions differed and the conference did not attempt to reach a consensus on any of the topics explored, there was much common ground among the participants. Lauterpacht, who was the chairman of the conference, gave impetus to the preparation of the papers and to the progress of the meeting, especially by preparing in advance a note that delimited the areas to be covered in the papers and during the discussions. That note, as well as the conclusions put down in writing by Caflisch, Seidl-Hohenveldern, and Shihata in their respective fields and the summary record of the conference,[1] were helpful guides in preparing the remarks that follow. The chairman, the rapporteurs, and all the participants in the debates will no doubt discover that their thoughts have penetrated into the introduction. To that extent the introduction reflects the work of the conference and is not an entirely original contribution. Nevertheless the text of this introduction is the responsibility of its author alone.

MOVEMENT OF NATIONALS

Does general international law confer on the nationals of a state the right to travel abroad, and in particular the right to leave their country for good? In other words, does there exist, under general international law, a duty of the state to allow its citizens to depart, temporarily or permanently?

The perusal of state practice shows that it is not uniform in this regard. Indeed, municipal regulations vary considerably: even a selective review of legislative and administrative activity such as the one presented in this book attests to the absence of identical or consistent standards. During the discussion in Bellagio, some categories of behavior were distinguished. There are states that prohibit freedom of movement only in certain clearly limited circumstances, such as to prevent the evasion of military service or to protect public health. Other states do not support freedom of movement as a matter of principle but are relaxed in their passport procedures and consequently give a fair or at least some chance to go abroad, at least temporarily, to practically any national. Some states may not be willing to permit departure abroad but are incapable of preventing their citizens from crossing the frontiers because of their geographical situation. There are also states that in fact and usually also in law prohibit most of their nationals from traveling into foreign countries, although they may occasionally permit the departure of some few individuals.

The foregoing categorization points to the variety of attitudes that governments adopt and establish in their regulations. However, the usefulness of such distinctions remains limited. When the procedural remedy that stands at the disposal of the individual becomes the yardstick, it is clear that even some of the states that have long traditions of respect for human freedom exercise considerable power in granting or denying the right of egress.

In the Universal Declaration of Human Rights, the General Assembly of the United Nations proclaimed, as a common standard to be achieved by all peoples and nations, that everyone had "the right to leave any country, including his own."[2] This principle has already been accepted, though not without restrictions, within the regional communities of states that initiated the European and U.S. treaties protecting human rights.[3] It remains to be seen to what extent the non-binding standards in "human contacts" as defined in the Final Act of the Conference on Security and Co-operation in Europe, Helsinki, Finland, 1 August 1975, will influence international obligations of the states whose representatives signed the act. The act, of course, is not a treaty.[4] However, present-day practice in the international community at large does not augur well for a more general acceptance of the principle. It figures in the International Covenant on Civil and Political Rights;[5] yet so far the universal conventions have been less effective in protecting individual rights than their regional counterparts.

It cannot be said that there is in existence a customary rule of international law whereby every individual, irrespective of the domestic regulations of his state, has a right to move freely across the frontiers of that state. Having stated this, one should not overlook the fact that such a right is now recognized by a growing number of treaties and resolutions of intergovernmental organizations. It is, therefore, possible to speak of a trend, though the legal connotation of the term is vague, in favor of accepting this right through arrangements that reach beyond regionalism and aim at universality. To contend that the principle conferring the right is binding as part of the general law of nations would fly in the face of legal reality, since it would ignore the requirements for the creation of custom.

We are faced here with a problem for which the making of a universally binding standard is a very difficult task. It is one of those questions on which ideological differences prove to be an obstacle to the establishment of uniform regulation. Nevertheless, such regulation should be sought. Freedom of movement is part of the personal freedom of the individual, and respect for this freedom can be reconciled with the interests of states and of the international community taken as a whole.

Conventions on human rights enumerate the reasons that authorize the state to restrict freedom of movement in peacetime. During an armed conflict the power of the state goes much further, but situations involving the application of the laws of war were not discussed in Bellagio in the context of the movement of individuals. Apart from these limitations, how far can a state go? The matter is one of domestic jurisdiction, though the competence of the state should not be identified as license to act entirely at will.

No doubt the enumerative method has its flaws, but it is not impossible to list the reasons for refusal fairly exhaustively, and the enumeration could be construed, in the interest of the individual, as implying that the burden of proof lies on the state, which would have to justify any extension of the prohibition. The state can always refuse permission to depart for one of the following reasons: (1) national security; (2) the security of another state, government, or authority, particularly to prevent the use of the territory of the state in an activity directed against the legally protected interests of another state; (3) maintenance of public order; (4) fulfillment of individual military obligations; (5) public health; (6) morals; (7) effective imposition of punishment for a criminal offense; and (8) implementation of the resolutions of intergovernmental organizations.

In some marginal cases there may arise a different kind of conflict of interest that is not between the state and the individual but between the individual and the interest of the international community. The individual's national state would then be called upon to prohibit his or her departure, such as in the case of the mercenaries traveling to Katanga during the Congo crisis of 1960.

The foregoing reasons limit freedom of departure, whether temporary or permanent. However, permanent departure, that is, emigration, has special features and consequences. Emigration cannot be treated by the law in exactly the same way as temporary travel. Through emigration the state and the nation lose their essential element of survival, which is the human element. Permanent departures on a large scale may put an end to the viable existence of the state.

An individual is, of course, physically able to go abroad for a temporary stay and then transform it into a permanent one. This possibility, however, does not remove the distinction between temporary and permanent departure of its relevance in politics and law. In most instances, for various family, property, or other practical reasons, emigration has to take place with the consent or cognizance of the individual's home country.

A mass exodus of some groups, such as in the professional fields, can have economic and social implications that might easily outweigh the arguments in favor of freedom of movement and the right to seek better material conditions. The solution lies beyond the realm of international law; the state should see to it that its policies do not force its citizens to look for permanent homes abroad. When the state persecutes certain minority groups or tolerates such persecutions, or when it fosters dissatisfaction and poverty through inept economic policies, by itself it creates the problem of, and the need for, emigration.

Probably the most difficult situation involves members of minority groups who can find a national home in another state or territory. The position becomes complicated when the interests of third states or peoples are at stake. Thus during the British mandate over Palestine the government of the United Kingdom limited the admission of Jews, and at some time, that government even promised to end the Jewish immigration, which had originated mainly in Central and Eastern Europe, in order to placate the Arabs of Palestine and the Arab states in the Middle East.[6] When the independence of Israel was proclaimed, the states from which the largest groups of Jewish immigrants came inherited the problem of taking into account the interests of third states.

In the present state of general international law, both the permission to emigrate and the admission of foreign immigrants remain within the domestic jurisdiction of the states. Unless the states have accepted specific treaty obligations, they are free to prohibit or regulate emigration and immigration. Nevertheless, this freedom should be exercised in a way that respects humanitarian considerations and common decency. A state that prohibits emigration in hardship cases, such as reuniting of families or helping old or disabled persons, may not act, technically, in violation of law, but it reverts to standards of behavior that morally disqualify it as a member of the international community. International law has a responsibility not only to regulate interstate relations, but also to protect human values and dignity.

The same considerations support the view that those few states that still expel or do not admit back their own nationals should abolish that practice. Insofar as the expulsion or nonadmission of a national results in the compulsory stay of that national upon foreign soil, the expelling or refusing state may easily find itself in breach of its obligation toward the foreign state concerned. A state that allows its citizens to travel abroad and, after their departure, deprives them of their nationality, is, again technically, under no duty to readmit these citizens. However, unless the individual himself has caused the deprivation of nationality by criminal conduct, the state cannot avoid the accusation that it has acted in bad faith toward the receiving state and in an inhuman way toward the individual.

On the other hand, voluntary emigrants or persons transferred to other countries by virtue of international agreements, as opposed to unilaterally operated population transfers, can be prohibited from immigrating if the state does not regard them as its citizens.

PROCEDURAL GUARANTEES AND FREEDOM OF MOVEMENT

It follows from the foregoing review of law and practice that the individual rights or interests discussed here still belong, to a large extent, to the sphere of domestic jurisdiction. To varying degrees, the slow penetration of international regulation shapes the limits of the exclusive competence of the state. These limits may not be restrictive. International regulation often results in the adoption of general principles or standards rather than specific obligations on which the individual can base an enforceable right. Indeed, enforcement is the crux of the matter. If there are domestic remedies whereby the individual can try to reverse the decision of the passport or emigration authorities, then even a broad formula defining the respective rights and duties of the state and the individual can become controllable in its effects. The same is true the other way around: substantive rules and protections lose much of their meaning if they are unaccompanied by procedural guarantees.

A comparison of the various national regulations and practices, especially as selectively shown by the reports collected in this volume, leads to the conclusion that in most if not all states the law indicates motives for which passports may not be granted or may be withdrawn. Decisions on passports can be reviewed in a majority of states, either by ordinary or administrative courts or by executive organs. However, in a number of countries the possibility of review is limited or doubtful. On the other hand, the prohibition of expulsion or nonadmission of nationals is enforceable on the domestic level.

Nonetheless, in spite of the sharp differences in the treatment of individual interests within the various systems of government, there is room for the view that municipal law and practice evidence a general trend toward granting individuals relief from decisions relating to their freedom of movement. Review by judicial bodies is to be preferred. These bodies should be empowered to verify whether the decisions under appeal conform to the law and in particular whether they might have been taken in excess of power. Some participants in the Bellagio discussions voiced their support or even preference for the access of individuals to international organs, possibly judicial, to seek observance by their home countries of treaty obligations relating to freedom of movement. It is true that the European Convention on Human Rights has created a working system of redress on the international plane; yet not all the parties to it recognize the right of individual petition to the European Commission and accept the compulsory jurisdiction of the European Court. Thus even in a regional community there is no unanimity about the acceptability of international, as opposed to domestic, remedies. Western European regulation is also a long way from being worldwide protection. The Optional Protocol to the International Covenant on Civil and Political Rights provides for a simple procedure that is at the mercy of the sovereignty and all the imaginable susceptibilities of the state concerned.[7] The protocol is open to members of the United Nations and some other states. However, the number of signatures under the protocol is very small. It clearly points to the reluctance of the great majority of states to submit the disputes between them and their nationals to international inquiry, let alone decision.

DIPLOMATIC PROTECTION

The question of direct access of individuals to international organs also arises in connection with diplomatic protection of nationals, which is characterized by the well-known duality of the right of the state and the interest of the citizen. As a concept, the duality goes back to the writings of August Wilhelm Heffter and Emer de Vattel, though the latter was careful to emphasize the indirect nature of the claim put forward by the state.[8]

The Hague Court still upholds the classical approach. As late as 1970, in the Barcelona Traction case (second phase), it repeated its previous opinion that in exercising diplomatic protection the state was always asserting its own right. The court denied that in this sphere there was any interaction of international and municipal law. Even if domestic legislation confers upon the national a right to demand protection abroad, the matter remains, in the words of the court, "within the province of municipal law and [does] not affect the position internationally."[9]

The fact is that the individual has no right to diplomatic protection either in international or municipal law. If there is a mention of the right in the constitution or a statute of the state, it amounts to nothing more than a statement of political intent; it does not create an enforceable right. There are states in which courts can review all administrative acts, and hence also refusals to grant diplomatic protection; but the latitude of discretion left to the foreign service is large. Consequently the whole idea of judicial control is highly speculative here. In inquiring into the merits of a refusal to grant diplomatic protection, the court would necessarily limit itself to the enforcement of equality before the law and to the prohibition of excess of power. A court of justice is unable to compel the executive actually to protect the individual, but it can grant damages, though the assessment of these damages might prove difficult. Retroactive control is also an unsatisfactory solution, since although in some countries the individual can sue the state and the official concerned, courts have no access to foreign office files and diplomatic correspondence and will not be in a position to examine the claim properly.

On the other hand, there is some merit in the Chilean practice, going back to the nineteenth century, whereby the government seeks advice from the Attorney of the Supreme Court before espousing the individual claim on the international plane. (See Chapter 6.) One might also envisage the appointment of two commissioners operating within the department of external affairs who would, in conjunction with the legal adviser, review requests for diplomatic protection in a regular fashion.[10]

However, the problem of remedies is not exhausted by devising one or another scheme for improving domestic procedures. Have individuals some means of direct action in the international sphere when they prefer not to enlist the help of their home states or when that help is not available? The answer to this question can be given in three contexts: access of the individual to adjudicating organs set up to deal with claims that arise in connection with some clearly defined circumstances and in a specific period of time; general protection and enforcement of human rights; and procedures relating to investment disputes.

1. Redress from special adjudicating organs is usually the result of a settlement related to the termination of a war or, generally, from a bilateral arrangement. The peace treaties concluded after the first world war provided for the creation of the Mixed Arbitration Tribunals, in which individuals had the capacity to institute proceedings. A tribunal organized under the German-Polish Convention Concerning Upper Silesia could entertain actions brought by nationals of one party against the other contracting state.[11] The Arbitral Commission on Property, Rights and Interests in Germany had jurisdiction over various claims put forward by Allied nationals and juridical persons against the Federal Republic of Germany

in the post-World War II period. The short-lived Central American Court was also available to individuals. On the whole it may be said that procedures dealing with claims connected with the peace settlement relieved diplomatic protection of its traditional task, but the bulk of other claims, and they are much more numerous, remains unaffected by this category of arrangements.

2. The position is not different in the case of petition and similar procedures established under the international instruments protecting human rights. In most cases one is faced here with claims arising out of violations of law by the claimant's own state, not a foreign state. These procedures could eventually assume the role and the place of diplomatic protection only in relationships involving a state that has a significant number of aliens and/or important foreign interests within its jurisdiction.

However, with very few exceptions, states submit only unwillingly, to international adjudication in the field of human rights. Another limitation is the fact that treaties in this field are rather reticent on the subject of property and proprietary interests.[12] While protecting the most fundamental values of the human person, these treaties are less concerned with the growing number of subjective rights, especially of an economic, commercial, or business character, recognized in the various conventions.[13] Diplomatic protection is not regulated in treaties relating to human rights; there is no "human" right to diplomatic protection. Thus the two instrumentalities, international procedures and traditional protection by the national state, complement each other. The view that, if there existed true international safeguards of human rights, diplomatic protection would become an out-of-date institution,[14] looks to a rather distant future. Besides, it cannot be denied that diplomatic protection also has a role in defending human rights, which it does not cease to play.

No doubt the limitations inherent in diplomatic protection call for some means of redress in the field of human rights. For instance, restrictions resulting from the doctrine of continuous nationality are not present in the type of safeguards, based on the concept of human rights, in which nationality is not the criterion for making and entertaining the claim. The doctrine of continuous nationality requires that the individual must have been the national of the espousing state continuously, both at the moment of the injury and at the moment of presentation of the claim by that state. There are some variations of the latter date. For instance, the day on which the treaty providing for the settlement of claims entered into force is sometimes used instead of the date of espousal. According to some practice the period of continuous nationality extends to the date of the award. Be that as it may, if the right of the state, as distinguished from that of the individual, is solely taken into consideration, then the existence of nationality in that state exclusively at the time of the harm should be the logical and adequate solution. Still, the state may not feel inclined to take up the claim of an individual who at the moment of espousal is no longer its national. There is obviously no justification in excluding "late" nationals from receiving compensation; yet today the matter is left to bilateral arrangements, and they usually adopt the doctrine of continuous nationality. It may be that the requirement of continuous nationality, as the very term "doctrine" already suggests, is not a rule of general law but belongs to the realm of treaty and arbitral practice. In any event, this practice is of decisive importance in the fate of individual claims.

3. In the matter of protecting investment abroad, attention has been focused on the Convention on the Settlement of Investment Disputes between States and Nationals of Other States.[15] The convention has created the International Centre for the Settlement of Investment Disputes, which provides facilities for conciliation and arbitration of investment disputes, on a strictly voluntary basis, between states and private investors having the nationality of other states. The center is meant to relieve the state of its function of intervening on behalf of its citizens. The convention expressly excludes diplomatic protection once the parties have consented to submit or have already submitted their dispute to arbitration in the framework of the center.[16]

On paper the scheme of the convention looks promising. The jurisdiction of the center has been accepted in numerous agreements between the developed and developing countries. However, in practice very little use has been made of the center. Nonetheless, recourse to the center has the specific merit of removing the dispute between the aggrieved foreigner and the state from the plane of interstate relations, or at least it achieves this effect for a period of time. The advantage is that the problem remains restricted to the issue of the individual claim, and the chances of avoiding broader political repercussions are great. It would be worthwhile to consider whether the model of the convention could be imitated by applying it to disputes that arise out of claims that originate in business and professional activities other than investment.

The abuses of diplomatic protection, particularly with regard to Latin America, gave birth in the past to ideas favoring the establishment of guarantees of individual rights through other means.[17] Today the heart of the matter is the fear that state protection might prove inadequate in defending individual or corporate persons. For the state, as the Hague Court put it in 1970, is "the sole judge to decide whether its protection will be granted, to what extent it is granted, and when it will cease."[18] The state "retains in this respect a discretionary power."[19] The picture becomes more complicated when economic considerations are taken into account, however. In contemporary economic relations the dichotomy and the oppositeness of the right of the state to extend diplomatic protection and the interest of the individual in having that protection fully granted have, in numerous instances, disappeared or at any rate considerably diminished. Even in a free market economy, the business activity of the national abroad is now more often than not controlled or supervised by his or her home state in various ways.[20] One may here quote the words of Judge André Gros: "The economic world today exhibits phenomena of State intervention in and responsibility for the economic activity of the subject within the national territory or abroad which are so frequent and thoroughgoing that the separation of the interest of the individual from that of the State no longer corresponds to reality."[21] In economic terms the state is rarely free to abandon the claims of its nationals.

THE STATE AND COMPENSATION

The fact that an individual may be able to count on the help of his or her state in the matter of procedure does not dispose of the substantive issue: Is the individual assured of satisfactory treatment when it comes to a decision on the merits of the claim?

An alien who suffered injury through acts that involved the responsibility of the state is entitled to reparation. As a rule the individual lacks standing in international law; so when he or she does not succeed by using local remedies, his or her home country can present the claim to the foreign state involved. However, at this very moment the dimension of the affair changes. The claim becomes an element in the state-to-state relationship, and it is possible that the individual will now be made a victim of foreign policy. Here, as in other domains, reconciliation of private and public interests is a difficult problem that defies a clear-cut solution.

Pursued logically to its conclusion, the duality of state and individual rights would safeguard the individual against the consequences of any waiver of rights by the state. Should not such a waiver be limited to the right of the state and not influence the position of the individual? The state may not choose to protect its citizen, but why should it bar that citizen from pressing an individual claim through means that might still stand at his or her disposal, such as in the domestic law of the delinquent state? Nonetheless, international law authorizes the state to "settle the claim on such terms as it may conceive proper."[22] Perhaps the recent treaties containing provisions that protect property rights, such as Article 1 of Protocol No. 1 to the European Convention on Human Rights, prescribing that "no one shall be deprived of his possessions,"[23] could restrict the operation of that rule, but so far practice has not justified this expectation, as in the unsuccessful argument based on the Fifth Amendment to the Constitution of the United States described in Chapter 20.

Waivers of claims in peace and similar settlements and provisions for the payment of lump sums below the value of actual losses in compensation agreements attest to the right of the state to effectively cancel the claims of its nationals. Such arrangements not only liquidate the claim on the international plane, but usually also prevent the individual concerned from seeking redress in municipal law. The impossibility of suing before domestic courts results from the effectiveness of the waiver in municipal law, through transformation or incorporation of the treaty into that law or through other devices.

Therefore no government has an international duty to make good such losses as the citizen may suffer because the government has forfeited his or her claim in its arrangement with the foreign country. The government is not obliged to pay the difference between full compensation and the lesser sum received from the state causing the injury.

However, payment of the difference would appear equitable, especially where the home state obtains definable advantages from the other contracting party in return for the settlement of the claims. The sacrifice that the holder of the right involuntarily makes for the good of the nation should be compensated. Compensation should here correspond to the value of the right impaired by the international delinquency of the foreign state, insofar as the home state of the individual failed, in the national interest, to secure the damages otherwise due.

There are situations in which the individual suffers damage as a result of the conduct of his or her own state; in other words, that conduct brought about the injury by the foreign state. Even in situations of this kind, "topping up" the funds received from the latter state is done only exceptionally and not as a matter of obligation, international or municipal. (See the cases referred to in Chapter 19, on the United Kingdom.)

Once compensation is paid by one state to another, the practice warrants the assertion that the individual may rest assured of receiving a fair share of the fund, though in lump-sum arrangements the individual share may represent only a fraction of what would cover the original loss. The money is the property of the state, which now distributes it among those entitled. In strict international law there is no duty to distribute the sum obtained. However, in Western practice, including the period of post-1945 nationalizations, there has not been a single instance in which a government refused to distribute a compensation and kept it as public money instead. In the light of that practice, it might appear that the rule that compensation belongs to the state is now obsolete. The rule could be modified or rephrased as conferring on the state, rights more limited than full ownership of the compensation money.

The state paying compensation no doubt has a legal interest in satisfying the aggrieved individuals. There have been instances in which compensation treaties played some role in the distribution of the money, even if the criteria and procedure of distribution were reserved for the domestic jurisdiction of the receiving state. In that sense the freedom of the latter is not so total as it might seem at first sight.

On the other hand, the rule that compensation belongs to the state retains its practical importance for states that have planned economies and in general for states that maintain currency controls and restrictions. Here the state acquires foreign currency through the compensation agreement, while it satisfies the individual claims through payments in local currency. Such an operation may prove advantageous to the public finances and can concurrently provide satisfactory damages to the persons concerned. At any rate, it would be rather difficult to subject the modalities of distribution to the control of international law unless there were specific treaty provisions regulating the matter.

Finally, one may point to various kinds of special protection. One example is payments made by the United States government to fishermen who have been fined by foreign states for fishing in areas that those states regard as their own territorial waters or exclusive fishing zones. (See Chapter 20, on the United States.) In turn, the United States, which does not recognize such wider maritime belts or zones, is supposed to collect the sum so paid from the foreign state. So far it has not succeeded in recovering any of the money it has paid to the fishermen.

The U.S. scheme has its politico-philosophical aspect. Since the source of the money is the taxpayer, the loss does not lie upon those who happen to be the immediate victims but is spread over the national community. However, it is unlikely that this pattern could be applied to other situations, especially where the losses to individuals are in higher amounts. When a state does not recognize the maritime jurisdiction of another state over a certain area, it has an interest in maintaining the presence of its vessels in the waters in question, and that interest overrides the inconvenience of a limited financial loss. It is a combination of public and private interest, with the former prevailing, that makes the scheme work. Its application to contingencies in which important property abroad is confiscated or nationalized would not be practical, nor would the situation offer parallel advantages to the compensating home state.

Cutting off aid or other advantages where there has been uncompensated taking of property has from time to time been resorted to with varying success. On the whole this method has not proved effective. It represents more of a policy sanction than a special measure protecting the individual against loss of property.

On the other hand, a more promising alternative that is preventive and not repressive in character is insurance on investments. Although this kind of insurance is sometimes looked upon by the developing countries with suspicion--they have described it as a measure of overprotection--it nevertheless encourages investors. Once the claim of the investor has been satisfied pursuant to the insurance scheme, the investor's home state will find itself in an easier position to waive its own claim for reparation.

It may be said by way of conclusion that problems of claims and compensation bring us into the wider context of the operation and recognition of foreign acts in the municipal spheres of other states. What is the latitude of these municipal systems in this respect? If an act tends to have effects abroad, to what extent is this regulated by, and subject to the supremacy of, international law? These questions will be considered in the next section.

THE ACT OF STATE DOCTRINE

This doctrine is undoubtedly an obstacle to the recovery of property or damages by individuals, and it questions the validity or applicability of the foreign law or executive act involved.

The Act of State doctrine resulted from various incidental opinions in municipal judicial decisions that slowly grew into a rule protecting acts of foreign states.[24] Sovereign immunity, though it concerned a different albeit related, issue, contributed to the birth of the doctrine.[25] According to the often quoted words of Chief Justice Melville Weston Fuller, "The courts of one country will not sit in judgment on the acts of the government of another done within its own territory."[26] In the opinion of Lord Justice Warrington, "The validity of acts of an independent sovereign government in relation to property and persons within its jurisdiction cannot be questioned in the Courts of this country."[27]

The scope of the acts enjoying immunity from review and scrutiny in foreign courts may vary from one municipal system to another. The subject is described in the following chapters and need not be summarized here. A more fundamental question arises concerning the relationship between international law and the foregoing opinions, and especially the rule they helped to establish. The question is, Is the doctrine one of municipal law only or does it also constitute part of the law of nations?

Chief Justice Fuller preceded the opinion quoted above with the assertion that "every sovereign state is bound to respect the independence of every other sovereign state."[28] Nobody will question that statement, yet an uncritical acceptance of any and every foreign official act is not the necessary corollary of the principle embodying respect for national independence. That indepence will not suffer if an official act does not find application abroad. In U.S. judicial practice the doctrine was formulated more out of deference to the executive branch and its freedom of action in external affairs than to protect the independence of foreign states.

The doctrine inevitably undergoes changes in the municipal system, and the legislation of the United States enacted in the aftermath of the Sabbatino case clearly shows the relativity of the doctrine's sacrosanctity. (See Chapter 20, on the United States.) Besides, municipal courts apply or do not apply foreign laws depending on what follows from the rules on conflict of laws. The criterion of public order is a powerful regulator of the extent to which foreign law finds effect. It is also a regulator that gives the judge a much wider measure of latitude than the test of conformity to international law.[29]

Protection of state sovereignty and independence by international law should not become self-defeating. That danger exists when acts contrary to that law are left immune. Organs of one state can assess, within the area of their municipal competence, the international legality of the acts of other states.[30] An organ, including a court, is not committing a breach of international law by engaging in such an assessment. In other words, the limitations that the Act of State doctrine imposes on the courts do not follow from international law. They are a matter of domestic law and domestic judicial practice.

The relevance of the domestic sphere explains why it is rather difficult to formulate inferences that would go beyond what has been said above, that is, the simple absence of prohibition to investigate the international lawfulness of the act. The (municipal) rules on conflict of laws and on the place of international law within the state complicate the task. If the conflict rule points to the foreign law, the court may not feel inclined to make any allowance for queries about its applicability except when it is incompatible with public order in the forum. Equally, when the court is one of a system in which the judicial branch of government refrains from inquiring into the conformity of domestic laws with the international duties of the state or in which the judge is obliged to give priority to the municipal regulation, then the chances that the international rule will prevent the application of the foreign law contrary to that rule will not be very great. The difficulty is that the impact and influence of municipal law cannot be eliminated here. In other words, the validity and applicability of internal acts of a foreign state are not regulated exclusively by the simple rule that the acts in question must conform to international law. The requirement of such conformity, whether regarded as a postulate of the law as it ought to be or as already part of the law, though unenforceable, cannot be put in doubt, yet practice shows that municipal organs still enjoy much freedom in recognizing or not recognizing the foreign act. Since this "question of recognition is governed in part by international law and in part by municipal law,"[31] much depends on the willingness of the court to give a decisive role to the test of conformity with international law.

In present-day municipal practice, whether the foreign act of state offends international law or not is not the sole criterion for the recognition of the act. A part of that practice clearly shows that it is not a test at all. The most that can be said is that a state does not violate any rule of international law if in assessing the legality of the act of another state it bases its assessment on international law and judges the foreign act by reference to its consistency with international law, provided it correctly applies international law. In an alternative formulation, a state does not violate any rule of international law if it adopts the position that public international law requires it to apply substantive international law in assessing the validity of acts of foreign states, especially when the rights of an alien are involved.[32]

The subject is one belonging to both the municipal and international systems, and the fact remains that what follows logically from the latter has not yet shaped the regulation existing in the former. The preeminence of international law is not questioned here; nor is the responsibility of the state for the acts of its organ. However, the enforcement of that preeminence in the municipal sphere is far from perfect.

When municipal courts refuse to take cognizance of foreign acts violative of international law, they often do it within the limits of their municipal law and not by virtue of international law.[33] Sometimes the basis is in international law. But their practice, in this respect, is not uniform. Thus it cannot be said that the reason why the courts of one state normally accept the efficacy of the legal acts of the organs of another state is international law.

On occasion the courts have not needed to recognize or apply the foreign act as such but have assumed a more limited role. They have merely acknowledged that the legislation or other acts have produced their effects in the territory of the foreign state involved.

One must agree with the proposition that "foreign laws should be recognized and enforced insofar as the private international law of the forum refers to the foreign law and insofar as the foreign law is formally valid according to its own law, not contrary to the public policy of the forum, and is in harmony with international law."[34] The combination of these criteria imposes reasonable limits on the operation of the Act of State doctrine, but frequent recourse to the test of international law is still a matter of future development. Domestic courts usually prefer to justify the nonapplication of a foreign law or executive act by relying on municipal law. Particularly, the reliance on the argument of public policy may prove an easier and less embarrassing solution in the court's view than an open review of the foreign act in terms of international law. Besides, a municipal court is, as a rule, better qualified to judge the act in the light of the public policy of its own juridical system than in the light of international law. Though occasionally public policy and international law may lead to similar or even identical results, they are different criteria and must remain so. The test of the international lawfulness of the foreign act should not be identified or confused with the test of public policy.

There are also other factors that influence the extent to which the Act of State doctrine is applied. One such factor is the nationality of the injured individual. The courts have not always been indifferent to the question of whether the individual is a citizen of the foreign state involved or of the country in which the court is held. Another factor is recognition of the foreign state or government by the state under which the court is. (See below.) The source of the international rule involved, whether custom or treaty, might equally influence the decision of the court. The same is true of the nature of the foreign act, whether legislative or executive, whether public or private law, and so on.

THE EXECUTIVE CERTIFICATE

By resolving whether to enforce a foreign act of state, the court no doubt enters the area of policy decisions. Here it may feel that it should seek help and guidance from the executive. This brings us to the subject of certificates or suggestions of the executive in connection with litigation in national courts.

The executive certificate is a statement issued by the executive department of government and addressed to the court in connection with specific litigation. The statement contains information on the international fact and, inevitably, on the international legal position. The information is relevant to the case.

Executive certificates deal with a practically limitless gamut of topics in international law: diplomatic and consular status, sovereign immunity, the legal position of states and territories, recognition, existence of the state of war, and many others.

In a number of states executive certificates can play an important and sometimes decisive role in litigation. The certification is not an act or concept of international law but belongs to practices evolved in the municipal systems. Its purpose is to facilitate adjudication and especially to avoid adoption by the court of a position that would conflict with the attitude of the executive in the field of foreign affairs. In other words, the aim is to influence the decision of the court.

Seen from the perspective of individual interest, the important point is the conclusiveness of the certificate. The question of whether, and if so to what extent, the statement of the executive binds the court is not uniformly answered in the various municipal systems. If the certificate is conclusive, then some due process should be followed in connection with its grant. In particular, the parties should be entitled to a hearing.

Generally, however, the nonconclusive nature of the certificate is to be preferred. The very need for executive statements or suggestions can be doubted. It should be the parties to a litigation who are responsible for providing the evidence relating to the international fact. The court would be free to examine it, to rely on its own investigations and to draw its own conclusions.

RECOGNITION

A frequent subject of certification is recognition of states and governments; but is recognition relevant in the judicial cognizance of foreign acts? Should not the two be divorced?

These questions can be approached in a larger context. Recognition of states and governments is a predominantly political function, and one may ask whether there is any actual need for the concept of recognition on the international legal plane. Although the establishment of diplomatic relations could be its substitute in interstate relations, in the national sphere foreign acts would be accepted or not by the courts, which would decide such issues for themselves, irrespective of international recognition. For the time being it would be difficult to get rid of the very term "recognition" in interstate and intergovernmental relations, but it seems both possible and desirable to limit the effects of recognition principally to the international plane and to restrict them when the individual rights and interests in municipal law are at stake.

The substitution of diplomatic relations for recognition was already part of the practice of some states in Latin America. The Estrada doctrine regarded recognition as a kind of intervention in the affairs of another state, and Mexico did not grant recognition but merely maintained or refused to maintain diplomatic relations. On the other hand, the decision on the establishment of diplomatic relations involves a process that is similar to recognition. However, the interpretation that was given to the Estrada doctrine some time after its formulation helped to circumvent the danger of that similarity. The mechanism is rather simple. Diplomatic relations are to be entertained with all countries, including those which have only de facto governments.

The Mexican government had followed this policy. Though it did not establish diplomatic relations with the Spanish government of Generalissimo Francisco Franco, Mexico had more relations with Spain than with some fully recognized governments. The Mexican example shows that it is possible to abandon recognition of governments; however, this would prove more difficult in the case of new states.

Latitude and elasticity are to be preferred in defining the powers of the court. The existence of a territorial entity or governmental organ always entails some legal consequences that concern the individual. Courts should not ignore the individual interests involved. Courts can give effect to certain manifestations of the foreign and unrecognized authority, while refusing in other respects. Thus some portions of foreign legislation can be applied without nullifying the policy of nonrecognition, while the grant of immunities, for instance, could depend exclusively on the opinion of the executive. Identification or assessment of the status of the territorial entity or government in question could be made either by judicial notice or evidence in the usual way; that is, the interested parties would be able to state their position or call on other witnesses. The litigation involving Rhodesia[35] illustrates this point.

IMPLEMENTATION OF INTERNATIONAL RESOLUTIONS

To what extent do resolutions adopted by international organizations affect individual rights and obligations? The answer requires consideration of the ways in which the various national systems are able to assist in the implementation of such resolutions. In other words, it is necessary to define the place they have in municipal law.

Some categorization may be useful here. International resolutions can be divided into acts that are binding on states, or some other addresses, and those that are not. Recommendations usually are not, though one must look behind the name: there are recommendations that contain an element of obligation, while other enactments, though called decisions and thus implying a binding force, can create no duties whatsoever.

Acts endowed with binding force can conveniently be subdivided into law-making and executive (administrative) resolutions. The former lay down general and abstractly formulated rules of conduct. These rules find application in an unlimited number of situations covered by the resolution. On the other hand, an executive resolution concerns a specific contingency or situation.

A law-making resolution is a source of international legal rules. It is a source that should be regarded as different from custom or treaty, though in the present stage of the development of the international community, an intergovernmental body cannot enact laws for states without prior authorization from them. Usually the authorization is to be found in the treaty that is the constitutive instrument of the organization. Therefore, faced with a regulative act of the organization, the member state is confronted with problems that to some degree are analogous to those that arise in connection with the place of treaties in the municipal sphere.

The procedures whereby international resolutions become effective inside the state vary from one municipal system to another. Fairly often various techniques are used within the same system. Constitutions rarely deal with the problem, which is just as well, since a constitutional provision on domestic implementation of the resolution of an organization raises problems of constitutional interpretation.

There are states in which the incorporation of the treaty into municipal law covers decisions adopted by the organization in conformity with and under, that treaty, provided the decision is self-executing.

A different system consists in adopting a law (statute) that expressly enables the executive branch to implement the decisions taken by an organization, such as the measures ordered by the Security Council by virtue of Article 41 of the UN Charter. Such a law or statute is characterized by the generality of its provisions. It does not concern a specific resolution or resolutions adopted at a specific date, but gives power to enforce any and every resolution within its ambit.

A law or statute may not deal with the international organization, yet it may prove instrumental in putting into effect the decisions or other acts of the organization. For instance, a law regulating foreign trade and import or export controls usually creates a sufficient basis for the government to enforce decisions on economic sanctions without resorting to the legislature. When the resolution in question does not quite fit into the framework of a law and the government is not willing to ask the parliament for additional legislation, the government may still be able to find adequate municipal foundation for its competence to implement the resolution. (The procedure is described in Chapter 5, on Canada.)

Not infrequently the executive seeks authorization on an ad hoc basis. Here, each time the state has an international duty or is asked by the organization to put a resolution into operation, the government refers the matter to the legislature. This solution is not satisfactory. It contains an element of improvisation, and the time gap between action by the international organization and national implementation tends to be larger than when other methods are used.

Another system, in contrast with all the foregoing procedures, dispenses with any legislative authorization and recognizes the competence of the executive to proceed with the enforcement of international resolutions. This system involves some delegation of sovereignty.

In supranational organizations there is delegation of part of the national legislative and executive powers to the bodies concerned, and consequently their acts are directly binding and applicable in the domestic legal systems of their members. Although it is sometimes maintained that this would be the ideal answer to the problems of implementing international resolutions, it is a method that presupposes a far-reaching uniformity of policy among the members. This feature is absent from many traditional organizations, including the United Nations; nor is it always present in all the fields in which supranational organizations are active, as shown by the history of the European Communities. Ideally, it could perhaps be proposed that the executive should have the competence to take steps necessary for the application of the decision adopted by the international organization. At the same time, these steps would be subject to subsequent parliamentary control, including invalidation, to protect against abuse.

At this point, we may turn to the consequences that national implementation of international resolutions has or can have for individual rights. The preceding survey of the various methods of implementation leads to the conclusion that none of them actually comprises adequate safeguards for the individual. Even the participation of parliament is not a guarantee, since the legislature can easily give priority to international decisions over individual rights. These rights are especially at stake when commercial transactions are affected through embargo or other economic sanctions. The harmony between the interests of the regional or world community and the interests of the individual could be established by instituting a procedure within the domestic sphere for granting of compensation to individuals, but such a procedure is not a practical possibility for the near future (late 1970s or early 1980s). Nor is there any chance that other organizations will imitate the remedies existing in the European Communities. There is a particular need for protecting individual rights in situations in which an organization oversteps the powers originally bestowed upon it by the constituent treaty and the treaty itself has thus been modified, in effect, by the gradual evolution of the organization.

In spite of these and similar difficulties, on the whole the activities of international organizations have proved beneficial to the interests of individuals, which always gives a deeper sense to the aims of the organizations. Their purposes, if limited to the strict context of interstate relations, often remain frustrated, since the achievement of its purposes by the organization is not necessarily the actual objective of national policies.

The papers that follow look at the various problems that arise between the state and the individual from the angle of national experience. The solutions and opinions vary, but a common thread runs through all the studies here published. This thread is the belief that reconciliation of state and individual interests is not beyond the reach of the law, international and municipal. It is also the assumption that at present international law assists and influences the national systems in their regulatory function in fields that are of direct concern to the individual. Within national boundaries the welfare of the individual is attained through mainifold and differing methods, but the matter is no longer in the exclusive domain of municipal law. While it is true that "men in general need their national law, but do not, in normal circumstances need international law,"[36] the latter protects the individual as such, and not only in the context and in consequence of state-to-state relations, as it begins to fulfill its new function as "the law of a welfare world."[37]

NOTES

1. The summary record of the conference was prepared by Vera Gowlland.

2. Art. 13, para. 2 of UN General Assembly, Universal Declaration of Human Rights (1948).

3. Art. 2, §§ 2, 3, protocol No. 4 of 16 September 1963 to the Convention for the Protection of Human Rights and Fundamental Freedoms, Rome, 4 November 1950, 213 U.N.T.S. 221, Europ. T.S. no. 46; Basic Documents on Human Rights 361 (I. Brownlie, ed., 1971); Art. 22, §§ 2, 3, American Convention on Human Rights, San José, Costa Rica, 22 November 1969, 9 International Legal Materials 673 (1970).

4. 14 International Legal Materials 1292, at 1313 (1975).

5. International Covenant on Civil and Political Rights, Art. 12, §§ 2, 3, annexed to GA Res. 2200 A (XXI).

6. See A. J. P. Taylor, English History, 1914-1945 500 (1970), Penguin).

7. International Covenant on Civil and Political Rights, op. cit.

8. E. de Vattel, Le droit des gens ou principes de la loi naturelle, Book 2, Chapter 6, § 71 (1758) .

9. Art. 44, § 78, [1970] I.C.J. Rep. 3.

10. This suggestion was made by S. M. Schwebel.

11. 15 May 1922, 9 L.N.T.S. 466. In Steiner and Gross v. Polish State, the tribunal held that nationals could also sue their home states. [4] Ann. Dig. (No. 188, 1927-28).

12. One such regulation is Art. 1 of Protocol No. 1, Convention for the Protection of Human Rights and Fundamental Freedoms, op. cit., 213 U.N.T.S. 262.

13. P. De Visscher, "Cours général de droit international public," 136 Hague Academy, Recueil des Cours 1, at 157 (1972, II).

14. C. W. Jenks, 2 Ann. Institut de Droit Int., 51, at 251 (1965).

15. 575 U.N.T.S. 159.

16. Art. 27. "Informal diplomatic exchanges for the sole purpose of facilitating a settlement of the dispute" do not fall under this prohibition.

17. See C. De Visscher, Théories et réalités en droit international public 305-306 (1970, 4th ed.).

18. Barcelona Traction (Second Phase), [1970] I.C.J. Rep. 3, at 44, § 79.

19. Ibid.

20. Separate opinion of Judge Gros, [1970] I.C.J. Rep. 268, at 269.

21. Ibid.

22. Dissenting opinion of Judge Moore, "Mavrommatis Palestine Concessions," P.C.I.J., ser. A, no. 2, 54, at 63 (1924).

23. 213 U.N.T.S. 262.

24. M. Zander, "The Act of State Doctrine," 53 A.J.I.L. 826, at 835 (1959).

25. See ibid., at 850-51.

26. Underhill v. Hernandez, 168 U.S. 250, at 252 (1897).

27. Luther v. Sagor, 3 K. B. 532 (1921) at 548.

28. Underhill v. Hernandez, op. cit.

29. Zander, op. cit., at 844, writes: "Public policy is a changing and relative concept, uncertain in its application, whereas international law provides a relatively more objective standard against which foreign acts may be measured."

30. Whether they can inquire into the municipal validity of acts of foreign states is a question that is not discussed here.

31. D. P. O'Connell, 2 International Law 794 2nd ed., (1970).

32. Both formulations are those by M. Leigh as stated during the discussion.

33. The Rose Mary litigation is a case in point. Anglo-Iranian Oil Co. v. Jaffrate, 1 W.L.R. 246 (1953); [20] I.L.R. 316 (1953). Cf. comments by O'Connell, op. cit., at 806.

34. Zander, op. cit., at 837.

35. Madzimbamuto v. Lardner-Burke and Baron v. Ayre, Bezuidenhout, Dupont and Lardner-Burke, 2 S. A. 284 (1968); A.C. 645 (1969); 39 I.L.R. 61. These cases concerned, among other things, the de facto nature of the Smith regime. The point in question, including the cases, was discussed by E. Lauterpacht.

36. G. Fitzmaurice, "The Future of Public International Law and of the International Legal System in the Circumstances of Today," Institut de Droit International, Livre du Centenaire 1873-1973: Evolution et perspectives du droit international 196, at 306 (1973).

37. C. W. Jenks, "Law for a Welfare World," Institut de Droit International, Livre du Centenaire 1873-1973: Evolution et perspectives du droit international 196, at 306 (1973).

CHAPTER

2

AUSTRIA

Ignaz Seidl-Hohenveldern

The protection of the individual against acts by the administration is almost over-perfect in Austria. In theory, at least, this protection extends also the activities of the administration in the field of international relations. An individual can appeal to the administrative court against any administrative act and in cases in which a violation of constitutional rights can be alleged, also to the constitutional court. Moreover, Austria adheres to the European Convention on Human Rights[1] and to its optional clauses concerning acceptance of the jurisdiction of the European Court of Human Rights and the right of access to the European Commission of Human Rights, which are granted to any individual alleging a violation of these rights regardless of nationality.

The European Court of Human Rights has interpreted Article 6, Paragraph 1 of the Convention, granting the right to a fair and public hearing in matters of civil rights and obligations, in a liberal manner. The court does not consider itself bound by the qualification of the national law concerned. It has thus held that the right to obtain permission to split up a rural estate constitutes a civil right, although under Austrian law this right is granted by administrative authorities.[2]

This chapter is substantially as it was written in 1972. However, it was carefully reviewed by the author in 1975, and brought up to date as of that time.

THE INDIVIDUAL

The Individual as a National

Movement

Passports. Under Article 4, Paragraph 3 of the Basic Law of 21 December 1867, Reichsgesetzblatt number 142, which has been maintained in force as constitutional law, "the state may restrict freedom of emigration only on account of military service obligations." However, a citizen's freedom to emigrate may also be restricted indirectly, under conditions that would restrict his or her freedom of movement inside Austria as well, by virtue of Article 5 of the Law Concerning the Protection of Personal Freedom of 27 October 1862, Reichsgesetzblatt number 87. This indirect restriction of emigration was approved by the decision of the constitutional court of 29 June 1949.[3]

In a decision of 5 October 1953, the constitutional court held unconstitutional the provision of the passport law of 9 January 1951, Bundesgesetzblatt Number 57/1951, which prohibited the issuing of passports to persons intending to emigrate who would be leaving behind them large arrears of unpaid taxes.[4] However, in this same decision the court approved the refusal to issue passports to persons under investigation for crimes or offenses or suspected of defrauding customs. By virtue of this decision the passport law was amended by a law of 24 December 1954.[5] Austrians may also enter many Western European countries without a passport, merely by showing their national identity card.

In 1945-46 various government decrees ordered that persons of German ethnic origin from the South Tyrol (Italy) who were residing in Austria and who had reopted for Italian citizenship after World War II should, upon their request, be "assimilated in administrative matters" as Austrian citizens.[6]

The attitude of Austrian courts in respect to South Tyroleans varies. The courts consider them Italians for the purpose of applying conflict-of-law rules, that is, in cases of alimony. On the other hand, the supreme court ruled on 11 April 1962 that the provisions according to which foreigners, having been punished in Austria, shall subsequently be expelled from the country do not apply to South Tyroleans.[7] South Tyrolean residents in Austria who had neither requested their assimilation pursuant to the above-mentioned decrees nor opted to reacquire Italian citizenship were treated as stateless persons.[8]

Departure. During the German occupation of Austria, a German ordinance of 28 June 1935, Reichsgesetzblatt I, page 903, was introduced in Austria. This ordinance prohibited newspapers from carrying advertisements offering work abroad unless they had previously obtained clearance with the national labor authorities. After 1945 this law was maintained in force in Austria and in the Federal Republic of Germany. However, by a decision of 4 April, 1967,[9] the FRG federal constitutional court declared this provision to be unconstitutional on the grounds that it conflicted with freedom of the press. Although Austrian constitutional law also guarantees freedom of the press, the Austrian constitutional court, by a decision of 27 September 1968,[10] held this law to be compatible with the Austrian constitution. Thereupon the Austrian administrative court, by a decision of 3 June 1969,[11] upheld a refusal to grant a newspaper permission to carry such advertisements.

The Austrian supreme court has held that Article 5 of the European Convention of Human Rights, which grants the right to liberty, does not grant individuals the freedom to leave any country, including their own. (See below.) Hence the law of the German Democratic Republic that prohibits emigration cannot be deemed to constitute a direct and grave attack against this right. The court rejected the plea of a defendant who had falsified an Austrian passport in an attempt to leave the German Democratic Republic that he had merely acted in the exercise of his legitimate right of self-defense against the above-mentioned law.[12] This plea was also rejected when it was advanced by Romanians who had hijacked a Romanian plane to fly to Vienna.[13]

Austria, as well as the Federal Republic of Germany, was criticized for allowing rocket experts who were its nationals to work on Egyptian military rocket projects. Austria had no legal tools to prevent such emigration. The rule of Article 9, paragraph 1, Number 2, of the Austrian Citizenship Law of 1949, which was then in force, provided for the loss of Austrian citizenship if an Austrian entered into the public service of a foreign state.[14] In order to avoid losing their Austrian citizenship, the contracts of employment of these experts were not concluded with the United Arab Republic as such, but with research institutes having a personality distinct from that of the state under UAR law. It was in order to avoid such circumventions of law that in Article 33 of the Austrian citizenship law of 15 July 1965 it is provided that Austrian citizenship shall be withdrawn in case of any activities on behalf of a foreign state that are detrimental to the interests or to the prestige of the Republic of Austria. The government memorandum to this article of the law alludes to the rocket expert cases.

Austrian citizenship law contains no provision authorizing the withdrawal of Austrian citizenship from a naturalized person on account of residence in a foreign country. According to Article 24 of the Austrian Citizenship Law of 1965, even an Austrian citizenship that is obtained under false pretenses can be withdrawn only if the person concerned does not thereby become stateless.[15]

Return. Articles 12 and 13 of the Austrian Citizenship Law of 1965 facilitate the reacquisition of Austrian citizenship by former Austrians by reducing the residence requirement from ten to three years (Article 12) and by renaturalizing ex-Austrian women who have lost their citizenship because of marriage, if they request renaturalization within two years after the end of their marriages. Returnees may be granted income tax reductions. These rules, however, do not apply to Austrians working in the Federal Republic of Germany close to the Austrian border and returning every day to their Austrian domiciles.[16]

In Austria there exists a law banishing members of the house of Habsburg-Lothringen who have made no declaration of loyalty to the Republic of Austria.[17] In view of this law Austria made a reservation when signing Protocol Number 4 to the Convention for the Protection of Human Rights and Fundamental Freedoms on 16 September 1963 (not yet in force), Article 3 of which provides that "no one shall be deprived of the right to enter the territory of the State of which he is a national." The eldest son of the last emperor was refused an Austrian passport "valid for entry into Austria" in spite of the fact that he had made the required declaration. By its decision of 9 September 1966, the administrative court ordered the minister of the interior to issue the claimant an Austrian passport without any restriction.[18] It held that the notion of an Austrian passport excludes its being made invalid for entry into Austria.

Expulsion. An Austrian citizen can not be expelled from Austria, nor can an Austrian be extradited abroad.[19]

The provision of Article 9, Paragraph 1, Number 2 of the Austrian Citizenship Law of 1949,[20] providing that the acquisition of foreign nationality entails the loss of Austrian citizenship, has given rise to a good deal of case law. The taking out of "first papers" as a first step to acquiring U.S. citizenship does not entail the loss of Austrian citizenship, nor even the loss of the Austrian domicile of an Austrian immigrant to the United States.[21]

The rule on acquisition of foreign citizenship was interpreted as applying only to voluntary acts of acquisition of such citizenship; for example, an Austrian minor who automatically acquired citizenship in the United Kingdom by operation of Section 7 of the British

National Act of 1948, with no chance of declining such citizenship, does not thereby lose his Austrian citizenship.[22]

When Israeli law bestowed Israeli citizenship automatically on all persons who had emigrated to Israel, this did deprive an Austrian emigrant to Israel of Austrian citizenship, since acquisition of Israeli citizenship by operation of the law was held to be voluntary because, pursuant to this law, the acquisition of Israeli citizenship could have been avoided by a simple declaration, which the emigrant had omitted to make.[23]

If an Austrian acquires foreign citizenship with retroactive effect, this does not entail a retroactive loss of Austrian citizenship. For this period of retroactivity the emigrant is considered to have been a national of both states.[24]

The large amount of case law generated by the provision of the Austrian Citizenship Law of 1949, which mandated automatic loss of Austrian citizenship by entry into the public service of a foreign state, became obsolete when this provision was replaced by the provision of Article 33 of the Citizenship Law of 1965. According to some of these decisions, any service rendered to the foreign state, except in diplomatic or consular representations in Austria or in cases in which the state acted in a non-sovereign capacity, was held to entail such loss--even service as a typist or teacher.[25] A decision by the Administrative Court of 28 June 1961 interpreted this provision restrictively to cases of a voluntary entry into such service. In the case concerned, an Austrian lost his citizenship by becoming a teacher in a state school of a foreign state. However, the court held incidentally that it would have allowed this citizen to retain his Austrian citizenship if he could have proved that he was forced to accept this job as his only means of making a living.[26]

Protection

Extent of Freedom of Activity Abroad. Since Austrian law does not permit the extradition of Austrians to foreign states, Austrian courts have jurisdiction over crimes and offenses committed by Austrians abroad if, and insofar as, such acts are punishable under Austrian criminal law, even if the act concerned (editing a pornographic book in the Federal Republic of Germany) is not punishable under the law of the country in which it is committed.[27] A cartel agreement concluded in the Federal Republic of Germany between Austrian and FRG firms, which was legal under FRG law because it was merely an export cartel, was held invalid in Austria insofar as it constituted a violation of Austrian antitrust law, although if the remaining parts of the agreement were valid according to FRG Law, they would also be valid in Austria.[28]

Unless otherwise stated, infractions, that is, acts punishable by administrative authorities, are punishable only if the acts are committed in Austria.[29] An Austrian had bottled water with labels declaring it to be a mineral water having curative effects. Austrian law forbids the utilization of such labels unless they are approved by the Austrian health authorities, but the Administrative Court held that the person concerned had committed no infraction of this law, since all the water concerned had been exported to the Federal Republic of Germany.[30]

In a somewhat similar vein, the Administrative Court interpreted the provision of the Austrian Air Law, granting neighbors and neighboring towns the right to be heard in proceedings concerning the enlargement of an airport, as concerning only those neighbors and neighboring towns of Salzburg Airport that were Austrian, but not residents and towns in Bavaria (Federal Republic of Germany) in close vicinity to this airport on the border between Austria and the Federal Republic of Germany.[31]

Right to Diplomatic Protection. Austria recognizes no duty of the state to grant diplomatic protection and to compensate Austrian citizens if their property is taken abroad.[32]

This refusal was shown, among other ways, by the rejection of a claim for compensation by an Austrian citizen against the Austrian Embassy in Egypt, which according to the claimant had been negligent in protecting her interests when she was expelled from Egypt. She claimed compensation by virtue of the Law of State Liability for Wrongful Acts of Officials.[33] The court went so far as to justify the inaction of the embassy by stating that any action on its part in this matter would have been incompatible with the sovereignty of the receiving state.[34]

A refusal by Austrian authorities to intervene with the occupying powers in Austria on behalf of an Austrian national was held to be an "official act" of the Austrian Authorities. Only official acts are reviewable by the Administrative Court.[35]

However, in an indirect way another decision has admitted at least certain duties of the state on behalf of its citizens in this regard. An Austrian law limited the right to receive certain allowances to Austrians resident in Austria. An Austrian citizen who had been abducted to the Soviet Union by the Soviet occupying forces in Austria was held to be a resident of Austria for the purpose of this law. The Administrative Court justified this by stating that where the state is unable to protect its own nationals, as in that particular case, this inability should not work to the disadvantage of the citizents concerned.[36]

Compensation. Austria has concluded lump-sum compensation treaties with the 14 countries listed in the appendix to this chapter. The last of these agreements, providing payment of 1.2 billion schilling by Czechoslovakia in compensation for nationalized Austrian property, was concluded on 19 December 1974, that is, the week after the adoption of the "Charter" of Economic Rights and Duties of States.[37] Dual citizens are excluded by implication from profiting by such agreements.[38] The Constitutional Court stated in its decision of 15 October 1966 that unless the indemnity to be paid by Poland for Polish nationalization measures were effective, full, and immediate, Austrian reprisals against Poland would be justified.[39] However, the lump-sum compensation agreement with Poland (see the appendix to this chapter), like all other lump-sum compensation agreements, remained well below this standard. The government memorandum concerned stated that Austria was entitled to waive parts of the claims of her citizens for full compensation and that the indemnity obtained was in agreement with international practice.[40]

The rights of claimants to participate in the lump sum received by Austria are held not to be civil rights but claims of a public law nature, which means that such rights exist only insofar as they are granted by Austria in its sovereign capacity, that is, by enacting a compensation law. Only rights of a civil law nature are considered property rights. However, the protection of such property rights against expropriation is weaker under Austrian law than under those of most other Western countries.[41] All that Austrian law requires as a protection against expropriation is that property may only be taken by virtue of a law. The payment of any compensation is not required. Hence, this distinction of claims under civil law and claims under public law made by the decision of the Austrian Constitutional Court on 28 November 1968[42] hardly weakens the rights, if any, of the claimant. This decision merely makes it clearer that in receiving and distributing a lum-sum compensation the Austrian State is not acting as the civil law agent of the individual claimants.

This clearly results from, among other things (see below), the decision of the Supreme Court of 20 February 1952 concerning the Austro-U.S. Claims Settlement agreement of 21 June 1947.[43] By this agreement the United States paid Austria a sum of 308,382,590 schillings in full, complete, and final settlement of claims incident to the operations of the United States Forces in Austria between 9 April 1945 and 30 June 1947. The Austrian government guaranteed the Government of the United States that it would adjudicate individual claims, "pay to individuals and settle with individuals, both Austrian nationals and others owning property, rendering service or residing in Austria, and--guarantee full protection to the United States against any (such) claims" (Article 6).

The Constitutional Court had held these claims to be of a private law nature, hence falling into the competence of the ordinary courts.[44] The Supreme Court, however, held these claims to be of a public law nature, hence not giving the individual claimants a right to receive an indemnity except on the basis of a special law to this effect.[45] In its decisions of 26 June 1951 and 8 October 1951 the Constitutional Court reaffirmed its earlier view.[46] Nevertheless, in its decision of 20 February 1952 the Supreme Court held that individuals could not base claims against Austria on this agreement. The agreement, under the Austrian constitution as interpreted by the Supreme Court, ought to have been approved by the Austrian Parliament. As long as this was not done, the agreement was not transformed into the domestic law of Austria.[47] The Vienna Court of Appeals held on 20 May 1953 that in failing to submit the agreement to Parliament after this decision of the Supreme Court of 20 February 1952, the Austrian government had acted contrary to moral dictates and that the plaintiff was accordingly entitled to damages.[48] The claims concerned were finally settled by the Austrian Requisition Compensation Law.[49]

The indemnities received under most of the lump-sum compensation agreements are distributed by the Austrian federal distribution commissions. These commissions are composed of judges and representatives of Austrian ministries and economic interests. The representatives of economic interests are chosen from among the interested parties as much as possible. These commissions enjoy a degree of independence similar to that of the courts. Their decisions are not reviewable by the Administrative Court. The Administrative Court held that this is compatible with the Austrian constitution and the European Convention on Human Rights.[50] However, the Constitutional Court is entitled to examine these decisions to prevent them from being arbitrary.[51] By its decision of 5 December 1968, a decision by the commission was annulled for arbitrariness, since the commission had decided on the basis of assumptions contrary to the facts contained in the files submitted to it.

Austria distributed the lump sums received without any additions from Austrian funds. If the sum received was insufficient to pay the claims in full, the amount of each compensation payment was reduced proportionately.[52] The only concession to the claimants was the fact that, in contrast with French practice,[53] the Austrian state does not ask the claimants to pay any administrative fees for handling their claims.[54] However, after Austria had concluded a Lump Sum Agreement with Italy providing for the payment of a lump sum expressed in lira,[55] the Austrian parliament adopted a distribution law distributing to the Austrian claimants a sum expressed in Austrian schilling corresponding to the lira amount provided in the agreement, converted at the rate of exchange in force at the time of the signature of the agreement.[56] By this arrangement the Republic of Austria bore the loss of approximately .1 million schilling because the lira was subsequently devaluated.[57]

The distribution law concerning Romania excluded Austrian-Romanian dual nationals from the distribution of the lump sum. Since the rule is in conformity with the drafting history and the intent of the property treaty with Romania, it was held compatible with the Austrian constitution.[58] However, when the distribution law concerning Poland imposed more test dates on which a claimant had to have enjoyed Austrian citizenship than the test date figuring in the property treaty with Poland, this rule was held to be incompatible with the equal rights clause of the Austrian constitution.[59]

The Republic of Austria guarantees Austrian exporters, in exchange for a payment of a fee ranging from .124 percent to .5 percent, compensation for 90 percent of their losses from political and currency risks.[60]

According to the decision of the Supreme Court of 14 February 1963,[61] the German Reich had distributed sums received under the German-Romanian Resettlement Treaty of 22 October 1940 in its sovereign capacity. Hence claims against the Federal Republic of Germany for a share in this sum are covered by the immunity of the Federal Republic of Germany and do not come under the jurisdiction of Austrian courts.

<u>Responsibility of the State for Injury Induced by Its Own Conduct</u>. Austria has not compensated Austrian citizens for actions in the field of international relations involving a responsibility of the Austrian state. In theory, however, such actions, if wrongful, could serve as a basis for a compensation claim, as was discussed above. As far as inaction or waiver of at least certain parts of claims are concerned, the Constitutional Court and the Administrative Court have held that in the absence of such legislation as was enacted at a later time, an Austrian could not claim compensation from Austria on account of requisition by members of the occupying forces in Austria. The particular claimant had contended in vain that by furnishing the requisitioned goods he had fulfilled an obligation incumbent upon Austria by virtue of the Hague Regulations of Land Warfare.[62]

Article 27, Section 2 of the Austrian State Treaty of 15 May 1955, which is also discussed below, reads as follows:

> The Federal People's Republic of Yugoslavia shall have the right to seize, retain or liquidate Austrian property rights and interests within Yugoslav Territory on the coming into force of the present treaty.

> The Government of Austria undertakes to compensate Austrian nationals whose property is taken under this paragraph.[63]

The Supreme Court, in a decision of 4 February 1960, held this provision to be self-executing.[64] Hence, even before the Eleventh Law to Execute the State Treaty,[65] the Supreme Court had awarded damages to such Austrian owners.[66]

Waiver. The government memoranda to all agreements, concluded by Austria with foreign states, that provide for lump-sum compensation for the nationalization of Austrian property maintain that the Austrian state has a right to waive a claim of its nationals. Hence it therefore follows that the Austrian state can conclude with a foreign state a settlement that provides for compensation that does not fully cover the losses suffered by the Austrian owners concerned.[67]

The terms of the treaty with Poland, which, as we have seen, provided for less than full compensation, are particularly instructive if read together with the above-mentioned decision of the Constitutional Court concerning reprisals against Poland for the nonpayment of its full indemnity. The exchange of letters, Number 4 annexed to the treaty with Poland, provides that these reprisal measures concerning the vesting of certain Polish restitution claims shall be lifted when the lump-sum compensation treaty enters into force.

Austria stopped negotiations with the USSR for the release of Austrian property held in the USSR, which the latter was obliged to return under Article 27, Section 1 of the Austrian State Treaty, when the USSR advanced the counterclaim that Austria, under Article 18 of the same treaty, was obliged to refund to the USSR the costs of transporting Austrian prisoners of war back to Austria. In the course of these negotiations the USSR had informed an Austrian owner of real estate in territories that had become part of the USSR after World War II that, for the purpose of returning the value corresponding to this real estate, the USSR valued this estate at 32,785 rubles. When the Austro-Soviet negotiations were broken off, the claimant required the Austrian State to pay this sum to him, insisting that, economically speaking, the Republic of Austria had paid part of a debt to be paid by her with the money that was due to claimant. The Supreme Court rejected this claim in its decision of 12 November 1969, stating that the claimant had not lost or sacrificed any amount belonging to him for the common good of Austria and could only make such a claim if and when the Austrian state were to enact a law distributing the compensation received by the USSR for Austrian property pursuant to Article 27, Section 1 of the state treaty.[68]

To a certain extent this attitude of the courts can be contrasted with a statement by Austrian Federal Chancellor Kreisky, made in the Austrian Parliament on 14 January 1971, that he would personally prefer to settle a case that the previous government had submitted to an Austro-FRG arbitral tribunal, in the interest mainly of German expellees, naturalized in Austria, who were dissatisfied with the fact that they received drastically smaller payments than expellees to the Federal Republic of Germany received there under the FRG Equalization of Burdens Law and under the FRG Reparations Damages Compensation Law. Kreisky stated that he would not feel authorized to drop and/or settle the case unless he had obtained the opinions of the persons really interested in this dispute or of their representatives.[69] In my view this statement should not be understood as a statement of the law, but as a statement of policy.[70]

The case Kreisky spoke of concerned the interpretation of Article 24, Section 2, of the Austro-FRG Finance and Compensation Treaty of 27 November 1961.[71] Having paid the lump-sum compensation provided in this treaty, and having received in exchange Austria's waiver of further claims, the Federal Republic of Germany felt free to provide, in subsequent FRG laws, higher compensation for German citizens and for citizens of third countries than the amounts distributed to the individual Austrian citizens by virtue of this treaty. The award rendered on 15 January 1972 drew a distinction between claims a state may advance on its own behalf and claims it brings on behalf of its citizens.[72] According to the interpretation given to Article 24, Section 2, of this treaty, Austria may continue to avail itself of its own right to protect the interests of Austrian citizens, although Austria had waived its right to interstate claims by receiving the sums paid by the Federal Republic of Germany under this treaty.

Under Article 23, Section 3 of the Austrian State Treaty, Austria waives certain claims against Germany that arose prior to 8 May 1945 and, under Article 24, Section 2, of the same treaty, Austria waives claims against the Allied and Associated Powers for acts done by them in the course of the war and the occupation. The waiver of Article 23, Section 3, of the Austrian State Treaty was held to be compatible with international law and also with the Austrian constitution, since the latter permits expropriations even without compensation.[73] This waiver clause does not provide for compensation to the persons affected thereby. (Contrast this with Article 24, Section 2, as discussed below.) The right of Austria to waive the claims of her citizens against the Federal Republic of Germany has also been upheld by the Austro-German Arbitral Tribunal instituted under the Austro-German property treaty of 15 June 1957.[74]

Article 24, Section of the State Treaty provides that Austria shall pay equitable compensation to the persons affected by this waiver of claims against the Allied and Associated Powers. The Constitutional Court, by its decisions of 19 June 1962 and of 27 June 1963,[75] has held this provision to be non-self-executing.[76] Moreover the Constitutional Court considered it immaterial that Article 24 speaks of "equitable compensation," whereas Article 27, Section 2, provided "compensation."[77] (See discussion above of compensation for requisitions by members of occupying forces.)

The Constitutional Court, in a decision of 21 June 1960,[78] rejected a claim that by virtue of Article 24 of the Austrian State Treaty, compensation granted by the Austrian Requisition Compensation Law[79] should be increased. This law was held to have fulfilled in advance the requirements of Article 24 of the treaty. The Constitutional Court, in its decision of 19 June 1962, held that it is immaterial whether Article 24, Section 2, of the treaty has constitutional rank, as the claimant had alleged in order to have the Austrian Occupation Costs Law declared unconstitutional on the grounds that the compensation provided therein remains below full compensation.[80] The court held that even if the provision of Article 24, Section 2 of the treaty should rank as constitutional law, and even if the words "equitable compensation" figuring therein should be understood as meaning full compensation, the Occupation Costs Law providing partial compensation could still not be held since it would be at least a step in the direction of full compensation. This reasoning, of course, is somewhat hypocritical, since there is very little likelihood that a further law will supplement the payments provided under the law concerned. However, such reasoning has also been advanced by the German Federal Court[81] concerning, for example, the law on the Final Settlement of the Consequences of the War, of 5 November 1957.[82]

The waiver of Article 24, Section 2, of the Austrian State Treaty was likewise upheld by the Supreme Court on 19 September 1967.[83] A very special type of indirect waiver of rights of Austrian residents resulted from the Austro-U.S. pay-as-you-go agreement of 21 June 1947.[84] Under this agreement the U.S. occupational forces in Austria derequisitioned, as of 30 June 1947, all premises hitherto requisitioned by them in Austria. The Republic of Austria, as a self-appointed trustee of the owners, agreed to rent these same premises to the U.S. forces for the duration of the occupation of Austria. On 9 October 1948 the Constitutional Court held that the Republic of Austria lacked any legal basis upon which to conclude such a rental agreement on behalf of the owners.[85] Thereupon the Austrian authorities requisitioned all these premises on the basis of the Reich Requisition Law, a German law maintained in force in

Austria that granted powers to requisition premises for the use of "the armed forces." The Constitutional Court and the Administrative Court approved these Austrian acts of requisition as a valid basis upon which to conclude the rental agreement,[86] although the indemnities paid to the owners under the Reich Requisition Law were vastly inferior to the rent received in U.S. dollars by the Republic of Austria from the U.S. occupational forces.[87] In a decision of 29 April 1953 the Supreme Court held that, in view of the lack of any legal basis for these rental agreements, the Republic of Austria was bound to account to each individual owner, upon his request, for the sums received by the Republic of Austria for his premises from the time of the conclusion of the pay-as-you-go agreement to the time of the requisition under the Reich Requisition Law.[88] All these matters were also settled by subsequent legislation.[89]

Special Protection. In reprisal for the confiscation of Austrian property in Poland and Czechoslovakia, Austria appointed Austrian administrators for property that ought to have been returned to the heirs or successors in title of absent or missing Polish or Czechoslovakian citizens under Austrian restitution law. In respect to Poland the vesting of these claims was approved by the Constitutional Court by its decision of 15 October 1966.[90] In respect to Czechoslovakia it was approved by the Constitutional Court decision of 28 December 1967.[91]

Austria adheres strictly to the seat theory to establish the nationality of corporations. Thus the assets of a 100 percent German-owned Swiss company in Austria were not considered German property by Austria.[92] An Austrian holding 100 percent of the shares of an Italian corporation could not claim compensation under the Eleventh Law for the Execution of the State Treaty,[93] since the property which had been confiscated in Yugoslavia was viewed as Italian, not Austrian, property.[94]

The Individual as an Alien

Movement

Entry and Stay. Austria has exempted citizens of most countries of the world from obtaining an entrance visa for entering Austria. On 17 June 1966 the administrative Court held that Article 31, Section 1, of the International Refugee Convention of 28 July 1951 prohibits the punishment of a refugee for illegal entry into Austria.[95] The rules on illegal entry are not otherwise obsolete.

In respect to the status of refugees, the Administrative Court in this same decision held it to be unsatisfactory that each Austrian authority determines for itself whom it considers to be a refugee. There is no instance that would establish a uniform recognition of the status of refugee and that would then allow the declaration of such status to be reviewed by the Administrative Court otherwise than, as in the case that was under consideration, on a case-by-case basis. (See below.)

Departure

Voluntary Departure. The Supreme Court has held it illegal to withhold the passport of a foreigner in order to compel him to pay a fine after a traffic accident.[96] Where the holder of a car presents the green car insurance card, his car may not be impounded if it is involved in an accident in Austria.[97]

Involuntary Departure: Expulsion and Deportation. A single unimportant infraction of the Passport Law does not justify expulsion.[98] There have been cases in which smuggling to the detriment of a foreign state has been held not to justify expulsion from Austria.[99] Recently, however, the Administrative Court has held in the opposite sense.[100] On 25 January 1965 the Administrative Court upheld the expulsion from Austria of a Belgian who was judged undesirable on account of having been sentenced by a Belgian court for bankruptcy and forgery of documents.[101] The court held that the Austrian authorities concerned were under no obligation to decide whether the Belgian judgment had been correctly adjudicated. The situation would be different, however, if the person concerned had been condemned abroad for an act not punishable in Austria, such as for interracial sexual relations.

The expulsion of a foreign smuggler was extended to his foreign wife and minor child so as not to leave them uncared for in Austria.[102]

On account of their administrative assimilation to Austria, South Tyroleans may not be expelled from Austria as a measure of punishment.[103]

Foreigners may be expelled from Austria for neo-Nazi statements.[104] An exiled Croatian living in Austria may be expelled from Austria to the Federal Republic of Germany after having been elected in the Federal Republic of Germany as an official of a foreign association intended to establish an independent Croatia.[105]

A refugee may be expelled from Austria, provided he or she is not expelled into the persecuting country.[106] A German whom

Austrian authorities wanted to expel on account of terrorist activities in the South Tyrol claimed that he could not be expelled into any of the countries neighboring Austria. Entry into Switzerland was forbidden to him, and prosecution had been instituted against him in the Federal Republic of Germany as well as in Italy. On account of his strong anticommunist opinions, he feared likewise that he might be persecuted in Czechoslovakia, Hungary, or Yugoslavia. The Administrative Court held that this fact could not constitute an obstacle to expulsion. He could leave by air to the country of his choice.[107]

Special Kinds of Protection. The Austro-U.S. Claims Settlement Agreement of 21 June 1947 and the Austro-U.S. pay-as-you-go agreement of 21 June 1947 are applied, among other ways, to damage caused to premises in Austria, regardless of the citizenship of the persons affected thereby.[108] Thus U.S. citizens were admitted as claimants under these agreements. In one case a U.S. citizen who was dissatisfied with the compensation offered to her by the Austrian authorities obtained additional compensation by appealing to the U.S. Court of Claims.[109]

NATIONAL IMPLEMENTATION OF INTERNATIONAL RIGHTS AND DUTIES

The Act of State Doctrine

In its decision of 22 December 1965, the Austrian Supreme Court held that the Austrian Courts have no jurisdiction to examine whether a foreign act of state is compatible with international law.[110] The courts would be obliged by virtue of the territoriality principle to accept the validity of the confiscation of an object situated inside the confiscating country, even if the confiscation were against international law. The Supreme Court did not mention any legal rule in laying down this particular interpretation of the Act of State doctrine, in a case of wood from a forest confiscated in Czechoslovakia and subsequently imported into Austria.[111]

On 13 May 1964 the Supreme Court held that in view of the opinion expressed in a document of the UN Secretariat of 7 April 1950, it may be doubtful whether the minority treaties of 1919 were still in force. In any event, if these treaties were to be superseded in Yugoslavia by subsequent Yugoslav law, the fact that such law would violate international law would not render it null and void.[112]

Implementation of Decisions of International Organizations

The federal structure of Austria is no obstacle to compliance with acts of international organizations, since under Article 16 of the Austrian federal constitution, all the legislative powers required to ensure compliance with Austrian treaty obligations pass to the federation if the legislative powers concerned are otherwise reserved to the Länder and if the latter fail to enact the legislation required. However, Article 18, Section 2, of the federal constitution drastically restricts the powers of parliament to delegate legislative powers to the executive. This prevents Austria from complying with the wishes of international organizations to facilitate compliance with their acts by means of enabling legislation authorizing the government to take the required measures by ordinance.

If self-executing, provisions of treaties establishing international organizations and the legislative acts and decisions of such organizations adopted pursuant to the powers granted in such a treaty are automatically part of the law of Austria. As such, the Constitutional Court may examine whether they are in conformity with the Austrian constitution.[113] Should this court find any such treaties unconstitutional, this does not free Austria from its obligations under them. Austria is bound either to reenact retroactively its ratification of the treaty concerned in a way compatible with its constitution,[114] which was the solution adopted when the Constitutional Court for formalistic reasons declared the European Convention of Human Rights unconstitutional,[115] or to compensate the citizens concerned for the violation of their constitutional rights. The Constitutional Court deemed it sufficient defense against the alleged arbitrariness of the decision to enlarge the airport at Salzburg, that the Austrian authorities had taken this decision in order to comply with an International Civil Aviation Organization (ICAO) plan for the enlargement of certain European airports.[116] Karl Zemanek quotes an Austrian statement that "without prejudice to the question of principle, whether Austria as a permanently neutral state Member of the United Nations is automatically bound by decisions of the Security Council."[117] Austria decided to cut off imports of Rhodesian tobacco, copper, and asbestos, the only items on the embargo list that had previously been imported by Austria from Rhodesia. Austria wants to decide this question on a case-by-case basis, weighing its obligation of UN membership against its obligation of permanent neutrality, of which all member-states of the

United Nations have been notified. Zemanek comments on this statement to the effect that the organization wielding power in Rhodesia does not qualify as state or as belligerent rebels; hence there exist no duties of neutrality. However, even if duties of neutrality exist, such rules may be incompatible with a ban on exports to a country engaged in war, but not with a ban on imports.

By a Federal Constitutional Law of 30 June 1965,[118] Austria took measures to facilitate placement of Austrian military personnel at the disposal of the United Nations. Among its other effects, this law extends the Austrian Law on discipline in the armed forces to acts by such military personnel abroad.[119]

I am not aware of any Austrian measures taken as a consequence of the termination of the mandate for Namibia (Southwest Africa).

In three decisions the Administrative Court has denied a person the status of refugee pursuant to Article 1F(c) of the convention relating to the status of refugees,[120] since the persons had committed acts contrary to the purposes and principles of the United Nations. Two decisions concerned a Swiss citizen, who, during World War II, had submitted to high Nazi officials proposals for a Nazi attack on Switzerland.[121] The third decision concerned an Italian citizen of German ethnic origin found guilty by an Austrian court of laying mines on South Tyrol. He protested against being denied refugee status, alleging that his acts were part of a fight for self-determination and thus for the purposes and principles of the United Nations. The Administrative Court rejected this plea, pointing to the fact that UN Resolutions had recommended a <u>peaceful</u> settlement of the South Tyrol controversy.[122] Incidentally, the court distinguished two types of terrorist activity within the context of decolonization. It held that such activities are compatible with the purposes and principles of the United Nations, but only as a last resource and only if the terrorist is acting in self-defense, exercising a right of resistance against an international delinquency, such as against the soldiers of a colonialist power. Attacks against persons not taking part in this struggle were said to be incompatible with the purposes and principles of the United Nations.

Procedures Relating to the Issue of Certificates or Suggestions of the Executive in Connection with Litigation in National Courts

According to Article 9, Section 3, of the Introductory Law to the Jurisdiction of Courts Law,[123] the Austrian courts, if in doubt whether a state or an individual enjoys diplomatic immunity, shall request a certificate from the Federal Minister of Justice. If the certificate of the minister is rendered upon the request of the court, it is binding on the court. However, if the minister submits such a certificate on his or her own initiative (probably upon the request of the foreign state or diplomat concerned), such an unasked-for certificate is not binding on the courts.[124]

On 27 March 1958 the Administrative Court dealt with the separation of powers problem involved in the administration's practice of issuing certificates concerning extraterritoriality. According to the Administrative Court, only the Supreme Court could in a specific case request the Constitutional Court to judge upon the question of whether the certificate involved in the case concerned would constitute undue interference with the activities of the court.[125] By a decision of 14 October 1970, rendered upon the request of the Supreme Court, the Constitutional Court held Article 9, Section 3 of the Introductory Law to the Jurisdiction of Courts Law to be unconstitutional on the grounds that the provision is contrary to the principle of separation of powers.[126] In a comment on this decision, former Austrian Minister of Justice Klecatsky reminds his successor to abrogate not only this provision, but also the nine other provisions in various fields of procedural law, bankruptcy law, and company law that bind the courts by such reciprocity certificates of the Federal Ministry of Justice.[127] In a book issued when Klecatsky was Minister, he had advocated leaving these matters to the decision of the courts.[128]

According to Article 7 of the Law of State Liability for Wrongful Acts of State Officials, Austrian courts may grant such rights to foreigners only if, upon request by the court, the Austrian Federal Chancellery certifies that the foreign state concerned grants similar treatment to Austrian citizens. The Austrian courts refused legal remedies against such a certificate where the certificate was addressed to the lawyer of the party concerned. The certificate was held not to constitute a decision but merely to give information.[129] Where the certificate was rendered upon request of the court, the Administrative Court in its decision of 24 February 1958 had nevertheless denied that such a certificate constitutes a "decision or official act."[130] Only decisions or official acts of the administrative authorities may be reviewed by the Administrative Court.

The Administrative Court, however, considered a certificate rendered by the Federal Ministry of Justice pursuant to Article 328, Paragraph 1, Number 4 of the German Code of Civil Procedure and to Article 24 of the Fourth Enabling Ordinance to the Marriage Law to be an act subject to review. By this certificate, which is binding on the courts, the ministry certifies that the legal requirements for the recognition of a foreign divorce have been fulfilled.[131] (See Chapter 9, on the Federal Republic of Germany.)

The fact that the Austrian police issued a person an identity paper pursuant to Article 27 of the International Refugee Convention, stating that the person is a refugee, is not binding on Austrian courts. The Austrian courts have to establish anew these facts for themselves.[132] (See above.)

Recognition

In Austria courts are not bound to obtain a certificate of the Ministry of Foreign Affairs concerning the existence or nonexistence of a state. Austrian courts did not hesitate to apply the law of the German Democratic Republic, even at a time when the latter was not recognized by Austria.[133] In a case concerning the entry into the service of a foreign state, the Administrative Court on 24 March 1954 spoke of the German Democratic Republic and of the Federal Republic of Germany as "the two German States,"[134] which even at that time, when the Hallstein doctrine was in full swing, did not lead to any protest by the Federal Republic of Germany. Such opinions of the courts are not held to engage the responsibility of Austria as a state. In another case, the Austrian Administrative Court held that an importer did not mislead the Austrian customs authorities when he stated that the imported goods came from "Germany."[135] The customs authorities erroneously assumed that the goods had been imported from the Federal Republic of Germany and had applied the lower tariff applicable to imports from the Federal Republic of Germany, although in reality the goods had come from the German Democratic Republic. The Administrative Court found that the use of the word "Germany" ought not to have misled the customs authorities, since this word nowadays is merely "a more or less specific historic and geographic conception"[136] but not a conception of public international or constitutional law that would allow one to ascertain whether the word is intended to refer to the Federal Republic of Germany or to the German Democratic Republic.

This liberty, thus left to the courts, has led to the advancement of some curious views. Thus, in a case decided by the Supreme Court on 21 March 1946, the appellants alleged that German citizens in Mecklenburg had become stateless as a result of the German defeat and of the fact that Mecklenburg was likely to be annexed by a foreign state. The Supreme Court, however, continued to apply German law to the divorce case between the German citizens concerned.[137] According to a decision by the Vienna Court of Appeals on 13 November 1948, the nonexistence of diplomatic relations between Austria and Israel does not free a claimant making an entry in the Austrian land register from the requirement that any document to be recorded therein, if established abroad before a notary public, shall be authenticated through diplomatic channels. The document concerned had been established before a notary public in Palestine on 13 December 1947 at a time when the state of Israel was neither de facto nor de jure. However, in this area, authentications were also carried out before the establishment of this state. At that time the area was under British sovereignty, and authentication was obtained through these channels.[138]

TREATIES AND THE INDIVIDUAL

Austria adheres to the World Bank Convention on the Settlement of International Investment Disputes. It has concluded numerous treaties of friendship, commerce, and consular rights, such as the Treaty of 19 June 1928 and Supplementary Agreement of 20 January 1931 with the United States.

For a list of the agreements for the payment of lump-sum compensation, see the appendix to this chapter. The list of reciprocal visa exemption agreements would be too long to establish. Austria adheres to the European Convention on Human Rights. Andreas Khol deems it inadvisable and superfluous for Austria to become a party to the UN covenants on human rights as well.[139]

By virtue of the Austro-German Property Treaty of 15 June 1957, Austria and the Federal Republic of Germany established an elaborate procedure concerning the settlement of claims arising from the seizure of German property in Austria for reparations purposes and the Austrian waiver of claims against Germany and German citizens. (See above.) Under this procedure an individual first had to bring his case to a conciliation committee consisting of high officials of both states. Nine-tenths of the cases were settled by this committee. If the committee did not reach an agreement, or if a party refused to follow the suggestions of the committee, the case could be brought before the competent ordinary Austrian or FRG court. This court, however, had to interrupt the case and obtain a binding opinion from an Austro-German Arbitral Tribunal on the interpretation of the treaty clauses concerned. Whether a lower court admitted or refused a suggestion by the parties to obtain such a binding opinion, the decision of the lower court had to be submitted by the appellate court to the Arbitral Tribunal for a binding opinion about whether or not the case actually came under the jurisdiction of the tribunal. The court, having requested a binding opinion, was bound to follow the views expressed therein. If a party considered the judgment rendered by the court under these conditions to be inequitable, the party concerned had a direct means of appeal to the Arbitral Tribunal, which then was empowered to reduce the burden imposed on the party for reasons of equity.[140]

In their decision on the waiver clauses of Article 23, Section 3, and of Article 24, Section 2, of the state treaty and on the lump-sum compensation agreements, the Austrian courts held, at least by implication, that there exists no direct right of the individual to compensation under general rules of international law. Hence Austria could waive such rights. (See the discussion on waiver above.)

On the nature of the rights granted to Austrians under Article 27, Section 2, of the state treaty obliging Austria to indemnify them for their property seized in Yugoslavia (see above), the Administrative Court held on 13 May 1964 that this provision contains elements of a treaty in favor of a third party, victims of expropriation, and of a constitutive recognition of indebtedness.[141]

The fact that Article 26, Section 1, of the state treaty provided for compensation of certain dispossessed owners does not oblige Austria to grant such a compensation as a claim under public law. A law adopted in execution of the obligation of Austria incurred under Article 26, Section 1, was held to grant such compensation constituting claims of a private law nature.[142]

The Austro-U.S. Dollar Bond Agreement of 21 November 1956 was an attempt to settle the payment of Austrian dollar bonds converted into German bonds after the occupation of Austria.[143] Under the German conversion law concerned, each bond holder had received a basic payment of 262 Reichsmarks, or $100. However, an additional "hardship allowance" of 116 Reichsmarks was provided for non-Jewish persons. The Austro-U.S. Dollar Bond Agreement provided that Austria should not issue substitute bonds to persons who had accepted payment for their dollar bonds by accepting the offer of the German authorities in July 1938. Persons who had accepted the payment of 262 Reichsmarks but had not qualified for the hardship allowance of 116 Reichsmarks applied to the Republic of Austria for substitute bonds, alleging that they had not received full payment. They wanted to obtain payment of the hardship allowance, at least. However, their claims were rejected. The words of the treaty applied. If the parties had wished to grant special treatment to persons who had not qualified for the hardship allowance they would have said so. These persons therefore were held to have no right to claim under the treaty. This was held to be justified in virtue of the rule <u>pacta sunt servanda</u>. The terms of the treaty must be interpreted as they stand, ruled the court, unless such obedience to the text of the treaty would lead to excessive results. This, however, was not the case here.[144]

According to Article 22 of the Austrian Bavarian Salt Mine Convention of 25 March 1957, consolidating an earlier convention of

18 March 1829, Bavaria granted the Austrian salt mine monopoly the right to mine salt under Bavarian territory from mine heads in Austria. As a counterpart, Austria is bound to offer employment in these salt mines to a certain number of inhabitants of bordering Bavarian villages.[145]

APPENDIX: LUMP-SUM COMPENSATION AGREEMENTS CONCLUDED BY AUSTRIA

This list was established by Richard Lillich with my assistance.

Austria-United States, 21 June 1947, 67 U.N.T.S. 89
Austria-Netherlands, 30 September 1959, 507 U.N.T.S. 111
Hungary-Austria, 31 October 1964, 605 U.N.T.S. 77
Hungary-Austria, 31 October 1964, 605 U.N.T.S. 63
Austria-Finland, 21 February 1966, 597 U.N.T.S. 273
Austria-Japan, 29 November 1966
France-Austria, Agreement of 18 July 1949 (still classified) and of 10 May 1965
Austria-Bulgaria, 2 May 1963, 535 U.N.T.S. 143
Austria-Romania, 3 July 1963, 588 U.N.T.S. 3
Austria-Hungary, 31 October 1964, 605 U.N.T.S. 3
Austria-Poland, 6 October 1970, [1974] BGBl. 74
Austria-Italy, 17 July 1971, [1973] BGBl. 635
Austria-Egypt, 18 December 1971, [1973] BGBl. 433
Austria-Czechoslovakia, 19 December 1974

NOTES

1. 213 U.N.T.S. 221.

2. European Court of Human Rights, decision of 16 July 1971, Ringeisen Case, ser. A, at 39, para. 94. See also Buergenthal and Kewenig, "Zum Begriff Civil Rights" in art. 6, abs. 5 der Europäischen Menschenrechtskonvention 13 Archiv des VR, 393 (1966/67). The Austrian Constitutional Court adopted the more restrictive view in its decision of 19 March 1968, 33 Sammlung (hereafter Slg.) No. 5684, at 151 (1968), denying that a right to an Austrian patent granted by public authorities could be a civil right.

3. 14 Slg. No. 1818, at 218 (1949), commented upon by Ermacora, Handbuch der Grundfreiheiten und der Menschenrechte, 119 (Vienna 1963), contra Pfeiffer, "Auswanderungsfreiheit," Juristische Blätter (hereafter Jur. Blätter), 421 ff. (1954).

4. 18 Slg. No. 2550, at 299 (1953).

5. [1955] Bundesgesetzblatt (hereafter BGBl.) 61; see also Weiler, Osterreichisches Pass-und Fremdenrecht (1956).

6. Goldemund-Ringhofer-Theuer, Das Osterreichische Staatsbürgerschaftsrecht 375 ff. (1969) and Manhardt, Das Internationale Familien-und Personenrecht Osterreichs, 220 ff. (1971).

7. 91 Journal du Droit International (hereafter Clunet) 138-39 (1964), and Supreme Court, 8 October 1968, 99 Clunet 649 (1972).

8. Supreme Court, 19 January 1949, 71 Jur. Blätter 394 (1949), 3 Osterreichische Juristenzeitung (hereafter O.J.Z.) 160, No. 197 (1949).

9. (FRG) 21 Federal Constitutional Court (hereafter BVerfG) 271, No. 36 (1967).

10. 33 Slg. No. 5777, at 484 (1960), 99 Clunet 650 (1972).

11. 24 Slg. No. 7585 (A), at 271 (1969), 99 Clunet 650 (1972).

12. 26 O.J.Z. 404, No. 224 (1971), 99 Clunet 654 (1972).

13. Supreme Court, 17 May 1972, 94 Jur. Blätter 623 (1972).

14. For discussion, see Goldemund-Ringhofer-Theuer, op. cit., at 315.

15. See text in UN Secretariat Legislative Series, Laws Concerning Nationality (ST/LEG/SER.B/4) 36 (New York 1954).

16. Administrative Court, 6 May 1970, 99 Clunet 651 (1972).

17. Law of 3 April 1919; Staatsgesetzblatt 209; and Art. 10 § 2 of the Austrian State Treaty of 15 May 1955, [1955] BGBl. 152, 217 U.N.T.S. 223.

18. 22 O.J.Z. 221, No. 91 (1967).

19. Art. 36 and Art. 235 of the old Austrian Penal Code. See Grassberger-Nowotny, The Austrian Penal Act, Vol. 12 of American Series of Foreign Penal Codes, Comparative Criminal Law Project (New York 1966).

20. [1949] BGBl. 276, Goldemund-Ringhofer-Theuer (1969), op. cit., at 315.

21. Administrative Court, 11 May 1960, 15 Slg. No. 5292 (A) (1960), 91 Clunet 136 (1964); Administrative Court, 30 June 1971, 27 O.J.Z. 219, No. 96 (1972).

22. Administrative Court, 25 November 1957, 12 Slg. No. 4484 (A), at 315 (1957), 12 O.J.Z. 335, No. 26 (1957), 24, I.L.R. 445, 86 Clunet 842-49 (1959); in re Ostritz (1957). The Austrian Citizenship Law of 15 July 1965, [1965] BGBl. 250, Goldemund-Ringhofer-Theuer, 1969, op. cit., at 37, clarifies this situation by providing that merely a voluntary acquisition of a foreign citizenship deprives an Austrian of his Austrian citizenship.

23. Administrative Court, 3 February 1955, 10 Slg. No. 3651 (A), at 103-04 (1955).

24. Supreme Court, 19 January 1966, 21 O.J.Z. 236, No. 187 (1966).

25. Goldemund-Ringhofer-Theuer, (1969), op. cit., at 347, 349.

26. Jur. Blätter 163-64 (1962), 91 Clunet 136-37 (1964).

27. Art. 36 and Art. 235 of the old Austrian penal code, see Grassberger-Nowotny, op. cit.; Supreme Court, 11 January 1972, 27 O.J.Z. 356, No. 196 (1972).

28. Supreme Court, 21 May 1968, 13 O.J.Z. 601 No. 375 (1968), 97 Clunet 360 (1970).

29. Art. 2 §2 of the Administrative Infractions Punishment Law.

30. Administrative Court, 9 May 1967, 23 Slg. No. 7142 (A), at 301 ff., 23 O.J.Z. 305 No. 110 (1968), 97 Clunet 348-49 (1970).

31. Administrative Court, 30 May 1969, 24 Slg. No. 7582 (A) 1969, 99 Clunet 647 (1972), Seidl-Hohenveldern, "A propos des nuisances dues aux aéroports limitrophes: le cas de Salzbourg et le traité austro allemand du 19 décembre 1967," 19 Ann. Fr. Dr. Int. 891 (1973), see also Federal Constitutional Law of 4 March 1964, [1964] BGBl. 51; von Grüningen, "Die österreichische Verfassungsnovelle über Staatsverträge vom 4 März 1964," 25 Zeitschrift für ausländisches öffentliches Recht und Völkerrecht (hereafter Z.a.ö.R.V.) 76 (1965), and Ohlinger, Der volkerrechtliche Vertrag im staatlichen Recht 338 (Vienna 1973). See also the reports on the FRG text discussed below.

32. Supreme Court, 13 May 1964, 86 Jur. Blätter 520 (1964), 19 O.J.Z. 462-63, No. 314 (1964), 94 Clunet 924 (1967).

33. [1949] BGBl. 20, as amended by [1959] BGBl. 38. See also the discussion below of the separation of powers problem in implementing the decisions of international organizations.

34. Supreme Court, 20 December 1968, 24 O.J.Z. 152-53, No. 93 (1969), 97 Clunet 347 (1970).

35. Administrative Court, 10 January 1951, Reference No. 2810/50/1.

36. Administrative Court, 6 February 1961, 16 Slg. No. 5849 (A), at 100-101.

37. The agreement with Czechoslovakia is No. 1479 of 13 Beilagen zu den Stenographischen Protokollen des Nationalrates GP (1974). The Charter is Res. No. 3281 (XXIX), 69 Am. J. Int'l. L. 484 (1975). See Seidl-Hohenveldern, "The 'Charter' of Economic Rights and Duties of States" in Studies in Honour of Giorgio Balladore-Pallieri (1975); Seidl-Hohenveldern, "Die 'Charta' der Wirtschaftlichen und Pflichten der Staaten," 21 Aubenwirtschaftsdienst 238-39 (1975).

38. Constitutional Court, 28 September 1967, 32 Slg. No. 5572, at 443 ff. (1967), 97 Clunet 338-39 (1970).

39. 31 Slg. No. 5379, at 635 (1966), 97 Clunet 357 (1970).

40. See Seidl-Hohenveldern, " The Valuation of Nationalized Property in Austria," in Lillich (ed.), The Valuation of Nationalized Property in International Law 78 (Charlottesville 1972).

41. See Seidl-Hohenveldern, Austrian-American Private International Law 42 (Dobbs Ferry, N.Y., 1963).

42. 33 Slg. No. 5838, at 750 (1968).

43. 5 Osterreichische Zeitschrift für öffentliches Recht (hereafter O.Z.O.R.) 563-64; Pokorny v. Republic of Austria (1952) 19 I.L.R. 459. See critique by Santner, "Amerikanische Besatzungsschäden aus der Zeit vor dem 1.7.1947 und ihre Wiedergutmachung," 74 Jur. Blätter 430 (1952). The settlement agreement is 67 U.N.T.S. 89.

44. Decision of 2 March 1950, quoted in 79 Clunet 581 (1952), accord Administrative Court, 4 April 1951, ibid., at 583.

45. Decision of 1 February 1951, (Bäcker v. Austrian Federal Treasury) I.L.R. 698 (1951), quoted in 79 Clunet 583, note 31 (1952).

46. 16 Slg. No. 2154, at 182 (1951); 16 Slg. No. 2201, at 305 (1951), Irresberger v. Republic of Austria (1951), 18 I.L.R. 9.

47. On these matters see Seidl-Hohenveldern, "Settlement of claims for damages arising out of the occupation of Austria," 79 Clunet 563 ff. (1952) and Seidl-Hohenveldern, "Relations of International Law to Internal Law in Austria," 49 Am. J. Int'l. L. 451 (1955).

48. Irresberger v. Republic of Austria (1953), 20 I.L.R. 433.

49. 27 Slg. No. 4213, at 281 (1962).

50. 27 September 1967, 97 Clunet 338 ff. (1970).

51. Decisions of 28 November 1968, 33 Slg. No. 5838, at 750 (1968), 99 Clunet 645 (1972), and of 5 December 1968, 33 Slg. No. 5848, at 793 (1968), 99 Clunet 645 (1972).

52. Seidl-Hohenveldern, op. cit., at 78.

53. See Burns H. Weston, International Claims: Post-war French Practice 48 (Syracuse 1971).

54. For example, see Art. 37 of the Austrian Distribution Law Concerning the Lump Sum Received by Bulgaria, [1964] BGBl. 129.

55. Treaty of 17 July 1971, [1973] BGBl. 635.

56. Law of 23 January 1973, [1973] BGBl. 636.

57. See the government memoranda to this treaty and this law, respectively Annexes No. 38 and 456 of Beilagen zu den stenographischen Protokollen des Nationalrates XIII GP, at 27 and 17.

58. Constitutional Court, 28 September 1967, 32 Slg. No. 5572, at 44 (1967).

59. Constitutional Court, 21 October 1975, 3 Europäische Grundrechte Zeitschrift 9 (1976).

60. Export Promotion Ordinance 1974, [1975] BGBl. 85.

61. 18 O.J.Z. 295, No. 210 (1963), 94 Clunet 914-17 (1967).

62. Austrian Hague Rules Case, Austrian Constitutional Court, 27 March 1952, 17 Slg. No. 2306, at 130-34 (1952), (1952) I.L.R. 626 ff., Administrative Court, 4 April 1951, ZL 500/51, 83 Jur. Blätter 349, No. A40 (1961), and 25 January 1951, ZL 2433/50, 73 Jur. Blätter 214, No. 17 (1951), and 9 January 1952, (1952) 19 I.L.R. 622 (1952) Austrian Supreme Court, 24 November 1950 (1950) 17 I.L.R. 424, quoted also in 79 Clunet 585, note 33 (1952).

63. [1955] BGBl. 152, 217 U.N.T.S. 223.

64. 40 I.L.R. 175 (1970).

65. [1962] BGBl. 195.

66. On the compensation provided under this law and its calculation, see Seidl-Hohenveldern, op. cit., at 72 ff., and Supreme Court, 29 October 1969, 99 Clunet 657 (1972).

67. Seidl-Hohenveldern, op. cit., at 78.

68. 25 O.J.Z. 151, No. 89 (1970); 99 Clunet 656 (1972).

69. Kreisky, written reply No. 319/A.B. submitted to the Nationalrat on 14 January 1971, 30th Session of the 12th Legislative Period in reply to Question No. 324/J submitted on 26 November 1970.

70. A reference to the statement may be found in my contribution to 65 Proceedings of the A.S.I.L. 337 (1971).

71. Austrian [1962] BGBl. No. 283, German [1962] BGBl. II 1041 (on background see Seidl-Hohenveldern, The Austro-German Arbitral Tribunal Established by Property Treaty of June 15, 1957, at 19-20. (Syracuse, N.Y. 1972).

72. 23 O.Z.O.R. 173-89 (1972). See Neuhold, "Das osterreichisch-deutsch Schiedsverfahren zur Auslegung des Art. 24 Abs. 2 des Finanz-und Ausgleichsvertrages 1961," 24 O.Z.O.R. 61 (1973). Mosler, "Das Osterreichisch Deutsche Schiedsgerichtsverfahren nach dem Finanz und Ausgleichsvertrag vom 27 November 1961," 32 Z.a.ö.R.V. 36 (1972), Seidl-Hohenveldern, "La sentence du Tribunal Austro-Allemand concernant la protection diplomatique," 18 Annuaire Français 323 (1972).

73. Supreme Court, 22 November 1961, 84 Jur. Blätter 260-61 (1962), 91 Clunet 128-29 (1964), 40 I.L.R. 184 (1970). To the same effect, Supreme Court, 7 February 1962, 3 Stanzl-Friedl, Handelsrechtliche Entscheidungen, 143 (13) (Vienna 1965), 94 Clunet 922-23 (1967), 17 O.J.Z. 69, No. 55 (1962), and Supreme Court, 21 December 1965, 22 O.J.Z. 65-66, No. 49 (1967), 95 Clunet 136-37 (1968).

74. See Binding Opinions No. 18, at 24, No. 25, at 31 and 40, No. 56, at 22; Seidl-Hohenveldern, The Austro-German Arbitral Tribunal, op. cit., at 125, 135-36, 171.

75. 27 Slg. No. 4213, at 280 (1962), 24 Clunet 920-23 (1967); 28 Slg. No. 4478, at 447 (1963), 91 Clunet 922-23 (1964).

76. To the same effect, Supreme Court, 12 January 1956, 40 I.L.R. 234 (1970).

77. 27 Slg. No. 4213, at 281 (1962).

78. 25 Slg. No. 3748, at 269 (1960), 91 Clunet 134-35 (1964).

79. Law of 3 April 1955. Austrian [1955] BGBl. 53, as amended by [1957] BGBl. 168.

80. 27 Slg. No. 4213, at 280-82 (1962), 94 Clunet 920-23 (1967).

81. 29 May 1967, 20 Neue Juristische Wochenschrift 1861 (1967 II).

82. See Seidl-Hohenveldern, "La Réparation des Dommages subis par les Nationaux à l'Etranger à la suite des Bouleversements Politiques: Comparaison des solutions françaises et allemandes," 21 Revue Internationale de Droit Comparé 774-75 (1969).

83. 23 O.J.Z. 209, No. 119 (1968), 97 Clunet 337 (1970).

84. 67 U.N.T.S. 99.

85. 13 Slg. No. 1701, at 254 (1948).

86. Decision of 28 June 1949, 14 Slg. No. 1813, at 206 (1949); decision of 16 November 1949, 4 Slg. No. 1092 (A), at 1033 (1949).

87. 4 Slg. No. 1092 (A), at 1039 (1949), and Appel, "Besatzungsrecht und Besatzungskosten in der US-Zone Osterreichs," 74 Jur. Blätter 313 (1952).

88. 40 I.L.R. 431 (1970), Der Staatsbürger, Folge 18, Supplement to "Salzburger Nachrichten," 1 September 1953.

89. Law of 3 April 1955. Austrian (1955) BGBl. 53, as amended by (1957) BGBl. 168.

90. 31 Slg. No. 5379, at 635 (1966), and No. 5382, at 643 (1966), 97 Clunet 357 (1970).

91. 32 Slg. No. 5565, at 421 (1967), 97 Clunet 340 (1970).

92. Chlorodent case, op. No. 1 of the Austro-German Arbitral Tribunal, established by the Austro-German Property Treaty of 1957, see Seidl-Hohenveldern, The Austro-German Arbitral Tribunal, op. cit., at 113.

93. [1962] BGBl. No. 195.

94. Supreme Court, 9 November 1966, 22 O.J.Z. 149, No. 128 (1967), 95 Clunet 139 (1968), Seidl-Hohenveldern, The Austro-German Arbitral Tribunal, op. cit., at 76.

95. 88 Jur. Blätter 632-33 (1966), 95 Clunet 148 ff. (1968).

96. Supreme Court, 23 November 1967, 90 Jur. Blätter 269 (1968), 97 Clunet 353 (1970).

97. Supreme Court, 6 May 1960, 15 O.J.Z. 402, No. 234 (1960).

98. Administrative Court, 4 November 1966, 90 Jur. Blätter 101 (1968), 97 Clunet 350-51 (1970).

99. Administrative Court, 8 March 1954, 9 Slg. No. 3340 (A) (1954), 84 Clunet 92-93 (1956).

100. 4 November 1966, 90 Jur. Blätter 101 (1968), 97 Clunet 350-51 (1970).

101. 20 Slg. No. 6559 (A), at 56 ff. (1965), 95 Clunet 152-53 (1968).

102. Administrative Court, 22 May 1963, 18 Slg. No. 6034 (A), at 477 (1963). Contrast this decision with the decision of the Münster Administrative Court of Appeals, 2 August 1960, quoted in the chapter on the Federal Republic of Germany.

103. Supreme Court, 11 April 1962, 17 O.J.Z. 439-40, No. 356 (1962), 91 Clunet 138-39 (1964).

104. Constitutional Court, 26 November 1965, 30 Slg. No. 5134, at 710 ff. (1965), 22 O.J.Z. 249 (1967), 95 Clunet 148 (1968).

105. Constitutional Court, 22 June 1962, 27 Slg. No. 4221, at 303 (1962), 91 Clunet 138-39 (1964), and Constitutional Court, 26 June 1962, 27 Slg. No. 4233, at 367 ff. (1962), 91 Clunet 932 (1964).

106. Supreme Court, 20 October 1958, 29 S. St. No. 61 (1958); to the same effect Supreme Court, 28 April 1961, 16 O.J.Z. 404, no. 315 (1961).

107. Decision of 16 December 1966, 22 O.J.Z. 414, No. 123 (1967), 95 Clunet 150-51 (1968).

108. 67 U.N.T.S. 89 and 67 U.N.T.S. 99, respectively.

109. See Seery v. United States, 127 F. Supp. 601 (Ct. Cl. 1955), 49 Am. J. Int'l. L. 410 (1955), adhered to 161 F. Supp. 395 (Ct. Cl. 1958), 53 Am. J. Int'l. L. 193 (1959) and Comments by Oliver, 49 Am. J. Int'l. L. 362 (1955); M. H. Cardozo, 49 Am. J. Int'l. L. 560-63, Sutherland 68 Harvard L. Rev. 1374 (1955), and Seidl-Hohenveldern, Austrian-American Private International Law, op. cit., at 91-92.

110. 21 O.J.Z. 204, No. 153 (1966).

111. The Supreme Court thus confirmed its earlier decision of 19 November 1958, 5 Aussenwirtschaftsdienst 129 (1959). Contra the recognition of acts of state violating rules of international law, see Seidl-Hohenveldern,

Völkerrechtwidrige Akte fremder Staaten vor innerstaatlichen Gerichten, Heymanns Verlag Festschrift, at 615-16 (Cologne 1965); "Expropriaciones des Estados Extranjeros y Tribunales Internos," Revista des Estudios Politicos 107-35 (1966), as well as in Seidl-Hohenveldern, "Confiscated Foreign Property and Public International Law," 56 Am. J. Int'l. L. 509 (1962).

112. 20 O.J.Z. 67, no. 44 (1965), 94 Clunet 926-27 (1967).

113. Seidl-Hohenveldern, "Probleme der Anerkennung ausländischer Devisenbewirtschaftungsmassnahmen," 8 O.Z.O.R. 92-93 (1957), "Relation of International Law to Internal Law in Austria," 49 Am. J. Int'l. L. 474 (1955); Ohlinger, op. cit., at 224.

114. Federal Constitutional Law of 4 March 1964, [1964] BGBl. 59. See also von Grüningen, op. cit., at 76; Ohlinger, op. cit., at 338.

115. Decision of 14 October 1961, 26 Slg. No. 4049 (1969). See Seidl-Hohenveldern, "Transformation or Adoption of International Law into Municipal Law," 12 Int'l. Comp. L.Q. 89, 106 (1963).

116. Decision of 10 October, 34 Slg. No. 6052, at 691 (1969); cf. Seidl-Hohenveldern, "A propos des nuisances dues aux aéroports limitrophes," op. cit., at 892.

117. Zemanek, The Problem of Participation of Permanently Neutral Austria in Sanction of the United Nations with Special Regard for the Case of Rhodesia, 28 Z.a.ö.R.V. 32 (1968), quoting from S/7795.

118. [1965] BGBl. 173.

119. Strasser, Osterreich und die Vereinigten Nationen 110-16 (Vienna 1967); Strasser, "The participation of national contingents in operations of international organizations," 34 Z.a.ö.R.V. 712 (1974) and Pernthaler Esterbauer, "Die Entsendung österreichischer Einheiten zur Hilfeleistung in das Ausland auf Ersuchen Internationaler Organisationen," 16 Jahrb. interna. Recht 8 (1973).

120. Convention of 28 July 1951, 189 U.N.T.S. 137.

121. Decisions of 16 December 1969, Ref. No. 876/69, and of 7 December 1971, Ref. No. 744/71. Both decisions are unreported. However, see Seidl-Hohenveldern, "Nichtanerkennung als Konventionsflüchtling wegen Handlungen gegen die Ziele und Grundsätze der VN," 22 Vereinte Nationen 107-108 (1974).

122. Decision of 16 May 1972, 27 Slg. No. 8235(A) (1972). See Seidl-Hohenveldern, "Nichtanerkennung als Konventionsflüchtling," op. cit., at 108-109, Seidl-Hohenveldern, "Kombattentenstatus für Terroristen?" 15 Neue Zeitschrift fur Wehrrecht 88 (1973); Alcook, The History of the South Tyrol Question 434-54 (London 1970).

123. See Seidl-Hohenveldern, Austrian-American Private International Law, op. cit., at 98, and Wahle, Ein neuer Zivilkommentar-Eine Buchbesprechung, 82 Jur. Blätter 35 (1960).

124. Supreme Court, 19 January 1962, 84 Jur. Blätter 271 (1962), 91 Clunet 144-45 (1964).

125. 3 Slg. No. 4615 (A), at 315 (1958), 86 Clunet 834 (1959).

126. 94 Jur. Blätter 37 (1972), 99 Clunet 650 (1972). To the same effect, Supreme Court, 28 April 1971, 101 Clunet 630 (1974).

127. Ibid., at 39.

128. Bundesministerium für Justiz, Gesamtreform der Justiz 122, note 14, and 125 (1970).

129. Constitutional Court, 27 September 1967, 32 Slg. No. 5556, at 395 (1967), 97 Clunet 364-65 (1970).

130. 13 Slg. No. 4575 (A), at 1958; 86 Clunet 834 (1959).

131. Administrative Court, 1 April 1954, 9 Slg. No. 3366 (A) at 228 ff. (1954) Seidl-Hohenveldern, "Non-Recognition of Reno Divorces," 4 Am. J. Comp. Law 245 ff. (1955).

132. Supreme Court, 3 February 1965, 20 O.J.Z. 347, No. 232 (1965), 94 Clunet 932-33 (1967).

133. Supreme Court, 3 April 1968, 23 O.J.Z. 488, No. 297 (1968), 97 Clunet 362-63 (1970).

134. 76 Jur. Blätter 599 (1954), 84 Clunet 668 (1957).

135. Administrative Court, 21 November 1962, in re Josef Delacher and Company, 17 Slg. No. 2745 (F), at 728 ff. (1962), 94 Clunet 912-15 (1967), 40 I.L.R. 5 (1970).

136. "ein mehr oder minder bestimmter historischer und geographischer Begriff."

137. 68 Jur. Blätter 185 (1946).

138. 4 O.J.Z. 21, No. 23 (1949).

139. Khol, Der Menschenrechtskatalog der Völkergemeinschaft 49 (Vienna 1968).

140. On this see Seidl-Hohenveldern, "Le Tribunal Arbitral institute par le traité austro-allemand du 15 juin 1957, portant règlement des Problèmes des biens," 15 Annuaire Français 1969 266-75, and my book on this Tribunal, Seidl-Hohenveldern, The Austro-German Arbitral Tribunal, op. cit.

141. 86 Jur Blätter 520 (1964), 95 Clunet 924-25 (1968).

142. Constitutional Court, 6 December 1963, 28 Slg. No. 4598, at 817 (1963).

143. 290 U.N.T.S. 181.

144. Supreme Restitution Commission, 17 February 1964. 19 O.J.Z. 353, No. 253 (1964), 94 Clunet 920, 921 (1967).

145. [1958] BGBl. 197; Günther Braun, Die volkerrechtliche Problematik des grenzüberschreitenden Bergwerkbetriebes 72 (thesis, Cologne 1967).

CHAPTER 3

BELGIUM

Michel Waelbroeck

THE INDIVIDUAL

The Individual as a National

Movement

Passports. A decree-law of 4 December 1939 still regulates the issuance and withdrawal of passports to Belgian nationals.[1] It provides that, subject to exceptions decided upon by the Minister of Foreign Affairs and Exterior Commerce, no one over 15 years of age may enter or depart from Belgium who does not hold a passport or document in lieu thereof. Passports are issued to Belgian nationals by the Minister of Foreign Affairs and Exterior Commerce; by an official appointed by him; or, in foreign countries, by Belgian diplomatic or consular agents. The minister may subject the issuance of passports to specified conditions and fix the duration of their validity.

A passport may be withdrawn by a decision of the Minister of Foreign Affairs and Exterior Commerce. The holder must be notified of the decision by registered mail and must return the passport within the period set forth in the decision to the authority specified therein. Failure to do so would subject the holder to an imprisonment of eight days to one year and/or a fine of 780 to 9,000 francs, or approximately $18 to $200. Any person who departs from Belgium or attempts to depart therefrom without a passport can be punished by imprisonment for eight days to one year and a fine of 780 to 30,000 francs, or approximately $18 to $680.

This paper is essentially as prepared in 1972. It was reviewed and somewhat revised by the author in 1974.

Although this decree, which is still in effect, seems to indicate that the minister has complete discretion in deciding whether to issue or to withdraw a passport to or from a given individual, in practice passports are granted as a matter of right. The only cases in which passports are denied are those in which the applicant is the object of a criminal prosecution or has been deprived of his or her freedom of movement by a judicial decision. It is generally recognized that, except in such cases, a decision to refuse to issue a passport or to withdraw a passport can be challenged before the Supreme Administrative Court on the ground that it constitutes a violation of Article 7 of the Constitution, which guarantees the right to individual freedom. However, according to information I have obtained from the Ministry of Foreign Affairs, no cases in which such an appeal has been brought are known to the ministry.

In recent years there have been several instances in which the minister has withdrawn passports from Belgian mercenaries engaged in operations in the Congo. According to information given by Pierre Harmel, Minister of Foreign Affairs, in reply to an oral question from a member of the House of Representatives, 137 passports had been withdrawn from mercenaries between October 30, 1961, and January 1, 1968.[2] It does not appear that this measure has always been very effective, if one may judge from the case of Jean Schramme, the leader of a group of mercenaries who led a revolt against the Mobuto government in the Kivu region. After Schramme returned to Belgium in April 1968, his passport was withdrawn. On June 10, 1968, he requested a passport to go to Brazil, where he said he intended to start a plantation. The passport was granted with the proviso that it was not valid for African countries. Nevertheless, Schramme apparently returned to the Congo under a false identity. In response to criticism, the government stressed that all Belgian citizens have a constitutional right to leave Belgium. Since Schramme was not under an order of arrest at the time the passport was granted, there was no reason why it should be refused. By specifically stating that the passport was not valid for African countries, the government claimed, adequate safeguards against a possible return of Schramme to the Congo had been provided.[3]

It must also be mentioned that, insofar as it provides that no Belgian national may leave Belgium without holding a valid passport, the decree-law of 4 December 1939 is no longer enforced. In order for a Belgian national to depart from Belgium, it is sufficient to hold an identity card. Since most other European countries do not require Belgians to hold a passport, a Belgian only needs a passport when he or she wishes to leave Belgium in order to go to a country that does not accept an identity card.

The need has been felt to amend the 1939 decree-law to adapt it to present practice. A draft bill was submitted to the Belgian Senate in 1966 that would abrogate the 1939 decree-law and provide that all Belgians have the right to leave their country except in cases of desertion or when they are under arrest or sentenced to prison. They could also obtain a passport to that effect.[4] Certain doubts have been voiced about whether the government should not continue to be entitled to refuse or withdraw a passport if its holder interferes in the domestic affairs of a foreign nation in violation of international law. This problem, which is exemplified by the Katanga mercenaries, reveals the difficulty of reconciling individual liberty with the duty of states to see to it that their nationals respect the rights of other states. To this day the draft bill has not been acted upon by either house of Parliament.

Departure. There are no restrictions of a general nature on the departure of citizens from Belgium, other than the requirement of obtaining a passport, to the extent that that requirement still applies. Of course, restrictions may be imposed in specific instances, such as during a criminal prosecution, or as a condition for liberation of a person before the expiration of a jail sentence. Restrictions may also arise indirectly, through the application of rules of a different nature. Thus, in a separation or divorce action, the court must decide which parent is to have custody of the children and how the visitation rights of the other parent are to be exercised. If the parent having custody leaves Belgium with the child and thereby makes it impossible for the other parent to exercise his or her visitation rights in the manner decided by the court, such parent commits a violation of Article 369 ff., last paragraph of the Penal Code, which provides for criminal penalties of eight days to one year of jail and/or a fine of 780 to 30,000 francs, or approximately $18 to $680.

During the Spanish Civil War, measures were taken to prevent the recruitment in Belgium of young men to serve in a foreign army. A law of 31 December 1936 punishes recruiters with imprisonment of eight days to six months.[5] A law of 23 June 1961 provides that recruitment of a minor child without the consent of the child's parents or guardian is punishable by one month to one year of jail and/or a fine of 30,000 to 300,000 francs, or approximately $680 to $6,800.[6] None of those provisions imposes any liability on the person recruited.

During the events of the Congo, an attempt was made to render the legislation more stringent. The government introduced a bill in 1965 "concerning services in an army or troup on the territory of the Democratic Republic of Congo."[7] This bill would have prohibited not only recruitment and all acts tending to provoke or to facilitate the recruitment of persons of non-Congolese nationality to serve in an army or troop in the Congo, but also the engagement, departure, or transit of the persons themselves. This bill was not adopted.

Return. Any person of Belgian nationality has the right to return to Belgium. No cases are known in which this right was denied.

Expulsion and Extradition. No Belgian national may be expelled from Belgium. This is a well-established rule of Belgian law.[8] It is also a well-established rule that a Belgian national may not be extradited.[9]

Protection

Extent of Freedom of Activity Abroad. Belgium is not among those states that try to give extraterritorial application to their laws and to regulate the conduct of their citizens abroad; nor does Belgium try to extend its control over foreign subsidiaries of Belgian companies. One instance in which this became apparent was the application given to the Security Council resolution of 20 November 1965 concerning the severance of all commercial relations with the Rhodesian government. The Minister of Foreign Affairs explicitly stated, in reply to a parliamentary question that the decisions taken by the Belgian government in compliance with the UN resolution only applied to physical and juridical persons established on Belgian territory and thereby subjected to Belgian legislation. "Subsidiaries of Belgian corporations established abroad are subject to the laws of the countries where they are established."[10] In a later reply to the same member of Parliament, who inquired about the activities of Belgian businessmen and the investments by Belgian firms in Greece after the 1967 coup d'état, the Minister of Foreign Affairs stated that "the Belgian Government has neither the right nor the possibility to control the activities of Belgian firms abroad."[11]

On the contrary, there have been cases in which the Belgian government and Belgian public opinion have gone against the exercise by other nations of extraterritorial jurisdiction. Thus Belgium has adopted a law prohibiting the supply of data and information concerning international maritime shipping to authorities of foreign states without the permission of the responsible minister.[12]

One specific instance in which there appears to have been some difficulties involved a Belgian subsidiary of a U.S. company specializing in the manufacture and sale of agricultural equipment. This firm had received from the Cuban government an order for 250 machines, plus spare parts, totaling 6 billion Belgian francs, or over $12 billion. The order had the support of the Belgian Office of

Foreign Commerce and of the official Export Insurance Agency. Since the majority of the directors of the subsidiary were U.S. nationals, the company was subject to the U.S. legislation concerning trade with Cuba by an order that had to be approved by the U.S. Treasury. The approval was withheld, and the board of directors decided to reject the order from Cuba. This decision caused considerable emotion in Belgian political circles, and several questions were put to the government about the attitude it would take in response to what was viewed as an inadmissible interference in domestic affairs. Foreign Minister Harmel replied cautiously, "The Belgian Government has explained the situation to the American authorities. Contacts are being pursued in view of finding a formula that would bring a satisfactory solution to this problem."[13] The present writer is not aware of the solution finally found.

The Rights to Diplomatic Protection and Compensation. The question whether a state has a duty to its citizens to exercise the right of diplomatic protection on their behalf is generally answered in the negative. The question was submitted to the Court of First Instance and the Court of Appeals of Brussels in the Manderlier case.[14] The action was brought by Manderlier for recovery of damages he had suffered from the action of the UN Emergency Force in Katanga. An agreement had been entered into between the Secretary-General of the United Nations and the Belgian government under which the United Nations was to pay the Belgian government $1.5 million, to be distributed by the Belgian government to the victims of the UN military action in proportion to the losses suffered by them. The plaintiff claimed that this amount was insufficient and asked the court to order the United Nations and the Belgian government to pay total compensation. To the extent that the claim was brought against the United Nations, both the court of first instance and the court of appeals rejected it on the basis of immunity from suit.[15] The action was also brought against the Belgian state, on the grounds that it had not adequately exercised its duty to protect its citizens. Here again the claim was rejected, both at first instance and on appeal, for the reason that, in the absence of an express undertaking to that effect, there exists no general obligation on the part of the state to exercise the right of diplomatic protection on behalf of its nationals. This solution is generally approved by Belgian authors.[16]

State Responsibility for Injury Induced by Its Own Conduct. Many Belgians suffered damage either to their persons or to their property after the accession of the Congo to independence. Although the Belgian state never acknowledged any responsibility for this damage, laws were enacted in order to provide compensation out of public funds for the victims. The enactment of these laws was based on the notion of "national solidarity," which had already been used to justify the laws passed after World War II to provide for indemnification of war damages.

As regards damage to persons, a law was passed on 6 August 1962 providing that Belgians, whether military or civil, who had suffered physical injury because of their participation in actions intended to protect, to save, or to evacuate endangered persons in the Congo after 1 July 1960, the date of Congolese independence, would receive a pension.[17] A later law, of 6 July 1964, provided for similar benefits for "passive" victims of the events that occurred in the Congo after independence. The acts giving rise to compensation were "(1) measures taken or facts accomplished by the de jure or de facto authorities of the territories covered by the law . . . and their agents" and "(2) military and police operations conducted by other authorities than those mentioned under (1)."[18]

As regards pecuniary damages, a law was passed on 14 April 1965 that provided for indemnification of "direct, material, and certain damages caused on the territory of the Democratic Republic of Congo to private tangible goods, whether movable or immovable" by acts giving rise to compensation under the law of 6 July 1964. Under Article 1, paragraph 2, subparagraph 2, any persons receiving compensation under the law waived all recourse against the Congolese government, other Congolese public authorities, or the United Nations with respect to any indemnification for the same damages caused by the same facts to goods of the same category.[19]

Waiver. Since according to the majority of authors and the bulk of the case law the Belgian state has no duty to grant diplomatic protection to its nationals, it is generally accepted that the state may refrain from prosecuting a claim against another state or an international organization under international law and that it may waive such a claim. The state may also agree to the payment of a lump-sum indemnity by the foreign state and waive all further claims against that state.

Numerous lump-sum settlements have been entered into by Belgium, on its own behalf and on behalf of the Grand Duchy of Luxembourg, most of them in connection with the nationalization of their interests by Eastern European countries.[20] Each agreement contains a clause whereby Belgium, or Belgium and Luxembourg, waive all claims concerning the effects of the nationalization that have arisen prior to the signing of the agreement. Special commissions set up under separate agreements between Belgium and Luxembourg are charged with the distribution of the indemnity to the individuals or corporations affected by the nationalization measures.[21] These commissions have the power to fix their own rules of procedure. Their decisions on the claims submitted to them are not subject to appeal but must be rendered upon the advice of the governments of Belgium and Luxembourg. The decisions are not published. It does not appear that grounds are given for the decisions adopted nor that an official record of them is kept.

The Individual as an Alien

Movement

Movement of aliens to Belgium is regulated by the law of 28 March 1952 on the policing of aliens. The basic principles enunciated in the law are further elaborated in a royal decree of 21 December 1965 on the conditions of entry, stay, and establishment of aliens in Belgium. Belgium is also party to a great number of international agreements dealing with movement of persons, the most important of which are the Benelux convention of 11 April 1960 on the transfer of control over persons to the external borders of the Benelux territory; the 25 March 1957 Treaty of Rome, instituting the European Economic Community (EEC); and the European Establishment Convention of 13 December 1955, which was adopted within the framework of the Council of Europe. As a result, the legal situation in Belgium in this area is rather complex.[22] I shall attempt to summarize it, however.

Entry and Stay. The entry of an alien into Belgium is subjected to the following conditions:

1. The alien must possess adequate means of living or have the possibility of acquiring such means by the lawful exercise of a lucrative activity. Such possibility is deemed to exist if the alien holds a work permit or a professional card.[23]

2. The alien must not be known as an Undesirable, which means, in practice, that the alien must not previously have been expelled from the country. (See below.)

3. The entry of the alien must not be considered as likely to jeopardize public tranquillity, public order, or the security of the country.

4. If the alien enters with the intention of staying less than three months, he or she must hold a valid passport and a transit or tourist visa. If the alien enters with the intention of staying more than three months, he or she must hold a valid passport and a temporary residence permit issued by the Belgian diplomatic or consular agent at the place of the alien's Belgian residence or stay.

Belgium has entered into a great number of bilateral agreements providing that, in the case of a stay of less than three months, nationals of the other contracting parties shall be exempted from the visa requirement. Many of these agreements also exempt the nationals concerned from the passport requirement and provide that presentation of an identity card shall be sufficient for admission to Belgium.[24]

These agreements do not exempt such nationals from the necessity of obtaining a temporary residence permit if they intend to remain in Belgium for more than three months. Since temporary residence permits may only be granted by Belgian diplomatic or consular agents abroad, the result is that if an alien who has remained in Belgium for three months wishes to extend his or her stay, the alien must leave the country and accomplish the formalities necessary to obtain the permit outside Belgium.

This requirement does not apply to nationals of other EEC member states. They may enter Belgium upon presentation of a passport or an identity card, even if they intend to stay longer than three months. The requirement that aliens must have sufficient means of living or the possibility of acquiring them is inapplicable to nationals of the Netherlands and Luxembourg.

Many aliens come to stay in Belgium without being aware that they are required to obtain residence permits before entering the country. In recent years the Minister of Justice, Alphons Vranckx, enforced the law with much vigor on this point, especially in regard to foreign students. This gave rise to much unrest in university circles during the winter of 1970-71.

In response to these reactions, a commission to study the condition of aliens in Belgium was instituted by a ministerial decree in 1971.[25] Its chairman was Henri Rolin, a former senator and an honorary professor of law of the University of Brussels. Its secretary was François Rigaux, a professor at the University of Louvain. On 24 February 1972 the commission delivered to the Minister of Justice the draft of a bill concerning access, stay, and establishment of aliens in Belgium.[26] If adopted, the draft will provide for a considerable improvement in the status of foreigners in Belgium.

All aliens except those staying at hotels for business or tourism for not more than three months per six-month period, must also register with the communal authority of the place of their stay within eight days after they enter Belgium. If no more than a three-month stay is intended, the communal authority delivers an "attestation d'immatriculation" certifying that the holder is entitled to remain in Belgium for the period indicated, which must be equal to the period of validity of the visa or, in case no visa is required, to three months. If more than a three-months stay is intended, the communal authority delivers a "certificat d'inscription au registre des étrangers," which is valid for one year and renewable thereafter.

If a stay of more than one year is contemplated, it is possible to apply for a "permis d'etablissement," which is delivered by the communal authority subject to the authorization of the Minister of Justice. The "permis d'établissement" is evidenced by a "carte d'identité pour étranger," which is valid for five years and renewable. This permit is usually granted when the presence of an alien has a certain degree of stability, such as when he or she has a work permit of unlimited duration, has already remained in Belgium for a continued period of five years, or is married to a Belgian. The "permis d'établissement" does not confer any special advantages with regard to the rights the alien enjoys during his or her stay; its principal effect is to confer on its holder certain procedural guarantees in case of expulsion. (See below.)

Nationals of other EEC countries are entitled to obtain an establishment permit automatically, unless reasons of public order, public security, or public health demand otherwise.

Instead of, or in addition to, obtaining an establishment permit, an alien may ask the King to authorize him to "establish a domicile" in Belgium according to Article 13 of the civil code. The granting of such an authorization is discretionary. Before a decision is taken, an investigation is conducted by the district attorney of the district in which the applicant resides, concerning such matters as the applicant's means of existence, reasons for settling in Belgium, property owned in Belgium and abroad, family and social relations and situation, and honor and morality. The effect of authorization is fully to assimilate the alien as a Belgian citizen insofar as the exercise of civil rights is concerned. This applies to the following rights, among others: (1) the right to institute legal proceedings without being required to furnish security for costs; (2) the right of successoral levy instituted by the law of 27 April 1965; and (3) the right to be a director of a professional union organized under the law of 31 March 1898.

According to the Conseil d'Etat, the requirement according to which all foreigners who exercise an independent lucrative activity in Belgium must hold a "professional card" is inapplicable to a foreigner who has been authorized to establish a domicile.[27] This decision has been criticized by Rigaux.[28]

In principle the above rights are reserved to Belgian citizens or to nationals of countries that have entered into reciprocity agreements with Belgium. Since Belgium has entered into reciprocity agreements with a large number of foreign countries concerning the exemption from the posting of security for costs, Article 13 has lost much of its significance in this regard.

Departure. No particular restrictions are imposed in case of voluntary departure. Involuntary or forceable departure may take place if the alien has entered Belgium without fulfilling the conditions described above. In such a case, an "order to take back to the border" may be issued against the alien by an official of the Ministry of Justice. Such an order does not prevent its addressee from entering Belgium later after having regularized his or her situation.

If the entry was regular but the alien did not comply with the conditions to which it was made subject, or if the Minister of Justice judges the presence of the alien as dangerous or likely to disturb public order, public safety, or the economy of the country, the Minister of Justice may "send back" the alien by decree.

If the alien has obtained an establishment permit from the Minister of Justice, he or she may be expelled by a royal decree if judged dangerous for the public order or the security of the country or if he or she is being prosecuted or has been convicted, whether in Belgium or abroad, for a felony or crime capable of giving rise to extradition. Thus the mere existence of a danger for the economy of the country is not sufficient to justify expulsion. If the expulsion is based on a political motive, the royal decree must be preceded by deliberation in the Council of Ministers.

The law does not provide for any obligation to give the alien a preliminary warning before a sending back or expulsion; however, such a warning is frequently given in practice. Normally the alien is not entitled to a hearing, but in a number of cases the decree may be taken only upon the advice of the Consultative Commission for Aliens, before which the alien must be heard. The opinion of the Consultative Commission is required if the proposed decree is directed against (1) a refugee or stateless person; (2) an EEC national; (3) a national of a country that has ratified the European Establishment Convention; (4) a person authorized by the King to establish a domicile in Belgium according to Article 13 of the Civil Code; and (5) a person who has special links with Belgium by reason of family status or length of stay.[29]

The Consultative Commission is composed of a judge, a practicing lawyer, and a person concerned or having been concerned with assistance to refugees. The first two members are appointed by the King for a term of three years, and the latter is selected by the alien from a list established every three years by royal decree. In the cases in which the Consultative Commission is called upon to give an opinion concerning the expulsion of an EEC national, the third member is an official of the Ministry of Foreign Affairs. The official explanation of this somewhat anomalous situation is that such officials are "specially competent in this area."[30] The opinion of the Consultative Commission is purely advisory.

The legality of refusing access to an alien or ordering that an alien be taken back to the border, driven out, or expelled from Belgium may be challenged before the Conseil d'Etat.[31] The Conseil d'Etat has refused to consider such decisions as "actes de gouvernement" not subject to review before it.[32] In the decisions it has rendered in this area, the Conseil d'Etat has developed the following rules for exercising its control over the government. It considers that it is not necessary that the decision should contain the full reasons of fact and law on which it is based, but that is sufficient if it indicates the general ground, such as danger to public order or public health. However, in order to be able to control the legality of the decision, it requires the defendant government to submit the full dossier and to give all pertinent information and explanations. If it finds that the decision was based on a misrepresentation of fact, that the facts could not reasonably be considered to justify the decision, or that the decision was based on a wrong interpretation of the law, the decision will be annulled.

The major drawback in the procedure before the Conseil d'Etat is that bringing an appeal does not suspend the applicability of the challenged decision. This constitutes a severe limitation on its utility, since several months are bound to elapse before the Conseil d'Etat decides the case, and in the meantime the appellant is obliged to leave the country. Several proposals have been made in order to empower the Conseil d'Etat to order a stay of execution in cases in which the execution of the challenged decision would cause an irreparable injury to the appellant.[33] The draft bill prepared by the commission to study the status of foreigners in Belgium provides for such a procedure.[34] As of the time of this writing, however, these proposals have not been adopted.

Protection. Except in cases in which it acts on behalf of another state not having diplomatic representation in a given country, Belgium never exercises the right of diplomatic protection on behalf of non-nationals.

NATIONAL IMPLEMENTATION OF INTERNATIONAL RIGHTS AND DUTIES

The Act of State Doctrine

Belgian courts have consistently applied the Act of State doctrine when measures taken by foreign governments have been challenged before them. The Cour de Cassation has decided on several occasions that it was not competent to control the validity or regularity of an extradition granted by a foreign state.[35] The same attitude was adopted by the Council d'Etat.[36]

The decisions concerning nationalization and expropriation measures taken by the Soviet Union, the satellite states, and Mexico follow the same line. In a judgment of 21 February 1939, the Civil Court in Antwerp stated that

> whereas the dispute . . . is the direct consequence of measures taken at the time by the Mexican State, acting as sovereign power, on its own territory, with respect to one of its subjects . . . concerning goods produced by Mexican soil and situated there;[37]

and whereas the legality of such measures is of no concern to

> Belgian public order and the legal disputes to which they may give rise . . . may not, under international law, be subjected to the authority of Belgian courts.[38]

Several decisions have also recognized the effectiveness of Soviet nationalization measures dissolving Russian companies.[39] However, Belgian courts have continually refused to acknowledge the effectiveness of nationalizations to the extent that property situated inside Belgium was concerned, on the grounds that such recognition would be contrary to Belgian public policy.[40]

The Brussels Court of Appeals rendered an interesting decision on 9 January 1968 concerning an action brought by a former official of the Colonial Service who had been discharged before the independence of the Congo by the colonial administration. He claimed that the discharge was illegal and that he had been deprived of the pension rights to which he was entitled. The Brussels Court refused to consider the legality of the discharge on the grounds that since "administrative acts performed by the Executive Power in the former Colony prior to this transfer," meaning the transfer of the exercise of sovereign powers from Belgium to the newly formed state, "must be considered as having, by reason of said transfer, been inserted in the legal order of the new state as of the date of independence, these acts are not subject to be reviewed by Belgian courts."[41]

It may be interesting to note in this context that the Belgian law of 19 May 1960 that established the new structure of the Congolese state conferred upon the Conseil d'Etat a transitory competence to pass on all appeals for annulment against acts of the future Congolese independent authorities, as long as a constitutional court was not organized in the Congo.[42] This transitory competence was suppressed by a Congolese law of 18 July 1963. Since the entry into force of this law, the Conseil d'Etat dismisses appeals brought before it against acts by the Congolese authorities.[43]

Belgian courts have never to my knowledge ruled on the validity of a foreign act of state under international law. The only control they have exercised has been limited to the effects of such acts on Belgian territory; the control has been exercised from the viewpoint of Belgian public policy and not that of international law.

Implementation of Decisions of International Organizations

In addition to being a member of a number of "traditional" international organizations, Belgium is a member of the European Communities. In view of the vast number of problems they raise and the extensive literature to which they have given rise,[44] it would exceed the scope of this paper to deal with the implementation and application of EEC regulations, directives, decisions, and other acts. I shall therefore limit myself to describing the manner in which the decisions of the so-called traditional international organizations are implemented.

In my opinion there is no fundamental difference between the manner in which traditional international treaties and the decisions of traditional international organizations are implemented in domestic law and the manner in which the EEC treaties and laws are implemented. The differences that do exist can be explained by the more elaborate development of EEC law and the more precise and coercive character of the obligations deriving therefrom, but not from a difference in nature between EEC law and international law. Therefore the solutions that have been developed in connection with EEC law can be applied, with the necessary changes, to international law and the decisions of international organizations.[45] One of the fundamental principles of interpretation that has been developed by the International Court of Justice and by the case law of the national courts with respect to the implementation of EEC law is that if a clear, precise, and unconditional obligation is imposed upon a state to act in a given manner, and if the state nevertheless adopts an act that is contrary to this obligation, any individual may invoke the existence of such obligation before a domestic court. The individual has three possible remedies.

1. If the violation by the state consists of an executive act, the individual may exercise a direct recourse to the Conseil d'Etat in order to have the act annulled.

2. If the violation consists of an act of a general nature, whether it is a statute voted by parliament or a regulation adopted by a governmental authority, and if the state attempts to apply this act to the individual, that individual may, by raising the "exception of illegality," request that the act not be applied to his or her case. This may be done before a civil, criminal, or administrative court.

3. If the violation has caused damage to the individual, he or she may bring an action for compensation before the civil court.

Thus, to the extent that the decision of an international organization imposes a clear and unconditional obligation upon the Belgian state, the individuals adversely affected by a legislative or administrative act in violation of such an obligation may avail themselves in the Belgian courts of the remedies described above against such act. There have been several examples of the successful exercise of such remedies in cases of violation of EEC law,[46] and there does not appear to be any reason to decide differently in the case of traditional international organizations.

It must be noted at this point that, by a judgment rendered on 27 May 1971, the Cour de Cassation has firmly established the principle according to which international treaties take precedence over national statutes, even over later statutes.[47] It does not seem doubtful that the court would apply the same principle to a decision of an international organization that is binding upon Belgium according to the charter of the organization, or that it would refuse to enforce a Belgian statute contravening such a decision. It is noteworthy that whereas the 27 May 1971 judgment involved a conflict between the EEC treaty and a later statute, the reasoning of the judgment is quite general and applies to all international treaties. The court thereby demonstrated its intention of regarding all treaties in the same way, without distinguishing between traditional treaties and EEC treaties.[48] It seems reasonable to assume that Belgian courts would follow the same line of reasoning with respect to decisions of international organizations and that they would decide that decisions imposing an obligation upon Belgium should have the same internal effects as decisions of the European Communities imposing similar obligations.

The situation is somewhat different with regard to decisions imposing obligations upon individuals. In the European Communities, only regulations and decisions may impose obligations directly upon individuals. In order to have such an effect, a regulation must be published in the Official Gazette of the European Communities,[49] and a decision must be notified to its addressee.[50] Traditional international organizations generally do not provide for the method of publication of their decisions nor for their notification directly to the individuals affected thereby. Such decisions are generally binding only upon the member countries, and it is up to the member countries to take appropriate steps to implement them among the individuals subject to their jurisdictions. Belgian practice and case law on this subject is described in the following sections.

ICAO Standards and Recommended Practices

The Cour de Cassation has held that the standards and recommended practices adopted by the International Civil Aviation Organization (ICAO) council can not restrict private property rights, such as by restricting the right to erect constructions of a certain height in the vicinity of airports, so long as these standards and practices have not been incorporated into Belgian legislation by Acts of Parliament.[51]

Rhine Navigation Commission Regulations

The regulations adopted from time to time by the Central Commission for Rhine Navigation are introduced into Belgian law by royal decree.[52] Such a method is appropriate to the extent that the regulations impose obligations upon individuals, since prior laws had already delegated to the executive branch the power to regulate the subject matter of the regulations.

World Health Regulations

The World Health Regulation adopted by the World Health Organization (WHO) assembly on 25 May 1951 was published in the Moniteur Belge, which is the collection of official legal texts.[53] Since such regulation does not directly impose obligations upon individuals, this form of introduction into Belgian law is to be considered appropriate.

Security Council Regulations Imposing Economic Sanctions

Article 2 of the law of 11 September 1962 authorizes the king "to regulate import, export, and transit of goods, among others, by the institution of a system of licences, . . . with a view to ensuring the performance of treaties, conventions, or arrangements pursuing economic aims or which relate to security, as well as (the performance) of decisions or recommendations of international or supranational organizations." According to Article 7, "when special circumstances so justify," the ministers authorized to this effect by the king may "suspend the validity or order the withdrawal of outstanding licences."

Pursuant to a UN Security Council resolution of 22 November 1965 imposing economic sanctions against Rhodesia, the Belgian government decided on 10 December 1965 that all imports and exports of goods to or from Rhodesia would be made subject to a license. The government also refused to issue any licenses for exporting arms, ammunition, war materials, or oil to Rhodesia, nor for importing sugar and tobacco from that country.[54] In February of 1966 Belgium decided to extend the import prohibition to all goods coming from Rhodesia except those imported under contracts entered into prior to 15 December 1965, for sugar, or 18 February 1966, for all other goods.[55] Instructions were given to the official export insurance agency, the Office National de Ducroire, to prevent it from insuring risks related to exports to Rhodesia of goods other than those the export of which had been prohibited. In April 1969, the government made the transit of all goods coming from or going to Rhodesia subject to a license.[56]

During the Biafran revolution it was realized that the conditions provided for in Article 2 of the law of 11 September 1962 were too narrow. On 11 July 1968 Foreign Minister Harmel declared in the Senate that the issuance of new licenses for export of arms to Nigeria had been suspended. He added, however, that under Article 7 of the law of 11 September 1962 the government did not have the authority to withdraw outstanding licenses if the conditions mentioned in Article 2 were not fulfilled. Since there had been no specific Security Council resolution dealing with the Biafran conflict, the withdrawal could not be justified as necessary to ensure "the performance of decisions or recommendations of international or supranational organizations."

Two days later, on 13 July 1968, a Sabena cargo aircraft crashed near Lagos, Nigeria. On board were 100 tons of arms destined for the Nigerian government. The public outcry that followed this incident prompted the government to submit to Parliament on 16 July 1968 a bill amending the law of 11 September 1962. Three days later, on 19 July, the law was enacted. It amends Article 2 so as to authorize the institution of a system of licenses when this is necessary "to ensure the observance of general principles of law and humanity recognised by civilized nations."[57] On 20 July 1968 a ministerial decree was adopted on the basis of the amended law to withdraw all export and transit licenses for arms and munitions to Nigeria.[58]

Procedures Related to the Issuance of Certificates or Suggestions

The procedure followed in many countries whereby the executive branch may issue a certificate to be used in court proceedings to determine questions such as the interpretation of a treaty, the recognition of a foreign state or government, or the granting of diplomatic immunity is unknown in Belgium. The courts have always decided such questions independently of any interference by the government. This has been regretted by many eminent authors,[59] but it is constant practice.

Just before World War I, the government attempted to convince the courts that they should follow the French practice of referring questions of interpretation of international treaties to the executive branch whenever the situation might have repercussions on the diplomatic level. However, the Belgian courts refused to follow this practice.[60]

Recognition and Nonrecognition

Although a number of older decisions attach paramount importance to recognition to determine whether the laws of a revolutionary government should be applied,[61] the modern trend is in favor of a less "political" and more "objective" approach. If a government effectively exercises its authority over a given territory, Belgian courts will recognize this effectiveness and will apply the laws enacted by the government in question to the situations they legitimately were intended to govern.

In 1935 Foreign Minister Paul Hymans made the following statement before the House of Representatives: "I incline to believe that where, in private law disputes, principles of international law dictate that foreign law should be applied, the legislation in force in Soviet Russia should be applied, except, of course, if it is contrary to Belgian public policy."[62] Since that time Belgian courts have followed this point of view.[63]

The judgment of the Brussels Court of First Instance of 24 November 1958 is particularly interesting in this respect.[64] It was rendered in a divorce proceeding between a Belgian plaintiff and a Chinese defendant. The defendant was living in Continental China. According to Belgian conflict-of-laws principles, the court had to inquire whether Chinese law permitted divorce. In so doing, it declared that it had to apply the law of Communist China and not of the Nationalist government. The following reasons are noteworthy:

> Whereas the thesis according to which a State exists legally vis-à-vis another State only if it has been recognized by it bases itself exclusively on principles of public international law, since such law specifies the conditions which a community must fulfill in order to constitute a State;

> Whereas the rules of private international law do not belong to this branch of law since they do not tend to safeguard the political interests of a State vis-à-vis other States (L. De Vos, Le problème des conflits de lois, 1947, p. 12);
>
> Whereas the object of private international law is to determine the proper law governing the rights and obligations of individuals;
>
> Whereas in passing from the national level to the international level, the essence of the civil law relationship to be governed is not altered;
>
> Whereas the adoption of a connecting rule, whether inspired by the necessities of a good social organization or whether it may be analyzed as constituting a manifestation of the fundamental respect for human persons in civilized societies, does not bring about an extension nor a narrowing down of the foreign State's sovereignty pursuant to an imaginary conflict of laws which would arise between it and the national sovereignty (R. Van der Elst, Conflits de lois et conflits de souveraineté, 1954);
>
> Whereas one may not disregard the fact that the People's Republic of China has been in existence for many years with its institutions, its legislation, its government and its territories, which extend to the quasi-totality of China. . . .

The judgment is interesting inasmuch as it affirms with clarity the principle of the autonomy of private international law in relation to public international law.

Two later decisions deal with the recognition of states, as distinct from recognition of governments. A judgment of the Commercial Court of Brussels of 15 February 1962, affirmed by the Court of Appeals of Brussels on 10 March 1964, refuses to apply an exchange control regulation adopted by the Katanga authorities for the reason, among others, that

> the existence of a State, in public international law, is dependent on the recognition made by other sovereign States; the defendant does not allege that one single State has effected such recognition, so that, as regards a foreign court, Katanga remains a province of the Republic of Congo and disposes only the powers conferred upon the provinces by the Fundamental Law of 19 May 1960.[65]

Another judgment of the Brussels Court of Appeals, of 20 January 1965, accepts the admissibility of an appeal brought by the government in exile of the Estado da India (Goa), notwithstanding the fact that the territory of that state had been annexed by India. The court declared

> that no legal consequences may be attributed to such an act of violence, as long as no international treaty is concluded; . . . that the recognition of such violence would be entirely contrary to the undertaking subscribed to by the Members of the United Nations (of which India and Portugal are a part) at the time of signing the Charter.[66]

As can be seen from these two cases, Belgian courts adopt the principle of effectivity when the question is whether the acts of an unrecognized government should be considered valid and given effect. However, when dealing with situations resulting from the creation of a new territorial entity or the annexation of one state by another, they still consider that recognition has an important role to play.

NOTES

1. Moniteur Belge (hereafter M.B.), 4-5 December 1939.
2. J. J. A. Salmon and M. Vincineau, "La pratique belge en matière de droit international," Revue belge de droit international (R.B.D.I.) 603 (1970).
3. R.B.D.I. 275-76 (1970).
4. Documents Parlementaires (hereafter Doc. Parl.), Chambre, 1965-66, no. 60, 1 February 1966.
5. M.B., 1 January 1957, at 2-3.
6. M.B., 7 July 1961, at 5577.
7. Doc. Parl., Chambre, 1964-65, no. 1005-1001, 15 March 1965.
8. The rule seems so evident to Belgian lawyers that it is seldom enunciated in a positive manner. See M. Verwilghen, "La condition des étrangers en Belgique," 30 Annales de droit (hereafter A.D.) 331, at 407-08 (1970); J. Verhoeven, "Droit du Benelux et de la Communauté européenne," 30 A.D. 331, 433 (1970). It is clear from the applicable legal texts that only foreigners may be denied access to Belgium or be expelled from it. See Law of 28 March 1952 on Police of Foreigners, M.B., 30-31 March 1952.
9. Réportoire pratique de droit belge, Extradition, no. 13.
10. J. J. A. Salmon and P. F. Smets, "La pratique belge en matière de droit international," R.B.D.I. 551 (1968).
11. J. J. A. Salmon and M. Vincineau, "La pratique belge en matière de droit international," R.B.D.I. 267 (1971).

12. Loi relative à la réglementation des transports maritimes, 27 March 1969, M.B., 17 June 1965.

13. Salmon and Vincineau, "La pratique belge," 1970, op. cit., at 348-50.

14. Civil Bruxelles, 11 May 1966, 81 Journal des tribunaux (hereafter J.T. 721 (1966); 1966 Pasicrisie belge (hereafter Pas.) (III) 103; confirmed by Appel Bruxelles, 15 September 1969, 1969 Pas. (II) 246.

15. The UN organization relied chiefly on Arts. 104 and 105 of the UN Charter and on Art. 2, §2, of the Convention on Privileges and Immunities of the United Nations.

16. J. Verhoeven, "Jurisprudence belge relative au droit international," R.B.D.I. 376 (1969); J. J. A. Salmon, "De quelques problèmes poses aux tribunaux belges par les actions des citoyens belges contre l'Organisation des Nations Unies en raison de faits survenus sur le territoire de la République Démocratique du Congo," 81 J.T. 713, 718-19 (1966).

17. J. J. A. Salmon and P. F. Smets, "La pratique belge en matière de droit international," R.B.D.I. 509 (1967).

18. Ibid.

19. M.B., 26 May 1965; Erratum, M.B., 1 June 1965.

20. See for example the agreements of 18 February 1949, 20 March 1950, and 12 April 1950 with France; 19 March 1947 and 13 September 1952 with Czechoslovakia; 1 February 1955 with Hungary; 15 April 1960 with Yugoslavia; 14 December 1963 with Poland; and 25 February 1965 with Bulgaria. The treaty between Belgium and the Federal Republic of Germany concerning compensation for victims of the war, signed in Brussels on 21 September 1962, should also be mentioned.

21. See for example the 14 January 1963 agreement between Belgium and the Grand Duchy of Luxembourg to ensure performance of the 14 November 1963 agreement with Poland. The agreement is described in Salmon and Smets, "La pratique belge," 1967, op. cit., at 528.

22. For an excellent description of the legal situation in Belgium, see the contributions by M. Verwilghen, J. Verhoeven, C. Huberlant, and M. De Kock in "La condition des étrangers en Belgique," 30 A.D. 33 ff. (1970).

23. A work permit is required if an alien wishes to exercise a lucrative activity in a salaried capacity. See Royal Decree no. 34, 20 July 1967. A professional card is required if an alien wishes to exercise a lucrative activity in an independent capacity. M.B. 19 February 1965.

24. A list of the countries with which such agreements have been concluded is to be found in 30 A.D. 605 (1970).

25. M.B., 22 May 1971.

26. The draft bill is analyzed and commented on in F. Rigaux, "Aspects actuels de la reforme des etrangers en Belgique," 87 J.T. 257 (1972).

27. Conseil d'Etat, 14 February 1956, Laane, Belge, 1957 Pas. (IV), 47.

28. F. Rigaux, Droit International Privé (Brussels 1968): 246.

29. M.B., 28 March 1952, amended 30 April 1964.

30. C. Huberlant, "Les garanties de procédure et de recours actuellement accordées aux étrangers," 30 A.D. 479, at 495 (1970).

31. H. Buch, "Les libertés individuelles dans la jurisprudence du Conseil d'Etat," 9 Travaux et conférences de la Faculté de droit de l'Université libre de Bruxelles 65, at 72 (1962); Verhoeven, "Jurisprudence belge," op. cit., at 690; R.B.D.I. 727 (1971); Huberlant, op. cit., at 505; M. Somerhausen, "La jurisprudence du Conseil d'Etat concernant les mesures d'eloignement des étrangers," 3 Miscellanea W. J. Ganshof van der Meersch 657 (Brussels 1972).

32. Conseil d'Etat, 19 May 1950; Bertholdi, no. 358, Garatti, no. 359, Saretto, no. 360, Recueil de la Jurisprudence du Droit Administratif et du Conseil d'Etat 202 (1950), with a note by Simonard; 1951 Pas. (IV) 4.

33. Huberlant, op. cit., at 518-20.

34. Rigaux, op. cit., at 262.

35. Cassation, 9 January 1911, Peeters, 1911 Pas. 78; 27 November 1967, Van den Branden, 1968 Pas. (I) 405.

36. Conseil d'Etat, 26 March 1969, Van den Branden, Recueil des arrêts et des avis du Conseil d'Etat (hereafter R.A.A.C.E.) 323 (1969).

37. Civil Antwerp, 21 February 1939, Propetrol, 1939 Belgique judiciaire 371 (1939), with a note by P. Wighy.

38. Ibid.

39. Commerce, Liège, 25 March 1938, Revue pratique des sociétés (hereafter R.P.S.) 220 (1939); 11 June 1938, R.P.S. 189 (1939).

40. In addition to the decisions cited in the preceding note, see Appel Bruxelles, 25 June 1947, 50 Clunet 864 (1950); J.T. 104 (1948); Appel Bruxelles, 14 October 1967, 1968 Pas. (II) 69.

41. Appel Bruxelles, 9 January 1968, 1968 Pas. (II) 136; 83 J.T. 129 (1968).

42. M.B. 19 May 1960, Art. 253.

43. Conseil d'Etat, 17 May 1968, 1968 Pas. (IV) 128; R.A.A.C.E. 398 (1968); R.J.D.A. 106 (1969).

44. See, among others, M. Waelbroeck, "The Application of E.E.C. Law by National Courts," 19 Stanford L. Rev. 1248 (1967).

45. I have elaborated this opinion more fully in M. Waelbroeck, "Effets internes des obligations internationales imposées à l'Etat," 2 Miscellanea W. J. Ganshof van der Meersch 573 (Brussels 1972).

46. Action for annulment: Conseil d'Etat, 7 October 1968, Corveleyn, 1969 Pas. (IV) 4. Setting aside a contrary provision of Belgian law, Cassation, 27 May 1971, 86 J.T. 471 (1971); 1971 Pas. (I) 886, with submissions by the Procurer General, W. J. Ganshof van der Weersch.

47. Cassation, 27 May 1971, op. cit.

48. Pescatore, Note under Cassation, 27 May 1971, 1971 Cahiers de droit européen 565, at 579-80; Salmon, "Le conflit entre le traité international et la loi interne en Belgique à la suite de l'aprêt rendu le 27 mai 1971 par la Cour de Cassation," 86 J.T. 500, at 533 (1971).

49. See for example, Art. 191, §1, of the EEC treaty.

50. See for example, Art. 191, §2, of the EEC treaty.

51. Cassation, 3 October 1957, 1958 Pas. (I) 88, with submissions by the Advocate General, P. Wahaux.

52. Institut Royal des Relations Internationales, Les conséquences d'ordre interne de la participation de la Belgique aux organisations internationales," 100 (Brussels 1964).

53. M.B., 11 October 1952.

54. 1965-66 Bulletin des questions et réponses (hereafter Bull. q.r.) no. 5, 28 December 1965.

55. Annales Parlementaires (hereafter Ann. parl.), Chambre, no. 84, 27 June 1967.

56. Ministerial Decree of 22 April 1969, M.B., 30 April 1969.

57. Law of 19 July 1968, M.B., 20 July 1968.

58. Ministerial Decree of 20 July 1968, M.B., 23 July 1968.

59. C. De Visscher, "Les gouvernements étrangers en justice," 1922 Revue de droit international et de législation comparée 300, at 331-32; J. Van Houtte, "L'interprétation judiciaire des traités internationaux," 2 Mélanges Mahain 372 (Paris 1935).

60. Civil Bruxelles, 21 June 1913, Revue de droit international privé 172 (1914).

61. Civil Bruxelles, 10 November 1923, 1924 Pas. (III) 54; 5 June 1925, 1926 Pas. (III) 131; 20 December 1930, 1931 Belgique judiciaire 182; Civil Liège, 21 March 1929, 1929 Belgique judiciaire 427, 428; Appel Liège, 20 February 1931, 1931 Pas. (II) 108.

62. Ann. Parl., Chambre, 29 January 1935, at 246.

63. Civil Bruxelles, 6 December 1934, 50 J.T. 156 (1935); Civil Anvers, 9 March 1935, Belgique judiciaire 600 (1935) Appel Bruxelles, 25 June 1947, op. cit.; Civil Bruxelles, 5 April 1951, 1952 Pas. (III) 40; 66 J.T. 688, with a note by M. Sluszny.

64. Civil Bruxelles, 24 November 1958, 74 J.T. 189 (1959), with a note by J. Ondel.

65. Jurisprudence commerciale de Bruxelles (hereafter J.C.B.) 103 (1962); J.C.B. 107 (1965).

66. 1966 Pas. (II) 19.

CHAPTER

4

CAMEROON

Joseph-Marie Bipoun-Woum

THE REASONS FOR AND THE IMPORTANCE OF THE PROBLEMS OF FREEDOM OF MOVEMENT AND RESIDENCE IN RELATIONS AMONG AFRICAN STATES

For essentially practical reasons, the ambit of this report has been restricted to Central Africa, as regards the examination of the juridical solutions applied to the problems of freedom of movement and right of residence. The territories that once belonged to French Equatorial Africa have, from their first years of independence, developed a special cooperation, due in part to historical accident, in part to ethnic ties, and of course the political good will of statesmen.[1]

As a result, in December 1964 an economic and commercial community was created: the Central African Customs and Economic Union (UDEAC) under the auspices of which the member states look for a solution to the question of freedom of movement and residence of their nationals in other member countries. In addition, these same states are members of the United Organization of Africa and Madagascar (OCAM), which includes most of the ex-French colonies south of the Sahara. Because of these factors, the search for a solution to the problems raised by the entry and exit of nationals among the member states has been a constant preoccupation.

Since I have been intimately involved with the work of OCAM experts regarding the legal aspects of the free movement of people

---

Originally written in French for the 1972 Bellagio Conference, this paper was translated in 1974 and reviewed and corrected by the author shortly thereafter.

and goods among the states of the organization, I have been able to gain an overall view not only of the solutions reached by OCAM but also of those of the states of Central Africa, both individually and as part of the Central African Customs and Economic Union.

However, although I thought that the introduction of solutions to the problems, whether being tried or only under consideration, would benefit from being confined within a strictly regional framework, the fact remained that the problem itself can validly be placed in the wider context of relations among the African states in general; it then becomes of interest to consider the juridical, social, and economic aspects of freedom of movement and right of residence in the perspective of cooperation among the less-developed countries.

THE LEGAL PERSPECTIVE: INDIVIDUAL RIGHTS AND STATE SOVEREIGNTY

The legal problem of free movement of people from one state to another raises the question of to what extent the domestic right of freedom of movement of citizens within the boundaries of their states, which constitutes one of their fundamental liberties, can be transposed into international law.[2] Insofar as this fundamental liberty may be restricted, like all other rights, by police and administrative authority under national law, by the same token, freedom of movement under international law may clash head-on with state sovereignty, since the international area is no more than a group of national areas, each of which is covered by different laws. Thus the problem of free movement of peoples and their right to reside in a land other than their own is perfectly applicable to the theme of this conference.

The most interesting aspect of the problem lies in the very strong pride that new states have in their sovereignty, at least in Africa. This can be demonstrated, if there is any need, by the doctrinal orientation and actions of the Organization for African Unity (OAU), which groups together all independent states in Africa except those ruled by whites, which follow a policy of racial discrimination against the black majorities.

In effect, if one analyzes the principles and aims stated by the OAU, it appears that the founders intended above all to create an instrument capable of protecting the state sovereignty of its member nations. They addressed much less thought to the idea of true regional integration, which would have resulted in a partial yielding of individual authority by each state. One of the aims of the OAU found in Article 2 of the Charter of Addis-Ababa is "the protection of the sovereignty, territorial integrity and independence" of member states. At the same time, prominent among the principles that, according to Article 3, should govern the actions of the OAU were "the sovereign equality of member states" and the "respect for the sovereignty and territorial integrity of each state and its inalienable right to an independent existence." (Emphasis added.)

My theory is that this bias of the organization toward consolidation of states in order to protect their individual existence is a very significant factor in the mechanics of present-day cooperation among African states. I have made a detailed and systematic study tracing the development of relations among African states, which includes legal, political, and sociological attitudes.[3]

The political character of African organizations helps to reinforce this tendency; thus it is that OCAM operates to ensure cooperation among its members "in the spirit of OAU."[4]

It follows from these principles that the African state system is one of protected sovereignty. This protection is guaranteed not by any kind of national force, but by the very real belief of the states in these principles. As a result, the member states in OAU have a common interest in ensuring that the rules of coexistence laid down by the Charter of the OAU are kept. The knowledge that all states will observe the same peaceful norms gives both small and new states the feeling of security necessary for them to concentrate on their own development.

However, this protection of state sovereignty, which has become the focal point of inter-African relations, has not been attained at the cost of individual rights within the nations. The legal protection of the individual, as much on the national as the international plane, does not involve any derogation from the principles of state sovereignty and equality.

As a general rule, the African states give no protection to movements that constitute, or could constitute, a danger to national development in their eyes. Certain countries for ideological reasons have banned the traditional chiefs, and all states are openly against tribes or ethnic groups. These latter receive neither official recognition nor any protection of the law, notwithstanding the principle of freedom of association. This policy is dictated only because of the uncertain foundations of African states and because of the need for a sense of nationality, which is indispensable if a society is to achieve homogeneity that includes people of differing ethnic backgrounds. The African laws are at least as liberal as those of other countries.

For example, the penal code of Cameroon severely punishes any "practice of minority cults"[5] and also "any outrage perpetrated against any race or religion to which many citizens or residents belong."[6] However, the laws protecting "goods" and peoples' "assets" are almost as liberal in approach as the French property law.[7]

In Africa, or at least in central Africa, the freedom of movement and the right of residence, insofar as they are exercises of individual rights, do not meet with any opposition that could be described as a deliberate attempt to thwart the exercise of individual rights and liberties. The high priority that African states give to the rights of individuals in international relations is known from other sources; our continent has suffered too much in the past, and indeed in the present, where these rights go unrecognized or violated.

A long time ago the Federal Republic of Cameroon decided to invest the 10th of December with particular emphasis by making it an annual public holiday in order to commemorate the Universal Declaration of Human Rights of 10 December 1948 in a worthy manner.

The restrictions on international mobility and residence that can be brought to bear in Africa are simply a normal expression of the African states in protecting their sovereignty, above all insofar as the notion of frontiers is an outward manifestation of such sovereignty. It was no accident that in July 1964, about a year after the creation of the OAU, the African heads of state met in Cairo and solemnly declared the principle of the inviolability of the frontiers inherited from colonial times. This is an essential preprequisite for the international protection of state sovereignty.

Leaving economic and political considerations apart for the moment, the legal problem of freedom of movement of people among nations is of special interest in that it brings into focus the convention's principle of inviolability of frontiers and the administrative limits in policing those frontiers.

The Economic Perspective: Protection of Labor and Attraction of International Investment

Two fundamental objectives govern the political outlook of the African states on the question of freedom of movement and right to residence: the protection of the national labor force against the influx of those from neighboring states and the encouragement of foreign capital to aid development. This second objective falls mainly into the framework of the relations of African states with industrialized nations, whereas the first is more current with relationships among the African states.

The protection of the national labor force is a little-acknowledged factor; however, it is often found to be the basis of the problem in question, particularly when there is an alleged inequality of education among the states concerned, and all the more where there is added the introduction of foreign investment, which generally leads to greatly increased employment opportunities, thus allowing for the establishment of large industrial or commercial enterprises in countries offering little in the way of professional expertise. It follows that many factors militate against equality of treatment in many fields among nationals of two or many countries.

In any case, concern for the social protection of a country's own nationals was one of the reasons for the veto in 1962 of an interesting project of the coordinational council that would have had the effect of conferring dual nationality by bilateral agreement on those who moved from one member state to another.[8]

On the other hand, African states openly welcome foreign investors. There is a natural insistence that this welcome be limited to investors coming from industrialized nations, which consequently limits it to capitalists, who are able to stimulate the financial aspect of economic growth of lesser developed countries. This restriction must not cause one to lose sight of the fact that, even in their reciprocal relations, African states have a tendency to encourage "foreign" investment; that is to say, much of the well-established African commerce is in states of which the investors are not nationals.

This is reflected in Article 9 of the General Convention of OCAM, which deals with freedom of movement and the right to residence, which will be discussed in greater detail later in this chapter in connection with the right of investment, which is regarded as a civil right in the same sense as the right of possession.

Investments of non-African origin, especially among the nations of one region of Africa, enjoy a very special position. The most characteristic aspect of this, and also doubtless the most internationally known, is demonstrated by the legal arrangements covering foreign investments.

The African states of French extraction have investment codes, the avowed purpose of which is to attract external capital. These codes give multiple guarantees that have the effect of minimizing as far as possible the risks to which international investments in new countries are unavoidably exposed. A Cameroonian economist has recently done an overall survey of this important question.[9]

By means of these liberal legal provisions, the ex-French African states, particularly those of Central Africa, are amenable to investments from foreign countries apart from those comprising the Common Market, with which there are special ties set up by a Convention of Association.

Finally, it is important to remember at this point that the majority of African states had no difficulty in either signing or ratifying the Convention of 18 March 1965 under the aegis of the International Bank for Reconstruction and Development, which provided for the peaceful settlement of disputes between states and private investors coming from other states. Our view is that as a result of this liberal attitude the African countries show that they have a very open approach to relations between states and individuals in the international field because this convention, like all other similar initiatives of the World Bank, is based on the premise of an individual right to private international investment. This in turn is a transference of the right of ownership under liberal states' legal systems into the international plane.

This brief analysis of the problems and agreements affecting freedom of movement and residence among the Central African countries shows that there are complex difficulties attendant upon a convention that would be acceptable to all ex-French colonies. However, continual attempts are being made that may be clarified by outlining the Cameroonian national legislation regarding the right to residence and freedom of movement.

CAMEROONIAN LAWS CONCERING THOSE ENTERING AND LEAVING CAMEROON

It is obvious that international law is concerned with the position of aliens, since it is they who lead to arrangements among states on the basis of reciprocity. However, the fate of those who leave Cameroon under national law is relevant to the central theme of this book because, as already stated in the introduction to this report, the individual's right to come and go as he pleases is not settled.[10]

The Departure of Nationals

Any Cameroonian is free to leave and reenter the country as he or she wishes. The right is limited by the public authorities because of two very reasonable factors. On the one hand, the state wishes to ensure that the national will return in such a manner that the state will not be required to pay the cost of such return. On the other hand, nationals ought not to be exempted from customs control at the frontiers. Therefore a deposit must be paid by the interested national when he or she applies for an exit visa, which is actually under the control of the border police. Normally the visa must be placed in a passport for it to be valid. Also, in conformity with international sanitary arrangements, Cameroonian legislation requires international vaccination certificates, depending of course on the destination of the traveler.

It would appear that in Cameroonian legislation the prevailing concern is the repatriation of departing nationals. An obligatory visa is waived for the benefit of state officials or others on foreign missions who have material reasons for failing to request a visa. Also, a national may leave the country without a passport as long as he has a "travel title," coupled with a safe-conduct pass stamped with an exit visa.

The same concern allows the authorities at police headquarters to dispense with the deposit of an exit payment, and in general they do so where there is an apparent intention to return, such as for people with business interests in the country or wives rejoining or accompanying their husbands abroad.

As far as I know Cameroon does not avail itself of the state power to dictate the countries to which its nationals may travel by limiting the validity of their passports. These are normally made valid for "all countries," thereby demonstrating an open-minded attitude about international relations.

Aliens' Entry Permits and Rights of Residence

Until 1967 the legislation governing entry permits and residence of aliens was somewhat restrictive, dating from the colonial era (Decree of 7 October 1930). However, the developing tourist trade and the need for foreign help in economic development called for less restrictive laws, and these were introduced by order number SO/CAB/PR of 6 April 1967. The most important reform, and the most interesting one for aliens, lies in the removal of the requirement for an entry visa, which used to have to be obtained at Cameroonian embassies or consulates abroad by all those wishing to visit the Cameroons.

This entry visa has been replaced by an entry permit granted by the national police force to would-be visitors who have satisfied certain prior requirements, which vary in accordance with categories of aliens.

By the provisions of the order of 6 April 1967, "foreigners" wishing to enter Cameroon are divided into three categories: residents, temporary visitors, and tourists. Residents are aliens who are authorized to remain in Cameroon for a period in excess of three months for professional reasons.

Conditions of Admission

An employer (the head of a company or director of an organization) who wants to employ foreign technicians must send a complete dossier to the central immigration-emigration office of the National Police Headquarters in Yaounde, detailing the following:

1. A request that an entry and residence permit be issued to the employee or agent; the members of the family of the employee or agent; and the people who will be under the employee or agent;

2. A contract of employment covering the period for which the request has been made, duly stamped and authorized by the national labor and employment office;

3. A repatriation allowance note for the employee or agent, the members of the family of the employee or agent, and eventually for his or her subordinates. In every case this note is required only for the employee or agent and the members of his or her family if the employing society does not have a general dispensation from such payments.

4. A reference form modeled on the form issued by the police headquarters, duly completed, dated, and signed by the employee or agent.

The residence permit is made out by the police headquarters to the employer, who must then send it to the employee or agent. This residence permit, which validates the entry visa to Cameroon, exempts the employee or agent from having to obtain a visa from a Cameroonian embassy or consulate abroad.

It should be noted that these provisions do not take the place of those listed previously but complement them. To put it another way, requests for visas deposited with Cameroonian embassies or consulates abroad will still be taken into consideration.

Visitors

Foreigners staying in Cameroon for a period not exceeding three months for a legitimate reason such as family visits or technical, commercial, educational, or cultural missions will be regarded as "visitors." An employer may ask a person interested in employment with his or her company to come as a visitor in either a professional or a private capacity.

The conditions of entry for visitors include a request for a temporary visitor's permit addressed to the general administration at police headquarters. This is a form along the lines set forth by the police. It must be duly completed, dated, and signed by the visitor and counterstamped by the competent authorities in the visitor's place of residence.

By the terms of the decree, visitors to Cameroon must not engage in any paid work during their stay. They are also precluded from making any arrangements for a definite stay, regardless of motive.

Any aliens coming to Cameroon on an organized visit around the country are regarded as tourists. They stay for a short time, which is not to exceed ten days, although in actual fact foreign tourists may apply for an extended tourist visa that allows them to stay for one month.[11]

In contrast to residents and visitors, tourists arriving at the borders without having a permit to stay must produce the following documents: a valid national passport or other travel document; a return ticket or a ticket for onward travel; and if they are traveling by car, a log book. Aliens who enter Cameroon under these provisions may not ask for either a temporary or permanent visa to stay, whatever the reasons may be.

Insofar as the extension of a tourist visa is concerned, it may be granted, depending on the circumstances, by the customs officials or the branch officers of the police force. As a general rule the extension is merely a formality and is free. In no case may the tourist visa be issued for more than one month.

Finally, with the exception of those who have exemption under the terms of international conventions, aliens of whatever category who enter Cameroon must show a certain number of documents, depending on their category.

A resident must produce a valid passport or other valid document; a permit to enter and stay issued by the administrative branch of police headquarters and a valid entry visa; and international certificates of vaccination against smallpox issued within the preceding three years, together with a vaccination against malaria issued within the preceding ten years. Insofar as the "repatriation guarantee" is concerned, a reference to it will be on the permit to stay. The permit will only be issued if a prior repatration guarantee has been made.

A temporary visitor must produce a valid passport or other travel document; an authorization to enter and stay temporarily, issued by the general administration of police headquarters, validating the entry visa; a repatriation guarantee, which may take the form of a return ticket; and international vaccination certificates against smallpox issued within the previous ten years.

A tourist must produce a valid passport or other travel document; a return or continuing ticket carrying a definite return date no later than the end of the maximum allowable time of staying; and if traveling by car, a log book.

As has been seen, the essential prerequisite to admission to Cameroon is a valid passport or travel document. This document must be visaed, the type of visa differing according to the length of stay, or it must be accompanied by a permit to enter and stay.

There are, however, exceptions to this rule, and people in certain categories are allowed to enter without producing a travel document or visa. These are the following:

1. Members of a ship or airplane crew, who may stay in the port of entry for the time they are docked or waiting to fly out again. They are covered by the ship's papers, under Articles 32 and 33 of the Chicago Convention, or by the Seaman's book. When such persons arrive by other transportation to join their plane or ship, their permits to enter are covered by the same documents.

2. Passengers on a plane making a stop to refuel. This stop is very short. Since the passengers do not leave the airport, no formalities are needed. However, if for any unforeseen reason this kind of stay has to be prolonged, then the passengers and crew are subject to the same requirements as other people coming into Cameroon. In the case of a stopover for a night or a short stopover caused by a malfunction of the plane or slight damage to the carrier, the passengers and crew would be allowed to leave the airport and go to the nearest town, provided they stayed within the town limits. Since they would be leaving by the same carrier, at the time of departure a "general declaration" and a "passenger manifest" would be given to the customs control, who would satisfy himself or herself about the identity of the passengers and crew by looking at the travel documents or identity cards shown.

This rule does not seem to have an equivalent counterpart with ships that have to dock for repairs or because their cargo is deteriorating. If the passengers are allowed to go into the town (on visits or outings), they must return to their ship in between times for lodging purposes.

In case of a long stopover, when major malfunctioning necessitates lengthy repair to a plane or a ship, the passengers and crew members leave by another plane, by ship, or by road transport. They are considered as regular transit passengers and must comply with the same formalities. The immigration service at the customs port will give transit visas to passengers continuing their travel in this case.

THE CONVENTIONAL LAW GOVERNING FREEDOM OF MOVEMENT AND RESIDENCE OF PEOPLE IN THE CENTRAL AFRICAN STATES

The juridical regime covering circulation of people among the Central African states has the common traits. OCAM adopted a general convention covering people and conditions of residence in the member states. This consists of a convention signed 8 September

1961 under the auspices of the old Union of Africa and Madagascar (UAM), to which OCAM succeeded in 1966. It became an OCAM convention as a result of a general resolution at a conference of heads of state, which decided to keep in force in the new organization instruments concluded under UAM.[12] Therefore this convention is still in force, at least among the states that have ratified it.

In fact, this convention is only applied sparingly. Some states hardly apply it at all, while others make great efforts to honor the provisions as far as possible, at least in spirit. This lack of effectiveness is perhaps attributable to the fact that the authors of the convention wanted to go a long way toward the assimilation of the civil and economic rights of those leaving member states with those of the nationals of the states into which they were entering.

For whatever reasons, some states have let the provisions lapse and wonder if there is a way to alleviate the faults or the insufficiencies of this convention either by adopting it, by bilateral agreements, by regional agreements, or by regional agreements confined to states bordering on each other. Cameroon, the Congo, the Republic of Central Africa, and Gabon, which are all members of OCAM, seem to favor this last alternative, for which they have been trying to work out an acceptable format under the auspices of UDEAC since 1970.

A pilot convention has been worked out, which has not yet become firm law but which nevertheless shows the feelings of the Central African States in regard to freedom of movement internationally and the right to reside within the framework of regional agreement. We will briefly outline the trends of these two documents.

The authors of the general convention of OCAM relating to the position of people and conditions of residence seem to have envisaged an almost complete assimilation of aliens and nationals among the member states. Certain articles limit this goal, but they do not substantially alter the somewhat unrealistic aims of the convention.

The principle of assimilation of aliens with nationals flows from the idea of equality of treatment and rights enunciated in Article 2 of the convention. This article states that the nationals of the country of one of the high contracting parties may freely enter the country of any other high contracting party for the purpose of travel or residence and may leave subject only to the same restrictions as that country's own nationals.

Article 3 of the convention also gives aliens the right to enjoy "the same rights and freedoms as the nationals," particularly those laid out in the Universal Declaration of Human Rights.

The articles relating to civil and economic rights are even more explicit. Hence by the terms of Article 9,

> the people leaving the territory of any one of the high contracting parties will benefit on the territory of any other high contracting party, from the same treatment as their own nationals insofar as civil rights are concerned, especially the right to invest capital, to acquire, own, manage, or rent all corporeal and incorporeal hereditaments, all rights and interests and the right of enjoyment or disposition thereof.

Article 11 forbids any discrimination in fiscal matters between nationals and nonnational residents where the latter are nationals of one of the contracting states. This prohibition protects both their physical and moral rights.

The equality extends also the rights of representation and of defense. In the articles of the convention, aliens are represented in the same way as nationals in the consular assembly and in organizations representing business interests. Moreover, they are guaranteed "free access to the courts in order to uphold and defend their rights."

Last but not least, the convention protects foreigners from eviction or unjust or discriminatory expropriation. "Each of the signatory states undertakes not to take any measures against the goods, rights and legally held interests of foreigners in their country which they would not take against their own nationals."

By Articles 10 (2) and 10 (3) any measures so taken by one signatory state against the nationals of another signatory state residing in their territory must be accompanied by the payment of a fair indemnity.

It seems true, therefore, to state that the dominating ideal in the OCAM convention is one of assimilating aliens and nationals among the signatory states. It would almost go so far as to create OCAM citizens, if certain restrictive articles did not limit the ambit of the provisions. These restrictive clauses concern political rights, expulsion, and some safety measures to protect the economy of member states against a rigid application of the principles when a state finds itself in difficulties.

Although as noted above, Article 2 of the convention sets out the principle of assimilation and equality of treatment, it also includes an exception covering "political rights."

In contrast to the rights guaranteed to foreign nationals, the text of the convention casts no light on what should be considered political rights. This omission could perhaps, in some cases, be attributed to an oversight, all the more so when it is noted that Article 4 permits the nationals of each member state to be employed in the government of another state as far as the legal provisions of the latter allow. This provision gives rise to problems of interpretation because if it were followed to its logical conclusion, aliens employed in government would enjoy the political rights attendant on their positions while at the same time being excluded from those rights by the fact that they were foreign.

The exclusion of political rights must therefore be narrowly construed as encompassing only voting rights, the contest for power or other exercise of national sovereignty, creation or open support of political parties, election to or eligibility for political assemblies, and participation in referendums or in the functioning of other constituent bodies.

The second factor limiting complete assimilation is that aliens living in another member state have no guarantee against being expelled from the country by the host state.

Article 5 of the convention clearly states that the rights and liberties allowed to foreigners cannot be considered to abrogate the sovereign right of each government to expel the members of another state. The African states are merely applying the traditional principles of international law, which allow governments to expel persons deemed to be "undesirable aliens" at their discretion. In addition, the expression "sovereign right" shows that such an act of expulsion would be an expression of sovereign will rather than of discretionary power, which would make it more subject to juridical control in the context in which it is exercised.

Given these conditions, one may well ask just how effective the provisions are that are drawn up to protect aliens who are expelled. The same article states that as soon as expulsion measures are taken they must immediately be notified to the government of the state whose national the person expelled is, and in addition the expulsion must be shown to be decided on an individual basis by the head of the government.

Finally, the expelling state must, under the provisions of the convention, "take all appropriate measures to safeguard the property and interests of the person expelled." The UDEAC draft convention has incorporated the OCAM provisions regarding expulsion.

Expulsion provisions are of very great interest because African states, including Central African states, resort to this measure fairly frequently. This constitutes one of the greatest stumbling blocks to agreement on freedom of movement and the right to residence. It even hinders increased cooperation in other fields. For example, it has been used to expel foreign students who were on a state's territory not only by virtue of their right to reside there but also because universities are more or less international institutions, a fact reflected in the make-up of their enrollments.

The governmental right to expel people, especially when not subject to other considerations, is also a grave limitation on the principle of equality of treatment of nationals and aliens in interstate relations.

Finally, a clause added to the convention by Resolution No. 17/ACS of 28 January 1969 at the Conference of Heads of States and Governments of OCAM allows a state to derogate from the principle of assimilation if the economic and social position of that country so dictates, insofar as industrial or agricultural development are concerned, as well as the needs of the fields of commerce, of artisans, or of those in the liberal arts professions.

To sum up, the OCAM convention remains strongly influenced by the idea of assimilation and equality of treatment and includes a vague definition of aliens that is unconnected to the reasons for their international travel or foreign residence. In this aspect it is undoubtedly less realistic than the UDEAC Convention.

THE DRAFT CONVENTION ON FREEDOM OF MOVEMENT AND THE RIGHT TO RESIDENCE IN THE MEMBER STATES OF THE CENTRAL AFRICAN ECONOMIC AND CUSTOMS UNION

The Heads of State of the Central African Economic and Customs Union decided to create an ad hoc commission in 1970 to study problems relating to freedom of movement of people and the right to residence in the member states of UDEAC. This commission met in Freetown (Gabon) from 17 to 23 March 1971 and studied, among other topics, a draft convention drawn up by the secretary general of the organization in 1970. The commission made suggestions for the amendment of certain articles that it hoped would be taken into consideration by the secretary general when drawing up the final treaty.

Certain remarks were made in the course of the discussions about the prejudicial problems of certain laws, which had nothing to do with freedom of movement and the right to residence except insofar as they had a bearing on the final form of the treaty and would affect the juridical balance among states, given that Article 6B of the treaty setting up UDEAC specifically refers to the OCAM convention of 8 September 1961 on all questions concerning freedom of movement and the right to residence in states belonging to the union. Obviously the final laws must bear this in mind.

The UDEAC draft has a long way to go before becoming positive law applicable to the interrelations of member states. However, it is indicative of the trend of Central African states governing their day-to-day relations with each other regarding the questions of freedom of movement and the right to residence.

The main preoccupation of the secretary general of UDEAC--a preoccupation shared by the ad hoc commission--is to have regulations the terms of which differ according to the category in which a person may fall, distinguishing between travelers and migrants, rather than one catch-all law covering all people moving from one country to another. The basis of the draft convention is similar in approach to the Cameroonian law and, like it, has many categories for foreign nationals. Thus it has been proposed that in view of the general preparations for creation of an effective right to residence within the UDEAC countries, the secretary general of UDEAC should concentrate on whether the right to residence is a particularly significant contribution to production and exchange (Article 21.5a).

The draft gained its inspiration from the OCAM convention, at least insofar as the definition of rights enjoyed by foreign nationals in common with a state's own nationals and the exclusion of political rights and the governmental right to expel foreigners are concerned.

However, the convention in the throes of preparation will categorize foreign nationals belonging to states that are members of the Union as follows:

1. Tourists, who are people traveling in another member state for tourism or personal reasons;

2. Business travelers, defined as people traveling in another member state for business reasons;

3. Workers, who the draft states are "people staying in the territory of another member state for salaried employment." One of the original aspects of the draft is the special mention of this category of foreign nationals.

4. Independent professionals, who are those who set themselves upon the territory of another member state to undertake non-salaried work of a freelance or artistic nature.

The difference between the UDEAC project and OCAM convention lies in the fact that in the UDEAC project the equality of rights and liberties among nationals and aliens only benefits "workers" and "independent professionals," rather than tourists and businessmen, who, it is true, cannot stay for more than one month so long as they remain in those categories. However, tourists whose normal residence permits are valid for 30 days may apply for an extension covering an equal length of time. This they may only do once.

Businessmen may travel and stay in member states for a period of 30 days per annum, renewable once (Article 10).

As a general rule the formalities of arrival and residence of aliens are extremely simple. A national identity card issued in the various member states, a valid passport, or a passport that has expired less than a year before allows a national to leave his or her country of origin and also allows that national to enter, stay, or reside in the territories of the other member states.

The freedom of residence of "independent professionals," which as already demonstrated underlines the realistic form of the draft, becomes effective after a trial period of one year from the time of the convention's entry into force. The administrative directors of the union must come to a decision, on a proposal from the secretary general, for a general phasing out of restrictions on the freedom of residence, the conditions to be attached thereto, and the stages to be gone through to achieve realization.

Finally, the project foresees the possibility that a state may put certain funds aside to support the activities of freelancers in the liberal arts. The text does not define what these activities might be; it is to be hoped that the member states will not over-use this provision, which would then run the risk of blocking the freedom, thus leaving the convention meaningless on this point.

The special interest of the draft provisions relating to the free passage and residence of workers lies in the fact, underlined in the first part of this report, that the desire of African states to protect their national work force has often, in the past, stultified projects aimed at liberalizing the international exchange of workers.

Once the draft convention becomes finalized, free movement of workers will be assured among the states of the union, at the latest within one year of the publication of the act adopting the convention, which will be published in the official journal. It will have the effect of removing all discrimination against workers who are nationals of member states, insofar as employment, remuneration, and other conditions of work are concerned (Article 13).

Once the right of workers to move freely has been established, every national will have the right to reply to advertisements for work, to move from country to country in search of a job, or to stay in another country and still be covered by the same laws, rules, and regulations of employment as if that national had been in his or her own country (Article 14).

In addition, the draft envisages a series of concrete measures and procedures, both administrative and legal, to be carried out by the administrative direction of UDEAC with a view toward making the free movement of workers effective in accordance with the spirit of the convention.

It must also be pointed out that in contrast with the OCAM convention the new convention activities of the "public administration" are not covered, which allows the member states to employ nationals of each others' countries in accordance with their own legislation or regulations (Article 17).

These are the legal bases and ideals of the Central African states as regards individual freedom of movement and residence. It is of great importance to look at the awareness and practice of governments in dealing with these questions, since judicial decisions are not made on the basis of semiformulated laws. There is no common jurisdiction among the Central African states, and so far as I know, there have been no national decisions covering freedom of movement internationally and the right of residence in a country not one's own.

NOTES

1. Cameroon, which was first a mandated territory under the League of Nations, then under the trusteeship of the United Nations, did not fall strictly within the colonial ambit. However, it was often included in the benefits of regional institutions in the French territories that became the Central African Republics of Congo, Gabon, and Chad after 1961.

2. All the constitutions of Central African states guarantee individual liberties and affirm that those states are parties to the Universal Declaration of Human Rights.

3. Joseph Marie Bipoun-Woum, Le Droit international Africain--Problèmes généraux, Règlements des conflits (Paris, Librairie General de Droit et de Jurisprudence, 1970).

4. Article 2(2) of the Charter of OCAM. See Secretariat Général de l'OCAM, Textes constitutifs de l'Organisation Commune Africaine et Malgache, Yaounde, 1964.

5. Loi no. 67-LF-1, Titres du Code Pénal de la Republique Fédérale du Cameroun, 12 June 1967.

6. Ibid.

7. Ibid.

8. The Council of the Agreement reunites the ex-French colonies of West Africa: Ivory Coast, Dahomey, Upper Volta, Niger, and Togo.

9. G. Ngango, Les investissements d'origine extérieure en Afrique Noir Francophone: statut et incidence sur le développement (Thèse, Lyon, Edit. de l'Agel), T. I. 199-254.

10. The headquarters of the police force in Yaounde produced a very practical paper, covering all the regulations and legal references to the question. We are grateful to the Commissioner Head of the Immigration Service for having so kindly put this paper at our disposal. It was the main source for this part of the chapter.

11. Circular No. 77/PS, 16 May 1967, Para. VI-d.

12. OCAM Resolution 1, 27 June 1966.

CHAPTER

5

CANADA

Jacques-Yvan Morin

THE INDIVIDUAL

The Individual as a National

There was no general definition of a Canadian citizen as distinguished from a British subject until 1946, when the Canadian Citizenship Act was passed by the federal parliament. Prior to that date the Immigration Act contained a definition of citizenship that applied for the purpose of that act only. Among the three groups of persons described as citizens were persons naturalized under the Canadian naturalization laws, so long as they retained a domicile in Canada. It was presumed that the domicile was abandoned if a naturalized citizen left Canada and remained abroad for more than a year without having his or her naturalization certificate endorsed to the effect that he or she wished to retain the Canadian domicile. Thus there were several cases involving loss of status following failure to seek the proper endorsement. As of this writing, the Immigration Act still provides that a naturalized Canadian will lose his or her citizenship if he or she has resided outside Canada for more than ten consecutive years.[1]

Another difficulty that existed prior to 1946 was the existence of Canadian "nationals" who were not Canadian "citizens," as was the case, for instance, with the alien wife of a Canadian citizen who had not "landed" in Canada. Thus a Canadian "national" may not have been entitled to enter Canada if he or she fell within the categories of prohibited persons, as defined in Section 3 of the Immigration Act. Such situations have been corrected by the 1946 act.

There are now, generally speaking, two categories of Canadian citizens: "natural-born" citizens, by right of birthplace or parentage, and persons who have been granted a certificate of naturalization.

Movement

Passports. Passports are issued by the Secretary of State for External Affairs in the exercise of the Royal Prerogative. There is as yet no statute governing the issue of passports, and the Minister has discretion in the exercise of this prerogative. No person has a legal right to a passport, although in practice the Minister has withheld or withdrawn passports only in very rare cases.

In response to a question in the House as to whether passports had been issued to a group of young Canadians to enable them to travel to Cuba, the Secretary of State for External Affairs stated as follows: "Canada has no regulations prohibiting the travel of Canadians to Cuba or to any other country, and Canadian passports are valid for all countries. Canadian passport application forms do not require applicants to specify the country or countries to which they intend to travel."[2]

In reply to an inquiry from a high commissioner in Ottawa requesting information on the policy and attitude of the government of Canada on the freedom of travel of Canadian nationals, with particular reference to passport endorsement, the Department of External Affairs issued the following statement on 21 December 1967:

> There are no . . . Government restrictions on travel. In peacetime, a Canadian citizen is normally free, so far as Canadian law is concerned, to leave Canada [and is readmissible as of right]. . . .
>
> There is no statute governing the issuance of Canadian passports and no person has a legal entitlement to one. In Canada, the legal position is that the Secretary of State [for External Affairs] has discretionary power to issue or withhold a passport.
>
> Passports are rarely withheld except when the applicant is indebted to the Government for repatriation expenses. At the request of the police or judicial authorities they may be withheld from a person who is charged with a serious criminal offence or is on bail while awaiting trial. In addition, it is sometimes necessary to withhold passport facilities for children under the age of sixteen years when there is a marital dispute involving custody and if it appears that the parent applying for the passport does not have a clear legal right to take the child out of Canada. . . .

> When financial assistance is given to a Canadian citizen at a post abroad, unless he is issued an Emergency Passport for return to Canada, his ordinary passport is endorsed [as being] valid only for travel to Canada and countries en route.[3]

To sum up, it may be said that legally the issue of a passport is a matter of grace in Canada. In practice, however, despite the fact that there is no judicial remedy against the ultimate decision of the Minister of External Affairs, a passport is virtually a right. Passports will be refused or withdrawn only in extreme cases and after careful weighing of the circumstances. Nevertheless, there are cases when the department is faced with difficult choices, and it would seem appropriate to submit the whole procedure to statute law.

Departure. As indicated above, Canadian citizens are normally free, in peacetime, to leave Canada and travel to the country of their choice. However, this freedom is not guaranteed by law, and circumstances could arise in which the government, in the exercise of its prerogative, might impede the departure of a citizen by withholding his or her passport.

In practice, departure has been prevented at the request of judicial authorities or the police in cases in which the person attempting to leave is charged with a serious criminal offence or in on bail while awaiting trial. There have also been cases in which passports have been withheld until repatriation expenses have been reimbursed to the government or in which there has been a dispute about the custody of children.

Return. Under Section 3(1) of the Immigration Act, "a Canadian citizen has the right to come into Canada." Before 1967 a citizen by naturalization ceased to be a citizen if, since acquiring Canadian citizenship, he or she had resided outside of Canada for a period of ten consecutive years, unless before the expiration of such period the citizen had satisfied the government that he or she intended in good faith to return to Canada for permanent residence.[4]

Thus persons other than natural-born Canadian citizens could, under certain circumstances, be prevented from returning to Canada. The Citizenship Act provided, however, that such persons could file a petition for resumption of citizenship and would, if the petition were approved by the Minister, be deemed to have resumed Canadian citizenship as of the date of such approval or as of such an earlier or later date as the Minister could fix in any special case.[5] These provisions were repealed in 1967,[6] and a naturalized Canadian citizen no longer loses his citizenship by reason of having resided outside Canada for a prolonged period of time.

Expulsion. A Canadian national may not be expelled from his own country. This rule may be inferred from Section 3(1) of the Immigration Act.

However, under former Section 19(1) of the Citizenship Act, there could arise situations that would result in de facto expulsion of naturalized citizens. The government could, at its discretion, order that any person other than a natural-born Canadian citizen ceased to be a citizen if, upon a report from the Minister of Citizenship and Immigration, it was satisfied that such a person had been charged with the offence of treason under the Criminal Code or with an offence under the Official Secrets Act and had failed or refused to return to Canada for trial.

This part of Section 19 was repealed in 1967.[7] Revocation of Canadian citizenship, entailing possible expulsion, can take place only in such cases as Canadian citizenship obtained by false representation, voluntary acquisition of a foreign nationality, or a declaration renouncing Canadian citizenship. Even then, an inquiry into the facts must be held before a special commission before the revocation can take place.[8]

Protection

Extent of Freedom of Activity Abroad. Although the Canadian government can influence directly the extent of the commercial and industrial activity of its citizens abroad, through such a device as the Export Development Corporation (see below), it has not attempted to control such activity, except to a limited extent where its security or the loyalty of its nationals are involved.[9]

Canada has often been on the receiving end of the extraterritorial application of U.S. antitrust laws and "guidelines." In the case of antitrust proceedings in the United States against the merger of a U.S. company and a Canadian company, the Minister of Justice made the following statement in the House of Commons on 26 February 1966:

> Having carefully studied the matter, I concluded that the situation does not appear to give rise to any conflict with Canadian anti-combines law and commercial policy, and that no action is contemplated in United States courts that would affect the commercial operations [of the Canadian

> company] in Canada. In my opinion, this is a matter of concern to the domestic economy of the United States: the United States authorities are seeking to restrain a United States company from acquiring or retaining assets that will increase its power in the United States domestic market.[10]

The 1965 U.S. guidelines for voluntary action on the part of U.S. investors and companies abroad to restrain the flow of their investment and bring back such funds as they reasonably could, caused some difficulties in the Canadian market for short-term securities and were the object of much criticism in the Canadian business community and in the House of Commons.[11] Commenting on the legal aspects of these guidelines, the Minister of Finance made the following statement:

> The American guidelines limiting direct investments have raised [the] issue . . . whether through them the United States government is interfering in the internal economic affairs of this country. . . . We pointed out to the United States government that this kind of measure as it applied to Canada was of very doubtful value as a means of relieving the United States balance of payments problem. . . . It must be recognized, however, that in attempting to limit the direct investment of its companies abroad the United States government is following well-established precedents. Other countries . . . have taken and do take measures to limit direct investments abroad of their international companies, and I have never heard any suggestion that [they are] thereby interfering in the internal affairs of other countries.[12]

The Canadian government thereafter issues its own "guiding principles of good corporation behaviour for subsidiaries in Canada of foreign companies," based on the "essential principle" that Canada expects the subsidiaries "to conduct themselves as good corporate Canadian citizens."[13]

<u>The Right to Diplomatic Protection and Compensation</u>. The Department of External Affairs has stated on a number of occasions that under well-established principles of international law, certain

prerequisites must have been fulfilled to justify the espousal of a claim by the Canadian government. On 18 May 1967 a statement of the general principles relating to Canadian practice in this field was issued by the department. It provided (in part) as follows:

> The Canadian Government can only espouse claims in respect of property, rights, interests or debts which belonged to Canadian citizens at the time of loss, confiscation, expropriation or nationalization. Furthermore, the claim must have belonged to Canadian citizens at all times since it arose, and the claimant must be a Canadian citizen at the present time.[14]

On 1 September 1965, in the course of the negotiations between Canada and Poland toward a lump-sum settlement of Canadian claims, the Department of External Affairs issued a statement concerning the procedure to be followed by claimants. This statement made it clear that the government, while anxious to obtain compensation for all claims against Poland, reserves its right not to espouse certain claims.[15]

More recently Canadian practice concerning lump-sum agreements was summarized in the following way by the Department of External Affairs:

> The decision on which course of action is to be followed depends in large part on the facts of the individual case. . . . It has been found useful to first obtain an agreement in principle with State concerned to negotiate a settlement of Canadian claims. Such preliminary agreements are then publicized and interested persons invited to file completed claims questionnaires with us. Following a period of assessment and preparation, those claims considered to be valid are made known to the other State and negotiations begin for a lump-sum settlement.[16]

To sum up, it would appear that a Canadian national does not have a right to require the Canadian government to intervene on his behalf, either by way of good offices or by way of espousal of his claim. However, the Department of External Affairs has not refused to intervene on behalf of Canadian nationals when it was felt that their claims were well established and met the requirements of international law.

The State and Compensation. There is no specific rule of law that obliges the Canadian government to distribute the amount of compensation obtained from a foreign country because of an injury done to its nationals. In practice, however, such amounts have always been remitted or distributed according to the number of claimants.

A good example of the distribution of claims settlements is provided by the procedure followed by the Canadian Claims Commission on Distribution, which was established after Canada had obtained a lump-sum settlement from Bulgaria in 1966.[17] The Commission was created to advise the Minister of Finance and the Secretary of State for External Affairs in the distribution of the fund. Of the claims, 8 were found to qualify under the agreement and 21 were rejected as not qualifying. A claimant whose claim had been disallowed requested a further review of his case. In reply, the Department of External Affairs wrote as follows:

> The question of whether a claimant is eligible to participate in any claims settlement between Canada and a foreign country is subject to the final decision of the Canadian adjudication authority. Advancement of the claim during negotiations and its acceptance as prima facie valid by the other side are not conclusive. . . . [The] recommendations [of the Commission] were accepted by the Minister responsible . . . and the proceeds of the Fund have now been completely distributed.
>
> . . .
>
> Canadian claims settlements with foreign countries are lump-sum settlements and while reflecting in a general way the number and value of claims submitted by the Canadian Government, they are not regarded as the sum total of a series of individually accepted claims.[18]

As indicated above, the department accepts as more or less normal the fact that the amount of a lump-sum settlement is usually inferior to the sum total of all the claims made against a foreign state. As a matter of fact, settlements usually represent only 20 percent or 30 percent of the "minimum sustainable value" of the claims. The Canadian government is not obliged to "top up" the compensation received to make it equal to the loss suffered by its nationals; it does, however, assume about 50 percent of the cost of distribution, and this might be considered to be a form of indirect subsidy.

The best summary of the law on the subject of claims as applied in Canada was provided as follows by E. Wang of the Department of External Affairs in an article published in the Canadian Bar Review:

> One should not lose sight of the fact that a government retains complete discretion as to whether it will espose a claim or category of claims. Nothing is clearer than that international law places no obligation on a State to take up the case of a national who has been wronged by another State; and it may, and sometimes does, decline to do so for reasons quite unconnected with the national in question (Waldock, Principles of Public International Law [1962], 106 Recueil des Cours 94). In exercising this discretion a government will normally give careful consideration not only to the legal merits of the claim but also to the political background in the relations between the claimant and respondent State. . . . Even if the claimant can establish his claim on the merits to the complete satisfaction of his government it may nevertheless be judged inopportune to espouse the claim and present it through diplomatic channels. . . .
>
> Under British law, the discretion of governments in espousing claims and negotiating their settlement is part of the Crown prerogative. This discretion is wide in scope. Even where the . . . executive has negotiated and concluded with a foreign government a settlement of claims on behalf of its subjects, it still retains full discretion as to how and to whom the funds obtained thereby should be distributed. . . .
>
> Similarly under Canadian law the prerogative of the Crown is the source of authority for the exercise of the treaty-making power, and the Canadian citizen cannot compel the Canadian Government to take up his claim at the diplomatic level. Nor under the same principle can he insist on the Government allowing him to share in any overall settlement of claims that it might negotiate (although, of course, he may have a moral right to participate in the proceeds negotiated on his behalf).[19]

The Responsibility of the State for Injury Induced by Its Own Conduct. There does not appear to have been any case in which the Canadian government has provided any measure of supplementary compensation for damage suffered by its nationals abroad on the ground that such damage was induced by the conduct of Canada.

With respect to Canadian claims arising out of World War II, the principal source of funds arose out of the Final Act of the Paris Conference on Reparation from Germany (December 1945). Under this agreement, an International Allied Reparation Agency (IARA) was established in Brussels. Its function was to allocate German reparations among the member governments. As far as Canada was concerned, the chief source of reparation was German external assets (Category A under the above agreement).

A War Claims Fund was established into which were deposited funds received under the German Agreement and the Treaty of Peace with Japan. The Canadian government did not provide any supplementary compensation. The ultimate distribution of the fund was described as follows in External Affairs:

> As it was impossible to foretell how much would eventually find its way into this Fund, let alone the total of the claims which would eventually be found to be valid. a strict system of priorities was established, in particular with regard to property claims. In practice this system has worked well: under it, all death, personal injury and maltreatment claims have been paid in full, while all valid property claims to an amount of $30,000 have been paid.[20]

The priorities referred to were established by Section 4 of the War Claims Regulations Schedule, which provided that if the fund were not sufficient to pay the claims in full, they were to be paid proportionately. In November 1963 the Prime Minister of Canada gave the following summary of the settlement of war claims against Germany (that is, the Federal Republic of Germany): "Since 1952, . . . some 7000 Canadians have received from the German war claims fund compensation for war losses under the Nazi regime, including maltreatment, amounting to almost $9 million."[21]

In the case of war claims against Italy, a lump-sum payment of .29 billion lire from the Italian government was negotiated, the distribution of this sum among interested claimants being left to the Minister of Finance. Under Appropriation Act No. 4,[22] the Minister was authorized to establish a special "War Claims (Italy) Account" in the Consolidated Revenue Fund, to which were credited the amounts received from Italy. Payment out of the said account was provided for in accordance with the War Claims (Italy) Settlement Regulations.[23] Section 6 of these regulations provided for the appointment of an advisory commissioner, but the Minister of Finance was not bound by the findings and recommendations of the commissioner. The only amount available for compensation was the sum of .29 billion lire paid by the Italian government except with respect to debts, bonds, and certain claims, which were dealt with separately.

Waiver. Lump-sum settlements concluded by Canada invariably provide that the payment agreed to constitutes satisfaction by the foreign state of its obligations to Canada and Canadian nationals. The claims covered by the agreement are extinguished; examples of this are the agreement between Canada and Bulgaria of 30 June 1966 and the note of the Secretary of State for External Affairs, addressed to the Minister of Foreign Affairs of Italy, of 20 September 1951. To the extent that the claims are in excess of the amount provided for in these agreements, the Canadian government may be said to have waived in part the claims of its nationals.

The Canadian government, as indicated above, has discretion to reject a claim of an individual Canadian citizen against a foreign government and to decline to espouse the claim even if it is well founded on the merits of the case or on the basis of international law.

Special Kinds of Protection. Of historical interest is the fact that the Royal Commission on Reparations, which was set up in Canada to report on war claims arising out of World War I, ruled that all claimants of British nationality who were resident in Canada on the date of ratification of the Treaty of Versailles (10 January 1920) were eligible for compensation.[24] As pointed out by J. G. Castel, this ruling may be regarded as a departure from the traditional requirement of continuous nationality.[25] However, it should be noted that the ruling was based upon the special terms of the Treaty of Versailles. Furthermore, before 1947 there was no general definition of a Canadian citizen as distinguished from a British subject.

A somewhat analogous tendency might be said to exist in modern Canadian practice with respect to claims by naturalized Canadians who were not Canadian nationals at the time of the events giving rise to the claims. E. Wang describes this practice as follows:

> The Canadian government, at its discretion, may in certain circumstances support and make diplomatic representations on behalf of a claim which is of uncertain validity on the merits or on the

> grounds of international law. For example, the Government might consider a request for assistance, in respect of a claim of a new Canadian who was not a Canadian at the time of the events giving rise to the claim. Under the rule of continuous nationality, . . . the Government would not fully espouse this claim, . . . but it might instruct the Canadian Embassy or Consulate in a foreign locality to lend assistance short of espousal by intervening informally, if such action were considered useful and appropriate.
>
> Such informal assistance . . . is often referred to as an exercise of good offices. It may take many forms including, for example, enquiries as to the present status of a dispute, as to the procedure which the claimant should follow, . . . or it may be in the form of a request for reconsideration or review of a decision of an agency of the foreign government. An intervention as an exercise of good offices may at the discretion of the government and depending upon the circumstances of the case be made at a high level and may be accompanied by strong representations.
>
> As a practical matter the distinction between formal espousal and an exercise of good offices may be somewhat blurred. It must be recognized, however, that also as a practical matter the possibility of effective assistance by the Canadian Government in cases which do not meet international standards will be severely circumscribed.[26]

The Individual as an Alien

An alien is defined in Section 2(a) of the Canadian Citizenship Act as "a person who is not a Canadian citizen, Commonwealth citizen, British subject or citizen of the Republic of Ireland." The status of British subject, which according to Section 23 of the Citizenship Act is the same as that of a Commonwealth citizen and applies indirectly to citizens of the Irish Republic, entitles a person to certain privileges with respect to obtaining Canadian citizenship, qualifying for certain public offices, or owning of a Canadian ship. British subjects other than Canadian citizens are subject to the same rules as aliens, particularly in relation to entering Canada. In other words, British subjects do not have a right to come into Canada.

Movement

Entry and Stay. The leading case on this point is still Musgrove v. Chung Teeong Toy,[27] a ruling to the effect that the government of the Colony of Victoria had authority to pass a law preventing aliens from entering the colony. In Papageorgiouv v. Turner, decided in the Supreme Court of New Brunswick, Judge Barker said:

> It is a received maxim of international law that the government of a State may prohibi the entrance of strangers into a country and may, therefore, regulate the conditions upon which they shall be allowed to remain in it or may require and compel their departure from it.[28]

There is, however, one feature of Canadian legislation that deserves mention because it confers a right of entry to domiciled aliens, subject to certain restrictions that have to do with disloyalty, subversion, or aid to the enemy. Section 3(2) of the Immigration Act provides as follows:

> Subject to subsection (3), a person who is not a Canadian citizen but has acquired, but has not lost Canadian domicile shall be allowed to come into Canada.
>
> (3) Any person with Canadian domicile other than a Canadian citizen, who
>
> (a) within or without Canada, performed any military service for or otherwise aided or abetted a country then at war with Canada;
>
> (b) within or without Canada, performed for or rendered to a country other than Canada any military service . . . that is prejudicial to any action taken by Canada under the United Nations Charter, the North Atlantic Treaty or other similar instrument for collective defence that may be entered into by Canada; or
>
> (c) left Canada for any of the purposes described in paragraphs (a) or (b); shall not be allowed to come into Canada unless authorized by the Minister to do so.

For the purposes of the Immigration Act, Canadian domicile is acquired by a person having his or her place of domicile for at least five years in Canada "after having been landed in Canada." Domicile is lost by a person voluntarily residing out of Canada with the intention of making a permanent home out of Canada and not for a mere temporary purpose.[29]

Departure

Voluntary Departure. An alien is free to leave Canada. In principle there are no limits to this right, the only constraints being those of a general penal nature applicable to both citizens and aliens. Under Section 25 of the Citizenship Act, an alien is subject to trial at law in the same manner as a natural-born Canadian citizen. Detention could therefore take place pending trial, and the alien, if convicted of an offence, can be imprisoned. Section 4(2) of the Immigration Act provides that no period during which a person is confined to penitentiary or prison shall be counted toward the acquisition of a Canadian domicile.

Under the Shipping Act, a deserting seaman can be prevented from leaving freely and returned to the authorities of his ship.

Under Section 33(2) of the Immigration Act, a person against whom a deportation order has been made may be allowed to leave Canada voluntarily, unless otherwise directed by the Minister or an immigration officer. A deportation order, however, will usually entail involuntary departure (expulsion).

Involuntary Departure: Expulsion and Deportation. A person other than a Canadian citizen or other than a person with a Canadian domicile who enters illegally or seeks permanent admission to Canada after entry while not meeting the conditions or requirements of the Immigration Act, or whose entry permit expires or is cancelled, may be expelled. Section 17 of the act describes in detail the various situations that may entail deportation, including conviction of an offence under the Criminal Code.

An alien having acquired Canadian domicile who engages in such activities as subversion of Canadian institutions or offences involving disloyalty to the Sovereign is subject to deportation.[30]

The procedure of expulsion and the remedies available constitute a rather complicated system, which will be described only in a general way. Every alien seeking admission to Canada has to appear before an immigration officer and is presumed to be an immigrant, that is, to be seeking permanent residence, unless the examining officer is satisfied that the alien is not an immigrant.[31] Subject to certain exceptions, aliens who have acquired Canadian domicile are allowed to come into Canada.

Where the immigration officer is of the opinion that it would or might be contrary to a provision of the Immigration Act, or the regulations, to grant admission to a particular alien, the officer may detain such person and report the case to a special inquiry officer.[32] This special officer is authorized, after such further examination as he deems necessary, to let the alien enter Canada or detain the alien for an immediate inquiry. In the case of persons coming from the United States, the special officer may make a deportation order against the person, who is then returned as soon as practicable to the place from which he or she came to Canada.

Similarly, if an alien who has been admitted to Canada is the object of a report to the effect that he or she is a member of a class of persons prohibited to come into Canada, if the alien engages in activities detrimental to Canadian security, if the alien has come in as a nonimmigrant and is now seeking to remain in Canada permanently, if the alien has been convicted of a criminal offence, or if there is some similar reason, the Director of Immigration may order an inquiry to be held before a special inquiry officer.

As a general principle, the Immigration Act therefore grants every alien a right to an inquiry by a special officer. Such an inquiry must take place "apart from the public" in the presence of the person concerned, who is entitled to be represented by counsel at the hearing. In the case in re Kokorinis, it was held by the Court of Appeal of British Columbia that the word "counsel" meant a professionally qualified lawyer but that the special inquiry officer was under no duty to insist that the alien be so represented; his sole duty was to inform the alien as to his right to representation.[33]

In an important 1967 decision of the Court of Appeal of Manitoba, it was held that the special officer must maintain an impartial and judicial attitude during the proceedings. In this particular affair his attitude had amounted to a denial of natural justice, since the alien had never learned the precise charge he had to answer. The court ruled as follows:

> The performance of the Special Inquiry Officer on this matter was not that of one engaged in an objective search for truth. Rather it appeared to be an attempt to find justification or support for a point of view to which, in advance of the relevant testimony, he was already firmly committed. Such conduct falls below the standard to which a person engaged in a judicial or quasijudicial task is expected to conform.[34]

The first remedy against a decision by a special inquiry officer that entails deportation is of a statutory nature. Prior to 1967 an appeal of a deportation order could be taken to the Minister, who could in turn order that the appeal should be dealt with by an Immigration Appeal Board composed of at least three persons nominated by him.[35] The special inquiry officer who had made the deportation order under appeal could not serve on this board to hear the appeal. There were exceptions to this right of appeal.

In 1967 a permanent Immigration Appeal Board was created, with the status of a court of record.[36] It consists of not less than seven and not more than nine members appointed by the Governor in Council. A person against whom a deportation order has been made under the Immigration Act may appeal to the board on any ground that involves a question of law or fact or mixed law and fact. The Minister may also appeal to the board from a decision made by a special inquiry officer.

The board has sole and exclusive jurisdiction to hear and determine all questions of fact or law, including questions of jurisdiction, that may arise in relation to an order of deportation. The act provides that a decision of the board can be appealed to the Supreme Court of Canada, if leave be granted by the court.

Prior to the creation of this new board, there were numerous cases of applications to the courts for certiorari or prohibition. In the case in re Edery in 1969, it was held by the Supreme Court of British Columbia that, in view of the creation of the board as a court of record, the ordinary courts lack jurisdiction in certiorari and in prohibition in relation to immigration matters; nor do they have jurisdiction to hear and decide any question of jurisdiction under the Immigration Act.[37]

The second remedy against a deportation order is the writ of habeas corpus, which is available to any alien admitted to Canada who alleges that he or she is being illegally detained, in order to test in court whether the detention of the alien is according to law. This is a common-law remedy.

Former Section 39 of the act attempted to preclude interference by the ordinary courts, as follows:

> No Court and no judge . . . has jurisdiction to review, quash, reserve, restrain or otherwise interfere with any proceeding, decision or order of the Minister, Deputy Minister, Director, Immigration Appeal Board, Special Inquiry Officer or immigration officer . . . made or given under the authority and in accordance with provisions of this Act relating to the detention or deportation

of any person, upon any ground whatsoever, unless such person is a Canadian citizen or has Canadian domicile.

In Masella v. Langlois, the Supreme Court of Canada held that this section closed the door to intervention of the courts, on condition that the deportation order be rendered in conformity with the provisions of the act. The court was precluded from reviewing findings of fact, but the applicant for a writ of habeas corpus could show that the proceeding of which he or she had complained had not been "made or given in accordance with the provisions of the Act."[38] A number of earlier cases also required compliance in substance with the provisions of the act and condemned "hugger-mugger" proceedings.[39]

On the other hand, if the deportation order has been issued in conformity with the act, the courts will not interfere and decide if in fact an alien is desirable or not; the writ of habeas corpus will then be quashed. In Hecht v. McFaul and the Province of Quebec,[40] it was held that Section 39 was not unconstitutional as being an arbitrary deprivation of basic rights guaranteed by the Canadian Bill of Rights.[41]

Protection

There is no reference in Canadian statutes to the possibility of affording protection to persons who are not Canadian nationals, apart from the practice, mentioned earlier, of providing "good offices" in favor of naturalized citizens who were not nationals at the time when their claims arose. On the other hand, subject to the ordinary rules of international law, there is nothing in Canadian statutes that would prevent the government from intervening to protect individuals who are not Canadian nationals, if it should deem proper to do so.

NATIONAL IMPLEMENTATION OF INTERNATIONAL RIGHTS AND DUTIES

In Canada the general position with respect to the relationship between international law and municipal law is that customary international law will be treated "as incorporated in our domestic law," provided it is not inconsistent with rules exacted by statutes or finally declared by the courts. This was held in the Foreign Legations case in 1943, citing Chung chi Cheung v. the King and Mortensen v. Peters.[42]

In Reference re Exemption of U.S. Forces from Canadian Criminal Law, Judge Taschereau said the following:

> Of course, I do not forget that international law has no application to Canada unless incorporated in our own domestic law. . . .
>
> The same principle has been held by this Court in the Foreign Legations Reference (supra), where . . . the Chief Justice [of Canada] said: "I think . . . that the proper conclusion from the legislation of the Imperial Parliament . . . in force, as some of the statutes were when the common law was formally introduced into Upper Canada [Ontario], from the decisions and judgments I have cited, and from the text-writers, is that this rule, recognized by France, is also implicit in the principles of international law recognized by the law of England; and, consequently, by the law of Ontario."
>
> If not accepted in this country, international law would not be binding but would merely be a code of unenforceable abstract rules of international morals. . . .
>
> I have come to the conclusion that there exists such a body of rules adopted by the nations of the world. . . . I have to acknowledge this existence, and treat them as incorporated in our domestic law. . . . And I see nothing in the laws of the Land inconsistent with their application within our territory.[43]

This "doctrine of incorporation" is completed by a rule of statutory interpretation based on the presumption that the legislature concerned did not intend to violate international law or to give a subordinate body the power to do so. Presumably this would apply to the Canadian parliament as well as to the provincial legislatures.[44]

Treaties do not generally affect private rights unless the appropriate legislation is enacted by the Canadian parliament or the provincial legislatures. In a federal state such as Canada, it may happen that a legislature will fail to implement a treaty lawfully made by the federal executive. See Labour Convention Case, in which it was decided that the succession of Canada to international status did not affect the distribution of powers as contained in the British North America Act of 1867, and therefore that a treaty made by the federal executive, if it related to a matter falling within any of the competence normally assigned to the provinces by that act, can only be implemented by the provincial legislatures.[45]

The Act of State Doctrine

With respect to the Act of State doctrine, there is not much authority, judicial or doctrinal, in Canada apart from the case of Brow, Gow, Wilson et al. v. Beleggins, Societeit N.V., in 1961, which is usually referred to as the Belso case.[46]

There the court had to determine the ownership of certain shares in a company incorporated in the Netherlands, which were held in trust in Canada for German nationals and which had been declared to belong to the State of the Netherlands by the wartime decrees of that government. The trustee from the Netherlands had come to Canada in 1939, bringing with him the share certificates and the assets of the company. A Canadian company was incorporated, and the shares of this company were issued to the company of the Netherlands in exchange for all its assets. Subsequently the government in exile of the Netherlands proclaimed decrees providing for the passing of enemy property into the ownership of the state in order to compensate its subjects who had suffered at the hands of the enemy during the war. These decrees had, according to the law of the Netherlands, the force of statutes. They came into force throughout the Netherlands when the German army withdrew.

Later the conflicting claims of the government of the Netherlands and of the trustee were put forward in Canada, and the banks in which the shares had been deposited applied to the courts for an order determining the ownership of the shares. The main question was whether the decrees were of such a confiscatory nature that the ownership should not be recognized by Canadian courts. The Ontario High Court held that the confiscation and transfer of the shares to the Netherlands government must be recognized. Although the Ontario Courts would not enforce the revenue or penal laws of foreign jurisdictions, the wartime decrees of the Netherlands were not of that nature, but rather were similar to foreign exchange laws, which had always been recognized by Canadian courts. The decrees could not be refused recognition as being confiscatory in nature and hence contrary to domestic public policy, inasmuch as Canada itself had precisely the same sort of legislation in force for the same purpose; moreover, the Dutch decrees accorded with international treaties and conventions to which both Canada and the Netherlands were signatories, such as the Bretton Woods agreement, which were designed to make German property available as reparation for devastated countries.

Chief Justice McRuer relied on the authority of Luther v. Sagor and Princess Paley Olga v. Weisz to the effect that, should any foreign government appropriate private property without compensation, the remedy was not for the courts to ignore the law of the foreign country but for the government to refuse to recognize it as a sovereign state.[47] The court stated that there is a class of cases in which the laws of a foreign country cannot be recognized because they are contrary to the public policy of the forum. However, the court was not prepared to hold that the Dutch decrees involved in this case fell into that class of legislation that was considered confiscatory without compensation; nor was it ready to offend against the public policy of Canada.

However, the Belso case does not deal with the question of whether the Act of State doctrine would preclude review of an act by a foreign state which allegedly violated international law. Canadian case law does not contain anything similar to the U.S. Sabbatino case, the Nissho Maru case, or the Rose Mary case.[48] It may be argued, on the basis of the principles laid down by Judge Upjohn in re Claim by Helbert Wagg & Co., that Canadian courts would be inclined to follow the reasoning in the Rose Mary case rather than that of the Nissho Maru case, provided of course that the property was within the jurisdiction of the court.[49] This means that Canadian courts would probably feel free to examine the validity of foreign legislation and acts in terms of international law.

Implementation of Decisions of International Organizations

The constitutions of a number of federal states provide that the central government shall have the necessary legislative power to implement the decisions and recommendations of international organizations. There is no such provision in the British North America Act. On the contrary, the power of the federal parliament to implement Empire Treaties even when the subject matter of the treaties falls within provincial competence was curtailed by the Judicial Committee of the Privy Council in the Labour Convention case,[50] and the present position with respect to implementing the decisions of international organizations appears to be that in general such decisions are subject to the same rules as the treaties upon which they are based.

Of course, if the international decision does not affect domestic legislation, either federal or provincial, or fall under the royal prerogative to conduct foreign affairs, the federal executive has all the power necessary to implement the decision (or recommendation). In order to make this absolutely clear in relation to sanctions under

Article 41 of the UN Charter, the Canadian parliament passed the United Nations Act. Section 2 of the act reads as follows:

> When, in pursuance of Article 41 of the Charter of the United Nations, . . . the Security Council . . . decides upon a measure to be employed to give effect to any of its decisions and calls upon Canada to apply such measure, the Governor in Council may make such orders and regulations as appear to him to be necessary or expedient for enabling such measure to be effectively applied.[51]

Section 3 provides that the government may prescribe a fine or a term of imprisonment as a penalty for a violation of an order or regulation made under the act. Any goods or merchandise dealt with in defiance of such an order or regulation may be seized and are liable to forfeiture at the instance of the Minister of Justice upon proceedings in the Exchequer Court of Canada or in any superior court. Under section 4, every order or regulation made under the act is to be laid forthwith before Parliament. If the Senate and House of Commons resolve that it be annulled within 40 days, it ceases to have effect, but without prejudice to its previous operation.

Following the unilateral declaration of independence by Rhodesia on 11 November 1965, the Canadian government announced a number of measures that were meant to implement the "statement" of the Conference of Commonwealth Prime Ministers held in June of the same year. These measures were nonrecognition, withdrawal from Salisbury of the Canadian Trade Commissioner; cessation of Canadian aid and export financing facilities, an embargo on arms and military equipment, and withdrawal from Rhodesian goods of the preferential tariff rates. Canadian teachers in Rhodesia under an external aid program were also withdrawn.[52]

In February 1966, the Secretary of State for External Affairs reported that approximately 90 percent of the trade between Canada and Rhodesia had been affected by the economic sanctions.[53] In the meantime the UN Security Council had adopted a resolution recommending the severance of all trade ties with Rhodesia. A member of the opposition raised the question of the authority of the government to impose sanctions. The Secretary replied as follows:

> We have acted under the Customs Tariff. We have acted under the Export and Import Permits Act. In that connection, under that act, as the Security Council resolution was not mandatory,

> it was possible to act under the various pertinent sections only provided there was an agreement between Canada and another power and that agreement would give rise to an obligation on Canada, pursuant to which we had authority, according to the law officers of the crown, to act under the Export and Import Permits Act.[54]

Thus, the United Nations Act not being applicable, the government had to resort to an "arrangement" between Great Britain and Canada (Great Britain being responsible for the external relations of Rhodesia) that made it possible to bring the action within the scope of the Export and Import Permits Act and provide for a total voluntary embargo on both imports and exports. When the Security Council decided to impose comprehensive mandatory sanctions against Rhodesia on 29 April 1968, no further action was required because the embargo was already complete.

To sum up, it may be said that the Canadian government has all the necessary power under the United Nations Act to implement decisions of the Security Council. When the measures envisaged are not mandatory, or when they stem from a recommendation of the General Assembly or of a Commonwealth Conference, the Canadian government, if it decides to support the measures on a voluntary basis, will resort to various legal devices in order to facilitate the implementation of the recommendation. The Rhodesian case has shown that it would be useful to envisage what would enable the government to act when the basis for such action is a simple recommendation emanating from an international organization to which Canada is a party, as distinct from a "decision" by the Security Council. Such legislation might also provide for some kind of compensation when the rights of individuals are adversely affected by the implementation of international sanctions.

Procedures Relating to the Issue of Certificates or Suggestions of the Executive in Connection with Litigation in National Courts

The issuing of certificates by the Secretary of State for External Affairs occurs only occasionally in Canada, and there is no comprehensive policy or practice on the subject.

It is not clear from departmental files who may ask for one, but in the past certificates have been issued at the request of the courts or of the parties to litigation. In a private action, the request would usually be concurred in by both parties, and the department would avoid getting involved on one side. The situation in which one of the parties would refuse to assent to the request has not been faced yet, but presumably the court itself would ask for the certificate if it proved to be essential to the proper hearing of the case.

The practice is to give an opportunity to each party to make representations to the department regarding the content of the certificate. A party could request that the certificate bear on specific facts and be drafted in specific language. Although no formal hearing is provided for, the department would listen to the other party and would certainly reserve its rights about the ultimate content of the certificate.

Some 10 or 15 years ago certificates took the form of simple letters. They have now become more formal, as shown by the language in the following certificate, issued on 18 December 1969:

> I, Mitchell Sharp, Secretary of State for External Affairs in the Government of Canada, refer to the certificate of the Hon. Paul Martin, of 10 November 1967 and the documents attached thereto, which . . . have been filed with the Exchequer Court of Canada. With reference to the treaty between Canada and France . . . which had been brought into force by the exchange of notes referred to in the certificate of the Hon. Paul Martin, and by the subsequent acts of Canada and France, I certify that while the instruments of ratification referred to in Article 16 of the treaty were not exchanged, the treaty was ratified by the exchange of notes and the conduct of the parties.

In the 1970 case of Château-Gai Wines v. Attorney General of Canada, the above certificate was accepted by the court as proof that a treaty between France and Canada had come into force as a binding international agreement, despite the fact that the formal instruments of ratification provided for in the agreement itself had not been exchanged.[55] P. Jackett said the following:

> In principle, . . . a question, whether of fact or law or both, as to whether an international agreement between Canada and another country has come into force . . . so as to create international rights and obligations, must be determined, in case of doubt, in the same way as

> (a) a question as to whether a person is a foreign sovereign power,
> (b) a question as to what persons must be regarded as constituting the effective government of a foreign territory,
> (c) a question as to whether a particular place must be regarded as being in Canada or as being under the authority of a foreign sovereign authority,
> (d) a question as to whether Canada is at peace or at war with a foreign power, or
> (e) a question as to whether a person in Canada is entitled to diplomatic privileges as being an ambassador of a foreign power or a member of the entourage of such an ambassador.
>
> All such questions are questions within the realm of responsibility of the executive arm of government and, being questions on which the state should speak with one voice, they are questions with regard to which the courts should accept from the appropriate minister of the Crown a certificate as to Canada's position.[56]

After citing a number of British decisions, including Luther v. Sagor (see above) and Carl Zeiss Stiftung v. Rayner & Keeler,[57] the court concluded that, even if on a proper interpretation of the agreement the exchange of formal ratifications were a condition precedent to bringing the agreement into force, nevertheless it would "feel constrained to accept the official view of the Canadian Government that the agreement had been brought into force without any such exchange of ratifications."[58]

TREATIES AND THE INDIVIDUAL

As the relations of Canada with the outside world have increased, especially since World War II, a great number of treaties that have benefited individual nationals have been concluded with other states. The agreements on double taxation, labor, visas, permanent residence, customs, road traffic, and trade, not to mention the older British treaties on extradition or on navigation to which Canada has succeeded, constitute a considerable body of law that is now to be found, to various degrees, in every state.

Of special interest are the recent agreements signed by Canada with nine other states concerning investment guarantees and providing for the payment of compensation in case of nationalization.

In 1970, the Export Development Corporation was established as an agent of the Government of Canada to act as guarantor of investments made abroad by Canadian nationals. Contracts of insurance are signed between the Corporation and the prospective investor with a view to covering any loss suffered by the latter by reason of war, insurrection, riot, rebellion, arbitrary seizure, expropriation or any action by a foreign government depriving him of any rights.

The agreements provide that, in the event of a payment to an investor by the Corporation under such a contract, the Corporation will be recognized by the foreign state as subrogated to all the rights of the investor for the purpose of recovering the amount of the loss. An example of an agreement of this kind has been included at the end of this chapter as an appendix.

In the event of "nationalization or expropriation of industry or business" the investor, or if the claim has been paid by the E.D.C., the Government of Canada, will be entitled to "fair compensation." However, no claim may be made under the agreement unless all local remedies have been exhausted.

In case of a dispute concerning the interpretation of the agreement or any claim arising out of the investments which, in the opinion of either government, presents a question of international law, and if the differences cannot be settled by negotiations, the dispute shall be submitted to an ad hoc arbitral tribunal "for settlement in accordance with applicable principles and rules of public international law." The agreement provides for the appointment of the members of the tribunal by the President of the International Court of Justice should the parties fail to comply with the appointment procedure established by the treaty. The decision of the tribunal is binding and definitive. The Canadian government expects to conclude between 20 and 30 similar agreements during the next few years.

APPENDIX

Canada/Singapore Bilateral Agreement, Foreign Investment Insurance

MINISTRY OF FINANCE
Fullerton Building, 5th Floor
Singapore 1, Republic of Singapore
30 July, 1971

Excellency,

I have the honour to acknowledge receipt of your Note dated 26th July, 1971 which reads as follows:-

I have the honour to refer to discussions which have recently taken place between representatives of our two governments relating to investments in Singapore which would further development of economic relations between Singapore and Canada, and to guarantees of such investments by the Government of Canada, through its agent the Export Development Corporation. I also have the honour to confirm the following understandings reached as a result of those discussions.

(1) In the event of a payment by the Export Development Corporation under a contract of insurance for any loss by reason of:

(a) war, riot, insurrection, revolution or rebellion in Singapore;

(b) the arbitrary seizure, expropriation, confiscation, or deprivation of use of any property by a government, or agency thereof, in Singapore;

(c) any action by a government, or agency thereof, in Singapore, other than action of the kind described in sub-para. (b) that deprives the investor of any right in, or in connection with, an investment; and

(d) any action by a government, or agency thereof, in Singapore, that prohibits or restricts transfer of any money or removal of any property from that country,

the said corporation shall be authorized by the Government of Singapore to exercise the rights having devolved on it by law or having been assigned to it by the predecessor in title.

(2) But to the extent that the laws of Singapore partially or wholly invalidate the acquisition of any interests in any property within its national territory by the Government of Canada, the Government of Singapore shall permit the investor and the Government of Canada to make appropriate arrangements pursuant to which such interests are transferred to an entity permitted to own such interests under the laws of Singapore.

(3) The Government of Canada shall assert no greater rights than those of the transferring investor under the laws of Singapore with respect to any interest transferred or succeeded to as contemplated in para. 1. The Government of Canada does, however, reserve its right to assert a claim in its sovereign capacity in the event of a denial of justice or other question of state responsibility as defined in international law.

(4) The legality of any expropriation by the Government of Singapore of investments insured by the Government of Canada, and the amount of compensation, shall be subject to review as prescribed by the law in force in Singapore.

(5) Should the Government of Canada acquire under investment insurance contracts, amounts and credits of the lawful currency of the Government of Singapore, the said Government of Singapore shall accord to those funds treatment no different than that which it would accord if such funds were to remain with the investor, and such funds shall be freely available to the Government of Canada to meet its expenditures in the national territory of Singapore.

(6) This agreement shall apply only with respect to insured investments in projects or activities approved in writing by the Government of Singapore.

(7) Differences between the two governments concerning the interpretation and application of provisions of this agreement or any claim arising out of investments insured in accordance with this agreement, against either of the two governments, which in the opinion of the other presents a question of public international law shall be settled, insofar as possible, through negotiations between the governments. If such differences cannot be resolved within a period of three months following the request for such negotiations, it shall be submitted, at the request of either government, to an ad hoc tribunal for settlement in accordance with applicable principles and rules of public international law. The arbitral tribunal shall consist of three members and shall be established as follows: each government shall appoint one arbitrator; a third member, who shall act as chairman, shall be appointed by the other two members. The chairman shall not be a national of either country. The arbitrators shall be appointed within two months and the chairman within three months of the date of receipt of either government's request for arbitration. If the foregoing time limits are not met, either government may, in the absence of any other agreement, request the president of international Court of Justice [sic] to make the necessary appointment or appointments and both governments agree to accept such appointment or appointments. The arbitral tribunal shall decide by majority vote. Its decision shall be binding and definitive. Each of the governments shall pay the expense of its member and

its representation in the proceedings before the arbitral tribunal; expenses of the chairman and other costs shall be paid in equal parts by the two governments. The arbitral tribunal may adopt other regulations concerning costs. In all other matters, the arbitral tribunal shall regulate its own procedures. Only the respective governments may request arbitral procedure and participate in it.

(8) I have the honour to propose that, if the foregoing is acceptable to your government, this Note, which is authentic in English and French, and your reply to that effect shall constitute an agreement between our two governments which shall enter into force on the date of your reply. This agreement shall continue in force until terminated by either government on six months' notice in writing to the other. In the event of termination, the provisions of the agreement shall continue to apply, in respect of insurance contracts issued by the Government of Canada while the agreement was in force, for the duration of these contracts; provided that in no case shall the agreement continue to apply to such contracts for a period longer than 15 years after the termination of this agreement.

Accept, Excellency, renewed assurances of my highest consideration."

In reply, I have the honour to inform you that the Singapore Government confirm the understandings as set up in your Note and will regard that Note and this reply as constituting an agreement between the Government of the Republic of Singapore and the Government of Canada, the agreement to enter into force on the date of this reply.

Accept, Excellency, the assurances of my highest consideration.

G. F. Bogaars
Permanent Secretary
(Economic Development Division)
Ministry of Finance

NOTES

1. Immigration Act, 1967, §18.
2. House of Commons Debate (hereafter H.C. Deb.) 5500 (1964).
3. 6 Can. Y.B. Int'l. Law 278 (1968).
4. Canadian Citizenship Act, 1946, former §18.
5. Ibid., former §18(4).
6. 16 Eliz. 2, at 4.
7. Ibid., §5.
8. Rules of the Supreme Court 1970, Criminal Code 19, §18.
9. See Criminal Code, §§5(2), 46(2), 240(1), 296(6).
10. H.C. Deb. 1398 (1964).
11. H.C. Deb., at 491 (1961).

12. Ibid., at 324-26 (1961).

13. 5 Can. Y.B. Int'l. Law 316 (1967).

14. J. G. Castel, International Law Chiefly as Interpreted and Applied in Canada (1976) 1118.

15. Department of External Affairs, 18 May 1967.

16. 7 Can. Y.B. Int'l. Law 315 (1969).

17. 5 Can. Y.B. Int'l. Law 269 (1967).

18. 8 Can. Y.B. Int'l. Law 362 (1970).

19. E. Wang, "Nationality of Claims and Diplomatic Intervention: Canadian Practice," 43 Can. B. Rev. 136 (1965).

20. 9 External Affairs 326 (1957).

21. H.C. Deb. 4902 (1963).

22. Court of Session Cases 1952, c. 55.

23. P.C. 1951:5818; P.C. 1954:1723 and amendments.

24. See Interim Report on Reparations 13 (1931).

25. International Law 1027 (1965).

26. Wang, op. cit., at 136.

27. A.C. 272 (1891).

28. 37 New Brunswick Reports 449 (1906).

29. Immigration Act, 1967, §4.

30. Ibid., §18.

31. Ibid., §§6, 19.

32. Ibid., §22.

33. 62 D.L.R. (2d) 433 (1967); 43 I.L.R. 225.

34. Gooliah v. Reginam and Minister of Citizenship and Immigration, 63 D.L.R. (2d) 224 (1967); 59 W.W.R. 705 at 713 (1967); 43 I.L.R. 219 at 223.

35. Canadian Citizenship Act, 1946, former §§31(2), 12.

36. Statutes of Canada c. 90, §§3, 7.

37. 70 W.W.R. 553 (1969).

38. 4 D.L.R. 347 (1955).

39. See Samejima v. the King, 4 D.L.R. 246 (1932) (Supreme Court) and R. & McDonnell v. Leong Ba Chai, S.C.R. 10 (1954); Violi v. Superintendent of Immigration, S.C.R. 232 (1964).

40. Quebec S.C. 392 (1961); 42 I.L.R. 226 (1971).

41. See also re Fraser, 47 Maritime Provinces Reports 81 (1962-63); 40 D.L.R. (2d.) 380 (1963) (Nova Scotia); 42 I.L.R. 229 (1971).

42. S.C.R. 208 (1943); A.C. 160 (1939); 14 Scots L.T.R. 227 (1906).

43. S.C.R. 483 (1943).

44. See G. V. La Forest, "May the Provinces Legislate in Violation of International Law?" 39 Can. B. Rev. 78 (1961).

45. A.C. 326 (1937).

46. Ont. 815 (1961); 42 I.L.R. 409.

47. 3 K. B. 532 (1921); 1 K. B. 718 (1929).

48. 376 U.S. 398 (1964); I.L.R. 305 (1953); ibid., at 316. Nissho Maru: Anglo-Iranian Oil Company, Ltd. Idemitsu Kosan Kobushiki Kaisha. District Court of Tokyo (Civil Ninth Division) 1953. High Court of Tokyo (First Civil Affairs Section) 1953.

Rose Mary: Anglo-Iranian Oil Company, Ltd. v. Jaffiate and (the Rose Mary) Aden, Supreme Court, 9 January 1953.

49. Ch. 323 (1956).
50. A.C. 326 (1937).
51. R.S.C. 1970, c. U-3, §2.
52. Office of the Prime Minister, press release, 11 November, 1965.
53. H.C. Deb. 499 (1966).
54. Ibid., at 644.
55. Exchequer C.R. 366 (1970).
56. Ibid., at 383-84.
57. 1 A.C. 853 (1967).
58. Exchequer C.R. (1970).

CHAPTER

6

CHILE

Francisco Orrego Vicuña

THE PRESENCE OF INTERNATIONAL LAW

Individual Rights and Social Values

Within the field of foreign affairs, the many problems related to individual rights against the state illustrate a very interesting contrast between the municipal legal orders of states, on the one hand, and international law, on the other. Most of the problems that will be examined here have been ruled so far by domestic jurisdiction and will probably continue to be so as long as the basic conditions underlying contemporary international law do not change. Nevertheless, the presence of international law in this field has been growing, perhaps as an inevitable result of the gradual reduction in the extent of domestic jurisdiction.

International protection of human rights in general, and the large number of international agreements that legislate on specific aspects, such as transit of persons, rights and protection of aliens, investment regulations, and other matters, are the advanced symptoms of this evolving phenomenon, which will undoubtedly lead to the establishment of a system of internationally protected individual rights before the state.

Perhaps, as Wolfgang Friedmann comments with regard to nationality, it is still Utopian to think in terms of universal standards of individual rights or of the suppression of state jurisdiction through the creation of a direct international apparatus under the

---

This chapter remains substantially as it was written in 1972. It should be read in the context of subsequent events in Chile.

rule of such an organization as the United Nations.[1] Although this is unlikely at the universal level, such a prospect should not be disregarded at the regional level, which already offers some good examples in this respect, such as the European Convention on Human Rights of November 1950.

Human Values and Legal Rule

The basic problem involved in the development of this and other essential aspects of law, both national and international, goes beyond the juridical field and is posed in the sphere of values and basic concepts concerning the human being. Charles De Visscher underlined this problem as follows:

> In the international as in the internal order, human values are the reason behind the legal rule. Based upon moral conceptions which are the very essence of civilization, they impose themselves upon the State, whose mission is to ensure their protection and their free development.[2]

To the extent that the states and their governments will reflect a common scheme of values concerning the individual, the eventual international regulation of their rights will pose no serious problems and, furthermore, will be the natural result of these values. This fact explains the progress attained by regional arrangements in this respect, since these arrangements are being developed among the states sharing common cultural values.

However, many states maintain and promote values that are exactly the opposite, according to which the individual is nothing but an object at the service of the only entity entitled to any rights, which is the state. All forms of totalitarianism offer a clear example of this destruction of values, which leads to the complete abolition of individual rights.[3]

In the absence of common values, any international regulation turns out to be impossible, for, as it was stated by l'Institut de Droit International, "An effective legal order among States is inseparable from respect for the human person in the internal order of each State."[4] Furthermore, when those called upon to administer the law are not profoundly convinced of the intrinsic value of human persons, any formal guarantee that the legal order may contain turns out to be a dead provision without real force, whether its source is municipal or international: only the state interest will prevail.

Values and the Evolution of International Law

From the point of view of international law, the values are of the greatest importance. Its evolution has been influenced to a great extent by the gradual incorporation of human values into its structure. Traditional international law, conceived as a body of rules among states, treated the individual more as an object than as a subject of international relations; gradually the individual reached the status of subject, for limited purposes, to the extent to which a person's own values were recognized.[5]

The writers who have recognized the individual as the only true subject of international law have not been few.[6] J. L. Brierly, for his part, has brilliantly shown that the state is nothing but a historical stage in the forms of social organization that individuals have decided to give themselves.[7] Therefore it is not an exaggeration to think of a gradual abolition of the state as a form of social organization, an abolition that in many aspects is already discernible.

However, as long as this process does not attain its full maturity, it is realistic to think with Jessup "that fundamental changes will take place only through state action, whether affirmative or negative."[8] Philip C. Friedmann, in this vein, wrote, "It follows from this premise that far and away the most important means of improving the position of the individual in international law must be the strengthening of the legal obligations of states to exercise their prerogatives and take action for the protection of legitimate individual interests."[9]

The preceding considerations allow one to state that any progress that individual rights might make, both at the municipal and the international levels, will depend substantially on the acceptance of the values inherent to the human person. Otherwise the basic contradictions will remain, in a world that at the same time that it proclaims a Universal Declaration of Human Rights proceeds to the forceable transfer of populations, collective expulsions, denial of the right of departure, systematic taking of private property, and destruction of nationalities. For this reason it is necessary to consider not only the formal provisions of law, but also its true spirit of enactment and application in relation to the values in force in a particular society.

Chile: A Case Study?

Chile is, perhaps, a unique case for the study of individual rights before the state in the field of foreign affairs, as well as in other fields that are not to be considered here.[10] On the one hand it presents the perspective of a country that throughout the nineteenth century underwent an important degree of economic development, trade expansion, and monetary strengthening, to the extent of becoming a capital-exporting country. Gradually this condition deteriorated until Chile had to face almost all the evils and problems of an underdeveloped country.[11] Its legal institutions have been basically the same in both periods, but their operation and implementation in practice has necessarily had to change.

On the other hand, it is the case of a traditionally democratic and liberal country, the government of which was achieved through elections by a Marxist-Leninist combination of political parties and president in 1970. Its legal institutions continued to be basically the same, and the government hoped and intended to build a socialist structure within the legal framework of a liberal and democratic society. However, the values of socialism and democracy are often opposites.

Therefore individual rights against the state can be assessed by the contrast of development to underdevelopment and liberal democracy to Marxism, and by the fact that the structure of the legal institutions has remained substantially unchanged from a formal point of view. This makes particularly interesting the examination of the real meaning of individual rights in the field of foreign affairs, in relation to the social values in force in each of these different stages. Such is the perspective of municipal law, which is to be combined with the one provided by international law already mentioned in the preceding section.

THE INDIVIDUAL

The Individual as a National

The Political Constitution of the State (1925) ensured the following to all the inhabitants of the Republic:

> the freedom to reside at any point in the Republic, to move from one place to another or depart from its territory, on condition that police regulations are observed and that no third party is prejudiced; no one may be detained, prosecuted, arrested or deported, except in the form provided by law.[12]

Thereby, in the same manner as previous constitutions and particularly that of 1833, personal and individual freedom and the rights of movement are guaranteed.

Individual freedom is mainly secured through the remedy of habeas corpus, established in Article 16 of the constitution. Through these procedures any individual who has been detained, prosecuted, or arrested in violation of constitutional guarantees may by himself or by anyone on his behalf demand the intervention of the corresponding court of appeal. The court, proceeding in a brief and summary manner, may order the immediate release of that individual, order that due process of law be observed, or place the individual at the disposal of the proper court. It must be noticed that procedures can be started by the individual affected by the violation or by anyone in his name, and this can be done even by telegraph.

It must be pointed out that both the individual freedom and the habeas corpus procedures also protect aliens, since these guarantees are ensured "to all inhabitants of the Republic." However, there are limitations on the rights of aliens, which are discussed later in this chapter.

The system of constitutional guarantees reflects typical democratic and liberal social values, in which the rights of the human person have reached their utmost expression. Traditionally the achievement of this was the object of a generalized consensus, both by those who govern and by those who are governed, which explains why the provisions of the constitution are only of a minimal character and do not try to enter the detailed regulation of each matter, as is frequently the case with Latin American constitutions that are not based upon such consensus.

For instance, freedom of movement has no other limitation than the observance of police regulations; these regulations are enacted by the government and might become very strict, but governmental discretion has been trusted, assuming that the juridically protected social value will be fully observed and safeguarded.

Nevertheless, this basic balance provided by the generalized consensus had been gradually undermined as a consequence of the appearance of different social values, which in time had led to the consideration and application of different standards to the same norms. This process was evident in such matters as property rights and some others. As will be examined further below, it also became apparent with regard to the right of movement.

Administrative procedures and the absence of administrative tribunals are factors that make this phenomenon even worse, since they are often necessary to put the guarantees into practice. Cases of intentional misapplication or distortion are not unknown. The Chilean legal system, broad and flexible though it is when granting large powers to the government that can be applied at will, makes the introduction of values contrary to individual rights easier, to the extent that the consensus mentioned will actually no longer be in force.[13]

The nature and extent of individual rights, such as departure from or return to the country, were to be examined within this system of constitutional guarantees. The presence of different social values and different interests are expected to explain the problems of interpretation and implementation that affect these rights in practice.

Movement

Passports. From the very moment at which the constitution guarantees the right of departure from the country, the state is bound to provide all its nationals with the necessary documentation for the exercise of this right. The usual document is a passport, except in those cases in which international agreements provide for other documents.[14] In exceptional cases Chilean passports may be granted to aliens.[15] This general obligation is to be complied with by the corresponding administrative bodies in the country and by Chilean consulates abroad.

The granting of passports is a right of the individual and an obligation of the state. Only exceptionally may the state refuse to grant this document, in such cases expressly provided for in the passport regulations. Among others, the reasons for such refusal would be cases of minors under certain circumstances, of persons who are not allowed to leave the country by provision of law or judicial order, of workers and employees holding a contract who must prove that they are entitled to prepaid return tickets to the country, of those repatriated at the expense of the state who have not paid the cost of repatriation, and of those who do not produce certificates proving that they have fulfilled their tax obligations and that they are not stopped from leaving the country.

These exceptions to the right to a passport will be commented upon further below in relation to the right to departure. However, it must be noted that passport regulations are set up by means of a simple decree from the Ministry of the Interior that may be modified at any moment by another decree issued by the same authority. Therefore the exercise of the right guaranteed by the constitution is left to a great extent to the discretion of the executive. The already-mentioned problem of the consensus in this regard is of essential importance, since a government upholding totalitarian values could perfectly well restrict freedom of movement through administrative action.

In general passports may not be withdrawn from Chilean nationals; but in practice there are administrative procedures that lead to the same results. Although Article 14 of the passport regulations requires, prior to the granting of a passport, that the petitioner must produce a certificate issued by the Bureau of Investigation stating that there are no judicial or police impediments to his or her departure from the country, in practice this procedure is also required for those who already have valid passports and wish to leave the country, by means of a registration of departure.

Anyone who does not obtain this registration cannot leave the country, and his or her passport will therefore be as useless as if it had been withdrawn. Restrictions for leaving the country will be examined further below; in general they are related to cases of prosecution or conviction for offences. The meaning of "police impediments" is not at all clear.

Chilean passports are valid for travel to any country. However, in practice passports are sometimes granted by Chilean consulates that are "valid only for the return to Chile." This is because of an effort to curb the frequent abuse of the right to a passport; often this document is misused, and then a new passport is requested from consulates with the excuse that the original one has become "lost."[16]

The right to a passport is not adequately protected by means of remedies. As has already been explained, in Chile there are no administrative tribunals. An adequate interpretation of habeas corpus should permit its application to this case, since the individual who is refused a passport is being prevented from the exercise of the right of movement guaranteed by the constitution.

The judicial decisions have been contradictory. In some occasions it has been held that habeas corpus is only admissible when there is "detention" in the restricted meaning of the term, that is, when the individual has been arbitrarily arrested.[17] On other occasions it has been stated that in the constitution "detention is opposed to the freedom thereby ensured to reside at any point of the Republic, to move from one place to another or to depart from its territory; therefore the word <u>detention</u> must be interpreted in its wider sense with the purpose of making habeas corpus admissible."[18] Legal doctrine is definitively inclined in favor of this latter intrepretation.[19] In any case, the problem has never been discussed in relation to the granting of passports.

Another interesting possibility is the one provided for by the penal code, which punishes offenses committed by civil servants against the rights guaranteed by the constitution and, particularly, civil servants who arbitrarily "prevent an inhabitant of the Republic from departing from its territory, in such cases in which there is no prohibition established by the law."[20] In cases in which there is no formal denial of passport but the passport is not granted, another provision of the code could also be applicable; this one punishes a civil servant "who should maliciously retard or refuse individuals the protection or service which he is bound to give in accordance to the law and regulations."[21]

Apart from these possibilities it would be of the greatest convenience if those remedies could guarantee the constitutional right under proper regulations, particularly if the broad discretionary powers that are actually enjoyed by the executive branch are taken into consideration.

Departure. The right to depart from a country is certainly one of the essential rights inherent to the human person, since no one should be retained against his or her will in a society that does not satisfy that individual for some reason, whether the reason is political, economic, cultural, or religious. Although the problem is certainly related to collective emigration, it should be treated separately because the consequences of individual and collective emigration are different. Collective emigration is a problem of general policy, both for the state of the emigrants' nationality and for the recipient state; this problem has serious economic and social aspects. Some of these problems will be briefly examined in relation to the rights of aliens.

In the case of noncollective expatriation, or even in the case of a collective expatriation that technically cannot be called "emigration," such as one motivated by political reasons, such problems of general policy are not posed in the same manner, and the rights of the human person must be fully safeguarded.

The right to expatriation has been the cause of problems for a long time. As early as 1868 the Congress of the United States passed a joint declaration that "whereas the right of expatriation is a natural and inherent right of all people,"[22] thus looking forward to opposing the restrictive policies enacted by European countries.[23] Today this problem has become critical, particularly because of restrictions imposed by the Soviet Union upon its nationals of Jewish origin and because of the restrictions imposed by Cuba. A growing concern for international regulation in this particular matter is already in sight.[24]

As has been mentioned, the Chilean constitution guarantees the right to depart from the country "on condition that police regulations are observed and that no third party is prejudiced." Of course, this broad guarantee has some restrictions provided by the law that constitute impediments to the exercise of this right. Penalties of imprisonment (prisión, presidio, reclusión);[25] restriction ("relegación");[26] and exclusion (deportation)[27] obviously prevent the individual from departing from the country. Some public officials cannot leave the country without special permission.[28]

It is also common that while a trial and proceedings are pending, an order to remain in the country will be issued by the court to prevent the frustration of the action of justice. Restrictions of public liberties may also be enacted in special circumstances by means of a state of siege, state of assembly, law of special powers, or state of emergency.[29] Some of these restrictions may eventually suspend the exercise of the right to depart. The constitutional condition that no third party be prejudiced is intended to prevent the exercise of the right from violating obligations to third parties, for instance in family law.

Aside from these natural and obvious restrictions, there are some other kinds of restrictions of the exercise of the right that are progressively being enacted, many of which are not quite compatible with the constitutional guarantee. Some of the exceptions included in the passport regulations that enable the state to deny passports are related to the legal impediments just examined. Such would be the case, for instance, of persons prevented from leaving by judicial order or of those repatriated at the expense of the government who have not paid for the cost of repatriation, since here a third party would be prejudiced. Other cases, such as those involving minors or workers, stem from the fact that these individuals need special protection to prevent a later prejudice.

In other cases, particularly those related to tax requirements, the situation is entirely different. One such requirement is to prove that taxes have been paid; there can be no objection with regard to such a policy. However, in practice someone is often required to make the declaration and payment of taxes before the dates set by the law, this being the only possibility of obtaining the certificate. Thus an illegal restriction has been created. At the same time, a declaration by a third person accepting responsibility for the payment of taxes during the absence of the traveler is also required, which is not clearly compatible with the constitutional provision.

Furthermore, the obligation to pay a travel tax of about $70 has been established for those traveling to countries outside Latin America.[30] This restriction is definitely against the constitutional guarantee, since its specific purpose is to discourage departures from the country and the reason invoked is the priority of economic necessities. Such restriction also discriminates against the low-income population sectors, which cannot afford extraordinary expenses of this nature. This is perhaps one of the effects that economic underdevelopment has had on the exercise of individual rights.

Even more dangerous was the tendency of the executive to restrict increasingly the exercise of the right of emigration and freedom of movement by means of its broad administrative powers. The quota of foreign currency to which each traveler is entitled has been constantly reduced, it being illegal to buy any such currency except in the state banks. High customs charges have also been established for those entering or leaving the country with Chilean currency.[31] This means that no one can move with any kind or amount of money, other than that sold by the state in accordance with the quotas and rates of exchange set at its own free will. Furthermore, the right to take personal belongings from the country was also restricted to $500 per capita; above this figure, high duties have been levied.

All these restrictions have gradually transformed the constitutional guarantee into an empty provision without real meaning. Given the enormous powers of the executive branch, at any moment a situation can be created in which the individual has the right to depart from the country but with no belongings or money, as is the case in Cuba for those who have obtained permission to leave.

Each new restriction has been justified by the government by many arguments of economic necessity, but in fact there has been a political conception behind these that does not place strong emphasis on the value of individual rights. This never was the intention of the constitutional guarantee, which was conceived in the framework of a democratic society and premised on the idea that the individual not only has the right to physical movement but also to the disposal of the means that are necessary to prevent such a movement from becoming a pilgrimage of misery. The emergence of these restrictions is illustrative of the different results that may emerge when different social values underlie the administration of the law.

The problem of remedies is similar to the one posed in relation to the right to obtain a passport. In terms of a broad interpretation, habeas corpus should always be obtainable when an individual is prevented from leaving the country, even if not arrested. However, in terms of a restrictive interpretation such as the one that construes detention as synonymous with arrest, the remedy of habeas corpus would not be admissible; but even in the case of a broad interpretation, such as the one supported by the general tendency of court decisions and by writers, all problems do not receive satisfactory solutions.

As a matter of fact, in accordance with the broad interpretation, recourse would be admissible when the individual is prevented from departing, although it is doubtful whether this would be so if departure were only permitted with no economic means, belongings, or money. A restrictive interpretation of the constitution would lead to a negative answer, in which case the protection would be related to an incomplete right, while a liberal interpretation would declare the recourse admissible, making a real and complete value of the right. Again, the problem has not been discussed in relation to the right to depart.

A second problem arises with regard to the extent of the remedy in cases of extraordinary restrictions upon the rights guaranteed by the constitution, such as a state of siege. Although the decisions of courts have admitted that habeas corpus should always be admissible, even when the law expressly refuses all remedy,[32] decisions are not clear with regard to these extraordinary restrictions. In several cases of state of siege the Supreme Court has rejected the admissibility of the recourse.[33] In spite of the fact that writers are in favor of admissibility,[34] it has been argued that the courts cannot examine the facts on which the executive bases its decisions to restrict individual freedom, since such an examination would be equivalent to a substitution of the functions of the executive by the judiciary. According to this proposition, courts can only examine whether the fact corresponds to those set by the law as the basis for restriction.[35]

Should this interpretation be admitted, a serious restriction to the objectives of habeas corpus would have been created, since the executive would be the only branch of government entitled to examine the facts and would even be entitled to do so arbitrarily. As will be shown further below with regard to the rights of aliens, this problem of qualification of facts has been raised often.

In some specific matters there are special remedies available. This is the case of the decisions of the Central Bank on imports, exports, and exchange regulations, which can be questioned in court.[36] The provisions of the penal code mentioned above would also be applicable.

An adequate regulation with regard to remedies is urgently required, since the right to depart guaranteed by the constitution is not satisfactorily protected. This is particularly urgent when initiatives to restrict the departure of professionals and technicians are being promoted. The economic value of these persons to a country is certainly important, but still more important is the moral value of their rights as individuals.

Return. For a long time, until 1971, the guarantee of individual freedom established in the constitution only covered the right to depart from the country, no mention being made to the right of Chileans to return. However, during this period, it was generally understood that the latter right was also protected by the constitution.[37] On 9 January 1971 a constitutional amendment was enacted that made Article 10, Number 15 of the constitution expressly provide for the right to return to the country; this was also the result of the guarantees that the Chilean democratic parties required from the new government.

The right to return is only restricted by those penalties imposed in Chile that have to be served abroad, it not being possible for these citizens to return until they have been fully served; these penalties are "confiñamiento" and "extrañamiento."[38] With regard to remedies the problem is posed in the same manner already mentioned, since the protection is related to the same guarantee of freedom of movement.

Expulsion. Expulsion of nationals from Chilean territory can only take place by means of a judicial decision imposing the penalties of confiñamiento or extrañamiento mentioned above. In general, both the penal code and the law of internal security of the state, as well as the code of military justice, reserve these penalties for the punishment of offenses against the external security of the state, its internal security, or public order.

I do not propose to enumerate the many applications of these penalties here.[39] As an example we may note that the penalty of confinamiento is applicable to those who commit armed insurrection against the government to promote civil war and to those who revolt to impede a popular election or to prevent the enactment or application of laws.

The penalty of extrañamiento is applicable to offenses such as obeying the orders or provisions of a foreign government directed against the independence or security of the state, providing assistance to a foreign power with a view to counteracting the self-determination of the Chilean people, and financing or assisting the organization of private groups with a view to substituting them for the public forces.

Every legal remedy is available against the decision of a court imposing any of these penalties, particularly the recourse to appeal. Should there be a violation of the constitutional guarantees related to detention, habeas corpus would also be admissible. For instance, if public officials should detain a Chilean national and expel him from the country, habeas corpus would undoubtedly be admissible, not only because the guarantees of detention and prosecution have not been observed but also because the constitutional guarantee of the right to reside in any part of the territory would have been violated.

With regard to habeas corpus, there have also been problems of interpretation in this matter. The tendency toward restrictive interpretation has led to the argument, at least on one occasion, that recourse is admissible when there is an arbitrary order of detention or imprisonment, but that holding the individual in custody to effect his expulsion does not technically constitute detention and that habeas corpus is therefore inadmissible.[40] As was already explained, in this view detention is synonymous with arrest, and habeas corpus would not be admissible for protection of the right to reside at any place in the republic or to depart from its territory, since in such cases there would have been no arrest.

As of this writing, this problem had lost some of its importance, since no Chilean may be expelled without trial. Should anyone be so expelled there would be a violation of the guarantee of prosecution, which makes habeas corpus admissible even upon the most restrictive view. However, as will be examined further below, the problem persists with regard to aliens.

Expulsion is possible only when a foreign country is willing to admit the one expelled, since otherwise the individual would lose his right to live in some place of the world, a right which, as De Visscher comments, was asserted a long time ago.[41]

Several aspects of the right of movement are already part of the concern of contemporary international law. In the field of human rights and their international protection, this concern is increasingly evident. The United Nations Covenant on Civil and Political Rights already has provided for an important implementation of the right. "Everyone shall be free to leave any country, including his own; . . . no one shall be arbitrarily deprived of the right to enter his own country."[42]

The same principle is supported by the American Convention on Human Rights, which is still not ratified by Chile, when it provides that

> Every person has the right to leave any country freely, including his own. . . . The exercise of the foregoing rights may be restricted only pursuant to a law to the extent necessary in a democratic society to prevent crime or to protect national security, public safety, public order, public morals, public health, or the rights or freedom of others.[43]
>
> . . .
>
> No one can be expelled from the territory of the state of which he is a national or be deprived of the rights to enter it.[44]

Obviously there is still much to be done to give to these guarantees and rights a real meaning. However, Friedmann pointed out that the most adequate means for the protection of individuals is to strengthen the obligations of the state with regard to the exercise of its prerogatives and to the protection of legitimate individual rights. This observation, which is also mentioned above, is evidently supported by an increasing practice and reality. The international protection of human rights is one of the means by which a state may be bound by precise obligations.

Although it is true that there are still many conflicting aspects in the domestic jurisdiction of states and in the desire for international regulation, which actually make the development of international regulation very difficult, it is also true that in certain aspects it is now possible to think of the harmonization of municipal systems by means of international agreement, which is another way of imposing precise obligations on the state.

The relative progress that has been registered so far with regard to refugees or nationality reveals a certain tendency in favor of international regulation in spite of the many difficulties that have been encountered. Could it not be possible to do the same in matters such as the right of the individual to live somewhere or the prohibition of expulsion in violation of this right, or in matters such as the right to obtain a passport and documentation?

The only indispensable requirement for reaching some progress in this matter is a realistic approach. It is useless to work on ideal solutions that states will never accept or that might even worsen the position of the individual instead of improving it.[45] Realism will reflect the values in terms of the human person that the respective states promote at home and the degree to which these values are further promoted by these states in the international agreements to which they are parties. It seems unlikely for the time being that the same obligations might be imposed upon states that are parties to the European Convention on Human Rights and upon the Soviet Union, for instance, since their respective value systems are in conflict.

In accordance with the preceding considerations, it is possible to conclude that any effort for improvement must be directed toward two objectives. On the one hand the cooperation among those states that share common values must be strengthened, since they will be capable of reaching harmonization or international regulation with greater facility. Some regional arrangements are already evidence of this harmonization.

On the other hand, the commitment to the task of promoting the value of the human person and defending that person against the irrational enlargement of the state function must be intensified. This will be the only way to create the necessary conditions on which international regulation may be based in the future and the only way to prevent the emergence of that world of horror anticipated by Aldous Huxley in Brave New World and by George Orwell in 1984. Wolfgang Friedmann has warned us that these nightmares might become a generalized reality through the world.[46]

Protection

The law and practice of Chile with regard to the protection of nationals is quite broad; however, a progressive diminution of such protection may be observed. As already noted, it is in this kind of regression, in which the effects of different levels and conditions of economic development or underdevelopment are demonstrated in the same legal institution, that the different values with which private initiatives are looked upon find their most typical expression. When Chile during the nineteenth century became a capital-exporting country and developed an active commerce all through the whole Pacific area, its protection of nationals was very intensive. To the extent to which these factors gradually disappeared, the practice of protection also diminished, leaving behind only a remnant.

Extent of Freedom of Activity Abroad. In general the Chilean state does not have jurisdiction over the activities of its nationals abroad. Therefore as a matter of principle Chileans are free to develop any activity that is not prohibited by the laws of the country in which they are residents or in which their action takes place. This general rule has, of course, several exceptions, particularly with regard to offenses committed abroad.

As a result of this rule the state cannot prohibit its nationals from establishing industries or businesses in foreign countries; nor can it lay down conditions in this matter. However, this will be so only to the extent that such nationals do not take capital from Chile but obtain it from some other place. The restrictions are so strong that it is virtually impossible to export capital for the establishment of industries or businesses. Only with the permission of state organs can this be done, under conditions set forth by the state. In practice this permission is only granted to government-owned enterprises.[47] During the nineteenth-century period of economic expansion, freedom of activity abroad, including the export of capital, was absolute, but since then, because of the deterioration of the economic situation, state controls have progressively become stronger, until at this writing they are total.

Therefore freedom of activity abroad is largely theoretical, since the state, by means of its control on exchange and foreign trade, will not allow the exportation of capital, will restrict it to those particular countries in which it might be interested, or may even lay down conditions. Freedom would only exist if capital were obtained from a non-Chilean source.

Because the Chilean economy has no significant activities abroad, antitrust legislation is only applicable to restrictive practices that are developed in the domestic market.[48]

However, a change in these conditions might eventually be expected by means of the operation of agreements of economic integration. The Agreement on Subregional Integration of the Andean Countries in particular provides for the enactment of an investment statute within the subregion, in the context of which Chilean nationals could eventually develop investment activities in the other countries of the area. In such a case the state will be bound to grant the corresponding facilities. A mechanism for the protection of freedom of competition is also sought by this agreement; thereby an antitrust control over activities developed abroad could eventually be established. The international regulation of the activities of the individual that are developed beyond the jurisdiction of the state is certainly one of the most significant symptoms of the evolution that international economic relations are undergoing.[49]

Chilean practice with regard to foreign enlistment reveals a concern about the problems posed by the enlistment of Chilean nationals in a foreign country. Protection has constantly been granted to those nationals who are compelled to enlist in foreign armed forces;[50] however, here also there is a gradual diminution in practice.

In accordance with this policy, Chile has encouraged and entered into treaties intended to prevent compulsory enlistment of the nationals of each of the contracting parties who are residents in the territory of the others.[51] Chilean nationality is not lost by foreign enlistment[52] or by compulsory adoption of the nationality of the country of residence as a condition of this residence.[53]

Chilean legislation prohibits and punishes enlisting or providing other kinds of military assistance to a foreign state engaged in a war with regard to which Chile has declared its neutrality,[54] and does not grant to nationals who violate this prohibition any protection whatsoever.[55] It also punishes a national who fights against his country under enemy command.[56] Nationality is lost by assisting the enemies of Chile during a war.[57]

Another area in which Chilean legislation shows a special concern is the one related to offenses committed abroad. Article 6 of the Organization of Courts Code enumerates many cases of offenses committed abroad that come under the jurisdiction of Chilean courts. Particular importance is given to those offenses that affect the sovereignty or the external security of the state, including treason, separatism, espionage, and such offenses against international law as violation of truce or neutrality.

On at least one occasion the violation of a treaty has also been made punishable. The 16 May 1832 Treaty of Commerce and Navigation between Chile and the United States established that in case of a violation of its provisions by the citizens of either of the contracting parties, both parties undertook not to grant protection to the offender and to punish the violation.[58]

The Right to Diplomatic Protection. Every Chilean national has the right to diplomatic protection from the government. This is expressly provided by the General Instructions to the Diplomatic Corps[59] and by the Consular Regulations.[60] The extent of this right and the manner in which it is to be implemented are not well established in Chilean legislation. Apparently the provisions just mentioned make a distinction between two cases. On the one hand it is provided as a general rule that "all Chileans residing in a foreign country are entitled to the protection of Chile"[61]; on the other hand it is provided that they are entitled to the protection necessary to obtain justice, of which the Ministry of Foreign Affairs is to be informed.[62]

On the other hand, it is provided that consuls shall take due care that the persons and properties of Chileans be granted the rights ensured by treaties or, in the absence of treaties, the rights that the laws and practices of that country grant to aliens.[63] Should these rights be affected, the consuls are to make the corresponding claims to the local officials. If no remedy is provided they are to make the necessary protest, of which the diplomatic mission or the Ministry of Foreign Affairs is to be informed.[64]

In all these cases only a minor form of protection is involved, which is the one usually provided by consular officials. In spite of the fact that terms such as "protection" or "claims" are used, this is obviously not the same as the institution known as "diplomatic protection" in international law. With regard to the latter, it is only provided that all claims must be previously authorized by the Ministry of Foreign Affairs, except in urgent cases.[65] Thus the government will always keep its powers to grant or not grant the protection requested by Chileans, thereby following the classical standards of international law. No legal provision compels the government to grant its protection automatically.

Therefore, the rule may be formulated as follows: all Chileans are entitled to the diplomatic protection of their government, which may grant it or not, entirely at will. Since no distinction has been made about the forms of protection, if the government decides to grant it, it can take the form of a presentation of a claim to a foreign government or that of the commencement of international judicial proceedings in the pertinent cases.

In Chile there are no special procedures for requesting diplomatic protection; it is only provided that all Chileans have the right of petition before public authorities.

Since there are no clear provisions of law in this matter, examination of practice is of the greatest importance in establishing the conditions under which the government has been willing to grant its protection. The first significant fact that Chilean practice shows is that the government has always been very cautious about granting protection and has only done so in very qualified cases. A good résumé of this policy is stated by the Attorney (Fiscal) of the Supreme Court of Justice, as follows:

> The Government of Chile, according to its desire to maintain foreign relations on a footing of perfect equality and justice, particularly with regard to neighboring nations of the same origin, shall not grant its protection except to those claims of its nationals that are fully justified in their motives, that have remained unheard without reason, that have been initiated after local remedies have been exhausted in accordance with the municipal laws of the country in which the injury takes place, and that are also supported by the principles of international law.[66]

With a view to strict compliance with this policy, which has also been supported by writers,[67] for a long time the government followed the practice of requesting prior advice from the Attorney (Fiscal) of the Supreme Court with regard to the admissibility of the claim.[68] Thereby it was also ensured that the institution of diplomatic protection be administered more as a judicial function than as a political function; for years the latter approach has vitiated the international practice of other states.

A second condition that has always been required by the government is the previous exhaustion of local remedies in the country where the injury has taken place. From this point of view, the practice that the government follows with regard to its own nationals is in perfect harmony with the practice followed with regard to aliens, who are also required to exhaust local remedies when presenting claims against the Chilean government. The policy of the Ministry of Foreign Affairs in this matter is well established, as follows:

> It is a well known rule of international law that the claims that a government presents to another government through diplomatic means, in favour of the individuals who complain of injuries or prejudices and of whose rights the Courts are called to judge, must be preceded by the corresponding judicial proceedings. Only in the case of a denial of justice or of a manifestly unjust ruling which is final and conclusive . . . only in such extreme case, according to the practice of nations, a claim from government to government will be admissible with view to compensate those injured.[69]

Chilean practice shows some other elements, closely related to the preceding requirements, that are in accordance with the generally accepted practice of international law. One of these elements is the principle that the individual who commits an offense abroad must be held responsible for it, claims not being admissible in this matter except by a request that due process of law be observed.[70] Also, in accordance with a well-established principle of international law, protection will not be granted to Chileans who have dual nationality, with regard to the states of their other nationalities.[71]

Another principle that the government has constantly upheld is that the rights of aliens are measured in accordance with the rights of nationals. That is, the principle of a national standard of treatment does not recognize special rights in favor of aliens. The government has applied this same standard to its nationals residing abroad, refusing to grant protection when they have been affected in the same manner as the nationals of that other country in which they reside.

However, the application of this standard must be strongly opposed when the refusal to grant protection will result in a violation of human rights. This was the case of Chilean Jews residing in Germany, to whom protection was refused with regard to the abuses of the Nazi regime.[72] The Chilean government only presented a "friendly request" to the German government.[73] Contrariwise, in the past, protection was always granted to Chileans who were affected by collective expulsion or hostility in a foreign country.[74]

The influence that the degree of development has on the institution of diplomatic protection is very evident. During the period of economic expansion in the nineteenth century, the government of Chile systematically protected its nationals and their interests abroad, even to the point of waging war in protection of its nationals injured by a foreign government.[75]

When this prosperity began to deteriorate, the practice of diplomatic protection also diminished, and nowadays it is almost no longer practiced. Furthermore, this phenomenon is coincident with the gradual change in the values upheld by different governments with regard to private initiative, ranging from the strong promotion and protection of the past to the obstruction and discouragement in present times, from the point of view of both national and of international action.

<u>The State and Compensation</u>. Chilean legislation is silent on the problem whether the state that secures compensation from a foreign country by reason of the injuries done to its nationals is bound to distribute it to these nationals. In the absence of an express provision

of the law, the problem has to be regulated by general principles of international law. However, none of these principles offer a satisfactory answer in this matter, since traditional standards in many cases are not coincident with those of modern trends. From the point of view of classical international law, only the state is entitled to claim the remedy, since it is assumed that the state has been injured by means of the injuries done to its nationals. Therefore, compensation belongs to the state, which is not bound to distribute it to its injured nationals.[76]

The modern view tends to hold that the one entitled to compensation is the one who has suffered the injury. If the injury is done to an individual, that individual is directly entitled to compensation, the state acting only as an agent on the individual's behalf and bound to distribute the compensation secured.[77] Only in the context of this modern approach is it possible to explain why the obligation to exhaust local remedies has to be complied with by the individual and to explain the fact that in some cases the individual has the possibility of suing a foreign government directly, or even his own government, before international tribunals.

In this matter Chilean practice shows at least one very interesting case. When the War of the Pacific came to an end, Chile and Peru signed a treaty of peace and friendship that provided that "compensations that are due by Peru to Chileans who have suffered injuries during the war shall be judged by an arbitral tribunal or by an international joint commission."[78] The government of Peru later argued that, although it was prepared to pay compensation, this was related to other debts that Chile on its part had undertaken to pay, thus achieving a clearance of reciprocal commitments.

In this situation the government of Chile was of the opinion that a debt from government to government, such as the one Chile had with Peru, should not be confused with a debt from government to individuals, such as the one Peru had with regard to Chilean nationals injured during the war. It further stated as follows:

> Therefore such provision is not a monetary obligation between both countries . . . but of the government of Peru with regard to Chileans who have suffered prejudice upon the occasion of the war. . . . The Government of Chile may sponsor the claimants, but the ruling of the tribunal shall order any payment by Peru, not to our government, but to the [individual] claimants.[79]

This thesis is truly revolutionary, particularly for the time when it was formulated, since it establishes that the one entitled to the claim and the compensation is the individual injured and that the state acts only as a sponsor. From this point of view the logical result is that the state is bound to distribute the compensation it secures to the individuals who are injured.

Another problem related to compensation is how the state is to proceed when it decides to distribute compensation and there are several nationals injured. Chilean legislation and practice are also silent on this matter.

Several laws provide for the distribution of certain properties among the creditors or injured persons, particularly with regard to bankruptcy[80] and maritime average.[81] In general, a priority of beneficiaries is established in accordance with the importance or categories of the respective credits. General principles could eventually be found in this legislation for their application by analogy to the distribution of compensation among several injured nationals.

In Chile the state is not bound to supplement the amount of the compensation secured in order to make it approximately equal to the real value of the loss suffered by the national; nor has the state ever done so voluntarily. This does not even happen with the taking of property by the state in the municipal sphere, such as agrarian expropriations, in which the individual affected normally receives a compensation that does not come anywhere near the real value of the taken property. It can hardly be expected, therefore, that there will be supplementary compensation in the international practice of the same state.

The Responsibility of the State for Injury Induced by Its Own Conduct. The progressive diminution of the practice of diplomatic protection has, among other effects, the result that Chilean practice has not received some problems or kinds of protection that are being developed in contemporary practice. Thus, for instance, Chilean legislation is silent regarding the problem of injury caused to nationals abroad that has been induced by the conduct of the state itself. No legal remedies exist for this purpose except the common remedies an individual has available with regard to state responsibility, which would probably lead to a negative result in this case.

Furthermore, the position, upheld by the Ministry of Foreign Affairs, that the rights of aliens are measured in accordance with the national standard probably would also lead to a complete refusal by the state of responsibility for injuries suffered by a national abroad in this situation.

Decisions related to the war of 1879 against Bolivia and Peru do not give any evidence that this problem was posed, both because by that time it had not yet been developed by practice and because both countries undertook to pay compensation for the injuries caused to Chilean nationals during the war. In any case, the Chilean state never did grant or supplement compensation to its nationals on this ground.

Waiver. What has been said poses an interesting problem with regard to the waiver by the state of claims presented because of the injury caused to its nationals. One of the effects of classical international law, which considered the state the only entity that was entitled to the claim and the compensation, was the possibility that the state might waive the right. However, if the one entitled to the claim is the individual directly injured, the state being only the individual's sponsor, is this waiver possible?

The problem is certainly of great complexity, since as was explained above, the state has an exclusive power to decide whether to accept the claims of its nationals and to grant the protection requested. From this point of view, in principle the state could refuse to give its sponsorship, since refusal would be one of the prerogatives of its exclusive power. However, if it is admitted that the state may refuse to sponsor, the effect would be exactly the same as if it had waived the claim, even though in the case examined, the state has no title of its own to the claim. The result would be that the individual is not protected and has no recourse against the responsible government.

This effect could only be prevented in two ways. (1) It could be provided by law that once the state has agreed to sponsor a claim of its nationals it will not be permitted to waive it later. (2) If international law clearly admitted the right of the individual to take action with regard to the foreign government responsible, the sponsorship of his or her government would no longer be required. There are already some manifestations of this tendency, and individual action has been admitted with regard to international organizations.[82]

Chilean legislation and practice do not offer any solutions to this problem, although there is evidence of a favorable approach to the exclusive power of the state, not only as acceptance of a claim is concerned but also with regard to its further pursuance. This has been stated as follows:

> The Government of Chile, in compliance . . . with its duty to protect the legitimate interests of Chileans injured by an act of a foreign government or by its authorities or troops, cannot refuse the protection requested by Mr. Rivas, although it will be subjected, in regard to procedures and the amount of the compensation, to the judgment that the consideration of this

> affair and the superior interest of our good relations with a friendly and neighboring republic will suggest.[83]

In the absence of a provision of law to the contrary, this broad discretionary power might eventually enable the state to waive a claim. However, in the case mentioned of the claim against Peru, the government of Chile refused to clear the claim with the public debts that it had incurred with regard to Peru.

A problem that has been common in Chilean practice has been that many times political considerations, such as the "superior interest" of the good relations with a foreign government, are taken into account when deciding on the admissibility of claims. This has often led to refusal of protection, even in cases in which the claim is manifestly just. This situation could be prevented if the institution of diplomatic protection were administered as a judicial and not as a political function, which was the approach the Chilean practice showed during a certain period.

Special Kinds of Protection. Finally, it must be noted that Chilean legislation does not provide for any kind of special protection, which might allow losses suffered by Chilean nationals abroad--for instance in cases of expropriation--to be spread over the whole community through government compensation or by other means.

Before drawing conclusions from this discussion, it is of interest to underline the close relationship existing between the economic and cultural status of a given community and the manner in which it tends to approach the corresponding problems of diplomatic protection and other related institutions in the international sphere.

When a satisfactory degree of economic development, and therefore of cultural amplitude, is reached, the state shows concern about the situation of its nationals abroad and about their rights as individuals. In contrast, states with underdeveloped economies are characterized by a lack of concern with regard to the interests and rights of nationals and by a strong parallel cultural limitation that undervalues the human person. The progress of international law in this field and its ability to control these institutions will therefore largely depend on the existence of a minimal base of a material and cultural nature.

Closely related to this phenomenon is another relationship of interest. In underdeveloped states the basic concern of legal institutions is inward-oriented within the respective community, and only in very exceptional cases will it be outward-oriented. Because of this there is less control over the economic activities of nationals abroad, thereby weakening the possibility of international regulation.

In a developed state the economy itself tends to move outward, and therefore legal institutions have a much broader perspective, thus facilitating international regulation. This perhaps will explain why the greatest developments of international law have always been principally induced by the necessities and orientations of the most developed countries.

Certainly the most well-established tendency in this field is the increased inability of the state to act as the central body of all regulations and forms of control. Because of the complexity of contemporary economic problems, in many aspects the state is no longer operative and efficient, since many kinds of action are already beyond state control.

If, for instance, the operations of a multinational corporation are examined, it will be evident that the state is no longer capable of controlling them, not even by means of extraterritorial application of its laws. This situation will gradually lead to the adoption of forms of control that will properly be international, upon the activities of both individuals and states. Thus a broad field is being opened for the development of international law.

This same tendency is also evident in the field of diplomatic protection. Because of the complexity of economic relations, the protective action of the state is no longer efficient. For this reason the direct standing of individuals before international courts is gradually being developed as a new kind of protection of individual rights, even with regard to the individual's own state. Certainly this tendency has eroded the status of diplomatic protection as the supreme institution that it was under classical standards.

Protection as a function of international organizations is part of this tendency, and its admission as a function of the individual, who will be able to proceed without the sponsorship of his or her government, is not an unknown phenomenon in contemporary international law. As a result of the different values prevailing with regard to private initiative, Latin American countries have been reluctant to accept the direct standing of individuals before international organs,[84] although in the past they created the first antecedent of significance in favor of this right of the individual.[85]

Individuals and Corporations. In spite of the fact that this tendency is basically positive, since it improves the implementation of the individual, it also has very serious deficiencies. In fact, as Friedmann points out,[86] the only individual who so far has a real possibility of benefiting from direct international participation is the big corporation, which by means of its strength and bargaining capacity can efficiently protect itself. However, the individual human being is still largely unprotected, being in the great majority of cases prevented from obtaining any benefit from such tendencies.

It is time that international law introduced a distinction between these two situations, which are basically different and which do not justify the indiscriminate application of the term "individual" to both. From this point of view the development of special kinds of protection for the human being is urgently needed. A significant first step would be to administer the institution of diplomatic protection as a judicial function, even under international control, to prevent the vicious political use and abuse that has been made of it and the lack of protection that it frequently generates.

The Individual as an Alien

Movement

Entry and Stay. All aliens entering Chile must, of course, have the relevant permission, be it of an individual nature, such as a visa, or of a general nature, such as the agreements on free transit mentioned above. The granting of this permission is a discretionary power of the state.

Chilean legislation has established some cases in which the entry of aliens might be prevented. These cases, in general, are related to those aliens who have been convicted or are actually being prosecuted for nonpolitical offenses, which the law qualifies as miscellaneous; to those who have departed the country by order of the government, which is a different case from that of expulsion; to those expelled from any other country by the proper authority; and in certain circumstances to minors.[87]

In addition to these cases, in which entry "might" be prevented, there are some other cases in which entry is prohibited. These prohibitions affect aliens who advocate doctrines intended to destroy or change by violent means the social order of the country or the republican and democratic form of government; those who promote such doctrines as activists; and those who perform acts that are contrary to the interests of Chile or that in the opinion of the government constitute a danger for the state. These provisions tend to protect the Chilean democratic organization, but as a result of the changes in values mentioned above, they have not been observed by the executive.

Other cases of prohibition affect those engaged in illegal traffic in narcotics, smuggling, or prostitution; those who have been convicted or are actually being prosecuted for nonpolitical offenses that the law qualifies as crímenes (felonies); those who do not have or cannot practice any profession or work or lack the means to support themselves in Chile; those who are afflicted by certain dangerous diseases; and those who have been expelled from Chile.[88]

In addition to the legal impediments, in the early 1970s there was also in Chile an increase in administrative practices intended to diminish the entry of aliens, particularly tourists. Among the regulations enacted, those related to foreign exchange were given the first priority, including an obligation to change a certain amount of hard currency for each day of sojourn, and application of the restrictions discussed above, with regard to entry or departure of Chileans with Chilean currency. In certain parts of the country, stores were prohibited from selling goods to aliens. This practice came to be known as the "paper curtain."

Two questions are particularly relevant with regard to the entry of aliens: that of whether there is any kind of vested right to return to the country and that of whether it is legitimate to discriminate racially in the granting of visas. Chilean legislation provides for several cases in which the alien holding a visa is entitled to reenter the country.[89]

In general, anyone holding a visa who wishes to leave the country and later return to it has the right to request the Ministry of Foreign Affairs for a "letter of reentry," which is valid for one year. By means of this letter, foreign service officials are instructed about the kind of visa to grant to the beneficiary for his or her return. This document does not exempt the beneficiary from the obligation to obtain a new visa, but the new visa will be granted automatically with no need for a new application.

For this purpose the applicant must prove that he or she is a resident in Chile. Those holding a visa on condition of a contract of work must prove that the contract is in force. Those who hold student visas must prove that they are actually students. When by reason of work an alien constantly has to leave and enter the country, that alien is not required to obtain a letter of reentry; instead the Ministry of Foreign Affairs authorizes his or her return by means of a note or declaration stamped in the passport. Those who hold a permit of permanent residence do not need to follow any of these procedures; they may reenter the country after filling out a simple tourist card.

An interesting problem is that related to racial discrimination by means of visas and other administrative permits. In a country like Chile, the legislation of which declares that both nationals and aliens are equal before the law and does not admit racial differences, is it legitimate for a government to discriminate by means of administrative procedures, for instance with regard to the granting of visas? Can it use its discretionary powers in a discriminatory manner? Apparently this problem is not posed in Chile, since there are no legal provisions that might be considered discriminatory in this sense, nor any administrative instructions, at least that are made public, that order any form of discrimination, a situation that would probably violate the UN covenants on economic, social, and cultural rights, on civil and political rights, and on the elimination of all forms of racial discrimination. However, the problem has existed in the past. Although it was principally related to problems of immigration, as indicated above this should in general be separated from the exercise of the individual right since the two are not coterminous.

The following instructions were issued in 1925 by the Ministry of Foreign Affairs:

> This Ministry has taken notice that a considerable number of individuals with bad antecedents and little skill for work have entered the country. One of the means of preventing such immigration is for consuls to comply with the provisions in force with regard to the granting of visas . . . and strictly enforce them in the case of individuals who have racial characteristics different from ours.[90]

In a more subtle form the Passport Regulations provided that "Chilean Consuls might not grant visas to individuals who in the consul's opinion might not be adaptable to the legislation and traditions of Chile."[91] The discriminatory intent of the latter provision became evident when other instructions by the Ministry of Foreign Affairs, which were based on it, instructed the consuls "to totally eliminate the granting of visas to Chinese citizens."[92] This, furthermore, was coincident with the point of view of the most important Chilean writers of international law at the time, who frequently made reference to "inferior races."[93]

Although this situation apparently does not exist any longer, there could be no doubt that it would be illegitimate. In fact, if the powers of the state in the legislative field have been limited by international law, by means of the covenants prohibiting all forms of racial discrimination, its administrative powers are still more limited, and could not be used validly in a discriminatory manner. Notwithstanding the fact that the covenants apparently are not applicable to this situation, even though the Spanish text leaves ground for doubt, the context within which they have been approved and brought into force is not really too different from the Chilean situation. In any case, this is a typical area calling for adequate international regulation, since it is a source of frequent disputes among states.[94]

Departure

Voluntary Departure. The constitutional guarantee examined above, by means of which the right to "depart from the territory" is ensured, exists for the benefit of "all the inhabitants of the Republic," thus also covering the situation of aliens. Habeas corpus and the other legal remedies that were then mentioned are also applicable in the case of the constitutional rights of aliens.

The exercise of these rights is subject to the same legal and de facto limitations that affect the rights of nationals. Thus, for instance, an alien who has been convicted and is serving a penalty is prevented from leaving the country. His or her rights may also be restricted on an occasion of extraordinary restrictions of constitutional guarantees, such as a state of siege. Also, in the case of war the government is empowered to proceed to the internment of enemy aliens,[95] and those who violate decrees of internment may be punished as for a criminal offense.[96] However, these are certainly not the kinds of restrictions that constitute a problem.

Both aliens and nationals are subject to a series of additional restrictions, such as the requirement of a permit for departure (registration of the passport) to prove that tax obligations have been complied with, and other restrictions related to foreign exchange and entering or leaving the country with Chilean currency, as well as some others that were mentioned above.

In some cases the regulations applicable to aliens are more liberal than those applicable to nationals. For instance, an alien departing from the country within 30 days following entry is not required to prove compliance with tax obligations nor to have a Chilean identity card. The registration of the passport can also be omitted when for reasons of work an alien frequently has to leave and reenter the country.[97] However, these exceptions do not change the general rule.

With regard to the extent of the rights of aliens, it is pertinent to raise the same question that was mentioned in relation to the rights of nationals, particularly when the rights of aliens who have been granted permits of permanent residence are involved. Does the constitutional guarantee cover only the physical departure of individuals, or does it also cover the right to leave with property?

As has been indicated, by the first alternative there would only be an incomplete right; a real and complete right can only be ensured by the second alternative. For this reason I definitively support the latter interpretation. Habeas corpus procedures should be applied to this situation and should protect individuals with regard to any restrictions that might affect their constitutional rights. So far this problem has not been discussed in the courts, but the liberal and restrictive tendencies of the decisions that were examined above with regard to the rights of nationals will probably also have an influence on this.

The Chilean Constitution has always ensured rights in their real meaning and extent. One of the first constitutions already provided with regard to aliens that "no one shall be prevented from coming to the country or leaving it when he desires with his property."[98] The fact that later constitutions were less explicit in this matter is not because of a restrictive purpose but rather because of the generalized consensus, which always understood that the full observance of the rights of the individual was the real meaning and extent of the corresponding provisions. Therefore it was not necessary to give details, and the right was sufficiently ensured by just saying that the individual could "depart from the territory."[99] Restrictive tendencies only appeared when the consensus began deteriorating and when contradictory social values with regard to the human person came into being.

The United Nations Covenant on Civil and Political Rights, ratified by the government of Chile, broadly ensures the right to depart freely from any country, since it declares that such right "shall not be subject to any restrictions except those which are provided by law, are necessary to protect national security, public order, public health, or morals or the rights and freedoms of others."[100] Many of the restrictions applied in Chile are not provided by law and have been enacted by means of administrative procedures of very doubtful legality.

Involuntary Departure (Expulsion and Deportation). Chilean legislation on the expulsion of aliens is broad indeed. The Law and Regulations of Aliens[101] provides that those aliens who by any circumstance or means should enter the country without complying with the requirements, conditions, and prohibitions of such legislation shall be subject to the immediate control of the authorities and moved to an inhabited part of the territory while their expulsion is decided. Only exceptionally, such as in the case of minor deficiencies in the documentation or in the case of political asylum, will the sojourn of these persons be regularized.

The requirements, conditions, and prohibitions established by the law are numerous and of a different nature. First there is the case of all those aliens entering the country in violation of the prohibitions with regard to entry that are established by the Regulations of Aliens, which were examined above. In this category we also have the case of those aliens who, after having entered the country, advocate doctrines or participate in activities that are contrary to democratic organization; affect external security, internal security, or public order; or engage in illicit traffic in narcotics, smuggling, or prostitution. These persons, as well as those who forge their documentation, are refused visas or their extension and are compelled to leave the country or expelled, in accordance with the procedure that will be examined further below.

In other cases requests for a visa may be refused. In this case the refusal is not obligatory, as in the preceding one. If the request is refused, the alien has to leave the country or be expelled. Examples, among others, are the cases of those convicted in Chile of felonies and other offenses; of those who make false declarations; of those who perform acts that may produce problems with regard to a country with which Chile maintains diplomatic relations or with regard to the authorities of such country; of those who become social problems by not being able to work, in terms that would have prevented entry into the country; of those who become afflicted by certain diseases that would also have prevented their entry; of residents whose visas are conditioned to a contract of work and who by their own fault bring about the termination of the contract; of those who have not complied with their tax obligations; and of those who by reasons of the convenience of the country do not merit the permit requested.[102] In some of these cases, particularly those that are more serious, visas in force may also be cancelled.

In addition to these particular requirements, aliens are also subject to some general requirements, the violation of which may also lead to their expulsion. Aliens who enter Chile are only allowed to perform activities that the law authorizes in relation to their specific visas; thus, for instance, a tourist may not engage in activities that might produce any sort of income.

Also, every alien is required to sign under oath a written declaration before the pertinent foreign service official that he or she will not engage in domestic politics or in acts that may constitute a problem to those governments with which Chile has friendly relations, and also that he or she will observe the Constitution, laws, decrees, and other provisions in force. In spite of the traditional enforcement of this requirement,[103] in the early 1970s it was no longer enforced with regard to certain aliens who advocated political doctrines that were coincident with those of the government.[104]

The Ministry of the Interior has broad discretionary powers in this matter. Applications for visas or their extension can be refused, and cancellations ordered by means of a simple administrative resolution. Only in the case of cancellation of a permit of permanent residence is a Supreme Decree signed by the Minister of the Interior required.

When the Ministry of the Interior orders a cancellation or refuses a permit, it must allow a period of at least 72 hours for the alien affected to leave the country. Should the alien not leave in this period, he or she will be expelled. The difference between leaving the country and being expelled in accordance with these procedures is very important. In the first case the alien's later reentry to the country "might" be prevented, while in the second case reentry is definitively "prohibited" as long as the decree of expulsion is in force.

What has been said presupposes that the alien has at least tried to clear his or her situation with the Ministry of the Interior or has a valid visa, which will enable the ministry to refuse the application or cancel the permit. In many cases the alien will actually be in the country, or will openly violate the legislation in force. In these situations, expulsion is the only pertinent measure.

In every case of expulsion the police must subject the alien to control and withdraw the alien's documentation. Expulsion requires a Supreme Decree stating the reasons why this measure is adopted. This will not only be omitted when the alien satisfactorily ensures that he or she will leave the country, authorities being bound to make sure that the alien does so. The Penal Code punishes the alien who has been expelled and later returns to the country while the decree of expulsion is still in force; in such a case he will be expelled once he has served his punishment without need of a new decree or of further procedures.

The Law of Internal Security of the State provides that when an alien is convicted for offenses against national sovereignty or external or internal security, the president must order his expulsion once the alien has served the penalty imposed. This will not be applicable to an alien who has a Chilean spouse or children.[105] Certain laws that are no longer in force were still more drastic. They provided that "aliens who . . . do not satisfy the conditions with regard to which the pertinent permit has been granted, shall be arrested by police authorities and expelled without further procedures, by means of a decree of the Ministry of the Interior."[106]

As already indicated above, expulsion will only proceed if another country will accept the individual expelled. In several cases the expulsion of aliens has not been possible because this elementary condition has failed. In any event, Article 13 of the United Nations Covenant on Civil and Political Rights should also be observed. This article reads as follows:

> An alien lawfully in the territory of a State Party to the present Covenant may be expelled therefrom only in pursuance of a decision reached in accordance with law and shall, except where compelling reasons of national security otherwise require, be

> allowed to submit the reasons against his expulsion and to have his case reviewed by, and be represented for the purpose before, the competent authority or a person or persons especially designated by the competent authority.

In addition to the reiteration of these rights, Article 22(8) of the American Convention on Human Rights further provides as follows: "In no case may an alien be deported or returned to a country, regardless of whether or not it is his country of origin, if in that country his right to life or personal freedom is in danger of being violated because of his race, nationality, religion, social status, or political opinions," and Article 22(9) prohibits the collective expulsion of aliens.

Remedies in Cases of Nonadmission and Departation. The legislation that has been examined is so broad that in fact any situation might, directly or indirectly, come under its provisions. Furthermore an important part of this legislation, such as the Regulations of Aliens, has been enacted by means of a simple degree, which may easily be enlarged. In these circumstances the only real guarantee of the individual rights of the alien, and his only protection against eventual arbitrary acts, will be by means of efficient judicial remedies. However, these remedies have not been satisfactory.

As indicated with regard to the rights of nationals, decisions of courts have accepted the admissibility of habeas corpus even when the law is silent or even when the law expressly provides that no recourse shall be available. This tendency has been reiterated in cases involving the rights of aliens, particularly with regard to the provision mentioned of the Law on Permanent Defense of Democracy, which allowed expulsion "without further procedures."[107] However, the extent of this remedy is not clear in the context of decisions. In addition to the problems of interpretation that were indicated with regard to nationals, which are also applicable with regard to aliens, two particular problems are posed here: What is to be understood by detention? and Who is competent to qualify the facts?

In decisions with a liberal tendency, habeas corpus is seen as necessary to protect individuals against restrictions that might impede their right to reside in any part of the republic, move from one place to another, or depart from the territory, as provided by the constitutional guarantee.[108] Detention would be all that restricts this guarantee, and this would be the meaning of the term as used by the Constitution. Expulsion prevents the individual from residing in the territory, and therefore recourse will be admissible. On the other hand, in decisions of a restrictive tendency, detention is only synonymous with arrest. Even though expulsion requires that the individual be held in custody and involves the restriction of the individual's freedom, this would not be the same as arrest and therefore recourse to habeas corpus would not be admissible.[109]

This last is the interpretation maintained by the Ministry of the Interior, which has stated:

> The provisions contained [in the Law and Regulations of Aliens] establish the power to enforce acts of apprehension and of restriction and deprivation of freedom which are necessary to effectively comply with a decree of expulsion: acts that . . . do not involve the detention or imprisonment established in Article 16 of the Constitution.[110]

Should this interpretation be accepted, aliens would be unprotected, and their constitutional guarantee would only be utopian. Decisions in the early 1970s have admitted this risk and have inclined in favor of the liberal tendency. The Supreme Court has stated as follows:

> The existence of an effective recourse before the courts of justice is a necessary element of the constitutional guarantee of personal freedom, which is involved in the right to freely choose the place of residence in the national territory, and which is insured by . . . the Constitution, . . . particularly when the alien is forcefully expelled from the country.[111]

The second basic problem is one related to the qualification of the facts on which the decision of the government to expel an alien is based. As indicated above, this problem is also posed with regard to extraordinary restrictions upon the constitutional guarantees, such as a state of seige.

The decisions with regard to the expulsion of aliens are also contradictory. In fact, on the one hand it has been said that both the Law and the Regulations of Aliens "grant to the government exclusive powers in this matter,"[112] which is the same as saying that the courts cannot examine the facts the government has considered in deciding upon expulsion. A tendency to the contrary has also become apparent, since "the power of the courts of justice to revise by their own means the restrictive decisions of personal freedom"[113] has been reaffirmed, and such facts have been qualified by the courts on some occasions.[114]

These contradictory tendencies in decisions have produced great confusion in the courts. On one occasion the Supreme Court admitted habeas corpus in favor of an alien because it considered that the facts invoked by the government could not be a basis for expulsion, but at the same time it declared that it could not deprive the decree of expulsion of its effects, since it lacked the constitutional and legal powers to do so.[115] The practical result of such a case is to permit the government the expulsion of an alien "without further procedures." This once again poses the need to construe habeas corpus in such a manner and with such amplitude as to protect the constitutional guarantee effectively.

In addition to habeas corpus there is only a limited remedy provided by Law Number 3.446 of 12 December 1918, by means of which entry into the country of aliens convicted or actually prosecuted for felonies, of aliens who could not work, and in other cases now incorporated to the Regulations of Aliens, was prohibited. In spite of the fact that all these aspects are actually regulated by the Law and Regulations of Aliens, the law of 1918 is still in force; therefore the remedy established in it is also in force and may be, and has been, invoked.[116]

By means of this remedy the alien affected may, alone or by anyone in his or her name, request a decision by the Supreme Court within five days following the publication of the decree of expulsion in the Diario Oficial. The Supreme Court must deliver its decision, proceeding as a jury.

The Limited Scope of International Law. The whole subject of the right of movement of aliens basically continues to be regulated by the full domestic jurisdiction of states. Curiously enough, in this field international law is still more limited and primitive than in the parallel field of the rights of nationals. For instance, the real timidity in the conception of the United Nations Covenant on Civil and Political Rights, which does not even require that the expelled alien be granted the right of recourse before the courts of justice but only permits approaching the same administrative authorities that have decided upon the expulsion, cannot be justified on any ground.

Although it is true that states are particularly jealous in this matter, it is nonetheless true that there is an urgent need to clarify, at least to a certain degree, the rights to which the individual is entitled as a part of the international protection of human rights.

International law could perfectly well introduce distinctions between situations that are essentially different. For instance, is it justifiable to expel an alien who becomes a social problem because he or she cannot work, in the same manner as one who has committed a criminal offense? Is the expulsion justified of an alien engaged in agriculture who has not complied with labor legislation and who has already been punished for this by the expropriation of his property, as in a case which has been registered by Chilean practice? Is the expulsion of one who has entered the country illegally more justifiable than that of one who has a permit of permanent residence?

Nothing seems to justify this, for situations that are so different also require different treatments. Although Chilean legislation takes a liberal approach in one kind of case and a stricter approach in another kind of case, this always depends on the discretionary opinion of the government, and it might lead to an expulsion in any alternative. It certainly would be better if the same international agreements that ensure the protection of human rights would also make explicit the different categories in which expulsion is or is not justified.

In this field, as well as with regard to nationals, the values that the respective governments uphold in relation to the human person will play a fundamental role. For this reason, the conclusion is equally justified that any progress will depend on the strengthening of the obligations of the state in order to effectively protect the legitimate rights of individuals. It will also depend on the advancement of international regulation by those states that share common values and on the strengthening of the conception of the fundamental rights of the human person.

Protection

For a long time Chilean legislation and practice has allowed for certain cases in which the protection of the government may be extended to individuals who have a foreign nationality but who are related to Chile by some particular link.

The consular regulations in force provide that, for the purpose of protection, consuls shall consider as Chileans those aliens serving on Chilean ships, but they shall not consider as Chileans those Chilean nationals serving on foreign ships except for very limited protection, such as to request that the conditions of the contract of service be observed or that they be contracted in accordance with Chilean legislation concerning the embarcation of Chileans in foreign ships.[117] In other words, protection is granted to aliens serving on Chilean ships but refused to Chileans serving on foreign ships, except for the purposes mentioned.

A different situation is the one provided for in the general instructions to the diplomatic corps. A friendly government that has no diplomatic mission where Chile does have one may entrust the protection of its nationals to the government of Chile, which requires the previous authorization of the Ministry of Foreign Affairs.[118] Likewise, Chile may entrust the protection of its nationals to a friendly government in a similar case.[119] However, this protection is performed in the name of the government that entrusts it and not directly.

Should there be no express provision, such as that in the consular regulations, that might authorize the granting of protection to aliens, the authorities are only bound to grant their protection to nationals. Already in 1864 the Ministry of Foreign Affairs stated, "I shall not omit mentioning to you the desire of the government that the consulates of Chile limit their acts of protection to the interests of the republic and of its nationals."[120]

Even though the provisions mentioned are principally related to protection by consular officials, which is different from diplomatic protection, there are no obstacles to the granting of diplomatic protection as well, should the case arise. Chilean practice does not show any antecedent that would shed light on how these provisions would have been applied if the problem had come up; nor are there provisions on the protection of aliens serving in the Chilean armed forces;[121] although since they are subject to an integral Chilean jurisdiction, the diplomatic protection of the government will also be applicable to their case.

NATIONAL IMPLEMENTATION OF INTERNATIONAL RIGHTS AND DUTIES

The Act of State Doctrine

Chilean legislation and the decisions of courts do not establish any limitation that might restrict the power of the courts to examine the validity of foreign legislation in terms of its compatibility with international law. In general, therefore, the problems that have restricted the action of British and U.S. courts by means of the Act of State doctrine, which on some occasions has prevented their judgment on this validity, are not posed in the case of Chile. It is true that there is no express provision or precedent that empowers courts for this purpose, but the interpretation of the legal system as a whole undoubtedly permits an affirmative response.

Chilean legislation frequently makes reference to public order (ordre public), which cannot be contravened. Thus, for instance, Article 1462 of the Civil Code provides that "anything which contravenes Chilean public law has an illicit object."[122] This will undoubtedly empower the courts to examine the validity of foreign legislation in terms of its compatibility with public order and to rule on whether such foreign legislation should be such considered in the courts as law[123] or as a mere fact,[124] a matter on which decisions have traditionally been divided. An application of these principles is that the enforcement of foreign judgments in Chile requires, among other conditions, "that nothing contained therein be contrary to the laws of the Republic."[125]

In some cases Chilean legislation itself orders the application of a certain foreign law,[126] which supposes an admission of its compatibility with public order. For this reason the remedy of annulment will be admissible for contravention of the foreign law when it has to be applied,[127] and with some frequency courts apply foreign law in their official capacity.[128] Although in general the Supreme Court has refused to rule on the constitutionality of a foreign law, it has accepted the admissibility of such a declaration should the foreign law contravene "a guarantee of public order."[129]

From this it is possible to conclude that at any moment Chilean courts may prevent the application of a foreign law if an examination of its validity leads to the determination that it is contrary to public order.[130] Thus, it is necessary to determine whether international law is a constitutive part of public order in Chile. If it is, the courts of justice should be empowered to examine the validity of foreign legislation in terms of its compatibility with international law, since if it contravenes the latter, it also contravenes public order. If it is not, the power of the courts to examine the validity of foreign legislation is uncertain.

Continuous practice and decisions have reaffirmed that in Chile international law is part of the law of the land. As early as 1833 the President and the Minister of Foreign Affairs declared that "general international law is really an integral part of the legislation of the state."[131] Undoubtedly this is so in the case of treaties and other conventional norms, whether they have been incorporated into municipal law by the traditional procedure of parliamentary approval[132] or by more modern procedures similar to executive agreements.[133] Furthermore, in all these cases international law has been admitted to be superior to municipal law.[134] Should a decision be delivered in contravention to a treaty, the remedy of annulment will also be admissible.[135]

Conventional international law is therefore part of Chilean municipal law. The extent to which international law is part of Chilean public order is basically a problem of interpretation. On the one hand it can validly be stated that international law is part of Chilean public law, even though its effects may often be directed to the field of private law. From the very moment at which public law is held to be part of the public order (for as it was indicated, the Civil Code declares illicit anything that contravenes it) it is possible to conclude that the whole of international law is part of the Chilean public order. In such a case, should the foreign legislation invoked be contrary to international law in force in Chile, the courts could prevent its application as being contrary to public order, in the same manner as if it were contrary to Chilean public law.[136] On the other hand, it is possible to consider that the strict application of this reasoning might lead to dangerous exaggerations.

Whatever might be the interpretation adopted, there is no doubt that Chilean courts are empowered to examine the validity of foreign legislation in terms of international law, since they are bound by the latter as part of municipal law. This is still more evident if it is remembered that for an important part of such decisions, foreign law is only a matter of fact and not of law. In the Sabbatino case one of the arguments given by Justice Byron White in his dissenting opinion was that "part of the law American Courts are bound to administer is international law."

The alternative that has been examined, which is related to conventional international law, probably will not be the most common in the courts. In such a case another question must be posed, which is whether Chilean courts are empowered to examine the validity of foreign laws in terms of their compatibility with the norms of international law that originates from sources other than treaties and agreements, such as custom and the general principles of law. According to Chilean decisions, the response is also affirmative.

There are cases in which the legislation itself orders the application of "rules of international law generally admitted."[137] Even when legislation is silent, the courts apply general rules of international law. It has been declared that "international law, the norms of which, coexistence with those of municipal law, are applicable in the order of the relations by it ruled, whichever be the form of its constitution,"[138] and that "principles of international law are of general application."[139]

Chilean decisions admit, therefore, "the doctrine of automatic incorporation, by means of which generally accepted rules of international law are automatically and globally incorporated to municipal law, and national courts are bound to apply them."[140] It has been understood that generally accepted rules include, of course, custom and general principles of law.[141] Exceptionally, international practice has also been included.[142]

The Supreme Court has expressly based this doctrine on the need to extend to the individual the rights that originate in the international order.[143] This tendency faithfully corresponds to the official statements indicated above, which admit that "general international law" is part of municipal law. This has also been formulated as follows: "General law of nations is a law of the Republic in all that its own laws or its agreements with foreign powers have not derogated from."[144]

Therefore it is possible to conclude that the courts are also empowered to examine the validity of foreign legislation in terms of general international law, which is also part of Chilean municipal law by means of its global incorporation and as such is to be applied by the courts. General international law also takes precedence over municipal law.[145]

Even if the norm of international law that is supposedly contravened were one of those that are controversial in international law (which was one of the arguments invoked in the Sabbatino case to support the application of the Act of State doctrine), the Chilean court would be bound to deliver its decision on the merits, since in the absence of an applicable provision of the law, equity is to be applied.[146] In any event the controversial matter has to be settled by the courts.[147]

The alternatives that have been examined so far, that is, conventional sources and general international law, permit the examination of the validity of foreign legislation because they are international norms that have been incorporated into Chilean municipal law. However, there is still one other possibility, which is that foreign legislation might contravene a norm of international law that is not part of Chilean municipal law. This, for instance, would be the case of a foreign law that contravenes a treaty to which the state enacting the law is a party, but to which Chile is not a party, the provisions of which are not part of general international law, which as such would be applicable in Chile. Are the courts empowered to examine the validity in this other case?

Writers admit that courts are empowered to examine the validity of foreign legislation in terms of the constitutional law of the country that has enacted that legislation.[148] Therefore, nothing will prevent the examination of its validity in terms of the international norms binding upon that other state.

When Chilean courts have been involved in a case in which the application of contradictory or mutually exclusive rules of international law is involved, such as one having its source in a treaty and the other in general international law, they have been inclined to apply those rules that have been approved by Chilean constitutional bodies.[149]

One such case was decided in 1969. On the occasion of the expropriation of Gulf Oil Company in Bolivia, an official agent of the company requested from Chilean courts an attachment and injunction against acts and contracts affecting certain machinery being routed to Bolivia across Chilean territory. Although the problem mentioned was not expressly discussed, the alternatives posed were the following: Should the court, in application of general international law, examine the validity of the Bolivian legislation, being empowered to uphold the validity and refuse attachment or to refuse validity and accept the attachment; or should the court, in application of treaties in force with Bolivia regulating free transit across Chilean territory, declare that it lacked jurisdiction and competence in the case, since such a matter should be decided by the Bolivian authorities. In both alternatives the application of international law was involved, but with regard to mutually exclusive norms. The court made its option for the latter solution, but more in consideration of political facts than of legal conviction.[150]

The Chilean courts have never declined competence in a case by reason of a problem of international law. The Ministry of Foreign Affairs has stated the following on this matter: "The fact that a matter within the jurisdiction of Chilean courts involves problems of international law does not prevent such jurisdiction from acting. The respective court shall consider the corresponding principles of international law and apply them as it deems convenient."[151]

The tendency in this matter has been to give jurisdiction to the higher courts of justice. Thus, for instance, the Organization of Courts Code provides that the President of the Supreme Court, in the first instance, and the Supreme Court in second instance, shall decide "the cases of . . . passive extradition and others which are to be decided in accordance with international law."[152]

The preceding considerations reaffirm the competence of Chilean courts to examine the validity of foreign legislation in terms of international law. The very few decisions that have been given in this matter have not made possible the development of a conception of international public order, which in other countries has a great significance, although the basic conceptions of the Bustamante Code with regard to private international law will always be applicable.[153] Express legislation on this matter would certainly be convenient, particularly as a means of preventing the courts from declining competence for political reasons, convenience of international policy, or governmental suggestions, since all of these would prevent the individual affected from having his or her legitimate rights protected by the judiciary.

The political problem is certainly the one underlying the whole of this matter, as was shown by the Sabbatino case and, in Chile, by the Gulf Oil Case Resolution of the Supreme Court. Again the solution will depend on the social values in force, because as a matter of fact, if the courts give greater importance to the political interests of the government they will very probably be inclined in favor of the application of the Act of State doctrine. Contrariwise, if greater importance is given to the rights of the individual, the courts will probably be inclined in favor of their protection when the rights of the individual have been unjustly affected. Between these two extremes there are many alternatives that can be developed to satisfy both purposes, such as, for instance, that the court will abstain from giving a decision while the government works out a diplomatic solution to the controversy.

In any event, it is very important that the courts be required to deliver their decisions in accordance with the merits of the cases and not according to other considerations, such as the political interest of the government. For this reason Chilean legislation clearly provides that "decisions shall be delivered in accordance with the merits of the procedures."[154] This was one of the strong suggestions of Justice White in the Sabbatino case and later was established in U.S. legislation.

If this is not so, the separation of public powers from the point of view that the exclusive administration of foreign policy belongs to the executive branch is far from being destroyed by means of the violation of judicial autonomy and the nonprotection of the rights of the individual. It must be remembered that the separation of the powers of the state was conceived as a guarantee of the rights of the individual.

Implementation of Decisions of International Organizations

The system of relations between international law and municipal law in Chile has not formally confronted the decisions of international organizations, for at the time of the enactment of the constitution now in force (1925) this source of law had not yet reached a significant development. However, contemporary international reality has brought about the development of a practice in this matter.

The first consideration that has to be made is that in Chile the decisions of international organizations are always implemented by means of executive authority and never by means of parliamentary approval, which is the procedure established in the Constitution. This, together with the case of agreements in a simplified form, which are not clearly contemplated by the Constitution, is one of the most important developments in Chilean practice. Thereby, the procedures for incorporating an international norm into the Chilean legal order have certainly been improved, but, as will be shown below, serious problems with regard to the rights of the individual also arise.

There are two principal fields in which this practice has been developed. These are decisions of international organizations imposing economic and other kinds of sanctions; and decisions of organizations of economic integration.

Sanctions. The implementation of sanctions has been permanently channeled through the authorities and bodies in charge of administering foreign trade, as requested by the Ministry of Foreign Affairs. The first time this practice was followed was on the occasion of the sanctions applied in 1935 to Italy by the League of Nations. The government of Chile implemented the economic sanctions through the International Exchange Commission, which was expressly requested by the Ministry of Foreign Affairs to permit no exports, among other measures.[155]

Already at this point several problems arose with regard to the rights of individuals, since the controls suggested by the government went beyond what had been agreed upon by the Geneva Coordinating Committee. The Ministry of Foreign Affairs itself was conscious of this, for at the same time that it requested that "no exports subject to compensation be permitted," it established an exception for those "very special cases in which the [individual] affected might go to court with a solid argument, since the prohibition of exports has not been contemplated among sanctions."[156] To a certain extent, therefore, this prohibition was subject to judicial control.

Years later this same procedure was followed with regard to the application of sanctions against Cuba by the Meeting of Consultation of the Ministers of Foreign Affairs of the Organization of American States. The executive committee of the Central Bank approved the following agreement on 23 April 1966.

> I certify that the executive committee of this Central Bank, in Session Number 403, . . . in compliance with the resolution approved by the Ministers of Foreign Affairs of the member countries of the Organization of American States, in the Ninth Meeting of Consultation, and with the authorization of the Ministers of Economic Affairs, Development, and Reconstruction, decided to prohibit direct or indirect commercial transactions with Cuba, except with regard to food, medical products, and equipment that for humanitarian reasons might be sent to that country.[157]

An identical procedure was followed with regard to the application of sanctions to Rhodesia by the United Nations.[158]

This system of implementing the decisions of international organizations that impose sanctions has been possible because of the broad powers granted to the executive and to some particular organs such as the Central Bank. However, this provokes serious problems for the rights of the individual, since, as was shown with regard to the movement of nationals, it is precisely through the utilization of these almost unlimited powers that the state organs have begun to restrict individual freedom.

Is it possible for the individual to effectively oppose the application of decisions of international organizations if they should restrict his or her rights, particularly those guaranteed by the Constitution? The answer to this problem is certainly difficult, for it must be remembered that such decisions are part of international law and, as such, will take precedence over municipal law. Before discussing this problem, it is necessary to examine the second major aspect of Chilean practice in this matter.

Decisions of Economic Integration. The practice of the Latin American Free Trade Association and of the Agreement of Subregional Integration of the Andean Countries shows that basically two kinds of decisions have been adopted by their organs. On the one hand there are those decisions that do not require any further action by the member states and that will be binding by their approval or their communication to the addressee. In general these decisions grant rights or impose obligations only upon states, but on several occasions this has also been so with regard to individuals. In the case of the Subregional Agreement this effect is normal and frequent. On the other hand, there is a kind of decision that does require further action by the member states before it can be implemented.

All these kinds of decisions have been accepted and admitted by the Chilean municipal legal order. Even the subregional agreement, which provides for a very complete system of economic integration in which both states and individuals have very important rights and obligations, was approved by means of a decision of the LAFTA agencies and brought into force through executive authority with no congressional participation.[159]

The amplitude that the legal order of economic integration has already reached is beginning to provoke serious problems in Chile[160] and in other member countries.[161] Although it is not possible to examine here the details of this problem, which are principally related to the observance of the respective constitutional systems with regard to the approval and ratification of international agreements, the basic aspect involved is protection of the rights of the individual. In fact, should the executive be permitted to develop with almost no limits the field of international commitments and obligations that will affect the individual, by means of its exclusive action and with no control by other state organs? What remedies does the individual have?

As has been shown, Chilean practice has broadly admitted the incorporation of the decisions of international organizations and in fact it has been able to implement them effectively. However, no one has been concerned about how individual rights might be protected effectively. The Agreement of the Central Bank might be resisted by means of some special remedies that are provided by the law, but that are very restricted. If the remedy should secure a decision in favor of the rights of the individual, the agreement of the Central Bank will not be applicable to that particular individual but will continue in force, and it is not derogated. Thus each citizen would be compelled to promote his or her own remedy for each particular case.

A still more serious problem arises from those decisions that do require further state action for their implementation. In fact, the state implements such decisions by means of its executive authority, which takes the form of a decree, a kind of administrative act. In Chile, because of the absence of administrative tribunals, there are no remedies against the administrative acts of the state, with very few exceptions. Thus the individual is unprotected with regard to international decisions even though they may affect his or her rights.

This situation is particularly anomalous because it exists only in the case of decisions of international organizations and not in the case of other major sources, such as treaties, which in Chile have the force of law. Against the law several remedies are available, which may also be used in the case of treaties. On some occasions it has been held that a decree is only a means of communication and publicity, the right or the obligation being derived from the international order and not from the administrative norm. If the right or obligation originates in the decision of an international organization, and this decision is a treaty, eventually it is possible that the recourse available against the latter would also apply against the decisions. However, it is not certain whether the courts would admit this interpretation.

With regard to those decisions that do not require further action by the state, individuals have no remedies unless the interpretation mentioned is admitted. The respective processes of integration do not provide for any judicial mechanisms that may enable the individual to have his or her rights protected by means of direct international standing. There are also no mechanisms of institutional control that might examine the validity of the acts of the organs, or define the limits to which their actions may be extended. Therefore, by utilization of their broad powers, regional organs might even go beyond the competence assigned to them by treaties, subject to no control whatsoever.

Effective remedies must be created at the national, regional, or international level. It is not intended that the development or the precedence of international law be questioned, for Chilean courts have accepted this very definitively, but only to prevent abuses that might affect the legitimate rights of the individual. International law, as well as municipal law, might also contain provisions that in given circumstances could violate the rights of the individuals; in such cases neither the superiority nor the precedence of international law could justify the violation, but on the contrary it would make it still more condemnable.

Probably this is not the case with the decisions on Rhodesia, Namibia, or Cuba, at least from the point of view of Chile, but the absence of control will certainly pave the road of precedents for future occasions, in which the problem might be conceived in a different manner or the sanction applied for different purposes.

Procedures Related to the Issuance of Certificates and Suggestions by the Executive in Connection with Litigation in National Courts

Traditionally the Chilean legal system has been very strict with regard to the effective separation of public powers. Because of this policy, in general, any form of intervention by the government that is intended to have a direct or indirect influence in the proceedings being conducted by courts will be inadmissible. On more than 50 occasions the Ministry of Foreign Affairs has stated that it is not competent to intervene by any means whatsoever in judicial matters.[162]

The organization of the judiciary tends to ensure this independence fully. In fact, among the auxiliary services of the administration of justice there is the Public Ministry, composed of the Attorney (Fiscal) of the Supreme Court and the attorneys of the respective courts of appeals, who are independent officials both with regard to the judiciary and with regard to the executive. The Public Ministry represents the general interests of the society before the courts of justice, the courts being bound to request its advice in several cases. Even when these officials are bound to provoke the action of the judiciary at the request of the government, they must do so in accordance with their own convictions, suggesting those conclusions that they consider to be in accordance with law.[163]

The Public Ministry is therefore a sort of buffer zone between the executive and the judiciary, entrusted with the defense of the general interest of the society in a broad meaning, including of course those aspects related to international affairs, of which practice gives evidence.[164]

Within this context is that the problem of certificates and suggestions by the executive in judicial matters has to be examined. Although the legislation does not provide for these mechanisms expressly, in practice they have been developed to a limited extent.

The Right of Courts. The courts are certainly empowered to request any kind of certificates from public authorities. When the procedure is prepared for giving a decision, the court for better resolving is empowered to order a certificate, but informing the litigants that it can order "the incorporation of any document deemed necessary to clarify the rights of litigants."[165] A certificate could very well be one of these documents. Furthermore, at any moment the courts may request the advice of the Public Ministry Attorney, who as was shown above will provide the point of view of the general interest of society.

The Right of Litigants. In this matter the right of litigants is not clear. Although the court, at the request of a litigant, may order the examination of any document existing in the hands of the other litigant or of a third party, provided that it has a direct relationship with the controverted matter and provided that it does not have a secret or confidential character,[166] this is not properly a procedure of certification. Eventually it might lead to the same result, but this will depend on the contents of the document. The document may be examined by a notary public when it is in the hands of a third party. This procedure has to be accomplished during the period of presentation of evidence.

This procedure is quite unsatisfactory, for it is subject to all kinds of eventualities. The court may or may not ask for a certificate; it may or may not accept the request of the litigant for the examination of documents; and the government may or may not grant the certificate, for it is not clearly bound to do so. As a result of this uncertainty the right of litigants to make representations to the executive with regard to the content of the certificate has not been defined, although all the inhabitants of the country enjoy the right of petition before public authorities.

The regulation of such mechanism is becoming urgent, since with each passing day the suggestions by the executive are more frequent, particularly when problems of international policy are involved. The case of Gulf Oil Co. mentioned above is particularly relevant in this matter.

A Surprising Case. As was shown, an official agent of Gulf Oil Co., the properties of which had been expropriated in Bolivia, requested the Court of Antofagasta to order attachment and other precautionary measures for machinery being routed to Bolivia across Chilean territory. The Ministry of Foreign Affairs requested the Supreme Court to adopt all measures necessary to apply in this case those agreements between Chile and Bolivia concerning free transit, "For the purpose of avoiding the emergence of conflicts with Bolivia that might affect the delicate relations existing between the government of that country and our own."[167] However important the political problem might be, can the Ministry of Foreign Affairs go to the extreme of suggesting to the Courts of Justice the law that they must apply in a certain case?

Even more serious has been the attitude of the Supreme Court, which, not even having examined the proceedings (which were before the Court of Antofagasta) and being informed of them only by means of the request by the Ministry of Foreign Affairs (which in turn had only been informed by local administrative authorities) accepted the request and declared as follows: "The precautionary measures . . . shall be voided, if already issued, and, in any event, any procedural steps taken in this case must be cancelled because the Court lacks jurisdiction and competence to hear such matters."[168] Can a court reach a decision in such a case without having examined the proceedings or in a case that has not reached its jurisdiction by the proper judicial channels, or of which it has been informed only by the executive?

Everything indicates that both the judiciary and the Ministry of Foreign Affairs overstepped their powers, for the least to which a litigant is entitled is to have his or her petition heard before any decision is given, which in this case did not occur. This might serve as a warning of the dangers involved in the practice of government suggestions when they are not channeled through well-established procedures.

TREATIES AND THE INDIVIDUAL

The Chilean practice with regard to treaties, from the point of view of their effects upon the individual, is the one that perhaps best reflects the double relationship that was mentioned at the beginning, that is, the influence that is exercised in a situation of development or underdevelopment, on the one hand, and by the different conceptions and values about the human person on the other hand.

Throughout the nineteenth and early twentieth centuries, the essential concern of the treaties entered into by Chile was the promotion of the interests of the individual in all those aspects that were relevant at the time. National development was based on a strong foreign trade and on the capacity and strengthening of private enterprise. Treaties were the instrument that ensured the fulfillment of this purpose at the international level.

Particularly relevant in this matter were the treaties of friendship, commerce, and navigation that were concluded with a great number of the most important states of the international community and with almost every Latin American country, even at the multilateral level.[169] Taking the treaty signed in 1854 with Great Britain as a model, it will be noted that it principally ensures freedom of commerce, navigation, and use of ports; freedom of residence; and freedom of establishment, all to the benefit of the respective nationals. Usually free competition for the industries of the respective nationals, freedom to set prices of their goods, and equality of treatment with regard to taxes were also ensured.

This concern also had its manifestation in fields other than commerce, such as to ensure the rights of the respective nationals in case of war between the contracting parties[170] or their exemption from enlistment in the armed forces when they had residence in the territory of the other contracting party,[171] among many others.

With regard to the protection of the property of aliens, practice was equally consonant with this prevailing value of private property, full compensation being provided for cases of taking. A typical clause was the following one contained in the treaty with Sardinia of 1856:

> Should the properties of a citizen or subject of any of the contracting parties, resident in the territories of the other, be taken, used or damaged by the legitimate authorities of that country, for use or service of public interest, a fair and full compensation shall be granted to the owner of such property, by the government of the contracting party adopting such measure.[172]

An arbitral procedure was also provided for the case of disagreement between the contracting parties. On some occasions compensation was also considered for cases of attachment of property or general closure of ports, with regard to the foreign merchant ships that might have been affected.[173]

Notwithstanding this broad and liberal policy, the government of Chile was always aware of the economic limitations of the country in relation to the potentiality of the great powers of the time, and it did not permit its nationals to be prejudiced by means of treaties that would bring about an absolute freedom of competence. Thus, while Chile proceeded to the consolidation of its process of development, the government did not enter into treaties that would establish the unconditional most-favored-nation clause. It always required compensation, and such compensation had to be real and effective.

Furthermore, a clause of exception known as the Bello Clause was always incorporated into treaties. By means of this clause the advantages and privileges granted by Chile to other Latin American countries would not be extended to third countries through the most-favored-nation clause.[174] Only when the country was entering into a relatively free competition, by the mid-nineteenth century, did it accept the most-favored-nation clause with no restrictions. The whole of this policy was expressly formulated with the purpose of protecting the industries and commerce of Chilean nationals.

In a different field, Chile also took care not to accept the pretensions of many foreign powers to immunity from Chilean justice with regard to claims presented by the nationals of those countries. It always required that the responsibility of the Chilean government be established before national courts in order that the rule of exhaustion of local remedies be fully complied with.[175] This did not prevent the making of agreements submitting claims to international arbitral tribunals, when the seriousness of the circumstances or the volume of the claims would justify it.[176] Thus an interesting body of arbitral decisions on state responsibility came into being.

As was shown further above, during this period Chile actively promoted the protection of the interests of its nationals abroad. As was also shown, for a time Chile even supported the revolutionary theory that the individual was the one directly entitled to the claim and the compensation and that the protection of the government, which in this specific case was incorporated in an international agreement, could only be understood as a sponsoring measure.

In short, the treaty practice of this period was characterized by a permanent concern for the interests and rights of the individual, within the context of political and economic realism, which was directed toward making this protection more effective.

Contemporary Practice: The Influence of Underdevelopment

To the extent to which the economic situation of the country began deteriorating, and as a result, also its culture, treaties gradually abandoned the individual as their principal concern. This phenomenon corresponded to a change of policy that could be noticed at every level, including, of course, municipal law.

The kind of concern that had previously been reflected in the treaties of friendship, commerce, and navigation ceased to be present in the treaties of Chile. It is true that this is so partly because some of their objectives became part of broader international regulation, at the multilateral level and even at the level of general international law. However, it is partly because the basic concern of the government was no longer related to the protection of the interests of Chileans abroad, which progressively became less significant. Therefore the government had no interest in the promotion of treaties that would ensure this purpose.

In the few cases in which this kind of treaty had been made at the request of a foreign government interested in the protection of its own nationals, its effect might be considered to be unilateral. In fact, it would only benefit those aliens residing in Chile; Chileans have few opportunities to obtain the same benefits in the territory of the other contracting party, since their interests are prevented from going there by the government restrictions.

Treaties of economic integration have certainly opened the commercial field to the interest of the individual. However, it cannot sincerely be said that this has been the basic purpose of such treaties, at least from the viewpoint of Chile. Instead they correspond to a strategy of foreign trade within which the individual has been integrated because of his or her part in the national economic system. This strategy would have developed even if the individual or private enterprise were not part of that national system.

Otherwise the increasing restrictions upon foreign trade, the expropriations of industries, and the proposals to create a foreign trade state monopoly could not be explained. Should treaties reflect a concern for the individual at the international level, national policies would reflect this concern with even a greater emphasis. Since the latter have no concern for the individual, it is not possible to suppose that the former will have other intentions.

The secondary role that has been assigned to the individual is further confirmed by the restrictive character of these treaties, which are principally concerned with commercial matters and do not regulate aspects such as movement or establishment of capital as well as the manner of their implementation.

Furthermore, according to the original conception of such treaties, the individual was not considered as having rights or obligations directly attributable to the international order. In the exceptional cases in which this effect has been admitted, it has been the result of the interpretation of writers who were not yet well established.

Where this phenomenon reaches its most typical expression is in the field of foreign investments. Since the very moment in which a country is requested to enter into treaties with capital-exporting countries in order to guarantee the investments being made in it, there is an implicit admission that those guarantees are not normally or seriously provided by the legal order or the practive of the recipient country. This is perhaps the most obvious indication that the rights of the individual are not adequately protected in that country. Chile has been requested on several occasions in the early 1970s to enter into this kind of treaty, and although it signed agreements with the United States, these have not entered into force.[177]

In this matter there is a well-defined government policy of not entering into commitments of this nature with foreign governments. Theoretically this situation may be inspired by one of two reasons: either the government considers that the national legal order offers enough guarantees of the rights of aliens or it prefers to retain its prerogative of protecting those rights at its own convenience. Only practice can give an answer to these alternatives. Chilean practice on nationalizations quite obviously redounds in favor of the latter alternative, as will be shown further below.

Chilean practice in this matter presents two aspects of interest. One aspect is the position of Chile and other Latin American countries with regard to the World Bank Convention on the Settlement of International Investments Disputes. Latin American countries have taken the position that all disputes on this matter are to be settled by the national courts of the recipient countries, submission to international procedures being inadmissible. This is the principal argument invoked for not signing the convention.

The second aspect is that the member countries of the Agreement of Subregional Integration, including Chile, have established at the multilateral level the common treatment applicable to foreign investments in the area.[178] This has been done by means of a decision by the highest organ of the agreement.

A very interesting legal problem has arisen with regard to this matter. The subregional agreement was approved by means of a decision of the LAFTA organs and brought into force by executive action in Chile and Colombia, countries in which the original parliamentary approval of the treaty of LAFTA was considered as also covering this other subregional development. However, the treaty of LAFTA does not allow the regulation of treatment of foreign investments so simply.

Can a decision by an organ, adopted within the framework of an agreement, which in turn has been approved by the decision of another organ, regulate a matter in a way in which the treaty that is the basis of the whole process does not authorize? As was mentioned above, this procedure has been objected to by the courts of Colombia and by the organs of administrative control in Chile. This is a typical case in which the rights and obligations of the individual are affected by a decision of international organs. In any event, this shows an interesting tendency in favor of the multilateral regulation of foreign investments.

In two kinds of treaties that have been concluded by Chile there has been real benefit for the individual. These are the treaties that ensure social security and other rights to migrant workers[179] and the agreements on free transit and on visas,[180] which eliminate restrictions on the international movement of individuals. (See the section on passports above.)

Although the state of underdevelopment has had a strong influence in the practice of Chile with regard to treaties and the individual, lately it has been possible to notice an even more negative influence, one originating in ideological factors, which puts the individual in the position of total dependence on the all-embracing powers of the state.

In the field of commercial treaties, the tendency has been to eliminate the participation of private enterprise. Agreements concluded with Cuba, which only permits trading through the respective state corporations, reveal this. This has also corresponded to the initiatives taken toward converting the Chilean foreign trade system into a state trading monopoly. Should this proposition have been implemented, the result would immediately have been a total incompatibility with the LAFTA and subregional agreement mechanisms,[181] which would nullify any benefit the individual might receive.

The preceding considerations lead to the formulation of a basic question. To what extent, if any, can a state, by means of its international agreements, affect the essential consumption of individuals or plan other forms of social life? An example will make the point clear. During 1971 Chile exported milk to Cuba by decision of the government, in spite of the fact that this was a product in short supply in the Chilean market and that, moreover, Chile was a country with serious nutritional problems. Rum and cigars were imported in exchange, although these are luxury products that the population could do without. Is this a legitimate decision or only a political abuse of governmental powers?

The response will depend on the prevailing conception of the functions of the state. If a liberal conception prevails, according to which the state is bound to satisfy the needs of society, the response will be that such a situation is an abuse with no possible justification and a misuse of power. On the contrary, if the conception prevails according to which the state is bound to express its solidarity with other countries that are ideologically coincident even at the expense of social welfare, the response will be to justify such a measure. This is one of the ways in which the ideological factor can influence the relationship between treaty and individual.

Although I do not propose to consider here the whole problem of human rights involved, this situation does illustrate the distortions that the ideological factor can introduce in the field of treaties and the individual.

The purpose of imposing certain forms of social organization leads to the violation of international commitments, often without any awareness that this is so. At one time the government sent a draft bill on Indian legislation to Congress creating a kind of state farm on which individuals would have no individual property nor right of succession. At the same time the United Nations Covenant on Elimination of all Forms of Racial Discrimination, which among other rights ensures the right of property and succession, was being ratified. The ideological factor tends to nullify the effects of treaties with regard to the individual.

Again, it is in the field of foreign investment that the problem is most evident. Today the right of states to nationalize natural resources is well established. Although there has been much discussion about the extent of the norms and standards of compensation, it is not questioned that compensation will always proceed, even in accordance with the practice of socialist states. However, Chilean practice broke with all precedents on the matter: the president was empowered to deduct from compensation what he deemed to be the excess profits of foreign corporations during their operations in the country, in spite of the fact that these profits having been obtained in accordance with the laws in force at the time. As a result of this, after expropriation the corporations ended up owing compensation to the government.

It is not our purpose to examine here the many problems of international law involved in this practice. Obviously there is a great contrast between this practice, which is influenced by typical ideological considerations, and the practice that was examined in relation to the treaties of Chile in the past, which was influenced by important values with regard to private rights. This clearly demonstrates to what extent economic, cultural, and political factors are capable of influencing the evolution of municipal law and international practice with regard to the rights of the individual. In such circumstances it is difficult to think of regulating compensation by means of an international agreement.

With regard to this problem of nationalization, there is one final point directly related to the effect of treaties on individual rights, as seen in a different perspective. Here again we find the problem of the responsibility of the state for those injuries to its nationals abroad that are induced by its own conduct.

Until the early 1960s there was in Chile an absolute respect for private property, be it property of nationals or of aliens. Private property could not be taken unless previous and full compensation was paid. The government of the United States, within the program of the Alliance for Progress, promoted and directly pressured for a series of changes that were considered to be necessary in Latin America, among which agrarian reform had first priority. In the specific case of Chile, the conclusion of agreements of financial assistance was conditioned upon the enactment of legislation on agrarian reform and its implementation, a policy that was not within the plans of the government of the time to such an extent or in such a manner.

The necessity for external financial resources compelled the government to sponsor this legislation. The only way in which this could be done, given the scarce resources available to pay previous and full compensation, was by modifying the principle that until then had protected the right of property. Payment in installments of up to 30 years, and no longer in anticipation, was then established.

Once the basic principle had been broken, deterioration continued progressively. The amount of compensation gradually decreased. With monetary devaluation and low rates of interest, those affected finally were to receive a symtolic compensation. The causes for expropriation were broadened, and arbitrary measures became common.

These same provisions, which were progressively enlarged and extended in their application to mining, were those that recently served for expropriating the copper properties of U.S. corporations. The principle having been breached, anything coming afterward was a natural result. If those norms had regulated the rights of nationals, nothing could have prevented their application to the rights of aliens, particularly since the government of those aliens was one that had promoted those norms for a decade. The condition written into the earlier agreements of financial assistance was the element that backfired on the rights of the nationals of the same government that had stipulated for it.

Can it be argued that the government of the United States has a responsibility to its own nationals because of this? If the problems of agrarian reform and of mining reform are considered separately, at the most there is a case of indirect induction; but if the problem is considered from the point of view of the right of property as a basic institution, of which agrarian and mining properties are only applications, then the connection seems more direct.

In the latter case there would be a most interesting relationship between an international agreement of financial assistance, conditioned for reasons of foreign policy, and the rights of nationals abroad. This would certainly not excuse the eventual responsibility of the government of Chile, but perhaps neither will it excuse the eventual responsibility of the government of the United States.

NOTES

1. W. Friedmann, The Changing Structure of International Law 236 (Columbia University Press, 1964).

2. C. De Visscher, Theory and Reality in Public International Law 180 (Princeton University Press, 1968).

3. Friedmann, op. cit., at 42-44; De Visscher, op. cit., at 182.

4. Resolution of L'Institut de Droit International, Lausanne Session, 1947, cited by De Visscher, op. cit., at 181.

5. Lauterpacht, "The Subjects of the Law of Nations," 63 L.Q. Rev. 438 ff. (1947) and 64 L.Q. Rev. 97 ff. (1948); P. Jessup, A Modern Law of Nations (1948), Chapters 2 and 5, cited by Friedmann, op. cit., at 234-35.

6. Georges Scelle, Précis de droit des gens 42-44 (1932), cited by Friedmann, op. cit., at 233.

7. J. L. Brierly, The Law of Nations 6-7, 54-55 (6th ed., 1968).

8. Jessup, op. cit., at 17.

9. Friedmann, op. cit., at 235.

10. For a general examination of how the Chilean legal order works, see Francisco Orrego Vicuña, La relación entre derecho y desarollo. El caso de Chile (Santiago 1971).

11. For an analysis of Chile in the nineteenth century, particularly from the point of view of international relations, see Robert N. Burr, By Reason or Force: Chile and the Balancing of Power in South America, 1830-1905 (The University of California Press, 1967). For a comparative examination between the situation of Chile in the nineteenth and twentieth centuries, see Francisco Orrego Vicuña, "The System of International Politics in Chile. Rise or Fall?" in Chile: A Critical Survey (Santiago, 1972).

12. Constitution of 1925, Art. 10.15.

13. One example of this was the right to property. While the generalized consensus was in force, protection of property, although guaranteed by the constitution, was mainly implemented in the civil code, where property was defined. No one thought of the risk that another law might modify such definition or implementation. When the consensus was broken as a consequence of the appearance of socialist values that directly opposed private property, the implementation of this right was raised to the category of a constitutional norm. When the Marxist government took office in 1970, a whole set of additional constitutional guarantees was imposed upon it by opposition parties, raising to the constitutional level several detailed provisions related to the protection of certain values, such as the freedom of the press. Within the traditional consensus, the basic principles provided by the constitution would have been and were enough guarantee; but since it was broken, a more explicit system of guarantees was sought.

14. Some agreements required only an identity card. These are the agreement with Argentina, 30 October 1947; Bolivia, 18 September 1937; Brazil, 5 July 1961; Paraguay, 1 June 1957; Peru, 13 December 1930; Uruguay, 31 August 1943; and Protocol of Transit of Persons of the Latin

American Free Trade Association, 12 December 1968. Chile is also a party to the 15 October 1946 agreement on travel documents for refugees of the Inter-Governmental Committee for Refugees.

15. Passport Regulations, Decree 676 of the Ministry of the Interior (15 February 1966), Art. 1. They can also be granted to foreign women who have lost their nationality by marriage with Chilean nationals, Consular Regulations, Decree 1.505 (4 December 1935), Art. 342.1.

16. In 1971 Chilean consulates reported the "loss" of more than 600 passports of Chilean nationals.

17. Supreme Court, ruling of 9 November 1942. This and other cases cited by Alejandro Silva Bascuñan, 2 Tratado de Derecho Constitucional 326 (Editorial Jurídica de Chile, 1963).

18. Supreme Court, 1 Gaceta de los Tribunales 222 (1936). Cited by Silva Bascuñan, op. cit., at 326-27 (my translation).

19. Mario Bernachina, 2 Manual de Derecho Constitucional 151 (1955); Silva Bascuñan, op. cit., at 327 (1955). Bascunan concludes that "Detention [for habeas corpus] would be every restriction or hindrance to freedom in the broad meaning that this word also has" (my translation). The Supreme Court itself, in the ruling of 19 December 1932 regulating procedures of habeas corpus, has given to detention this broader meaning.

20. Penal Code, Art. 158.4.

21. Ibid., Art. 256.

22. Cited by De Visscher, op. cit., at 184-85.

23. Elihu Root, "The Right to Expatriation," speech to U.S. Senate, 19 December 1911, Cong. Rec., Senate, 483 (19 December 1911), cited by De Visscher, op. cit., at 185.

24. "El derecho de irse," 10 Boletín del Centro de Relaciones Internacionales (Universidad Nacional Autónoma de México, September 1971).

25. All these penalties involve imprisonment for different periods of time.

26. "Relegación" compels residence in a certain part of the territory.

27. "Deportation," in the meaning given to the term by the penal code, involves expulsion from a certain place in the territory, the individual being free to reside in any other part of the country.

28. This is particularly the case of the president, ministers of state, and members of Congress.

29. All these restrictions involve cases of public emergency, such as war or rioting. See Silva Bascuñan, op. cit., at 339-72.

30. Regulations on Travel Taxes to Foreign Countries, Decree 2.191 (8 October 1966).

31. Agreement of the Executive Committee of the Central Bank (29 October 1971). The legality of this agreement is being challenged in court, but so far no decision has been given in this case. One of the bases of illegality that has been invoked is precisely the violation of the constitutional guarantee of the right to depart.

32. Supreme Court, ruling of 8 November 1935, 2 Gaceta de los Tribunales 282 (1935).

33. Supreme Court, ruling of 22 April 1932, 48 *Gaceta de los Tribunales* 174 (1932); Supreme Court, ruling of 14 April 1936, cited by Silva Bascuñan, op. cit., at 332.

34. Silva Bascuñan, op. cit., at 331.

35. Ibid., at 332.

36. Regulations to the Law of International Exchanges, Decree 2 of the Ministry of Economics (January 1962).

37. Silva Bascuñan, op. cit., at 327. Also Carlos Andrade Geywitz, *Elementos de Derecho Constitucional Chileno* 194 (Editorial Jurídica de Chile, 1963).

38. "Confinamiento is the expulsion of the one convicted from the territory of the Republic to a forced residence in a certain place," Penal Code, Art. 33; "entrañamiento is the expulsion of the one convicted from the territory of the Republic to the place of his choice," Penal Code, Art. 34 (my translation).

39. Penal Code, Art. 118, 121-26; Law of Internal Security of the State, Arts. 1, 4, 6.

40. Supreme Court, ruling on the recourse of habeas corpus in favor of Daniel Schweitzer, expelled by the government for alleged violation of the security of the state. Cited by Silva Bascuñan, op. cit., at 326.

41. De Visscher, op. cit., at 186. President Jefferson in his address to the United States Congress in 1801 stated that "every man has a right to live somewhere on the earth." Cited by De Visscher, op. cit., at 186.

42. International Covenant on Civil and Political Rights, opened for signature 19 December 1966; *International Legal Materials* 368 (1967).

43. Art. 22, §§2, 3, American Convention on Human Rights, San José, Costa Rica, 22 November 1969, 9 *International Legal Materials* 673 (1970).

44. Ibid., Art. 22, §5.

45. This would have been the result of the solution proposed in the Hague Protocol of 12 April 1930, by means of which the state that proceeds to deprive human groups of their nationality is bound to receive them back. This would have meant the delivering of political refugees to their worst enemies. See De Visscher, op. cit., at 186.

46. Friedmann, op. cit., at 44.

47. This is the case of the Corporación de Fomento de la Producción (Production Development Corporation), which has established fishing industries in Ecuador.

48. Law 13.305 (April 1959), Art. 172.

49. Francisco Orrego Vicuña, *El Comercio de Estado: Alternativa de la cláusula de la nación más favorecida en la estructuración jurídica del comercio internacional*? (Carnegie Endowment for International Peace, Inter-American Study group, 1971).

50. Address by the President, Joaquín Prieto, and the Minister of Foreign Affairs, Ramón Luis Irarrazabal, to Congress, 17 July 1841, in Alberto Cruchaga Ossa, *Jurisprudencia de la Cancillería Chilena* 164, no.

349 (Santiago 1935); also, note by the Minister of Foreign Affairs, Manuel Antonio Tocornal, to the consul in Guayaquil, 17 November 1863, in ibid., at 589-90, no. 1259.

51. Treaty with Great Britain (4 October 1854), Art. 11, in Cruchaga Ossa, op. cit., at 361, no. 724. Also Convention on the Conditions of Aliens, signed in Havana at the Sixth International American Conference, (1928), Art. 3.

52. Note 14.183 from the Minister of Foreign Affairs, Manuel Barros, to the Consul General in the Netherlands (10 December 1972), in Manuel Fuentes Herrera, Jurisprudencia de la Cancillería Chilena, 1926-1932 80 at 78-79 (Santiago 1958).

53. Supreme Court, ruling of 11 January 1937, cited by Andrade Geywitz, op. cit., at 88; also Constitutional Amendment of September 1957.

54. Law 5.478 (14 September 1934), Art. 1.

55. Note from the Minister of Foreign Affairs, Antonio Varas, to the Chargé d'Affaires of New Granada in Lima, 15 May 1852, in Cruchaga Ossa, op. cit., at 288, no. 615.

56. Penal Code, Art. 107.

57. Constitution, Art. 6.3.

58. Treaty of Commerce and Navigation with United States (16 May 1832), Art. 31.2, in Cruchaga Ossa, op. cit., at 61, no. 148.

59. Decree 93 of the Ministry of Foreign Affairs (13 December 1948).

60. Supreme Decree 1.505 (4 December 1935).

61. General Instructions to the Diplomatic Corps, Art. 496 (my translation).

62. Ibid., Art. 497.

63. Consular Regulations, Art. 302.

64. Ibid., Art. 303.

65. General Instructions to the Diplomatic Corps, Art. 499.

66. Supreme Court, ruling of 15 October 1889, on claims and charges of a Chilean citizen against the Government of Peru and request for diplomatic protection in Ambrosio Montt, Dictamenes del Fiscal de la Corte Suprema de Justicia 263 (Santiago 1894, my translation).

67. Miguel Cruchaga Tocornal, Nociones de Derecho Internacional 124 (Santiago 1902).

68. Cases in Montt, op. cit.

69. Statement by the Minister of Foreign Affairs, Ramón Luis Irarrazabal, in annual report of the Ministry of Foreign Affairs (1844). In Cruchaga Ossa, op. cit., at 188, no. 418 (my translation). Also note from the Minister of Foreign Affairs, Geronimo Urmeneta, to the Minister of Peru, 5 November 1859, in ibid., at 500, no. 1078; Note of the Minister of Foreign Affairs, Felix Nieto del Río, to the Chargé d'Affaires of Chile in Paraguay, 14 September 1931, in Fuentes Herrera, op. cit., at 108-09, no. 118.

70. Note from the Minister of Foreign Affairs, Geronimo Urmeneta, to the Consul in Iquique, 30 January 1858, in Cruchaga Ossa, op. cit., at 458, no. 989.

71. Note from the head of the Consular Department to the Consul General of Chile in Germany, 28 March 1938, in Roberto Carmona Klemm, Jurisprudencia de la Cancillería Chilena, 1933-1938 113, no. 118 (Santiago 1959).

72. Note from the Minister of Foreign Affairs, José Ramón Gutierrez, to the Ambassador of Chile in the United States, 15 June 1938, in Carmona Klemm, op. cit., 117-18, no. 123.

73. Note from the Minister of Foreign Affairs, José Ramón Gutierrez, to the Ambassador of Chile in Germany, 8 July 1938, in ibid., at 118-19, no. 124.

74. Note from the Minister of Foreign Affairs, Antonio Varas, to the Minister of Chile in Peru, 28 September 1855, in Cruchaga Ossa, op. cit., at 390, no. 806. Also note from the Minister of Foreign Affairs, Miguel Luis Anumategui, to the Chargé d'Affaires of Chile in Peru, 5 January 1869, in Benjamín Lister Minister, Jurisprudencia de la Cancillería Chilena, 1866-1870, 65, no. 136 (Santiago 1956).

75. In April 1879 Chile disembarked troops in Antofagasta, then under the jurisdiction of Bolivia, to protect the Chilean nitrate industries, which had been damaged by acts of the government of Bolivia in violation of treaties in force. This began the War of the Pacific.

76. For the classical approach, see "Mavrommatis Concessions in Palestine," P.C.I.J. Ser. A., no. 2, 12 (1924): also Nottebohm I.C.J. Reports 24 (1955), and Dickson Car Wheel Co., Commission of General Claims, U.N. Rep. Int'l. Arb. Awards 678 (1931).

77. On contemporary tendencies, F. V. Garcia-Amador, Principios de Derecho Internacional que rigen la responsabilidad 68-71 (Madrid 1963).

78. Treaty of Peace and Friendship with Peru, 20 October 1883, Art. 12 (my translation).

79. Note from the Minister of Foreign Affairs, Carlos Balmaceda, to the Ambassador of Chile to Peru, No. 2649/26 (18 May 1932), in Fuentes Herrera, op. cit., at 116-18, no. 127 (my translation).

80. Law 1297 on Bankruptcy (23 June 1931), Tit. X.

81. Commercial Code, Arts. 1104-28.

82. "Reparations for Injuries Suffered in the Service of the United Nations," I.C.J. Reports 174 (1949).

83. Decision of the Attorney (Fiscal) of the Supreme Court on the request for diplomatic protection by a Chilean citizen injured by acts of the Bolivian troops in a war (28 May 1889), in Monti, op. cit., at 169-70 (my translation).

84. The mechanisms for the settlement of disputes in the Latin American Free Trade Association and in the Agreement of Subregional Integration and Central American Common Market are only open to the participation of states.

85. This was the case of the Central American Court of Justice, established in 1907, in which the individual had a direct standing after exhaustion of local remedies.

86. Friedmann, op. cit., at 232-34.

87. Regulations of aliens, Decree 5.021 of the Ministry of the Interior (16 September 1959), Art. 14.

88. Ibid., Art. 15.

89. Ibid., Arts. 75-79.

90. Instruction No. 16 from the Minister of Foreign Affairs, Antonio Hunneus (28 August 1925), in Annual Report of the Ministry of Foreign Affairs 1215-16 (1923-26) (my translation, emphasis added).

91. Passport Regulations, Decree 4.072 (11 October 1933), Art. 22 (my translation). An identical provision was contained in the regulations established by Decree 315 (25 January 1937). Legislation in force no longer contains this provision.

92. Note from the Director of the Consular Department to the Consul of Chile in Shanghai, no. 7.601 (19 December 1933), in Carmona Klemm, op. cit., at 30, no. 33 (my translation).

93. Cruchaga Tocornal, op. cit., at 146.

94. De Visscher, op. cit., at 187-90.

95. Law 7.401, Art. 8.

96. Penal Code, Art. 116.

97. Regulations of Aliens, Arts. 73, 74, 76. Tourists and residents with diplomatic and other official visas enjoy a more favorable treatment.

98. Provisional Constitutional Regulations (27 October 1812), Art. 24. In Cruchaga Ossa, op. cit., at 15, no. 10 (my translation).

99. The constitution of 25 May 1833 contained in its Article 12 an identical provision to the one actually in force in the constitution of 1925, ensuring the right to "depart from the territory"; in the former constitution this provision never had a restricted meaning.

100. UN Covenant on Civil and Political Rights, Art. 12, op. cit.

101. Regulations of Aliens, Law 13.353 (28 July 1959). The constitution prohibits slave traders from living in Chile, Arts. 10.1, 10.2.

102. Invoking this broad legislation, in 1965 the government expelled an alien who worked in agriculture for not observing certain provisions of the labor legislation with regard to benefits to which his workers were entitled. His farm was expropriated.

103. Declaration of the Ministry of the Interior (28 November 1960), in Jonás Guerra Araya, Derecho y practica consulares 9-10 (Santiago 1969).

104. Between September 1970, the date on which the socialist coalition was elected to government, and December 1971, 21,000 aliens from socialist countries, particularly the USSR and Cuba, entered Chile. An average of 1,500 socialist aliens entered Chile per month. These figures were made public by a congressional investigation in January 1972.

105. Law 12.927 on Internal Security of the State (6 August 1958), Art. 3.5.

106. Law 6.026 on Internal Security of the State (12 February 1937), Art. 17; Law 8.987 on Permanent Defense of Democracy (3 September 1948), Art. 26 (my translation).

107. Supreme Court, ruling of 2 October 1953, confirming the decision of the Court of Appeals of Santiago of 16 September 1953 on habeas corpus of Antonio Ferrán Sabaté. Cited by Silva Bascuñan, op. cit., at 325.

108. See, Supreme Court, 1 Gaceta de los Tribunales 222 (1936) cited by Silva Bascuñan, op. cit., at 326-27. See also Supreme Court ruling of 9 November 1954, on habeas corpus of Salvador Medalla. On this occasion the Supreme Court eliminated a consideration of the decision of the Court of Appeals of Valparaiso, which gave a restricted meaning to detention. Silva Bascuñan, op. cit., at 327.

109. Supreme Court, ruling of 9 November 1942, habeas corpus of Antonio Klaiber. Cited by Silva Bascuñan, op. cit., at 326.

110. Note from the Ministry of the Interior to the Court of Appeals of Santiago on habeas corpus of Diaz Guerra y de los Rios, 7 January 1961 (my translation). The Court of Appeals refused habeas corpus by its decision of 9 January 1961. The Supreme Court confirmed the refusal by its decision of 13 January 1961.

111. Supreme Court, ruling of 1 July 1965, confirming the decision of the Court of Appeals of Santiago of 24 June 1965 on habeas corpus of Víctor Catán (my translation). Habeas corpus was not admitted on other grounds.

112. Court of Appeals of Santiago, ruling of 22 April 1965, refusing habeas corpus of Cuban citizen Silvia Urrutia de Undurraga (my translation).

113. Supreme Court, ruling of 2 October 1953, op. cit. Cited by Silva Bascuñan, op. cit., at 327 (my translation).

114. Supreme Court, ruling of 1 July 1965, op. cit. The court declared that "the order of expulsion issued by the government . . . and the facts on which it is based correspond to the provisions of law." Dissenting opinions stated that the facts were not in accordance with law "creating causes which the latter does not establish and, thereby, it results that the detention prior to expulsion is illegal." In any event, the facts were expressly qualified by courts.

115. Silva Bascuñan, op. cit., at 331.

116. Ibid., at 316, 326; also Andrade Geywitz, op. cit., at 198.

117. Consular Regulations, Arts. 237, 270. Guerra Araya, op. cit., at 251. An identical provision was contained in the Consular Regulations of 1860. Cruchaga Ossa, op. cit., at 527, no. 1149.

118. General Instructions to the Diplomatic Corps, Art. 500.

119. For this purpose several treaties have also been signed, including the treaties with Mexico (1831), Ecuador (1855), and Nueva Granada (1844). In Cruchaga Ossa, op. cit., at 46-47, no. 118, 376, no. 765, and 593, no. 1268, respectively.

120. Note from the Minister of Foreign Affairs, Manuel Antonio Tocornal, to the Consul of Chile in Caracas, 15 March 1864. In Cruchaga Ossa, op. cit., at 594, no. 1272 (my translation).

121. The legislation has many references to aliens serving in the Chilean armed forces. For example, Code of Military Justice, Art. 377.

122. Among other provisions that make reference to public order, see Arts. 1461, 1467, and 1682 of the Civil Code.

123. Court of Appeals of Valparaiso, Compañía Inglesa de Vapores v. MacGregor, 2 January 1908. This and other cases cited by Federico Duncker Biggs, Derecho Internacional Privado 347, Note 2 (Santiago 1956).

124. Supreme Court, Fisco v. Compañía de Salitres de Antofagasta (7 September 1923). This and other cases in Duncker Biggs, op. cit., at 348, note 2.

125. Code of Civil Procedure, Art. 242.1. Decision cited by Alfredo Etcheberry, American-Chilean Private International Law 89, note 360 (Parker School of Foreign and Comparative Law, Dobbs Ferry, N.Y.: Oceana 1960).

126. Duncker Biggs, op. cit., at 343-47.

127. Ibid., at 385-91.

128. Etcheberry, op. cit., at 84-85.

129. Supreme Court, Junta Provincial de Beneficencia de Sevilla v. Guxmán y otros (10 August 1936). Cited by Duncker Biggs, op. cit., at 342, note 1, and by Etcheberry, op. cit., at 85, note 339.

130. Etcheberry, op. cit., at 85, note 339.

131. Addresses of the President, Joaquín Prieto, and the Minister of Foreign Affairs, Joaquín Tocornal, to Congress, 21 November 1833. In Cruchaga Ossa, op. cit., at 84, no. 194 (my translation).

132. Santiago Benadava, "Las relaciones entre Derecho Internacional y Derecho Interno ante los tribunales chilenos," 59 Revista de Derecho, Jurisprudencia y Ciencias Sociales 1-2 at 7-9 (January-April 1962).

133. Francisco Orrego Vicuña, "La incorporación del Análisis de la práctica chilena," 7 Derecho de la Integración 53 (Instituto para la Integración de América Latina, October 1970).

134. Supreme Court, as cited by Benadava, op. cit., at 27. Only on one occasion has the Supreme Court supposedly contradicted this superiority; this was Duncan Fox y Cia. v. Dirección General de Impuestos Internos (1932), cited ibid., at 26.

135. Cases and comments ibid., at 22-24.

136. The Civil Code of Argentina expressly provides that foreign legislation is not to be applied when it contravenes "public law," Art. 14, cited by Duncker Biggs, op. cit., at 417.

137. Code of Criminal Procedure, Art. 1.

138. Supreme Court, 1932. In Benadava, op. cit., at 5 (my translation).

139. Court of Appeals of Santiago, 1949, ibid. (my translation).

140. Benadava, loc. cit., at 2 (my translation).

141. Ibid., at 7; Cases at 9-10.

142. Ibid., at 3.

143. Lauritzen v. Fisco, ibid., at 5.

144. Note from the Minister of Foreign Affairs, Joaquín Tocornal, to the Chargé d'Affaires of Chile in France, 4 July 1833. In Cruchaga Ossa, op. cit., at 73, no. 171 (my translation).

145. Cases in Benadava, op. cit., at 15-16, 19.

146. Code of Civil Procedure, Art. 170.5.

147. Ibid., Art. 170.6.

148. Duncker Biggs, op. cit., at 342.

149. Benadava, op. cit., at 11-13.

150. Supreme Court, resolution of 10 December 1969, 10 International Legal Materials 1 at 1-5 (1971).

151. Note from the Minister of Foreign Affairs, Conrado Ríos Gallardo, to the Ambassador of the United States, 4 September 1928, in Fuentes Herrera, op. cit., at 51, no. 45 (my translation).

152. Organization of Courts Code, Arts. 53.3, 98.5. This has also been the tendency in classical practice and legislation. In Cruchaga Ossa, op. cit., at 39, no. 100, and 572-73, no. 1225.

153. Covenant and Code of Private International Law, signed in Havana at the Sixth International American Conferences, 20 February 1928.

154. Code of Civil Procedure, Art. 160 (my translation).

155. Note from the Minister of Foreign Affairs, Miguel Cruchaga Tocornal, to the President of the International Exchange Commission, no. 7.532 (5 November 1935). In Carmona Klemm, op. cit., at 64-65, no. 68. Sanctions became effective on 18 November 1935.

156. Ibid., at 65 (my translation).

157. In Official Journal, 30 April 1966 (my translation).

158. Agreement of the Central Bank of 7 February 1967, in compliance with Resolution 234 of the Security Council of the United Nations of 10 December 1966.

159. For the system of Latin American Free Trade Association and of the Subregional Agreement, particularly in relation to the decisions of these agencies and the problems that have arisen, see Francisco Orrego Vicuña, "Contemporary International Law in the Economic Integration of Latin America," Académie de Droit International, Recueil des Cours, Colloque 1971; Francisco Orrego Vicuña, "La incorporación del Análisis de la practica chilena," op. cit.

160. Serious problems were posed by the procedures followed to bring into force Decision 24 of the Commission of the Subregional Agreement on Regulation of Foreign Investments, which were rejected by the Contraloría General de la República, an organ of administrative control.

161. Before the courts of Colombia, more than five recourses have been presented requesting that several decisions of the Subregional Agreement and the Agreement itself be declared contrary to the constitution. See Francisco Orrego Vicuña, "La incorporación del ordenamiento jurídico subregional al derecho interno: Análisis de la práctica y jurisprudencia de Colombia," 11 Derecho de la Integración (INTAL, October 1972).

162. Materials in Cruchaga Ossa, op. cit.

163. Organization of Courts Code, Art. 362.

164. The participation of the Supreme Court Attorney (Fiscal) in cases of diplomatic protection was mentioned further ibid. above. In the Gulf Oil case mentioned in ibid., Sect. 6.1, the attorney also gave his advice with regard to the request of the Ministry of Foreign Affairs.

165. Code of Civil Procedure, Art. 159.1 (my translation).

166. Ibid., Art. 349.

167. Note from the Minister of Foreign Affairs, Gabriel Valdés, to the President of the Supreme Court, 4 December 1969. In 10 International Legal Materials 1 at 1-5 (1971).

168. Ibid., at 5.

169. Text in Fernando López Rubio and Germán Carrasco Dominguez, Recopilación de tratados, convenciones y acuerdos internacionales bilaterales celebrados por la República de Chile, 1810-1860 (Ministry of Foreign Affairs, Santiago 1960).

170. Treaty with the United States (16 May 1832), Arts. 23, 24.

171. Treaty with Great Britain (4 October 1854), Art. 11.

172. Treaty with Sardinia (28 June 1856), Art. 26 (my translation). An identical provision was contained in the treaty with Great Britain (4 October 1854), Art. 17, and with Germany (1 February 1862), Art. 18, among others.

173. Treaty with Great Britain (4 October 1854), Art. 11.

174. For this practice, Francisco Orrego Vicuña, "Estudio sobre la solidaridad Latinoamericana en el Sieglo XIX," in Francisco Orrego Vicuña, ed., América Latina y la Cláusula de la Nación más Favorecida (Carnegie Endowment for International Peace, Santiago 1972).

175. For the many declarations of the Ministry of Foreign Affairs in this matter, see Cruchaga Ossa, op. cit., nos. 104, 107, 108, 123, 212, 418, 1219.

176. Arbitral tribunals were constituted to judge the claims presented based on the War of the Pacific in 1879 and the civil war of 1891.

177. General Secretariat of the Organization of American States, El régimen de las inversiones privadas en el mercado común centroamericano y en la Asociación Latinoamericana de Libre Comercio. Antecedentes para un trato común 476 ff. (1964).

178. Commission of the Agreement, Decision 24 (December 1970).

179. Agreements of this nature were signed with Argentina in September 1971 with regard to Chilean workers residing in Argentina.

180. Guerra Araya, op. cit., at 5.

181. Francisco Orrego Vicuña, El Comercio del Estado. Alternativa de la Cláusula de la Nación más Favorecida en la Estructuración Jurídica del Comercio Internacional? (Carnegie Endowment for International Peace, Inter-American Study Group, 1972).

CHAPTER

7

DENMARK

Isi Foighel

THE INDIVIDUAL

As a National

Movement

Passports. The provisions relevant to the movement of Danish nationals are contained in the Passport Act.[1] The basic principle is that any Danish citizen has a right to obtain a passport. There are, however, certain situations in which the issuance of a passport may be denied or in which a passport already issued may be withdrawn. Among the situations mentioned in the Passport Act are the following:

1. The person is charged with a criminal offense that presumably will result in imprisonment, and there are cogent reasons to believe that the person will leave the country or remain abroad in order to avoid punishment.

2. The person has been sentenced to imprisonment but has not yet served the sentence or has been fined or had property confiscated without having performed the financial actions required or put up security, and there are cogent reasons to believe that the person will leave the country or remain abroad in order to avoid imprisonment or payment.

3. The person's departure would violate legislative provisions, the purpose of which is to secure a person's presence in Denmark until obligations owed to public or private parties are fulfilled.

Passports are issued by the police authorities, and if they decide to withdraw a passport or if they refuse the granting of a passport, their decision may be appealed to the courts, which shall sustain or overrule the police decision as expeditiously as possible.

Departure. Normally a Dane is free to leave Denmark at any time. Exceptions to this rule are made only in the situations outlined above.

Return. It is part of the rights of Danish citizenship that a citizen is free to return at any time. Should the immigration authorities refuse the citizen entry upon arrival, their decisions may be appealed to the courts.

Expulsion. As a manifestation of the same basic principle of citizenship, a Danish citizen can never be expelled from Denmark. Should any authority nonetheless decree an expulsion, the decision may likewise be appealed to the courts.

Protection

Extent of Freedom of Activity Abroad. As a basic principle, Danish authorities do not interfere with the activity of a Danish citizen abroad, it being left to local authorities to take whatever steps may be called for. There are, however, various exceptions to this general principle in which Danish authorities will still exercise some jurisdiction over Danish citizens staying or residing abroad.

Thus, in the financial field there are a number of complex restrictions on capital movements. Furthermore, Danish citizens who have been subject to Danish taxation remain Danish tax-subjects after their departure from Denmark until they submit evidence that they have become subject to taxation in another state.

Danish male citizens may be drafted for military service at the age of 17. The obligation to serve does not lapse with departure from the country. Denmark does not interfere with enlistment abroad, but even if such enlistment is due to the fact that the person in question has acquired citizenship in another country without losing his Danish citizenship, military service in Denmark will still be required of him unless there happens to be a mutual exemption agreement between Denmark and the country of his new citizenship.

Enlistment abroad would become objectionable, and even punishable, if it resulted in a Danish citizen actually participating in military actions against the Danish state or one of its allies. Such activity is punished by up to 12 years imprisonment.

The Danish government exercises no control over the participation of a Danish citizen in an election abroad, nor does it otherwise curb or restrict the activities of the citizen outside Denmark, with the exception of a few instances in which Danish penal legislation may be applied to criminal offenses committed outside Denmark, such as crimes committed on Danish ships on the high seas and crimes against the Danish government or public authorities committed outside the country.

As for judicial jurisdiction, the basic rule of the Danish Administration of Justice Act of 1916 is that court actions must be brought in the district where the defendant has his or her residence. However, if a Danish citizen has no residence in Denmark, an action may also be brought before the court in the district where the citizen is currently staying or, should information on the current whereabouts of the citizen not be available, in the district of his or her last known residence or place of sojourn.

The Right to Diplomatic Protection. A Danish national's right to diplomatic protection by his government is not regulated by any law or statutory provision. It is, however, the general opinion that no Danish citizen has such a right. In the following situations this opinion is clearly correct:

1. A claim may arise against a state that is not recognized by the Danish government or with which Denmark has no diplomatic relations.

2. A claim may be based on illegal behavior on the part of the national, such as smuggling, fraud, or a war crime, and it may therefore be politically embarrassing for the government to represent the national. The evaluation of such a situation must rest in the executive branch, under the Foreign Minister.

3. Even where a claim against a foreign state may be justified, there could be a situation in which raising a claim could jeopardize a delicate political situation. Also, in such a situation the assessment of the case must rest with the foreign minister.

Apart from these three situations, in which diplomatic protection is either impossible from a technical point of view or inexpedient from a foreign-policy point of view, there could be cases in which it would be justifiable to recognize the existence of a right to diplomatic protection. Even if such a right is not expressly stated in Danish law, practice shows that the Danish authorities very seldom, if ever, deny a citizen diplomatic protection in cases in which there is a reasonable chance of success. Even in situations like that mentioned above in which Danish citizens were involved in illegal acts such as smuggling, the Danish diplomatic service has tried, by direct negotiation, to help them. The position can be summarized by stating that in all cases in which there are no technical or political obstacles, diplomatic protection will be afforded to Danish citizens if there is a reasonable chance of obtaining a satisfactory result.

If, however, the Foreign Minister decides not to assist a Danish citizen or his efforts to do so fail, that citizen can not claim any sort of compensation from the Foreign Ministry.

A corollary to the nonexistence of a legal right to diplomatic protection is found in the fact that the government cannot impose on any citizen a duty to abstain from advancing a claim against any foreign government.

The right of diplomatic protection is sometimes exercised indirectly for persons other than citizens. The action by the Danish government against the Greek government at the European Human Rights Commission was motivated by concern over the treatment of Greek citizens in opposition to their government. Even if this is very far away from traditional diplomatic protection, it is an interesting example of concern by a government for human beings who, in the eyes of that government, are victims of injustice. The legal basis for the Danish action was, however, to be found in special treaty relations, namely the European Convention on Human Rights.

The State and Compensation. If the Danish government, in exercising diplomatic protection for a citizen, receives compensation from a foreign government, this amount, after deduction of costs, fees, and so on, has to be handed over to the claimant. This is not dictated by law but stems from general legal principles and has never been questioned.

If compensation has been received for a group of citizens, as has been the practice in the postwar compensation agreements concerning nationalization, the situation is different. The very fact that the government represents a group of claimants whose claims vary in quality and legal foundation raises many problems when, as is usually the case, only partial compensation is received. This complex problem raises at least two important questions: To what extent does international law play a role in the distribution of compensation to individual claimants? and How is the distribution administered?

It follows from the compensation agreements that the state receiving the compensation, rather than the paying state, has the right to decide how the compensation shall be distributed. This must mean that the distribution formally takes place according to the municipal law of the receiving state. The question is, however, to what extent the general rules of international law, the compensation treaty, and its preconditions are to be taken into account.

The rules of international law are sometimes applied to avoid claims for repayment by the state that has paid compensation. In individual cases the distribution of compensation in another country is of direct financial importance to the state paying compensation. In the compensation agreement between the United States and Yugoslavia of 19 July 1948 it was provided that Yugoslavia should pay total compensation of $17 million to the United States. In accordance with the express provisions of the treaty, the United States was to set up an agency for the management of the distribution, the decisions of which should be final.[2]

It was, however, laid down in Article 1 of the compensation treaty that if there should be a balance remaining after all claims had been met and expenses connected with the distribution of the compensation had been deducted, it should be returned to Yugoslavia.

In this instance Yugoslavia had a direct financial interest in ensuring that the U.S. distribution of compensation took place in close agreement with the wording and preconditions of the agreement for global compensation. The treaty of 1948 also contained a provision that the United States would make available to Yugoslavia confirmed copies of the decisions made by the distribution agency. At the same time, in connection with decisions on the individual cases, Yugoslavia was empowered to submit advice to the U.S. courts.[3]

If in this situation the United States had compensation outside the terms authorized by the compensation treaty and international law, and if this had resulted in a claim for the repayment of surpluses, Yugoslavia would have been entitled to receive compensation from the United States. In this case a distribution of the global sum received in conformity with the terms of the treaty was a legal necessity.

The rules of international law are sometimes applied in the incidental interests of the state paying compensation. Instances can occur in which the state paying compensation has directly stipulated in the compensation treaty that the distribution must follow a course set out therein in detail.

The state paying compensation may have a particular interest in this. It is, for example, conceivable that the nationalizing state, even after the nationalization, is in some degree dependent on a group of claimants or individuals. Consequently, it may be important for the state paying compensation that, with its future economic policy in mind, it be able to point to the sums of compensation that have actually been paid to the claimants in question.

Although it is not possible to pronounce with certainty on the motives behind the global agreement concluded between France and Romania on 9 February 1959, it can be said that just such a distribution is laid down in that agreement. Article 11 states that the amount of global compensation shall be distributed in accordance with certain detailed guiding rules.

Similar detailed provisions on distribution of compensation are to be found, for example, in Article 1(2) of the agreement between Great Britain and Hungary of 27 June 1956, in Article 1, Clause 4 of the agreement between Sweden and Poland of 16 November 1949, and in Article 1 of the Danish-Polish Protocol No. 2 of 26 February

1953, in which it is similarly laid down that certain claimants, expressly named in the treaty, are to receive definite sums.

There is no doubt that in these cases the state paying compensation must be able to demand that the rules in the treaty concerning the distribution of compensation be accurately observed. This demand was also met in the national regulations for distribution.

The rules of international law are sometimes applied in the general interests of the state paying compensation. In addition to cases in which the distribution of compensation directly affects the relations between the two contracting states and in which this has been expressed in detail in the text of the treaty, it is conceivable that the distribution of the global sum by the state receiving the compensation is of essential importance to the state paying the compensation, both insofar as it affects other states and insofar as it affects the nationals of the state receiving compensation.

Since the signing of an agreement for global compensation is often the final step in protracted negotiations, in the course of which the parties to the treaty have discussed individual claims with a view to determining the approximate size of the global sum, it will obviously be unreasonable if the state paying compensation is not released from all material liability to the claimants in respect to the claims that have been recognized and that consequently have influenced the amount of the global sum.

If the state paying compensation is not released, it may be possible that claims already recognized and paid to the receiving state may be raised afresh, for example by a third state that may assert that the claimants are also (or only) nationals of that state or that some of its nationals are shareholders in companies that have the nationality of the state receiving compensation. As pointed out, doubt can arise both from questions about the nationality of the claimants and from questions about the indirect ownership of the nationalized property.

With these cases before it, the state paying compensation is vitally interested in seeing to it that the receiving state distributes the global sum in conformity with the treaty and with the rules of international law in general. Even though the renunciation clauses in the treaties on global compensation will scarcely have much influence in the case of the third state, they will of course be an extraordinarily weighty argument in any negotiations with that state concerning compensation, that for the property for which the third state desires compensation compensation has in fact been paid to the natural or juridical persons entitled to it under international law.

This interest in the distribution of compensation is clearly stated in the compensation treaty between the United States and Poland of 16 July 1960, in the appendix to which it is expressly specified that it is "for the purpose of the distribution of the sum to be paid by the Government of Poland" for the claims in respect of nationality and ownership that are covered in the treaty. Further, Article 5 of the treaty states:

> With a view to protecting the Government of Poland from the possible assertion through third countries, or otherwise, of claims settled by this Agreement, the Government of the United States will furnish to the Government of Poland copies of such formal statements of claims as may be made by claimants and copies of decisions with respect to the validity and amounts of claims.

According to Article 7 of the treaty, this appendix is a constituent part of the treaty. Although Article 3 entrusts the distribution of compensation to the government of the United States, the provision quoted appears to imply that during the distribution the United States should pay due regard to the interests of Poland in being released from all material obligations to individual claimants. Whether the United States would incur legal responsibility if it ignored the alleged interests of Poland during the distribution must be regarded as doubtful, however.

The material release of the state paying compensation is also important in another way in direct relation to the individual claimant. Although the state paying compensation discharges its obligations to the receiving state with the conclusion and implementation of the treaty of global compensation, this is not always the case relative to individual claimants.

The effect of a relative renunciation of this kind is simply that the state receiving compensation expressly binds itself to refrain from supporting claimants in their demands against the state paying compensation. The private person who is affected by the action of the foreign state is not thereby excluded from raising the claim for compensation with the foreign state if he finds it opportune. The precondition for this is, however, that the individual has not received full payment of a claim for compensation in the distribution of the compensation made by his or her home state.

Consequently the state paying compensation will in these cases, too, be directly interested in knowing that the distribution takes place in agreement with the treaty and its preconditions, since the distribution of the global amount decisively affects the degree to which the state paying compensation is released from financial obligations to the foreigners whose property has been affected by nationalization. It would therefore be natural if in such a case the state receiving compensation were to follow the rules of international law in making its distribution. This to a considerable extent takes place in practice, though no legal obligations for doing so exist in these cases.

It must, however, be recognized that the arguments produced by the interest of the state paying compensation in being released materially from any obligation to the claimants is predominantly hypothetical and not of great practical importance in the arrangements for distribution by the receiving states. First of all, the views quoted depend on the assumption that there will be a decisive change in the attitude of the state paying compensation toward the treatment of individual claims for compensation. This in most cases presupposes a change of regime, a factor that states scarcely include in their deliberations when concluding compensation treaties. It must also be observed that the situation described here, in which the state receiving compensation gives only a relative renunciation, occurs extremely rarely, since the relative renunciation is often accompanied by a guarantee from the state receiving compensation to the paying state. Thereby the interest in maintaining the rules of international law in the distribution of the compensation passes from the state paying compensation to the state receiving it.

The rules of international law may be applied for the purpose of the guarantee of the state receiving compensation. The agreement between Sweden and Czechoslovakia of 22 December 1956 declares in Article 4 that

> the Swedish Government guarantees that the Czechoslovak Republic together with Czechoslovak physical and juridical persons, following the payment in full of the sum of 5 million Swedish kroner, shall not be called upon to make any further payments for the Swedish claims and demands made in art. 1.

Similar provisions are to be found in other agreements for global compensation concluded by Sweden and in the treaties concluded by some other states. A guarantee against further claims is often a condition required by the state paying compensation for accepting only a relative renunciation from the claimant state.

The effect of such a guarantee is that in a case in which a person affected by nationalization in some way obtains additional compensation from the nationalizing state, the other party to the treaty with the state paying compensation shall pay the same amount. There are thus no financial reasons why the state paying compensation should be interested in the distribution of the compensation, and the distributing state need not consider the paying state during the distribution.

The state receiving compensation has itself, however, a vital interest in ensuring that the distribution of the global sum takes place in the closest possible conformity with the compensation treaty and with the rules of international law in general, since it can be concluded with certainty that when the treaty was concluded and implemented a settlement took place, at least for those claims for which the evidence of losses and the basis for compensation under international law was satisfactory.

To the extent that distribution takes place in conformity with the compensation treaty and the rules of international law in general, the risk that the guarantee contained in the compensation treaty will be invoked is reduced for the state receiving compensation. The rules of international law may also be applied out of other considerations. In the cases described above, the compensation treaty and the assumptions behind it, which to a large extent means the rules of international law on the working out of liability to pay compensation (which were examined in the previous section), were thus important for the distribution of the compensation. Clear disregard of the rules of international law will, in various ways, cause the state receiving the compensation to incur legal or financial responsibility relative to the state paying compensation.

There are, however, examples in which the payment by the nationalizing state of the global sum under the terms of the treaty finally put an end to all problems of compensation between the two contracting states. If the state paying compensation pays a global sum in full and definitive settlement of its liability, irrespective of whether the compensation paid in individual cases is of the same size as the claim that arose from the nationalization, if the state paying compensation completely, that is, also in material affairs, hands over the distribution of compensation to the receiving state, and if the receiving state can give, and has given on behalf of its nationals, an absolute renunciation of further claims, then it must be taken that the distribution of compensation is the sole concern of the state receiving compensation and its nationals and that no obligation exists to apply the rules of international law to the distribution of the compensation.

These preconditions are fulfilled in some of the earlier British global agreements for compensation, such as the treaty with Yugoslavia of 23 December 1948; the treaties with Poland of 14 January 1949 and of 11 November 1954; the treaty with Bulgaria of 22 September 1955; and the treaty with Hungary of 27 June 1956. Similar absolute renunciations are to be found, for example, in the agreement between Belgium and Czechoslovakia of 30 September 1952 and between Denmark and Poland of 26 February 1953.

In this situation the rules of international law, as they may appear from the treaty and its preconditions, are without importance.

The state receiving compensation can, without fear of legal or financial consequences relative to the paying state, distribute at its discretion the compensation it has received.

Nevertheless, the practice shows that even in these cases the rules of international law bear on the settlement of many of the legal questions arising from the distribution of compensation. The causes are various. Some of them may possibly be found in the constitutions of the states receiving compensation. Other causes lie in the fact that the application of rules of international law will be appropriate, if only because the individual states frequently lack traditional rules on the distribution of compensation. It is natural to apply to the distribution of the compensation the rules that formed the basis of the payment of the compensation. However, no legal necessity for this has ever existed.

The first lump-sum agreement was concluded with Poland on 26 February 1953. It was then possible to distribute the compensation received by the Danish government without any serious difficulties. All the claims were known in advance, and the number of claimants was so small that these could be kept informed of progress and thus had an opportunity to approve the results that could be obtained during the negotiations with Poland before the signing of the treaty. The amount of global compensation that Poland undertook to pay was thus fixed on the basis of a list of the Danish claims submitted. It was then also possible to use this list as a basis for the distribution of the money received.

On 27 January 1957, however, the Ministry of Commerce put before Parliament a bill concerning the distribution of certain compensations received from abroad. In this bill it was suggested that a board be set up to organize the distribution. According to the notes accompanying it, one reason for the bill was that other countries had created similar boards and that the distribution of the global sum had given rise to a number of difficult legal questions demanding thorough knowledge of such matters as the law of probate and the procedure for negotiations with the foreign state. "During the distribution there will, therefore, be a call for expert legal knowledge of different kinds, and this objective can best be attained by entrusting the distribution to a board set up for that purpose, in which the various branches of legal expert knowledge can be represented."

As a further reason it was claimed that the setting up of a board would result in the establishment of uniform practice in the distribution of the global compensation received from various countries. It is probable that certain problems of procedure and evidence were being thought of here, since the law, as far as material legal questions are concerned, makes the individual treaty the decisive factor. These material legal questions include which persons have claims to part of the distribution and what kind of claims can be met.

With a few alterations the bill was adopted and became Law Number 179 of 7 June 1958. In accordance with Section 2 of the law, a board was to be set up consisting of a chairman, who must possess the qualifications for appointment as judge, nominated by the Minister of Commerce in consultation with the Minister of Justice, and three other members representing the Foreign Ministry, the Finance Ministry, and the Ministry of Commerce.

Thus, in the Danish board, the procedure used in some other countries, in which representatives for the claimants or experts from industry and commerce are represented on the board, was not followed.

The board was to undertake the distribution of global compensation received by the Danish state in accordance with treaties for losses sustained as a result of measures taken by the state paying compensation, "among them that the property has been nationalized, seized or in some similar way abstracted from the owners."[4] It may be taken that this also covers, for example, losses sustained as a result of property being placed under national control, although the rights of ownership still rest with the original owners, as may be seen by the alteration in the text of the bill carried out in committee. The amendment was directed to Section 1, Clause 1, in such a way that there could be no doubt that any and every financial loss was covered by the law.

Paragraph 3 authorized the issue of official notices. In Section 5 it was further provided that if the claim submitted was rejected in whole or in part, the decision was to be accompanied by reasons for the rejection. The decision of the board could be brought before the courts by the applicant.

Expenses in connection with the work of the committee were to be met from the global compensation unless other arrangements were authorized by the parliamentary finance committee.[5]

With reference to the work of the board in distributing the global compensation and its material basis for doing so, Section 4 provided that the board should undertake an examination of the claims submitted and determine, among other things, whether the documentary evidence provided was satisfactory. Thereafter, on the basis of the claims received and the information available to the board, coupled with the guidance in the agreement and its preconditions, the board was to fix the sum of money that should form the basis of the distribution of the global compensation. All persons sharing in the distribution should have the same proportional cover, unless other provisions existed from the agreement, from the negotiations, or from the preconditions for the agreement.[6]

No guidance was given in the law on the question of the persons included in the distribution, but the notes on the bill contained an express provision that "this question must be decided separately for each agreement." This must mean that the board was not empowered to waive the provisions that were laid down on this point in the treaty.

Similar reference to the compensation treaty is only to be found in the notes to Section 4 of the bill, in which the legal inquiries by the board were to include the question of whether the documented claim was included in the agreement.

It thus appears that the comparatively few material legal rules that are given in the law as guidance for the board all refer back to the basic treaty and its preconditions. On this point the Danish legislation corresponds entirely with the practice in other countries.

A claimant who is dissatisfied with the decision of the board can instigate legal procedures against the board at the ordinary courts. One such case has been decided on by the Danish Supreme Court. The facts of the case were as follows. A Danish-born woman married a Czech citizen, acquired Czech citizenship, and lived with him in Czechoslovakia until 1947, when he died. She left Czechoslovakia in 1950 and reacquired her Danish citizenship without losing her Czech citizenship. During the negotiations between the governments of Denmark and Czechoslovakia, the Danish government had included her claim among the other Danish claims. The Czech government dismissed her claim on the basis of her dual nationality. The claimant argued that the Czech government, even if it dismissed her claim, did not specify what claims were covered by the lump-sum agreement. The compensation has to be distributed in accordance with Danish law, and in this respect the woman was entitled to the same treatment as any other Danish citizen.

The Supreme Court held, however, that the rules of international law as expressed by the compensation agreement and its preconditions were binding upon the board.

<u>The State's Responsibility for Injury Induced by Its Own Conduct.</u> There is an extensive practice and literature on government liability for injury in general, but it deals only with internal facts and situations, and therefore, given the context and framework of the question posed, it is not germane to the question at hand. As for liability for conduct exercised or provoked abroad, Denmark has had no experience similar, for instance, to the Belgian experience in the Congo or the U.S. sugar problem with Cuba. Seeing that, among other things, any government action must presumably be based on an assumption that it is for the benefit of the state in general and that, as mentioned above, there is no obligation to "top off" foreign compensations, it seems unlikely that there would be a claim against the Danish state, should a situation of this type arise.

Waiver. The State is entitled to waive the claims of its nationals in respect to injury caused by foreign states.

Special Kinds of Protection. As was mentioned above, a Danish citizen is not generally considered as having a right to diplomatic protection. Since there is not even a right to a general protection, it follows that Denmark does not provide any special kind of protection.

The Individual as an Alien

Movement

Entry and Stay. Non-Danes are generally allowed to enter Denmark, but the Minister of Justice may make a visa a condition for entry. During the last 20 to 25 years there has, however, been a constant decrease in the number of countries in which a visa is required. In most cases the requirement of a visa has been rescinded on the basis of mutual agreement, but in certain cases Denmark has even rescinded this requirement unilaterally; for instance, citizens of the United States have for many years been allowed to enter Denmark without any visa, although the United States, with insignificant exceptions, still makes a visa a condition for Danish citizens entering the United States.

Under the Foreigner's Immigration Act the immigration authorities shall refuse a foreigner entry into this country (1) who is not in possession of a passport, visa, or other documentation required; (2) who there is a reason to believe is not financially able to sustain himself or herself for the period to be spent; (3) who there is reason to believe intends to seek employment or remain permanently or for an extensive, undefined period in Denmark without having secured the work permit required; (4) who there is reason to believe intends, wholly or in part, to make a living in an illegal or fraudulent manner; (5) who is known to the authorities as a professional criminal or who circumstances indicate intends to enter Denmark for the purpose of committing crimes; (6) whose entry is undesirable on account of previously committed crimes; or who has previously been expelled and is attempting to reenter Denmark without having obtained the permission required.[7]

The fact that an alien has previously stayed or resided in Denmark does not give that alien a special vested right to reentry. He or she will either come under the general rule of unrestricted entry or will fall into one of the exceptional categories enumerated above, in which case it makes no difference whether the situation is one of first entry or of reentry.

If the immigration authorities apprehend an alien and put that alien under arrest beyond a specified time limit, he or she may request that the case be brought before a court. Furthermore, the decisions of the immigration authorities may, in general, be brought before the court.

Departure. As for departure, an alien is free to leave Denmark at will. Expulsion is possible in certain situations, of which the most important are the following:

1. Entry into Denmark could have been refused for the reasons mentioned above, and the reasons there given still obtain.
2. The alien intentionally, or in spite of warnings by the police, repeatedly violates the rules on registration with the police.
3. The alien violates regulations on work permit, visa, or residence permit or does not fulfill the conditions under which such permits are given or has obtained a permit through fraudulent misrepresentation or nondisclosure.
4. The continued stay of the alien is undesirable for various reasons, such as participation in actions of a hostile nature against the Danish government or Danish institutions.

An expulsion order may be contested before the courts.

Protection

As outlined above, even Danish citizens do not have a right to diplomatic protection. It consequently follows that no such right is available to aliens.

NATIONAL IMPLEMENTATION OF INTERNATIONAL RIGHTS AND DUTIES

The Act of State Doctrine

In Denmark the issue of foreign legislation is considered an issue of fact and not an issue of law. Consequently, Danish courts ruling on a case involving foreign legislation will take the contents of such legislation as a fact and thus as something that cannot be examined in terms of validity, regularity, or the like. Danish courts would take a position on the merits or nonmerits of foreign legislation only in extreme situations, such as one involving a foreign law that is contrary to principles of Danish public policy.

Implementing Decisions of International Organizations

In general Denmark may be counted upon to secure implementation of the decisions of international organizations, assuming of course that Denmark is a member of the international organization in question and is bound by its decisions. Thus the sanctions adopted by the Security Council of the United Nations against Southern Rhodesia resulted in Danish legislative provisions in 1968 prohibiting the import from or export to Southern Rhodesia of goods, as well as payment to Southern Rhodesia or capital movements, personal services, and the like for the benefit of Southern Rhodesia--all in conformity with the provisions of the particular Security Council resolution. For violation of these regulations, a punishment ranging from a fine to up to three years' imprisonment is prescribed. One case involving violation of the legislation outlined has been brought before the courts, resulting in a fine.

As for the termination of South Africa's mandate over South West Africa, the situation at this state does now appear to be clear. After the Advisory Opinion on Legal Consequences for States of the Continued Presence of South Africa in Namibia,[8] which states that members of the United Nations are under obligation to recognize the illegality of South Africa's presence in Namibia and that South Africa's acts on behalf of or concerning Namibia are invalid, Denmark will accordingly comply with this direction.

As is well known, the relationship between the law of the European communities and the national laws of their member states creates a special and complex problem, but the date of Danish accession to the European Community not yet having been reached, it appears premature to go into this far-reaching problem.

Procedures Related to the Issuance of Certificates or Suggestions by the Executive in Connection with Litigation in National Courts

Adhering strictly to the fundamental principle of complete independence of the courts, Denmark does not normally allow the executive branch of government to interfere in any litigation, be it on its own initiative or at the request of third parties. The general regulations provided by the various offices of the executive branch may play a role as providing data of interpretation, but they will never have a determinative role, and they will never be issued with a view to a specific case before the courts.

The above remarks naturally do not refer to a situation in which a department of the executive branch is itself involved in litigation nor to a situation in which a government office has particular and specific interest in a court action between other parties pending before a court. If the latter situation arises, the government may intervene in the case under certain procedural rules of the Danish Administration of Justice Act of 1916.

TREATIES AND THE INDIVIDUAL

The subject of treaties and the individual is one of broad ramifications involving a vast material. It is therefore hardly possible to do more than to point to a few quite general facts and figures.

Denmark enters extensively into international bilateral and multilateral treaties or agreements covering a wide scope. In 1971, for instance, Denmark entered into almost a hundred international agreements. In the nature of things, some of these treaties involve only the state as such. This is the case, for instance, when dealing with cultural agreements, agreements on government loans, conventions on the protection of archaeological heritage, and treaties regarding air passage. A large number of treaties, however, will affect the individual either directly or indirectly.

The indirect repercussions to the individual of treaties that appear to affect merely the state should not be overlooked. For instance, the treaty of early 1972 entered into by the Danish government on the accession of Denmark to the European Community was basically a treaty at the constitutional level, dealing with problems and regulations of international cooperation in various important fields. Nevertheless, it is evident that this was a treaty of vast significance to every member of Danish society, as also demonstrated by the fact that accession or nonaccession to the community was subsequently made the subject of a referendum. The many well-known provisions of the EEC treaty on import and export, customs duties, competition, community rules, superseding of national law, freedom of movement for workers and capital, liberalization of restrictions, and so on, are clearly provisions that in one way or another have a bearing upon the living conditions of most or all Danes. The philosophy behind this kind of treaty and related treaties is that what is good for the government is good for the citizens, their progress and benefit being the ultimate, recognizable goal of all government.

Denmark has entered into numerous treaties more specifically related to the benefits and protection of individual interests. As a pertinent example may be mentioned treaties on double taxation. Since World War II, when this type of treaty began to be a common one, Denmark has entered into some 40 treaties of this nature. Some of these treaties were entered into as late as 1972, and their number is constantly on the increase. Other examples of treaties aiming at the protection of individual rights may be mentioned, including conventions in the field of human rights; reciprocal visa agreements; treaties on fishing rights and other maritime affairs; conventions on inspection in respect to the manufacture of pharmaceutical products; agreements providing rules on international air carriage; and multilateral conventions concerning hygiene in commerce and offices, narcotics control, and protection of the rights of artists.

NOTES

1. Passport Act (7 June 1952), no. 223.
2. Treaty between the United States and Yugoslavia (19 July 1948), Art. 8, 89 UNTS 43, 62 STAT. 2658, TIAS 1803.
3. Ibid., Art. 9.
4. Law no. 179 (7 June 1958), § 1, clause 1.
5. Ibid., § 8.
6. Ibid., § 6.
7. Foreigner's Immigration Act, Act no. 20 (7 February 1961).
8. ICU Reports 1971, p. 58.

CHAPTER

8

EGYPT

Ibrahim Shihata

This is by no means a comprehensive study of the attitudes of the Egyptian legislative bodies and courts in matters related to individual rights and the state in foreign affairs. It is merely a treatment of some points that may be of special interest, either because of the peculiarity of their substantive regulation or because of their special importance on the national or international plane.

Since the division of topics dealt with in this book follows the simple distinction between "nationals" and "aliens," it may be relevant to point out from the outset of this chapter the special position in the present Egyptian legal system of certain groups of individuals who, though not nationals, are not treated in all respects as aliens. At this writing (in 1972) these include in particular the Palestinian refugees and nationals of the other members of the newly established Union of Arab Republics, which are the Syrian Arab Republic and the Libyan Arab Republic. Special attention will therefore be given to the treatment of these categories. There are also some points of special interest that are not covered in the aforementioned divisions and that will be inserted here where it is deemed appropriate to include them.

In reading the materials presented in this chapter, it may be relevant to recall some important facts. First, for the major part of its recent history, Egypt has been under martial law. The liberal democratic system introduced by the 1923 constitution prevailed with some interruptions until the participation of Egypt in World War II, when martial law was imposed on 1 September 1939. Martial law was lifted in October 1945 but reintroduced in May 1948 on the eve of the Egyptian involvement in the Palestine conflict. The partial lifting of martial law in April 1950 lasted for less than two years, as martial rule was reinstituted in January 1952, to be annually renewed until June 1956. In November 1956 the country was put in a state of emergency, which was reinstituted in 1958 and has prevailed ever since. The 1923 constitution was formally abandoned after the 1952 revolution, which introduced instead a series of constitutional declarations and provisional constitutions, five in number, before a new, "permanent" constitution was finally adopted by a popular plebiscite in 1971. The proclamation of this new constitution, which included a much greater emphasis on individual liberties, has not resulted, however, in the termination of the state of emergency, because of the situation prevailing in the Middle East. It is in the light of this background that the less than liberal and at times repressive attitudes of Egyptian legislation and practice in the matter of individual rights may be viewed.

Second, Egypt, although a developing country and a net importer of capital, is also an exporter of tens of thousands of professionals and technicians to its neighboring countries. Its apparent interest in narrowing the scope of protection according to aliens in its territory is matched by its interest in securing a wide protection for Egyptians residing abroad.

Third, it may be noted that the attitudes shown in Egyptian legislation and court decisions often have their impact in other Arab countries. Many of the Egyptian codes are simply copied in other Arab states, and the pronouncements of Egyptian courts are sometimes cited as precedents in the judicial decisions of their courts. Egyptian regulations relating to rights of individuals, especially nationals, thus find similar counterparts in other Arab countries, particularly those known as the "revolutionary" countries, in which government has a fuller control over individual activities and a greater share in the ownership of the means of production.

THE INDIVIDUAL

The Individual as a National

Movement

Passports: The Right of Movement. The successive constitutions of independent Egypt have consistently provided for the "right of movement" by prohibiting "the confinement of the residence of any citizen in any particular area, except under the conditions determined by law." Furthermore, the Constitution of the Union of Arab Republics mentions this right as one of the "basic liberties and principles" to be provided for in the constitution of every member republic.[1] Such a constitutional right has been limited, however, in the higher judicial interpretation to "movement within the territorial limits of the state,"[2] despite some language to the contrary in earlier decisions of the lower Court of Administrative Adjudication.[3] Even within such territorial limits, administrative courts have held that martial orders declaring some areas as "prohibited" and restricting entrance thereto were valid, if based on considerations of public interest.[4]

To this right of movement within the territory of the state there must be added the right of movement among the territories of the members of the Union of Arab Republics, which is guaranteed by the constitution of the Union to all its citizens.[5] Although this right is yet to be regulated by a Union law, travel among the territories of the member republics is now possible for their nationals by means of official identity cards. Departure of Egyptian citizens to other member republics has also been freed from the exit-visa requirement under unilateral regulations issued by the Egyptian Ministry of the Interior in May 1972.

Travel abroad has been described in a few decisions of the Egyptian Conseil d'Etat as a "basic freedom"[6] and even as one aspect of the constitutional right of movement.[7] As a result, compensation was awarded by the Court of Administrative Adjudication for "deprivation of this freedom" by means of refusal to issue a passport to the national requesting it "when it was justified by the desire to avoid a contingent and uncertain danger."[8] This is, however, a unique precedent, which, it must be noted, dates back to the period before the 1952 revolution. However, the principle established in that period, to the effect that the decision to withhold a passport is an ordinary administrative decision, the annulment of which may be requested from the Conseil d'Etat,[9] has been maintained up to the present.

The passport law now in force specifies in clear terms that the Minister of the Interior may refrain from issuing or renewing a passport and may withdraw a passport already issued "for important reasons that he estimates."[10] This has not, however, influenced the established trend of the Conseil d'Etat to the effect that the power of the executive branch in withholding passports may be based only on "the protection of public interest" and must not be vitiated by turnovers in power."[11]

The Supreme Administrative Court chose, however, to express this doctrine in broader terms. After referring to the provision on "right of movement" in the Constitution and in the Universal Declaration of Human Rights, the court upheld the right of the executive to regulate the "freedom to travel abroad," subject only to the condition that such regulation be "general in character and not arbitary."[12] It thus reversed the decision of the lower court, which had upheld "the right of the individual to travel abroad for purposes of medical treatment." Restriction of the right to travel abroad "for reasons related to the good of the society and to its protection" was furthermore found by the Court of Administrative Adjudication to be well established in the "principles of international law."[13]

Under such a broad criterion the refusal by the ministry to issue a passport to someone who failed to present a "certificate of nationality" was held as valid,[14] although the presentation of such a certificate is not required in the normal procedure. The same judicial attitude was followed in another case in which the withholding of the passport had been based on the fact that the person requesting it was suspected of smuggling narcotics (though never prosecuted),[15] although similar grounds (suspicion of smuggling gold and dealing in foreign currencies) were found to be inadequate for withholding a passport in an earlier case.[16] The court also upheld the right of the executive to withdraw the passport of a person who while in Yemen was in the habit of "spreading rumours that were calculated to prejudice the reputation of the country and to undermine the political relations between it and the Kingdom of Yemen," as evidenced by a statement of the Egyptian ambassador to that country, the truth of which was not challenged by the applicant.[17] A broader discretion in the matter of renewal of passports was approved by the court in a case in which such renewal had been rejected because the interested person had previously "disgraced the reputation of the nation" by leading an unworthy show group to Sweden.[18] In yet another case the court approved the withholding of the passport of a young woman simply because she wanted to travel abroad to work as a show girl in a night club, whereas "she had no reputation in show business, had worked before only as a waitress in a bar, and her travel abroad would lead her to follow undignified means of subsistence."[19]

At times the Conseil d'Etat has shown more inclination to preserve the freedom to travel abroad against such extensive intrusion on the part of the state. It thus annulled a decision withholding a passport on the basis that the applicant had been convicted, more than 25 years earlier, of the charge of acquisition of narcotics.[20] It also annulled a similar decision based on the fact that the applicant had been convicted of a felony, but ignoring the fact that he had by the time of the application been reinstated in his civil rights.[21]

Issuance of Passports. It has been the practice of the Ministry of the Interior to request the opinion of the Advisory Section of the Conseil d'Etat before making a decision to refuse to issue or renew a passport upon a valid application submitted to it by a person not among those who are excluded from travel abroad, to whom reference will soon be made. Such an opinion is not binding on the ministry and has no bearing in case the decision of the ministry is later appealed before a court of the Conseil d'Etat. It is, however, an important guarantee against possible abuses of the minister's "right" to withhold passports.

Ministerial Arrêté Number 63 of 1959, on passports, includes some provisions that are interesting, especially as they figure in a decree by the Minister of the Interior that was issued only to implement the Passport Law. Without a specific authorization in the text of the law, the arrêté requires the additional approval of certain persons or entities for the granting of passports in the following cases:

1. A wife may not be granted a passport, or have her name added to the passport of her husband, without the approval of the latter.

2. Government employees, both civilian and military, must submit evidence of the approval of the government entity that employs them among the documents needed for obtaining a passport.

3. Minors and incapacitated persons must submit evidence of the approval of their legal representatives.

None of these provisions has been challenged before the courts as unconstitutional or illegal. Although the requirement of approval by the husband may well run counter to the constitutional principle of equality of the sexes, its challenge on this ground may now be all the more doubtful, since the present constitution provides that such equality is upheld "without prejudice to the rules of Islamic law."[22]

The arrêté further provides that, in case of the deportation of an Egyptian from abroad at the expense of the government, the passport of that citizen will be valid only for a return trip to Egypt and may not be renewed thereafter except with special permission from the Ministry of the Interior.

Another practice provided for in the arrêté is the listing in passports of the names of the states for which they are valid. These will ordinarily be the states requested by the passport holder "unless their inclusion is contrary to the security of the state or its safety or is in contradiction with its higher policy." In practice, states not recognized by Egypt are never listed, while special permission is usually needed to list states with which Egypt has no diplomatic relations and states known as centers of immigration. The practical difficulty of listing the names of all the states that exist at present is usually solved by mentioning them as geographical categories, that is, as European states, African states, and so on. Diplomatic and special passports issued by the Ministry of Foreign Affairs are often designated, however, as valid for "all countries." The refusal by the Passports Department to include the name of a state requested by the passport holder is again an administrative decision subject to the judicial review of the Conseil d'Etat if appealed within 60 days. However, no instance of such an appeal is to be found in the published reports.

Reciprocal arrangements with Iraq, Syria, and Libya allow Egyptians to travel to these countries using their national identity cards. Also, the Council of Arab Economic Unity, the membership of which includes Egypt, Syria, Jordan, Iraq, Kuwait, Sudan, and Yemen, has been working since 1965 on the establishment of a "unified identity card" as a valid document for travel by the citizens of all members among their territories. Several decisions have since been adopted by the council relating to the principle and the procedures of issuing such cards,[23] but their actual implementation still awaits "mutual consultations on the technical problems involved."

An interesting question arose in relation to the power of the recently established Union of Arab Republics to issue travel documents. Although each of the member republics has retained its international personality, the Union is described by its constitution as a state, with powers in the legislative, executive, and judicial fields. Furthermore, the constitution speaks categorically of the "people of the Union" and the "sovereignty of the Union." As to nationality, it includes a rather circuitous provision that reads, "Until a Union law is issued to regulate the unitary citizenship of the Union, each member republic shall regulate the nationality of its citizens within the general principles to be issued by a Union law."[24] Under this provision two stages are envisaged. In the first stage each republic retains its own nationality, while regulating it under general principles equally followed in the other republics. Such different nationalities will, in the second stage, give way to a unified citizenship in the Union. The Union government has considered issuing passports for its employees at this first stage, in order to emphasize their independent character in relation to their national governments. Theoretically there may be different methods for reaching this objective. The Union government could either follow the practice of international organizations, which issue laissez passer documents for their officers with the approval of their member states, or it might institute a general "Union subjecthood" along with the citizenship of each republic, on lines similar to those devised in the British Nationality Act of 1948, which distinguished between Commonwealth citizens (British subjects) and the citizens of the United Kingdom. The trouble with both solutions is that the validity of travel documents issued by the Union will be admitted only by the states recognizing them. Besides the difficulties involved in the acceptance of Union travel documents by the member republics at this stage, it should be noted that no other state has so far recognized the Union as a "state"; nor has any foreign power dealt with it as an "international person." The question of issuing Union passports or other travel documents may therefore be an attempt at a premature solution at the present stage, although it is likely to be raised again with the regressive development of the constitutional ties among the member republics.

Departure: Exit Visas. The present Egyptian constitution includes, for the first time, a provision for the "right of permanent and temporary emigration outside the country," adding that "this right, the procedures and conditions of emigration as well as departure from the country, shall be regulated by law."[25] The last statement came to confirm the preexisting practice and fell short of the demand of many Egyptian jurists, including myself,[26] that it be provided in the constitution that restriction of departure from the country is a penalty that may be imposed only by a judicial order.

In 1956, Law Number 254 authorized the Minister of the Interior to require all individuals leaving the country to obtain a permit as a precondition for their departure, an authority that the said minister did not hesitate to exercise by issuing an arrêté regulating the "exit vis" procedure. Such a repressive procedure, required before only under martial rule, was justified in the explanatory note of the law by considerations of "public security, safety of the country, and protection of national economy." Its constitutionality was soon challenged before the Court of Administrative Adjudication, which held, however, that

> the law did not exceed the regulation of the freedom of individuals to move and travel abroad, such regulation being based on the necessity of maintaining public security, the safety of the nation in and outside its territory, and the protection of national economy. . . . This does not violate the liberty in itself, but merely defines its limits so that its absolute character shall not prejudice the interests of the community.[27]

The exit visa procedure was authorized anew in the Passport Law of 1959 and regulated in further detail in Arrêté Number 65 of 1959 by the Minister of the Interior. This arrêté requires all Egyptians, with negligible exceptions (holders of passports for pilgrimage to Mecca or Jerusalem, military personnel and their families, civil servants leaving for the Gaza strip, and military personnel traveling on a "movement order" from the General Military Command) to obtain exit visas before leaving the country. It provides that such a visa will be issued "in the limits justified by the higher interests of the state or by the requirements of public security."[28] Recently, however, some relaxation was introduced in this respect exempting from the exit visa procedure persons exceeding 60 years of age, students traveling on their summer vacations with special passports valid for one trip, and all citizens carrying government permits for employment abroad or for emigration. Travel by Egyptian nationals to both Libya and Syria, the other members of the Union of Arab Republics, has also been freed from the exit visa requirements, as of May 1972.[29]

Black Lists for "Prohibited Persons." The power of the executive to "regulate" the departure of nationals is understood to include its power to prohibit such a departure in certain cases, subject always to possible review by the Conseil d'Etat. Such a prohibition is regulated by the provisions of Arrêté Number 183 of 1964 of the Minister of the Interior, which provides for the establishment of a Commission for the Lists of Prohibited Persons. This commission is composed of ten government officials including a delegate from the office of the Public Prosecutor. It receives requests from the interested government departments to include or exclude names from the four types of lists it maintains. These include a list of persons prohibited from traveling abroad, a list of persons who need special permission before they are granted exit visas, a list of persons prohibited from entering the country, and a list of persons needing special permission before they are granted entry visas. Those on the first two lists remain on the lists for three years unless a special request is made for keeping them for a further period, but they must be automatically deleted from the lists after ten years of inclusion.

The arrêté provides categorically for certain cases in which persons may not be included in the lists related to departure from the country, except under a special procedure. No one may be listed because of tax evasion unless such is requested in writing by the office of the Public Prosecutor. No one may be included merely because he or she is under investigation or trial for committing a crime, except on the written request of the said office and only for important crimes, the punishment of which exceeds one year of imprisonment. Persons convicted by criminal procedure may only be listed on the request of a certain competent authority for reasons acceptable to the commission and provided they have been subject to the penalty of imprisonment for at least one year.

The same arrêté also establishes an appellate commission to look into the appeals presented to it by persons whose names figure in the lists. This is a five-member commission that includes a counselor from the advisory section of the Conseil d'Etat, whose presence is necessary for a valid quorum. It is, however, an administrative commission, the decisions of which are subject to appeal before the courts of the Conseil d'Etat. Furthermore, the Supreme Administrative Court has ruled that the decision to prohibit a person from traveling by refusing to grant that person an exit visa is independent of the decision to include his or her name in the list, which means that the former decision may be subject to appeal before the courts even if the latter decision has not been appealed in time.[30]

Prevention of departure on the basis of inclusion in the "black lists" was found invalid by the Court of Administrative Adjudication in a case in which, as a result of this procedure, the person involved requested permission to waive his Egyptian nationality and was actually deprived of it and given the laissez passer accorded to stateless persons. In that particular case the person concerned was described by the administration as "Zionist" (a term different in Egyptian law from the term "Jewish," as will be seen) and was prevented from departure on the grounds that he was involved in financial investigations of a company under sequestration. He was not, however, heard in any investigation, despite his formal requests to give testimony. The court annulled the decision that prevented him from leaving the country, since "it was, under the circumstances, devoid of cause."[31]

No exit visa is given to a wife without the approval of her husband, nor to a minor without the approval of his or her legal representative. Furthermore, government employees must obtain the approval of the competent minister before they can apply for an exit visa. The ministerial approval itself must be preceded by a confirmation from the Security Bureau in the ministry. Obviously such complex procedures, and the bureaucratic complications they are likely to entail, are a source of constant complaint, but the exceptional conditions prevailing in the country have often been cited in justification of them. However, some relaxation is developing in this area. Persons whose work involves a great deal of traveling are usually granted exit visas valid for several trips. All approvals required for government employees are given automatically, in most cases within a period of about two weeks. The exit visa itself is issued within 24 hours of a valid request and may be issued immediately on payment of a certain fee. Thus the exit visa requirements, though formidable on paper, have been gradually adapted to the pressing needs of rapid travel in the modern age.

Limitations on the Right to Emigrate. The right of emigration, which was recently provided for in the Egyptian constitution of 1971, is yet to be "regulated" by law. At present there is only an Emigration Commission established by a presidential decree to draw up the national policy in the matter of emigration and to look into applications for emigration abroad. The commission has already issued certain restrictions on the subject by listing the professions for which emigration is limited to certain quotas, to be determined annually by the commission. The approval of other governmental authorities is also required in the case of applications submitted by certain categories of professionals; for instance, the approval of the Ministry of Health is required for applications submitted by medical doctors.

The decisions of the commission, like other administrative decisions not qualified as "acts of sovereignty," are subject to the judicial review of the Conseil d'Etat. Such a review is, however, limited by the traditional attitude adopted by the Conseil d'Etat in refraining from questioning the exercise of the discretionary power of the Executive, if the administrative decision is valid in form and is issued by the competent authority, unless it is vitiated by a change in government. The Supreme Administrative Court has confirmed that conclusion by holding as valid a decision of the Ministry of the Interior to refuse an application for emigration on the basis of the regulations in force.[32]

Return. The Egyptian constitution interdicts in clear terms the prevention of any citizen from returning to the country.[33] Such a prevention may be practiced, however, under the provisions of the Nationality Act if it is preceded by the deprivation of the national's citizenship, which is extensively authorized under the same act. While abroad, and in part because of being abroad, an Egyptian may be deprived of his or her nationality who has left the country "with the intention of not returning to it," has stayed abroad for more than six months, and has been officially requested to return but "did not reply or gave unconvincing answers," provided that deprivation of nationality in such a case is based on "important reasons to be estimated by the President of the Republic."[34] Such a deprivation automatically extends to the wife and minor children who left with the person concerned.

Though drafted in general terms, the provision authorizing deprivation of nationality in such circumstances was first devised in 1956[35] and was mainly intended to enable the government to deprive of their Egyptian citizenship the members of the former royal family who were residing abroad. In practice this provision has been applied in a few cases to individuals who have long been in residence abroad, many of whom had in fact renounced their Egyptian nationality (such renunciation being in itself without effect from the viewpoint of Egyptian law). The provision is, however, criticized in all doctrinal writings, especially because of the very short period provided in it for residence abroad. The Court of Administrative Adjudication annulled a decision applying the provision to the case of an individual who, though working abroad under a valid government permit, was deprived of his nationality for reasons the government declined to submit to the court. The court emphasized in particular that "the intention not to return" is not to be presumed and must be based on valid grounds.[36]

Deprivation of nationality is also possible under the Nationality Act in the more familiar cases of nationals who acquire foreign nationalities without the prior approval of the President, who voluntarily join the armed forces of foreign countries without the permission of the Minister of War, who work for foreign states or governments that are in a state of war with Egypt or whose political relations with Egypt are severed, who have been convicted by a court of law for violating the law requiring the acqisition of a government permit before working in a foreign entity, who remain in the employment of foreign governments or entities abroad despite orders from the Egyptian government to resign such employment, or who have been convicted of crimes for which the judgment states that such crimes prejudice loyalty to the country or involve a betrayal of it. Naturalized citizens may also be deprived of their citizenship in case of residence abroad for two successive years "without an excuse acceptable to the President of the Republic."

It is to be noted that the decision of deprivation of nationality under the 1956 and 1958 acts was left to the Minister of the Interior until Law No. 282 of 1959 introduced the requirement of the issuance of a presidential decree in every case of deprivation. Such a requirement undoubtedly introduces an element of guarantee against possible abuses. Presidential decrees are also subject to the judicial review of the Conseil d'Etat. Needless to say, however, the attitude of Egyptian law in this respect is a long way from the liberal standards adopted in the UN Convention on Reduction of Statelessness (1961), to which Egypt is not a party. The harshness of the provisions of the law is probably meant to have a deterrent effect, however, and they have rarely been applied in actual cases.

Expulsion. The constitution interdicts the expulsion of any citizen.[37] However, extradition of citizens is optional under one of the two extradition treaties to which Egypt is a party[38] and is excluded under the other.[39] In practice no such extradition has ever taken place, since extradition has been prohibited by the regulations of the Ministry of Justice since 1901.

The prohibition of the expulsion of nationals was sanctioned several times by the courts of the Conseil d'Etat even when the national was also a citizen of a foreign state[40] or was a confirmed Zionist.[41] The invalidity of such an expulsion was found to be based not only on the constitutional provision, but primarily on "general constitutional principles that derive their force from the human conscience and the international conscience."[42] However, the court held as valid the expulsion of a "Sudanese national" at a time when the Egyptian government claimed title over the Sudan. "Acquisition of such a Sudanese citizenship," said the court, "was based on [British-enacted] legislation not issued by a legitimate power within its proper jurisdiction and in the issuance of which neither Egyptians nor Sudanese were consulted."[43]

Individuals deprived of their Egyptian citizenship may be deported as aliens with the travel documents issued by Egyptian authorities to stateless persons. One of the important reasons of deprivation, which is usually followed by expulsion, is "Zionism." The rule was first introduced by the Nationality Act of 1956, issued in November of that year, soon after the first Israeli invasion of Sinai and after the famous Lavon affair, in which a number of Egyptian Zionists were involved in subversive activities in Egypt in collaboration with Israeli intelligence. The explanatory note to this law, however, clearly distinguished between Zionism and the Jewish faith. "It is obvious," the note said, "that Zionism is not a religion, since Egyptians are all equal before the law; it is a spiritual and material tie established between the person adopting it and Israel," an entity with which Egypt has been technically and at times actively in a state of war since 1948.

The Court of Administrative Adjudication further elaborated this point by stating that "the establishment of a spiritual and material tie with Israel is an objective question that has to be proved by established facts to that effect while giving the person described as Zionist the opportunity to resort to court to prove his innocence from such a description." As a result, the court maintained that the basis on which the applicant was considered a Zionist must be submitted to it for examination. It thus annulled a decision to deprive a citizen of her nationality on that account because she had subsequently been granted a residence permit for ten years, a fact found by the court to contradict the previous decision and to show its fallacy.[44]

The Supreme Administrative Court seemed, on the other hand, to be less concerned with the preservation of the "title" to nationality when the higher interests of the state were at stake. It did not hesitate to defend the validity of the provision authorizing deprivation of the Egyptian citizenship of Zionists on the basis that the regulation of nationality is a matter left to the discretion of the legislature. "There can be no vested right or personal legal status for the individual vis-à-vis the state in the acquisition of its nationality." The court went further to say that

> in such a domain, which pertains to the sovereignty of the State and its public order and is related to the safety of the nation and its security in a critical period such as the one following the Israeli aggression, it was not necessary to allow the applicant a hearing and to carry out an investigation in her presence, as long as the reasons justifying denationalization were proved in her case.[45]

Protection

Extent of Freedom of Activity Abroad. Law Number 173 of 1958 prohibits the employment of nationals in any foreign entity, including an international organization, a foreign government, or a foreign private or public corporation, in Egypt or abroad, before they are so authorized by means of special government permits. Violation of this general requirement is an offense punishable under law by imprisonment of not more than two years or a fine of not more than 1,000 Egyptian pounds. Furthermore, conviction of such a crime renders the convict liable to denationalization under the Nationality Act, as seen above.

A national who is properly authorized to enter the employment of a foreign entity may later be ordered by the Egyptian government to resign such employment, under the sanction of possible deprivation of citizenship. Permits are usually issued on an annual basis but may be granted for longer periods, subject to conditions specified by a Ministerial arrêté. It may be noted, however, that the constitution of the Union of Arab Republics secures "the right of work" for the "citizens of the Union" in all member republics, subject to regulations to be issued by virtue of a Union law.

Voluntary enlistment in a foreign army can only be authorized by the Minister of War. Otherwise, such enlistment may entail denationalization. The same sanction may apply if the national is employed in the service of a state at war with Egypt or with which Egypt has severed diplomatic relations.

Nothing in the law prohibits a citizen from establishing a business abroad or lays down conditions in this regard. Income derived by an Egyptian from a business or employment in a foreign country is not subject to Egyptian taxes as long as the income earner resides outside Egypt. An arreté of the Minister of the Economy requires, however, that Egyptians employed abroad repatriate a percentage of their income, 10 percent for married persons and 25 percent for single. Respect for such an ordinance, which is not based on any supporting legislation, is ensured because pursuant to the requirements of the Ministry of the Interior, the above-mentioned percentage must be transferred before the government permit for employment abroad can be obtained. Renewal of permits is also dependent on the submission of evidence of such a transfer. The legality of such a practice is rather questionable. It has not, however, been challenged before the courts.

Competence of Egyptian Courts Over Activities Abroad. The Egyptian penal code confers on Egyptian courts competence over crimes committed by nationals abroad, provided such crimes are punishable in the country in which they are committed and not characterized under Egyptian law as minor infractions. Such jurisdiction may not be exercised, however, before the return of the offender to Egypt or if he or she, upon return, has already been prosecuted before a foreign court for the same act and either has been acquitted or has completed the punishment.

The jurisdiction of Egyptian courts also extends to the trial of certain categories of crimes committed abroad by any person. These include violation of the security of the state, forgery of official Egyptian papers, and counterfeiting of currencies accepted as legal tender in Egypt. Egyptian courts may also exercise jurisdiction over any Egyptian who, while abroad, has been involved in a crime committed in Egypt. On the other hand, these courts do not enjoy a general jurisdiction over crimes committed abroad against Egyptian citizens.

Civil suits may be brought against Egyptians before local courts in all cases related to their activities abroad, with the sole exception of suits concerning immovables situated abroad, in which cases jurisdiction is conceded to the courts of the areas in which the immovables are located.

The Right to Diplomatic Protection. Egyptian doctrinal writings adopt the traditional view that diplomatic protection is a prerogative of the state, not a right of the individual. There is very little practice in this field, however. When I investigated the matter with the Foreign Office, I was reminded only of the inaction of the Egyptian Embassy in one African state after the sequestration there of a modest industrial complex owned by an Egyptian businessman. The injured party was informed that his treatment in the host country was a matter within the domestic jurisdiction of the latter, in which the Egyptian government might not intervene. At times a more active role has been adopted to protect Egyptian professionals employed in other Arab countries. At times claims have also been made through Egyptian embassies by state-owned companies operating in other countries. However, no published material is available on this subject, and I could not find any of a national resorting to courts with a claim for compensation for the failure of the state to protect him or her from the actions of another state. At any rate, such a claim would probably be considered to be beyond the jurisdiction of the judiciary, since the exercise of diplomatic protection can easily be characterized by the courts as an act of sovereignty.

However, a decision by the Court of Administrative Adjudication rejecting the claim of an alien resident to a return visa on his Egyptian laissez passer included a dictum to the effect that "only the bond of nationality entitles the individual to the protection of his state wherever he goes and creates in particular the obligation of that state to take care of his interests abroad."[46]

It may be noted that the Egyptian government has also entered into a number of labor agreements with the neighboring countries, which regulate on a reciprocal basis the rights of the nationals of each party employed in the territory of the other. Unlike the investment agreements to which reference is made later on, these labor agreements find application mainly to Egyptian nationals, since Egypt is an exporter of manpower. They represent one important form of protection of Egyptians abroad. Their violation readily gives room for governmental involvement in the ordinary course of administering treaty relations.

<u>The State and Compensation</u>. Egyptian nationals have not been in the position of having large economic interests abroad that are likely to be threatened by measures calling for compensation. Consequently, no compensation has been secured from foreign governments in respect to financial losses or damages sustained abroad by Egyptian nationals; nor has the Egyptian government obtained any compensation for the losses sustained by it and its nationals as a result of the repeated invasions of its territory by Israel or of the military adventure of France and the United Kingdom in 1956.

No recent precedent may therefore be cited for the distribution by the state of compensation received from other states, let alone any "topping up" of such compensation in favor of affected nationals. However, the compensation received by the government from Germany after World War I for the material losses inflicted in Egypt was ordinarily distributed among affected persons. The Conseil d'Etat rejected the claim of the creditor of an affected national to seize part of that compensation, on the technical ground that the claim was not based on an administrative decision but on the provisions of the Treaty of Versailles, whereas "disputes over the interpretation and application of treaties to the State and to individuals constitute a political matter and an acte de souveraineté for which the government may not be sued."[47]

There were on the other hand, numerous instances in the 1960s of payment of compensation by Egypt to European and Arab countries for the nationalized and sequestrated properties of their nationals and also to the Sudan, under the Nile Waters Agreement of 8 November 1959, for the losses resulting from the execution of the Aswan High Dam project. In such cases the compensation was normally distributed among the affected individuals by the receiving states and was often topped off by these states in favor of their nationals.

Expropriation of private property has always been authorized under successive Egyptian constitutions, subject to only two conditions: it must be done for the purposes of a public utility, and it must be accompanied by the payment of compensation. The constitution of 1971 adds in Article 35 that nationalization can only be imposed by virtue of a legislative act issued in the public interest against the payment of compensation. General confiscation is explicitly prohibited, while confiscation for a specific property may be effected only by means of a judicial decision.[48] Sequestration is also made subject to a judicial trial, and only in cases to be defined by law.[49] These provisions apply to nationals and aliens alike.

In the early 1960s (the "Socialist Transformation Period"), before the adoption of such detailed provisions, many properties were nationalized or put under sequestration by administrative decrees. Although nationalization was always accompanied by some compensation, this normally took the form of long-term government bonds with low interest rates. Foreign investors, however, were able to receive cash payments by virtue of the lump-sum agreements concluded with their governments.

Compensation for War Damage. The advisory section of the Egyptian Conseil d'Etat had several occasions to discuss the extent of state responsibility for loss or damage resulting from acts of war. In 1954 the council expressed the view that such acts are acts of sovereignty, over which courts have no jurisdiction. Since the state could not be sued for the effects of its own military acts, of course it could not answer for damage resulting from the acts of its adversaries. The state may, however, compensate voluntarily both kinds of damage on considerations of equity.[50]

This view was slightly modified in later opinions of the assembly of the advisory section of the Conseil d'Etat in 1960 and 1964. Commenting on Military Orders Number 9 and Number 10 of 1956, which had been issued for the compensation of victims of the war of that year, the assembly distinguished among Egyptian nationals,

nationals of neutral states, and nationals of the enemy. Egyptian victims of the war may be "entitled" to compensation under the constitutional principle of social solidarity, regardless of the source of the damage sustained. Nationals of neutral states may also be compensated on the basis of equity, but the state is under no legal obligation to do this. Enemy subjects may not be compensated by the state, since reparation for war damages sustained by them is a matter for their own state to decide. As a result, the assembly advised against compensation of a British oil company for the losses sustained by it as a result of British and French air raids.[51] Under the same principle the assembly advised that the military orders related to compensation, the application of which was not confined to Egyptian nationals, may be validly applied to citizens of neutral states affected by the war. It thus authorized the payment of government compensation to Mobil Oil Company of Egypt, which was then a U.S. corporation, "on the basis of equity."[52] Although it sanctioned the payment of the compensation offered by the state for war damages even to neutral aliens, the Supreme Administrative Court held that the state was under no legal obligation to compensate material losses that may result from war and that the payments provided by it were more in the nature of insurance, which need not correspond with the actual loss sustained.[53]

The Responsibility of the State for Injury Induced by Its Own Conduct. As a general rule, any interested person may appeal to the courts or the Conseil d'Etat against administrative decisions and may request annulment of the decision involved and/or compensation for the damage ensuing therefrom. No such appeal is authorized, however, against the acts of sovereignty of the state, which include conclusion of treaties with foreign powers and acts of war. Thus the advisory section of the Conseil d'Etat expressed in its opinion of 18 August 1954 the view that "it is inadmissible to allow individuals, in the course of the protection of their personal interests, to introduce evidence before the courts to the effect that the state has erred by declaring war or has continued it unduly or has committed certain military failures."[54] This view had support in the Conseil d'Etat law then in force, which excluded from the jurisdiction of administrative courts "claims related to measures of external security and military acts and, in general, all claims related to any acte de souveraineté."[55] The latter acts are still excluded under the present law, but without reference to specific examples in the text. The Supreme Administrative Court has also excluded the possibility of state responsibility for material losses resulting from war.[56]

The state cannot be held liable, on the other hand, for damage resulting from its legislative acts.[57] Such acts will only bring into play the doctrine of government actions unhampered by legal restraints if they result in special damage to a contractant with the administration, causing the contract to be modified or otherwise adversely affected by the new legislation. Compensation in such a case will be due, however, from the contracting administration, not the state as such.[58]

The courts of the Conseil d'Etat are also without jurisdiction to entertain claims for the compensation of damage resulting from material acts of the state. Their competence in this respect is limited to claims based on damage resulting from administrative decisions. On this basis alone, the Court of Administrative Adjudication has rejected a claim for damages caused by the material conduct imputed to the employees of the Egyptian government in the Republic of the Congo.[59]

Such is the legal position, but it should be noted that the state has, as seen above, provided compensation to nationals and neutral aliens for damages resulting from the 1956 war even when such damages were not caused by its own conduct. The government also made a special effort to secure jobs for Egyptians expelled from Saudi Arabia during the Yemen war in the early 1960s. Although the constitutional principle of "social solidarity" may be cited in justification of such conduct, it is quite doubtful whether the courts would have entertained claims against the government if it had acted otherwise.

Waiver. No precedent can be cited for the waiver by the Egyptian government of the claims of its nationals against foreign states. However, doctrinal writings adopt the traditional view of the Permanent Court of International Justice that by espousing the claim of one of its nationals, the state will be "in reality asserting its own rights."[60] It is commonly stated, as a result, that the state may waive its right to diplomatic protection and may reach agreement with foreign states on the settlement of the claims of its nationals even through the waiver of all or part of these claims. The Egyptian government has indeed concluded some 15 lump-sum compensation agreements with foreign states related to the settlement of the claims of these states and their nationals against the Egyptian government. These agreements included standard provisions for the payment by Egypt of partial compensation for the claims of the nationals of the other parties, which in return waived all such claims. (Further reference to these agreements is made at the end of this chapter.)

Special Kinds of Protection. Apart from such advantages as may be accorded to Egyptian nationals in other countries on the basis of reciprocity, no arrangements seem to exist in Egyptian law whereby a special type of protection is conferred on Egyptian nationals residing or doing business abroad. In the opposite situation, however, the Egyptian legal system has long known the privileged treatment of aliens (mainly Europeans) under the Capitulations System, to which reference will be made below.

As a general rule government employment is confined to Egyptian nationals and nationals of other Arab countries on the basis of reciprocity.[61] Sudanese nationals who were in the service of the Egyptian government on 1 January 1956 are treated like Egyptian nationals in this respect.[62] Libyan nationals have been given the same rights to employment (in government or otherwise) as Egyptian nationals and the same rights to professional practice, pursuant to a law issued in September 1972. Other aliens may only receive temporary assignments under special conditions. Naturalized citizens may not, on the other hand, enjoy the "special rights of nationals" and other "political rights" before the passage of five years after acquisition of nationality, and they must wait ten years to be eligible for election or appointment to a representative body.[63] Such a condition applies to employment in the service of the government, this being a "political right" and "one of the special rights of nationals."[64]

Employees of the Foreign Service and officers of the Armed Forces, as well as members of the Conseil d'Etat, may not be married to aliens. However, exemption from such a requirement may be authorized by a presidential decree in case of marriage to a national of another Arab country.

Under Article 75 of the 1971 constitution, the President of the Republic must have Egyptian parents. No similar requirement obtains, however, for the Vice Presidents, the Prime Minister, or the other members of the cabinet; nor are any of those high officials not permitted to be married to an alien.

Under Companies Act No. 26 of 1954, foreign workers in joint stock companies may not exceed 10 percent of the total number of workers or receive more than 25 percent of their total pay, whereas foreign employees other than workers may not exceed 25 percent of the total number or receive more than 35 percent of the total pay. The first of these requirements applies also to partnerships limited by shares and companies of limited liability without qualification, but the requirement related to employees applies to these companies only when their capital exceeds 50,000 Egyptian pounds. In all cases the Minister of Industry may waive one or both requirements if no Egyptian nationals are available for the job.

The Individual as an Alien

Movement

Entry and Stay. Aliens were admitted into Egypt without any prior authorization until the country began its independent diplomatic representation after World War I. At present, Law Number 89 of 1960, on the entrance, residence, and departure of aliens requires the alien to carry a valid passport (or an equivalent document allowing the alien to return to the country of issue), accompanied by the proper authorization by the Egyptian government, as a precondition for entry. This requirement may, however, be waived in individual cases by the Director-General of Immigration and Passports. The Minister of the Interior is also authorized to waive the entrance visa requirement for all or some of the nationals of other countries. Ministerial Arrêté Number 31 of 1960 authorizes the issuance of "collective" and "transit" visas along with the "ordinary" and "diplomatic" visas. Under several ministerial arretés, no entrance visa is required for entry of the nationals of Arab countries and of some other countries, including Finland and the Soviet Union. The exemption of non-Arab citizens is made subject to reciprocal treatment, however. As a result this exemption has not been implemented in all cases. Exemption of citizens of other Arab countries was issued, on the other hand, in implementation of a decision of the League of Arab States, supported for some of these countries by decisions of the Council of Arab Economic Unity. Not all Arab countries grant reciprocal treatment to Egyptian nationals, whose entry to the Sudan, Saudi Arabia, Kuwait, and the Union of Arab Emirates is still subject to prior authorization.

Before the establishment of the Conseil d'Etat, the Court of Cassation held that it was beyond the jurisdiction of the judiciary to discuss the power of the executive to permit or refuse entry to an alien.[65] Such is not the case at present, and the Conseil d'Etat exercises judicial review over administrative decisions issued in this respect.

Ministerial Arrete Number 31 of 1960 specifies three categories of persons for whom an entry visa may not be issued. These include the following.

1. Persons whose names figure in the lists of persons prohibited from entry issued under Arrêté Number 183 of 1964, referred to earlier in this chapter. The lists include all persons who have

been deprived of their Egyptian nationality, as well as Jews from 10 to 60 years of age who used to have a "special" or "ordinary" residence in Egypt but have definitively left the country. The inclusion of such persons is obviously based on the fact that by leaving Egypt under the prevailing circumstances they have opted to cut their ties with it and may well have become Israeli nationals. The lists may also include members of "organizations hostile to the social system in the country," but only when investigations show that the person involved "has established international activities or has close links with similar organizations in Egypt." The decision to include a name in the lists is subject to appeal before the same appellate commission mentioned previously, and the decisions of that commission are also subject to appeal before the courts of the Conseil d'Etat.

2. Persons whose passports are issued by a state not recognized by Egypt, or who carry travel documents other than passports that are issued in accordance with a convention to which Egypt is not a party.

3. Persons who, after having been residents, have definitively left the country and are requesting entrance before the passage of one year from the date of their departure, with the exception of "high-ranking businessmen and employees of transnational corporations."

All other persons may be granted an entrance visa on request, "regardless of their nationality or religion." However, if the request is made for the purpose of employment in Egypt or of conducting a "show business" there, the approval of the Ministry of the Interior must be obtained before issuance of the visa, subject to some exceptions provided for in the above-mentioned arreté.

Under Law Number 89 of 1960, an alien may have one of three types of residence in Egypt: special residence, ordinary residence, or temporary residence.

The following persons are entitled to special residence for ten years, renewable, upon request, for similar periods:

1. Aliens who were born in Egypt before the publication of Law Number 74 of 1952, that is, before 26 May 1952, and who uninterruptedly resided there until the publication of Law Number 89 of 1960, that is, until 3 March 1960.

2. Aliens who legitimately entered Egypt, had resided in it for 20 years before 26 May 1952, and continued their residence there until 3 March 1960.

3. Aliens who have legitimately entered Egypt and have resided there for more than five years, if they are engaged in a business beneficial to the national economy or are rendering scientific, cultural, or technical services to the country.

4. Scientists, men of letters, artists, industrialists, economists, and others who may render important services to the country. In their case the condition of previous residence in Egypt is waived.

The right to special residence, including the right to return to Egypt in case of travel abroad during its period, and the right to renewal are lost, however, in case of unauthorized absence from the country for more than six months. Any absence for more than two years produces the same effect, unless it is justified by the pursuit of education or by conscription abroad. However, absence caused by conditions beyond the traveler's control was found by the courts to be immaterial in preventing such an effect.[66]

Ordinary residence is authorized, as a matter of right, for a period of five years to aliens who legitimately entered Egypt, resided in it for 15 years before 26 May 1952, and continued their residence there until 3 March 1960. Renewal of this residence is, however, subject to the discretion of the Minister of the Interior.

Aliens other than those qualified for special or ordinary residence may be granted "temporary residence" for a period not exceeding one year.

In addition to the above-mentioned types of residence, a fourth type may eventually develop in favor of the citizens of other nations in the Union of Arab Republics, since the Union constitution secures for all "citizens of the Union" the right of residence in all member republics.[67] This right will be implemented only after it is regulated by Union law.

Employment and acquisition of assets: As an overpopulated developing country that was for a long time exploited by foreigners enjoying a privileged position on its territory, Egypt has introduced many restrictions on the freedom of aliens to work or to acquire assets.

With the exception of Libyan nationals, who are now treated as Egyptian nationals in respect to employment conditions,[68] employment of aliens in any Egyptian concern is subject to the authorization of the Ministry of Manpower. Article 35 of Labor Law Number 91 of 1959 provides that such authorization may be granted only to "aliens having a residence permit subject to reciprocal treatment in their country and to the same extent as such treatment." Details of the issuance of the 'employment permit" are regulated by Arrêté Number 9 and Arrêté Number 81 of 1963. Government employment, which is open to aliens only in exceptional cases, is now available for nationals of other Arab countries that give Egyptian nationals the same treatment. Presidential Decree Number 114 of 1968 states the special conditions of the employment of aliens in government departments. In addition, the Conseil d'Etat has ruled that aliens would benefit from the general rules of government employment in matters in which the special law regulating their service is silent.[69] It has also indicated that discrimination in favor of nationals in the privileges of the civil service is legally valid.[70]

At present the practice of the medical, legal, and accountancy professions is restricted to nationals under the laws regulating these professions, although exceptions are usually provided for on the basis of reciprocity and in the case of aliens who were practicing these professions in Egypt before the issuance of such restrictive laws. Libyan nationals have been given the same treatment as Egyptian nationals in the practice of all professions.

Other restrictions are imposed on the acquisition of certain kinds of property. Aliens may not acquire arable or desert land.[71] An alien may not own a ship flying the Egyptian flag nor become a member of a company operating such a ship.[72] Aliens may not initially subscribe to more than 51 percent of the share capital of any Egyptian joint stock company and may not form the majority of the board of directors of such a company, unless it is engaged in an economic development project benefiting from the law applicable to foreign investments,[73] nor may they hold shares in companies licensed to carry on banking, insurance, and reinsurance operations in Egypt.[74] Under Law Number 33 (1972), however, Libyan nationals are entitled to acquire all types of movable and immovable property in Egypt.

Voluntary Departure. Under the authorization of Law Number 89 of 1960, Arrêté Number 186 of 1964 issued by the Minister of the Interior explicitly provides that no alien shall be authorized to depart from Egyptian territory without a special permit to do so. Such a condition does not apply, however, in the case of aliens who have entered by virtue of an entry visa and have not resided for more than six months in Egypt; nor does it apply to members of the diplomatic and consular legations accredited to Egypt nor to the UN employees in the service of UN offices in Egypt or in the offices of UN specialized agencies, provided that they are not Egyptian nationals and that they carry the UN laissez passer.

The Minister of the Interior is authorized by Law Number 89 of 1960 to designate "the forms and conditions of the travel documents that may be given to certain categories of aliens and refugees." Such documents are now regulated by Arreté Number 179 of 1964, which authorizes issuance of laissez passer documents to four categories of aliens. These categories include

> (i) stateless persons and persons without a proved nationality, (ii) refugees recognized as such,

(iii) persons who, though having a proved nationality, cannot obtain travel documents from the state to which they belong or in which they reside for reasons to be appreciated by the Ministry of the Interior, and (iv) wives of the above mentioned persons and their minor children under sixteen years of age.[75]

The documents are issued for two years, are renewable, and do not entitle their holders to enter Egyptian territory or to pass through it before obtaining the required visas. On the other hand, under Arrêté Number 181 of 1964 Palestinian refugees residing in Egypt or in the Gaza Strip are given "provisional travel documents" in the form of Egyptian passports with the designation of "Palestinian Refugee." These documents are treated as Egyptian passports by the local authorities, except that they are less costly and their holders need to obtain visas for entry into Egypt. Each document ordinarily includes the names of the refugee, his wife, and his children under 16 years of age.

Involuntary Departure: Expulsion and Deportation. By an agreement concluded in 1866 between the Egyptian government and representatives of the states whose nationals enjoyed a privileged position under the Capitulations System, local authorities were only authorized to request expulsion of the undesired alien through the consul of the state to which that alien belonged. If the consul refused to take such a measure, the government was to resort to a committee composed of nine consuls accredited to Egypt. However, the Mixed Court of Appeals, which began its work in February 1876, recognized the right of the state to expel aliens who were a threat to its public security. This practice was codified in the Fourth Declaration annexed to the Montreux Convention of 1937, which limited the expulsion of aliens who were subject to the jurisdiction of the mixed courts to three categories of persons, those convicted of certain crimes, those who have committed acts against the public interests of the state, and those who have become a financial burden thereon. The same conditions were later adopted in a decree issued on 22 June 1938, which remained in force until the abolition of the Capitulations System on 14 November 1949.[76] Law Number 49 of 1940 regulating the residence of aliens nevertheless provided that aliens authorized to reside in Egypt for a limited period were under an obligation to leave the country after the lapse of that period under the sanction of possible expulsion.

After the termination of the Capitulations System, the Conseil d'Etat recognized the unfettered power of the state to expel any undesired alien in the public interest of the state, regardless of nationality. Such a power was found to be a corollary of the principle of state sovereignty and of the rules of public international law.[77] However, Law Number 74 of 1952, the first to be issued on the subject after the legislature restored its freedom in this respect, restricted the expulsion of aliens resident for 20 years in the country to certain specified cases. This law was replaced by Law Number 89 of 1960, which is now in force.

Deportation Order Subject to Judicial Review. The plea that the expulsion of an alien is an act of sovereignty and not subject to judicial review was rejected from the outset by the Conseil d'Etat.[78] In their review of the discretionary power of the state in the matter of expulsion, its administrative courts required serious grounds justifying that procedure as a measure taken "in the public interest within the limits of the law."[79] The expulsion of an alien whose period of residence had terminated without being renewed was held to be valid, however, even when no other reasons were given to indicate the threat involved in the continued presence of the alien.[80]

Thus the Court of Administrative Adjudication upheld the expulsion of an alien who had taken up usury as a profession,[81] opened a brothel (even though the alien in question had been acquitted in criminal proceedings on technical grounds,[82] traded in narcotics,[83] engaged in the smuggling of gold,[84] acted as a spy for a foreign power,[85] was a threat to public morals,[86] was promoting the interests of Israel,[87] or was performing Zionist activities in Egypt, including the encouragement of young Egyptian Jews to emigrate to Israel and join the Israeli army.[88] Conversely, expulsion orders were annulled by the same court when they were not based on any specific accusation[89] or when the orders were based on such shaky grounds as the collection of signatures denouncing atomic tests in the world[90] or the taking up of employment other than that authorized in the residence permit.[91] In other cases the court clearly stated that the executive had absolute discretion in weighing the objective reasons establishing the danger involved in the presence of the alien, so long as no abuse of power on the part of the executive is found by the court.[92] The Supreme Administrative Court further emphasized this point by indicating that judicial review in the matter of expulsion should be limited to the examination of the legality, not the propriety, of the deportation order without interfering in the evaluation of the seriousness of its grounds so long as the order is free from abuse of power.[93]

The expulsion of an enemy subject in time of war seems to present a special case. The Conseil d'Etat considered it a valid measure even when there were no special grounds related to the particular individual involved,[94] while the Mixed Court of Appeal characterized it as an act of sovereignty and not subject to judicial review.[95]

<u>Certain Restrictions on the Expulsion of Aliens</u>. Law Number 89 of 1960 lays down two limitations on the expulsion of aliens who have a special residence in Egypt. First, they may not be expelled unless their "presence threatens the security of the state, its internal or external safety, its national economy, public health, public morals, or public tranquility, or if [they become] a financial burden on the state." Such grounds may be too broad to constitute an additional guarantee. Even temporary residence could not be interrupted without a reasonable justification related to the public interest of the state.[96] The second and more important condition is that the matter must first be submitted to the Expulsion Commission. This commission is composed of six high-ranking officials, including two counselors from the Conseil d'Etat, and its approval is a precondition for the expulsion of any alien with a special residence permit. The Supreme Administrative Court has held that resort to the commission is necessary in case of expulsion during the authorized period of special residence, but not in case of refusal to renew it.[97] This attitude is criticized in some doctrinal comments, however.[98]

<u>Extradition of Political Refugees</u>. The Egyptian Constitution interdicts the extradition of political refugees.[99] The same principle is provided for in the two extradition treaties to which Egypt is a party at present: the treaty with Iraq signed on 20 April 1931 and the Arab League Extradition Convention, which is now in force between Egypt, Saudi-Arabia, Jordan, Syria, Libya, Iraq, Kuwait, and South Yemen. Former extradition agreements related to the Sudan (17 May 1902) and Palestine (1 October 1922) have lapsed. Both the treaty with Iraq and the Arab League Extradition Convention leave it up to the state from which extradition is requested to characterize the crime involved, while making extradition compulsory for certain defined crimes. In actual practice, however, Egypt is a well-known haven for political refugees from other Arab and African countries. Within recent years it has risked its good relations with China out of respect for the principle of nonextradition of political refugees.

No national legislation on the matter of extradition exists in Egypt, however. Extradition is still regulated by international custom, supplemented by Regulations Number 8 of 1901 and Number 38 of 1914 of the Ministry of Justice. Under these regulations, extradition may take place only for common-law crimes of a certain importance, including felonies and, in case a judgment has already been issued, other crimes punished by at least one year of imprisonment. In practice the state does not feel obligated to extradite offenders except on the basis of reciprocity.[100]

Protection

Apart from the special case of the Palestinians of the Gaza Strip, who have been treated in many ways as they were citizens, the Egyptian government has not attempted to extend its diplomatic protection to any other aliens. An alien resident who carried an Egyptian laissez passer after his government refused to renew his passport was not granted a return visa, lest this should give him a right to the diplomatic protection of the state. Such a practice was upheld by the Conseil d'Etat on the basis that the only obligation the state had toward such a person under Egyptian law was "to provide him with departure documents without the obligation to grant him a return visa" and that the "obligation of protection" was only due to nationals.[101]

Former privileged aliens in Egypt: Until the establishment of the Mixed Courts of Egypt, which was brought about by the judicial reform of 1875,[102] nationals of 15 European states and of the United States, as well as some Egyptian nationals who were protégés of these foreign powers, were immune from the jurisdiction of Egyptian courts in civil and criminal matters because they could be sued or tried only before their consular tribunals, which applied their own laws. With the establishment of the mixed courts, such aliens became subject to their jurisdiction in civil and commercial matters, except in cases between aliens of the same nationality, which do not involve immovable property in Egypt, and in a limited number of criminal offenses. Other matters remained subject to the jurisdiction of consular tribunals. Mixed laws were not to be amended without the approval of a special majority of the assembly of the Mixed Court of Appeal. Under the Montreux Convention of 1937 this "exceptional system" was to terminate after a transition period of 12 years, during which the Mixed Courts continued to operate. The convention provided that Egypt was not to discriminate against aliens and that they were not to be subject to legislation violating the principles commonly adopted in modern legislation. Such provisions were to apply, however, only in the transition period "except insofar as they are considered as established rules of international law."[103]

The special system recognizing legislative and judicial privileges for aliens in Egypt, which started early in the sixteenth century, had thus continued in force until 1949, that is, 27 years after formal independence.

NATIONAL IMPLEMENTATION OF INTERNATIONAL RIGHTS AND DUTIES

The Act of State Doctrine

The Act of State doctrine as developed and applied in the Anglo-American legal system is not known in the practice of Egyptian courts. A legislative act of a foreign sovereign does not constitute a "rule of decision" for such courts unless it is applicable under the relevant conflict-of-laws rules of the Civil Code and subject to the limitations defined by these rules. Two remarks may be borne in mind in this respect. First, the principle of sovereign immunity as it now stands before Egyptian courts is applied only to foreign states enacting public acts. Its application is therefore dependent on an objective element related to the nature of the act of the foreign state. Second, Egyptian courts are entitled to exclude application of a foreign law or to ignore its effects when such a law runs counter to "the public policy and morals" of Egypt.

The following is now established before Egyptian courts:

> When the judge is asked to review an act of a foreign government, he will first have to determine its nature. If the act is one that may only be issued by the state or in its name, the judge will have to decline jurisdiction. If, on the other hand, the nature of the act is such that any legal person may perform it, such as a contract or a loan and the like, the court may look into it regardless of the motive behind it or the purpose for which it was made.[104]

This principle has been applied only in relation to the executive acts of foreign governments, in suits brought against a government or one of its public agencies. Since immunity has not been recognized as inherent in the person concerned in all suits brought against foreign sovereigns, apparently such immunity as is applied is in substance an immunity from the acts themselves.

Article 28 of the Civil Code explicitly interdicts the application of a foreign law that would otherwise be applicable under the general provisions of the code, when it runs counter to public order or public morals in Egypt. Obviously this implies the power of the court to examine foreign legislation from that angle. Whether such an examination also entails the review of the validity of such legislation in terms of international law is a matter of interpretation, depending on the extent to which international law may be considered as part of the public order before an Egyptian court. Doctrinal comments suggest that examination by the court under the said article may be limited to the question of the conformity of the foreign legislation to "the society's higher order" and the "vital interests of the state," without reference to any international law.[105] The explanatory note of the Civil Code confirms such domestic overtones of public order by referring to "the general beliefs of the community." The Court of Cassation followed the same attitude, defining public order in this respect in terms of the "principles related to the basic structure of the state and to the public and fundamental interests of the community" and rejecting its invocation for the purpose of excluding a foreign law that is merely "different from, or less beneficial than, national law."[106]

It is worth noting, however, that resort to the doctrine of public policy may enable courts to exclude the application of foreign legislation depriving individuals of their property without compensation, which, it seems, is the major occasion for invoking international law in this respect. Thus one doctrinal comment indicated that Soviet laws violating private property rights would not have been applicable before Egyptian courts under Article 28 of the Civil Code.[107] According to another author, foreign nationalization cannot be ignored on the basis of public policy if it has been done in accordance with the rules of international law.[108]

Implementation of Decisions of International Organizations

Boycott of Israel. In its fourteenth session (May 1951) the Council of the League of Arab States issued a resolution establishing the Principal Office for the Boycott of Israel, to supervise regional offices established in each member state for the same purpose. Several subsequent decisions, especially the decision dated 11 December 1954, have culminated in the institution of a sophisticated system of boycott implemented by member states under the constant supervision of the Arab League office. This system was introduced in Egypt by virtue of Law Number 506 of 1955, which is meticulously followed.

Sanctions against South Africa. In implementation of UN General Assembly Resolution 1761 (17), dated 6 November 1962, and the Resolution on Decolonization adopted by the Conference of the Heads of States of the Organization of African Unity in Addis Ababa, 22-25 May 1963, the Egyptian government was quick to sever diplomatic relations with South Africa, on 30 May 1963. A few months later it responded to the policy outlined by the UN Security Council[109] by cutting all economic ties with South Africa[110] and by closing its ports to ships and planes flying the South African flag.[111] It made sure, however, to provide in the above-mentioned instruments that such measures would not affect freedom of passage through the Suez Canal and the direct facilities related to this passage, thus suggesting the primacy of its treaty obligations under such an important instrument as the Constantinople Convention of 1888.

Since all relations with South Africa had been severed and all transactions outlawed since 1963, no further step had to be taken in implementation of Security Council Resolutions 276 and 283 (1970), which included a call on the states to refrain from any relations with South Africa that would imply recognition of its authority over Namibia and to discourage all trade and investment activities in that territory. The same was true of the similar "obligation" suggested by the advisory opinion of the International Court of Justice of 21 June 1971.

Sanctions against Portugal. The Egyptian government severed its diplomatic relations with Portugal on 29 June 1963 in implementation of the Resolution of the Heads of States of Organization of African Unity (OAU), adopted in May of that year. Following the steps outlined by the Security Council,[112] it later severed all economic ties with Portugal[113] and closed its ports to Portuguese ships (without prejudice to the freedom of passage through the Suez Canal) and to Portuguese airplanes.[114]

Rhodesia. Egypt has not recognized Rhodesia as a state and has not had any economic or other relations with it. On the contrary, at one point it severed diplomatic ties with the United Kingdom over the hesitant policy of the latter on Rhodesia in 1965. Here again the Egyptian action was taken on 15 December 1965 in implementation of a resolution of the OAU passed ten days earlier.

Procedures Related to the Issuance of Certificates or Suggestions by the Executive in Connection with Litigation in National Courts

There is no established system in Egyptian practice for the issue of certificates from the Ministry of Foreign Affairs for communication with the courts in respect to matters of international importance. However, different government departments are authorized to issue certificates "to whom it may concern," that provide such unclassified information as may be requested by a person having a direct interest in obtaining it. Such certificates are usually given with the advice of the advisory section of the Conseil d'Etat. Courts themselves do not ask for certificates from the executive, although they may seek expert opinion and may summon government officials to give testimony in any case.

In a recent decision of the Giza Court of First Instance,[115] the court recognized the diplomatic immunity of the Commercial Center of the German Democratic Republic in Cairo, partly on the basis of a certificate of the Ministry of Foreign Affairs, presented by the director of that center, indicating that it was part of the embassy and enjoyed immunity under the 1961 Vienna Convention. The court referred to that certificate as one item of evidence among others, including a formal legislation conferring immunity on the center. In another case, however, the same court ruled in favor of the immunity of the director of the Soviet Cultural Center in Cairo on the basis of a certificate conforming his diplomatic status issued by the Soviet Embassy and not by the Egyptian Ministry of Foreign Affairs.[116] The latter decision made no reference to Presidential Decree Number 1418 of 1960, which provides explicitly that foreign cultural centers are not part of foreign embassies, do not enjoy diplomatic protection, and do not benefit from the international conventions that apply to such embassies. In a later decision issued by the same court against the same defendant, the court declined immunity on the basis of the above-mentioned presidential decree alone.[117]

Egyptian courts undertake the interpretation of treaties when necessary in order to reach a decision in the disputes submitted to them, without attempting to obtain an official interpretation from the Ministry of Foreign Affairs for each case. It is this ministry, in fact, that often requests the advisory section of the Conseil d'Etat to give legal opinions on the interpretation of treaties and other questions of international law. Even in such political matters as the status of the Gaza Strip, the opinion of the Conseil d'Etat was sought when legal issues were involved, such as the extent to which Egyptian law applied there.[118] The same issue was discussed by the Court of Cassation as a purely legal matter in the course of deciding a case involving the transfer of Egyptian currency to the Gaza Strip.[119]

On the other hand, the Prize Court of Alexandria has consistently discussed the legal nature of the relationship between Egypt and Israel as a decisive factor in the exercise of its jurisdiction.[120] Although the court concluded in every case that this relationship was a state of war, it did not simply rely on the official attitude of the government but went into a detailed discussion of the subject matter under international law, an approach that I criticized in an article published in Arabic in 1965.[121] The Court of Cassation has also held that, for the purpose of application of certain provisions of the Penal Code, Egypt was in a state of war with Israel that had not been terminated by the conclusion of the Armistice Agreement in 1949.[122]

Recognition and Nonrecognition

Normally recognition of the foreign state or government is merely a matter of political convenience, and Egyptian practice has shown a great deal of flexibility in this regard. Although the German Democratic Republic was recognized by Egypt on 11 July 1969, a law issued seven years earlier (Law Number 16 of 1962) conferred diplomatic immunity on the members of the GDR Commercial Center in Egypt.

The conflict-of-laws rules of the Egyptian Civil Code do not specifically exclude application of the foreign laws of unrecognized states. Such exclusion, if adopted, would have to be based on the public order of Egypt or on the negation of the legislative character of such acts. In 1931 the Mixed Court of Appeals refused the application of Soviet legislation on the grounds that it was issued by a government not recognized by Egypt at that time.[123] It is doubtful, however, whether Egyptian courts in the 1970s would adopt a similar attitude with respect to laws issued by an unrecognized government or even by an unrecognized friendly state, as was the case of the German Democratic Republic before its recognition and as is, as of this writing, the case of Bangladesh.

Israel presents a case apart, however. As matters presently stand, it is not to be expected that Israel would be admitted as applicant or defendant before the Egyptian courts; nor is it likely that legislative character would be imputed to purported legislative acts of Israeli organs. Recognition of the legislative character of such acts by Egyptian courts would entail, in their view, recognition of the legitimacy of forcible territorial occupation, accompanied by wholesale expulsion of the inhabitants and the purported exercise of sovereign privileges based merely on a territorial possession forcibly acquired by military occupation. In other words, the political facts that govern the issue of recognition are likely to have their bearing on the determination of related legal questions by the courts.[124]

TREATIES AND THE INDIVIDUAL

Treaties before Domestic Courts

According to Article 151 of the Constitution, treaties that have been properly ratified and published "have the force of law" before the courts. Influenced by this language, most doctrinal writings equate treaties and domestic legislation in this respect and suggest that subsequent legislation prevails over conflicting treaty provisions.

However, laws regulating matters likely to have international effects often include a "without prejudice clause" in favor of relevant treaty provisions.[125] Furthermore, with respect to the service of judicial notice between Egypt and the Sudan, which has been regulated since 1902 by a bilateral agreement between the two governments, the Court of Cassation held that such a service was to be made in accordance with the treaty provisions even if they were in conflict with domestic law, whether the domestic law was issued before or after the conclusion of the treaty.[126] However, when the treaty provision was deemed to run counter to legislation related to public policy, such as that outlawing the gold clause in all transactions, the court ruled in favor of domestic legislation even when it was issued before the treaty came into force. Payment of compensation to shippers under the 1929 Warsaw Convention was thus found by the court to have been properly effected when paid in Egyptian currency under the official rate of exchange, without regard to the gold value clause provided for in the two conventions.[127]

As has been mentioned earlier, the Conseil d'Etat declined jurisdiction in a suit brought against the government for the seizure of parts of the compensation received from Germany after World War I under the applicant's claim that his debtor was entitled to receive a share of that compensation pursuant to the provisions of the Treaty of Versailles. Although the judgment adopted the reasoning that in compensation cases the jurisdiction of the court was limited to damages resulting from administrative decisions only, it added that the denial by the government of the title of the applicant's debtor to compensation under the Treaty of Versailles was also an act of sovereignty and therefore beyond the jurisdiction of the judiciary.[128] This, it is true, seems to be the only judicial pronouncement in that direction, but no other precedent can be quoted to the contrary.

The text of the declaration annexed to the Montreux Convention of 1937 provoked an interesting controversy related to the right of the individual to rely on the preparatory works and the original foreign language of a treaty ratified and published locally in Arabic. This declaration, as ratified, authorized the expulsion of aliens convicted of felonies and other crimes, the punishment of which exceeded three <u>months</u>' imprisonment. A claim was made in an expulsion case before the Conseil d'Etat to the effect that expulsion was not valid, since the crime involved was punished by imprisonment for less than three years (though more than three months), while the original French text of the declaration and the preparatory works of the Montreux Convention all indicate the adoption of the three <u>years</u> limitation in this respect. In rejecting this claim, the Court of Administrative Adjudication held that the applicant had no right to invoke the preparatory works of a treaty, this being the exclusive prerogative of the states party to it, and that a domestic court may only apply the text ratified by the national legislature.[129] The question was moot, however, for the purposes of the case involved, since the expulsion order under review had been issued after the termination of the system introduced by the Montreux Convention.

Investment Treaties

Apart from the labor treaties, agreements on cultural or commercial exchange, and agreements on the reciprocal abolition of visas, which have their bearing on individuals, Egypt is a party to a host of treaties related to foreign investments within its territory.

A Convention on the Payments on Current Transactions and the Facilitation of Transfer of Capital among the States of the Arab League was signed on 7 September 1953. It was later modified in 1959, to add a few advantages to the modest ones accorded by it to investments by the nationals of one member country in the territory of another. This convention, as amended, is now in force among Egypt, Jordan, Lebanon, Iraq, and Syria. Saudi Arabia is a party to the original convention but not to its amendment. Egypt also concluded a bilateral agreement with Kuwait on 2 February 1966 that provides for a greater measure of protection for the nationals of each party investing in the territory of the other but is actually meant to encourage Kuwaiti investment in Egypt. A more general multinational convention prepared in August 1970 by the Council of Arab Economic Unity, the Convention on the Investment and Transfer of Arab Capital, was signed by Egypt on 11 December 1971.[130]

Egypt has also signed and ratified the Convention Establishing the Arab Investment Guarantee Corporation, which introduces the first comprehensive international multinational investment guarantee program.[131] This convention has been signed by ten other Arab countries and ratified by four of them. It will enter into force upon ratification by five countries subscribing to 60 percent of the share-capital of the proposed corporation.

Outside the Arab sphere, on 29 June 1963 Egypt entered into an agreement with the U.S. government allowing the application of the U.S. Investment Guaranty Program to U.S. investments in Egypt. In November 1971 the country ratified the Convention on the Settlement of Investment Disputes between States and Nationals of other States signed on 18 March 1965. On 4 August 1967 it also signed the two UN Human Rights Conventions.

Finally, Egypt was particularly successful in reaching agreed upon settlements of the claims of aliens whose properties were nationalized or sequestrated in its territory. Some 15 bilateral lump-sum agreements have been concluded with European and Arab states, providing for a substantial partial compensation for the properties concerned against a final waiver of the claims related to them.[132]

NOTES

1. Art. 12(g), Constitution of the Union of Arab Republics, approved by popular plebiscites in the Arab Republic of Egypt, the Syrian Arab Republic, and the Libyan Arab Republic on 1 September 1972. Original Arabic text of the constitution is published in 1 Official Journal of the Union of Arab Republics 4 (1972).

2. See, for example, decision of the Supreme Administrative Court (hereafter SAC) of the Conseil d'Etat, dated 8 May 1965. Judicial decisions are herein cited by their dates. Their text is available in Arabic in the respective annual reports of the courts issuing them. No English translation is readily available, however, for any of the decisions cited in this report except one case reported in I. L. R.

3. See, for example, decision of the court of Administrative Adjudication (hereafter CAA) of the Conseil d'Etat, 24 November 1959.

4. CAA, 3 March 1954, 21 April 1959.

5. Constitution of the Union of Arab Republics, op. cit., Art. 13.

6. See, for example, CAA, 8 April 1952.

7. CAA, 24 November 1959.

8. CAA, 8 April 1952.

9. CAA, 22 April 1952.

10. Passport Law No. 79 (1959).

11. CAA, 2 March 1955, 20 December 1955, 27 November, 1956, 11 December 1959.

12. SAC, 8 May, 1965.

13. CAA, 10 May 1960.

14. CAA, 20 December 1955.

15. CAA, 27 November 1956.

16. CAA, 9 June 1953.

17. CAA, 10 May, 1960.

18. CAA, 7 March 1955.

19. CAA, 11 December 1956.

20. CAA, 29 January 1957.

21. CAA, 27 November 1956.

22. Constitution of the Union of Arab Republics, op. cit.

23. See Decisions of the Council of Arab Economic Unity, Nos. 77, 88, 96, and 113 of 1965, Nos. 281 and 282 of 1966; No. 33 of 1968, and No. 477 of 1970. Official Records of the Council of Arab Economic Unity (not published).

24. Constitution of the Union of Arab Republics, op. cit., Art. 10.

25. Art. 52, Constitution of the Arab Republic of Egypt, 1971.

26. See I. Shihata, "Guarantees for Civil Liberties in the Permanent Constitution" (in Arabic), in the daily Al-Ahram, 28 May 1971, p. 5.

27. CAA, 24 November 1959; 17 May 1960. See also SAC, 12 November 1966.

28. Arrêté of the Minister of the Interior No. 65 (1959).
29. The exit visa requirement was abolished as of 15 May 1974--Ed.
30. SAC, 1 December 1962.
31. CAA, 24 January 1961.
32. SAC, 12 November 1966.
33. Constitution of the Arab Republic of Egypt, op. cit., Art. 51.
34. Nationality Act No. 82 (1958).
35. Law No. 391 (1956).
36. SAC, 28 March 1961.
37. Constitution of the Arab Republic of Egypt, op. cit., Art. 51.
38. Art. 7, Extradition Convention between Members of the League of Arab States, signed at Cairo in 1953.
39. Art. 7, Extradition Treaty between Egypt and Iraq, 20 April 1931.
40. See, for example, CAA, 27 January 1948.
41. CAA, 17 February 1953.
42. CAA, 24 May 1953.
43. CAA, 31 May 1953.
44. CAA, 30 June 1959.
45. SAC, 22 April 1961.
46. CAA, 18 January 1955.
47. CAA, 26 May 1949.
48. Constitution of the Arab Republic of Egypt, op. cit., Art. 36.
49. Ibid., Art. 34.
50. Advisory Section of the Conseil d'Etat, Legal Opinion No. 74, dated 18 August 1954.
51. General Assembly of the Conseil d'Etat, legal opinion, 10 August 1960.
52. Ibid., 28 October 1964.
53. SAC, 19 May 1962.
54. Advisory Section of the Conseil d'Etat, op. cit.
55. Law No. 9 (1949).
56. SAC, 19 May 1962.
57. Mixed Court of Appeal, 4 June 1945, 57 Bulletin de Legislation et de jurisprudence égyptiennes (hereafter Bulletin) 172; see also CAA, 3 March 1957.
58. See, for example, CAA, 9 December 1956; 3 March 1957; General Assembly of the Conseil d'Etat, legal opinion, 20 July 1960.
59. CAA, 8 November 1964.
60. Mavrommatis Palestine Concessions Case (Jurisdiction), P.C.I.J., Ser. A, No. 2, at 12 (1924).
61. Art. 7, Law No. 58 (1971).
62. Law No. 283 (1960).
63. Art. 16, Nationality Act (1958).
64. CAA, 22 June 1959.
65. Court of Cassation, Chamber of Civil and Commercial Affairs (hereafter Cass. Civ.), 16 May 1935.
66. See, for example, CAA, 12 May 1952, 7 December 1953.

67. Constitution of the Union of Arab Republics, op. cit., Art 13.
68. Law No. 32 (1962).
69. CAA, 8 January 1953.
70. CAA, 9 April 1962.
71. Law No. 47 (1951); Law No. 15 (1963).
72. Code of Maritime Commerce.
73. Arts. 11, 28, Law No. 26 (1954).
74. Law No. 163 (1957); Law No. 195 (1959).
75. Arrêté of the Minister of the Interior No. 179 (1964).
76. For the effects of termination of the 1938 decree as a result of the abolition of the Capitulations System, see, for example, CAA, 12 December 1950; CAA, 30 May 1951.
77. See, for example, CAA, 31 May 1953.
78. See, for example, CAA, 30 November 1948; 8 April 1952.
79. SAC, 28 March 1964.
80. See CAA, 12 April 1953; SAC, 4 August 1956.
81. CAA, 27 November 1951.
82. CAA, 27 November 1956.
83. CAA, 22 February 1954.
84. CAA, 23 November 1952.
85. CAA, 14 January 1954.
86. CAA, 30 January 1956.
87. CAA, 17 February 1955.
88. CAA, 25 February 1954.
89. See, for example, CAA, 18 January 1953; 7 March 1954.
90. CAA, 12 March 1953.
91. CAA, 7 January 1954.
92. CAA, 7 November 1955; 6 December 1958.
93. SAC, 28 March, 1964.
94. CAA, 17 November 1959.
95. Decision of 6 March 1940, 52 Bulletin 37.
96. See CAA, 18 December 1956.
97. SAC, 4 August 1956, 10 November 1956.
98. See, for example, F. Riad and S. Rashed, Manual of Private International Law 345-46 (1971) (in Arabic).
99. Constitution of the Arab Republic of Egypt, op. cit., Art. 53.
100. This principle was officially expressed in the Response of the Ministry of Foreign Affairs to the U.S. Delegation in Cairo, dated January 1933 (not published), and in its Response to the Austrian Embassy, dated 1 March 1934 (not published).
101. CAA, 18 January 1955.
102. The Mixed Courts were created by a reglement d'organisation judiciare that received the adherence of the principal capitulatory powers. 66 British and Foreign State Papers, 1874-1875 593. For an English translation see Brinton, The Mixed Courts of Egypt (1930).
103. As so described by the Egyptian Court of Cassation in Cass. Civ., 20 April 1950.

104. See Mixed Alexandria Commercial Court, 29 March 1943, 55 Bulletin 114. See also Alexandria Civil Court, 12 May 1951 (English translation in [1951] I. L. R. 225, Case No. 54); Giza Court of First Instance, 10 March 1960.

105. See, for example, E. Abdallah, 2 Private International Law 487-97 (5th ed., 1965, in Arabic); H. Sadek, Conflict of Laws 512-15 (2nd ed., 1971, in Arabic).

106. Cass. Civ., 5 April 1967, 26 July 1967.

107. See Abdallah, op. cit., at 500, note 1.

108. A. El Kohberi, "Nationalization in Private International Law," 11 Review of Juridical and Economic Sciences 233, 311 (Cairo 1969, in Arabic).

109. UN Doc. S/5386, 9 August 1963.

110. Arrêté of the Minister of the Economy No. 718 (1963).

111. Presidential Decree No. 1066, 19 March 1964.

112. UN Doc. S/5380, 31 July 1963.

113. Arrêté of the Minister of the Economy No. 960 (1963).

114. Presidential Decree No. 1066 (1964).

115. Third Civil Division, 12 March 1972.

116. Giza Court of First Instance, summary decision, 11 October 1970.

117. Ibid., 1 March 1971.

118. Legal Opinion No. 646, 7 February 1954 (advising that Egyptian law does not apply automatically in the Gaza Strip).

119. Court of Cassation, Chamber of Criminal Affairs (hereafter Cass. Crim.), 29 May 1961.

120. See J. Trappe, "On the Jurisdiction of the Egyptian Prize Court, 1948-1960," 15 Revue Egyptienne de Droit International Public 60 (1960).

121. I. Shihata, "Justiciability of Disputes of International Character before National Courts," 9 Review of the Department of Government Disputes 1-24 (Cairo 1965, in Arabic).

122. Cass. Crim., 13 May 1958; 16 January 1967.

123. Decision of 10 March, 1931, 43 Bulletin 283.

124. This also seems to be the case in international law, where no hard and fast rules can be said to have been universally developed in this field. However, this is not to deny the legal value of the act of recognition as such. Such an act still plays an important legal role, especially in the relationship between a mother country and a territory claiming independence. The doctrinal claim that recognition is becoming devoid of legal significance in international law and should therefore be replaced by mere "acknowledgment" seems to go beyond the present stage of the development of that law, although the use of the latter term may be politically more convenient in certain situations. It is relevant in this respect to note that Egypt has accepted, under Security Council Resolution 242, 22 November 1967, the "acknowledgment" of the sovereignty, integrity, and independence of "every state in the area," only as part of a global settlement that involves Israeli withdrawal from occupied territories and a just settlement of the problem of the Palestinian refugees.

125. See, for example, Art. 23, Civil Code (1949); Art. 301, Code of Civil Procedure (1968); Art. 30, Nationality Act (1958).

126. Cass. Civ., 8 March 1956.

127. Cass. Civ., 11 February 1960 and 4 April 1967, respectively.

128. CAA, 26 May 1949.

129. CAA, 15 May 1951.

130. For the Arabic text of these conventions see I. Shihata, Treatment of Foreign Investments in Egypt, Annexes (1972, in Arabic). In September 1971 a new investment law was issued in Egypt securing greater advantages for "Arab capital" than those provided for in any of the abovementioned treaties and authorizing the extension of such advantages to "non-Arab foreign capital" by virtue of a presidential decree in each case. Law No. 65 (1971).

131. See I. Shihata, "Arab Investment Guarantee Corporation," 6 Journal of World Trade Law 185-202 (March-April 1972).

132. Other than the lump-sum compensation agreements concluded between the Egyptian government and such private parties as the representatives of the stockholders in the Suez Canal Company (29 April 1958), the Compagnie Financière de Suez (13 July 1958), and the French Lebon Company (28 July 1966), the government reached bilateral settlements with the United Kingdom (28 February 1959, August 1962, and 24 April 1967); Switzerland (20 June 1964); France (5 November 1964 and 28 July 1966); Lebanon (18 November 1964); Italy (23 March 1965); Denmark (12 June 1965); Sudan (1 June 1966); Greece (26 September 1966); Saudi Arabia (4 November 1969); The Netherlands (25 February 1971); Sweden (10 November 1971); and Austria (23 December 1971).

CHAPTER

9

FEDERAL REPUBLIC OF GERMANY

Ignaz Seidl-Hohenveldern

THE INDIVIDUAL

As far as judicial redress against administrative action is concerned, the present system of the Federal Republic of Germany is almost overperfect. According to Article 19, Section 4 of the Basic Law (Constitution) of the Federal Republic of Germany,[1] Administrative Courts have unlimited power to review all administrative acts. In case of any infraction of rights guaranteed by the constitution, individuals may also bring their cases before the Federal Constitutional Court. This right is guaranteed to domestic judicial persons but not to foreign ones.[2] (See the section below on treaties and the individual.)

The Federal Republic of Germany adheres to the European Convention on Human Rights and to its optional clauses. (See Chapter 2, on Austria.)

Some authors in the Federal Republic of Germany complain that even these ample means of judicial review could be dangerous in the field of foreign relations. German commentators on the Sabbatino case have recommended de lege ferenda that the judicial branch in the Federal Republic of Germany should follow the example of the U.S. Supreme Court and abstain from deciding political questions.[3]

Originally written in 1972, reviewed and revised by the author in 1975.

The Individual as a National

Movement

Passports. According to Article 7, Paragraph 1, Article 8 of the Passport Law of 1972,[4] a passport will not be issued, or may be withheld, if the holder of the passport would endanger considerable interests of the Federal Republic of Germany. Article 11 of the Basic Law guarantees freedom of movement only inside the Federal Republic of Germany. However, the Federal Constitutional Court has held the above provision of the Passport Law to be compatible with the Basic Law.[5] Dieter-Dirk Hartmann criticizes these decisions,[6] but he would admit certain restrictions as compatible with the constitution. These would include restrictions in order to protect young persons from neglect, to prevent disease, to ensure the fulfillment of military obligations, and to prevent crimes from being committed abroad by persons previously convicted.[7]

A peculiarity of the law of the Federal Republic of Germany is the recognition of a class of persons who are treated "as if they were German citizens." Article 116, Section 1, of the Basic Law of 23 May 1949 reads as follows:

> Unless otherwise regulated by law, a German within the meaning of the Basic Law is a person who possesses German citizenship or who has been admitted to the territory of the German Reich, as it existed on 31 December 1937, as a refugee or expellee of German stock or as the spouse or descendant of such person.[8]

Such persons are issued passports by the Federal Republic of Germany with the mention "German" in the space indicating citizenship.[9] These persons are entitled to receive diplomatic protection by FRG authorities.[10] However, they are not German citizens. The Federal Administrative Court[11] sees a distinction in the fact that they could not avail themselves of Article 16, Paragraph 1, of the Basic Law, which protects only German citizens against denaturalization.[12] The status of "Article 116 German" is granted very liberally. For instance, it was given to a German-speaking Italian citizen who had been expelled from a formerly German-speaking area of Czechoslovakia, in spite of the fact that he was the holder of an Italian passport.[13]

A proposal to clarify the situation of these persons by requiring them either to obtain naturalization within a certain time limit or to forego their status under Article 116 was rejected in 1955 on the grounds that it would endanger the right of the expellees to return to the places from which they had been expelled.[14] Ruby refers to misgivings on the part of France and the Saarland, which at the time did not belong to the Federal Republic of Germany, in respect to the notion of "Germans according to Article 116."[15]

Teppert refers to a decision by the Netherlands Raad voor Rechtsherstol of 17 July 1956, which considers this article not as part of German citizenship law but as part of German law regarding aliens, granting to some persons who are and remain aliens a special status in order to protect their persons and property.[16]

The Reich Citizenship Law of 22 July 1913,[17] in spite of many amendments, is still the citizenship law in force in the Federal Republic of Germany.[18] The Federal Republic of Germany considers this law as a last common bond with the German Democratic Republic. Actually, until 1967 this same law was also in force in the German Democratic Republic. However, Article 19, Paragraph 2, of the Citizenship Law of the German Democratic Republic has repealed the 1913 Reich Citizenship Law,[19] retroactively bestowing GDR citizenship on all German citizens who were residents of the German Democratic Republic on 7 October 1949.[20] However, according to G. Zieger the Federal Republic of Germany does not recognize this "separatist" citizenship any more than it had recognized the Saarland citizenship.[21] This practice continues.[22] The Federal Constitutional Court held on 31 July 1973 that the Treaty concerning the Bases of Relations between the Federal Republic of Germany and the German Democratic Republic of 21 December 1972 will be compatible with the Basic Law of the Federal Republic of Germany only, if, notwithstanding the GDR rules on GDR citizenship, any citizen of the German Democratic Republic coming into the Federal Republic of Germany shall be treated there as a German within the meaning of Articles 16 and 116 of the Basic Law, thus conforming with the mandate of the latter to achieve the reunification of Germany.

Persons who are GDR citizens under the GDR citizenship law continue to receive FRG passports upon request when coming into the Federal Republic of Germany. This creates difficulties in cases in which, as in the Austro-German Property Treaty of 15 June 1957,[23] the Federal Republic of Germany tries to reserve advantages only to such persons as would be considered by objective observers to be FRG citizens. However, under FRG doctrine there are no such persons, only Germans. Article 3 of the treaty therefore uses a circumlocution. It calls these persons "Germans, whose diplomatic interests are protected by the FRG." The Austro-German Arbitral Tribunal had held quite logically that a GDR resident would not qualify as such a person, although during a short stay in Munich he had obtained an FRG passport.[24]

Departure. Against a refusal to issue a passport there lies an appeal to the Administrative Courts. In spite of heavy press criticism, Article 7, Paragraph 1, of the Passport Law of 1952[25] was not used to prevent the departure of FRG rocket experts to work in the UAR armaments industry.[26] Apart from the restrictions rendered possible by the above-quoted provision of the passport law, a German may leave the country temporarily or permanently and may also travel to most Western European countries without a passport, by simply presenting a national identity card.

Return. Article 13 of the German Citizenship Law of 1913 facilitates the reacquisition of German citizenship by former Germans (Lex Delbrück). During World War I this provision was invoked by Allied enemy property custodians to extend the notion of German property also to the property of such former Germans.[27] However, a German having lost his German citizenship by acquiring Austrian citizenship in 1950 did not automatically reacquire German citizenship when his acquisition of Austrian citizenship was annulled in 1958 on account of having been obtained under false pretences.[28]

Expulsion. An expulsion in the strict sense of the word appears inconceivable in the Federal Republic of Germany, as far as nationals are concerned. This also applies in the case of extradition, since under Article 16, Paragraph 2, of the Basic Law a German citizen shall not be extradited to a foreign country.[29]

This provision in turn has been relaxed in order to permit the authorities to reextradite a German who had been arrested abroad and sent to the Federal Republic of Germany under an express or implied condition that he would subsequently be handed back to the authorities of the state that arrested him.[30] However, there exists no general obligation to return a person of doubtful nationality to France who, while being extradited from France to Austria, claimed while in transit in the Federal Republic of Germany, to be a German citizen.[31]

Under Article 16, Paragraph 1, Clause 1, of the Basic Law, a German shall not be deprived of his or her German citizenship. In its decision of 30 October 1954,[32] the Federal Administrative Court concluded from this provision that an Austrian citizen may not be deprived of German citizenship acquired by virtue of the Anschluss, even if that citizen is claimed by Austria as an Austrian citizen. This decision was reversed by the decision of the German Constitutional Court of 9 November 1955,[33] which held this provision inapplicable to persons claimed as citizens by a state in the course of de-annexation.

It may be presumed that the German Democratic Republic will try to draw an analogy to this case in order to claim that the Federal Republic of Germany should discontinue regarding all GDR citizens as "German citizens." (See discussion above of the Reich Citizenship Law.)

Article 16, Paragraph 1, of the Basic Law does not protect "as if" citizens under Article 116 against loss of this status.[34] (See above.)

Article 16 of the Basic Law will also cause difficulties in the case of the Warsaw Treaty of 7 December 1970.[35]

An opinion by Armbruster and Klein made upon a request by the Christian Democratic Party (CDU) stated that the recognition by the Federal Republic of Germany of the territories east of the Oder-Neisse Line as Polish Territory will deprive the indigenous population of the territories between the Oder-Neisse Line and the German frontiers of 1937 of their German citizenship.[36] In 1945 these persons were German citizens. In the meantime they have acquired Polish citizenship. Under Article 25 of the German Citizenship Law of 1913, a person does not lose German nationality merely by acquiring a foreign citizenship. Such loss ensues only if, in addition to acquiring such citizenship, that person no longer has any domicile or residence in Germany. This passage has always been understood as limiting the loss of German citizenship to cases in which the person concerned also emigrates. For this reason the Celle Court of Appeals, 3 December 1951, denied that these persons lost their German citizenship by acquiring Polish citizenship.[37] They continued to reside in a territory that was at that time considered by the Federal Republic of Germany as still German territory. Hence they had not emigrated. According to Armbruster and Klein, the recognition by the Federal Republic of Germany that the territory concerned is no longer German territory will entail the loss of German citizenship of the persons concerned.[38] I question the soundness of this reasoning. After all, a person remaining in his or her place of residence cannot be said to have emigrated because territorial sovereignty over that place of residence is acquired by another sovereign.[39] The FRG government considers these persons, as well as persons of German ethnic origin who are residents of Czechoslovakia and who reacquired their Czechoslovak citizenship since 1953, as dual citizens.[40] Hence the Federal Republic of Germany can intercede in their favor before the Polish or Czechoslovak authorities only in an informal manner.[41]

Protection

Extent of Freedom of Activity Abroad. Since the German Basic Law forbids the extradition of a German citizen, the old version of the

German Criminal Code (in force until 31 December 1974) provided in Article 3, Section 1, that the code shall apply to acts of German citizens irrespective of whether the act was committed in Germany or abroad. This also applies in principle to acts that under the domestic law of the foreign country concerned are not punishable, like abortion. Some doubts have been raised in the Federal Republic of Germany as to whether this rule is compatible with the principles of international law. These views are refuted in the leading German commentary.[42] However, Article 7, Paragraph 2, number 1, of the Second Law to amend the Criminal Code of 4 July 1969 limits this jurisdiction of the German court to acts that would also be punishable under the law of the state in which the act was committed.[43] This Amendment Law entered into force on 1 January 1975.

A peculiarity of the German Criminal Code is the so-called passive personality principle embodied in Article 7, Paragraph 1 of the Criminal Code,[44] according to which a foreigner may be punished in the Federal Republic of Germany for acts committed abroad against a German if the act concerned was punishable also under the law of the state in which the act was committed.[45] This law aims at punishing the acts punishable by German standards. Although this law was enacted during National Socialist times, it is not held to be a typical Nazi product.[46]

The German courts may inflict punishment by virtue of their own function upon acts that in the country concerned would be punishable only upon the request of the damaged person.[47] There has been some dispute about whether German citizens can be punished according to the German highway code for minor infractions committed abroad in traffic accident cases. This was denied by some courts,[48] but the German highway code was held applicable to such acts committed in Austria by virtue of the Austro-FRG Treaty on Legal Assistance in Criminal Matters.[49]

Even in absence of such a treaty, the Bavarian Supreme Court of Appeals punished a German according to the German provisions (which are very strict) for having fled after causing an accident abroad.[50] However, the court voiced some doubts about whether it would really have the power to punish the defendant under this German law, if after the accident he had done all that local law would have required him to do.[51]

The rules of Article 3 Strafgesetzbuch and Article 7 of the Second Law to Amend the Criminal Code also extend to "as if" Germans under Article 116 of the Basic Law.[52]

Article 98, Section 2, of the German law against restriction of competition also holds illegal the conclusion of cartel agreements by foreigners abroad if the agreements influence the FRG market.[53] However, no clear-cut case of that nature has come before the courts.[54]

The Right to Diplomatic Protection. In the FRG literature there is some dispute about whether a citizen has a right to diplomatic protection by his or her state or not. K. Doehring denies such a right.[55] U. K. Geck believes in the existence of such a right but concedes to the administration a very wide range of discretion.[56] Moreover, if a court decision has asserted a citizen's right to such protection, the administration cannot be forced to actually grant such protection. All that can be done in this respect is to grant the citizen a right to compensation for having been denied such a right of protection.

In practice the Federal Court has held that there is no individual right to diplomatic protection.[57] In a decision of 30 October 1961, the Administrative Court of Appeals at Münster rejected the claim by Adolf Eichmann that the FRG Foreign Office should be forced to pay his defense costs.[58] This refusal was held not to be an abuse of the discretionary power granted in this respect to the FRG Foreign Office. The court likewise denied any right of the individual to claim diplomatic protection.

There is no right of diplomatic protection for dual nationals against the other state of which they are citizens.[59]

The rules of diplomatic protection do not apply by analogy to residents of one German land (Hamburg) against another German land (North Rhine-Westphalia).[60]

Insofar as a right to diplomatic protection exists in the Federal Republic of Germany, this right on principle should also be due to citizens of the German Democratic Republic. In support of this view, Oberthür quotes decisions by the FRG Federal Constitutional Court[61] that grant to former residents of the German Democratic Republic and to Saarlanders constitutional rights (freedom of movement and freedom of opinion) equal to those of Germans having their residence in the Federal Republic of Germany.[62] According to Oberthür, if diplomatic protection is refused the citizen concerned has a claim for compensation for an act assimilated to expropriation in virtue of Article 14, Section 3, of the Basic Law.[63]

In two cases, German citizens at the end of the war left property in the care and protection of the German embassy, in one case in Italy and in the other in Portugal. These sums were seized as Reich property by the countries concerned. Claims by the depositaries for the return of their deposits were rejected by German courts.[64]

The State and Compensation. Hitherto the Federal Republic of Germany has received compensation only under one lump-sum compensation agreement with Israel, that of 1 June 1962, concerning compensation instead of the return of property owned prior to World War II by the Tempelgesellschaft in Palestine.[65] The distribution law concerned provided for distribution of this sum in proportion to the losses incurred. (See below.) The distribution of the lump sum received by Israel has not led to any reported litigation.

The distribution of the lump sum received is left to the discretion of the receiving state. Usually only nationals of the state concerned who were also nationals at the time of damage are entitled to a share of this sum. However, a German court held that France did not violate any rule of public international law when it admitted a person to participate in this distribution of a lump sum paid by the Federal Republic of Germany to France, who was a Polish citizen at the time of the damage and who had acquired French citizenship only after the conclusion of the FRG-French lump-sum compensation treaty concerned.[66]

In its Decision Number 143 of 5 November 1965 in the Baron Brincard case, the Arbitral Commission for Property, Rights and Interests in Germany held that the Federal Republic of Germany was obliged to "top up" the sum received by the French claimant in this case as his share of the lump sum paid by the Federal Republic of Germany to the Netherlands in compensation for certain damages caused by the German occupational forces in the Netherlands.[67] This FRG-Netherlands Compensation Agreement contained a waiver clause (Article 15) whereby the Netherlands waived all further claims in respect to the objects covered by the treaty,[68] which concerned, among other things, compensation for the securities of German issuers removed from the Netherlands during World War II. Baron Brincard, a Frenchman, had deposited such shares in the Netherlands, which were thus removed. The sum he received under this lump-sum settlement was below the value of his claim, but the Arbitral Commission awarded him a claim against the Federal Republic of Germany for the remainder of the value of his shares.[69]

An indirect means whereby the Federal Republic of Germany tops up a compensation received from foreign states is the Hermes-Insurance Scheme. Hermes, an insurance company owned by the Federal Republic of Germany, offers to FRG exporters, for a moderate premium, insurance against political risks such as devaluation, moratoriums, and nationalization. In case the compensation received from the nationalizing foreign state concerned should prove inadequate, Hermes Insurance will make up the difference to the insured amount of the venture.[70] Rather amazingly, until February 1972 Hermes Insurance did not work at a loss. Heavy claims, especially owing to the events in Chile, made it probable that in 1972 Hermes would work at a loss for the first time, its deficit to be made up by the FRG taxpayers.

The Responsibility of the State for Injury Induced by Its Own Conduct. Article 5 of Chapter 6 of the Convention on the Settlement of Matters Arising out of War and the Occupation reads, "The Federal Republic shall ensure that the former owners of property seized pursuant to the measures referred to in Articles 2 and 3 of this Chapter shall be compensated."[71]

This provision was held to be non-self-executing by the Cologne Court of Appeals on 20 May 1955,[72] and by the Austrian supreme court in its decision of 4 February 1960,[73] which contrasted this provision with that of Article 27, Paragraph 2, of the Austrian State Treaty. The Federal Republic of Germany has fulfilled at least parts of the promise made in this article by the Reparation Damages Compensation Law of 12 February 1969.[74]

On 31 January 1966 the federal court refused to grant compensation to an FRG knäckebrot manufacturer who was of the opinion that a trade agreement of the Federal Republic of Germany with Sweden allowing for additional knäckebrot imports from Sweden was detrimental to his business interests.[75] The court rejected his claim but stated incidentally that a claim for state liability for wrongful acts by officials (under a law reminiscent of the British Crown Proceedings Act) would have been possible if the Federal Republic of Germany Bundestag had ratified the treaty with Sweden upon false information furnished by the administration.

During the planning of the enlargement of Salzburg airport, residents of the Federal Republic of Germany had been excluded from a hearing pursuant to the Austrian Air Law. (See Chapter 2, on Austria.) After these events the Federal Republic of Germany and Austria ratified the Salzburg Airport Treaty,[76] which was based obviously on the existence of the enlarged airport. The residents concerned challenged the treaty as unconstitutional, since it denied them their right to a fair hearing in any administrative or judicial procedure guaranteed in Article 103 of the Basic Law. In summary proceedings the Federal Constitutional Court denied that these persons had been deprived of any such right by the conclusion of the treaty.[77] Prior to the coming into force of the treaty, this right had been denied to them by the Austrian Administrative Court. Thus they were now not worse off than before.

Having obtained a German forum in virtue of this treaty (see below), these persons thereupon claimed that the airport should be closed down, since the airport operation license had not been granted in a procedure ensuring due process of law. The Landgericht Traunstain (Bavaria) rejected this plea.[78] (See below.) The planning and the official licensing of the enlargement of Salzburg Airport had been accepted as a fact by the conclusion of the Salzburg Airport Treaty. The court shared the view of the Federal Constitutional Court, which had deemed this treaty compatible with the Basic Law. Hence, the Landgericht held, the Airport was an "approved installation." Also, under FRG law its neighbors could no longer challenge its existence. They may, however, be entitled to damages for the nuisance of airport noises.

Waiver. The Federal Court held in a decision of 26 February 1963 that the existence of provisions waiving individual rights to claims for compensation for acts arising out of the war and occupation, such as they figure in the several peace treaties or treaties concluded in substitution for peace treaties or in compensation treaties, prove that as a matter of principle such individual rights could exist.[79]

The 2 August 1952 treaty between the Federal Republic of Germany and Switzerland concerning the liquidation of German assets in Switzerland, which waived parts of the claims of German citizens for the restitution of such property,[80] was upheld by the FRG Federal Constitutional Court on 21 March 1957.[81] The Federal Republic of Germany accepted this taking as a Swiss act of state.[82] In view of the fact that the peace treaties with the satellite countries and the Austrian State Treaty contain clauses obliging these countries to waive certain claims against Germany and German citizens, FRG courts have had to rule on the meaning of such clauses.

The FRG courts accepted the waiver in the Hungarian Peace Treaty as also extinguishing in the Federal Republic of Germany the rights of the Hungarian citizens concerned. The acceptance of the effect of this waiver by the Federal Republic of Germany was said to result from Article 5, Paragraph 4, of the London Agreement Concerning German External Debts of 23 February 1953.[83] This waiver clause also includes the waiver of rights of Hungarians who did not live in Hungary at the time of the conclusion of the peace treaty,[84] but it does not extend to claims by Hungarian citizens whom Hungary had failed to protect against persecution.[85]

The Kammergericht (West Berlin Court of Appeals) held on 2 July 1965 that under international law Hungary is obliged to compensate Hungarian citizens for the damage caused to them by the acceptance of the waiver in the peace treaty.[86]

Special Kinds of Protection. In practice the Equalization of Burden Law, adding a certain compensation to the losses suffered by expellees and bomb victims, can be considered as a special kind of protection.[87]

Another special kind of protection to German citizens is the passive personality principle. (See above.)

Foreigners may be drafted into the FRG armed forces in reprisal if their states draft Germans into their forces.[88] Such reprisals may be imposed by an ordinance issued by the FRG government.[89] No such ordinance has as yet been issued.[90]

The difficult situation caused by the enlargement of Salzburg Airport was solved when the Salzburg Airport Treaty of 19 December 1967 (see above) came into force on 17 May 1974.[91] By a fiction of law, as far as effects in the Federal Republic of Germany are concerned, the Federal Republic of Germany will now treat this Austrian airport as if it were located in the Federal Republic of Germany. Thus, on the one hand, the FRG authorities will establish safety (building prohibition) zones in the Federal Republic of Germany to protect this airport. On the other hand, FRG authorities and courts will deal with all complaints by FRG residents concerning flight noises and other hazards from Salzburg Airport. In doing so they will apply FRG law. Any compensation awarded by them will be refunded by the Republic of Austria to the FRG authorities. A separate agreement under Austrian law, concluded between the Republic of Austria and Salzburg Airport Company, ensures that this company will refund to the Republic of Austria any sum spent for this purpose.

The Individual as an Alien

Movement

Entry and Stay. Citizens of 85 states may enter the Federal Republic of Germany without having to obtain visas.[92]

Voluntary Departure. In refutation of allegations advanced by the USSR, the FRG Ministry of the Interior, by a letter of 15 November 1955, solemnly recognized the right of any foreigner (including a displaced person of Soviet origin) to leave the Federal Republic of Germany when and if the person wanted to leave it.[93]

Involuntary Departure: Expulsion and Deportation. The fact that a refugee has crossed the borders of the Federal Republic of Germany illegally does not justify expulsion.[94]

A person who has resided for more than 60 years in Germany can no longer be expelled.[95] The court in this case applied, even prior to its coming into force (1965), the 13 December 1955 European Convention on Establishment, according to which after ten years of residence expulsion is possible only for reasons of national safety or for other compelling reasons.[96]

The expulsion of a foreigner cannot actually be carried out until it has been established that the expulsion does not violate any rights guaranteed under the Refugee Convention, unless the nonexecution of the expulsion constitutes a danger to public safety.[97]

According to a 2 August 1960 judgment by the Munster Administrative Court of Appeals, a Belgian bigamist could not be expelled if the expulsion would violate his right to family life with his second "wife," which is guaranteed under Article 8 of the European Convention on Human Rights.[98] In practice this means that a foreigner married to a German wife cannot be expelled.[99]

An expelled foreigner can rely directly on an establishment convention with his or her home state.[100] A foreigner who by mistake was treated as a German citizen by German authorities for more than ten years was held to have acquired German citizenship by estoppel.[101] The German Federal Court has held that it had been abusive of Hungary to have expelled a Jewish immigrant, forcing him to return to Nazi Germany.[102]

A Turkish citizen condemned for treason against the Federal Republic of Germany may be expelled from the Federal Republic of Germany. Articles 32 and 33 of the International Refugee Convention, which permit expulsion of refugees in such cases, are merely declaratory of international law. The safety of the state enjoys priority over the individual's right of asylum. However, it was stated in this case that the person concerned must not be expelled to a country where he risked the death penalty.[103] Nevertheless, on 30 June 1964 the Federal Constitutional Court held that a Yugoslav-born member of the French Foreign Legion might be expelled even to France, where he risked the death penalty for the murder of 11 Algerians.[104] This does not appear to be prohibited by Article 102 of the Basic Law, abolishing the death penalty in the Federal Republic of Germany.

An alien may not be expelled for a political crime, if such expulsion is merely intended as a substitute for extradition, which would not be permitted by law.[105]

Protection

Diplomatic protection is granted to "as if" Germans (see discussion of "Article 116" at the beginning of this chapter) and to GDR citizens (although a court decision to the contrary is discussed in the section above on passports). The FRG claim to protect GDR citizens is not recognized by the United States, insofar as residents of the German Democratic Republic are concerned.[106] This claim has also led to an exchange of notes between the Federal Republic of Germany and the USSR.[107]

A rather curious case was reported in the Hamburg newspapers in 1971. A German citizen, having taken out first papers, had been drafted into the U.S. Army for service in Vietnam. He had obtained leave to visit his relatives in Germany. Upon his own request he was thereupon drafted into the FRG Armed Forces, which automatically freed him from danger of prosecution by U.S. authorities in Germany.[108]

During the occupation of Polish territory by Germany, Polish citizens had no right to expect diplomatic protection by the German authorities. Hence a Polish citizen who was ill-treated and imprisoned in the USSR between 1939 and 1940 had no claim against the Federal Republic of Germany on account of the fact that the German embassy in Moscow had neglected to take care of his interest.[109]

By virtue of an FRG-Israel undertaking to negotiate a treaty of 10 September 1952, the Federal Republic of Germany was authorized to negotiate a lump-sum settlement agreement with Israel for the compensation of all the members of Tempelgesellschaft.[110] The members of this group originally came from Germany. After the war some of them had retained German citizenship, while others had migrated to Australia and had been naturalized there. The Federal Republic of Germany, with the consent of the Australian and Israel authorities, subsequently concluded the Agreement of 1 June 1962, which provided compensation for all members of the group.[111] The lump sum agreed upon between the Federal Republic of Germany and Israel, however, in virtue of an exchange of letters attached to this agreement, was split up in two parts, one part going to Australia and the other to the Federal Republic of Germany. Only this latter part was distributed pursuant to the FRG distribution law.[112]

NATIONAL IMPLEMENTATION OF INTERNATIONAL RIGHTS AND DUTIES

The Act of State Doctrine

The courts of the Federal Republic of Germany recognize the Act of State doctrine. However, in an incidental opinion the Hamburg Court of Appeals held on 8 May 1951 that a foreign expropriation that is carried out in violation of international law should be considered null and void.[113]

In its decision of 10 May 1961, the Federal Administrative Court held that the Polish Land Reform Law of 1925 was compatible with international law.[114] In the Bremen Tobacco case, the Hanseatic Court of Appeals held on 21 August 1959 that the Indonesian nationalization measures did not violate international law.[115] In its decisions in the Chilean copper cases, the Landgericht Hamburg held that the Chilean takings were contrary to international law and contrary to German public policy, but it refused to restore the copper concerned to claimant (the non-nationalized ex-Chilean "split company") for lack of a sufficiently close connection of the case with FRG jurisdiction. (See below.)[116] However, it results from these cases that the German courts consider themselves to have jurisdiction to pass judgment on the compatibility of foreign law with public international law. On 20 December 1968 the German Federal Court held that German courts cannot examine whether extradition by a foreign state is in conformity with the law of that state.[117]

Implementation of Decisions of International Organizations

In the Federal Republic of Germany the treaty-making power of the federation does not authorize it to enact by federal law any legislative measures required by the fact that it adheres to an international organization if, under the constitution, the legislative powers concerned are vested with the Länder and not with the federation. For instance, this would be the case in the field of cultural affairs. However, no difficulties in this respect have occurred in practice.

The strict provisions of the federal constitution against any not strictly specified enabling law prevents the Federal Republic of Germany from complying with the wishes of certain international organizations and supranational communities by providing by an FRG law that the government be authorized to change any existing legislation necessary in order to ensure compliance with an act of the organization concerned. (See Chapter 2, on Austria.)

The compatibility with the constitution of treaties and self-executing acts of international or supranational organizations may be reviewed by the Federal Constitution Court. Should this court hold such rules unconstitutional, they would become inapplicable in domestic law, yet the Federal Republic of Germany would remain bound by them on the international level. (See Chapter 2.) The Federal Constitutional Court hitherto has held all such rules, especially those of the EEC treaty,[118] to be compatible with the constitution, but it has asserted its right of review in spite of the fact that the Court of the European Communities denies such a right to domestic constitutional courts.[119]

Article 87a of the Basic Law provides that FRG armed forces shall act only in those specific situations in which the Basic Law authorizes such action. The Basic Law does not mention actions on behalf of the United Nations. Since the United Nations was aware of this situation when the Federal Republic of Germany applied for membership, E. Klein concludes that the United Nations would be estopped from asking for a participation of FRG armed forces pursuant to Article 43 of the UN charter.[120]

Rhodesia

Even at a time when the Federal Republic of Germany was not yet a member state of the United Nations, the Federal Republic of Germany had declared its willingness to participate in sanctions against Rhodesia.[121] This was effected by two ordinances of 14 February 1967.[122] These ordinances are based on Article 7, Section 1, Number 2, of the German Law on Trade Abroad of 28 April 1961, which enables the federal government to restrict imports or exports into the Federal Republic of Germany if a considerable disturbance of the foreign relations of the Federal Republic of Germany is apprehended.[123]

H. P. Ipsen doubts the constitutionality of these ordinances.[124] According to him the Constitutional Court ought to be able to examine in each individual case whether the specific import demand concerned would endanger the foreign relations of the Federal Republic of Germany. This view is shared by Linde.[125]

Namibia

Recently the Hermes Insurance contract for FRG investment in Namibia, which is also discussed above, was not renewed. I do not know whether this was done in compliance with the various UN resolutions on Namibia or for other reasons.[126] According to Frankfurter Allgemeine Zeitung of 15 March 1972, the FRG government for political reasons has threatened to cut off the financial support of the Max Planck Gesellschaft (the FRG counterpart to the Centre National de la Recherche Scientifique) if the Max Planck Gesellschaft builds its Southern Hemisphere observatory in Namibia.

UNESCO

On 22 June 1972 the German Federal Republic refused to enforce a contract for insurance on the export of African works of art exported in violation of the legislation of the country of provenance. The court held this contract to be contrary to German public policy, since it violated the principles recommended by UNESCO concerning protection of the cultural inheritance.[127]

Procedures Relating to the Issue of Certificates or Suggestions of the Executive in Connection with Litigation in National Courts

Owing to a strict conception of the separation of powers, certificates by the administration are not binding on the courts but are merely a means of information.[128] Habscheid states that certificates by the German Foreign Office on the immunity of foreign states and diplomats are not binding on the courts.[129] The German Foreign Office itself does not require that courts comply with its certificates.[130] A circular of the Federal Minister of the Interior of 5 March 1958 on exterritoriality[131] is binding only on the administration.

Article 24 of the Fourth Enabling Ordinance to the German Marriage Law of 25 October 1941 gave the Reich Ministry of Justice certain powers in respect to the recognition of foreign judgments in matrimonial relations cases.[132] These powers have been held inapplicable in the Federal Republic of Germany, as an invasion of the rights of German judges.[133] (See Chapter 2, on Austria.) Other courts were ready to accept such certificates by the Federal Ministry of Justice but considered them open to appeal to the German Administrative Courts[134] (see Chapter 2) or to appeals to ordinary courts.[135]

Similar powers granted to the German Minister of Justice to certify the existence of reciprocity in patent matters have been held incompatible with the principle of separation of powers by the appeals board of the German Patent Office.[136]

On the other hand, in the absence of certificates concerning the existence of reciprocity according to the law concerning state liability for wrongful acts of officials, German judges may not start their own investigations of the facts even if such proof is offered by the parties.[137]

A German court was held not to be bound by a certificate of the U.S. treasury to the effect that gold-dollar coins are still legal tender in the United States. Contrary to this certificate, the Hamm Court of Appeals found on 5 November 1962 that such gold coins are no longer legal tender in the United States.[138]

Recognition

According to the federal court, there existed no duty to recognize the German Democratic Republic.[139] The nonrecognition of the German Democratic Republic by the Federal German Republic did not entail the entire nonrecognition of its laws.[140]

However, in view of the fact that the Federal Republic of Germany did not recognize the German Democratic Republic, the German Democratic Republic was held not to be a member of the Madrid Agreement on Trade Marks, in spite of the fact that the German Democratic Republic had declared its willingness to accede to this agreement. The court, although not bound by the attitude of the executive, took note of the factual situation created by the nonrecognition policy of the FRG executive.[141]

The German courts have recognized the status of Poland[142] and of Czechoslovakia[143] as states, deducing that status from their existence and from the fact that they possessed a territory, a population, and a stable government, even at a time when the German Reich had not yet recognized these two states.

German courts, contrary to widely held opinions, consider that during the war years Slovakia and Croatia were independent states.[144]

The existence of Israel as an independent state prior to the establishment of diplomatic relations between the Federal Republic of Germany and Israel was deduced from the fact that the Federal Republic of Germany had concluded international law agreements with Israel.[145]

Thus the courts sometimes appear to be in advance of the government in their recognition of foreign states. I have found no trace of a decision in the opposite sense, that is, of a court denying the existence of a country or government in spite of the fact that it was recognized by the government of the Reich or of the Federal Republic of Germany. The Supreme Court of the British Zone of Occupation in Cologne, 10 February 1949 did not consider itself retroactively bound by the view that had been advanced by the National Socialist Government that Poland had ceased to exist as a state (case of Landwirtschaftszentrale Cracow).[146]

TREATIES AND THE INDIVIDUAL

The Federal Republic of Germany adheres to the World Bank Convention on the Settlement of International Investment Disputes. It has concluded reciprocal visa arrangements with numerous states, and it has concluded 40 treaties establishing investment guarantees. (See the appendix to this chapter.)

It has also concluded several treaties of friendship, commerce, and navigation, among other things, with the United States, Treaty of 29 October 1954.[147] This treaty has been held to guarantee to U.S. citizens a right of full indemnity in the case of the taking of building sites for reconstruction purpose in West Berlin,[148] although a decision of the Kammergericht (West Berlin Court of Appeals) had held that the law concerned providing for less than full indemnity in such a case was not incompatible with the guarantee of the right of property of Article 14, Section 3, of the Basic Law of the Federal Republic of Germany.[149] However, such protection is granted only in case of interference with U.S. property rights by German authorities. According to the Hamburg court, the treaty does not authorize U.S. citizens to recover their property in the Federal Republic of Germany nationalized by Chile.[150] (See the discussion above of the Act of State doctrine.) There would have been a sufficiently close contact with the forum only if German citizens had been the victims of such Chilean nationalization.[151] (See above.)

An FRG government legislative project to grant workers and trade union representatives an equal share with the owners in the management of all big German firms[152] has been held incompatible with the FCN Treaty in an expert opinion by Wilhelm Wengler.[153]

Mann complains that the Federal Constitutional Court in a decision of 1 March 1967[154] gave priority to Article 19, Section 3, of the Basic Law, reserving the protection of the rights guaranteed under the Basic Law merely to German juridical persons but not to foreign juridical persons, over Article 6 of this treaty, granting U.S. nationals equal rights concerning the access to the courts along with German citizens.[155]

The Federal Republic of Germany adheres to the European Convention of Human Rights. It has also ratified the covenants of the United Nations on human rights.[156] (See Chapter 2.) It has thus accepted the coexistence of these rival rules.[157]

On the jurisdiction of the Arbitral Tribunal, instituted by the Austro-German Property Treaty of 15 June 1957, and on the award of the Arbitral Tribunal of 15 January 1972, established under the Austro-German Finance and Compensation Treaty of 27 November 1961, see Chapter 2, on Austria.

Under Article 77 of the EEC treaty, courts of last resort in the EEC countries shall obtain a preliminary ruling of the Court of the European Communities concerning the interpretation of the EEC treaty and the rules enacted pursuant thereto.[158] According to the practice of the Court of the European Communities, national courts of last resort are not bound to obtain a new preliminary ruling if such a court merely intends to follow a ruling rendered by the Court of the European Communities in a similar previous case. For this reason the FRG Federal Finance Court had in a given case omitted to obtain such a preliminary ruling. Thereupon the claimant turned to the FRG Federal Constitutional Court, invoking the protection of Article 101, Paragraph 1, Clause 2, of the Basic Law, which guarantees to everybody access to the judge provided by law. In its decision of 9 June 1971, the Federal Constitutional Court rejected this claim merely on account of the fact that the refusal of the Federal Finance Court to submit the case for a preliminary ruling to the Court of the European Communities could not be considered to be arbitrary under the circumstances of the case concerned.[159] At least by implication the Federal Constitutional Court thus admitted a constitutional right under FRG law of the individual to have his or her case submitted to the Court of the European Communities.

APPENDIX: TREATIES OF THE FEDERAL REPUBLIC OF GERMANY ON THE PROMOTION AND MUTUAL PROTECTION OF INVESTMENTS

(as of 31 December 1973)

Country	Signed	In Force	Bundesgesetzblatt Number
Cameroon	29 June 1962	21 November 1963	1963 II 991 and 1537
Central African Republic	23 August 1965	21 January 1968	1967 II 1657 1968 II 48
Ceylon	8 November 1963	7 December 1966	1966 II 909 1966 II 1526
Chad	11 April 1967	23 November 1968	1968 II 221 1968 II 1095
Chile	30 March 1964		--
Colombia	11 June 1965		1967 II 1552
Congo (UR)	13 September 1965		1967 II 1733 1967 II 2367
Ecuador	28 June 1965	30 November 1966	1966 II 825 1966 II 1522
Ethiopia	21 April 1964		--
Gabon	16 May 1969	22 March 1971	1970 II 657 1971 II 212
Ghana	19 May 1967		1968 II 1251
Greece	27 March 1961	15 July 1963	1963 II 216 1963 II 914
Guinea	19 April 1962	13 March 1965	1964 II 154 1965 II 408
India	(Exchange of Notes of 15 October 1964 covering the protection of German Investments, in force after ratification)		Notification dated 27 November 1964; Bundesanzliger 235 of 16 December 1964
Indonesia	16 June 1970	19 April 1971	1970 II 492 1971 II 214
Iran	11 November 1965	6 April 1968	1967 II 2549 1968 II 171

Country	Signed	In Force	Bundesgesetz-blatt Number
Ivory Coast	27 October 1968	10 June 1968	1968 II 61
Kenya	4 December 1964		1966 II 899
Korea	4 February 1964	15 January 1967	1966 II 841 1967 II 736
Liberia	12 December 1961	22 October 1967	1967 II 1537 1967 II 2373
Madagascar	21 September 1962	21 March 1966	1965 II 369 1966 II 178
Malaysia	22 December 1960	6 July 1962	1962 II 1064 1963 II 1153
Mauritius	25 May 1971	27 August 1973	1973 II 615 1973 II 1511
Morocco	31 August 1961	21 January 1968	1967 II 1641 1968 II 8
Niger	29 October 1964	10 January 1966	1965 II 1402 1966 II 54
Pakistan	25 November 1959	28 March 1962 28 April 1962	1961 II 793 1962 II 172
Philippines	3 March 1964	--	1966 II 549
Ruanda	18 April 1967	28 February 1969	1968 II 1260 1969 II 191
Sambia	10 December 1966	25 August 1972	1968 II 33 1972 II 1018
Senegal	24 January 1964	16 January 1966	1965 II 1391 1966 II 10
Sierra Leone	8 April 1965	10 December 1966	1966 II 861 1966 II 1564
Singapore	3 October 1973	--	--
Sudan	7 February 1963	24 January 1967	1966 II 889 1967 II 908
Tanzania	30 January 1965	12 July 1968	1966 II 875 1968 II 584
Thailand	13 December 1961	10 April 1965	1964 II 687 1965 II 368
Togo	16 May 1961	21 December 1964	1964 II 154 1965 II 39
Tunisia	20 December 1963	6 February 1966	1965 II 1377 1966 II 53
Turkey	20 June 1962	16 December 1965	1965 II 1193, 1631
Uganda	29 November 1966	19 August 1968	1968 II 449 1968 II 785
Zaire	18 March 1969	22 July 1971	1970 II 509 1971 II 1099

NOTES

1. Peaslee, Constitutions of Nations: Europe 365 (the Hague 1968).
2. Contra Mann, 65 Am. J. Intl L. 793 (1971).
3. Vogel, Der gerichtliche Rechtsschutz des einzelnen gegenüber der vollziehenden Gewalt in der BRD, 1 Judicial Protection Against the Executive 136 (Max Planck Institut, Cologne and Dobbs Ferry, 1969) and Gurski, "Ausländische Enteignungen und Spaltgesellschaften," Wertpapier-Mitteilungen, Part 4, at 1144-45 (1964).
4. [1952] Bundesgesetzblatt (hereafter BGBl.) I 290.
5. Decision of 16 January 1957, 6 Entscheidungen des Bundesverfassungsgerichts (hereafter BVerfG) 32 (1957), and of 10 October 1961, 13 BVerfG 153 ff. (1961).
6. Hartmann, "Ausreisefreiheit" in 17 Jahrbuch für öffentliches Recht 471 (1968).
7. Ibid., at 465 ff.
8. Peaslee, op. cit., at 391.
9. Schaetzel, Deutsches Staatsangehörigkeitsrecht 96 (Berlin, 1958).
10. Ibid.
11. 25 September 1957, Neue Juristische Wochenschrift (hereafter N.J.W.) 473 (1958).
12. In its decision of 31 July 1973, BVerfG 36, 1 N.J.W. on the compatibility of the Treaty concerning the Bases of Relations between the FRG and the GDR of 21 December 1972, [1973] BGBl. I 427, with the Basic Law of the Federal Republic of Germany, the Federal Constitutional Court seemed to grant this protection also to "Article 116 Germans."
13. German Federal Administrative Court, 24 February 1966, 19 N.J.W. I 1529-30.
14. G. Zieger, Das Staatsbürgerschaftsgesetz der DDR 17, note 44 (Frankfurt 1969).
15. Ruby, L'Evolution de la Nationalité Allemande d'après les textes, 1843-1953 328 (1954)
16. Teppert, "Die Rechtsstellung der Deutschen ohne die deutsche Staatsangehörigkeit im Sinne des Artikels" 116 Abs., 1 des Grundgesetzes 18 (thesis, Cologne, 1969).
17. 11 N.J.W. I 320 (1958).
18. Ruby, op. cit., at 494, UN Secretariat Legislative Series, Laws concerning Nationality (ST/LEG/SER.B/4) 178 (New York 1954).
19. Law of 22 July 1913, [1913] Reichsgesetzblatt (hereafter RGBl.) 583, as last amended by the Federal Law of 8 September 1969, [1969] BGBl. I 1581.
20. Law of 20 February 1967, [1967] Gesetzblatt (hereafter GBl.) 3; von Münch, Dokumente des geteilten Deutschland 369 (1968).
21. Zieger, op. cit., at 36, 58. In respect to this latter see also Münch, "Zur Staatsangehörigkeit im Saarland," 19 Zeitschrift für ausländisches öffentliches Recht und Völkerrecht (hereafter Z.a.ö.R.V.) 318 (1958).

22. Zieger, Die Staatsangehörigkeit im geteilten Deutschland, 62, note 224 (1971). Zieger proposed a solution more in conformity with the new "Ostpolitik." Ibid., at 66.

23. [1958] BGBl. II 130.

24. Opinion No. 65, Seidl-Hohenveldern, The Austrian-German Arbitral Tribunal 181 (1972); Seidl-Hohenveldern, "Le Tribunal Arbitral institué par le Trâité Austro-Allemand du 15 juin 1957 portant règlement des problèmes des biens, 15 Annuaire Français de Droit International 273, note 55 (1969).

25. [1952] BGBl. I 290.

26. 25 Z.a.ö.R.V. 247, No. 20 (1965) and 26 Z.a.ö.R.V. 115, No. 19 (1966).

27. McNair, The Legal Effects of War, Cambridge: 1966, 4th ed., 29; Weber case (1916) A.C. 421; Liebmann case (1916) 1 K. B. 268 (1948).

28. Federal Administrative Court, 1 June 1965, 43 I.L.R. 194 (1972). However, under the present Austrian Citizenship Law such annulment would no longer be admissible. See Chapter 2, on Austria.

29. In conformity with the decision of the Federal Constitutional Court of 31 July 1973, BVerfG 36, 1 N.J.W., the Kammergericht (West Berlin Court of Appeals) held that the German Democratic Republic is not a "foreign country" within the meaning of this article. Hence the Kammergericht intends to hand over to the GDR authorities Ingrid Bruckmann, an 18-year-old GDR girl who fled to West Berlin after having killed her father, who had raped her, in the German Democratic Republic. As of this writing, the case is pending before the European Commission on Human Rights.

30. Federal Court, 7 February 1968, 22 Entscheidungen des Bundesgerichtshofes in Strafsachen (hereafter BGHSt.) 62 (1968); 21 N.J.W. I 1056 (1968), 31 Z.a.ö.R.V. 322, No. 86 (1970).

31. German Constitutional Court, 20 October 1959, 10 BVerfG 136, revising Federal Court, 7 January 1959, 12 BGHSt, 262 (1959), 28 Z.a.ö.R.V. 195, Nos. 181 and 182 (1968).

32. 21 I.L.R. 175 (1954), 1 Entscheidungen des Bundesverwaltungsgerichts (hereafter BVerwG) 206 (1954), 20 Z.a.ö.R.V. 194, No. 10a (1959).

33. 4 BVerfG 323 ff. (1955), 22 I.L.R. 430 (1955), 16 Z.a.ö.R.V. 676 (1955-56), and 20 Z.a.ö.R.V. 219, No. 89 (1959).

34. Teppert, op. cit., at 77-78, and Federal Administrative Court, 9 June 1959, 8 BVerwG 340 (1959).

35. 10 International Legal Materials 127 (1971).

36. Frankfurter Allgemeine Zeitung, 25 January 1972, Zahl D 2954 A.

37. 5 N.J.W. 475-76 (1952), 21 Z.a.ö.R.V. 566-667, No. 423 (1961), 81 Journal du Droit International (hereafter Clunet) 840 (1954).

38. Frankfurter Allgemeine Zeitung, op. cit.

39. In respect to these problems, see also Stoll, Die Rechtsstellung der Deutschen Staatsangehörigen in den polnisch verwalteten Gebieten 244 (Frankfurt 1968).

40. To the same effect, Austrian Supreme Court, 20 June 1974, 97 Juristische Blätter (hereafter Jur. Blätter) 34 (1975).

41. Seidl-Hohenveldern, "Das Münchener Abkommen im Licht des Prager Vertrages von 1973," in Festschrift für E. Manzel (Rauschning, ed., Göttingen 1975).

42. Schönke-Schröder, Strafgesetzbuch, Kommentar, § 3, note 6, at 79 (München, 16th ed., 1972).

43. In the version of the Second Law to amend the Criminal Code of 4 July 1969, [1969] BGBl. I 717, quoted by Lackner-Massen, Strafgesetzbuch 753 (München, 6th ed., 1970).

44. Art. 4, para. 2, No. 2 of the old version of the Criminal Code. By virtue of Art. 5, no. 6, of the Criminal Code, this restriction does not apply in cases of kidnapping or political denunciation.

45. Obiter Federal Court, 22 February 1963, 19 Juristenzeitung (hereafter J.Z.) 380 (1964), refusing to convict a Dutchman for living on the immoral earnings of his consenting German wife in Lebanon.

46. Federal Court, 12 July 1951, 4 N.J.W. 769-70 (1951). In this latter case both the defendant and his victim were Germans. The compatibility of the passive personality principle with international law is doubted by Oehler, Internationales Strafrecht 139, 307, 412-13 (Cologne 1973), giving a comparative survey, ibid., at 407-08. In Austria the passive personality principle introduced during the German occupation was abrogated after 1945 without even a debate about whether its retention would serve any useful purpose. The Austrian Supreme Court in a decision of 7 February 1974, 29 Osterreichische Juristenzeitung (hereafter O.J.Z.) 397, No. 180 (1974) referred to this fact when rejecting a plea to take this principle into consideration for equitable reasons in a trial concerning an accident in Hungary in which both the defendant and the victim were Austrian citizens.

47. Federal Court, 1 June 1954, 7 N.J.W. II 1086 (1954).

48. Frankfurt Court of Appeals, 30 September 1964, 18 N.J.W. I 508 (1965), and by the Bavarian Supreme Court of Appeals, 21 July 1965, 18 N.J.W. II 2166 (1965).

49. Treaty of 22 September 1958, [1960] BGBl. II 1347, Federal Court, 26 July 1967, 20 N.J.W. II 2069 (1967).

50. 21 August 1963, 13 Entscheidungen des Bayrischen Obersten Landesgerichts-Strafsachen (hereafter Bay. ObLGSt.) 195 (1963).

51. 28 Z.a.ö.R.V. 94-95, No. 89 (1968).

52. GBL, Art. 116, Abs. 1.

53. Federal Court, 12 November 1957, 11 BGHSt. 63-64 (1957).

54. Gesetz gegen Wettbewerbsbeschränkungen, 3 January 1966, [1966] BGBl. I 37.

55. Die Pflicht des Staates zur Gewährung diplomatischen Schutzes 94 (1959).

56. "Der Anspruch des Staatsbürgers auf Schutz gegenüber dem Ausland nach deutschem Recht," 17 Z.a.ö.R.V. 516-17 (1956-57).

57. Federal Court, 12 July 1963, Rechtsprechung zum Wiedergutmachungsrecht (hereafter R.z.W.) 76 (1964) and two other cases, 28 Z.a.ö.R.V. 112-13 (1968).

58. 77 Deutsches Verwaltungsblatt (hereafter DVBl) 139 (1962).

59. Federal Court, 12 July 1963, 15 R.z.W. 76 (1964), 28 Z.a.ö.R.V. 116, No. 136 (1968).

60. Deutsches Obergericht für das Vereinigte Wirtschaftsgebiet, 14 December 1949, 3 N.J.W. 142 (1950), 14 Z.a.ö.R.V. 253, No. 1 (1951).

61. 7 May 1953, 2 BVerfG 277 (1953), and 4 May 1955, 4 BVerfG 176 (1955).

62. Oberthür, Der Anspruch des deutschen Staatsbürgers auf diplomatischen Schutz und konsularischen Schutz gegenüber anderen Staaten 71 (1965).

63. Contrast however, these views of Oberthür with those held by the Austro-German Arbitral Tribunal in opinion No. 65, which are given in the discussion of passports in the early part of the text of this chapter.

64. Federal Court, 10 January 1963, Ernst-Jung-Kellmereit, Allgemeines Kriegsfolgengesetz, Kommentar, looseleaf edition, Art. 12, Note 2b (Portugal 1969).

65. [1965] BGBl. I 189, 448 U.N.T.S. 227. On these claims see also 16 UN Rep. Int'l. Arb. Awards 1 (1969).

66. Cologne Court of Appeals, 29 August 1973, 24 R.z.W 479 (1973).

67. 8 Official Collection 67.

68. Finance Treaty, 8 April 1960 [1963] BGBl. II 629, 509 U.N.T.S. 195.

69. On this case see Seidl-Hohenveldern, Der Barcelona Traction Fall, 22 Osterreichische Zeitschrift für öffentliches Recht (hereafter O.Z.ö.R.) 295 (1971).

70. See Christopeit, Hermes-Deckungen (1968).

71. Uberleitungsvertrag, [1955] BGBl. II 405, 332 U.N.T.S. 219.

72. 8 N.J.W. II 1635 (1955); see also Seidl-Hohenveldern in Seidl-Hohenveldern and Ispen, Entschädigungspflicht der Bundesrepublik für reparationsentzogenes Auslandsvermögen 152 (1962).

73. 40 I.L.R. 175 (1970).

74. [1969] BGBl. I 105; on the latter see Seidl-Hohenveldern, "La Réparation des Dommages Subis par les Nationaux à l'Etranger à la suite de Bouleversements Politiques--Comparaison des Solutions Françaises et Allemandes," 21 Revue Internationale de Droit Comparé 763-78 (1969).

75. Aussenwirtschaftsdienst (hereafter A.W.D.) 100 (1966), 45 Entscheidungen des Bundesgerichtshofs in Zivilsachen (hereafter BGHZ) 83 ff (1966).

76. [1974] BGBl. II 15.

77. Decision of 11 December 1974, Ref. No. 1 BVR 242/73.

78. Landgericht Traunstein, 16 April 1975, 24 Zeitschrift für Luft- und Weltraumrecht 160 (1975).

79. 14 R.z.W 527 (1963), 28 Z.a.ö.R.V. 83, No. 66 (1968).

80. [1953] BGBl. II 127.

81. 6 BVerfG 290 (1957); 18 Z.a.ö.R.V. 121 (1957-58); 24 I.L.R. 542 (1957).

82. Ibid., Point 5(b).

83. 333 U.N.T.S. 3. Such decisions include the decision of the Kammergericht (West Berlin Court of Appeals), 2 July 1965, 16 R.z.W.440 (1965), and of the German Federal Court, 2 October 1963, 15 R.z.W. 34 (1964), 28 Z.a.ö.R.V. 76, No. 47 (1968). For further such waiver cases, see German Federal Court, 14 December 1955, 17 Z.a.ö.R.V. 312 (1956-57), German Federal Court, 21 June 1955, 17 Z.a.ö.R.V. 323.

84. Federal Court, 22 June 1960, 11 R.z.W. 553 (1960), 28 Z.a.ö.R.V. 98, No. 200 (1968).

85. Obiter Kammergericht (West Berlin Court of Appeals), 1 February 1965, Entscheidungen der Oberlandesgerichte in Zivilsachen (hereafter O.L.G.Z.) 207 (1965), 29 Z.a.ö.R.V. 110-11, No. 126 (1968).

86. 16 R.z.W. 440 (1965), 28 Z.a.ö.R.V. 83, No. 65 (1968). Contrast the Austrian interpretation (in Chapter 2) of an identical provision in Art. 23 § 3 of the Austrian State Treaty.

87. On this law see Blocq, Aperçue de la législation allemande sur la péréquation des charges et de ses incidences sur les étrangers et leurs biens (1966).

88. Art. 2 § 1 of Wehrpflichtgesetz as consolidated by the Law of 28 September 1969, [1969] BGBl. I 1773.

89. Hahnenfeld, Wehrpflichtgesetz, Art. 2, note 5 (looseleaf edition, 1969).

90. Ibid., Art. 50, note 5.

91. [1974] BGBl. II 7831.

92. Kimminich, "Kommentar zum Bonner Grundgesets," Bonner Kommentar, Art. 74, No. 4, note 51, at 20 (2nd ed., 1950).

93. 23 Z.a.ö.R.V. 258-59 (1963).

94. Federal Administrative Court, 30 September 1958. 7 BVerwG 231 (1958), 28 Z.a.ö.R.V. 130, No. 170 (1968).

95. Administrative Court of Appeals, Münster, 16 May 1961, 16 Entscheidungen der Oberverwaltungsgerichte Münster und Lüneburg 300-301 (1961), 28 Z.a.ö.R.V. 58, No. 13 (1968).

96. [1959] BGBl. II 998.

97. Federal Administrative Court, 30 September 1958, 7 BVerwG 331 (1958).

98. 13 Verwaltungsrechtsprechung 199-200, No. 58 (1960).

99. To the same effect Bavarian Constitutional Court, 25 October 1956, 72 DVBl. 57 (1957) and Federal Administrative Court, 27 February 1962; Buchholz, Sammel-und Nachschlagwerk des BVerwG. 402.20 §5, APVO No. 8 (1957), 28 Z.a.ö.R.V. 118, No. 142 (1968), and Federal Constitutional Court, 18 July 1973, 35 BVerfG 382; contrast Austrian Administrative Court 22 May 1963, as given in Chapter 2.

100. Münster Administrative Court of Appeals, 18 November 1965, 81 DVBl. 645-46 (1966), 28 Z.a.ö.R.V. 73, No. 40 (1968), and seven more cases.

101. Federal Administrative Court, 14 December 1972, 26 N.J.W. I 146 (1973). See Bleckmann, Staatsangehörigkeitserwerbkraft Vertrauensschutzes, 34 Z.a.ö.R.V. 320 (1974).

102. Federal Court, 4 April 1962, 13 R.z.W. 361 (1962), 29 Z.a.ö.R.V. 118, No. 141 (1968).

103. Bavarian Supreme Court Decision, 23 March 1964, Bay. ObLGSt. 127 (1964), 79 DVBl. 588 (1964), 28 Z.a.ö.R.V. 59, No. 14, and 130, No. 170 (1968). For a different opinion see Klottschen, Die Rechtsstellung des politisch verfolgten Fremden nach deutschem Recht 69-70 (thesis, Cologne, 1965).

104. 18 BVerfG 112-21, 28 Z.a.ö.R.V. 134, No. 180 (1968).

105. Münster Administrative Court of Appeals, 1 October 1968, 20 Verwaltungsrechtsprechung 98, at 232 (1969), 31 Z.a.ö.R.V. 323 (1971). See Buschbeck, Verschleierte Auslieferung durch Ausweisung (1973).

106. 57 Am. J. Int'l. Law 410 (1963).

107. 18 Z.a.ö.R.V. 713-16 (1957-58).

108. According to information I received from the German Federal Ministry of Defense, there were two such cases, one in 1968 and the other in 1970.

109. Federal Court, 13 February 1963, 14 R.z.W. 368 (1963).

110. 23 Z.a.ö.R.V. 248 (1963), 345 U.N.T.S. 92.

111. 448 U.N.T.S. 227, 24 Z.a.ö.R.V. 675-76 (1964).

112. [1965] BGBl. I 189, 448 U.N.T.S. 227. See also 16 UN Rep. Int'l Arb. Awards 1 (1969).

113. 6 J.Z. 444 (1951), 89 Clunet 373 ff. (1954).

114. 14 N.J.W. 225 (1961), 28 Z.a.ö.R.V. 54, No. 6 (1968).

115. 9 Archiv des Völkerrechts 318 ff. (1961-62), 28 I.L.R. 16 (1963), Seidl-Hohenveldern, 5 A.W.D. 272 ff (1959).

116. Landesgericht Hamburg, 22 January 1973, 12 International Legal Materials 251 (1973); 19 A.W.D. 163 (1973), Rabelszeitschrift 578 (1973); and Obiter-LG Hamburg, 13 March 1974, 20 A.W.D. (1974); 13 International Legal Materials 1115 (1974). See Seidl-Hohenveldern, "Chilean Copper Nationalization Cases before German Courts," 69 Am. J. Int'l. Law 110-19 (1975).

117. 22 BGHSt. 309 (1968), 31 Z.a.ö.R.V. 304, No. 55 (1971).

118. Federal Constitutional Court, 7 July 1967, 22 BVerfG 134, at 152 (1967), 5 C.M.L.R. 302 (1967), and Federal Constitutional Court, 29 May 1974, 27 N.J.W. II 1967 (1974), leading to a protest by the Commission of the European Communities in Kommission der Europäischen Gemeinschaften, 8 Gesamtbericht über die Tätigkeit der Gemeinschaften 306, No. 465 (1974). Federal Constitutional Court, 18 October 1967, 22 BVerfG 293 (1967), 5 Comm. Mkt. L.R. 483 ff. (1967), Federal Constitutional Court, 9 June 1971. 31 BVerfG 145 (1971).

119. Court of the European Communities, 17 December 1970, Case 11/70, 16 Slg. GL.EG 1125 (1970). See Seidl-Hohenveldern, "Britain's Entry into the Common Market," 25 Current Legal Problems 28 (1972).

120. Klein, "Legal Problems of German Participation in the Establishment of Military Forces of the UN," 34 Z.a.ö.R.V. 450 (1974).

121. See von Schenk, "Das Problem der Beteiligung der Bundesrepublik Deutschland an Sanktionen der Vereinten Nationen besonders im Falle Rhodesien," in 29 Z.a.ö.R.V. 257 (1969).

122. German [1969] BGBl. I 193, amending the FRG ordinance on trade abroad of 28 April 1961, German [1961] BGBl. I 481.

123. German [1961] BGBl. I 481. In the version of the law of 28 October 1964, [1964] BGBl. I 821.

124. Ipsen, Aussenwirtschaft und Aussenpolitik, Rechtsgutachten zum Rhodesian-Embargo 65 (Cologne 1967).

125. Aussenwirtschaftsgesetz und zwischenstaatliche Vereinbarungen 135 (Göttingen 1970).

126. Frankfurter Allgemeine Zeitung, February 1972.

127. German Federal Court, 22 June 1972, 59 BGHZ 83 (1972). See Bleckmann, "Voidness of a Private Contract Because of Breach of the International Ordre Public," 34 Z.a.ö.R.V. 132 (1974).

128. See German Federal Court, 25 February 1960, 32 BGHZ 76, 88 (1960), and several other cases, quoted in 28 Z.a.ö.R.V. 77, No. 51 (1968).

129. Habscheid, Schaumann and Habscheid, "Die Immunität ausländischer Staaten nach Völkerrecht und deutschem Zivilprozessrecht," 8 Berichte der Deutschen Gesellschaft für Völkerrecht 179-80 (1968).

130. To this effect Darmstadt Court of Appeals, 20 December 1926, 56 Juristische Wochenschrift 2324 III (1927); Ann. Dig. 323 (1925-26).

131. 20 Z.a.ö.R.V. 684 (1959-60).

132. [1941] RGBl. 654.

133. Federal Court, 9 May 1956, 20 BGHZ 323 (1956), and Federal Administrative Court, 19 December 1957, 6 BVerwG 86-94.

134. Bavarian Constitutional Court, 4 April 1955, 71 DVBl. 763-64 (1956).

135. Kammergericht (West Berlin Court of Appeals), 18 March 1957, 10 N.J.W. I 1406 (1957).

136. Decision of 4 February 1953, Die deutsche Rechtsprechung auf dem Gebiete des internationalen Privatrechts 501 (1952-53) and of 27 May 1953, ibid., at 484, 20 Z.a.ö.R.V. 200-201, Nos. 30, 30A (1959-60).

137. Federal Court, 1 October 1956, 9 N.J.W. 1836 (1956), 23 I.L.R. 379 ff. (1956), Federal Court, 10 May 1954, 13 BGHZ 241 (1954), 21 I.L.R. 208-209 (1954), 20 Z.a.ö.R.V. 200, No. 28 (1959).

138. 18 Betriebsberater 37 (1963), 28 Z.a.ö.R.V. 99, No. 103 (1968).

139. Decision of 17 December 1963, 17 N.J.W. 650 (1964), 28 Z.a.ö.R.V. 85, No. 68 (1968).

140. Federal Court, 28 October 1954, 7 BGHSt 53 (1954), and 17 February 1960, 5 Recht in Ost und West 211 (1961), 20 Z.a.ö.R.V. 85, No. 68 (1968).

141. Federal Court, 18 December 1959, 31 BGHZ 374 (1959), 28 I.L.R. 82-88 (1963), and Federal Court, 19 December 1960, 24 BGHZ 91 (1960), 28 Z.a.ö.R.V. 85, No. 67 (1968).

142. Reichsgericht, 10 May 1921, 56 Entscheidungen des Reichsgerichts in Strafsachen (hereafter RGst.) 6 (1921), Fontes Juris Gentium A.2, 1. No. 224.

143. Reichsgericht, 29 June 1920, 55 RGSt. 82 (1920), Fontes Juris Gentium A.2, 1, No. 202.

144. 28 Z.a.ö.R.V. 79, Nos. 55, 56 (1968), Slovakia: BVerwG 30 April 1959, 10 R.z.W. 421-22 (1959), Neustadt Court of Appeals, 20 March 1964, 15 R.z.W. 446-47 (1964), Neustadt Court of Appeals, 6 November 1964, 16 R.z.W. 218 (1965), Kammergericht, 24 March 1964, 15 R.z.W. 296 (1964). Croatia: Kammergericht, 25 October 1965, 17 R.z.W. 58 (1966), Koblenz Court of Appeals, 17 November 1965, 17 R.z.W. 268 (1966).

145. Federal Court, 23 October 1963, 15 R.z.W. 130 (1964), 28 Z.a.ö.R.V. 85, No. 69 (1968).

146. OGHZ 2.1, Fontes Juris Gentium A II 3; Deutsche höchstrichterliche Rechtsprechung in Völkerrechtlichen Fragen, 1945-49 85, at 198.

147. 273 U.N.T.S. 3, [1956] BGBl. II 487.

148. Federal Court, 19 December 1957, 26 BGHZ 202 (1957).

149. Decision of 3 April 1956, 9 N.J.W. 1358 (1956).

150. For an opposing opinion see Seidl-Hohenveldern, "Die Verstaatlichung von Kupferbergbaubetrieben in Chile," 20 Aussenwirtschaftsdienst 428 (1974).

151. An opposing opinion is found in Seidl-Hohenveldern, "Chilean Copper Nationalization Cases," op. cit., at 117-18.

152. Time (Europe), 21 April 1975, at 9.

153. Wengler, Völkerrechtliche Zulässigkeit der Anwendung des geplanten Mitbestimmungsgesetzes auf amerikanische Beteiligungen in der Bundesrepublik Deutschland, Eine Untersuchung im Auftrag der American Chamber of Commerce in Germany (Frankfurt 1974).

154. 21 BVerfG 207 (1967).

155. Mann, "The U.S. Treaty of Commerce with Germany and the German Constitution," 65 Am. J. Int'l. L. 793 (1971).

156. [1973] BGBl. I 1533 1569.

157. See Eisen, "Convention Européenne des Droits de l'Homme et Pacte des Nations Unies relatif aux droits civils et politiques: problèmes de coëxistence," 30 Z.a.ö.R.V. 239 (1970). The differences between these conventions are explained by de Meyer, La Convention Européenne des Droits de l'Homme et le Pacte international relatif aux droits civils et politiques (Heule, Belgique, 1969).

158. 295 U.N.T.S. 23.

159. 24 N.J.W. II 2122 (1971) commented on by Seidl-Hohenveldern, The Austrian-German Arbitral Tribunal, op. cit., at 103-04.

CHAPTER

10

FRANCE

Prosper Weil

THE INDIVIDUAL

The Individual as a National

Movement

The liberty of every French citizen to go abroad has only rarely been studied. Works dealing with what are called "public freedoms" in France generally only devote a few pages to this subject,[1] if in fact they mention it at all.[2] Those who teach international or administrative law or "public freedoms" in the universities seem equally unconcerned about the problem. The reason for this apparent lack of interest is clear: the freedom of every French citizen to enter and leave the country is so well established that no discussion of the matter is necessary.

However, this does not mean that all restrictions on this freedom have been abolished. It must be stressed, however, that such restrictions as do exist are purely marginal and are applied only in exceptional cases that have no real importance, quantitatively or qualitatively.

Passports. Astonishing as this may seem in a country in which regulations of all types abound, French legislation concerning passports draws essentially on a few archaic provisions dating from the revolutionary epoch. The provision actually in force is found in a decree of 26 February 1793 that states, as follows:

This chapter was reviewed by the author in late 1975, and no changes were deemed necessary.

> The national assembly, considering that it is extremely important to set out terms so that they may be understood by the appropriate authorities, so that they may arrest and punish violators traveling around the Republic inciting others to break laws, and to put a stop, insofar as possible, to all criminal activities encouraged by enemies abroad, decrees that the decrees of 1 February-28 March, 28-29 July and 7 December 1792 relating to passports will remain in force until otherwise notified.

The decrees referred to provided that everyone wishing to go abroad must have a passport. The 1 February 1792 decree extended this obligation even to those who were traveling around within France.

The obligation to have a passport for foreign travel was set aside from the time of the First Empire, that is to say, in the first years of the nineteenth century, and was not reinforced until 1871, after which time it rapidly fell into disuse. The provisions were only reestablished at the time of World War I, still on the basis of the 1793 decree.

A certain amount of updating has been done to determine what authority should deal with the issuing of passports, but the 1793 text remains the juridical basis.

Thus one must turn to law and practice to seek the outer limits of the powers of the administration, insofar as the issuing of passports is concerned, as well as the extent of judicial control in this area. In the last two centuries the courts have dealt with cases involving the refusal of a passport perhaps half a dozen times, which shows how rare such cases are.[3] However, there are certain regulations governing the issuance of passports.

1. The issuance or renewal of a passport cannot be considered as a right in the strict sense. The administrative authority may refuse to issue or prolong a passport to a French national if it has reason to believe that it would not be in the interests of state security to do so. For the same sort of reason, the administrative authority may specifically except certain countries from the passport and limit the travel time allowed. The reasons for this decision are obvious.

2. Once refused, the interested party may find a remedy before the administrative courts on the grounds of "abuse of powers," in which case the refusal will be set aside if the decision was taken by a body other than the one so competent or if the prescribed formalities have not been complied with. Nevertheless, the judge is likely to require stricter compliance than the administration; however

little the administration has used the excuse of national safety, so long as the facts leading to the decision really existed, there would be no effective control over the decision, an appreciation of which tends to indicate that the administrative authority could not be brought before a judge for excess of powers.

The appreciation of the dangers or otherwise of allowing a French citizen to go abroad becomes a question of pure chance, with which it is not the judge's province to interfere. The article in the Universal Declaration of the Rights of Man according to which "every person has the right to leave any country including his own, and the right to return to his own country"[4] cannot curb the powers of the administration in this case, since the said declaration, although published in the French Official Journal, does not have the status of a treaty or international agreement duly ratified or approved, which would give it an authority over and above French national laws.

The recent case of Fouéré is an interesting example of this principle. The administration refused to renew the passport of an industrialist who had a large crustacean factory in Ireland, and the administrative court of Rennes rejected the industrialist's appeal against this decision. The Minister of the Interior raised the question of Fouéré's activities as a ringleader in the Breton autonomy movement, especially his involvement in its underground fight for freedom, which contributed largely to the tribunal's decision not to set aside the administration's refusal to renew Fouéré's passport. The plaintiff's argument was that the refusal interfered with his rights of freedom of thought and freedom of movement, but the tribunal concluded that these liberties could not stand in the way of a valid exercise of the duty of the administrative authority to protect national security.[5]

In law, as we have just seen, only questions of national security can be a valid ground for the refusal to grant a passport. However, in practice other considerations sometimes interfere.

On occasion, the Ministry of the Interior will at the bidding of the Finance Minister, refuse to grant a passport to anyone who owes the state a large amount of money. Parents may ask that a passport not be granted to their children if they are minors, this being especially applicable in the case of a divorced person who has custody of a minor. Passports may also be refused to drug traffickers. Again, the French, by agreement with the government of Ruanda, decided not to grant passports to French mercenaries from Katanga who had taken refuge in Ruanda (this being a precondition for the Ruandan decision not to hand the mercenaries over to the Congolese but to return them to France). However, the importance of these exceptions should not be overemphasized; they give rise to perhaps ten cases of refusal a year. No legal precedent seems to have been framed from these cases.

The limited case of refusal of a passport for which provision is made in the penal code of 1960 should be cited. This concerns those who are convicted of white slave trading. The sentence may include the removal of the passport and also the driver's license of the individual for a maximum period of three years.[6]

Finally, by a law of 17 July 1970, the trial court judge may enjoin certain accused to hand their passports over to the registry or the police.

The refusal of a passport in both law and practice is exceptional in France. However, the problem of French citizens abroad cannot be fully understood by discussing the passport question alone, since it is becoming less and less important as evidence of freedom to leave.

Departure. A French citizen furnished with a passport may not in principle be stopped from leaving France, since the exit visa no longer exists.

By virtue of international conventions, many countries are readily accessible to a French person, either by a passport valid for five years or by a single identification card. The granting of an identification card is the inalienable right of every French citizen, and the administration cannot issue it with the proviso that it must not be used for foreign travel, any more than the administration can take away the identity card. All countries bordering on France, as well as all European countries other than Eastern Europe, have the same arrangement; thus one can see how easy it is for the French to go abroad. For example, Fouéré, whose passport had been refused, as seen above, could easily go to Ireland using his national identity card, without anyone being able to stop him. One may usefully add, at this point, some observations on what is being done within the European Economic Community to facilitate the free movement of people among its member states.

A French citizen who owes a large amount of money or a ward of court may be stopped at the frontier, by means of long practice that has virtually acquired the force of law. However, this is very rarely applied. A person under warrant for arrest may legally be stopped at the frontier. In fact, however, the controls exercised at the frontiers are extremely lax, partly because of the increase and rapidity of travel, thereby rendering any such arrests very rare.

The administration no longer has the means to distinguish between temporary and permanent departure.

The law of 17 July 1970, which reinforces the guarantee of citizens' individual rights, allows the trial judge, among the other measures he may take if the accused runs the risk of a term of imprisonment, to prohibit the person concerned from moving away from a certain place or enjoin that person to hand over to the registry or police all "legal identity documents especially his passport in return for a receipt which may serve as valid identification."[7] An accused person may therefore be deprived of the right to leave France for all or part of the time in which he or she is being proceeded against.

Return. Although it is not spelled out in any legal document, every French citizen has an absolute right to return to France. Moreover, there have never been any problems in this respect, French practice showing a marked liberalism on this matter. A directive issued by the European Economic Community on 25 February 1964, calling upon all member states to take back their own nationals has never been difficult for France to follow. In fact, in the late 1960s and early 1970s, the French authorities had to deal with the application of this directive by the British government, in order to put an end to the problems caused by the British Commonwealth nationals who, having passed through France, are then not allowed into Britain.

Administrative agreements have been made by France with Benelux, West Germany, Switzerland, and Austria by which each country agrees to accept its own nationals even when their nationality is open to question.

Needless to say, the right of every French citizen to return to France applies equally to those coming from French possessions overseas. This leads to some Cameroonians being allowed to return to Cameroon despite the certainty of the French authorities that they would engage in seditious activities as soon as possible thereafter.

Those who have left France in an irregular manner, such as deserters or minors in flight, may have their passports removed by the consular authorities, but they will always be given documents allowing them to return to France.

Exile. It is absolutely unheard of for a French citizen to be exiled, in either law or administrative practice in France.

It may be noted that during the Algerian war, and by virtue of special rules, the administration could regulate the arrival, departure, or stay, in all or part of the territory of Algeria, of any person, even a Frenchman, and could prohibit the arrival or stay of those whose presence was likely to hinder the exercise of those in power in any way whatsoever.[8] As a result some French citizens were not allowed to enter or return to Algeria or were expelled therefrom. These provisions, which covered people's rights to enter or stay in provinces of Algeria, did not act to limit their right to stay in any other part of France but in fact were extraordinary measures to limit travel within France, rather than measures to limit travel abroad or restrict people coming from abroad. The administrative tribunal was called upon many times to rule on the legality of the measures so taken.[9]

Protection

Extent of Freedom of Activity Abroad. With the exception of regulations concerning economic matters, especially the control of foreign exchange, French authorities have no powers to regulate, limit, or control the activities of French nationals abroad. Registration with a French consulate does have certain advantages, since the consulate can issue passports, establish proxy, and participate in the choice of members of the French Superior Council abroad, but these advantages are purely administrative and give the consular authorities no right to curb the activities of French nationals, especially on the economic plane.

Contrary to traditional legal practice, in 1963 the State Criminal Court condemned Colonel Antoine Argoud, who had been brought back from West Germany in a somewhat mysterious manner, together with his aide Curutchet, who had been arrested on his way to Uruguay while bearing normal French papers by the Senegalese, who handed him over to the French. These two were being sought for having participated in the Algerian insurrection against the policies of General de Gaulle in Algeria. The position taken by the French judiciary in this case has been criticized.[10]

The regulations governing French investment abroad are too complex to be studied in detail here. The details vary depending on the economic and financial situation and especially the exchange control position. Let us say simply that, by virtue of a decree of 27 January 1967, direct investments by French citizens were subjected to a statement giving the Minister of Finance the right to oppose them within two months. However, by a decree of 22 February 1971, all countries forming part of the European Economic Community are exempt from these provisions except insofar as their own exchange controls operate.

The Right to Diplomatic Protection: Waiver. When a French national is subjected to pressures abroad that the French government considers illegal or arbitrary, the French authorities normally intervene on behalf of the national. The forcefulness of the intervention varies according to the case in point. Consular protection is hardly ever withheld; for example, in case of arrest the French consul always tries to visit the accused and find out whether the conditions of arrest and detention are in conformity with legal and humanitarian principles.

As for diplomatic protection properly so called, this is more rare and is subject to varied manifestations. In most cases the French authorities are called upon only if the national interest is in some way at stake; these efforts, which are not of a formal diplomatic nature and are made before local remedies have been exhausted, are intended to satisfy the foreign government without bringing in the concept of diplomatic protection in the strict sense. There are innumerable examples of these interventions, but I will limit myself to a discussion of the arrest of a French diplomatic agent by the Algerian authorities on 6 November 1970. This agent was subsequently released on 19 November as a result of great pressure from the French government.[11]

As for diplomatic protection in the technical sense of the term, which may go so far as the international courts, it is used but rarely and only as a result of a variety of factors, the importance of which only the government can gauge. The agreements on petroleum between France and Algeria, especially when the French oil companies were nationalized on 24 February 1971, caused several shifts in the attitude of the French government, so much so that the companies resorted to negotiating in their private capacities with the Algerian government, whereas at other times the government had taken the main role.[12]

Therefore it is hardly surprising that the French often complain that their government does not give them any protection, either because intervention is not in its favor or because it fails to intervene until too late, or that the intervention is too half-hearted or stops short of the desired objective. The principles followed by France in this connection are very clear.

1. It must be in conformity with international law. It is recognized that diplomatic protection extends only to relations among states and that individuals have no right to interfere.[13] It is also recognized that it forms part of the discretionary powers of a government, as illustrated by a bulletin from the judiciary to the Minister for Foreign Affairs on 11 July 1938, which stated as follows:

> A State alone is the judge . . . to the point of knowing if and in what manner it may extend its protection to a national. This latter cannot bring the State to account before a tribunal even where he feels his right to protection should have been exercised and was not.[14]

The right of a government to give or not to give its protection is not contested. The individual has no right to demand it.

2. The position of the French authorities relative to diplomatic protection amounts to an Act of State in the same way as all other national actions taken by France, and as such is not subject to any reviews favorable or otherwise.[15]

The combination of these two principles leads to a lack of jurisdictional control over measures taken for the representation, defense, or protection of French citizens or French interests abroad with regard to foreign authorities. It especially leads to refusal, default, insufficiency, lateness, or withdrawal of diplomatic and consular protection of French interests. Jurisprudence on this point is abundant; it suffices to outline a few examples. For instance, the Council of State decided as follows, on the question of the protection of a French woman's property after the Agadir earthquake:

> The accomplishment of the mission of protection of the goods of French citizens which is incumbent on the French diplomatic or consular services abroad was, in the circumstances, time and place where the damage occurred, inseparable from the exercise of powers of the French government in its international relations. . . . In those conditions, the request raised a question which, by directly involving relations between France and a foreign state, was not justiciable by its very nature before the administrative courts.[16]

An identical refusal was overruled by the Haute Assemblé on the question of a society that complained of the insufficiency of the support it was given by the French authorities vis-à-vis the Vietnamese authorities.[17] In an analogous position the Council of State refused to recognize any decision admitting that there had been insufficient protection of French nationals in Egypt in the aftermath of Suez in 1956.

> If Mr. L. brings up the insufficiency of the measures of protection taken on behalf of French nationals in Egypt, the question to be answered is, always supposing this insufficiency is established, was it of such a nature as to necessarily implicate the responsibility of the public power which leads to an appraisal of the relations between France and a foreign

> state; such a question is outside the ambit of the administrative courts, so no conclusions may be reached.[18]

To these cases there may be added those in which the Council of State refuses to act on the complaints of individuals who complain that the French government has not sufficiently protected their interests or granted them protection in the courts of international negotiation. For instance, when the Geneva Accords of 20 May 1954 put an end to the Indochinese war; a group complained that the accords did not adequately protect their interests. In answer to this the Council of State replied that it was a question of "a problem which by its nature was not justiciable by the courts."[19] The Zurich Accords of 22 August 1958 between France and the United Arab Republic gave rise to similar complaints, to which the Council of State replied that "the alleged inadequacy of the terms of the Accords could not be laid at the door of the French State."[20] Finally, concerning the Evian Accords of 1962, which put an end to the Algerian War and established Algerian independence, the Council of State, dealing with a request for indemnity from the French State based on "the actions of the French authorities who brought about, negotiated and countersigned the Evian Accords," decided that "the negotiations and the decisions which formed the basis of the wrong complained of were not severable from the action taken by the French government when a new state gained independence" and that the question therefore was one with which the courts could not deal.[21]

Apart from cases in which the French government has agreements with other countries relating to indemnification, French citizens who suffer losses abroad have virtually no means of recouping their losses from the government by obtaining a favorable finding in the French courts.[22] This is (1) because in traditional international law, actions taken by a foreign power do not automatically involve the French state; (2) because the inadequacy of protection granted by the French authorities either in proceedings with a foreign government or in the course of negotiating treaties with the said government may not be questioned before the courts; and (3) because treaties once concluded are in case of doubt interpreted by the French government, and that interpretation does not generally favor the plaintiff. For instance, when the question of interpretation was referred to it by the Council of State, the government decided that the 1962 Evian Accords did not include any disposition allowing French people living in Algeria to recoup their losses from the French government.[23]

One may always point to certain recent decisions that have made the French state responsible to French people who have been victims of acts of foreign powers. These decisions are not based on the absence of protection by French diplomatic or consular authorities but on the principle of responsibility without fault. In the Perruche decision of 19 October 1962, this principle was established by the decision that an order given to the French consul to stay at his post in Seoul after the departure of the South Korean authorities put him "in an exceptionally dangerous situation regarding both his person and his property" and further that he had a right to compensation on the principle of equality of citizens with public offices. Another recent decision applied this reasoning to the case of French supporters in Laos, who stayed there during the 1960 troubles, effectively at the request of the French authorities. "Because of the legal liens which existed between them and the state, the Martins found themselves obliged to stay at their posts; taking into consideration the seriousness of the situation in Vientiane at that time, this involved them in great personal risk of a type which entitles them to compensation."[24] The difficulty of protecting French supporters abroad has its own particular problems, and in fact the French government goes out of its way to put special clauses into conventions concluded with other states giving supporters the same immunities accorded to United Nations assistance personnel.[25]

However, this remains a very limited category of jurisprudence. It doubtless allows reparations to be made where there has been insufficient protection of French nationals or business interests abroad, but for the moment it is restricted to French government officials in service abroad who are exposed to exceptional risks in the exercise of their duties by reason of the juridical links uniting them with France.

The State and Compensation. When the French government receives insufficient compensation from a foreign government for losses suffered by a French national, it is under no obligation to make up the difference, and the national may not so argue on the grounds of state responsibility. The law cited above shows clearly that, on the one hand, there can be no litigation on the way the French government conducts its foreign relations and, on the other, that there is no obligation on the part of the French government to compensate its nationals for losses incurred overseas. Following nationalization in Eastern Europe after World War II, the treaties with Poland (12 March 1948), Czechoslovakia (2 June 1950, Hungary (12 June 1950), and Yugoslavia (14 April 1951) that awarded the French government only partial compensation, there was no question of any responsibility of the French state to make up the amounts so received. Total reparations also were not provided for in the Zurich Accords between France and the United Arab Republic in 1958, and the French government could not be held accountable for the losses suffered by the French in Algeria. In other words, the French government is free to negotiate with foreign states in a way that best protects its own interests and openings, and the people affected can neither claim complete compensation nor claim the balance from the government because of the way in which the negotiations were conducted.

The question of whether the state is under a legal obligation to hand over the compensation received by it from the foreign government to those who have suffered the loss is controversial. In the first place, the reasoning is that diplomatic protection is purely a matter of relations among states, the individual having no standing in this matter. The attitude of the French government in this respect is considered as intimately tied to its international actions, brooking no interference by the courts because of the "Act of State" doctrine. Following the Baden-Baden agreements by which Germany agreed to pay compensation to France for all people from Alsace-Lorraine who had been arrested, interned, or banished for their political beliefs in the 1914 war, even the commission set up to distribute this money was not subject to the jurisdiction of the courts because of the international character of the governing agreement.[26]

Over the last 20 years the law on this question has been becoming more tractable. When the amount of the reparations for nationalization of interests in the Eastern Bloc was too low, in effect the Council of State calculated what could be divorced from French international actions and counted as an individual's own enterprise, and the commission appointed to deal with the matter acted accordingly.[27] The same solution applied to the compensation paid in 1960 by Germany to France on behalf of French nationals who had been subjected to National-Socialist harassment.[28] The rights of individuals were safeguarded in relation to the French government where global reparations were concerned. The question of whether an individual would have the same recourse if compensation were received by the French government from a foreign state because of that individual's personal losses does not seem to have arisen before a court and appears to be hypothetical.

In certain cases special legislation is drawn up to remedy the undesirable effects of the principles outlined above. The most outstanding example is the law of 15 July 1970, passed after eight years of hesitation, unfulfilled promises, and juridical controversy, which provides for "a national contribution to compensate French people whose property is in a territory once under the sovereignty, protection or trusteeship of France." The content, which is mainly of interest to French citizens who were victims of expropriation measures in Algeria following its independence, has been extended to provide for complete compensation. The government stated very precisely during the debates in the National Assembly that the French government did not accept any responsibility for the measures taken and had no intention of standing in for the state of Algeria. It was only a question of an "act of solidarity" among Frenchmen, of a "national contribution," which even in legal terms has the appurtenances of "an advance on credit held by foreign states."[29] The law adds that "before January 1, 1972, the government will account to the parliamentary commissions on foreign affairs for negotiations undertaken with expropriating states with the aim of getting compensation."[30] This clause, which has, needless to say, remained a dead letter, is significant in that it excludes reparations properly so called in favor of terms such as "contribution" or "advance." The sum total of this "contribution" represents only about 14 percent of the value of the property lost, which as may be imagined, has caused those involved to be critical.[31]

The Responsibility of the State for Injury Induced by Its Own Conduct. As we have seen, the French state does not hold itself responsible for the possible consequences to its nationals of measures taken by it to further its international relations. The question was raised before the Council of State after the Suez crisis of 1956. A French national had asked for state compensation for injury suffered as a result of the Anglo-French action of 1956, which in turn had led the Egyptian government to confiscate his property in Egypt, the Council of State decided that in the absence of any clear legal text to the contrary the French state could not be held liable for such loss. Furthermore, the inadequacy of the compensation agreed to in the Zurich Accord did not imply any state responsibility to compensate or to augment the reparations.[32] In other words, in the absence of an express provision to the contrary, the French must put up no compensation for losses caused by French foreign policy.

The Individual as an Alien

Movement

Entry and Stay. As noted in the questionnaire, in this matter the regulations are extremely complex, and there can be no possibility of dealing with them in detail. However, certain observations may be made.

In principle foreigners are allowed to enter France, provided that they are carrying valid passports stamped with entry visas. These visas are varied in form: travel visas for a stay of less than three months (transit or "short stay"), or long-term visas for longer periods. The administration has a discretionary power to issue visas. For example, in the late 1960s, Mrs. Leopold Trepper was refused a visa; according to the press, this refusal was not because the government had anything personal against Mrs. Trepper, who had been to France some time before, but only in the then current campaign to procure permission for her husband to leave Poland. Trepper had had an expulsion order served on him in 1967, and since that time his presence in France had not been considered desirable.[33]

There is a growing number of exceptions to the principle that everyone seeking to enter France must have a valid entry visa. The European Agreement of 13 December 1957 dispensed with the requirement on behalf of all the member countries of the Council of Europe. Measures have also been taken by the French government to enable nationals of the European Economic Community to enter and stay more easily.[34] To these must be added (1) bilateral and international conventions; (2) transit agreements, which have been concluded with some degree of success with countries in Western Europe, dispensing with visas if the stay proposed is less than three months (that is to say, the exemption covers tourists and businessmen); (3) special travel agreements concluded with certain of the African countries in an attempt to limit the influx of workers who were entering under the guise of tourism; (4) agreements reached on employment and labor with some countries whose nationals wish to come to work in France; and (5) agreements to allow residence, which have been concluded with many European and African countries. These conventions mainly limit the entry of foreign labor, either seasonally or permanently. There are, as may be imagined, problems in dealing with their application.

The relatively open regulations governing the entry of foreigners into France sometimes lead to unexpected consequences. For instance, in response to a question raised in Parliament about why a Brazilian policeman had been allowed to visit France when he had come with the avowed purpose of checking up on Brazilian refugees in France and had used his normal passport instead of being required to apply for a visa, the Ministry of Foreign Affairs replied that the French authorities had no legal means of refusing to allow the policeman to enter France.[35]

This reply is the more surprising because on other occasions the government has not been slow to state that it has a discretionary power to exclude all foreigners whose presence on French soil is considered undesirable.[36] A large body of law from the Council of State backs up the wide powers of the administration in this respect. For instance, on the question of whether an Italian national could enter France without a visa, the Council of State held that "this circumstance is no obstacle to the administration's police-type powers, with which it controls the entry, travel and stay of foreigners, in the interests of national security, by which they could refuse to let the Italian enter France.[37] Bernadette Devlin was sent back to London on 14 March 1972 for having attended a public meeting on "the Irish resistance movement." English trade unionists were not allowed to disembark in Calais on 16 April 1972 when they arrived to join French trade unionists in a protest against the Common Market.[38]

In theory the procedure of refusing and returning people should be distinguished from expulsion. Refusal and return covers foreigners who have not entered France legally and covers only a refusal to allow regular entry, while expulsion refers to persons who have entered France legally but who are guilty of matters other than those pertaining to their entry. In practice this distinction is sometimes blurred, since there are fewer formalities to be observed in refusal and return than in expulsion, and therefore there is a tendency to use the former.

The powers of the administration in this respect should not be overestimated, but they are rarely used, and in practice France has a very liberal attitude with regard to entry by foreigners.

This liberalism is manifested by the growing and already large procedure of regularization. Foreign workers wishing to immigrate have less and less respect for the legalities. They come into the country in clandestine fashion and then ask that their presence be regularized. The statistics published by the National Immigration Office reveal that two-thirds of the foreign workers in France have used this means of entry.

Voluntary Departure. In order to leave France, a foreigner theoretically must have an exit visa. If the foreigner has any intention of returning to France, he or she should have an exit-entry visa. However, this now only applies in very rare cases. The exit visa, like the entry visa, is hardly ever required. The foreigner may leave freely and return, provided that the allotted time in France has not expired. Sometimes absence from France may not exceed a certain time unless special permission has been obtained from the administrative authorities. For instance, Algerian nationals leaving France without permission for more than six months are treated as new immigrants on their return. However, the principle has not proved easy to apply in practice.

It goes without saying that a foreigner may be refused the right to cross the border if there is a warrant for his arrest or if he owes the state a large amount of money. Here the law and practice is the same as that applicable to French nationals.

The principle is that "foreigners are free to travel and stay in France,"[39] subject only to the production on request of documents showing that the stay is authorized. However, the liberality of this principle is hampered by some restrictions. Special permission is required if the foreigner wishes to establish residence in the frontier district of the Maritime Alps. The administration may refuse to allow a foreigner to travel or stay in certain areas or limit the stay to one area.[40]

Such measures, over which the courts have minimal control, are rarely invoked.[41]

When Leonid Brezhnev visited France in October 1971, the administration "invited" a certain number of aliens, originally from Central and Eastern Europe, to spend the time of his visit in Corsica. These measures of separation had been effected before for the visits to France of Marshal Tito and Nikita Khrushchev, but they were obviously illegal and gave rise to severe criticism.[42] However, those involved appear to have made no complaint to the court.

Involuntary Departure: Expulsion and Deportation. Expulsion of foreigners[43] is a very emotional issue in France and often gives rise to tirades in the press. However, the number of expulsions is minimal. In 1969, for example, out of a foreign population estimated at about 3.2 million people, the expulsion rate was less than .09 percent. According to the figures given to François Mitterand by the government, 2,949 expulsion decrees were made in 1969, of which more than half concerned foreigners not resident in France who had performed some criminal act during their brief stay in France. Only 20 expulsion orders had been made under emergency procedures.[44] (See below.)

By the terms of the ordinance of 2 November 1945 an expulsion order can only be made "if the continued presence of the foreigner on French territory becomes a menace to public order." The order may only be made by the Minister of the Interior except in the frontier provinces, where the police chiefs are also competent. Eight days must elapse between the order and actual expulsion, to allow time for the foreigner to appeal before a commission presided over by the chief justice of the civil courts and give reason why the expulsion should not take place. The foreigner has the right to see his dossier, may speak in his or her own defense, and may have a lawyer's assistance. These rights are strictly observed "except in case of extreme emergency."[45]

The application of this ordinance has given rise to extensive litigation, especially following on the disturbances of May 1968, during which a state of extreme emergency was declared. However, taken as a whole, one may say that the Council of State, although recognizing a discretionary power on the part of the administrative authorities, is beginning to exercise tighter control over expulsion measures. Nevertheless, this control is feeble compared to the amount exercised in other measures taken by the administration. The following are examples of this increased control.

1. An expulsion order may be made against a foreigner temporarily out of France. This was decided in the case of Daniel Cohn-Bendit, who discovered that he had been expelled when, after a short visit abroad, he tried to re-enter France.[46]

2. The judge of the administrative court cannot ask the administration to suspend an expulsion decree.[47]

3. The judge of the administrative court regards a decision made by the minister of "danger to public order" as a result of a foreigner's presence in France as a matter of fact not reviewable by the court (established law).

It is on the question of procedural guarantees that the Council of State has made the biggest inroads into administrative discretion. It has held that these guarantees apply to all foreigners, including those who, like Algerians, stay in France by means of a simple identity card.[48] However, the most important decision has yet to be made. Having for a long time refused to commit itself about whether the declaration of "extreme emergency" allowed the government to dispense with all procedural guarantees, a fact that encouraged the administration to claim an emergency in every case, the court now decides in each individual case whether a state of emergency exists.[49] In a similar fashion, the Council of State is charged with the execution of the Franco-German convention of 27 October 1956, which provides that, in the absence of questions of state security that cause special powers to be invoked, nationals of either country who stay for more than a year in the other country may not be expelled without being given a chance to appeal against expulsion before the competent authorities. This was used to set aside an expulsion order against a German student in which these procedures had not been observed. The minister was not able to establish imperative reasons of state security necessitating the student's immediate expulsion.[50]

Criticisms and suggestions for the reform of the current laws and practice in this field are directed at procedure rather than form, especially procedures for independent review.

As pointed out, a foreigner is only heard before the commission if he or she so requests. Many foreigners are ignorant of their rights in this respect, and the general consensus of opinion is that the hearing should be automatic.

There has also been a suggestion that the commission, the composition of which could be better organized to safeguard the interests of aliens, should be given powers to make decisions, creating in effect an appeal mechanism.

Some have even gone so far as to advocate that no expulsion should be made before the government of the subject has been consulted. The West German government asked to be so consulted in 1968 concerning German students in France; this suggestion was somewhat indignantly received by the French government.[51] It is beyond argument that the expelling state has full powers in this respect that can only be limited by reciprocal international conventions.

While awaiting these not inconsiderable reforms, some easing of the situation could be brought about by strengthening jurisdictional control. As has been seen, the Council of State appears to be acting along those lines already, and one can only hope it will continue to do so.

Protection

From the information available, it is almost certain that the French government would act to protect foreigners serving in the French armed forces, especially the Foreign Legion. However, no such problems have arisen directly. Sometimes, officers and sergeants of the Foreign Legion have been given French passports to facilitate their travel (for example, during the time of French nuclear testing in the Pacific), which they have undertaken to give back on their return.

NATIONAL IMPLEMENTATION OF INTERNATIONAL RIGHTS AND DUTIES

The Act of State Doctrine

There is no equivalent in French law of the American Act of State doctrine. French legal rules on this point can be summed up as follows:

1. In certain cases, by application of principles of private international law (theory of conflict of laws), foreign legal rules are applied.

2. The foreign law that would be applicable by French conflict laws is always set aside if its terms are not in harmony with the French public order, that is to say with social or legal mores

that are too inherently different from French ones to be applied.[52] For example, it has been held that violent acts of dispossession, such as those resorted to by the National Socialists in Germany against non-Aryan citizens, cannot be upheld in French territory.[53] It was even decided that, as a matter of public policy, resale of furniture that had been expropriated by Spanish authorities without payment of compensation and then imported into France, would not be allowed.[54]

The most remarkable example is still the one furnished by Algerian measures of dispossession. After long controversy the Court of Cassation decided effectively, by statements of principle on 23 April 1969, that these measures, whatever they were called (nationalization, appropriation of empty property, and so on), were contrary to the concept of public order in France because they were not accompanied by a just and fair indemnity, and therefore could not be upheld in France. From there the highest court ensured the principle that the title to the goods had not validly passed to the Algerians either actively or passively and the people concerned were still liable for their debts.[55] Special legislative measures had to be taken to avoid a rash of creditors seizing goods of Algerian expatriates in France to recover debts incurred before Algerian independence.

3. Thus the application of foreign law and the legal effects of acts of foreign authorities in France is limited by the concept of French public order. It is unusual, indeed, almost accidental, that these judgments are in conflict with international law. Thus France refused to apply a Brazilian law conferring Brazilian nationality on all aliens present in Brazil at a given date because it would have been "a grave violation of public international law."[56] By the same token the Court of Cassation refused to give effect to rights created when Germany annexed Alsace in 1940, since this annexation had been made "in violation of human rights and against the armistice provisions of 23 June 1940."[57] A court of appeal refused to confirm a mayor put into office by the Germans, since the action was contrary to the terms of the armistice, as well as the Hague Convention of 1899.[58] A lower court refused to recognize Algerian expropriation measures as fraudulent and "against the French law understanding of international public order."[59]

Implementation of Decisions of International Organizations

Rhodesia

Although France abstained on the question of sanctions against Rhodesia because it questioned the efficacy of these measures,

France has strictly observed the decrees of the Security Council because it maintains that member states have an obligation to do so.

The enforcement of Resolution 232 (1966) was achieved by a notice to importers and exporters published in the Official Journal.[60] Further, an order dealing expressly with Articles 25, 39, and 41 of the UN Charter and Resolution 253 of 29 May 1968 put the general sanctions involved against Southern Rhodesia into effect. A note the same day overruled the previous notice.[61] By the terms of this order, which entered into force only 15 days after its publication, only medical, teaching, and public information materials (an order from the Minister of Economics and Finance listed about a hundred articles covered by this exemption) were exempted from a total ban on even indirectly importing goods from or exporting goods to Rhodesia. Some foodstuffs were also exempted. The French government told the Secretary-General of the United Nations that there was no means of transportation between France and Rhodesia.[62]

Namibia

On the question of Namibia, France has not hesitated to express its disapproval of the actions undertaken by the United Nations. She did not vote on Resolution 2145 (1966), proclaiming the end of the mandate; on Resolution 2248 (1967), creating a UN council for South-West Africa; on Resolution 2372 (1968), substituting the name "Namibia" for "South-West Africa"; nor on Resolution 276 (1970), calling on states to abstain from all relations with South Africa. France regards the resolutions of the Security Council in this regard as recommendatory only, and thereby not binding on member states. Thus no attempt has been made to give effect to any of these resolutions in French law. However, in order to comply with the wishes of many African states, France has instituted a limited embargo. Exporters of arms may not sell weapons to South Africa that could be used for civil strife, such as small arms, automatic rifles, helicopters, or low-flying aircraft, although exports of fighter planes and other armaments are still allowed.

Procedures Relating to the Issue of Certificates or Suggestions of the Executive in Connection with Litigation in National Courts

It is unknown in France for the executive to issue "certificates" during the course of judicial proceedings. The only role the authorities have to play before the national courts is in interpretation of international treaties.

It has become customary that administrative tribunals may not interpret international treaties, even though the decisions of such tribunals have the force of law and they normally interpret legal texts. The administrative judge must apply treaty provisions when they are "clear," on the understanding that the judge determines when this is so, but the judge cannot interpret these treaties. When the judges are faced with stipulations that are not clear to them and that must therefore be interpreted, they must ask the Minister of Foreign Affairs for an interpretation and then decide the case on that basis. An examination of the mass of cases dealing with this question shows that in general the judges do defer to the Minister of Foreign Affairs whenever a treaty is in question. It should be added that the judge accepts and applies the government interpretation in its entirety.[63]

This delegation of the judge's normal duty of interpreting the laws he applies has often been criticized. It amounts in effect to a recognition that the government may effectively settle a case to which it is a party (before the administrative courts the government is always a party) in the manner most favorable to itself. The strength of the executive makes itself felt in a particularly regrettable fashion in this area.

The compensation of French people from Algeria furnished an outstanding example of governmental interpretation favoring government policy. This interpretation weighed heavily against the individual. Many Algerian French had petitioned the government for compensation for damage and losses incurred in Algeria as a result of its independence. The Council of State in an early decision decided to wait until the Minister for Foreign Affairs decided whether the Evian Accords had the force of an international convention and, if so, whether they gave French residents in Algeria the right to claim compensation for damage suffered from the French state.[64] When it had received the governmental interpretation requested, it then ruled as follows:

> Considering that as a result of the communication by the secretariat on the question before the Council of State regarding this decision [of 27 March 1968], . . . the Minister of Foreign Affairs made known . . . the interpretation to be given . . . on the questions asked by the Council of State; that the Minister reveals that [the Evian Accords] . . . amount to an international convention but do not contain any provisions which would allow French residents in Algeria the right to compensation from the French government for losses incurred; that, it follows, the request . . . cannot be granted.[65]

For reasons that are not easy to determine, the judicial tribunals adopted a somewhat different position. The Court of Cassation decided that in principle judicial tribunals had the duty to interpret international treaties and that this was only abrogated "when provisions failing to be interpreted brought up questions of public international law." That, at least, was the formula evolved by the courts, after much hesitation.[66]

Despite appearances the law followed by the Court of Cassation comes to much the same conclusions as that followed by the Council of State. In the former as in the latter court, it is generally left to the government to decide the question of interpretation of international conventions raised before the judge.

It may also be mentioned, although this was exceptional, that in one case the Paris Court of Appeal agreed to apply a provision of the Vienna Convention (18 April 1961) on diplomatic immunity which had not, at that time, been ratified by France because the Minister of Foreign Affairs testified by letter that the provision merely codified a customary rule of international law. This letter amounted to a "certificate of custom," it was held.[67]

Recognition and Nonrecognition

The question of the effect in French courts of the nonrecognition of a foreign government by France is one of great controversy. One thing is certain: there is no need for a prior executive act (the issuing of a certificate, for example) of any kind to show that a foreign government has been recognized or even exists. That is for the courts to decide, taking into consideration the surrounding circumstances. (An example will be cited below.) This being so, there has been a growing tendency for France to extend the rules governing recognized governments and states to nonrecognized governments.

On the question of whether to give effect to foreign decisions, it has been written that "it does not appear to be necessary when the question of whether to give effect to foreign decisions arises, for the French government to have recognized the state or government in question."[68]

Insofar as a French judge is called upon to apply foreign law, where this is dictated by French conflict-of-laws rules, it appears to be accepted today that the nonrecognition of a government or state is no bar to applying its laws, so long as the principle of effectiveness is upheld.[69] After some hesitation the law came round to this view, especially on the question of recognition of Soviet laws before

France had recognized the Russian government. In this connection, the judgment of the court of the Seine of 12 January 1966 stated unambiguously that "the lack of recognition of a foreign government could not result in French courts ignoring private laws made by the government before its recognition over a territory where it unquestionably was exercising sovereignty."[70]

This tendency is most marked when questions of immunity from the court's jurisdiction arise. The noted Clerget affair has given the courts a chance to decide the question definitiely. A private creditor seized the effects of the commercial attaché of North Vietnam, which had been deposited in a bank in Paris. The Court of Cassation decided in a statement of principle on 2 November 1971 that the Court of Paris had correctly looked at the actual situation of the North Vietnamese government and decided

> that the Democratic Republic of North Vietnam, although not recognized is represented in France, is an independent sovereign state whose assets . . . cannot be seized, having regard to this sovereignty and independence which international courtesy forbids us to breach even to obtain payment of debts incurred in a private capacity.[71]

This case shows in a particularly striking manner the sovereign powers recognized by the courts in these cases. It also states the extension of rules covering recognized governments or states to nonrecognized governments that are deemed effective by the judge.

In the light of the developments just noted, the question of the capacity of a nonrecognized state of government to make laws or enjoy rights seems to be answerable in the affirmative.

NOTES

1. See, for example, J. Robert, Libertés publiques (Paris, Montchrestien, 1971), who, after having studied "L'étranger en France" (pp. 283 ff.), briefly considers the case of the French citizen abroad (p. 293).

2. See, for example, G. Burdeau, Les libertés publiques (Paris, Librairie generale de droit et de Jurisprudence, 4th ed., 1972); C. A. Colliard, Libertés publiques (Paris, Dalloz, 4th ed., 1972).

3. Conseil d'Etat (hereafter C.E.), 13 August 1836, Bureau de la Buffardière, Jurisprudence générale, See Passeport, No. 10; C.E., 22 April 1921, Leloutre, Recueil des décisions du Conseil d'Etat et du Tribunal des Conflits (hereafter Rec.) 381; C.E., 14 May 1948, Imbach, Dalloz 226, note by Cujonin; C.E., 11 May 1960, Car, Rec. 319; Tribunal administratif (hereafter Trib. adm.) Rennes, 23 November 1971; Fouéré, Le Monde, 25 November 1971.

4. Universal Declaration of the Rights of Man, Art. 13-(2), Journal Officiel de la République Française (hereafter J.O.).

5. See Le Monde, 25 November 1972.

6. Penal Code, Art. 355-1.

7. New Code of Criminal Procedure, Art. 138.

8. Law of 16 March 1956, Decree of 17 March 1956.

9. See, for example, C.E., 21 February 1964, Manville, Rec. 118; C.E., 20 January 1967, Chevallet, Rec. 701; C.E., 22 December 1967, Trape, Rec. 701; C.E., 25 October 1968, Douzon, Rec. 517.

10. See Robert, op. cit., at 296 ff.

11. On Maurois, see la chronique de M. Rousseau, Revue Générale de Droit International Public (hereafter RGDIP) 1080 (1971).

12. Ibid., p. 762. In the mid-1960s the Minister of Foreign Affairs came to the conclusion, concerning the detention in Algeria of French nationals who had become Algerian, that diplomatic and consular protection could not be officially extended unless the foreign government agreed in favor of those who had retained their French nationality at the same time. Reply to written question, J.O., 18 May 1966, at 1348. Cited in Annuaire Française de Droit International (hereafter AFDI) 897 (1966); insofar as concerns the efforts of the French government to claim compensation in Tunisia, see AFDI 1025 (1965).

13. Court of Cassation (hereafter Cass.), 4 June 1964; Argoud, Journal de droit international (hereafter Clunet) (1965), rapport Comte.

14. Cited in A. Kiss, 3. Répertoire de la pratique française en matière de droit international 821.

15. In French law certain actions of the executive that are not subject to legal control are known as "government acts." These actions, which are becoming less numerous, deal either with relations between the executive and Parliament, such as a decree dissolving the National Assembly, or with international relations.

16. C.E., 2 March 1966, Dame Cramencel, 157; RGDIP 791 (1966), note by Rousseau.

17. C.E., 28 June 1967, Société des transports en commun de la région d'Hanoi 279; 2 Juris-Classeur Périodique (hereafter JCP) 15393 (1968), note by Ruzié.

18. C.E., 4 October 1968, Lévy 473; see C.E., 18 December 1968, Beinisch, Clunet 361 (1969), note by Ruzié.

19. C.E., 8 March 1963, Société Rizeries Indochinoises 167.

20. C.E., 30 March 1936, Guyot 259; C.E., 4 October 1968, Lévy 473.

21. C.E., 29 November 1968, Tallagrand 607; Dalloz 386 (1969), note by Silvera; Clunet 382 (1969), note by Ruzié; Revue de Droit Publique et de Science Politique (hereafter RDP) 686 (1969), note by Waline.

22. For complete coverage of the problem, see Morand, "La responsábilité de l'Etat français pour les dommages subis par ses ressortissants a l'etranger," Actualité Juridique, Droit Administratif (hereafter AJDA) 588 (1970).

23. C.E., 31 January 1969, Moraly 50; Dalloz 326 (1969), note by Silvera; 2 Juris-Classeur Publique 15832 (1969), note by Ribs and Manesse; Revue de droit Public 686 (1969), note by Waline; Clunet 322 (1970), note by Ruzié; Revue Critique 461 (1969), note by Kovar; RGDIP 1151 (1969), note by Rousseau.

24. C.E., 16 October 1970, Epoux Martin, Rec. 593; 2 Juris-Classeur Publique 16577 (1971), conclusions of Braibant. For the hardships endured by French magistrates working in Algeria when exercising their functions, see C.E., 6 November 1968; Benejam, Rec. 545; RGDIP 218 (1969), note by Rousseau; 10 January 1969, Grafmuller, Rec. 16; 2 Journal-Classeur 15832 (1969), note by Ruzié. See also Touscoz, "La situation juridique des coopérants techniques et la jurisprudence française," RDP 287 (1970).

25. A few of the clauses written in order to ensure the immunity of French technical experts abroad are found in Convention with Jordan, 16 June 1965, Art. 8; Convention with Sierra Leone, 19 October 1964, Art. 7; Convention with Paraguay, 10 December 1963, Art. 19; Convention with Guinea, 22 March 1963, Art. 6; Accord with Honduras, 13 January 1968, Art. 10. On the subject of refusal of diplomatic immunity to a French supporter by the Supreme Court of Chile, 25 November 1969, see "Affaire Fabre: Chronique Rousseau," RGDIP 1054 (1970).

26. C.E., 15 May 1935, Strauss, Rec. 548.

27. C.E., 16 December 1955, Epoux Deltel, Rec. 592; Dalloz 44 (1956), conclusions of Laurent, RDP 150 (1956), note by Waliné.

28. C.E., 13 March 1964, Vassile, Rec. 179; ASDA 484 (1964), note by A.D.L.

29. Law of 15 July 1970, Art. 1.

30. Ibid., Art. 66.

31. On the law of 15 July 1970, see Morand, op. cit., at 660 ff. "Chronique Rousseau," RGDIP 470-71 (1971).

32. C.E., 30 November 1966.

33. See Le Monde, 1 April 1972.

34. See especially the circular of 24 January 1972, J.O. 1570, 7 May 1970.

35. Ibid.

36. On the refusal of France to allow the Greek journalist and politician Brillakis to enter France following the 1967 revolution, see the reply of the Minister of Foreign Affairs, O.J., 21 March 1970, at 648, and that of the Minister of the Interior, 6 June 1970, at 2319.

37. C.E., 21 November 1952, Marcon, Rec. 524.

38. See Le Monde, 15 March 1972 and 18 April 1972.

39. Decree of 18 March 1946.

40. Ibid.

41. C.E., 12 June 1953, Dame de Savitch Ritchgorsky, Rec. 281.

42. See Le Monde, 29 October and 7-8 November 1971.

43. There is no question here of expulsion by administrative authorities. In certain cases the expulsion complements the sentence announced

by the judge. Thus a law of 31 December 1970 provides that foreigners convicted of certain crimes related to drug peddling or usage may be barred from France for a fixed length of time or indefinitely.

44. J.O., 19 September 1970, at 3991; see AFDI 973 (1970) and RGDIP 1153 (1971).

45. In order to facilitate the return to their own countries of aliens expelled from France, agreements known as "prise en charge" have been concluded with Benelux, Germany, Austria, and Switzerland.

46. C.E., 9 January 1970, Cohn-Bendit, Rec. 15.

47. C.E., 26 November 1954, Van Peborgh, Rec. 627.

48. C.E., 16 January 1970, Mihoubi, Rec. 25.

49. C.E., 18 March 1955, Hamon ben Brahim, Rec. 168; 16 January 1970, Mihoubi, Rec. 25. Since the person concerned in the Mihouki case was in prison, his expulsion was not an urgent matter.

50. C.E., December 1970, Demoiselle Benz, Rec. 763.

51. See Le Monde, 22 June 1968 and 3 July 1968.

52. See I. Batiffol, Droit International Prive 420 (5th ed., 1970).

53. Tribunal de Commerce de la Seine, 18 January 1940, cited in Kiss, op. cit., at 17, No. 29.

54. Cass., 14 March 1939, at 1982.

55. Blondeau; Rev. crit. 713 (1969), note by Schaeffer; JDI 912 (1969), note by Chardenon.

56. Trib civil Seine (13 July 1915), cited by Kiss, op. cit., at 21.

57. Cass., 8 December 1954, 1 Bulletin de la Cour de Cassation, Chambre Civile (hereafter Bull. civ.) 298 (1954), cited by Kiss, op. cit., at 30, No. 56.

58. Colmar, 16 January 1952, cited in ibid., at 31, No. 56.

59. Le Mans Court, 25 June 1969, 2 Gazette du Palais 262 (1969), AFDI 912 (1970).

60. J.O., 25 May 1967, at 1999.

61. J.O., 27 August 1963, 8215, 8236.

62. Ruzié, Organisations internationales et sanctions internationales 126-27 (1971).

63. For a complete view of the problem, see Repertoire Dalloz de droit international, V° Traité international, no. 172 ff.; Virally, "Le Conseil d'Etat et les traités internationaux," 1 JCP 1098 (1953); Auby and Drago, Traité de contentieux administratif 34 (1962); Kiss, op. cit., at no. 837.

64. C.E., 27 March 1963, Moraly Rec. 205; Dalloz 678 (1968), note by Silvera; 2 JCP 15847 (1969), note by Ribs and Manesse; Revue Critique du Droit International Privé (hereafter Rev. crit.) 461 (1969), note by Kovar; RDP 686 (1969), note by Waline; AFDI 827 (1969), observation by Lachaume.

65. C.E., 31 January 1969, Moraly, Rec. 50; Dalloz 326 (1969), note by Silvera; 2 JCP 15847 (1969), note by Ribs and Manesse; RDP 686 (1969), note by Waline; JDI 322 (1970), note by Ruzié; RDGIP 1151 (1969), note by Rousseau; AFDI 877 (1970), observation by Lachaume.

66. Cass., 19 March 1963, JDI 1046 (1963), note by P.G.; 2 JCP 13270 (1963), note by Ancel; Dalloz 529 (1963), note by Milaurie; 7 November 1969, 2 JCP 16248 (1970), note by Ruzié; Rev. crit. 105 (1971), note by H.B.; AFDI 898 (1970), observation by Lachaume. The exact content of this formula is far from clear; on the full problem, see Batiffol, op. cit., Benoist, "L'interprétation des traités diplomatiques par les tribunaux judiciares," JCP 1133 (1953).

67. Paris, 30 June 1967, Rev. crit. 478 (1968). Normally "certificates de couture" designate statements by foreign judges about the position of a law on a certain point when French conflict of laws operated.

68. Batiffol, op. cit., vol. 2, no. 773, at 415.

69. Batiffol, op. cit., vol. 2, no. 256, at 308.

70. Rev. crit. 120 (1957), note by Loussouarn.

71. Cass., 3 November 1971, Clerget, 2 JCP 16969 (1972), note by Ruzié; see Paris, 7 June 1969, 2 JCP 15954 (1969), conclusions of Fortier, note by Ruzié; Rev. crit. 483 (1970), note by Bourel; JDL 894 (1969), note by Pinto; RGDIP 522 (1969), note by Rousseau; AFDI 931 (1970), observations by Lachaume.

CHAPTER

11

ISRAEL

Yehuda Blum

"Palestine law, though not Mosaic, is a mosaic." This statement, which is attributed to the late Norman Bentwich, the first Attorney-General of Mandatory Palestine, is as true of the law of Israel today as it was of Palestine law when it was thus characterized by Bentwich some 50 years ago.

The British Mandate, while retaining the Ottoman law that existed at the time of the British occupation of the country, superimposed on it British Common Law and Equity. Article 46 of the Palestine Order in Council of 1922 provided that the jurisdiction of the civil courts, as distinct from religious tribunals, which retained their jurisdiction in matters of personal status affecting members of their respective communities, should be exercised in conformity with Ottoman law in force, and "so far as the same shall not extend or apply, shall be exercised in conformity with the substance of the common law and the doctrines of equity in force in England."

These 30 years of British Mandatory rule also left an indelible mark on the law of Palestine, and British law became the dominant element in the law of the country during that period. It was carried over into the law of Israel by virtue of Section 11 of the Law and Administration Ordinance of 5708-1948 of 21 May 1948, adopted by the Provisional Council of State, which was the interim parliament of Israel between May 1948 and January 1949. This ordinance stipulates that "the law which existed in Palestine of the 5 Iyar 5708 (14 May 1948) shall remain in force, insofar as there is nothing therein repugnant to this Ordinance or to the other laws which may be enacted by or on behalf of the Provisional Council of State."

Essentially as written for the 1972 Conference, this paper was reviewed and approved by the author in late 1975.

Thus the reader will frequently encounter in this chapter reference to the legislation and judicial practice of Mandatory Palestine as well as those of Israel.

THE INDIVIDUAL

The Individual as a National

Movement

Passports. Section 2(a) of the Passports Law, 5712-1952, lays down the general principle that a passport shall be issued to an Israel national upon application.[1] This general provision, which at first appears to entitle a national to a passport as of right, is, however, subject to the stipulation contained in Section 6 of the Law which authorizes the Minister of the Interior, at his discretion, to refuse to grant a passport or to extend its validity; to attach conditions to the granting of a passport or the extension of its validity; to cancel or shorten the period of validity of a passport and order the surrender thereof; and to limit, either at or after the issue of a passport, the range of countries for which it is to be valid.[2]

In 1966 the Knesset amended the Passports Law with a view to making it more difficult for Israel nationals to remain abroad for extended periods.[3] Section 6A of the Law authorizes the Minister of the Interior, with the approval of the government and after consultation with the Home Affairs Committee of the Knesset, to determine by regulations those cases in which Israel nationals abroad, who have severed their links with the state, shall not have passports issued to them or shall not have passports in their possession extended except for the purpose of returning to Israel, unless there are circumstances that, in the opinion of the minister, otherwise justify the issue or extension of a passport. In many cases implementation of this provision would have meant a limitation of the period during which the national could remain abroad. In fact, no such regulations have been promulgated, and the period of validity of a passport was extended, under a 1969 amendment of Section 4 of the law, from two to five years, thus making it easier for a national to remain abroad for extended periods without having recourse to the Israel authorities.[4]

The criteria by which the Minister of the Interior was to exercise his discretion under Sections 6 and 6A of the law have not been spelled out in the law, nor, for that matter, in the regulations made thereunder. There does, however, exist a cabinet decision of 23 February 1964, approving certain directives that would appear to be relevant here. According to these guidelines, a passport will be issued to a new immigrant who has acquired Israel nationality by return[5] only after the immigrant has been in the country for a period of at least one year, unless special circumstances warrant a departure from the general rule. This provision was intended to reduce the number of "fictitious immigrants," that is, persons who come to Israel as immigrants when their real intention is to acquire an Israel passport and to leave with it for abroad. Gouldman takes the view that "it would be a valid exercise of the minister's discretion to refuse a passport to a new immigrant who had no real intention of living here but wished to use his newly-acquired Israel nationality as a means of helping him settle abroad."[6] Even in those cases in which a passport is issued to a new immigrant who has spent less than one year in the country, its validity is to be limited, under the cabinet directives, to a period of one year and should not be extended except for the purpose of the holder's return to Israel.

Furthermore, under the said cabinet directives, passport services shall not be granted, with the exception of the issue of an Israel laissez passer valid only for return to Israel, to the following categories of persons:

1. A person who has failed to return to Israel to fulfill military duties under the Defense Service Law;

2. A person who has violated a court injunction[7] against the departure from Israel of himself or herself or of a minor;

3. A person whose stay abroad is likely to endanger the security interests of the state (the Minister of the Interior is to exercise discretion with regard to persons falling within this category only if an appropriate request has been made by the Director-General of the Ministry of Defense);

4. A fugitive offender; or

5. A person causing damage to the "good reputation" of the State of Israel, namely a person who has been convicted of a crime involving moral turpitude; a person who has committed an offense involving immorality, such as procuration and instigation to an act of prostitution under the Law on Prostitution Offenses of 1962; a person lacking financial means of support abroad and likely to become a burden on public institutions; or a person engaged in fund-raising activities under false pretences.

Also, passport services are not to be granted, except for an Israel laissez passer valid only for return to Israel, to Israelis who have stayed abroad continuously for a period of five years and have failed to establish contact at least once yearly with the nearest Israel consular office. In Gouldman's view, while Section 6 of the Passports Law empowers the Minister of the Interior to refuse to extend the validity of a passport or to attach conditions to its extension, a power that in Gouldman's opinion is not exercisable upon a group but only in those individual cases in which there exist adequate grounds for refusal, "it is doubtful whether mere absence from Israel as such is a sufficient reason for refusing to extend the validity of a passport."[8]

Indeed, the main purpose of the 1966 amendment of the Passports Law was to empower the Minister of the Interior, who under Section 6 of the law, which remains unaffected by the change, had to be satisfied in every individual case that there existed grounds for refusal or nonextension of the passport, to prescribe by regulation certain categories of persons to whom the grant or renewal of passports will be automatically refused unless they can show that there are special reasons for excluding them from the application of such regulations. However, no such regulations have been forthcoming.

> After pushing the Law through a somewhat reluctant Knesset, the Government has not so far utilised its main provisions. Perhaps the reason is that the Government is anxious to attract rather than antagonise nationals living abroad in the hope that they may one day decide to return to Israel.[9]

In practice, however, the Cabinet directives of 1964, which it will be recalled were aimed at regulating the passport policy with regard to Israelis abroad, are also applied, with the necessary changes, to the issue or extension of passports in Israel.

Section 9(a) of the Passports Law enables the Minister of the Interior to delegate to another person all or any of his powers under the law except the power to cancel a passport and the power to make regulations.[10] A person aggrieved by a decision regarding the granting of a passport; its extension; or the conditions attached to its granting or extension, made by a person to whom the minister's powers have been delegated (such powers have been delegated to the director-general of the Ministry of the Interior, the deputy director-general in charge of Immigration and Registration, and the directors of the District Offices of the Ministry), may apply to the minister "for a final decision."[11] However, the "final" decision of the minister is not final; it may be regarded as final only on the administrative level, and the applicant, once having exhausted the administrative remedies available, may petition the High Court of Justice (the Supreme Court also sits as High Court of Justice), which, under Section 7(a) of the Courts Law, 5717-1957, "shall deal with matters in which it deems it necessary to grant relief in the interests of justice and which are not within the jurisdiction of any other tribunal"[12] and which, under Paragraph (b)(2) of the same section, is competent "to order State authorities . . . and officials of State authorities . . . and such other bodies and individuals as exercise any public functions by virtue of law to do or refrain from doing any act in the lawful exercise of their functions."[13] With a view to facilitating the high court's supervisory functions, the Knesset in 1958 passed the Administrative Procedure Amendment (Statement of Reasons) Law, 5719-1958,[14] Section 2 of which lays down the rule that "where application has been made to a public servant in writing, to exercise any power conferred on him under any law, and he refuses the application, he shall notify the applicant, in writing, of the reasons for the refusal."

However, Section 3(1) of the law does exempt a public servant from this duty "if the law which vests the power in him provides that he is authorised to exercise it at his discretion." It will be recalled that the refusal to grant a passport, to extend its validity, and the other powers vested in the Minister of the Interior under Section 6 of the Passports Law are powers to be exercised "at his discretion" and thus are not subject to the provision imposing on a public servant the duty to state the reasons for refusing an application.

Nevertheless, the public servant will have to state his reasons for refusal if the High Court of Justice has issued a conditional order at the request of the unsuccessful applicant so as to enable the court to exercise its supervisory function and to examine whether the discretionary power was exercised for the purpose for which it was granted; whether relevant considerations were taken into account and irrelevant ones disregarded; whether discretion was exercised without discrimination; whether it was exercised in good faith and not arbitrarily and capriciously; and whether it was exercised in a reasonable manner.[15] Thus, in Kardosh v. Registrar of Companies,[16] the High Court of Justice exercised its supervisory functions in respect of a refusal by the Registrar of Companies to register a company, a power that, under Section 14 of the Companies Ordinance, is in his "absolute discretion"[17] (emphasis added).

Therefore it is clear that the High Court of Justice is competent to review any decision made by the Minister of the Interior in the exercise of his discretionary powers under Section 6 of the Passports Law. As far as could be ascertained by the present writer, there has been no judgment by the High Court in connection with the refusal of the minister to grant a passport or to extend its validity. The possible explanation for this is that rejected applicants (and their counsel) have obviously felt that the minister and those to whom the minister has delegated authority have been on firm legal ground in rejecting their applications and consequently saw little chance of success in petitioning the High Court with a view to having those administrative decisions reversed by the court.

Departure. Departure from Israel was first regulated by the emergency regulations of 24 August 1948.[18] Since under Section 9(c) of the Law and Administration Ordinance, 5708-1948,[19] an emergency regulation expires three months after it is made "unless it is extended or revoked at an earlier date, by an Ordinance of the Provisional Council of State [now a Law of the Knesset], or revoked by the regulation-making authority." The Provisional Council of State, which functioned until the elections to the First Knesset were held in January 1949, passed, with certain amendments, the Emergency Regulations (Foreign Travel) (Extension of Validity) Ordinance, 5709-1948,[20] on 18 November 1948. Subject to some slight changes, this ordinance was to remain in force until 1961, and after some significant modifications in that year, has been in force ever since.

No Israel nationality existed in 1948. The Nationality Law, 5712-1952[21] was only passed four years later, when it conferred Israel nationality retroactively, as of the date of the establishment of the state, on various categories of persons. The original emergency regulations did not distinguish between foreign nationals and those who were not. Accordingly, Regulation 1 of the 1948 Emergency Regulations provided that "no person shall go abroad save under an exit permit from the Minister of Immigration [now Minister of the Interior]"[22] (emphasis added). The general policy in those days, the period of Israel's War of Independence, was a rather restrictive one, and the authorities endeavored to dissuade the inhabitants of the state from going abroad unless imperative reasons warranted their journey. The purpose of this policy was twofold: (1) to avoid the depletion of manpower and the demoralization usually accompanying an exodus in time of war and (2) to prevent the depletion of the meager resources of the state in foreign exchange. The only general exemptions from the exit permit requirement, provided for in the Emergency Regulations, applied to persons enjoying diplomatic immunity (including UN representatives) persons belonging to the regular consular service of a foreign state, and persons in possession of diplomatic or service passports of Israel.

Generally speaking, the Minister of Immigration in those days seems to have made extensive use of his powers under Regulation 2 to refuse to issue a permit, to attach conditions to its issue, or to subject permits to special or general conditions, including a limitation of the time for which the holder of a permit could stay abroad. Thus persons of military age, and this included males aged 17-49 and unmarried women aged 17-35, as well as those approaching military age, were generally not permitted to leave the country. Equally, exit permits that were requested by entire families would occasionally be refused to one of their members, apparently on the assumption that this was an effective means of ensuring the family's eventual return to Israel.

However, even while those stringent restrictions on the right to leave the country were in force, the right to leave Israel was declared by the Supreme Court to be a fundamental right that could not be adversely affected unless there existed good grounds for so doing. In considering the nature of the Minister of the Interior's discretionary power to refuse the issue of an exit permit, Justice Silberg in Kauffman v. Minister of the Interior (1953) raised the question of whether the exit permit was

> a special privilege which the competent authority may grant to a citizen who has been found fit and worthy of it or does the opposite situation apply, i.e. that the citizen in his capacity as citizen, is entitled to the permit, and the competent authority, before refusing to grant a permit, must find a reason for so doing.[23]

Although the wording of the regulation pointed to the first approach, the second was held by Justice Silberg to be its correct interpretation, as follows:

> The national's freedom of movement to go abroad is a natural, recognised and inherent right in every State which possesses a democratic regime and our country is one of them. The citizen does not require any special qualification in order to win such a "grant."[24]

A gradual relaxation of the foreign travel restrictions was effected in the years following the termination of the War of Independence in 1949. In 1955 the Knesset abolished the hitherto absolute power of the Minister of the Interior to refuse at discretion the granting of an exit permit, by limiting the minister's discretionary power in this matter to those cases in which "there is reason to apprehend that the going abroad of the person applying for the permit may prejudice the security of the State."[25] In 1956 the Knesset passed another amendment to the regulations, regarding the issue of exit permits to persons of military age who belong to the reserve forces. Under the new Regulation 2A, an exit permit can be granted to a reservist "if the Minister of Defense . . . has consented in writing to the grant of the permit" and subject to the latter's power, under new Regulation 2B, to prescribe conditions for his consent.[26]

The major breakthrough in the process of liberalization of exit procedures came in 1961 when the Knesset abolished the exit permit system. Following the amendment of Regulation 1 by the Knesset, the regulation has required the following:

> a person leaving for abroad shall, at the time of leaving, produce to a frontier control officer a valid passport or laissez-passer or any other document issued to him for that purpose by the Minister of the Interior.[27]

The latter retains the power to "prohibit the departure of any person from Israel if there is reason to apprehend that his departure may impair the security of the State" (Regulation 6). Under Regulation 5

> a person shall not leave for any of the countries specified in Section 2A of the Prevention of Infiltration (Offenses and Jurisdiction) Law, 5714-1954, save with the permission of the Minister of the Interior, and an Israel national or Israel resident shall not enter any of those countries in any way save with such permission as aforesaid.

Section 2A of the Prevention of Infiltration Law had made it a punishable offense to leave Israel knowingly and unlawfully for Lebanon, Syria, Egypt, Transjordan, Saudi Arabia, Iraq, Yemen, or any part of Eretz Israel (the Hebrew name of Mandatory Palestine outside Israel.)[28] Following the June War of 1967, this prohibition was waived in February 1968 in respect to all those territories that had come under Israel control as a result of the said hostilities, provided entry into them was permitted by the military commanders of the areas concerned.[29]

The Minister of the Interior also retains the power to lay down conditions, restrictions, and limitations in those cases in which the law authorizes the minister to grant, or refuse, exit permits or to impose a prohibition on the exit of a given person. Persons of military age belonging to the reserve forces are required to produce to the frontier police an exit permit from the Minister of Defense; those who do not belong to the reserve forces are required to produce a certificate to that effect. Although the Minister of Defense, or a person appointed by him, may subject the grant of an exit permit to a person of military age to conditions, restrictions, and limitations, including a limitation of the length of stay abroad,[30] it has been the practice over the past decade to issue such permits to persons of military age as a matter of routine, by the applicants' army units and usually without any delay.

There is also the possibility of preventing the departure from Israel of persons against whom a judgment has been given in a civil suit or against whom a civil action is pending.

Section 14(a) of the Execution Law, 5727-1967, reads as follows:

> if the Chief Execution Officer has reason to believe that the judgment debtor is about to leave Israel and thereby to frustrate any proceeding or to render the execution of the judgment more difficult, he may order the prevention of his departure from Israel and the deposit of his passport or travel document.[31]

If the judgment debtor refuses to deposit his or her passport or travel document, under Section 14(b) the Chief Execution Officer may also substitute for an order preventing the departure of the judgment debtor from Israel an order making such departure conditional upon the giving of security, to his satisfaction, in order to ensure the execution of the judgment.

As amended in 1966, Regulation 254 of the Civil Procedure Regulations of 1963 provides that where a civil action has been brought and it has been proved to the satisfaction of the court or the registrar that the defendant intends to leave Israel forever or for an extended period, and where his absence from Israel may frustrate any proceedings or render the execution of the judgment more difficult, the court or registrar may order the prevention of the defendant's departure from Israel or lay down conditions for his departure, subject to the qualifying provision of Regulation 255, according to which no order preventing departure shall be issued in connection with actions not exceeding 500 Israel pounds, with the exception of maintenance claims.[32]

With regard to criminal proceedings, Section 39 of the Criminal Procedure Law, 5725-1965, provides that the release on bail of a person suspected of an offense, or of an accused, or of a person whose appeal against a sentence is pending, may be made conditional by the court on the deposit of his passport. The court may also prohibit the exit of such person from Israel.[33] It is to be noted that the police have no power to compel the person to deposit his or her passport and have to ask for an appropriate court order. In practice, however, the police frequently confront a suspect with the alternative of either voluntarily surrendering his or her passport to the police or being brought before a magistrate by them for the issue of an appropriate order to this effect.

Passing reference may also be made here to another requirement, fiscal in character, the fulfillment of which is a prerequisite for departure from Israel, by a national or resident of the country. Under the Foreign Travel Tax Law of 1950, as amended, a "foreign travel tax" shall be charged on the acquisition of travel tickets in Israel and also on the travel tickets of Israel nationals and residents acquired abroad.[34] The Minister of Finance may exempt specific classes of persons from the payment of all or any part of the tax.[35] Accordingly, nonresident foreigners and Israelis residing abroad, provided a specified minimum period of time has elapsed since their last visit to Israel, are exempted from the payment of the tax. Also a wide range of persons belonging to some 50 odd categories enumerated in the regulations made by the Minister of Finance are entitled to a total or partial exemption from the tax, which is fixed "at a percentage of the price of the travel ticket, or at a specific amount, or both, but shall not exceed 100 per cent of the amount of the price of the ticket plus IL 500."[36] As of May 1977, the tax stands at a lump sum of IL 1000 plus 15 percent of the price of the travel ticket. Tickets purchased by foreign governments or by international organizations are exempted from the payment of the tax. Partial exemptions are granted to among others, students, businessmen on business trips, and persons traveling for medical reasons.

Return. The right of an Israel national to return to Israel is not spelled out specifically in any law. According to Gouldman, this right "may . . . be deduced from those statutory provisions limiting the right of residence of the non-national, and from case law."[37]

The Entry into Israel Law, 5712-1952, requires that admission to the country be by visa.[38] However, it is specifically provided that the above provisions shall not apply to an Israel national.[39] In a number of applications to the High Court of Justice, all of them heard shortly after the coming into force of the Nationality Law, 5712-1952,[40] namely Yehie-Kalef v. Inspector of Police, Hadera; Bader v. Minister of Police; and Mustafa v. General Officer Commanding Northern Command,[41] the judgments were devoted entirely to determining whether the person concerned had acquired Israel nationality. However, in each case the real point at issue was the right of the aspirant to nationality to enter or remain in Israel. The answer to this question was wholly dependent on whether the person was or was not an Israel national.[42] Therefore the case law may also be relied upon as authority for the proposition that a national is always entitled to enter Israel.

This proposition was somewhat qualified by the High Court of Justice in Naima Hakim v. Minister of the Interior,[43] where the petitioner asked for an order absolute against the authorities to permit her son to return to Israel from Lebanon. The parties and the court proceeded on the assumption that the petitioner's son was an Israel national. In spite of this the court held that the authorities were entitled to prevent his return to Israel, since he had voluntarily chosen to stay in an enemy country and had advocated views hostile to the state, and thus constituted a threat to its security. Therefore refusal by the authorities to permit his return could not be regarded as arbitrary.

Another possibility of preventing the return of an Israel national to Israel would appear to exist under Regulation 112 of the Defense (Emergency) Regulations of 1945. The Regulation enables the Minister of Defense (then the High Commissioner) to make an order for the deportation of "any person" from Israel (then Palestine), as well as to make an exclusion order requiring "any person" who is out of the country to remain out of it. A person concerning whom a deportation or exclusion order has been made shall remain out of the country as long as the order remains in force. While a more detailed discussion of Regulation 112 will be found below in connection with the expulsion procedures, it is worth mentioning here that in Khalil v. Minister of Police[44] and Bader v. Minister of the Interior[45] the High Court of Justice held that the entry into Israel of a person against whom an unlawful deportation order (by way of analogy we may infer that this also applies to an unlawful exclusion order) has been made, shall not be regarded as illegal. This could conceivably legitimize entry into Israel otherwise than at one of the frontier stations prescribed by the Minister of the Interior, in pursuance of his powers under Section 7 of the Entry into Israel Law of 1952, as amended in 1966.[46]

Expulsion. Reference has already been made to Regulation 112 of the Defense (Emergency) Regulations of 1945,[47] which is an unrepealed residual of the British Mandate. That regulation, it will be recalled, empowers the Minister of Defense to make a deportation order in respect to any person in Israel (even a national); but Regulation 108 provides that such order shall not be made unless the Minister of Defense "is of the opinion that it is necessary to make the order for securing the public safety, the defence of Palestine [now Israel], the maintenance of public order or the suppression of mutiny, rebellion or riot." An Advisory Committee set up under Regulation 111(4), and consisting of persons appointed by the Minister of Defense from among persons holding or having held high judicial or senior government offices, may, under Regulation 112(8), if so requested by a person against whom a deportation order has been made, consider and make recommendations to the government in respect to any such deportation order. At present this committee, the main function of which is to consider detention orders made under Regulation 111, is headed by a justice of the Supreme Court.

A deportation order made under Regulation 112 is subject to the supervisory authority of the High Court of Justice, which will probe into the propriety of the order and of the motives underlying it.[48]

The question is, however, largely academic, since as far as I have been able to ascertain, no deportation order against an Israel national has been made under Regulation 112, ever since the commencement of the Nationality Law in 1952. It may also be asked whether Regulation 112, insofar as it applies to Israel nationals, can be reasonably reconciled with Section 13(a) of the Entry into Israel Law of 1952,[49] which empowers the Minister of the Interior to issue an order of deportation "in respect of a person other than an Israel national or an oleh [immigrant] under the Law of Return." This provision, it is submitted, would appear to reflect the conviction of the legislature than an Israel national ought not to be deported from his country of nationality.

Another largely theoretical possibility for expelling an Israel national from Israel appears to exist under the Prevention of Infiltration (Offenses and Jurisdiction) Law, 5714-1954.[50] Under Section 30(a) of this law, the Minister of Defense, or a person authorized by him, may order in writing the deportation of an "infiltrator," whether or not he had been charged under the law.[51] The definition of "infiltrator" in Section 1 of the law includes a person who has entered Israel knowingly and unlawfully and who at any time between 29 November 1947 (the date of the UN resolution of the partition of Palestine) and his entry was a resident or visitor in Lebanon, Egypt, Syria, Saudi Arabia, Transjordan, Iraq, Yemen or, prior to the June 1967 War, in any part of Palestine outside Israel. In view of the fact that Section 7 of the Entry into Israel Law of 1952, as amended in 1966, requires every person, "whether or not he is an Israel national," to refrain from entering Israel "otherwise than at one of the frontier stations prescribed by the Minister of the Interior . . . and after reporting there to a frontier control officer and producing to him a valid passport or laissez passer,"[52] it follows that an "infiltrator" secretly crossing into Israel at a place that is not a prescribed frontier station is liable to be expelled even if he happens to be an Israel national.

Protection

Extent of Freedom of Activity Abroad. Following the British pattern, Palestine criminal law (and hence Israel criminal law) has been basically territorial in its outlook. The central provision on this matter was contained in Section 6 of the Criminal Code Ordinance, 1936, which provides that "the jurisdiction of the Courts of Palestine [now Israel] for the purposes of this Code extends to every place within Palestine [Israel] or within three nautical miles of the coast thereof." (In 1956 the territorial sea of Israel was extended to six nautical miles.)[53] There were, however, certain offenses that were extraterritorial by their very nature, such as piracy, under 78 of the Criminal Code Ordinance. Still, the provisions of criminal law also applicable beyond the boundaries of the country were considered the exception rather than the rule.

This basic concept has not changed over the past 40 years, but the tendency has been to widen the scope of the exceptions. Through the combined application of the protective principle, which is the principle of universality, as well as of the active and passive nationality principles, an increasing number of laws, and indeed entire categories of laws, have provided that they shall apply irrespective of the place of commission of the acts referred to in them. Some of these provisions apply abroad only to the nationals (or residents) of Israel, while the extraterritorial application of others is extended to "every person."

Chronologically, it is worth mentioning first in this connection the Defense (Finance) Regulations of 1941, enacted by the Mandatory Government in the early part of World War II and, subject to modifications, still in force. The regulations introduced into Palestine the foreign exchange control, which also extends to certain activities of Israel nationals and residents abroad. Thus Regulation 10E, entitled "Offenses Committed Abroad," provides that "where an Israel resident does outside Israel, for the purpose of realising a right, the ground for claiming which arose or existed while he was in Israel, an act which, had he done it in Israel, would have been contrary to these Regulations, he shall be deemed to have done the act in Israel."

The question of the precise meaning of this provision has been raised before the courts on numerous occasions. In Schwarzbaum v. Maziz (1964),[54] the respondent claimed to have given the appellant a short-term loan of U.S. $400 while both of them had been in London. The appellant denied having received such a loan and claimed, alternatively, that even if he had, by virtue of the principle that a base cause will not be enforced by the courts, the respondent could not rely on a transaction violating Regulation 3(1) of the Defense (Finance) Regulations, which provides as follows:

> Except with the permission of the Minister of Finance or a person appointed by him, no person other than an authorized dealer shall buy, borrow

> or otherwise obtain control of foreign currency or gold from, or shall sell, lend or otherwise transfer control of foreign currency or gold to any person not being an authorised dealer.

This provision the appellant took to mean also a prohibition of a foreign currency loan granted in London by one Israel national to another. The District Court rejected the appellant's argument, and its decision was confirmed by the Supreme Court, which held that "the application of any law is confined to the territory of the State unless its provisions indicate a contrary intention. . . . The language of Regulation 3(1) does not indicate that the legislator intended it to apply also beyond the State's frontiers."[55]

The extraterritorial effect of some of the laws enacted since the establishment of the state flows from the duty of allegiance that an Israel national, and on occasion even a resident, owes to the state, not only when in Israel but also while abroad and even while residing in enemy territory. Thus, in Hakim v. Minister of the Interior,[56] the High Court of Justice held that "in a period of war the link between a State and its nationals is not severed even though they are living in the enemy's country. The duty of allegiance of the 'enemy' national to his homeland continues in force."[57]

The duty of allegiance of a national or resident of Israel to the state, even while abroad, is clearly reflected in the Penal Law (State Security, Foreign Relations, and Official Secrets), 5717-1957.[58] Under this law it is an offense to commit any act calculated to impair the sovereignty or territorial integrity of the state; to bring about military action against Israel; to assist an enemy of Israel in war against Israel; to spread defeatist propaganda at a time of actual fighting; to commit acts prejudicial to the armed forces, such as the instigation of mutiny, willful endangering of military property or supplies, or incitement to evasion of duty and to disobedience; to commit acts of espionage, including the establishment of contact with foreign agents and entry into military places; to deliver official secrets; and to impair foreign relations. On their face, these provisions seem to apply to everyone, irrespective of his or her connection with Israel. Section 41 also provides that "a person who has committed an offence under this Law abroad shall be tried for it in Israel." The scope of the extraterritorial effect of the law is, however, qualified by a proviso in Section 41, under which a person shall not bear criminal responsibility for offenses relating to the impairment of the sovereignty of the state, for the causing of war against it, for the spreading of defeatist propaganda at the time of actual fighting, or for the impairment of Israel's foreign relations if such offenses were committed abroad and if at the time of their commission the person was not an Israel national or resident or under allegiance to the State of Israel, either because he or she had served in the state service or from any other cause. In other words, persons owing allegiance to Israel by virtue of nationality, residence, state service, or any other reason will be subject to all the provisions of the law, irrespective of the place of commission of offenses under it.

Section 11 also makes it a punishable offense for an Israel national or any other person who owes allegiance to Israel, either because that person is liable to defense service (this also applies to the residents of Israel of military age) or because the person has served in the state service, to serve in the armed forces of the enemy. In Section 32(a) volunteering to serve in the armed forces of a foreign state that is not an "enemy State" is, however, prohibited only for the nationals of Israel, not its residents, and an Israel national serving in an armed force of a foreign state shall be deemed to have volunteered to serve. By Section 32(c), enlistment of an Israel national in the armed forces of a foreign (nonenemy) state shall not entail criminal responsibility if done under an agreement between Israel and another state or an international agency or organization or with the permission of the government of Israel.

Israel nationals who have committed an act constituting a breach of allegiance to the State of Israel may be deprived of their Israel nationality. Section 11(a)(2) of the Nationality Law, 5712-1952, as amended in 1968, enables a District Court, upon the application of the Minister of the Interior, to annul the nationality of such persons.[59]

Mention should also be made here of Section 13(a) of the Military Justice Law, 5715-1955,[60] which confers on Israel courts-martial the jurisdiction to try "soldiers" who have committed acts constituting military offenses, whether such acts were committed in Israel or outside it. It is to be noted that the definition of "soldier" in Section 1 of the law includes persons belonging to the regular or reserve forces of the army, by virtue of the Defense Service Law, 5719-1959, as well as on a voluntary basis, whether under an engagement for permanent service or in any other manner, although the Military Justice Law applies to reservists only while they are in active service. However, certain obligations are also imposed on reservists who are not on active service, by virtue of the Duties of Reservists Off Service Regulations, 5711-1951.[61] Among those duties is the obligation listed in Regulation 2(b), namely, "to report, while he is abroad, with the nearest Israeli representation." This provision applies to reservists who stay at one given place abroad for a period exceeding one month but not to tourists.

A more comprehensive catalogue of Israel laws with extraterritorial effect may be found in the Penal Law Revision (Offenses Committed Abroad) Law, 5716-1955, as amended over the years (as of this writing, the most recent amendment was passed by the Knesset on March 21, 1972). Under this law, courts in Israel are competent to try a national, resident, or public servant of Israel who has committed abroad a bribery offense or an offense under certain sections of the Criminal Code Ordinance harming the property or rights of the state, the World Zionist Organization, the Jewish Agency, the Jewish National Fund, the United Jewish Appeal, or any supervised body within the meaning of the State Comptroller Law of 1949. The 1972 amendment to the law has also added to this category of extraterritorial offenses acts under the Penal Law Amendment (Deceit, Blackmail, and Extortion) Law of 1963 and the related sections of the Criminal Code Ordinance of 1936.[62]

Section 1A of the law confers jurisdiction on Israel courts to try a national or resident of Israel who has committed abroad an act constituting an offense under the Penal Law Amendment (Bigamy) Law, 5719-1959,[63] which prohibits entering into a bigamous marriage as well as to performing such a marriage. British Mandatory legislation had forbidden such a marriage for Christians, permitted it for Moslems, and permitted it, under certain circumstances, for Jews.[64] Section 1A now extends the absolute prohibition of the 1959 law also to bigamous acts of Israel nationals and residents abroad.[65]

The protective principle is clearly reflected in the provisions of Section 2 of the Penal Law Revision (Offenses Committed Abroad) Law. Paragraph (a) of this section, which was passed by the Knesset in March 1972, confers on Israel courts jurisdiction to try under Israel law any person, including of course, a national of Israel, who has committed abroad an act that, if committed in Israel, would have constituted an offense under its laws, if that act has harmed or was calculated to harm the state of Israel, its security, property, economy, or lines of transportation or communications with other countries. The insertion of this paragraph was necessitated by the increasing frequency of attacks on Israel offices, airliners, and so on abroad in the wake of the hostilities of June 1967. Although the law was primarily intended to punish the non-Israeli perpetrators of such attacks, the wording of the paragraph makes it equally applicable to Israelis who may commit such acts abroad.

The same considerations have also prompted the Knesset to insert into said law the new Section 2B, which through the application of the passive nationality principle, confers on Israel courts jurisdiction to try under Israel law any person who has committed an act abroad that would have been an offense if committed in Israel and that has harmed, or was calculated to harm, the life, limb, health, freedom, or property of a national or resident of Israel. However, with regard to such offenses Section 2B(b) introduces the "double criminality" test by providing that no person shall be prosecuted in Israel for an offense committed under Section 2B(a) at a place within the jurisdiction of another state unless that act is also an offense under the law of that state. Again, this provision was intended primarily to cover offenses committed by non-Israelis, but it equally covers acts referred to in Paragraph (2) committed abroad by nationals or residents of Israel.

Under Section 2 of the law, Israel courts are also competent to try persons who have committed offenses abroad under the Flag and Emblem Law of 1949 or the State Seal Law of 1949 and certain offenses against the security of the state under the Criminal Code Ordinance,[66] as well as acts of perjury committed abroad.[67]

Extraterritorial effect has also been given to Section 8 of the Passports Law of 1952, which prohibits forging a passport; to unlawfully adding, altering, or deleting any entry therein; tearing off any part thereof; using such passport or possessing it; unlawfully using the passport of another person; or permitting another person to unlawfully use one's own passport; as well as to making false statements with a view to obtaining, extending, altering, or correcting a passport. It is also an extraterritorial offense to supply false information in order to obtain for any person a visa for a permit of residence in Israel or an immigrant's certificate or visa, or to use such certificate or visa.[68]

A 1969 amendment of the law has added to the list of extraterritorial offenses the nonreporting by nationals and residents of Israel abroad of the birth or death of a member of their family, as well as the adoption of a child by them, as required by the Population Registry Law of 1965.[69] Also, offenses under the Knesset Elections Law (Consolidated Version), 5729-1969, have been added to this list.[70]

The principle of universality finds expression in Section 2A of the law, entitled Crimes against Humanity, which confers on Israel courts the jurisdiction to try persons for offenses committed abroad under the Prevention and Punishment of the Crime of Genocide Law, 5710-1950; the Nazi and Nazi Collaborators (Punishment) Law of the same year; the Dangerous Drugs Ordinance of 1936; as well as for piracy (Section 78 of the Criminal Code Ordinance of 1936) and for offenses under the Air Navigation (Offenses and Jurisdiction) Law, 5731-1971,[71] which is modeled along the pattern of the 1963 Tokyo Convention on Offenses and Certain Other Acts Committed on Board Aircraft (the "Hijacking Convention").

Reference should be made here also to Regulation 5 of the Emergency Regulations (Foreign Travel) Amendment Law, 5721-1961, which contains a prohibition for Israel nationals and residents to enter any of the enemy countries (Egypt, Syria, Lebanon, Iraq, Transjordan, Saudi Arabia, and Yemen), even if such entry is not done directly upon leaving Israel.[72]

Finally, it is worth mentioning the Emergency Regulations (Offenses Committed in Israel-Held Areas--Jurisdiction and Legal Assistance) (Extension of Validity) Law, 5728-1967,[73] which has been renewed annually by the Knesset. Under Regulation 2(a) a court in Israel is competent to try under Israel law any person who is in Israel for an act or omission that occurred in any region that came under Israel control in the course of the June 1967 hostilities (the Golan Heights, Judea and Samaria, the Gaza Strip, and Sinai) that would constitute an offense if it had occurred in the area of jurisdiction of the courts in Israel.

The Right to Diplomatic Protection. Although it was said incidentally by the Supreme Court, by Justice Sussman, in Hakim v. Minister of the Interior[74] that the state owes protection to a national resident in an enemy country "insofar as it is able to defend him through the good offices of a friendly government," there is no law in Israel requiring the state to afford protection to its nationals abroad. Whether or not such assistance is granted is a matter for government discretion. There is, though, an isolated dictum by the Haifa District Court, by Judge (now Justice) Kister, in which it was said that "it is a cardinal rule that a State has a duty to protect its citizens abroad."[75]

The State and Compensation. The question regarding the right of the state to dispose of money secured from a foreign country in respect to its nationals came up in Richuk v. State of Israel.[76] Richuk was a member of the Palestine police force for more than 22 years. After the termination of the British Mandate and the establishment of the State of Israel, the U.K. government confirmed his entitlement to an annual pension for his service. Between 15 May 1948 (Israel's accession to independence) and 31 May 1950, the British government paid an annual pension in sterling and Richuk received the pension in Israel in local currency at the rate of one Israel pound per pound sterling. By Article 3 of the Anglo-Israeli Agreement of 30 March 1950,[77] the government of Israel agreed with the U.K. government to pay the pensions of former officials of the Mandatory Government resident in Israel up to an amount not exceeding .2 million Israel pounds annually, the capitalized value of which was estimated at 2.4 million pounds sterling.

Commencing on June 1, 1950, the government of Israel paid to the plaintiff an annual pension of 124,101 Israel pounds. On 31

December 1953 a new rate of exchange was fixed, namely 5,040 Israel pounds per pound sterling. Following this devaluation, Richuk demanded a pension of 625,460 Israel pounds per annum, but the government of Israel continued to pay the same annual pension as before, plus a small discretionary premium. His claim for the payment of the balance having been rejected by the Tel Aviv District Court, he appealed to the Supreme Court, whose attitude on the question here under consideration is well reflected in the following passages from President Olshan's judgment.

> Let us assume that money is owing from a foreign country to a citizen and he authorises his Government to claim the money, and that Government takes upon itself to do so. If a treaty is concluded between those two States, by which the debt is settled, the citizen will be entitled to bring an action against his Government, and even if he refers in his Statement of Claim to that Treaty, it will be no answer to him to say that he is basing his claim on a Treaty between two States. . . . The reason is that the action will be based on the agreement between the citizen and his Government and not on the Treaty between the two Governments, despite the reference to the Treaty in the Statement of Claim. . . . Had an agreement been concluded between the appellant [Richuk] (or all the recipients of pensions) and the British Government and the Government of Israel, by which this latter would take upon itself the payment of the pensions, then clearly the contention . . . that there is here a transfer of debt . . . would be well founded, and the fact that the two Governments decided to include the transfer in a treaty regulating outstanding financial matters between them would not have placed any obstacle in his way. . . . I would go further and say that if the two Governments had inserted in the Treaty a stipulation to the effect that the arrangement made between them would come into effect after the pension holders had consented thereto, then I think that the appellant could have based his claim on the transfer of debt. But the mere receipt of money by the appellant from the Government of Israel, only because

> that Government made payment of money to him as a result of its obligation undertaken towards the British Government and not as a result of an obligation undertaken by it towards the appellant--gives no right of action against the Government of Israel.[78]

The case was returned to the District Court to enable the parties to amend their pleadings and bring their evidence. However, no further proceedings took place because agreement was subsequently reached between the parties. In any event, the decision by the Supreme Court seems to indicate that the state is not bound to distribute to its nationals compensation secured from a foreign country in respect to them unless it has pledged itself toward them on the domestic, as distinct from the international, level. Naturally, therefore, there is certainly no duty on the part of the state to "top up" such compensation in the absence of an undertaking by the state, under domestic law, toward its nationals.

The State's Responsibility for Injury Induced by Its Own Conduct. Although the government of Israel does not seem to admit an inherent obligation to compensate nationals for losses suffered abroad as a result of the political and military situation of the state, the vulnerable position of Israel nationals abroad, especially in the light of attacks abroad on Israel nationals and Israel property since the June War of 1967, has prompted the Knesset to pass a number of legislative provisions with a view to ensuring compensation for injuries to life, limb, and property, caused to Israelis abroad by virtue of their nationality.

The Foreign Trade Guarantees Law, 5719-1959, Section 2, as subsequently amended in 1963 and 1968,[79] authorizes the Minister of Finance to guarantee on behalf of the State of Israel a guarantee given by a person in respect of losses arising from "export transactions" or to guarantee against such losses directly, provided that a guarantee of an amount exceeding .5 million Israel pounds for a capital investment abroad by an Israel resident shall require the approval of the Finance Committee of the Knesset.[80] "Export transaction" is defined in Section 1 of the law as meaning

> the export of goods for a consideration receivable in Israel from a person outside Israel, and the production or marketing of goods or the rendering of a service, whether in Israel or outside Israel, for a consideration receivable as aforesaid, and capital investments abroad by Israel residents, and includes the grant of credit to finance such operations.

A guarantee under Section 4 of the law is given if in the opinion of the Minister of Finance it is likely to contribute to the encouragement of export transactions. Guarantees granted by the state under this law have made possible investments, enterprises, and services by Israelis in foreign countries where doubts existed with regard to the stability of the regimes or their relations with Israel and where, as a result of such doubts, Israelis would have hesitated to engage in such projects. When, prior to breaking off diplomatic relations with Israel, the government of Uganda in March 1972 abruptly terminated contracts with Israel firms, it was announced in Jerusalem that the various projects under those contracts had been guaranteed by the Israel government under the Foreign Trade Guarantees Law and that the Israel firms involved in those projects would accordingly be compensated by the government of Israel for the losses suffered as a result of the measures taken by the government of Uganda.

Further legislative measures taken with a view to meeting the contingencies that arose after June 1967 included an amendment in 1970 of the Property Tax and Compensation Fund Law, 5721-1961,[81] as well as the passing by the Knesset in the same year of the Victims of Hostile Activities (Pensions) Law. Under the former law a Compensation Fund had been set up for the payment of compensation for various kinds of damage, including war damages, drought, and so on. In 1970 the new Section 46C was inserted into the law, under which the Minister of Finance was authorized to make regulations with a view to compensating for damage caused to "Israel property abroad," which is defined as "immovable property, stock-in-trade or equipment situated outside the area of the state, the owner of which is an Israel national or Israel resident or a body corporate registered in Israel."[82] Under a further amendment of the same law in 1969, "Israeli property abroad" was widened to include a vessel or aircraft chartered by a national or resident of Israel or by a body corporate registered in Israel, a vessel or aircraft operating for the benefit of the state economy (as certified by the Minister of Finance or on his behalf), as well as goods transported in such a vessel or aircraft.[83]

No such regulations have so far been made by the minister. The Victims of Hostile Action (Pensions) Law, 5730-1970[84] accords the social security benefits granted under the National Insurance Law also to the "victims" of "enemy-inflicted injury." Under Section 1 of the law, a "victim" includes a national or resident of Israel who has sustained an enemy-inflicted injury, whether in Israel or abroad. An "enemy-inflicted injury" is defined in the same section as "an injury caused through hostile action carried out in aid of one of these or upon its instructions or on its behalf or to further its aims." Thus, under this law, a national or resident of Israel who is harmed by the activities of anti-Israel military, semimilitary, or irregular forces or their sympathizers will be entitled to the social security benefits normally paid under the National Insurance Law, irrespective of whether the national or resident has been harmed in Israel or outside it. Accordingly, it was announced following the murder by Arab terrorists in Munich, on 5 September 1972, of 11 members of the Israel team in the Olympic games, that the survivors of the murdered athletes were entitled to the benefits accorded under this legislation.

Waiver. Reference has already been made in a different context to the Anglo-Israel Agreement on 30 March 1950, which regulates certain financial matters that were outstanding on the termination of the British Mandate over Palestine. Under that agreement, it will be recalled, the government of Israel assumed from the U.K. government the obligation to pay the pensions due to former officials of the Mandatory Government who were resident in Israel and simultaneously relieved the United Kingdom of its obligations toward such persons.

A provision to similar effect may be found in Letter No. 1a, addressed to Konrad Adenauer, then Chancellor of the Federal Republic of Germany, by Moshe Sharett, the then Minister of Foreign Affairs of Israel, appended to the Israel-German Agreement concluded in Luxembourg on 10 September 1952.[85] Under this agreement the FRG government undertook to pay to the State of Israel the sum of 3 billion deutsche marks, in view of the fact that Israel had assumed the burden of resettling a great number of uprooted and destitute Jewish refugees from Germany and the German-occupied territories of Europe, victims of the National-Socialist regime. Under Article 14 of a protocol concluded simultaneously between the Federal Republic of Germany and the Conference on Jewish Material Claims against Germany ("Protocol No. 1"), the Federal Republic of Germany undertook to pay to persons persecuted by the Nazis for their political convictions, race, faith, or ideology and who became stateless or acquired a new nationality after the end of persecution, appropriate compensation for deprivation of liberty and damage to health and limb, as well as annuities to the survivors of such persecutees.

However, with regard to Israel nationals, Paragraph 2 of Sharett's above-mentioned letter, as confirmed by Adenauer, stated as follows:

> The Government of Israel is here proceeding on the assumption that claims of Israel nationals under legislation in force in the Federal Republic of Germany on internal restitution, compensation,

> or other redress for National Socialist wrongs, and the automatic accrual of rights to Israel nationals from any future legislation of this nature, will not be prejudiced by reason of the conclusion of the [Luxembourg] Agreement, provided, however, that the provisions of Article 14 of Protocol No. 1 . . . shall apply to Israel nationals only insofar as the payment of compensation for deprivation of liberty and the payment of annuities to survivors of persecutees.

The government of Israel thus waived any claims of Israel nationals against the Federal Republic of Germany other than claims for the payment of compensation for deprivation of liberty and the payment of annuities to survivors of persecutees.

The legal effects of the said waiver on the domestic legal plane were discussed by the Supreme Court in Friedlander v. Competent Authority under the Invalids (Nazi Persecution) Law, 5717-1957 and Others.[86] The purpose of the Invalids (Nazi Persecution) Law, which was passed by the Knesset in April 1957,[87] was to secure certain benefits for persons who, but for the waiver contained in Sharett's letter referred to above, would have been entitled to a pension or other compensation from the Federal Republic of Germany. Among these benefits, Section 21 of the law provides for the payment to an invalid, at the expense of the state and in accordance with such rules as shall be prescribed by regulations, of his or her medical expenses. In November 1958 regulations concerning medical expenses were published, with retroactive effect from April 1957. Mrs. Friedlander, a persecutee of the Nazis, maintained, however, that she was also entitled to reimbursement for her medical expenses incurred before 1957. On this the Supreme Court, through Justice Sussman, had the following to say:

> Counsel for the petitioner argues that but for the waiver by the Israel Government regarding compensation due to a persecutee for damage to his health, the petitioner would have received this compensation from the German Government. The Invalids (Nazi Persecution) Law does restore to her some of the benefits she would have enjoyed but for the [Luxembourg] Agreement and the waiver. Yet the Israel law does discriminate against an Israel national in that it has not granted him all those remedies to which he would have been entitled under [the legislation passed by] the

> German Government. It follows that a Jewish persecutee who is not an Israel national is in a better position than an Israel national who is subject to the waiver made in connection with the reparations arrangement. Of this argument of Counsel for the petitioner is correct, it is a matter for the legislature who should give some thought to the fact that an Israel law and a treaty to which the Government of Israel is a party have deprived Israel nationals, survivors of the Nazi persecutions, of compensation which they would have received from the German government. It follows that a Jew benefits from the fact that he is not an Israel national, for the arrangement made by the Israel Government does not apply to him.[88]

Although Justice Sussman does not hide his indignation and displeasure at this state of affairs, it is clear that he does not question the right of the Israel government to waive the claims of its nationals.

Special Kinds of Protection. The Foreign Trade Guarantees Law, 5719-1959, the Property Tax and Compensation Fund Law, 5721-1961, and the Victims of Hostile Action (Pensions) Law, 5730-1970[89] have already been mentioned in connection with the responsibility of the state for injury induced by its own conduct. Similarly, mention has been made elsewhere of Section 2B, inserted into the Penal Law Revision (Offenses Committed Abroad) Law in March 1972.[90]

To this list of legislative provisions granting different kinds of special protection to Israelis abroad, it appears pertinent to add yet another legislative measure, which indirectly affords protection to Israelis abroad through the application of the principle of reciprocity. Section 191 of the National Insurance Law (Consolidated Version), 5728-1968, authorizes the Minister of Labour to enact by regulations special provisions affecting the insurance of a national of a state the laws of which discriminate against Israel nationals in branches of insurance dealt with by the said law. In the same vein, Paragraph (2) of Section 190 (added in 1969) provides that a multilateral convention relating to national insurance acceded to by Israel shall be regarded as an agreement between Israel and each of the other states that are parties to the convention, provided that the state in question does not discriminate against Israel nationals in branches of insurance dealt with by the law.[91]

The Individual as an Alien

Movement

Entry and Stay. The ideology of the "ingathering of the exiles" underlying the establishment of the State of Israel is perhaps best expressed in the legislative field by the Law of Return, 5710-1950, Section 1 of which proclaims that "every Jew has the right to come to this country as an oleh."[92] ("Oleh," it will be recalled, is a Jew immigrating to Israel, while "aliyah" is immigration of such a person). In introducing the proposed law to the Knesset, the first Prime Minister of Israel, David Ben Gurion, explained its special nature in the following words:

> This Law does not provide for the State to bestow the right to settle in Israel upon the Jew living abroad; it affirms that this right is inherent in him from the very fact of his being a Jew; the State does not grant the right of return to the Jews of the Diaspora. This right preceded the State; this right built the State; its source is to be found in the historic and never-broken connection between the Jewish people and the homeland.[93]

Every Jew, irrespective of his nationality, has therefore a vested right to an "oleh's visa," which is to be granted to him once he has expressed his desire to settle in Israel, by Section 2 of the Law of Return.

When the Law of Return was passed by the Knesset in 1950, it did not contain a definition of "Jew." This question has plagued the State of Israel since its inception, and no really satisfactory solution to it has so far been propounded. Under Jewish religious law (the "Halacha"), a Jew is a person born to a Jewish mother or converted to Judaism. Since for most of the time since 1948 the Ministry of the Interior, which is in charge of the laws of Return, Entry into Israel, Passports, Nationality, and Population Registry, has been headed by ministers representing the National Religious Party, there has been a tendency to issue directives to the lower echelons of the ministry with a view to applying the traditional Halachic concept of "who is a Jew." This naturally has proved unsatisfactory to agnostics, atheists, and those who in an attempt to secularize the definition of "Jew" wanted to divorce this definition from the Halacha. Material objections to the application of the traditional definition pointed to the fact that the religious law test would exclude from the operation of the Law of Return the offspring of mixed marriages in those cases in which the wife was not Jewish, even where such children had been brought up as Jews; had been regarded by their parents and outsiders as such; and more important, had regarded themselves as Jews. By contrast, if the completely "liberal" test, stipulating that any person who considered himself a Jew should be accepted as such, had been adopted, this would have been far too subjective and would have left the matter exclusively in the hands of the individual, who then could have acquired, even without any previous connection with Judaism, immigrant's rights under the Law of Return as well as Israel nationality.

The confusion surrounding the problem of "who is a Jew" was well illustrated in two celebrated cases that reached the Supreme Court in the 1960s, that is, the Rufeisen and Shalit cases.

In Rufeisen v. Minister of the Interior,[94] the facts were somewhat unusual. The petitioner, Rufeisen, was born in Poland to Jewish parents and brought up as a Jew. During the German occupation of Poland in World War II, Rufeisen many times risked his life to save fellow Jews. In 1942 he converted to Christianity and in 1945 joined the Carmelite Order of monks. In 2958 he reached Israel, coming from Poland on a travel document of the kind issued by the Polish authorities to Jews emigrating to Israel, and, as Brother Daniel, joined the Carmelite monastery on Mount Carmel, near Haifa. Soon thereafter he applied for an immigrant's certificate under the Law of Return. Under the Jewish religious law test, Rufeisen, the son of a Jewish mother and now a Catholic monk, should have been considered a Jew. The "liberal" test, curiously enough, leads to the same result: since Rufeisen considered himself as a Jew, he should be considered as such, despite the fact that he stood before the court in the robes of a Catholic monk. However, common sense recoiled from the paradox inherent in the application in this case of the traditional and subjective tests alike, and the Supreme Court, by a majority of four to one, propounded a judicial test of its own based on what it believed was a common-sense interpretation of the Law of Return. The court pointed out that the said law was a wholly secular law. Consequently, the term "Jew" in the law was not subject to the Halachic definition but was to be interpreted in accordance with its ordinary, everyday meaning, taking into account the legislative purpose that had led to the enactment of the law. The ordinary, everyday meaning of the word "Jew" was held not to include a Jew who had converted to Christianity and was, at the date of the petition, a practicing Catholic monk. After the dismissal by the Supreme Court of Rufeisen's petition, the Minister of the Interior repeated his offer, which had initially been rejected by Rufeisen, to grant him Israel nationality by naturalization rather than "by return"; this time Rufeisen accepted the minister's offer.

The question that arose in 1968 in Shalit v. Minister of the Interior[95] was not directly concerned with the Law of Return. The point at issue was whether the petitioner's children, who had been born in Israel to a Jewish father and a non-Jewish mother, could be registered as Jews under the Population Registry Law of 1965. The Haifa Registration Officer, in accordance with directives issued by the Minister of the Interior, had refused to register the petitioner's children as Jews. The petitioner alleged that such refusal derived from religious, and hence improper, motives. He contended that the law was to be interpreted by secular criteria and that by such standards a child born in Israel to a father who was Jewish, an Israel national, and an officer serving in the Israel defense forces (Lieutenant-Colonel Dr. Shalit served as the Chief Psychologist of the Israel defense forces), brought up and educated in Israel and speaking Hebrew as his mother tongue, ought to be registered as belonging to the Jewish ethnic group. The problem of the nationality of Shalit's children did not arise; as the children of an Israel national, they acquired Israel nationality by birth.

In its decision handed down in January 1970, the Supreme Court, by a majority of five to four,[96] made absolute the order calling upon the Minister of the Interior to register the Shalit children, in accordance with their father's declaration, as belonging to the Jewish ethnic group. The majority judges were at pains to stress that their judgment did not constitute a decision on the "who is a Jew" question. They held that the Minister was not empowered by the Population Registry Law to lay down criteria for determining whether or not a person belongs to a particular ethnic group. The registration officer's duty was to accept an informant's declaration given in good faith unless it was obviously wrong, such as if an adult man declared himself to be five years of age.

Within two weeks of the handing down of the Shalit judgment, the government introduced a bill for the amendment of the Law of Return, which was passed after a bitter debate in the Knesset.[97] Under new Section 4B of the Law of Return (and new Section 3A[b] of the Population Registry Law), a Jew is henceforth to be defined as "a person born of a Jewish mother or converted to Judaism who is not a member of another religion." According to Gouldman, on whose research the foregoing analysis of the Rufeisen and Shalit cases is largely based, to a large extent this definition "gives statutory effect to the religious law test, rejected by the majority in the Shalit case," by laying down certain objective criteria for determining who is a Jew.[98] At the same time, Gouldman points out that the new statutory definition departs from the religious test in at least two particulars.

1. A member of another religion is not to be regarded as a Jew even though born to a Jewish mother or previously converted to Judaism, thus giving statutory authority to the Rufeisen decision.

2. The reference to persons "converted to Judaism" does not specify in accordance with which rules the conversion must be effected, thus preserving the right of the official (orthodox) rabbinical courts and institutions in Israel to refuse to recognize conversions performed abroad by nonorthodox (conservative, liberal, reform) rabbis, who do not always comply with the exact--and exacting--requirements of Jewish religious law. It may well be that the definition in the Law of Return is intended to include every convert to Judaism, however converted, since as Gouldman points out, the Knesset rejected a proposal to replace the words "converted to Judaism" by the words "converted to Judaism in accordance with the Halacha."[99]

Moreover, new Section 4A(1) of the Law of Return extends the operation of the law also to the non-Jewish spouses, children, and grandchildren of a Jew, provided the Jew has not changed his religion of his own accord.[100] Thus, such non-Jewish members of a Jewish person's family are now also granted the rights of immigrants under the Laws of Return and Nationality, together with the rights of immigrants under any other enactment. The 1970 amendments to the Law of Return are thus in the nature of a compromise: although they in substance overrule the majority decision of the Shalit case by adopting the religious law test, at the same time they widen the scope of the law by also granting its privileges to a non-Jewish member of a Jewish person's family.

However, under Section 2(b) of the law, as amended in 1954,[101] the Minister of the Interior may refuse the granting of an immigrant's visa to a person who would normally be entitled to it if he is satisfied that the applicant (1) is engaged in activity directed against the Jewish people; (2) is likely to endanger public health or the security of the state; or (3) is a person with a criminal past, likely to endanger public welfare.

So far the first two exceptions have not caused serious problems. The first refers to persons who at present engage in activities against the Jewish people, thus not covering, for instance, persons who collaborated with the Nazis during World War II. Such persons could, however, according to Gouldman, be refused the status of immigrants under the third exception (persons with a criminal past) if the minister were satisfied that they were still likely to endanger public welfare.[102] It could conceivably be used today to prevent the immigration of persons actively engaged in helping Arab terrorist organizations or their supporters.[103]

Little use has been made over the years of the second exception. For one thing, Section 3(b) of the Law of Return expressly provides that a person shall not be regarded as endangering public health on account of an illness contracted after his arrival in Israel. This applies to persons who having initially arrived in Israel as nonimmigrants, subsequently wish to change their status to that of immigrant. Repeated suggestions to widen the minister's powers and to authorize him to refuse an immigrant's visa to a physically or mentally sick person have been rejected; Israel's policy of full implementation of the concept of return of the Jews to the country in spite of the financial burden involved in accepting sick and ailing immigrants has been retained. Regulation 6 of the Return Regulations of 1956, as amended in 1960, does, however, empower the minister to refuse the granting of an immigrant's visa to a person who refuses to undergo a medical examination, to have a smallpox vaccination administered to him, and so on.[104]

The most controversial of the three exceptions is undoubtedly the one relative to persons "with a criminal past likely to endanger public welfare." In Yoanovici v. Minister of the Interior,[105] the High Court of Justice held that the one and only conviction of the petitioner by a French court was sufficient to turn him into "a person with a criminal past" within the meaning of the Law of Return. Difficulty arises where a person with no previous criminal record is charged with the commission of a serious crime but flees to Israel before he or she can be brought to trial. According to Gouldman, the dilemma in such a case stems from the fact that "on the one hand, it is unreasonable to allow the Law of Return to be used by the suspected offender as a means of escaping justice. On the other, the principle that a man is innocent until proved guilty requires that he should not, in the absence of a conviction, be subjected to any disabilities, penal or otherwise."[106]

The High Court of Justice was confronted with this problem in Gold v. Minister of the Interior.[107] A warrant for Gold's arrest had been issued in Cleveland, Ohio, because he had been suspected of having dealt in Canadian government bonds, knowing them to have been stolen. However, prior to the issue of the warrant, Gold had left the United States using a second passport obtained by means of a false declaration. Having reached Israel, he applied for an immigrant's certificate under the Law of Return. The Minister of the Interior rejected his application after taking into account the charges against Gold in the United States, particulars of which had been submitted by the U.S. embassy.

The majority of the court upheld the minister's decision. Justice Sussman held that Israel was not established to attract those who have broken the laws of their countries of residence, even if they are Jews. He saw no difference, from the point of view of immigration to Israel, between a man who has committed a crime and been convicted of it and one who has committed a crime but has not been convicted. If the charges against Gold were true, Justice Sussman went on to say, then by ordering the minister to grant Gold an immigrant's certificate, the court would become a party to the settling of a fugitive criminal in Israel. If Gold were to stand trial in the United States and be acquitted, he could always renew his application for an immigrant's certificate. In the circumstances of the case, Justice Sussman found that the minister was justified in refusing Gold's application even in the absence of a criminal conviction.

Justice Landau reached the same conclusion though through a different line of reasoning. He agreed in principle with the minority view of Justice Cohn that a man is presumed to be innocent as long as he has not been convicted and that the mere bringing of a charge against him does not deprive him of the benefit of this presumption. However, Justice Landau argued, Gold had admitted to the frontier police at Lod (Tel-Aviv) Airport that his second passport had been obtained by means of a false declaration, and this admounted, in the judge's view, to an admission of the commission of a criminal offense justifying the minister's negative decision on Gold's application.

The matter came up again in the case of Lansky v. Minister of the Interior, which because of the importance of the decision was heard before a bench of five of the High Court of Justice. Meyer Lansky, reputedly one of the former chiefs of organized crime in the United States, came to Israel in 1970 as a tourist and a year later applied for an immigrant's certificate. This request was rejected by the minister because of Lansky's alleged past association with the U.S. underworld; he did, however, offer to give Lansky an Israel laissez passer to any country willing to admit him, in order to avoid his indirect extradition to the United States, which had revoked Lansky's passport, thus making it valid for him only for his return to the United States. (The United States had not requested Lansky's extradition.) Upon receiving the minister's negative reply to his application, Lansky sought and obtained a conditional order from the High Court of Justice against the minister.

When the hearing of the case opened on 22 March 1972, the State Attorney admitted that Lansky's convictions were relatively minor (disorderly conduct in 1918 and 1920, contravening Prohibition in 1931, illicit gambling activities in 1950 and 1953). The reason Lansky had never been charged with major offenses, the State Attorney argued, was that law enforcement officials were under Lansky's influence and witnesses were afraid to testify. The State Attorney supported his allegations with documentary evidence, including the report of the U.S. Senate Kefauver Committee, which had investigated U.S. organized crime in 1950 and which had attributed to Lansky, along with other well-known figures of the U.S. underworld, "the organization and integration of criminal activities (especially gambling) throughout the country." The State Attorney further recalled that when Lansky had appeared before the Kefauver Committee, he had answered nearly every question with the Fifth Amendment, including questions about what his business was and whether he had any legitimate business, while admitting to the committee that he "knew" some 28 leading American gangsters. Lansky had been equally evasive when asked similar questions by New York grand juries in 1963 and 1966 and also refused to obey a subpoena issued against him to appear before a grand jury.

The State Attorney also rejected the argument that even if Lansky had a criminal past, he was "not likely to endanger public welfare" (it will be recalled that the third exception to the Law of Return applies only if both conditions are fulfilled, to the minister's satisfaction), since Lansky, aged 70 at the time of the hearing, was now "retired." The State Attorney countered this argument by producing evidence of an underworld "summit meeting" that had been planned for Tel Aviv in 1971 with Lansky's participation and that had been called off after three of the would-be participants were barred from entering Israel by the Israel police, who were acting on tips from Interpol and the New Scotland Yard.

All this, as well as other evidence cited before the High Court of Justice, was sufficient in the State Attorney's view to "satisfy" the minister that the third exception was applicable to Lansky even in the absence of recent criminal convictions, since the minister was entitled to rely on evidence that would not necessarily stand up in a court of law.[108]

In a unanimous decision handed down on 11 September 1972, the High Court discharged the conditional order issued against the Minister of the Interior. The court, through President Agranat (Justices Sussmann, Landau, Berinson, and Cohn concurring), held that although the right of return was a fundamental right, the exceptions to which had to be narrowly interpreted, such exceptions could not allow Israel to become a magnet and refuge for fugitives from justice. In deciding whether a person was entitled to invoke in his favor the provisions of the Law of Return, the Minister of the Interior could also take into account facts and evidence not directly concerned with a "criminal past" that could indicate the likelihood that the subject would be a danger to public welfare. According to the court, "criminal past," within the meaning of the law, included any conviction of an offense of a disgraceful nature, regardless of the punishment that had been meted out to the convicted person. An admission made to the police could be regarded by the minister as a substitute for a formal conviction, provided the applicant was given a fair hearing by the minister based on evidence that reasonable persons would have regarded as being of probative value. Such evidence, however, does not necessarily have to comply with the rules of admissibility applicable in a court of law. The court added that it was within the minister's discretion to decide whether a person was likely to endanger public welfare and found that in the circumstances of the case the minister was justified in concluding that such a danger existed. In any event, his assessment of the situation was not unreasonable. The fact that Lansky had only been convicted of mild offenses was a result of the corruption of the law enforcement machinery and the fear by some law enforcement officers that Lansky could prevent their reelection.[109]

Before concluding this survey on the right of entry to Israel under the Law of Return and the exceptions to it, it should be noted that the Minister of the Interior has no power to withhold an immigrant's visa or certificate from a Jew on the grounds of age, poverty, or general inability to maintin himself or herself, even when it is more than probable that the burden of the upkeep of such a person will eventually fall on the state.

The entry of persons wishing to enter Israel otherwise than under the Law of Return is governed by the Entry into Israel Law, 5712-1952[110] and the regulations made thereunder. The Entry into Israel Regulations of 1974,[111] which replace those of 1955, as subsequently amended, authorize the Minister of the Interior to refuse or to cancel, at his or her discretion, an entry visa to a person who (1) is or was engaged in activity directed against the Jewish people; (2) is likely to endanger the security of the state; (3) is a person with a criminal past, likely to endanger public welfare; (4) is likely to hurt public feelings; (5) is likely to become a burden on public institutions; (6) violates or has violated any law in force in Israel; (7) has obtained an entry visa or a permit of residence by giving a false statement or has failed to comply with any of the conditions set out in such visa or permit under the law, regulations, or otherwise that are specifically attached to his visa or permit; (8) is a person in respect of whom there exists adequate evidence that he or she has come to Israel to evade the payment of debts abroad; (9) is likely to endanger public welfare or public health. This includes persons who suffer from dangerous or contagious diseases, persons afflicted with grave mental diseases, drug addicts, persons unable to prove that they have been vaccinated against smallpox or other contagious diseases and refuse to permit such vaccination to be administered to them, and persons who refuse to be quarantined or otherwise to submit to medical supervision.

Although persons who have acquired immigrant's status in Israel under the Law of Return have a right to be in Israel, and hence also a right to reenter Israel after leaving it, irrespective of whether or not they chose to acquire Israel nationality, permanent residents who do not fall within this category and who have not acquired Israel nationality have no vested right to return to Israel after leaving the country. Under Section 5 of the Entry into Israel Law of 1952, the Minister of the Interior may grant a return visa to a person who, being permitted to reside in Israel permanently, either wishes to leave Israel with the intention of returning, or is abroad and wishes to return to Israel.

It will be recalled that Section 9 of the Administrative Procedure Amendment (Statement of Reasons) Law, 5719-1958,[112] exempts the Minister of the Interior, when making a decision under the Entry into Israel Law, from the general duty imposed on a "public servant" to give in writing the reasons for refusing an application to exercise any power conferred on him under any law.[113] However, a permanent resident who is aggrieved by the refusal of the minister to grant him or her a return visa will still be able to petition the High Court of Justice and will be permitted to show that in rejecting the application the minister has taken into account irrelevant and extraneous considerations and has thus exercised the power of discretion improperly.

Voluntary Departure. As has been pointed out above, the legislation regarding departure from Israel originally applied to "every person" irrespective of nationality. However, over the years a clear distinction has been drawn between the residents of Israel, nationals and nonnationals alike, on the one hand, and nonresident foreigners on the other.

There are, generally speaking, no restrictions on the voluntary departure of nonresident foreigners from the country. However, their departure may be prevented under Section 14(a) of the Execution Law of 1967, under Regulations 254 and 255 of the Civil Procedure Regulations of 1963, and under Section 39 of the Criminal Procedure Law of 1965. It should be noted, however, that in Scmech v. Erzer[114] the Supreme Court held that when the court is requested to order the prevention of departure, in accordance with Regulation 254 of the Civil Procedure Regulations, of a nonresident foreigner against whom a civil action has been brought, because of the drastic character of such order in respect to a foreigner, especially weighty grounds have to be shown to persuade the court to exercise its power of ordering the prevention of departure of a nonresident alien.

Nonresident foreigners are also subject to the provision contained in Regulation 5 of the Emergency Regulations (Foreign Travel)

(Amendment) Law of 1961, which prohibits "any person" from leaving Israel for any of the hostile countries specified in the Prevention of Infiltration Law of 1954. Under Regulation 5 of the said Emergency Regulations, the Minister of the Interior retains the power to prohibit "the departure of any person from Israel if there is reason to apprehend that "his departure may impair the security of the State" (emphasis added).

The position of resident foreigners with regard to departure from the country is on the whole assimilated to that of nationals, including the requirement that those of military age produce upon their departure appropriate permits from the military authorities, as well as the requirement of compliance with the provisions of the Foreign Travel Tax Law of 1950.

However, one particular provision of the Emergency Regulations (Foreign Travel) (Amendment) Law of 1961 specifically concerns the departure of resident aliens from Israel. Regulation 2 provides that a resident alien shall not leave for abroad unless he or she has given the Minister of the Interior, or a person appointed by the minister for that purpose, notice of his or her departure at least 14 days in advance.[115] Under Regulation 4 the minister may, if he sees a reason for doing so, permit the departure of such a person even if the required notice has not been given. For a better understanding of the rationale underlying this provision, it has to be remembered that it was passed by the Knesset simultaneously with the abolition of exit permits in general and was prompted by the consideration that, while the authorities concerned, such as the police and the income tax authorities, can usually be advised by the Ministry of the Interior in advance of an Israel national's intention to leave for abroad because of the national's application for a passport or passport extension, no such possibility exists with regard to resident aliens because the latter are holders of foreign passports. Hence the requirement in Regulation 2 for advance notice. Under Regulation 3, the receipt of this advance notice is acknowledged by stamping the resident alien's passport or, if necessary, a separate sheet.

Involuntary Departure: Expulsion and Deportation. The powers conferred on the Minister of Defense to order the deportation from Israel of "any person" under Regulation 112(1) of the Defense (Emergency) Regulations of 1945 or of an "infiltrator" under Section 30(a) of the Prevention of Infiltration (Offenses and Jurisdiction) Law of 1954 have already been mentioned elsewhere. It has also been pointed out that although those powers may theoretically be exercised in respect to both Israel nationals and aliens, in practice no use is made of them in respect to nationals. Likewise, their use in respect to aliens is of a limited nature, primarily because of the restrictive character of the two provisions.

Powers of deportation of a considerably wider scope are conferred on the Minister of the Interior under Section 13(a) of the Entry into Israel Law of 1952, which expressly excludes from its operation "an Israel national or an oleh under the Law of Return."[116] With regard to persons not belonging to either of those categories, the minister may issue an order of deportation if they are in Israel without a permit of residence.

Before discussing at greater length the questions arising in connection with the deportation powers of the Minister of the Interior under the Entry into Israel Law, a clear distinction must be drawn between deportation, on the one hand, and nonadmission to Israel, on the other. Section 10(a) of said law enables the minister to "remove" from Israel a person coming to Israel without having been permitted to enter the country. This provision applies primarily to persons who have arrived in Israel without being in possession of a valid entry visa.

Nationals of most Western European and American countries, as well as those of some other states, are not required to obtain a visa prior to their arrival in Israel and are issued their entry visas on their arrival at an authorized port of entry. The frontier police may, in such cases, refuse to issue an entry visa. Although physically on Israel territory, such persons are not deemed to have entered Israel before having been permitted to do so by the frontier control officer. If permission is refused, such persons will have to depart from Israel without delay. Section 10(3) of the law imposes on the master of any ship or the person in charge of any aircraft, train, motorcar, or other means of transportation that has come to Israel to take out of Israel, on the demand of a frontier control officer, any person who has arrived by that means of transportation with the intention of entering Israel, if it has been found that such person is not permitted to enter. Under Section 10(b) of the law, a frontier control officer may detain such a person until his or her departure or removal from Israel. Such detention usually takes place at the police station of the port of entry.

As has already been stated above, a deportation order may be issued against a person other than an Israel national or an immigrant under the Law of Return who is in Israel without a permit of residence. This usually happens either because the alien's visa has expired and has not been renewed or because the Minister of the Interior has exercised the power under Section 11(a) of the Entry into Israel Law to cancel, at his or her discretion, a visa granted under the law. A person whose visa is about to expire is supposed to leave Israel prior to its expiration, under Reguation 20 of the Entry into

Israel Regulations of 1974,[117] to avoid the possibility of being deported. If the visa of the alien about to be deported has not yet expired, the cancellation of the visa for the unexpired period will have to precede the deportation order (the two are usually issued simultaneously).

Under Regulation 9 of the Entry into Israel Regulations of 1974,[118] the Minister of the Interior may cancel the visa and residence permit of a person belonging to any of the categories of persons to whom he may refuse such a visa or residence permit in the first place. (See above.)

According to Section 13(d) of the Entry into Israel Law, the Minister of the Interior may direct that an order of deportation be carried out at the expense of the person on whom it has been issued. A frontier control officer or police officer may arrest and detain such person until his or her deportation from Israel, according to Section 13(c) of the law and Regulation 22 of the Entry into Israel Regulations.

In practice, deportation orders are issued under Section 13(a) of the Entry into Israel Law in respect of the following two broad categories of persons:

1. Persons with a criminal past. This includes both persons who have violated Israel law while in Israel and those whose criminal past has become known to the Israel authorities after their arrival in the country and who are deemed to constitute a menace to its public order. On the average, every year about 90 percent of the 90 to 100 deportation orders issued fall into this category. A deportation order may be issued in respect of more than one person, and this is usually done when the order is issued in respect of whole families. The majority of deportees on account of a criminal past are violators of the Israel antidrug legislation. About one third are common criminals, and the remainder are involved in crimes against the security of the state.

2. Persons who constitute a public health risk or are likely to become a burden on the public purse because of their inability to maintain themselves. This category accounts for about 10 percent of the total of deportees.

Under Section 16(b), a person aggrieved by a deportation order issued by the power delegated by the minister may apply to the latter for a final decision. Having exhausted this administrative remedy, they may then challenge the minister's decision by petitioning the High Court of Justice. This right of prospective deportees to judicial remedy is now specifically laid down in Regulation 21 of the Entry into Israel Regulations of 1974.

The provisions contained in this regulation were first included in 1963 in the wake of the Soblen controversy of 1962, which had exposed the shortcomings of the situation then existing and the inadequacy of the legal safeguards available to would-be deportees at the time. Dr. Robert Soblen, a U.S. national, was convicted by a federal court of espionage for the Soviet Union and sentenced to life imprisonment, both conviction and sentence being upheld by the U.S. Supreme Court. Before he began to serve his sentence, Soblen, who was afflicted with leukemia in an advanced stage, jumped $100,000 bail put up by his wife and friends and, using a Canadian passport in the name of his deceased brother, flew from Montreal to Israel.

At the time of his arrival in Israel in June 1962 there was no extradition treaty in force between the United States and Israel. (Such a treaty was signed in December 1962 and went into force in December of the following year.) Even if there had been such a treaty in force, it probably would not have applied to Soblen because of the arguably political nature of his crimes.

Shortly after Soblen's arrival in Israel, the U.S. Assistant Secretary of State for Near East Affairs, Philips Talbot, met with the Israel ambassador in Washington, Harman, and requested that Soblen be returned to the United States. Although both sides denied American pressure in this matter, it soon became obvious that Soblen's presence in Israel became an embarrassment for its government, which apparently also feared that as a Jew Soblen might apply for Israel nationality under the Law of Return and thus cause a serious political and legal controversy.

Some 36 hours after Soblen's arrival, when his true identity and whereabouts became known, he was arrested at a Tel Aviv hotel, taken into custody, and brought before a magistrate, who issued a detention order pending an inquiry into a suspected crime (that of illegal entry into the country) and granted a remand of ten days.

On the following day, after consultations on the highest government levels, including the Prime Minister, the Minister of the Interior issued a deportation order according to which Soblen was to be deported after the intervening Jewish Sabbath (the order was issued on Friday). In the meantime Soblen was held practically incommunicado in a government hospital and prevented from contacting his lawyer (the latter learned of the deportation order issued in respect of Soblen only several hours after Soblen's departure from Israel). His Canadian passport having been found invalid, Soblen was provided with an Israel laissez passer and on the morning of Sunday, 1 July 1962, was placed on board an airliner en route to Athens, where he was transferred to another plane en route to New York under the custody of a U.S. marshal. It was believed that a number of F.B.I. agents were also on the two airliners.

On approaching London, Soblen slashed his wrists and stabbed himself in the abdomen. Having unsuccessfully exhausted all legal remedies available to him in the United Kingdom, Soblen committed suicide in order to frustrate a deportation order issued against him.[119] A petition to the Israel High Court of Justice filed after Soblen's arrival in London and seeking an order for his return to the country failed on the ground that the petitioner was no longer within the effective jurisdiction of the court.

The official government communiqué, according to which Soblen had entered Israel on the basis of a tourist visa obtained on a passport belonging to another person and was deported from Israel because he was found to be on Israel territory without a valid and legal permit,[120] did not meet with wide public acceptance. Among the foremost critics of the government version was Yaakov Shimshon Shapira, then a practicing lawyer, who had been Israel's first Attorney-General in 1948 and who was to serve as Minister of Justice in 1966-73.[121] It was argued that irrespective of the merits of Soblen's conviction, the circumstances surrounding his removal from Israel were not worthy of a country committed to the rule of law, since he was not given a fair chance to challenge the deportation order; he was prevented from seeking legal advice; and the circumstances of his deportation amounted to a de facto extradition to the United States.

It was also argued that Soblen could not be deported so long as the ten-day remand by the magistrate was in force. In fact, the Courts Administration Authority, in an official statement, publicly denounced this aspect of the deportation, as did the magistrate who had issued the remand.

On 11 July 1962, the Knesset, after a heated debate, defeated an opposition nonconfidence motion in connection with the Soblen affair by 53 to 28.[122] However, the outcry that followed the government's handling of the matter eventually resulted in the insertion into the Entry into Israel Regulations in 1963 of three new regulations, with a view to ensuring that a Soblen-type situation could not recur. Regulations 14 through 16,[123] since replaced by Regulation 21 of the 1974 Regulations,[124] provide as follows:

> 14. A person in respect to whom a deportation order has been given, shall be served such order in writing and shall not be deported within three days after the delivery to him of such order.
>
> 15. A person in respect to whom a deportation order has been given and who has been detained pending his deportation, may submit a petition to a court and may contact a lawyer for this purpose. However, the filing

of such petition shall not delay the implementation of the deportation order unless the court otherwise decides.

16. Every deportation order shall specify the right under Regulation 15 of the person in respect to whom it has been made.

Protection

Although as a rule the government of Israel confines itself to protecting the interests of its nationals abroad, there is at least one instance in which it also assumed the representation of persons who were not Israel nationals. In its memorial submitted to the International Court of Justice in the Aerial Incident of 27 1955 (Israel v. Bulgaria) case, the Israel position regarding the representation of the interests of the stateless passengers of the El-Al airliner attacked and brought down by Bulgarian air defenses was explained in the following words:

> The Government of Israel considers that it is justified in this case in putting forward claims in respect of losses incurred by persons who are stateless. . . The Government of Israel submits that it is entitled to adopt the cause of persons whose cause is not otherwise adopted, when the damage which those persons suffered was incurred when the victims of an illegal action were flying in a commercial airliner on a scheduled international flight under the Israel flag. In the Reparations for Injuries Suffered case the Court stated that "even in inter-State relations there are important exceptions to the rule [that diplomatic protection is exercised only on behalf of nationals], for there are cases in which protection may be exercised by a State on behalf of persons not having its nationality."[125]

Although in the said memorial the right of diplomatic protection by Israel was claimed only on behalf of Israel nationals (not having another effective nationality) and stateless persons, on the obvious assumption that the interests of the passengers having an effective nationality other than that of Israel would be represented by their respective countries of nationality, there is nothing in the wording of the memorial to preclude the argument that Israel might consider itself justified in certain circumstances in affording diplomatic protection to persons having a nationality other than that of Israel if the cause of such persons is not embraced by their countries of nationality.

NATIONAL IMPLEMENTATION OF INTERNATIONAL RIGHTS AND DUTIES

The Act of State Doctrine

On a number of occasions Israel courts have rejected pleas that certain acts or transactions committed abroad be given recognition by them and regarded as valid on the grounds that they were legal and valid under the laws of the countries in which they took place. The "Act of State" plea has been rejected by the courts in those cases in which the foreign legislation relied upon for a justification of such acts or transactions was regarded by the courts as contrary to international law, "natural justice," "international morality," public order, and so on.

The best-known Israel decision rejecting the "Act of State" plea with regard to acts contrary to international law is unquestionably the Supreme Court judgment in Eichmann v. Attorney General, about which the court had the following to say.

> Counsel for the appellant proceeded to plead that the acts attributed to his client were committed within the framework of the anti-Jewish decrees of the Nazi regime . . . which, for all the injustice they entailed, had at the time the force of law. To this argument there are two replies. First, . . . it would appear . . . that the dominant tendency in the jurisprudence of West Germany today is to invalidate ab initio the discriminatory and destructive decrees of the Nazi regime, to deny them any legal validity from the day they were issued and enforced. . . . It follows that, according to the said jurisprudence, not only is the present contention of counsel for the appellant completely untenable even in German law, but that also . . . the acts in question cannot be accorded the nature of "Acts of State." However, we need not resort to modern German judgments as support for rejecting this contention. The second and principal reason for our doing so is that the discriminatory and plunderous

> decrees of that evil State and the murderous edicts of the autocrat who directed its affairs are not laws in the contemplation of international law and can in no manner render these terrible crimes valid or absolve those who participated in committing them from the personal responsibility they bear. . . .
>
> To conclude this aspect of the matter we can do no better than repeat the words of the District Court: "The very contention that the systematic extermination of masses of helpless human beings by a Government or regime could constitute an "act of State," appears to be an insult to reason and a mockery of justice."
>
> The plea of "Act of State" is rejected.[126]

This view of the invalidity of the discriminatory anti-Jewish legislative measures taken by the Germans during the Nazi occupation of various European countries is also reflected in the Supreme Court judgment in Mazor v. Kirschenbaum. Here the court had to pass on the validity or otherwise of a transaction involving gold and U.S. dollars, a transaction that had been concluded in occupied Poland in 1943. On this the court, through President Olshan, had the following to say:

> It has . . . been argued by counsel for defendant that the transaction was made in Poland and was forbidden there under the law, and that, therefore, the plaintiff is not entitled to any remedy by this Court. . . .
>
> It is true that as a rule the courts will not be inclined to sanction transactions that were illegal under the law of the country where they were made, subject to certain exceptions provided for by the principles of private international law. However, the recognition by our courts of the legislation of foreign countries is a matter affecting public order and the public interest. It seems to me that, having regard to the circumstances that prevailed under the Nazi occupation of Poland, when the Jewish inhabitants were put outside any law, when millions of them were exterminated, it is only reasonable to say that public order and public international morality alike do not require that a transaction of the

> kind here under consideration, the purpose of which was to save the lives of those unfortunate people, shall be declared invalid because it was regarded as such by the law enacted by the Nazi tyrants. I do not think that public policy imposes on Israel courts the duty to permit counsel for defendant to raise a plea of this kind.[127]

A similar approach has been adopted by the courts with regard to the anti-Jewish legislation passed by various Arab countries subsequent to the establishment of Israel in 1948.[128] In Elimelech v. Bazini the Tel Aviv District Court refused to entertain a plea by the defendant that a transaction in foreign currency made between himself and the plaintiff in Egypt should be considered as invalid because it was contrary to Egyptian law. The view of the court was as follows:

> It is a strange argument that in the present situation Israel courts have a duty to enforce Egyptian law. Even if there is no state of war between the two countries, in any event there are no "friendly relations" between them. In the present circumstances I agree with counsel for plaintiff that it is not contrary to public policy but rather in the interests of Israel-Jewish public policy in Egypt and Israel alike to enable Egyptian Jews to rescue their money from that country.[129]

A similar conclusion was reached by the Jerusalem District Court in Twik v. Gliko.[130] The defendant relied on an Egyptian law of 1948 prohibiting owning of immovable property situation in Israel, with a view to invalidating a transaction reached between himself and the plaintiff while both had still been in Egypt. To this argument the court replied in the following words:

> It is true that the courts will normally decline to sanction a transaction which is invalid under the lex loci contractus. . . . But . . . this rule is subject to certain exceptions, . . . and in those cases in which public interest or public international morality do not require the annulment of a given transaction, in spite of its being illegal at the place where it was concluded, we shall enforce such transaction here.

> Israel did not declare war on Egypt in 1948 and was not hostile to her. In those circumstances the Egyptian law which prohibited the owning of property in Israel is illegal and immoral. Therefore I believe that the transaction should be given legal effect here and that we should disregard the lex loci contractus.

Implementing Decisions of International Organizations

The measures taken by the Government of Israel in connection with the unilateral independence declaration of the white minority regime of Southern Rhodesia in November 1965 largely precede the UN resolutions on this matter. In a letter dated 13 November 1965, from the Permanent Representative of Israel to the President of the Security Council,[131] the following was pointed out: "The Government of Israel will not recognize this illegal regime and is taking immediate steps to prohibit all ties with it, including economic relations. The Government of Israel . . . will give its support to such action as the United Nations may take for that purpose."

Pursuant to this declaration of intention, the Israel consular missions abroad were advised in December 1965 that Israel does not consider passports issued by the Salisbury regime on or after 11 November 1965 (the date of the unilateral declaration of independence) or passports extended after that date, as valid for travel to Israel and that therefore no Israel visa whatsoever should be stamped in such a passport. This was done in accordance with the standing instructions of the Consular Section of the Israel Ministry for Foreign Affairs to the Israel missions abroad that no entry visa be granted to a person holding a passport of a country that has no diplomatic or consular relations with Israel without the prior approval of the application by the Consular Section in Jerusalem. As far as I could ascertain, no person holding a passport issued or extended by the Salisbury regime has sought to enter Israel on such passport so far.

The steps taken by Israel by January 1966 were recapitulated in a verbal message of 10 January 1966, addressed to the Secretary-General of the United Nations, as follows:

> Israel has not recognized the Salisbury regime and consequently does not entertain diplomatic or other relations with it. The Government of Israel has forbidden all ties with the above-mentioned regime and, accordingly, the supply

> of arms, equipment and military matériel to Southern Rhodesia has been prohibited and all economic relations with Southern Rhodesia, including the supply of oil and petroleum products, have been broken.
>
> In conformity with the above, the Bank of Israel has severed all relations with that part of the Bank of Rhodesia which is controlled by the Salisbury regime, and has recognized the new Governor of the Reserve Bank of Rhodesia in London as the only duly constituted authority, which was established in order to ensure that assets of the Reserve Bank of Rhodesia held abroad be safeguarded from the illegal regime in Southern Rhodesia.[132]

In May 1966 it became clear that the Israel ban on economic ties with Southern Rhodesia extended also to goods passing through third countries on their way to or from Rhodesia. In a press release by the Israel Government Press Office of 4 May 1966, it was revealed that the government of Israel had learned that the ship S.S. Maya, on its way to Haifa and carrying cargo for Israel, included shipments that after further investigation had proved to have originated in Rhodesia, although they had not been bought there. The press release then stated as follows:

> In accordance with the policy of the Government of Israel which was expressed in its announcement of 12 November 1965, of non-recognition of the illegal regime in Rhodesia and the severance of all contact with it, including economic ties, the Government used its full authority and took the necessary steps to prevent the import of this cargo into Israel. The Minister of Trade and Industry has taken the necessary action to prevent a repetition of similar occurrences in the future.

Following the adoption by the Security Council on 16 December 1966 of Resolution 232 (1966), in which the council, acting in accordance with Chapter 7 of the UN Charter, decided that all member states should prevent activities by their nationals or in their territories affecting commodities originating in Southern Rhodesia, as well as the supply to Southern Rhodesia of certain vital items, the Acting Permanent Representative of Israel in a verbal message of

13 January 1967, addressed to the Secretary-General of the United Nations, recalled the various measures that had been taken by Israel and assured the Secretary-General that "the Government of Israel will implement fully Security Council Resolution 232 (1966) of 16 December 1966 and, having examined the provisions in force, has reached the conclusion that no further legislative steps are necessary in order to give effect to this resolution."[133]

This position of Israel was reaffirmed in a verbal message of 13 August 1967 addressed to the Secretary-General, following the adoption by the Security Council, on 29 May 1968, of Resolution 253 (1968). The government of Israel informed the Secretary-General that it was

> again reviewing the situation with the intention to give full effect to Security Council Resolution 253. While it appears that the provisions of that Resolution are virtually covered by existing legislation and administrative regulations, this has not yet been finally established. A further report on the matter will be furnished shortly to the Secretary-General, if that should be necessary, in order to supplement the information contained in the present letter.[134]

More recently this position of Israel was reiterated by Foreign Minister Abba Eban, in a statement made on 20 March 1970, when he said the following:

> We have no political, economic, commercial or other relations with the present regime [in Southern Rhodesia], and it is our resolve to maintain that stand. . . . It is not in our mind to change one iota in our attitude until there is established in Southern Rhodesia a Government based upon the will of the people, and one that honours the tradition and practices that ought to prevail in human and international relations.[135]

Procedures Related to the Issue of Certificates or Suggestions by the Executive in Connection with Litigation in National Courts

According to Shablai Rosenne, an executive certificate was first introduced into a court in Palestine in 1940.[136] In <u>Tetsema</u>

and Others v. The Royal Italian Consul General and Others,[137] the Italian government brought action in the Jerusalem Land Court claiming certain property by reason of the Italian conquest of Ethiopia. In an order of 3 July 1940, the Land Court adjourned the action, without striking it out or dismissing it, "until the end of the war with Italy." Between the issuance of the Land Court's order and the judgment of the Supreme Court of 11 December 1948, the High Commissioner informed the Chief Justice, in writing, that "I have been acquainted by the Secretary of State for the Colonies that the de jure recognition of His Majesty's Government of the Italian conquest of Ethiopia has been withdrawn." The Supreme Court therefore concluded that "the title of the Italian Government to the property in question can no longer be recognised as existent," and the appeal was accordingly allowed.

It is noteworthy that in this case the executive certificate was submitted after the court of first instance had concluded its proceedings, during the appeal stage. Clearly it was submitted at that late stage because a new fact, that is, the withdrawal by the United Kingdom of its de jure recognition of the Italian conquest of Ethiopia, had occurred after the Land Court's order had been given. However, there would appear to be nothing in the law to prevent the Court of Appeal, in other circumstances as well, from receiving executive certificates at any stage of its proceedings prior to the handing down of judgment. Thus, in El-Turani v. Attorney General the Supreme Court requested a Foreign Office Certificate during the appeal stage even in the absence of any new facts. El-Turani was charged with offenses alleged to have taken place in the demilitarized zone established between Israel and Syria under Article 5 of the Israel-Syria General Armistice Agreement of 20 July 1949,[138] and the question arose whether the criminal jurisdiction of Israel extended to the demilitarized zone. The Haifa District Court replied to this question in the affirmative, basing its decision on Israel legislation and judicial practice. The Supreme Court dismissed El-Turani's appeal and agreed with the District Court's reasoning, with the following qualification:

> Since the question related to the foreign relations of the State, we found it necessary to approach the Ministry for Foreign Affairs, notifying both parties, asking it to inform us if the village which is in the demilitarised zone is inside the frontiers of Israel or not, and the reply of the Ministry was in the affirmative. From this it follows more clearly that the offenses of which the appellant was accused

> were committed within the area sovereignty over which is vested in the State of Israel.[139]

The Supreme Court does not appear to have had any scruples with regard to eliciting the Foreign Office Certificate in the appeal stage. The notification of the parties of its intention to do so was presumably motivated by its desire to enable the parties to make any suggestions they might see fit with regard to the phrasing of the questions to be put to the executive. As a general practice, however, Foreign Office Certificates are requested and submitted in the course of the deliberations of the court of first instance; this practice would seem to be a reasonable one in view of the fact that Foreign Office Certificates are sought with a view to determining questions of fact.

It is worth mentioning, though, that on at least one occasion, Heirs of Shababo v. Heilen and Others,[140] the Jerusalem District Court sought a Foreign Office Certificate even prior to the hearing. Shababo had been run over and killed in Jerusalem in June 1952 by a car driven by Heilen, a soldier in the Belgian Army on duty with the Belgian Consulate-General in Jerusalem. The action for damages was brought by the widow of Shababo against Heilen, as well as against the Consulate-General and Consul-General. The car belonged either to the Consulate-General or to the Consul-General and was being driven on duty at the time of the accident. Before the defendants entered a conditional appearance in December 1952, in which they claimed that for a number of reasons the court lacked jurisdiction in respect to them, Judge (now Justice) Witkon on 23 November 1952 sent a letter to the Foreign Ministry in which he had written the following:

> It is possible [emphasis in original] that the defendants will argue that the Court lacks jurisdiction to hear the action brought against them. I would therefore be grateful if you could kindly inform me whether the defendants or any of them are entitled to diplomatic [sic] immunity from civil jurisdiction.

Rosenne has criticized Judge Witkon's request, saying that while the court may seek a Foreign Office Certificate even prior to the court hearing,

> it is desirable, as a rule, to refrain from submitting it prematurely. Since the certificate is supposed to state facts, and such statement in turn, entails a political commitment, the Foreign

> Ministry should not be confronted with such necessity unless it is truly indispensable. A fortiori, the Minister should not be asked hypothetical questions.[141]

The practice of the Israel Foreign Ministry ever since 1948 has been to issue Foreign Office Certificates only at the request of the court and not of the litigants or their representatives.[142] However, in appropriate cases the ministry may advise the litigants of its reply in an informal manner and without committing itself, even before a formal request has been submitted to it by the court.[143]

At the same time, the litigants will be given the opportunity to suggest to the court the precise phrasing of the question to be put to the executive.

As a rule the Foreign Ministry advises the court in writing of its position. However, occasionally its views are brought to the attention of the court in the form of an oral statement by the Attorney-General or his representative. Thus, for example, in Attorney-General v. Kamiar the Deputy State Attorney, who was representing the Attorney-General in the extradition proceedings instituted against Kamiar at the request of the Swiss government, advised the Jerusalem District Court orally that the Israel government regarded itself bound by an extradition treaty between the two countries. Counsel for Kamiar had disputed the validity of the treaty on the grounds that it had not been properly ratified by Israel.[144]

Similarly, in Heirs of Shababo v. Heilen and Others,[145] the second enquiry of the Foreign Minister by the District Court was answered orally on his behalf by the Attorney-General's representative.

It is also worth mentioning in this connection that on at least one occasion, in the Kamiar case, the government departed from its declared position that executive certificates (or suggestions) are submitted only in response to a request by the court. There the District Court was presented with a statement by the government regarding the validity of the Israel-Swiss extradition treaty without any request by the court that it do so.

As to the conclusiveness or otherwise of a Foreign Office Certificate, it is worth starting the survey on this matter with the first Israel case in which a Foreign Office Certificate was requested, that is, El-Turani v. Attorney General. There, it will be recalled, there arose the question of Israel criminal jurisdiction in the demilitarized areas established under the Israel-Syrian General Armistice Agreement of 1949. The Haifa District Court answered this question in the affirmative, on the strength of various provisions of Israel law analyzed by it. The Supreme Court, while upholding the

District Court's judgment as well as its reasoning, asked for a Foreign Office Certificate because "the question related to the foreign relations of the State." The reply of the ministry confirming the conclusions reached independently by the District Court was regarded by the Supreme Court as the "conclusive answer to the argument raised by counsel for appellant to the effect that in so far as concerns the demilitarised zone, Israel's frontiers have not yet been determined and that there is still doubt whether the zone is within the territory or not."[146]

The Supreme Court's approach has been criticized by Rosenne, who takes the view that if an analysis of the provisions of Israel law was sufficient to determine the juridical status of the demilitarized zone, and if the Supreme Court upheld the District Court's conclusion on this point, there was no reason to request a Foreign Office Certificate and, at any event, there was no ground to request a Foreign Office Certificate on a matter already determined in the judge's mind before submitting his request to the executive. Rosenne further argues that the Supreme Court was wrong to ask for a Foreign Office Certificate on a matter that was regarded by both the District Court and the Supreme Court as a question of law, as distinct from a question of fact.[147]

The principle that Foreign Office Certificates should be sought only on questions of fact pertaining to the foreign relations of the state and that such a certificate should be regarded as conclusive on those questions was forcefully reiterated by Justice Cohn in Kamiar v. Attorney General. There, it will be recalled, the Attorney General's representative transmitted orally to the District Court dealing with the Swiss extradition request the Foreign Ministry's statement that in her relations with Switzerland Israel regards herself as bound by the Israel-Swiss extradition treaty of 1958. Justice Cohn expressed this as follows:

> It is true that in the United States courts have regarded State Department certificates as binding also on substantive questions of international law, . . . and there are also certain dicta of British judges widening the determinative scope of Foreign Office Certificates so as to cover also legal questions. . . . But it should not be forgotten that a Foreign Office Certificate is always in the nature of evidence and is always intended to prove a fact; and as proof of a fact it is conclusive, i.e. it constitutes a final and conclusive evidence of the fact to which it attests. Sometimes that fact stems from the operation of international law,

> and in such cases the court will not cast doubt on the Foreign Office Certificate, which proves that fact by going into the origins under international law of the act that preceded the certificate or was its cause. Occasionally the fact attested to by the certificate may necessitate some legal action (such as the granting of immunity) and then the Court will refrain from casting doubt on the certificate and will take the [required] legal action. However, wherever the question that comes up for determination by the Court is one of a purely legal character and all the facts are properly proven or undisputed--the decision has to be made by the Court, and the Executive Branch has no right to arrogate to itself any judicial authority, irrespective of whether the ultimate decision will be based on international law or domestic law. The statement of the Foreign Minister on the matter before us, as transmitted to the District Court, constitutes conclusive evidence that in her relations with Switzerland the Government of Israel regards itself bound by the [extradition] treaty.[148]

Justice Cohn then went on to reject the well-known "two-voices" theory. He took the view that constant unanimity between the executive branch and the judiciary smacks of totalitarianism and to the extent that courts will remain independent of the executive branch and speak in their own voice, they will be better able to discharge their duties toward the citizens.[149]

Justice Cohn's approach to the matter here under consideration appears to be open to criticism on several grounds.

First, he seems to assume a clear-cut dichotomy between questions of fact and questions of law, whereas "the question ordinarily asked of the executive is one of mixed law and fact."

Second, whenever there arises a mixed question of law and fact, there is also the problem of "whether the Executive should confine itself to statements of fact and refuse to draw legal conclusions therefrom."[150]

Third, Justice Cohn apparently did not take into account those instances in which the Foreign Office Certificate cannot be regarded as conclusive even on questions of fact because "the statement of the Foreign Office lacks clarity on account of the novelty or complexity of the facts which it is requested to certify [and] the Court is presumed to have the power--and the duty--to interpret the certificate in accordance with the principles of International Law applicable to the situation."[151]

It might be added that occasionally a Foreign Office Certificate is deliberately equivocal, and then it certainly falls upon the court to interpret it. This seems to have happened in Heirs of Shababo v. Heilen and Others, which is generally regarded as the leading Israel case on the question of the role and scope of a Foreign Office Certificate in an Israel court. In reply to Judge Witkon's letter inquiring about the immunity to which the Belgian Consulate-General and Consul-General, respectively, were entitled, the Foreign Minister, in a letter of 8 January 1953, replied in the following terms:

> Comte Thiery de Lichtervelde, in charge of the Belgian Consulate-General in Jerusalem, was sent to Jerusalem on behalf of the Belgian Government and with the knowledge of the Israel Government as representative of the Belgian Government as well as serving as Consul-General of Belgium in Jerusalem; but the Israel Government had not been asked to issue an exequatur, and no consular exequatur has been issued to him. The name of Roger Heilen appears on the list of official employees of the said representative of the Belgian Government which has been submitted to the Ministry of Foreign Affairs.

Some doubt having arisen concerning the correct interpretation of that certificate, the court inquired further of the minister as follows:

> Have the defendants in this case, all or any of them, been recognised by the Israel Government as diplomatic representatives or as belonging to the staff or suite of a recognised diplomatic representative?

An oral reply was delivered to the court on this question by the representative of the Attorney General, who had intervened in this case because of the public interest involved. In that reply it was stated as follows:

> I have been instructed by the Foreign Minister to inform the Court in reply to the question put by the Court . . . that the facts regarding the

> defendants are as has been described in the certificate dated January 8th, 1953, submitted by the Legal Adviser of the Foreign Ministry on instructions from the Foreign Minister, and that the Foreign Minister regrets his inability to furnish the Court with any reply to the specific question asked of him.

It consequently fell upon the court to interpret the apparently deliberately ambiguous certificate submitted to it by the Foreign Ministry, which it accordingly did.[152]

Fourth, it would seem that a Foreign Office Certificate is <u>not</u> required even on a question of fact pertaining to the foreign relations of the state where those facts are within the judicial notice of the court. This question arose in <u>Kassem and Ziara v. Attorney General</u>. In that case a national of Israel had been killed in April 1956 in one of the Egyptian-inspired fedayeen actions. The first appellant, Kassem, at the time was a civilian policeman in charge of a police station near Gaza, about 2 kilometers on the Egyptian side of the Armistice Demarcation Line with Israel. The second appellant, Ziara, was a farmer who lived near the police station. On the day of the crime the appellants proceeded to a ditch that indicated the Armistice Demarcation Line. The first appellant and the Egyptian soldiers were armed, and the second appellant carried the ammunition. When the victim was making his morning rounds on horseback, Ziara rose and began to run toward the ditch. The victim followed into the ambush, where Kassem and the soldiers shot at and wounded him. The victim fell to the ground four meters from the ditch. Kassem and the soldiers then went up to him and killed him. Kassem and Ziara were arrested by the Israel police some time after October 1956, during the Israel occupation of the Gaza Strip. Convicted of murder by the Jerusalem District Court, which relied on a Foreign Office Certificate stating that the ditch was one meter within Israel territory, Kassem and Ziara appealed to the Supreme Court, arguing, among other things, that it had not been proved that the crime took place in Israel territory. The appeal was rejected and the Supreme Court, through Justice Landau, pointed out that the Foreign Office Certificate had been submitted to the District Court without opposition by the accused and that it was too late to object to its admissibility during the appeal. Justice Landau then went on to say the following:

> The certificate, in that part of it which deals with the description of the Armistice demarcation line, repeats Article VI, paragraph 1, of the General Armistice Agreement between Israel

> and Egypt. This agreement was published in the Israel Treaty Series, and its contents are therefore known even without the Foreign Minister's certificate. . . . Furthermore, the lower court also heard evidence from Major N., who was Vice-Chairman of the Israel Delegation to the "Israel-Egyptian] Mixed Armistice Commission and who had personally dealt with the delineation of the Armistice demarcation line by the ditch. In his evidence he confirmed what was stated in the . . . Foreign Minister's certificate regarding the situation of the ditch, and accordingly the District Court had sufficient evidence on this matter even without the . . . Foreign Minister's certificate.[153]

In other words, the Foreign Office Certificate was deemed unnecessary by the court, partly because its contents were within the judicial notice of the court and partly because the facts stated in it could be proved in the normal manner. Thus it may legitimately be asked why, in the light of these considerations, the District Court should have resorted to the Foreign Office Certificate in the Kassem and Ziara case in the first place.

In light of Justice Landau's remarks concerning the lack of need for a Foreign Office Certificate with regard to facts that are within the judicial notice of the court, it is also difficult to follow the reasoning of the majority of the Supreme Court in Ravidi and Meches v. The Hebron Military Court and Others. The petitioners were two Jerusalem antiquity dealers whose store is in the eastern part of the city, which was under Jordanian rule until June 1967. Under the Jordania Antiquities Law of 1966 it is prohibited to export antiquities from Jordan without a permit from the competent authority. In Order No. 117 of 1967, the commanding officer of the Israel defense forces in Judea and Samaria decreed that the said Jordanian Law should be taken to prohibit the export of antiquities from Judea and Samaria. On a number of occasions in 1968 the petitioners transferred antiquities from the Hebron region (in Judea) to their store in Jerusalem. They were brought before the Hebron Military Court for having violated the said law as modified by the Order of the Military Commander.

In a preliminary plea they claimed that no violation of the Jordanian Law had occurred, the implication being that Eastern Jerusalem was also part of the territory to which the law applied and consequently the transfer of antiquities from Hebron to Jerusalem constituted no offense under it. When that preliminary plea was rejected by the Military Court, Ravidi and Meches petitioned the High Court of Justice, which dismissed their petition.

However, both Justice Witkon and Justice Cohn took the view that the proper approach to the question would have been to request a Foreign Office Certificate on the question of whether Eastern Jerusalem was within Israel territory or not, since, in their view, this was a political rather than a legal question. The two justices stated that they had refrained from requesting such a certificate merely because the question of the juridical status of Eastern Jerusalem had not been brought into issue by the parties.[154]

In my opinion, however, there was no reason even to contemplate a request for a Foreign Office Certificate in this case, even if the parties had not been in agreement on this matter, since under Israel law the juridical status of Eastern Jerusalem was clearly within the judicial notice of the court. More specifically, the Supreme Court obviously had judicial notice of the Law and Administration Ordinance (Amendment No. 11) Law, 5727-1967 of 27 June 1967,[155] Section 1 of which provides that "the law, jurisdiction and administration of the State shall extend to any area of Eretz Israel designated by the Government by order." It also had notice of the order made in pursuance of the law in respect of Eastern Jerusalem the following day. This attitude, which is the correct one in the present view, was expressed by the minority (Justice Kahn), who stated as follows:

> There is no need for any certificate by the Foreign Minister or any other executive authority in order to ascertain that Eastern Jerusalem constitutes a part of the territory of the State of Israel. Nor do I need for this purpose the admission of the petitioners. . . . On June 28, 1967, the Government issued an order . . . [pursuant to the Law of the previous day] . . . and it is not disputed that the petitioners' store is located within the area described in the annex to that order.[156]

In contrast, there have also been cases in which the courts have refrained from requesting Foreign Office Certificates when such requests would have been justified from the legal point of view. A case in point is Jiday v. Chief Execution Officer, Haifa District Court, and Others. There the High Court of Justice was petitioned with a view to overruling the decision given by the first respondent in favor of the second respondent (the wife of the petitioner), pursuant to the judgment for the payment of maintenance rendered by the religious court of the Greek Catholic Melkite Community (the petitioner and the second respondent were members of that community) and confirmed by the Melkite Appellate Tribunal appointed by the Melkite Patriarch, whose residence is in Lebanon. Before the High Court of Justice, the counsel for the petitioner argued, among other things, that since Lebanon was in a state of war with Israel and her residents were consequently enemy aliens under Israel law, the Melkite Patriarch was not entitled to appoint judges to determine any matter in Israel, and the Appellate Tribunal's judgment was therefore invalid.

The court, through Justice Goitein, rejected this argument, basing itself on the assumption which the present view would hold to be erroneous, that pursuant to Articles 33 and 37 of the UN Charter, "states members of the United Nations cannot be in a state of war so long as they have made no effort to reach agreement with their enemy or so long as the Security Council has not reached a decision concerning the state of affairs which has come into existence between the two States."[157] Justice Goitein then proceeded to analyze various provisions of the Israel-Lebanon General Armistice Agreement of 23 March 1949[158] and reached the conclusion that "our situation might properly be described as one of termination of war."[159]

In the present view, and having regard to the controversial character of armistice agreements in general and their impact on the termination or otherwise of the state of war between the parties to such agreements, the High Court of Justice should have sought a Foreign Office Certificate on the matter under consideration. That this was not done is perhaps to be explained by the fact that Justice Goitein, who had been a member of the Israel diplomatic service prior to his appointment to the bench, apparently considered that he had judicial notice of the Israel claim referred to in his judgment, namely, that Egyptian interference with Israel navigation in the Suez Canal on the ground that a state of war existed between the two countries was unacceptable in view of the fact that the Israel-Egyptian Armistice Agreement had terminated the state of war that had existed between them.

TREATIES AND THE INDIVIDUAL

By virtue of Article 46 of the Palestine Order in Council of 1922[160] and Section 11 of the Law and Administration Ordinance, 5708-1948,[161] Israel law follows English common law in regarding customary international law as part of the domestic law of Israel. (See Shimshon Palestine Portland Cement Factory v. Attorney General[162] and Stamfer v. Attorney General.[163]) As ruled in Steinberg v. Attorney General, this holds true only as follows:

> Where we are dealing not with the Common Law but with a written statute which expresses the will of the legislator, the Court must carry out the will of the legislator, without considering if there exists contradiction between the statute and international law. It may well be that international law imposes a certain obligation on the State. But since international law concerns not the relations of a State to its citizens but a State's relations with other States, it follows that such obligations are for the benefit of other States, while the individual citizen is granted no right to insist upon the carrying out of the obligation.[164]

Likewise, in Eichmann v. Attorney General, where a conflict exists between the provisions of municipal statutory law and a rule of international law, the Supreme Court held as follows:

> It is the duty of the Court to give preference to and apply the laws of the local Legislature. . . . True, the presumption must be that the Legislature strives to adjust its laws to the principles of international law which have received general recognition. But where a contrary intention clearly emerges from the statute itself, that presumption loses its force and the Court is enjoined to disregard it.[165]

Israel law has also adopted British practice with regard to the domestic status of treaties to which Israel is a party, that is, that such treaties do not automatically become part of domestic law and their effect on the domestic plane depends on a specific act of transformation. The leading Israel case on this matter is Custodian of Absentee Property v. Samra. The respondent, an Arab farmer whose lands had been transferred to Israel under the Israel-Jordan General Armistice Agreement of 3 April 1949,[166] was relying vis-à-vis the Custodian of Absentee Property on the provisions of the said agreement. In rejecting his argument, the Supreme Court, through Justice Berinson, had the following to say:

> The Rhodes [Armistice] Agreement is a Treaty between Israel and another State. Whatever its force and validity according to international law, it is not a law which the Israel courts will or can enforce. The rights which it grants and the duties

> which it imposes are the rights and duties of the States which concluded the Treaty and its implementation is a matter for them alone to secure by those special means which are usual to ensure the implementation of international treaties. Such a Treaty is not given to the jurisdiction of the courts of this country except and to the extent that it, or the rights and duties which flow from it, have been embodied in the law of the land and have acquired the force of binding law. In such circumstances, it must be pointed out, the Court would then have reference not to the Treaty as such but the the law which alone gives it validity for domestic purposes. . . . What is more, even when an inter-State or international agreement provides that certain individuals should have defined rights, such an obligation remains an international obligation binding upon the State, and nothing more. The individuals concerned obtain no substantive right on the basis of the agreement and have nothing which they can secure in a court of law, whether on the ground that they are beneficiaries under the agreement or on some other basis.[167]

A similar question arose more recently in Richuk v. The State of Israel, reference to which has already been made elsewhere. The three justices on the bench in that case unanimously rejected any attempt by the appellant to rely in his favor on the provisions of the Anglo-Israel Financial Agreement of 1950.[168] The opinion of Justice Witkon was as follows:

> There is no necessity to expatiate on the respondent's argument to the effect that the individual cannot bring a claim against the Government on the basis of an international treaty. That argument is sound in itself.[169]

Likewise, President Olshan stated as follows:

> The rule that an individual cannot claim from the Government on the basis of an international treaty is not disputed--that is to say, on the basis of a treaty concluded between the State of which the individual is a national and another

> State. In such a case, if as a result of such a treaty the Government pays to one of its citizens a sum of money, that in itself is not sufficient to prove that legal privity has been created between it and the citizen.[170]

Justice (now President) Agranat followed suit by stating as follows:

> The making of the Treaty by the Government of Israel with the British Government was an act performed by the Government of Israel in virtue of its sovereign authority and therefore it is not possible to see the Treaty as part of the domestic law or as granting rights on which any citizen of the State can base a claim.[171]

In the latter part of the 1960s an attempt was made by Justice Cohn--on at least two occasions--to restrict the scope of the rule as enunciated in the Samra and Richuk cases. In Kurz and Another v. Kirschen, the Supreme Court was faced with the problem of ascertaining the law of personal status applying in Israel to stateless persons. Under Article 64 of the Palestine Order in Council of 1922, the law of personal status of foreign nationals is that of their country of nationality. Justice Cohn took the view that the answer to this question was to be found in the International Convention Relating to the Status of Stateless Persons of 1954,[172] to which Israel had become a party in 1958.[173] Article 12(1) of that convention provides that "the personal status of a stateless person shall be governed by the law of the country of his residence." Justice Cohn pointed to the fact that this provision was identical with the one contained in the 1951 Convention on the Status of Refugees,[174] which had also been acceded to by Israel,[175] and then added the following:

> Although it is true that an international treaty does not have per se the force of a binding [domestic] law, . . . it must be said that this rule applies to any specific provision found in a given treaty which does not conform with domestic law and does not reflect general international law as accepted . . . by the overwhelming majority of the world's nations. But it does not apply to a provision that does not contradict domestic law and reflects international law, accepted . . . in the manner described above. For in such a case the fact that

> it is laid down in an international treaty to which Israel has acceded and by which Israel has become bound cannot weaken such a provision; on the contrary, this fact only gives it added force and significance. . . . The Israel Legislature has not seen fit or necessary to pass a law in order to give the force of a binding rule to the provision contained in Article 12 of the Convention [on Stateless Persons] which is already a provision of general [international] law. But it must be remembered that this provision found the general acceptance of the nations of the world. It is immaterial for our purpose whether they acceded to it formally or not, since . . . the Convention was drafted by, and with the knowledge of, legal experts from all over the world, international lawyers and representatives of all the existing legal systems alike. There has been no reservation on their part. Moreover, the very fact that this provision has been included for the second time in an international treaty, bears witness to the fact that it is a recognised and accepted rule of international law. And if we add to this a further consideration--which to me is the weightiest of them all--namely, that there is a lacuna in our domestic law precisely on this question of the law of personal status of stateless persons, I cannot refrain from reaching the conclusion that the provision contained in this Convention, which accurately reflects an accepted rule of international law, in indeed intended to fill this gap.[176]

In other words, the very adoption of an international treaty by the vast majority of nations is regarded by Justice Cohn as creative of general international law, which thus becomes part of the domestic law of Israel, at least in those cases in which there appears to be a gap in the domestic law, even though the treaty in question has not undergone the process of transformation normally required for the provisions of treaties to become binding rules of domestic law.

This tendency of Justice Cohn was carried even further by him in The American European Beth El Mission v. The Minister of Social Welfare and Others.[177] In that case the petitioners challenged the validity of the regulations made by the minister under the Homes (Supervision) Law, 5725-1965,[178] on the grounds that they violated the principle of freedom of religion since they provided that a minor should not be sent to a home operated by a religious community other than his or her own. While dismissing the petition, Justice Cohn held as follows:

> Any regulation that violates fundamental principles of the freedom of religion or of any other human right recognised as such by international law, will be regarded by this [High] Court [of Justice] as unreasonable and will thus be declared invalid by it. I need no explicit authority on this point; I regard as sufficient the long-standing rule according to which the norms of international law, to the extent that they have been accepted by the majority of nations and do not contradict a law passed by the Knesset, are part of the law of Israel. . . . The principle of the freedom of religion, as well as other human rights, as laid down in the Universal Declaration of Human Rights and the Covenant on Civil and Political Rights of 1966, are nowadays the heritage of all enlightened nations, whether or not members of the United Nations, irrespective of whether or not they have already ratified the 1966 Covenant; for they were drafted by legal experts from all over the world and adopted by the U.N. General Assembly of which the overwhelming majority of nations are members.[179]

Feinberg has criticized this approach--rightly, I believe--on the ground that Justice Cohn apparently fails to distinguish between declaratory and constitutive treaties. Although principles contained in declaratory treaties could properly be regarded as reflecting general international law and, as such, also principles of Israel domestic law, it could not be maintained that constitutive treaties intended to create new norms of international law could become by their very adoption part of general international law, binding also those states that have not become parties to them. Consequently, Feinberg goes on to argue, they cannot be regarded as part of the domestic law of Israel, even if Israel is an adherent to the treaties in question, unless they have been transformed by the Israel legislature into norms of the domestic law of Israel.[180]

It would appear that Justice Cohn's pronouncements in the Kurz and Beth El Mission cases do not reflect the mainstream of Israel legal thinking. Certainly his statements in the latter case must be regarded as irrelevant to the decision, since he found no fault with the regulations made by the Minister of Social Welfare and dismissed the petition.

Abbreviations Used in Citations

D.K. Divrei HaKnesset, Record of Knesset proceedings (in Hebrew)

I.R. Iton Rishmi, the Official Gazette during the tenure of the Provisional Council of State (in Hebrew)

K.A. Kitvei Amana (Treaty Documents), Israel Treaty Series (in Hebrew)

K.T. Kovetz HaTakanot (Collection of Regulations), Subsidiary Legislation (in Hebrew)

L.S.I. Laws of the State of Israel, authorized English translation of Israel laws, prepared by the Ministry of Justice

P.D. Piskei Din (Judgments), law reports of the Israel Supreme Court, published by the Ministry of Justice (in Hebrew)

P.E. Psakim Elyonim (law reports of the Supreme Court), published by the Israel Bar Association (1948-61) (in Hebrew)

P.L.R. Palestine Law Reports, law reports of the Supreme Court of Mandatory Palestine

P.M. Psakim Mehoziim (law reports of the District Courts, published by the Israel Bar Association (in Hebrew)

S.H. Sefer Hallukkim (Book of Laws), Principal Legislation, containing the laws passed by the Knesset (in Hebrew)

1. 6 L.S.I. 76. The official English translation ("A passport is issued to an Israel national upon his application.") uses a less mandatory language than the original Hebrew.

2. The provisions of Section 6 equally apply to an Israel laissez passer, which under Section 2(b) of the law is issued (1) to a person who is not an Israel national or whose nationality is undefined or doubtful or (2), in special cases, to an Israel national upon application.

3. 20 L.S.I. 64. The main purpose of this amendment was to eliminate, or at least minimize, the phenomenon of the "fictitious immigrant." See on this Gouldman, Israel Nationality Law 45-61 (1970).

4. 23 L.S.I. 50. A passport may be extended for an additional period not exceeding five years. The total period of validity of a passport is not to exceed ten years. The fee for the issue of a passport is 300 Israel pounds. For the extension of its validity the fee is 100 to 200 Israel pounds, depending on the period of extension. Lower fees apply to various categories of pass-

ports, including those issued to organized groups traveling on collective passports.

5. Section 5 of the Law of Return, 5710-1950, 4 L.S.I. 114, grants every Jew "the right to come to the country as an oleh." ("Oleh" is a Jew immigrating, or literally, "ascending," to Israel.) Section 2 of the Nationality Law, 5712-1952, 6 L.S.I. 50, entitles every oleh to become an Israel national "by return," subject to the right of such person who holds a foreign nationality to declare, within three months after arrival in Israel, in written notice to the Minister of the Interior, that he or she does not wish to become an Israel national. 22 L.S.I. 241. Under an amendment of the law passed by the Knesset in 1971, Israel nationality by return may be granted also to "a person [who] has expressed his desire to settle in Israel, being a person who has received, or is entitled to receive, an oleh's visa under the Law of Return." 25 L.S.I. 1171. Persons falling within this category may apply to the Minister of the Interior, who may then confer on them, at his discretion, Israel nationality prior to their arrival in Israel. Ibid.

The purpose of this amendment was to enable Jews wishing to settle in Israel who are prevented from doing so because of the emigration policies of their countries of residence (primarily Soviet Jews) to acquire Israel nationality "by return" even prior to their arrival in Israel. As of May 1977, some 600 applications of this kind have been received by the Minister of the Interior; all but very few of them have been approved by him.

6. Gouldman, op. cit., at 49.

7. This includes injunctions issued by the religious tribunals of the various communities, which under the law dating back to the Ottoman period and inherited by Israel from the British Mandate, have jurisdiction in matters of personal status.

8. Gouldman, op. cit., at 102.

9. Ibid., at 50.

10. 6 L.S.I. 77.

11. Ibid., § 9(b).

12. 11 L.S.I. 158.

13. Ibid.

14. 13 L.S.I. 7.

15. See the paper by H. Cohn, "Judicial Protection of the Individual against the Executive in Israel," 1 Judicial Protection Against the Executive 442-43 (1969). See also Pelley-Karp, "Judicial Limits of Administrative Discretion," Israeli Reports to the Seventh International Congress of Comparative Law, 1966 105-106.

16. 15 P.D. 1151 (1961).

17. For a recent decision to similar effect see Al-Kurdi v. National Labour Tribunal, 26 (II) P.D. 66 (1972).

18. I.R. 5708-1948, Supp. II, at 81.

19. 1 L.S.I. 8.

20. 2 L.S.I. 16.

21. 6 L.S.I. 50.

22. 2 L.S.I. 17.

23. 7 P.D. 534 (1953).
24. Ibid., at 536.
25. 9 L.S.I. 105, amending Reg. 2(a) of the Emergency Regulations.
26. 10 L.S.I. 33.
27. 15 L.S.I. 179.
28. 14 L.S.I. 56.
29. K.T. 5278-1968, at 911.
30. 15 L.S.I. 180-81 (Regulations 7-10).
31. 21 L.S.I. 114.
32. K.T. 5727-1966, at 1044.
33. 19 L.S.I. 163.
34. 5 L.S.I. 13, § 2; 16 L.S.I. 28-29.
35. 5 L.S.I. 14, § 11.
36. 15 L.S.I. 49; 24 L.S.I. 164, § 3(b).
37. Gouldman, op. cit., at 102.
38. 6 L.S.I. 159, § 1.
39. Nor does the need for an entry visa exist for the holder of an immigrant's visa under Section 2(a) of the Law of Return of 1950, 4 L.S.I. 114, even if the immigrant has decided, in accordance with Section 2(c)(2) of the Nationality Law, 22 L.S.I. 241, to opt out of nationality by return.
40. 6 L.S.I. 50.
41. 12 P.E. 246 (1953); 8 P.D. 970 (1954); 7 P.D. 587 (1953).
42. See Gouldman, op. cit., at 104.
43. 6 P.D. 638 (1952).
44. 7 P.D. 49 (1953).
45. 7 P.D. 366 (1953).
46. 20 L.S.I. 47.
47. Palestine Gazette, 1945, Supplement 2, at 1055; Palestine Gazette, 1946, Supplement 2, at 1963.
48. See, for example, Bader v. Minister of the Interior, 7 P.D. 366 (1953).
49. 6 L.S.I. 161.
50. 8 L.S.I. 133, 136.
51. Ibid.
52. 20 L.S.I. 47.
53. 11 L.S.I. 3.
54. 18 P.D. 769 (1964).
55. Ibid., at 776; see also Amsterdam and others v. Minister of Finance, 6 P.D. 945, at 983 (1952); 19 I.L.R. 229, at 237 (1952).
56. 6 P.D. 638 (1952).
57. On the duty of allegiance of an Israel national in general, see Yeridor v. Chairman of the Central Elections Committee to the Sixth Knesset, 19 (III) P.D. 365 (1965) where the Supreme Court, in the words of President Agranat, held that "it is clear that the status of Israel nationality contains within itself the duty of allegiance to the State of Israel." Ibid., at 386.
58. 11 L.S.I. 186. The original name of the law was Penal Law Revision (State Security) Law, until renamed by the Knesset in 1967, 21 L.S.I. 39.

59. 22 L.S.I. 243.

60. 9 L.S.I. 184.

61. K.T. 5711-1951, at 1146.

62. S.H. 5732-1972, at 52.

63. 13 L.S.I. 152.

64. On the legal situation that obtained prior to the passing by the Knesset of the Penal Law Amendment (Bigamy) Law of 1959, see Yosifof v. Attorney-General 5 P.D. (1951), 481; for an English translation see 1 Selected Judgments of the Supreme Court of Israel (Goitein, ed., [1962], 174). The amendment of 1959, while prohibiting bigamy in general, still recognizes a new marriage contracted by a person to whom Jewish religious law applies, without such person having divorced his former spouse, if permission to contract it had been given by a final judgment of a rabbinical court and the judgment has been approved by the two Chief Rabbis of Israel. 13 L.S.I. 152, § 5. This provision was necessitated by the fact that under Jewish law a divorce is effected not by a court decree but by the mutual consent of the spouses to dissolve the matrimonial bond. Thus, if one of the spouses is unwilling to obey a court order to have the matrimonial bond dissolved or is incapable of giving his or her consent (by reason of insanity, for example), the first marriage cannot be validly terminated under Jewish law. It is in these cases that rabbinical permission will be granted for a new marriage, prior to the termination of the first.

65. S.H. 5732-1972, at 52.

66. 10 L.S.I. 8.

67. 15 L.S.I. 121.

68. Ibid.

69. 19 L.S.I. 288.

70. 23 L.S.I. 110.

71. 25 L.S.I. 55.

72. 15 L.S.I. 179, 180.

73. 22 L.S.I. 20.

74. 6 P.D. 638, at 642 (1952).

75. Attorney-General v. Steiner, 9 P.M. 473, at 489 (1954).

76. 13 P.D. 959 (1959); 28 I.L.R. 442 (1963).

77. 86 U.N.T.S. 231.

78. 28 I.L.R. 451 (1963).

79. 13 L.S.I. 244, amended by 17 L.S.I. 133; 22 L.S.I. 193.

80. Approval by the Finance Committee is also required for guarantees of smaller amounts if the aggregate amount of guarantees given by the minister without the approval of the committee exceeds one hundred million Israel pounds. 13 L.S.I. 24.

81. 15 L.S.I. 101.

82. 24 L.S.I. 10-11.

83. Ibid., at 130.

84. 24 L.S.I. 131.

85. 162 U.N.T.S. 205.

86. 14 P.D. 2390 (1960).

87. 11 L.S.I. 111.
88. 14 P.D. 2392 (1960).
89. 13 L.S.I. 214; 15 L.S.I. 101; 24 L.S.I. 131.
90. S.H. 5732-1972, at 52.
91. 22 L.S.I. 114, 162; 23 L.S.I. 221, at 233.
92. 4 L.S.I. 114.
93. 6 D.K. 2037.
94. 16 P.D. 2428 (1962).
95. 23(II) P.D. 477 (1969).
96. The Israel Supreme Court has eleven members. The bench usually consists of three judges, but the President of the Supreme Court or his or her Permanent Deputy may direct, before the beginning of the proceedings in a particular matter, that such proceedings shall be before a greater uneven number of judges. Section 3(1) of the Courts Law, 5715-1957, 11 L.S.I. 157. Also, in further hearings of the Supreme Court the bench consists of five or more judges. The significance attached to the Shalit case is well attested to by the fact that it is the only instance in which the bench of the Supreme Court has consisted of as many as nine judges.
97. 24 L.S.I. 28.
98. Gouldman, op. cit., at 31.
99. Ibid., at 32.
100. This does not apply to persons who converted to another religion in order to save their lives. The fact that a Jew converted to Christianity in order to escape from Nazi persecution would not necessarily mean that he could not again be regarded as a Jew, for, to quote Gouldman, "it is very doubtful whether, in such cases, there was a meaningful spiritual adoption of the new religion. There is nothing to prevent such a convert from re-identifying with his Jewish origins and from being accepted as a Jew under the Law of Return." Gouldman, op. cit., at 26. In Basan v. Basan, 47 P.M. 41 (1965), an application for maintenance, the District Court said that "the allegation that the petitioner was baptized during the [Second World] War can make no difference whatsoever. It is well known that such things were done in Italy in order to save the lives of Jews."
101. 4 L.S.I. 114, amended by 8 L.S.I. 144.
102. Gouldman, op. cit., at 33.
103. Ibid.
104. K.T. 5716-1956, at 820, amended by K.T. 5720-1960, at 1270.
105. 12 P.D. (1958) 646.
106. Gouldman, op. cit., at 36.
107. 16 P.D. 1846 (1962).
108. Jerusalem Post, 23 and 24 March 1972.
109. 26 (II) P.D. 337 (1972). For a commentary on this case, see Klein, "The Lansky Case," 8 Israel Law Review (1973) 286.
110. 6 L.S.I. 1959.
111. K.T.5734-1974, at 1518, Regulation 9.
112. 13 L.S.I. 7, at 8.

113. Thus, in Lafi v. Minister of the Interior, 28 (I) P.D. 13 (1974), the Supreme Court reaffirmed the absolute discretion of the minister, under the Entry into Israel Law, to permit or refuse the entry into the country of any person who is not an Israel national or a person entitled to enter Israel by virtue of return. See also to the same effect Clark v. Minister of the Interior, 27 (I) P.D. 113 (1973).

114. 24 (II) P.D. 799 (1970).

115. 15 L.S.I. 179-80.

116. 6 L.S.I. 161.

117. K.T. 5734-1974, at 1520, 6.

118. Ibid.

119. See Alona E. Evans, "Reflections upon the Political Offense in International Practice," 57 Am. J. Int'l. Law 1, at 9-11 (1963).

120. Jerusalem Post, 2 July 1962.

121. See Shapira, Tel-Aviv Ha'aretz, 9 July 1962.

122. 34 (II) D.K. 2670, at 2684.

123. K.T. 5724-1963, at 94.

124. K.T. 5734-1974,at 1521, K.T. 5724-1963, at 94.

125. Memorial of the Government of Israel in Aerial Incident of 27 July 1955, Pleadings, Oral Arguments, Documents, at 106; I.C.J. Rep. (1957).

126. 16 P.D. 2033 (1962); 36 I.L.R. 277, at 311-12 (1968).

127. 10 P.D. 1479 at 1482 (1956).

128. See, for example, the Iraqi Law on the Control and Administration of Jewish Property of 1951, published in the Iraqi Official Collection of Laws for 1951, p. 23. Another pertinent example is the 1958 amendment of an Egyptian decree providing in Article 8 that "there will be inscribed on the lists of persons to whom access [to the territory of the U.A.R.] is forbidden, Jews who have forfeited Egyptian nationality in case of definitive departure. . . . The case of Jews having temporary residence who ask to quit the country definitively and who are between 10 and 65 years of age will be examined separately, in order to consider the inscription of their names on said lists." Decree of April 1958, published in the Journal Officiel of the U.A.R., 15 April 1958. Occasionally the legislative intentions are couched in different, and less explicit, terms. Thus, for example, the Law on Nationality of the United Arab Republic of June 22, 1958, empowers the Minister of the Interior to withdraw nationality in the republic from any person "who was known at any moment as being a Zionist." Section 22(7), Journal Officiel, 3 July 1958. The law does not give a definition of a "Zionist." Other legislative measures, while formally of general application, are in fact directed against the Jewish minorities in Arab countries. A case in point is the Egyptian Government Decree of 11 October 1948, Journal Officiel, 11 October 1948, concerning the obligation to declare any property situated in "Palestine."

129. 11 P.M. 229 (1956).

130. 24 P.M. 3 (1960).

131. S/6930.

132. S/7093.
133. S/7679.
134. S/8775; see also the Secretary-General's Report, 28 August 1968, S/8786.
135. S/9719.
136. Rosenne, "The Foreign Office Certificate," 11 *Mapraklit* (Israel Bar Journal) 33 at 37 (1955), in Hebrew.
137. 7 P.L.R. 597.
138. 42 U.N.T.S. 327.
139. 6 P.D. 1145 (1952). 18 I.L.R. 164 at 166-69 (1951).
140. 8 P.M. 455 (1953). 20 I.L.R. 391 (1953).
141. Rosenne, op. cit., at 44.
142. Ibid.
143. Ibid.
144. For the judgment of the Supreme Court, see 22(II) P.D. 85, at 94 (1968); for that of the District Court, see 51 P.M. 13 (1966).
145. 20 I.L.R. 392 (1953).
146. 18 I.L.R. 164, at 169 (1951).
147. Ibid., at 39.
148. 22(II) P.D. 93-94 (1968).
149. Ibid.
150. O'Connell, 1 *International Law* (2nd ed., 1970) 116.
151. Oppenheim, 1 *International Law* (8th ed., Lauterpacht, 1955), 767, note 2.
152. 20 I.L.R. 391 and especially at 392, 393-95 (1953).
153. 32 I.L.R. 80 at 82 (1966); 14 P.D. 1065 (1960).
154. 24 (II) P.D. 419, at 421, 423 (1970).
155. 21 L.S.I. 75.
156. 24 (II) P.D. 423-24 (1970).
157. 22 I.L.R. 699-700 (1955).
158. 42 U.N.T.S. 287.
159. 22 I.L.R. 701 (1955); 9 P.D. 135 (1935).
160. Drayton, 3 *Laws of Palestine* 2580 (1934).
161. 1 L.S.I. 9.
162. 4 P.D. 143, at 146 (1950); 17 I.L.R. (1950), Case No. 19.
163. 10 P.D. 5 (1956); 23 I.L.R. 284 (1956).
164. 5 P.D. 1061, at 1065-66 (1951); 18 I.L.R. 10 (1951).
165. 16 (III) P.D. 2033, at 2040 (1962); 36 I.L.R. 277, at 280 (1968).
166. 42 U.N.T.S. 303.
167. 22 I.L.R. 5, at 7-8 (1955); 10 P.D. 1825 (1955).
168. 86 U.N.T.S. 231.
169. 28 I.L.R. 446 (1963); 13 P.D. 959 (1959).
170. 28 I.L.R. 450 (1963); 13 P.D. 959 (1959).
171. 28 I.L.R. 458 (1963); 13 P.D. 959 (1959).
172. 360 U.N.T.S. 130.
173. 8 K.A. 545.
174. 189 U.N.T.S. 150.

175. 3 K.A. 5.

176. 21 (II) P.D. 20 at 26 (1967).

177. Ibid., at 325.

178. 19 L.S.I. 44.

179. 21 (II) P.D. 333 (1967).

180. Feinberg, Declaratory and Constitutive Treaties in International Law (in Hebrew) 443, 24 Hapraklit, 1963.

CHAPTER

12

ITALY

Gaetano Arangio-Ruiz

THE INDIVIDUAL

As a National

Movement

Passports. Freedom of temporary or final exit from the country is qualified as a right under the Constitution. The exercise of this right is subject to an authorization (passport), the granting of which is understood to be an act of administrative authority that is due to all individuals enjoying the right.[1] In general, therefore, every citizen is entitled to obtain a valid passport[2] in order to travel to any other country of his or her choice,[3] the enjoyment of this right being subject only to the onus (onere) of showing that he or she has fulfilled the requirements of the law by producing the necessary documentation. The opinion that a full right to a passport does not exist is an isolated one,[4] and the prevalent judicial practice confirms the dominant view.[5]

In certain cases "equivalent documents" may be accepted in lieu of passports.[6] Persons leaving the country without a valid passport or an equivalent valid document are subject to sanctions ranging between "ammenda" (pecuniary sanction) and arrest, according to the situation.[7]

As stated above, the right to leave the country, which is covered by Article 16 of the Constitution and Article 1 of Law No. 1185 of 21 November 1967, and the consequent right to obtain a passport

---

Reviewed and revised by the author in 1975.

or equivalent document are subject to compliance with legal onera and obligations.[8] The prerogative of competent organs to withdraw a passport is strictly connected with this principle. It follows that the passport may or must be withdrawn in the following situations:

1. whenever the person is found to be in circumstances that would have justified the denial of a passport (see below);

2. in other "personal" situations contemplated by the law, such as judicially ascertained noncompliance, in given circumstances, by the person concerned, with maintenance obligations toward relatives (ascendants, spouse, or descendants) or habitually immoral activities or dangerous or unhealthy work carried out by a minor abroad;[9]

3. in cases in which residence or travel by nationals abroad may be of prejudice to the external or internal security of the state or whenever the life, economic interests, or health of nationals may meet with serious danger in given countries. In such cases passports may be either withdrawn or territorially restricted.[10] (Further elaboration of the latter rule is given below.)

Those who can withdraw a passport are the Minister of Foreign Affairs and, on his behalf, (1) at home, "questori," and, in exceptional cases, "frontier inspectors" for nationals abroad and (2), in foreign territories, diplomatic envoys and consular officials.[11]

The legal remedies available against refusal or withdrawal of a passport are "ricorso" to the Minister for Foreign Affairs under Article 10 of Law Number 1185, 21 November 1967, or "ricorso" to the territorially competent Regional Administrative Tribunal according to the same article.[12] Against the minister's decision an appeal can be brought to the Regional Administrative Tribunal of Lazio, under Law Number 1034, 6 December 1971. A further remedy against the decisions of regional administrative tribunals can be sought before Consiglio di Stato. According to A. Sandulli, the appeals before regional administrative tribunals could be made directly to the minister regardless of prior recourse. According to the same author, regional administrative tribunals have an exclusive jurisdiction that also permits examination of the substance of these appeals.[13]

Appeals of passport revocations remain within the jurisdiction of ordinary tribunals for up to three months; after this they are transferred to the regional administrative tribunals. The decisions of the tribunals are final.

In addition to these "administrative" remedies within the framework of the executive branch, legal action may also be taken against the administration before ordinary civil courts. Since leaving the country and obtaining a passport or equivalent document are matters of full right, it follows that both matters are as justiciable before ordinary courts as any other matters of right, on the basis of a general rule, even where no express provision is made for action before the civil courts.[14]

Departure: Temporary or Permanent Restrictions. A category of restrictions follows from Article 3 of Law Number 1185. According to this provision a passport is not to be granted to unaccompanied or unauthorized minors. The authorization is to be given to the parent exercising parental responsibility, to the warden, or to the tutelary guardian. It is not to be given to the parent of minor children who is not authorized to go abroad by the tutelary guardian or by the other parent; to persons against whom an arrest warrant has been issued; to persons subject to military service;[15] and to other persons listed in the subparagraphs a through g of the provision quoted.[16]

Further limitations may derive from legal obligations connected with governmental employment or tax law obligations. Where affected persons are in possession of a passport, the restrictions with regard to departure are equally operative. Indeed, as noted above, the same circumstances would justify the withdrawal of a passport.[17] A further possibility of restriction derives from the bankruptcy legislation,[18] insofar as it restricts the freedom of movement of the physical person of the bankrupt or of the administrators or liquidators of a bankrupt company. Although departure abroad is not expressly mentioned, it is implied in this restriction.[19] A passport may also be withdrawn because of membership in a jury;[20] or an obligation to act as a witness in legal proceedings.[21]

A different category of restrictions follows from those provisions of Law Number 1185 that are prompted by the exigencies of public order in a wide sense, specifically Article 9, Paragraphs 2 and 3, according to which the Minister for Foreign Affairs may, in exceptional circumstances, temporarily suspend or restrict by decree the granting of passports or reduce the territorial validity thereof (1) for causes connected with the external security of the state; (2) for reasons of internal security (in consultation with the Minister for Internal Affairs); or (3) when the lives, economic interests, or safety of nationals are seriously endangered in given countries.

Under the same provisions, travel abroad by nationals who may be subject to military service obligations may in exceptional circumstances be suspended as provided for by legislation concerning military service and recruitment of the armed forces.[22]

Restrictions of similar kinds are to be found in Article 9 of Royal Decree Law (RDL) Number 2205, 13 November 1919; in Article

28 of Law Number 306, 1 February 1962, concerning the ratification and execution of the New York Convention on the Status of Stateless Persons of 28 September 1954; and, less specifically, in Article 9, first paragraph, Law Number 1185.

An issue has arisen, in doctrine and practice, with regard to the constitutionality of some of the above restrictions. According to one opinion, the legislation envisaging those restrictions confers upon administrative authorities a discretionary power that is in contrast with Article 16, Paragraph 2, of the Constitution, according to which freedom of departure from the country is only subject to compliance with the obligations deriving from the law.[23]

With regard to possible remedies against abusive denial of exit or passport or abusive restriction of the territorial spheres of passports or equivalent documents, the situation is the same as that described above in the section on passports.

All the restrictions contemplated in the legislative rules mentioned in the present section might be remedied by the plea of unconstitutionality of the relevant legislative enactments. This would be in conformity with the mentioned view according to which Article 16, Paragraph 2, of the Constitution excludes or limits any discretionary powers of administrative authorities in the matter.

Return. For nationals, return is unquestionably covered by an absolute right.[24] This is based essentially on Article 16, Paragraph 2, of the Constitution and Article 1 of Law Number 1185, 21 November 1967.

Expulsion. From the point of view of Italian law, it does not seem possible to conceive expulsion of a national. Forcible physical expatriation is conceivable in the form of extradition.

Under Italian law, a national may be extradited only if the extradition is expressly provided for in an international convention;[25] the fact with regard to which extradition is requested is qualified as a delict by Italian law as well as by the law of the applicant state; and the matter is not one of political crime.[26]

By Article 661 of the Code of Criminal Procedure extradition is subject to further conditions. The extradited person must not be judged on charges prior to the extradition and or on charges other than those with regard to which the extradition is requested. The person must not be subjected to a penalty other than provided in the judgment in consideration of which extradition is granted (or offered). The same article provides that the Minister of Justice may make further conditions if he or she deems it appropriate.

The judicial remedy is double. First the granting of extradition is subject, under Article 662 of the Code of Criminal Procedure, to a favorable decision by the territorially competent Court of Appeals. It is the responsibility of this court to decide whether the essential conditions for extradition exist. No discretionary power of the administration is thus admitted unless it is in favor of the accused or condemned party.[27] Second, the judgment of the Court of Appeals may further be appealed before the Court of Cassation, on the merits as well as on procedure.

With regard to stateless persons, it is necessary to recall the provision of Law Number 306, 1 February 1962, concerning the ratification and execution of the quoted New York Convention on Stateless Persons. According to Article 31.1 of that convention, stateless persons who have legally entered the territory of one of the contracting parties will not be subject to expulsion except for reasons of national security or public order.

Protection

Extent of Freedom of Activity Abroad. In this section, as in the section concerning foreigners, criminal responsibility for acts committed abroad is left out. As in a number of other legal systems, Italian criminal law, and possibly jurisdiction, does cover some categories of criminal acts committed abroad by citizens, and in given instances by foreigners.

Article 5 of Decree Law Number 476, 6 June 1956,[28] which was later converted into, and modified by, Law Number 786, 25 July 1956,[29] prohibits all residents, unless authorized, from owning "participation quotas" in companies having their headquarters outside the territory of the republic or shares originating or payable abroad. It must be added, however, that it is the practice of the Ministry of Foreign Trade to enact "general authorizations" on the basis of which the condition of "administrative authorization" is fulfilled once and for all.

By Article 5 of the same legislation, residents possessing the foreign assets indicated above are also obliged to declare them to the Bank of Italy in the form and within the time requirements indicated by the Ministry of Foreign Trade. By virtue of the same article, the Minister of Foreign Trade may also provide, with binding effect, that the assets in question be deposited with the Bank of Italy or with authorized agencies thereof.[30]

A special restriction of the freedom of activity of nationals abroad is provided by Decree Law Number 1007, 3 October 1968,[31] converted into, and modified by, Law Number 1188, 19 November 1968,[32] concerning the prohibition of economic relations with Southern Rhodesia and the prohibition of activities aimed at promoting emigration to Southern Rhodesia. Among the prohibited activities are the assignment or transfer of funds to Southern Rhodesia in favor of natural or other persons, private or public, residing therein (Article 1, f); air navigation to South Rhodesia on the part of companies having their headquarters in Italian territory or by aircraft registered in Italy, and so on (Article 1, g). Article 5 provides sanctions against persons, expressly including nationals abroad, who contravene the said prohibitions.

The Right to Diplomatic Protection. It does not seem that Italian nationals enjoy a "diritto soggettivo" (full right) to diplomatic proection by the state.

I am inclined to believe, however, that some legal (judicial and/or administrative) remedy against inaction or inadequate action by the executive could perhaps be asserted in given circumstances. This could be done either on the basis of a very wide, albeit problematic, interpretation of Article 10 of the Constitution and other constitutional rules or, more plausibly, by the indirect device of a claim for damages against the state and its responsible officials.[33]

The State and Compensation. It would seem at first sight that in the matter of compensation the situation is equally unsatisfactory, except in cases that are specially provided for. In Italian law there do not seem to be general rules governing claims by private parties, natural or juristic, as a matter of right, any compensation or part of a compensation obtained or to be obtained by the Italian state from a foreign state for damage suffered by such parties as a consequence of an international wrongful act of the foreign state or in circumstances of a similar nature. The situation seems to be not different from the situation resulting in the United Kingdom from such decisions as Baron De Bode v. the Queen, 1851;[34] Rustomjee v. the Queen, 1876;[35] Civilian War Claimants Association v. the King, 1931;[36] and Administrator of German Property v. Knoop, 1932.[37] Here again, however, it is felt that judicial or administrative remedies might be made available, under certain conditions, through the operation of general rules or principles. In addition to the same rules or principles considered above in the discussion of departure, recourse might be had, for example--circumstances permitting--to the constitutional rules or principles concerning equality of persons before the law and nondiscrimination.

The situation is different under certain special rules. Provision has been made, for instance, for Italian property, assets, and interests in territories ceded to Yugoslavia under the Treaty of Peace. This applies both to the assets in Yugoslav territory contemplated by Law Number 1064, 5 December 1949, and assets in Zone B of the former Free Territory of Trieste, covered by Law Number 269, 18 March 1958.

Article 4 of Law Number 1064 provides that nationals who have suffered loss as a consequence of nationalization, agrarian reform, or any other measure affecting property in Yugoslavia shall be indemnified to the extent to which an indemnification shall have been paid by the government of Yugoslavia in compliance with the Italo-Yugoslav agreement signed in Belgrade on 23 May 1949 and executed in Italy by Law Number 121, 10 March 1955. This and other provisions of the law have been interpreted by the Corte di Cassazione in Judgment Number 1017, 28 April 1964 (against the judgment of the Rome Court of Appeals, 27 February 1961), to mean that the agreements between Italy and Yugoslavia and the internal legislation executing such agreements had created a "special mechanism" through which Yugoslavia paid the indemnity to the Italian government instead of directly indemnifying the dispossessed Italian owners. Consequently the Italian government fell under the obligation to distribute the sum among the interested parties. The Court of Cassation further stated that the distribution of the indemnities by the Italian government was thus regulated by the law, not on the basis (or "by reason") of the general or public interest, but more specifically with a view to the safeguard of the individual interests themselves, such interests thus enjoying the full legal protection that is typical of "diritti soggettivi perfetti" (full individual rights).[38]

A different situation seems to result from legislation concerning loss of property, rights, and other assets situated in the former Free Territory of Trieste.[39] The relevant rules provide for indemnification by the Italian government for nationalized assets on the basis of given quantitative criteria,[40] subject to the condition that an indemnification had not been received by the parties from Yugoslav authorities or in any other manner.[41] For assets other than those subjected to Yugoslav measures against private ownership, indemnification by the Italian government was subject to the condition that the private parties concerned had not been in a position to protect their rights with regard to the relinquished assets and to the further condition that the parties themselves cede to the Italian state any indemnities obtained otherwise.[42]

Another set of special rules has been adopted by Law Number 607, 5 July 1964, concerning the application of the first part of the Italian-German agreement signed at Bonn on 2 June 1961 and approved by DPR Number 1233, 14 April 1962, and DPR Number 2043, 6 October 1963, concerning the distribution of sums paid by the Federal Republic of Germany, in compliance with the above agreement of 1961, for the indemnification of Italian nationals who had suffered from Nazi persecution. Law Number 607 authorizes the payment of indemnities to natural or juristic persons of Italian nationality enjoying laws and rights toward the German State, or

German citizens or entities belonging to the Federal Republic or the Berlin Land, such laws and rights having arisen in the period between 1 September 1939 and 8 May 1945.[43] Article 7 provides that if the lump sum obtained from the German government were to prove not sufficient for the complete satisfaction of claims deemed to be valid, the indemnities would be reduced in proportion, while any residual sum would remain with the Italian state. Here again a full right seems to be envisaged.

DPR Number 2043, 6 October 1963, provides for the distribution of the sum paid by the Federal Republic of Germany in favor of Italian nationals who had been the victims of Nazi deportation by reason of race, religion, or ideology, up to the exhaustion of the lump sum in question. The quantitative criteria of the distribution are indicated in Article 10. A full right also seems to be envisaged here.

Indemnities are finally provided under Law Number 1265, 20 December 1967, containing the rules for the application of the Frankfurt German-Italian agreement of 20 December 1964 for the settlement of the disputes contemplated in Part V, Article 4, of the convention for the settlement of issues arising from the war and military occupation. Here again a diritto soggettivo was provided, specifying an indemnity compatible with the "ceiling" amount indicated in Article 1 as the lump sum agreed upon at Frankfurt between the two governments.

<u>Responsibility of the State for Injury Induced by Its Own Conduct</u>. The responsibility of the state for injury induced by its own conduct is a matter not covered by general rules. It is possible, however, although not very likely, that the nature of the claim and the nature and circumstances of the conduct (positive or negative) from which the injury has derived might be such as to justify recourse to constitutional provisions such as those in the section above on departure. We refer in particular to Article 28, concerning the liability of the state and civil servants, and Article 3, on equality and nondiscrimination.

Ad hoc legislation, on the contrary, is adopted by parliament to meet given situations after they occur. Examples of such legislation are Law Number 1050, 29 October 1954, concerning private losses resulting from the application of Articles 74 and 79 of the peace treaty of 1947, and Law Number 968, 27 December 1953, concerning war damages.

Law Number 1050 indemnifies private parties whose property or other assets abroad were totally or partly lost as a consequence of the implementation of Articles 74 and 79 of the peace treaty of 1947. It could be, and was, argued from the terms of these provisions that the indemnity claims of Italian nationals abroad covered by the provisions themselves were to assume the nature of full individual rights. As such, the claims in question could have been brought before ordinary civil courts in the same way as any common claims for damages.

It was argued to the contrary, however, that the claimants were only entitled to a reasonable expectation of a right or a "legitimate interest" (in the sense of Italian administrative law) against the state. The state, in other words, would provide indemnities as a matter of discretion. According to this view, the claims of Italian nationals covered by the two quoted provisions were not justiciable as full individual rights.

The terms used by the legislators in Law Number 1050, and the remarks and observations made before Parliament during the discussion of the text,[44] show that the Italian parliament adopted the second interpretation. In providing for indemnification, it was felt, the Italian state has not proceeded on the basis of a strict compliance with the relevant parts of Articles 74 and 79 of the peace treaty. The signature and ratification of the peace treaty were to be considered as having been given by the Italian state as a matter of necessity. In particular, the provisions of the treaty that concerned confiscation of the property of Italian nationals presented some of the features of an abuse of power. Therefore, it was further maintained, the Italian state provided for indemnification only because it deemed it just and socially equitable that the burden deriving from the claims of other powers should not be imposed upon a single category of citizens. According to a general principle of equitable distribution of the _onera_ of war, the latter should be the responsibility of the whole nation. On this basis private claims were not to be treated as full individual rights.

The same view was taken by the courts, which only admitted the existence of legitimate interests. For example, according to the Consiglio di Stato in _Facher v. Ministero del Tesoro_, the indemnity to be paid for the loss of Italian assets abroad as a consequence of the implementation of Articles 74 and 79 of the peace treaty derives from the discretion of the state, and as such it will be the object of a "diritto soggettivo" only after its determination and as a consequence thereof. The beneficiary can only claim a reasonable expectation.[45]

War Damages. Under Law Number 968, 27 December 1953, natural and juristic persons of Italian nationality are entitled to indemnity and "contributions" for loss or damage of movable or immovable property as a consequence of the war. See in particular Articles 23, 26, and 28.

It is questionable, however, whether and under what conditions the damaged party has a full legal right to indemnification, actionable before ordinary tribunals, or just a legitimate interest. The point is discussed in two judgments of Corte di Cassazione, in Costantino v. Ministero Lavori Pubblici[46] and Societa Immobiliare Palazzo via Carducci v. Marelli.[47]

Italian law seems to admit the power of the state to renounce, by international agreement, claims that it might otherwise put forward against a foreign state for damage suffered by Italian nationals. It is submitted, however, that this doctrine is based on the assumption that the treaty is accompanied or followed by the legislation necessary for its implementation.

Examples of agreements of this kind are as follows:

1. Treaty of Peace between Italy and Allied and Associated Powers, Paris, 10 February 1947, Articles 76 and 77;

2. Agreement with Rumania for the settlement of pending financial matters, Rome, 23 January 1968, Article 4;

3. Agreement with Egypt concerning reparation for damages suffered by Egypt as a consequence of war operations on its territory and of the release of Italian assets in Egypt, Paris, 10 September 1946, Article 3;

4. Agreement with Czechoslovakia on financial and patrimonial questions, Prague, 27 July 1966, Article 5, Article 2;

5. Memorandum of Understanding with the United States of America concerning the settlement of certain claims for the war period and questions connected therewith, Washington, D.C., 14 August 1947, Article 1.

The implementation of international agreements of this kind is generally considered to be sufficient to extinguish any claim the national may have against the foreign state with which the agreement is concluded or, as the case may be, against the subjects of a foreign state. Practice seems to support this view. According to the Corte di Cassazione in Soc. Ilva v. Ditta Cavinato, renunciation made by Italy in an international agreement is fully operative with regard to private claims of Italian nationals by virtue of the implementation of the treaty.[48] This decision concerned claims against Germany renounced by Italy under Article 77 of the peace treaty. The same view was taken by Tribunale Aquila, in Ditta Pomante v. Federal Republic of Germany.[49]

Special Kinds of Protection. One special kind of protection is envisaged by Law Number 131, 28 February 1967, which contains provisions concerning (1) the insurance and financing of the credits of Italian nationals arising from the export of goods or services or from building and other works undertaken abroad and (2) assistance to developing countries. Among other things, this legislation provided for the following:

1. Institution of a special fund consisting partly of insurance premiums and partly of public moneys (Article 32);

2. Coverage by this fund of the risks that Italian firms may face when operating abroad as a consequence of such occurrences as war, revolution, rebellion, riot, or natural catastrophe in a foreign country;

3. Coverage of risks deriving from a moratorium or suspension of payments due on contracts as a result of action by the foreign state in connection with the above occurrences;

4. Coverage of similar risks, such as lack or suspension of compensation, increase of costs, or destruction or damage of machinery and equipment (Article 5).

The benefits of these rules extend to persons or firms meeting the conditions indicated by the law.

The Individual as an Alien

Movement

Entry. The admission of an alien into the territory, whether for temporary residence or settlement, is subject to authorization to be granted by diplomatic or consular agents. Foreigners so admitted must comply with the requirements of Article 142 of "Testo Unico" of the law of "Pubblica Sicurezza." The most important of these is the registration required for all aliens, with the exception of tourists or other people staying in the country for a period not exceeding two months. Whenever an authorization of temporary residence or settlement has been secured from consular or diplomatic agents, the requirement of registration does not imply a discretionary power of the police authorities to which the declaration is to be submitted. The registration may be dispensed with (Article 143) in special cases provided for in "Regolamento per l'esecuzione del Testo Unico delle Leggi di Pubblica Sicurezza."

Under Article 145 of the Testo Unico and decree law Number 50, 11 February 1948, persons giving hospitality to foreigners or employing an alien (foreign citizen or stateless person) are obligated to notify the police. This provision was found to be not unconstitutional by Corte Costituzionale.[50]

Departure. Any alien visitor or residence may be subject to measures of expulsion. Under the Codice Penale, expulsion must be ordered by a court whenever the person has been condemned to imprisonment for more than ten years (Article 235) or for any "delitto contro la personalità dello Stato" (Article 312). Under the Testo Unico expulsion may also be ordered as a consequence of any other criminal offense, for reasons of public order (in a wide sense), or following a violation by the alien of rules concerning the admission and residence of aliens (Article 150). Expulsion for reasons of public order must be ordered by the Minister of the Interior in consultation with the Minister of Foreign Affairs and with the consent of the Prime Minister. Aliens who are expelled are not allowed to reenter the country without special authority from the Minister of the Interior (Article 151).

In addition to the indicated expulsion measures, the Testo Unico provides that for reasons of public order and in case of urgency, prefects of provincial departments may "avviare alla frontiera" aliens present within their respective provinces (Article 152).

When expulsion is ordered as an accessory of a criminal penalty, legal remedy is admitted by way of analogy under Article 212 of the Codice di Procedura Penale.[51] In other words, the measure of expulsion can be appealed against, together with the judgment of which it is an accessory.

When expulsion has been ordered by a local prefect, a remedy can be sought by referring the matter to the Minister of the Interior. Against the decision of the latter a complaint can be brought before the Administrative Tribunal for Lazio and, against the decision of the latter, before the Consiglio di Stato. (On recourse to the minister, see Sandulli's opinion, which is discussed in the section on passports at the beginning of this chapter.)

The practice of Consiglio di Stato in the matter seems to be based on the assumption that once final (Minister of the Interior), an order of expulsion does not require motivation. According to Consiglio di Stato, evaluation of the order of expulsion by that tribunal must be confined to a control of the legitimacy of the measure and does not extend to its merits.[52] This interpretation seems to find support in the decision of Corte Costituzionale, which is discussed below in connection with the Act of State doctrine.

Special Rules for Entry. The onera provided by general law for the entry, sojourn, or establishment of aliens are reduced by special provisions of municipal law, mostly enacted in compliance with bilateral or multilateral agreements with foreign states. Besides Article 149 of Testo Unico (concerning diplomatic envoys and other persons exempted from the registration requirement, these provisions include DPR Number 1656, 30 December 1965, concerning the movement and sojourn of nationals of member states of the European

Economic Community (EEC), and other provisions, considered in the section below on treaties and the individual.

Asylum. According to Article 10, Paragraph 3, of the Constitution, the right of an alien to enjoy asylum in Italy is limited, since the alien is not allowed the effective exercise of the democratic liberties provided for by the Italian constitution. The provision states formally that (further) conditions of such right of asylum are to be determined by statute. However, notwithstanding the fact that no statute determining such conditions has been passed as of the writing, the prevailing doctrine maintains that the constitutional rule is applicable, and the alien's right of asylum derives directly therefrom.

Protection

Under the Treaty of Friendship with San Marino, signed at Rome on 31 March 1939,[53] Italy grants diplomatic protection abroad to San Marino nationals in relation to third states in which the Republic of San Marino has no diplomatic or consular agents of its own.

THE ACT OF STATE DOCTRINE

The problems related to the Act of State doctrine may be expressed in the following questions: To what degree can Italian judicial organs evaluate the conformity with international law of the foreign legislation to be applied by them? What is the position of Italian judicial organs in relation to the Italian executive branch with regard to the above evaluation? How can Italian courts deal with unrecognized governments or states?

In various countries the national courts are precluded by doctrine and practice from effectively investigating the conformity of foreign legislation with international law, on the basis of three kinds of arguments, which may be summarized as follows: (1) national courts are technically "not prepared" to evaluate the conformity of foreign law with international law. (2) The result of the evaluation of foreign law by judicial organs might conflict with the diplomatic action of the executive, in particular with the acquiescence by the latter to the wrongful act of the foreign state whose legislation is in question or the renunciation by the same executive of claims consequent to such a wrongful act. (3) The state as a whole must abstain from intervening in the internal affairs of other states.[54]

In the Italian legal system it does not seem possible to find any general rule in support of such a doctrine or of the arguments upon which it is based.

Italian courts have solved the problem in positive terms, namely by admitting the possibility for them to judge the conformity of foreign law with international law, on the basis of Article 10 of the Constitution. As mentioned above, this article states that Italian law conforms to the generally recognized rules of international law.

An example of this is to be found in the 13 September 1954 decision of Tribunale di Roma in Anglo-Iranian Oil Co. v. Supor.[55] According to the tribunal, it is the power and the duty of the Italian judge to examine foreign law from the point of view of legitimacy, in order to determine whether it is in contrast with the constitution of the foreign country, with public order or with generally recognized rules of international law. This is by virtue of Article 31 of "disposizioni preliminari al Codice Civile" and Article 10 of the Constitution. On this basis the tribunal decided as follows: "The judge [must] deny expropriation against a foreigner without indemnity, notwithstanding the fact that [the foreign law in question] had been adopted for non political or [non] odious motives."[56]

It is debated in doctrine whether conformity with international law is absolutely necessary to the application in Italy of foreign law referred to by Italian conflict-of-laws rules or whether that conformity is relevant only indirectly as a consequence of the operation of the general limit of public order as in Article 31 of the preliminary provisions of the Civil Code.[57] The latter view seems to be favored. Its supporters maintain that conformity (or a lack of disagreement) with international law constitutes one of the fundamental principles of the Italian legal system by virtue of Article 10. As such, conformity with international law is to be used together with the other principles of public order.[58] It is in this way that its nonconformity with international law would make foreign law inapplicable by Italian courts.

The decision of the Court of Appeals of Genoa in Petrolifera Muntenia v. Child is in accordance with the latter view. The Genoese court moved from the notion that Article 31 of the preliminary provisions of the Civil Code of Italy aims at safeguarding, against the application of the foreign law, referred to by the Italian rules on conflict of laws, those "concepts of a moral and political order which, having imposed themselves within the national community as the common heritage of all the members of the society, may be assumed to be the fundamental principles and directives of our legal system."[59] Such principles, according to the court, are to be found "by virtue of Article 10 of our Constitution, also the generally recognized rules of International Law." One of these rules, according to the court, was the rule that forbade those nationalizations that, although inspired by motives of public utility and general policy, assume the character of a confiscation.

The doctrine was applied by the Corte di Cassazione in Pitassi v. Fichbein.[60] The same doctrine, that conformity with international law is a principle of public order in the sense explained above, also underlies the decision of the Corte di Appello in "Archimedes" Glashuetter etc. v. Società Ornati.[61] In the latter case the court has referred to international law in order to assert that according to that law, and in spite of the Italian rules on conflicts of laws, expropriations and confiscations are effective only within the state by which they are decided.[62]

In the Italian system there are no general rules governing the position of courts in relation to the executive with regard to the evaluation of the conformity of foreign norms or acts with international law. The question can only be solved on the basis of the rules of the constitution, the general principles concerning the relationship of the judiciary with the executive, and the adaptation of such rules and principles to the exercise by the courts of their functions with regard to cases affecting, or affected by, the external relations of the state.

Three fundamental principles seem to govern the matter, the principle that the courts are only subject to the law;[63] the principle that the judiciary constitutes an autonomous order independent of any other power;[64] and the principle according to which "the individual private interest" is not subordinate to the interest of the community and is at most, in exceptional cases especially provided for by the law, harmonized therewith.[65] Besides Amministrazione del Governo britannico, Pubblico Ministero, Comune di Venezia v. Guerrato ved. Arcagniolo, these principles seem to have been followed in the Rissman case.[66]

In the case before the Constitutional Court the issue was the constitutional legitimacy of the legislation of 1926 concerning executive measures against foreign states, according to which such measures were subject, on condition of reciprocity, to the authorization of the Minister of Justice. According to the party that instituted the proceedings before the Constitutional Court, the provisions of that legislation, according to which no remedy was allowed against the decisions rendered by the Minister of Justice, were not in conformity with the Constitution. In rejecting the government argument that the minister's decision was an act of a political nature and as such not susceptible of judicial control, the court asserted that the exclusion of judicial remedies would constitute a violation of Article 113 of the Constitution, according to which all acts of the public administration are subject to judicial control.

In the Rissmann case, which involved a German consul, it is remarkable that at one point the Ministry of Foreign Affairs sent a note to the tribunal calling its attention to the general rules of international law concerning consular immunity and to the principle of "adaptation" of Italian law to international law embodied in Article 10 of the Constitution, explaining the intervention of the ministry itself as the exercise of an "institutional duty." This duty, according to the ministry, was directed, among other things, at avoiding the negative international consequences that might derive from the disregard of the opinion of the Administration of Foreign Affairs. After the Genoese and national press had called public attention to the episode, the Executive Committee of the Genoese section of the National Association of Judges protested against the "undue and unconstitutional" interference by the Ministry of Foreign Affairs with the function of a court. It thus seems that the Italian judiciary feels entitled in such matters to the widest independence from influence.

The attitude of Italian courts toward the legislation and the acts of unrecognized foreign states or governments seems to be prompted by a similar preoccupation with the independence of the judiciary.

This tendency is clearly revealed, for instance, in a number of decisions involving the effects in Italy of legislation or acts emanating from the German Democratic Republic; two such cases before the Corte di Appello of Milan were Volks Eigener Betrieb Zeiss Ikon e Società Coproma v. Zeiss Ikon, A.G.,[67] and "Archimedes" Glashuetter etc. v. Società Ornati.[68] By these decisions the Milanese court rejected the claim of Eastern German companies to inhibit the use of their trade marks in Italy, in the belief that to uphold such claims would imply the admission that foreign "confiscatory" measures could have an effect in Italy. In both cases, however, although the German Democratic Republic was not recognized by the Italian government, the court did not consider that element relevant. As these and other cases indicate, Italian courts do not follow in these matters the doctrine of so-called "recognition" as was followed in England in Luther v. Sagor.[69] However, the application of the doctrine according to which courts should ignore the laws and acts of a state that the government does not recognize seems to have been made by Tribunale di Genova, 19 May 1923, in Captain Katsikis v. Società Fati Svoroni di Pallone, etc.,[70] and by Commissione dei Ricorsi in materia di Brevetti, 22 February 1969, in VEB Kamera und Kino werke Dresden.[71] The latter commission, the jurisdiction of which has been questioned, rejected a claim based upon a GDP patent because, according to the commission itself, "the Ministry of Foreign Affairs has notified that the Government of Italy does not recognize the German Democratic Republic."[72] The commission admitted that recognition is a legal act "which States are at liberty to perform or not, unless they are otherwise bound by a special rule of the Law of Nations."[73] Therefore lack of recognition did not imply "the nonexistence of the international personality of the unrecognized State."[74] However, nonrecognition results in the nonexistence of the state in question for the domestic law of the nonrecognizing state. This view is authoritatively rejected by doctrine.[75]

Implementing Decisions of International Organizations

In implementing the decisions of international organizations, three types of guidelines should be used: resolutions of international organizations constituting useful elements in the determination of the contents of rules of general international law; resolutions creating international duties of the state under treaty law; and nonbinding resolutions.

Resolutions Relevant for the Determination of the Content of Rules of General International Law

There have been cases in recent Italian practice of the use of international resolutions in determining the rules of general international law. The general rules of international law involved were applied by the courts by virtue of Article 10 of the Constitution.

One such case is Petrolifera Muntenia v. Child,[76] in which was stated by the court, among other things, to demonstrate the existence of a general "permissive" rule of international law with regard to nationalizations, that in addition to judgments of Italian courts with regard to Iranian Oil nationalization, one could "quote the deliberation adopted, on the same subject, by the General Assembly of the United Nations at its meeting of December 21, 1952."

Resolutions Possessing a Binding Character under Treaty Law

Italian practice is very consistent in maintaining that Article 10 of the Constitution, in providing for the "adaptation" of Italian law to international law, only covers customary international law. With equal consistency, Italian courts consider the "adaptation" of Italian law to treaty obligations as a prerogative of Parliament. The latter principle is extended to binding resolutions of international organizations, exclusive of European Community regulations (the internal effect of which is automatic) and inclusive of European Community directives. Common binding resolutions of international bodies seem thus to require ad hoc "incorporation."

An example of this attitude is Law Number 1188, 19 November 1968, converting into legislation (with amendments) Decree Law Number 1007, 3 October 1968, containing, among other things, norms prohibiting economic relations with Southern Rhodesia. (See above.)

Nonbinding Resolutions

Italian courts seem to be very cautious with regard to nonbinding resolutions. It seems clear that while the courts do refer to such acts for the purpose of their decisions they do not envisage their content as a part of Italian law.

Cases in which important international resolutions have been invoked--occasionally not without some consequence--are the Krüger case, decided by the Court of Appeals of Bologna on 4 February 1963;[77] and Grsetic, Pukoc, Nesek e Hizar, decided by the Court of Appeals of Milano on 27 November 1964.[78]

In the first case the court refused the extradition of a German citizen accused of genocide to the Federal Republic of Germany in view of the "political" nature of the crime of which he was accused. The decision was rendered at a time subsequent to the 1948 UN Assembly Resolution on Genocide and to the Italian ratification of the Genocide Convention, both acts being expressly referred to by the court in its decision. Neither the ratification nor the Assembly resolution were deemed by the court to be sufficient in the face of the fact that the Act of Parliament by which the ratification of the convention had been authorized stated expressly that the convention "shall be fully and completely executed" at the "entry into force of the legislation to be enacted" in accordance with Article 5 of the convention itself, since such legislation had not yet been passed.

It should be noted that the Bologna Court of Appeals was also led to its negative conclusion because the Constitution as it then stood prohibited the extradition of an alien for crimes of a political nature.[79] The matter is now covered by an amendment according to which "the last paragraph" (the same as above) "of Article 10 and the last paragraph of Article 26 of the Constitution do not apply to the crime of genocide."[80]

In Grsetic, Pukoc, Nesek e Hizar, the question was whether a foreigner derives a full individual right from the provision of Article 10, Paragraph 3, of the Italian Constitution, according to which the foreigner who is barred in his country from the exercise of the liberties guaranteed by the Italian Constitution is entitled to asylum in Italy. In arguing in favor of the existence of a full individual right for the foreigner on the basis of Article 10 and without necessity of a further legislative enactment, the court considered, among other things, that as a member of the United Nations Italy had pledged itself to Article 14 of the Universal Declaration of Human Rights.[81]

Procedures Relating to the Issue of Certificates or Suggestions of the Executive in Connection with Litigation in National Courts

As indicated above, it is not the practice of Italian courts to have "certificates" or "suggestions" by the executive produced in the proceedings with regard to the content of international rules or with regard to facts relating to the external affairs of the state. It therefore follows that such statements have no binding value for the judge.

Under Article 213 of the "Codice di Procedura Civile," a court may "request of its own initiative from the Public Administration written information concerning acts and documents of the Administration which may be of relevance for the proceedings." The court, however, remains free to evaluate any such elements.

Further possibilities for courts to address themselves to the executive are envisaged under Article 55 of the Disposizioni di Attuazione del Codice di Procedura Penale and under Article 49 of DPR Number 200, 5 January 1967, on the functions and power of consuls.[82]

These rules concern particularly the acquisition by the judge of knowledge of foreign law. In both instances, however, the general principle of the independence of the judiciary is preserved.[83]

The first rule envisages cooperation by the Ministry of Justice and the second provides for the cooperation of Italian consular authorities abroad. In both cases it is a matter of duty and not a matter of power on the part of the executive bodies concerned. In both cases the final decision rests solely with the court.[84]

The situation is very similar to that of a case in which the parties in litigation cooperate with the court in the acquisition, when necessary, of knowledge of foreign law.[85]

TREATIES AND THE INDIVIDUAL

In addition to participating in the multilateral (Washington) Convention of 18 March 1965 for the settlement of disputes with regard to investments,[86] Italy has concluded numerous bilateral agreements concerning investments, nationalization, and so on.

Investments

Investments Abroad

A first group of agreements, and the most numerous, concerning investments abroad consists of treaties dealing with economic and technical cooperation with countries such as Afghanistan, Chile, Morocco, Ruanda, Somalia, Tunisia, Uruguay, and Yemen. The obligation of Italy under these agreements is usually (1) to authorize Italian firms to supply goods or services against deferred compensation (in the Yemen agreement, however, Italy is only committed to consider requests of that kind); (2) to extend to the credits for such supplies guarantees provided by Italian law (up to $20 million for Somalia, under given conditions); and (3) to favor investment of Italian capital (Chile, Ruanda, Somalia, and Yemen). The other party's obligation is (1) to guarantee the transfer of sums due to Italian firms and (2) to consent to the transfer of salaries or other income on a most-favored-nation basis.

Foreign Investment in Italy

Italy has concluded various agreements with the United States affecting foreign investment. There is also an agreement with France concerning certain Italian loans.

Commercial Credits in Favor of Italian Nationals

The protection by Italy of these credits, and particularly of credits covered by export credit guarantees, assumes a variety of forms. Examples that might usefully be considered are the 1964 exchange of notes with Cuba for the settlement of Italian "frozen" credits, the 1965 agreement with Chile, and the agreements with Indonesia of 17 July 1968.

Nationalization and Expropriation Indemnities

In the matter of nationalization and expropriation indemnities, Italy has followed either the classical method of "lump" settlement, at the interstate level, of the claims of nationals following foreign nationalization or expropriation measures or a system of direct indemnification by the foreign state. The first method was followed in the agreements with Tunisia in 1967, which covered not only lump indemnity but also future economic and financial cooperation; with

Bulgaria in 1965; with Yugoslavia on 3 July 1967; and with Czechoslovakia in 1966.

The method of direct indemnification of Italian nationals by the foreign state had been adopted in the 1947 agreement with Czechoslovakia and in the 1956 agreement with Lybia.

Treaties of Friendship, Commerce, and Navigation

These treaties are significant, within the present context, especially with regard to protection of persons and property; freedom for foreigners to exercise industrial, trade, and professional activities; guarantees in case of expropriation or requisition; and freedom of transfer of capital, income, or indemnities. In these and similar fields, the treaties in question are usually characterized by rigorous reciprocity and by the constant use of the most-favored-nation clause[87] and/or the "treatment of nationals" principle.

With regard to protection of nationals and their property of the other contracting state, the most-favored-nation treatment is provided for under Article 6, Paragraph 2 of the treaty with the Federal Republic of Germany. The "treatment of nationals" principle is embodied in the agreements with Nicaragua and Greece (Article 3, Paragraph 2), and that with Thailand (Article 1, Paragraph 3). Article 5, Paragraph 1 of the 1948 treaty with the United States envisages a treatment in conformity with international law as to the treatment of nationals and most-favored nation status.

For the exercise of commercial, industrial, and professional activities (the latter including "métiers"), the rule generally envisaged in the agreements under scrutiny is the most-favored-nation clause. Such is the case of the treaties with France (Article 2), Germany (Article 8, Paragraph 2), Iran and Lebanon (Article 2),[88] Greece (Article 4), and Panama (Article 8). The treaty with the Netherlands contemplates the treatment of "nationals" instead. The 1948 treaty with the United States, in its turn, utilizes <u>cumulatively</u> the treatment of "nationals" with the most favored nations (Articles 1 through 4 and Article 24, Paragraph 7).[89] "Full freedom" in the activities in question is envisaged in the agreements with Nicaragua and Thailand.

The commercial and industrial activities of the companies of each party are entitled to most-favored-nation treatment according to the agreements with Greece (Article 10, Paragraph 3), Iran and Lebanon (Article 8, Paragraph 2), France (Article 7, Paragraph 3), and Thailand (Article 5, Paragraph 3). The Agreement with France (same paragraph) extends to companies the same treatment reserved to nationals if the company is under Italian or French "control," as defined in an annex protocol.

With regard to the possibility of employing people, as dependents or otherwise, most favorable treatment is envisaged in Article 2, Paragraph 1, of the almost identical treaties with the Federal Republic of Germany and with Panama. For a combination of most-favored-nation with "national" treatment, see Article 2 of the 1948 treaty with the United States.

For requisitions, the most common pattern of guarantees is equality with nationals. See for instance the treaties with the Federal Republic of Germany (Article 3), Panama (Article 4, Paragraph 3), Iran and Lebanon (Article 6), and France (Article 5).

For expropriations, equality with nationals is used, in conjunction with most-favored-nation treatment, only in the agreements with Greece (Articles 6 and 8), France (Article 4), and the United States (Article 5).[90] In all the other cases only most-favored-nation treatment is envisaged. Such is the case of the agreements with Germany (Article 6, Paragraph 4), Panama (Article 5, Paragraph 4),[91] and Iran and Lebanon (Article 4).

There must be an adequate provision for transfer of invested capital, income derived from investment, and compensation obtained for expropriation or requisition (Article 15, Paragraph 3, of the agreement with the Federal Republic of Germany and Article 16, Paragraph 3, of the agreement with Panama). The agreements with the United States further provide for the transfer in the currency of the beneficiary (Article 5, Paragraph 2, of the treaty of 1948 and Article 3 of the 1961 agreement). The latter agreement also provides for a rate of exchange approved by IMF or otherwise "equitable and reasonable."

A few special remarks on the 1948 and 1961 agreements with the United States may be of interest.

The treaty of friendship, commerce, and navigation of 1948 is without prejudice, in particular, to the laws and regulations of either High Contracting Party prohibiting direct or indirect ownership by aliens or foreign corporations and associations of the shares in, or instrument of indebtedness of, corporations and associations of such High Contracting Parties carrying on particular types of activities (Article 7, Paragraph 3, last part). As regards financial transactions (as defined in Article 17, Paragraph 1) between the two countries, the most-favored-nation clause shall cover the financial transactions between the two countries. Financial transactions made by nationals of the other party between the two countries or between nationals of one country and a third state, are covered by the "national treatment" rule combined with the most-favored-nation clause (Article 17, Paragraph 3). In any case, governmental control of financial transactions must be such as not to prejudice the competitiveness of the investments and of the commercial position of the other party in relation to third countries.

Article 24, Paragraph 1 (f), creates the parties' obligation not to avail themselves of the privileges deriving from Article 6, Paragraph 3 of the Articles of Agreement of the IMF (namely not to practice the exchange restrictions under Article 7, Paragraph 3-b of the articles or during the transitional period envisaged in Article 15-2). It is otherwise provided, however, in Article 4 of the 1961 agreement. According to the latter, each High Contracting Party reserves the right, at times of monetary difficulties, to apply "particular exchange restrictions especially authorized . . . by IMF."

According to Article 24, Paragraph 5 of the 1948 agreement, each contracting party remains free to exclude companies subject to the "control" from the sphere of application of the agreement. By paragraph 6 of the same article, the parties waive any immunity from prosecution of public or state-owned companies admitted to the exercise of economic, industrial, or commercial activities in the territory of the other contracting party.

The Additional Agreement of 1961 specifies in Article 1 the reciprocal obligation of the contracting parties to admit individual nationals or companies of the other party to participate in economic activities and in Article 3 the obligation to treat in the most liberal possible manner the transfer of any capital or income (in the currency of the beneficiary).

Visas

With regard to visas, the agreements concluded by Italy reveal a tendency toward abolition of visas for persons provided with valid passports.[92] This result, however, is fully applied only to stays not longer than three months.[93]

In most cases the abolition is reciprocal. In the cases of given countries, Italian visas are waived for stays not exceeding three months in exchange for duty-free visas for longer periods (12 months, 24 or more) and for multiple entries. In the cases of Argentina, Ecuador, and the United States a three-months extension of sojourn without visa is permitted.

In cases of longer stays, agreements abolishing visas for periods not exceeding three months often provide for free visas (Austria, Japan, Morocco, and New Zealand).[94] Free visas are also contemplated in the agreement with Brazil for residents, for a stay not exceeding three months, or for permanent settlement.

In the cases of Upper Volta and Morocco, the reentry is granted to resident citizens of both parties without visa within 90 days after departure from the state of residence.

Visa agreements with special features have been concluded by Italy with Belgium, Greece, and the USSR. The agreement with

Belgium does not provide for reciprocity with regard to the visa-exempt period of stay. Italian nationals enjoy the exemption for two months, any longer stay requiring a (free) temporary "settlement" visa. Belgians are exempt for three months, any longer stay requiring a (free) visa. In any case, and on a basis of reciprocity, Article 8 requires a special authorization for nationals of either country to carry out any remunerative activities in the other.

The Treaty with Greece abolishes visas for a period not exceeding one month, subject to a three-month extension by (discretionary) permission of the respective local authorities. Visas remain necessary for those who carry out remunerative activities.

The agreement with the USSR provides Soviet nationals with either transit visa, with a five-day stay, at request, or an entry visa within six days to official delegates or persons designated by the Soviet government for congresses, commercial meetings, and sports competitions. Visa applications for other purposes shall be considered by the Ministry of Foreign Affairs within one or two weeks. Italian nationals are entitled to obtain, at request, transit visas for a five-day stay. The same rule applies to entry visas to delegations, "public" persons, businessmen, and so on, who are invited to the USSR. The Soviet authorities shall give benevolent consideration within one week (or two weeks for other purposes) to entry applications for purposes such as tourism or exhibitions.

Agreements abolishing visas were concluded by Italy with Cyprus in 1962; Colombia in 1965, Denmark in 1950, Chile in 1957, the Federal Republic of Germany in 1954, Yugoslavia in 1966, Malaysia in 1964, Niger in 1964, Paraguay in 1965, Spain in 1959, Sweden in 1949, Togo in 1966, and Uruguay in 1960.

NOTES

1. Constitution, Art. 16, Para. 2; Art. 35, Para. 4; Law No. 1185, 21 November 1967, Art. 1, relating to passports; Royal Decree No. 2205, 13 November 1919, Norme sulla emigrazione, Art. 9, Para. 1, Art. 15, Para. 1. Mention should also be made of the European Convention on Human Rights, to which Italy is a party.

2. Jurists are generally in agreement on both its status as a right and the fact that it is subject to authorization. G. Biscottini, 2 Diritto Amministrativo Internazionale 30 ff., 148 ff. (Padua 1966); V. di Benedetto, "Diritto al passaporto: Procedura e tutela giurisdizionale," 2 Il Consiglio di Stato 353-57 (1968); P. Barile, "La libertà di espatrio e il rilascio del passaporto," Il Foro Amministrativo 200-04 (1956); V. Crisafulli, "Libertà personale, costituzione e passaporti," Archivio Penale excerpt, at 11 (1955).

3. The fact that the government of a country is not recognized by Italy is not an obstacle. Law No. 1185, 21 November 1967, Art. 22.

4. For a view opposing the prevailing doctrine, see Anaslone, "Ritiro di passaporti e rimedi giurisdizionali," 2 Giur. Ital. 218-20 (1955); a similar opinion in E. Vitta, 1 Diritto Amministrativo 368 (Turin, 1962).

5. Some of the exceptions are quoted by Anaslone, op. cit., and Vitta, op. cit.

6. Royal Decree No. 773, 18 June 1931, carrying approval of "T.U. delle leggi di pubblica sicurezza," Art. 3, Para. 3, as modified by Law No. 224, 18 February 1963, Para. 4, and by DPR No. 1656, 30 December 1965, Art. 10. See also Presidential Decree No. 851, 28 July 1967, Art. 2, Para. 1, and Law No. 306, 1 February 1962, Ratifica della Convenzione relativa allo status degli apolidi, New York 18-9-1954; Art. 28, Para. 1 of the Convention.

7. See, for example, Law No. 1185, Art. 24. See also Royal Decree No. 773, 18 June 1931, and Art. 158 (Art. 160 of Testo Unico of 1926). It will be noted that Judgment No. 19 of the Constitutional Court, 5 March 1959, published in Gazzetta Ufficiale 70 special issue, 21 March 1959, declared the "constitutional illegitimacy" of the first paragraph of the quoted Art. 158, in view of its nonconformity with Art. 16 of the Constitution. Following this pronouncement, the amount indicated in the first paragraph stands reduced to 20,000 lira as a consequence of nonapplication of the increase provided for in Law No. 603, 12 July 1961, Art. 3. See also Legge di Pubblica Sicurezza, Art. 220.

8. See Law No. 1185, 21 November 1967, Art. 8.

9. Law No. 1185, 21 November 1967, Art. 12.

10. Law No. 1185, 21 November 1967, Art. 9, Para. 2.

11. See ibid., Art. 5.

12. According to ibid., Arts. 10-12; Law No. 1034, 6 December 1971 (Istituzione dei tribunali amministrativi regionali).

13. A. Sandulli, I tribunali amministrativi regionali 40 (Naples 1972).

14. This follows from Constitution, Arts. 103, 113.

15. In connection with Subparagraph f, Art. 3, see Also Art. 22, DPR No. 237, 14 February 1964.

16. Law No. 1185, 21 November 1967, Art. 3.

17. Law No. 1185, 21 November 1967, Art. 12.

18. Royal Decree No. 267, 16 March 1942.

19. Ibid., Arts. 49, 146. The constitutionality of Art. 49, in connection with Articles 13 and 16 of the Constitution, has been recently affirmed by Corte Costituzionale in Judgment No. 24, 20 February 1969.

20. On the above restrictions, see P. Barile, Il soggetto privato nella Costituzione italiana 124 (Padua 1953).

21. See Biscottini, op. cit., at 155. This writer, however, does not include obligations under tax law among the causes of restriction of the freedom to go abroad. (See ibid., at 150-51.) A similar position is taken by Cossiga, "Note sulla libertà d'espatrio e di emigrazione," 1 Rassegna di Diritto Pubblico 62 ff. (1953). Crisafulli, op. cit., at 113 ff., specifically 115-16, holds that the list of legal obligations limiting freedom to go abroad results from Regulation No. 36, 31 January 1901, insofar as the latter is not in contrast with the Constitution.

22. In connection with this provision, see also DPR No. 237, 14 February 1964, Arts. 17-19, concerning military draft and recruitment of the army, navy, and air force.

23. On this issue see Barile, "La libertà di espatrio," op. cit., and the literature mentioned therein and Barile, "Il soggetto privato nella Costituzione," op. cit., at 125. In a similar sense, see Crisafulli, op. cit., at 120. See also Biscottini, op. cit., at 149, 151-52, 153. According to Biscottini, on the contrary, Art. 19, Decree Law 1964 (military draft) is compatible with the Constitution. Ibid., at 155-56. In support of the validity of the restrictions in question, see Consiglio di Stato, decision of 3 February 1956, 2 Il Foro Amministrativo 199 ff. (1956). A similar line is taken by Cossiga, op. cit., at 84-85. Cossiga, ibid., at 67, also maintains that the state would be under the obligation to prevent 'l'espatrio di cittadini che si rechino in altri Paesi per fomentare o per sostenere disordini o la cui circolazione possa essere di nocumento per la situazione sanitaria mondiale."

24. See, for example, Biscottini, op. cit., at 161. See also Cossiga, op. cit., at 78, note 97.

25. Codice Penale, Art. 13.

26. Constitution, Art. 26. "Political crimes" are defined in the last paragraph of Codice Penale, Art. 8. For the crime of genocide, see, however, supra, page 594.

27. The procedure is governed, in addition to the quoted constitutional rule, by Codice di Procedura Penale, Arts. 661-70.

28. Official Journal 137, 6 June 1956.

29. Official Journal 192, 2 August 1956.

30. See Law No. 786, 25 July 1956, Art. 1, for the definition of "residents."

31. Official Journal 252, 3 October 1968.

32. Official Journal 304, 19 November 1968.

33. See Constitution, Art. 28.

34. 3 H.L. Cas. 449, 10. Eng. Rep. (H.L.) 176 ff., especially 184.

35. 1 Q.B.D. L.R. 487 ff. (1875-76) and 2 Q.B.D. L.R. 69 ff. (1876-77).

36. Lauterpacht, Annual Digest and Reports of Public International Law Cases 237-39 (1931-32), Case 118.

37. Ch.D. L.R. 439 ff. (1933).

38. It should be noted on the other hand that the same Article 4 of the legislation in question clearly implies that the government of Italy would be under no obligation to ensure total indemnification of its nationals whenever the sums paid by the Yugoslav government were inadequate to ensure total compensation of private losses. This same principle, that no such obligation exists, has been asserted with regard to the indemnification of losses suffered by nationals as a consequence of the application of Articles 74 and 79 of the peace treaty. See Law No. 1050, 29 October 1954, Art. 1.

39. Law No. 269, 18 March 1958.

40. Ibid., Art. 1.

41. Ibid., Art. 2.

42. Ibid., Art. 3.

43. Law No. 607, 5 July 1954, Art. 1.

44. Atti Parlamentari del Senato, page 6 of the "Relazione" on Law No. 1050.

45. Consiglio di Stato No. 19, 16 January 1963, 1 Foro Amministrativo 276 ff.

46. Judgment No. 990, 23 April 1964, 1 Giustizia Civile 2067 (1964).

47. Judgment of 13 July 1963, 1 Giustizia Civile 356 (1964).

48. Corte di Cassazione, 2 February 1953, Giustizia Civile 388 (1953).

49. Tribunale Aquila, 7 December 1960, Foro Italiano, Repertorio 1133 (1961), No. 18.

50. Corte Costituzionale, Judgment No. 144, 16 July 1970, 2 Giur. Ital. 1, at 1585 (1970).

51. See M. Mazzanti, 'Espulsione dello Straniero," 15 Enciclopedia del diritto 915 (Giuffrè 1958--).

52. Decision of Consiglio di Stato, Sez. sec. 4, No. 208, 27 February 1952, 3 Foro Italiano 107 ff. (1952).

53. Put into effect by Law No. 1320, 6 June 1939.

54. See, for example, P. Mengozzi, L'efficacia in Italia degli atti stranieri di potesta pubblicà su beni privati 225 ff. (Milan 1967).

55. Tribunale di Roma, 13 September 1954, 1 Foro Italiano 256 ff. (1955).

56. Ibid. In the specific case, however, the court did not find that the expropriation had been made without indemnity.

57. Namely "ordine pubblico internazionale italiano."

58. To be understood in the sense of "ordine pubblico internazionale italiano."

59. Revista di diritto internazionale privato e processuale (hereafter Revista) 642 (1964).

60. Corte di Cassazione, Judgment No. 2124, 26 July 1962, Revista di diritto internazionale 263 (1963).

61. Corte di Appello of Milan, 22 February 1957, 1 Foro Padano 834 (1957), 2 Rivista di diritto industriale 337 ff. (1958), with a comment by Venturini.

62. For the indication of further decisions in the same sense and a critique of this position, see Mengozzi, op. cit., at 126-30.

63. Constitution, Art. 101, Para. 2.

64. Constitution, Art. 104, Para. 1.

65. The first two principles are stressed, among others, by Giuliano in tema di opposizione," Revista. The third principle was asserted by the Constitutional Court in Amministrazione del Governo britannico, Pubblico Ministero, Comune di Venezia v. Guèrrato ved. Arcagniolo, Judgment No. 135, 4 July 1963, quoted in Revista 713 (1969).

66. Tribunale di Genova, 6 May 1970, Revista 702 ff. (1971). For comments on both decisions and on the general problem see Mengozzi, Esecutivo ed autorità giudiziaria nella determinazione dei poteri dello Stato sulla piattaforma continentale, in Rivista di diritto internazionale 609 ff. (1972).

67. Corte di Appello of Milan, 10 August 1956, 1 Foro Padano 896 (1958), with comment by Ruini.

68. Corte di Appello of Milan, 22 February 1957, 1 Foro Padano 834 (1957), 2 Revista di diritto industriale 337 ff. (1958), with a comment by Venturini.

69. Luther v. Sagor (1921), 3 K.B. 532.

70. Journal de Droit Internationale (hereafter Clunet) 1021 (1923).

71. 2 Giustizia Civile 223 (1969).

72. Ibid.

73. Ibid.

74. Ibid.

75. See, for example, Morelli, Nozioni di diritto internazionale 129-30 (Padua 196); B. Pallieri, Diritto internazionale pubblico 331-32 (Milan 1962).

76. Corte di Appello of Genoa, 29 January 1964, Revista 642 (1964).

77. Rivista 320-21 (1964).

78. 2 Foro Italiano 122 ff. (1965).

79. Constitution, Art. 10, Para. 4.

80. Legge Costituzionale No. 1, 21 June 1967.

81. According to V. Arangioriuz, "La Dichiarazione Universale dei Diritti dell'Uomo," in La Comunità Internazionale 10 (1965), in cases such as these a decided preference for a solution in keeping with the declaration should be the only way in which the judge can adhere to the moral and social exigencies of our time.

82. Gazzetta Ufficiale No. 98, 19 April 1967, Suppl. ord.

83. See, among others, Bernardini, "Sulla richiesta di informazioni circa il dirit to straniero," Rivista 649 (1961).

84. This is also stressed in "Relazione ministeriale," accompanying DPR No. 200, 5 January 1967.

85. See G. Morelli, Elementi di diritto internazionale privato, 24-25 and cases quoted therein (9th edition, 1968).

86. See Law No. 1093, 10 May 1970, Official Journal 8, at 155-81, 12 January 1971.

87. Article 8, Paragraph 2 of the treaty with Siam of 1937 provides for reciprocal most-favored-nation treatment in the field of commerce and navigation "whether . . . [the most favored] State shall have been accorded such treatment gratuitously or in return for reciprocal compensatory treatment." Other treaties consider relevant, for the application of the most-favored-nation clause, only the most favorable treatment due to a third state on the basis of a treaty.

88. The treaties with Iran and Lebanon are identical.

89. Curiously enough, this agreement expressly excludes the legal profession and specifically allows the exploitation of mines.

90. Article 5, Paragraph 2 of the treaty with the United States provides that the expropriation of property or of interests held directly or indirectly by nationals (Additional Protocol, Para. 1) may take place only

by due process of law and with prompt payment of just and effective compensation, with the additional requirement of transferability within a certain period. Article 5, Paragraph 3 provides for the same protection in case of nationalization of companies in which nationals of the other party possess a "substantial interest."

91. This agreement specifies that expropriations of property of nationals of the other party may only take place for purposes of "public utility," with prompt, adequate, and effectively available compensation. It is stated that the determination and the payment of compensation must be adequately provided for at the latest at the time of expropriation.

92. In many instances simpler identification documents may be substituted for passports.

93. In only one case, which was the agreement with Ireland of 1949, now superseded by the 1960 agreement, the abolition of the visa was subject to a stay of not less than three months. This agreement also made it possible for an Italian national to enter Ireland, for purposes other than work, with a simple identity paper or tourist card from the Bord Failte Eireann.

94. The agreement with Peru envisages free visas only in the case of permanent settlement in Italy.

CHAPTER

13

MEXICO

Cesar Sepúlveda

THE INDIVIDUAL

The Individual as a National

Movement

Passports. For Mexicans the granting of passports is a right derived from the individual guarantee of freedom of movement in Article 11 of the Constitution.[1] The Passport Regulations of 1938 merely confirm this right and establish the regulations for its exercise.[2]

The regulations state that the passport is only "an internationally accepted proof of nationality and identity of persons."[3] (It may also be observed that a passport is a very useful document for entering and leaving the country.) The regulations continue, "The ordinary passport will be issued to the individuals of Mexican nationality who request it and comply with the requirements that these regulations demand."[4] From this it follows that the granting of a passport to any individual citizen is an obligation of the state and that the citizen has a correlative right to demand it.

This is also confirmed by the text of Article 53 of the regulations, which reiterates, "Every person of Mexican nationality by birth or naturalization may solicit from the Secretariat of Foreign Relations the grant of an ordinary passport, after the compliance with the requirements set by these regulations."

The requirements are merely formal and have to do with the application and proof of nationality. There are only a few restrictions,

---

Revised by the author in 1975.

such as that on minors, who need the consent of those who exercise the parental responsibility. Another restriction is concerned with the completion of military service.[5] In cases in which the interested party does not comply with the requirement of proof of national status or where this is doubtful, a passport valid for only one journey will be awarded, according to Article 62 of this ordinance.[6]

The passport is granted for two years, and it may be renewed twice for like periods; therefore it covers a maximum period of six years.[7] A passport valid for one trip cannot be renewed.

The passport may be confiscated if there is suspicion that it has been issued in contravention of the regulations. This action may be exercised at the moment of application for renewal[8] or through the diplomatic representative in the country or countries where the holder is going,[9] if the latter is willing to act in these cases.

Once confiscated, the passport is cancelled in the following circumstances: When a felony has been committed; when improper use is made of the document; or when the proof of nationality is counterfeit.[10]

A peculiar situation must be mentioned. In the days when the agreements with the United States on migratory workers were in force, the latter were not granted passports so as to avoid their penetrating further than their place of work and to prevent them from being victims of exploitation because of their unpreparedness. A copy of the labor contract served as a limited passport.[11] In this case the visa of the country of destination was endorsed on the document.

I do not know of any case of refusal or arbitrary revocation of a passport. Any arbitrary act or excess of power is remedied by means of a constitutional Ampara action.[12]

Departure. Temporary or permanent departure from the territory is also free, in accordance with the constitutional right of free movement cited earlier. However, there exists a misleading decree. In Article 40 of the Population Act of 1947 it is stated that the Secretariat of the Interior "may close the maritime and border entrances, prohibit the entry or departure of nationals . . . when it is estimated necessary." This is in flagrant contradiction of the Constitution. This regulation surely would not pass the test of a constitutional challenge, since constitutional rights can only be limited or restricted by the Constitution itself, in the cases and under the conditions that it establishes in Article 1. That is, "in cases of invasion, disturbance of the public peace, or any other that places society in grave danger of conflict."[13]

Particular limitations on departure from the territory may only be imposed by judicial authority, for example when arraigo (bail) is imposed on someone scheduled to answer a judicial charge or when there is an arrest warrant.

State territory may be left without need of a passport. However, difficulties may be met upon reentering the territory without this document, for which reason it is convenient to carry one. Naturally there are the requirements of international civil aviation regulations and those of the shipping lines, which necessitate a passport for departure from the national territory by these means of transportation.

Of course, an Amparo action is the most suitable way to challenge any arbitrary or anomalous act with respect to free departure. No case is known in which a Mexican has been forbidden to leave the national territory.

The cases of diplomatic asylum must be carefully examined. In exceptional cases Mexican citizens have sought refuge in foreign embassies under the pretext of political persecution, under the cover of the Inter-American Conventions on Asylum.[14] In all these cases the Mexican government has granted a safe-conduct pass.[15]

Return. In accordance with Article 11 of the Constitution (see above), there is complete freedom for Mexican nationals and their relatives to return to the national territory. Here we again encounter Article 40 of the Population Act, which cannot impede the return of a national except in the case of an immigration prohibition, which is possible but unlikely unless it were connected with a public disaster, such as is contemplated by Article 29 of the Constitution.

Any violation of the right of return can be attacked by means of the Writ of Amparo.

Expulsion. Expulsion of nationals does not exist in Mexican law; nor does that law allow the extradition of a Mexican citizen. Those having asylum in the embassy of an American nation that recognizes the right of asylum may leave the national territory with a safe conduct, in accordance with the Inter-American Conventions on Diplomatic Asylum of 1928, 1933, and 1954, to which Mexico is a party.

Protection

Extent of Freedom of Activity Abroad. In general no limitation is placed upon the activity of a Mexican abroad, with the exception of the usual rules that specify loss of citizenship for service in a foreign army or power or, as is provided in Article 3 of the Law of Nationality and Naturalization of 20 January 1934, by voluntarily acquiring a foreign nationality. A change in citizenship is not considered voluntary when the foreign citizenship is acquired by simple residence or when it constitutes a prerequisite for obtaining work or keeping it.[16] A Mexican by naturalization loses his or her nationality by residing for five continuous years in the country of origin.[17]

A certain limitation on freedom of action is the possibility of punishing a Mexican who has transgressed on foreign territory, if the alleged criminal is within the republic, if he or she has not been judged in the country in which the act was committed and if the act is criminal by both the law of Mexico and that of the other country.[18] Apart from this, there are no limitations upon activity abroad.

However, there are special recommendations, contained in presidential declarations with reference to Central and South America, that are directed toward Mexican investors. When investing in those countries, according to these declarations they should agree to minority participation with respect to local capital, since only in that manner will they obtain official Mexican financial aid.[19]

The Right to Diplomatic Protection. Mexico does not recognize the right to diplomatic protection, nor does it practice it. There is only what may be called diplomatic or consular assistance for the individual, but never in property matters. Protection is exercised by the Secretariat of Foreign Relations through its diplomatic or consular personnel.[20]

On not a few occasions the executive has called on the people not to discuss the measures of foreign governments that affect the property of enterprises, since the Mexican state has resolved not to espouse any claim for economic damage by a national abroad, who must be content with the local remedies.[21]

On the one hand this position of the Mexican government is the result of its noninterventionist policy, firmly maintained. On the other hand it is a product of history, since Mexico has been afflicted by numerous unjust pecuniary claims and its attitude constitutes a rejection of the "right to diplomatic protection."[22]

William R. Manning, who carefully investigated the Mexican national archives, wrote in 1916 that judging by the mountains of correspondence accumulated in the Secretariat of Foreign Relations of Mexico, one must conclude that adjustment of foreign claims had been the principal occupation of the Mexican chancellery up to that time.[23] This more than justifies the aversion of Mexico toward any kind of diplomatic protection.

The State and Compensation. Until now the Mexican Republic has not obtained compensation from any foreign government for damage caused to its nationals. During World War II the Mexican government decreed the taking of enemy property among other purposes, for compensation for damage caused to Mexicans.[24] At the end of the conflict the property or the proceeds of its sale were returned to its owners without any discount and without a demand for compensation. I know of no other cases of compensation requested by Mexico.

We may examine the cases of the 1941 global adjustment of the claims covered by the Mexico-United States General Claims Commission of 1923-34. In the agreement for global adjustment of 19 November 1941,[25] Mexico agreed to pay the United States a lump sum of $40 million, equivalent to 2.64 percent of the total claims filed by North Americans, and to pay to its own nationals the amounts of their claims. This sum, whatever it might have been, acted as compensation in reaching the agreed amount. From this one might deduce that Mexico would take care of the paying of the claims of its nationals from compensation received from the other country.

Later, on 9 December 1941, in relation to this agreement, a presidential decree was issued to the effect that it was "the duty of the Government to attend the demands of our nationals in order to satisfy them in accordance with the role they fulfilled in the recently concluded Agreement . . . in accordance with the maxims of equity," and that these had "lost their international character in becoming internal obligations of our Government," and were "only part of domestic pecuniary obligations."[26]

In the decree the Secretariat of the Treasury was instructed to study and draw up a projected law for adjustment, appraisal, and payment of Mexican claims.

Nevertheless, these steps were never taken, nor was an explanation ever given, and prescription of the debts was allowed to operate. I have not been able to find why this generous idea was abandoned. The inevitable conclusion is that the Mexican state, notwithstanding its desire to comply, has assumed that it may arbitrarily dispose of the claims of Mexicans against foreign countries, this being confirmed by the fact that it was not questioned in this single instance. Thus it can be said that there was acquiescence to the measures taken.

The question of the responsibility of the state for injury induced by its own conduct has not arisen in Mexico because up to this time the Mexican state has not acted beyond its frontiers, nor has any important case been found concerning the property of Mexican nationals in enemy territory that could involve the responsibility of the Mexican state.

Waiver. In accordance with the doctrine prevailing in Mexico, which maintains that the sovereign state is not subject to responsibility, it must be admitted that Mexico has the right to waive the claims of its nationals presented against other countries for damage caused by the latter. The Agreement of 1941 is an eloquent example of this.

There is another precedent, though it is hardly conclusive because of its age. By virtue of Article 11 of the Treaty of Guadaloupe Hidalgo of 1848, the United States agreed to make an indemnity for damages caused by pillage by the Indians of Mexicans who remained in the territories ceded by the treaty (California, Arizona, New Mexico, and Texas). By 1851 the estimated damages caused by the incursions of these Indians had already risen to $8 million. By Article 2 of the 1853 Mesilla or Gadsden Treaty between Mexico and the United States, the United States was exempted from the obligations imposed by the treaty of Guadeloupe Hidalgo. The disposal of the rights of Mexican citizens in this claim is evident.

For this reason, the right of the Mexican state not to espouse a claim of one of its nationals against a foreign nation if it considers it should not do so, seems unquestionable. There exists no legal or administrative remedy for compelling the Mexican government to act in espousing a claim when it has declined to do so.

Special Kinds of Protection. The question of special kinds of protection also does not exist in Mexican law. I do not know of any case of damage of a special nature against a national because of an international competence that Mexico would not recognize.

The Individual as an Alien

Movement

Entry and Stay. Though from Article 2 of the Constitution, which was cited earlier, it is understood that everyone, even a foreigner, has the right to enter the country, the truth is that foreigners only enjoy a privilege that the law grants subject to the requirements of immigration statutes and some other circumstances.[27]

There is no discrimination with respect to any nationality, race, or creed. Mexican ordinances are quite generous in permitting the entry of tourists, visitors, and transmigrants.[28] There are only a few limitations because of immigration policies[29] or in the case of persons who wish to take up residence in the country, particularly foreigners who want to work there. Pursuant to Article 60 of the Population Act, there is the possibility that a foreigner may be denied entry into the country (1) when there is no international reciprocity; (2) when there is no equivalence of population interchange; (3) when quotas are filled in those cases in which they have been set; (4) when it is regarded as injurious to the economic interests of nations, as in the case of foreign laborers; (5) when faultless conduct has not been observed during previous residence in the country; or (6) when the migration regulations have been infringed upon.

With regard to persons who wish to earn a living in the country, the Population Act[30] and practice show that a foreigner may enter the country as an immigrant as an investor, in which case it is necessary (1) to make an investment in the securities of official banking institutions, (2) to receive a permanent income from abroad; or (3) to invest in the agricultural or cattle industries or commerce, but not in stock companies; or as a technician in specialized occupations that cannot be performed by residents in the country; or in exceptional cases, to practice a profession or to assume a position of confidence in enterprises or institutions established in the republic. It is also possible to enter as a dependent of relatives within the second generation and, finally, to study in educational centers.

It is worth commenting that Mexico grants a resident foreigner the right to return after visits abroad, pursuant to Article 68 of the Population Act,[31] as long as he or she does not remain abroad for two consecutive years and as long as his or her absences do not add to more than five years within a period of ten years. If the absences amount to that much, the foreigner will lose his or her immigrant status and on entering the country will only be allowed to do so under one of the other categories indicated by the law (tourist, visitor, transmigrant, and so on). Mexican laws are generous in permitting the reacquisition of Mexican nationality by Mexicans by naturalization who have lost it because of absences.

Voluntary Departure. There is no statutory limitation placed upon the departure of foreigners. The exception is the particular limitation referred to in the section on departure of nationals.

Involuntary Departure: Expulsion and Deportation. Article 33 of the Constitution places the right to expel foreigners in the hands of the executive, a power that in this respect is subject to no control. In fact, even though in theory constitutional judicial review of an expulsion decree is possible, there is no precedent of an Amparo being granted because of an action of this kind. Since expulsion is effected immediately, without any previous judgment, it is an executed act, against which the constitutional suit is technically not admissible. Moreover, the letter of the precept is definitive, as follows: "The Federal Executive shall have the exclusive power to compel any foreigner whose remaining it may deem inexpedient to abandon the national territory immediately and without the necessity of previous legal action."[32]

Another aspect of involuntary departure is extradition requested by another country, in accordance with the treaties in force. It is pertinent to note that Mexico does not grant extradition of political offenders, since this is forbidden by Article 15 of the Constitution.

Protection

If, as said above, Mexico refuses diplomatic protection even in the case of its nationals, it is to be assumed that it would not exercise it in the case of foreigners.

NATIONAL IMPLEMENTATION OF INTERNATIONAL RIGHTS AND DUTIES

The Act of State Doctrine

In Mexico the question of the Act of State doctrine, as it is known in North American practice, does not exist, since Mexican courts are not qualified to examine whether the act of a foreign state is compatible with international law. In its fundamental aspect the Act of State doctrine is applied to the acts and decrees of a nonrecognized government. In Mexico recognition is an entirely political question, and acts of this nature are not susceptible to judicial control. Moreover, the recognition of, and maintenance of diplomatic relations with, other governments is a matter exclusively for the executive, in accordance with Article 89 of the Constitution. All these relations are handled by the executive branch.

Another aspect of the Act of State doctrine is seen in relation to acts of confiscation or expropriation by a foreign government that is recognized, when it is considered that the act violates principles of international law. However, few examples of this are to be found.

Nevertheless, in certain cases, in spite of the general principle accepted in Mexico, a foreign government and its public institutions are immune to local jurisdiction even though that jurisdiction is not recognized. Notwithstanding the principle of the territoriality of foreign public law, domestic law may find some application.

For example, in the case of expropriation of property or confiscation dictated by another government, if the property is situated in the expropriating country or in a third state, Mexican courts have no opportunity to exercise jurisdiction; nor can the invalidity of the expropriation be argued before them. On the other hand, if the property is found in Mexico and, let us say, belongs to an interested individual, then there is the possibility that the expropriation measures would not be effective because the foreign sovereign would have to litigate, thus subjecting itself to the local jurisdiction. In that case there would be occasion for applying the principle of public policy.[33]

In accordance with the principle stated in the Mexican Civil Code, in principle foreign public law is not applicable and is unenforceable.[34] Exception is made for those cases in which there is no legal regulation or when a treaty requires its application.

It may be interesting to note, on the other hand, that when the oil expropriations of 1938 were discussed with Great Britain and the United States the Mexican government insisted that there existed no clear and definite rule of international law that prohibited expropriation without compensation or that established the obligation of "prompt, effective and adequate" indemnity. From this it may be deduced that an expropriatory legislation or act, even damaging a Mexican, would not be regarded as contrary to public policy in Mexico.[35]

However, with reference to legislation concerned with the status or capacity of persons, a law enacted by a foreign government, though recognized, may not be applied normally in Mexico if it is in conflict with the territoriality of Mexican law or with public policy. Insofar as other matters are concerned, conflicts of this kind do not usually involve diplomatic relations with other states.

In conclusion, in Mexico the Act of State doctrine is interpreted as the exclusive capacity of the executive for finding solutions by diplomatic negotiations to problems concerning acts of foreign governments, if such acts are contrary to local law.

Implementation of Decisions of International Organizations

In discussing the implementation of decisions of international organizations, it is convenient to consider the problem of the status of treaties in the Mexican legal order, since some of the decisions of intergovernmental organizations are similar to international agreements, are derived directly from a treaty, or are incorporated into domestic law in a manner similar to the law contained in treaties.

Article 133 of the Constitution lays down the fundamental principle for determining the authority of international treaties with respect to the different Mexican municipal laws with which they may come into conflict. This provision states as follows:

> This Constitution, the laws of the Congress of the Union that emanate therefrom, and all treaties that have been made and shall be made in accordance therewith by the President of the Republic, with the approval of the Senate, shall be the supreme law of the whole Union. The Judge of Each State shall conform to the said Constitution, laws and treaties, in spite of any contradictory provisions that may appear in the constitutions or laws of the States.

Certain similarities with Article 6, Paragraph 2, of the U.S. Constitution can be observed, but the comparison is somewhat pointless, since the international experience of Mexico shows that most international agreements present practically no problems of conflict with the constitutional order.

The case of an agreement entered into in violation of the Constitution, although it is rejected by the Constitution and by international law at the same time, is a true exception, being more a matter of selection of the applicable law. However, this rule is not useless, since it continues to constitute a healthy provision for preventing the conclusion or the ratification, whichever is the case, of certain treaties that could affect or annul the political organization, territorial integrity, or individual rights.

Undoubtedly the most acceptable rule is that if a collision between a treaty or a decision of international organizations and the fundamental laws arises, the latter should prevail.[36] This results from the following considerations:

1. The Constitution is a general rule of political order that was produced after long-thought-out elaboration, during which all the social factors were taken into consideration; while an agreement is a concrete and specific rule, as is a resolution of an international organization.

2. A treaty should conform to the Constitution, and not the latter to the former. This is to be derived from the text of Article 133 and from the practice of nations.

3. If the supremacy of the agreement is admitted, the executive branch is unjustifiably given the capacity to reform the constitutional order through its power to conclude treaties or can alter the constitutional precepts in whatever matter convenient to its program of international relations, which is inadmissible for a correct constitutional technique. In a regime of separation of powers such as that established in the Mexican system,[37] the executive cannot step outside its own sphere of action nor assume legislative functions.

Article 133 of the Constitution should be interpreted more as a prescription, insofar as its requirements must perforce be observed in concluding and ratifying international treaties. Thus in the first place it establishes that the capable and authorized organ for making agreements is the President of the Republic, by virtue of the powers expressedly recognized in Article 89, Section 10.[38] In the second place, it is necessary that treaties be in harmony with the Constitution, because if they conflict the next step cannot be undertaken. The third requirement is approval by the Senate of the Republic. Though the Constitution does not regulate this aspect of the matter, it is necessary that the international instrument be ratified and that there be an exchange and deposit of ratifications or of the instrument of adhesion, as the case may be. Other formalities are the promulgation and publication of the agreement.

We may comment that in the field of public administration of Mexico the immediate application of international pacts is observed most strictly, as is the punctilious and undisputed compliance with them, without the introduction of problems of hierarchy or of questions of application. This is understandable, since the greater number of treaties are concluded in the sphere of so-called "international cooperation," which has an essentially administrative content. It should also be borne in mind that the executive power is the organ that conducts international relations and concludes treaties. Therefore its adherence to them must be taken for granted.

A very interesting phenomenon can be observed between treaties and the internal order, in that on some occasions agreements have a direct application without the need of legislation to implement them. In other cases, by a virtue of the treaty, effect is given to the laws of another state or to the resolutions of international organizations. Under these circumstances the treaty becomes a source of municipal rules, and on not a few occasions the agreement has brought about the creation of new administrative institutions so as to fulfill the agreement. In such cases there is an interesting combination of the law of treaties and domestic Mexican law, which is just beginning to be observed but which possesses dynamics that must translate themselves into more cogent rules in the future.

On the other hand, the powers of the executive in international matters "to direct diplomatic negotiations," contained in Article 89, Section 10, of the Constitution, give it sufficient room for application and compliance, or for nonapplication if it judges this to be more in accordance with the national interest and with the resolutions and acts of international organizations. Moreover, since the executive possesses the faculty of dictating administrative decrees in the sphere of its administrative functions without the need of legislation by the federal congress, and since for the most part acts of international organizations are essentially administrative if they do not require a law for their implementation or at most a simple administrative decree, it is clear that they can easily be implemented in Mexico.

With this in mind, we may now examine what has happened with respect to some resolutions of international organizations.

The Sanctions against Cuba by the OAS

The 8th Meeting of the Organization of American States (OAS), held in Punta del Este, Uruguay, on 22 January 1962, decided in its Resolution 6 to "exclude" the government of Cuba from participation in the Interamerican System,[39] and in Resolution 8 to suspend the trade in arms and in other articles.[40]

The Mexican Republic declared that it did not consider the exclusion of a member state legally well founded, since it was not provided for in the charter of the OAS.[41]

Later, in 1964, the 9th Meeting of the Consultation of Ministers of Foreign Affairs, in its Resolution 1, decided upon the rupture of diplomatic and consular relations and upon direct or indirect interruption of commercial interchange, as well as of maritime transport with Cuba, until "the moment when the government of Cuba has ceased to constitute a danger to the peace and security of the Continent."[42]

These dispositions resulted in obligations for all members of the OAS by virtue of Article 20 of the Treaty of American Reciprocal and Mutual Assistance of 1947 (Treaty of Rio de Janeiro).[43]

Once again the Mexican government dissented from these measures, because the Rio treaty did not include measures "having the nature and characteristics of those that have been decided upon at the Meeting of Consultation."[44]

Mexico has continued to maintain diplomatic relations with the Cuban government to date, but as far as commercial relations are concerned, these had to be interrupted because of the circumstances and because of fears of Mexican exporters of being placed on the "black list" of the United States.

In this manner parties interested in trade with Cuba were affected, notwithstanding the position of Mexico with respect to sanctions.

Recommendations and Conventions of The International Labour Organization

As is well known, in its early years the International Labour Organization produced some 130 recommendations and conventions, which constituted its principal activity.[45] Since the Constitution of 1917 (Article 123) and the Labor Law of 18 August 1931, Mexico has been distinguished for its advanced labor and social legislation. It not only has adopted and applied the 51 conventions on working conditions that it has ratified (by the time of this writing) and the recommendations it has accepted, but it has also been an important factor in the advance of laborer-employer relations. The new federal labor law adopted in 1970 incorporated all the decisions of the ILO and even went beyond them.[46]

In the interval between the old and the new labor laws, the conventions were applied directly without legislation to implement them. They were incorporated in the collective labor contracts and in the so-called law-contracts for federal industry, giving them a self-executing character, without major problems.

It is interesting to note that in a 1966 Official Review the texts of the conventions ratified by Mexico and the corresponding norms of the federal labor law were published in order that it could be objectively seen that such conventional rules had acquired the force of law in the country.[47]

It should be noted, on the other hand, that the International Labor Organization has abandoned its role as a producer of conventions and recommendations relative to labor rules and has converted itself more and more into a technical assistance organ, dealing with such matters as industrialization, development of resources, and training of workers. Since its purpose is to promote acceptable working conditions around the world, the problem of the application of its decisions has therefore been overcome.

This is a clear example of participation by a nation in the formation of the decisions of an international organization. It is also an example of the application and observance of such decisions; the incorporation of them in internal law; and the discharge, for the benefit of individuals, of the obligations derived therefrom.

Conventions and Agreements of the World Health Organization

The World Health Organization (WHO) issues conventions, agreements, and regulations on the subject of health. All these have been complied with by Mexico. The recommendations and suggestions of this specialized international organization have been adopted, as well as those of the Pan-American Sanitation Organization in Washington, which is established as a regional organization in the terms of Chapter 11 of the constitution of WHO and at the same time as a specialized organ of the Organization of American States.[48]

In 1960 WHO made its decisions more flexible,[49] abandoning its former legislation in favor of a recommendatory procedure that made its measures more easily acceptable.

Resolutions of the Latin American Free Trade Association

The organs of LAFTA can make decisions that require no action whatever on the part of the governments in order to operate but are obligatory once they have been adopted by those organs and have been communicated to the member states.[50]

LAFTA produces resolutions that affect the rights of private persons, since they limit their rights of export and import and their freedom to invest in certain branches of industry. These resolutions may also place them in a situation of increased competition because of authorization privileges for merchandise coming from free-trade zones.[51]

The resolutions and agreements are implemented directly in the states by administrative decree and are incorporated into national law without any special procedure, given their self-executing character.

Possible Remedies against the Application of the Decisions of International Organizations

The greater part of the decisions of international organizations that we have examined benefit the individual person, the private person, or the social conglomerate as a whole. However, some of them, such as those of LAFTA, could entail injury to the interests of some affected party.

The policy of acceptance by the state of resolutions and acts of international organizations has not been accompanied by remedial devices to protect private parties if they sustain some undue injury when the state discharges its obligations or when, on the contrary, it does not comply with them when obligated to do so. A well-shaped mechanism for the defense of private persons does not exist for challenging the decrees incorporated into internal law.

Though the writ of Amparo, which is referred to above, could serve to challenge one of these measures, it can only be used when actual and tangible damage has been done and when the measure effectively violates individual rights guaranteed by the Constitution. In other words it is very difficult, if not impossible, to secure redress by an action of Amparo because the constitutional violation or the arbitrary act of authority is not established clearly.

I do not know of any case in which a decision by an international organization that has been adopted by the Mexican Republic and put into practice in its territory has been challenged.

Procedures Related to the Issue of Certificates and Suggestions by the Executive in Connection with Litigation in National Courts

In Mexico executive certificates, an institution familiar in Anglo-Saxon public law, are not known.

According to my experience, the federal courts, which have always shown great independence in respect to the executive, have not on any occasion requested, in matters of relevance to international law, a document equivalent to the certificate that has been employed in U.S. or British practice.

Exception is made for the information furnished by the Secretariat of Foreign Relations in cases in which some matter is before the court that involves diplomatic immunity of persons or of domicile.

When the executive appears in Amparo suits, it does so as a party. It then issues what is known as Informecon Justificacion (the report with justification),[52] a document in which it gives reasons and legal foundations to sustain the constitutionality of the act being impugned or the lack of merit of the action of Amparo against it. However, this instrument is far from being a certificate.

Recognition and Nonrecognition

Nonrecognition of a foreign government produces unpleasant effect for nationals as well as foreigners in the domestic forum of the country that does not recognize the other. For example, it creates difficulties in proving the status and capacity of persons coming from the country the government of which is not recognized. It also makes it difficult to establish the validity of acts or decrees that affect that civil status or capacity. Without consular relations, there is no authority to give formality to the documents that are issued by the nonrecognized government.

Such a situation is notoriously unjust to the individual. Even tacit recognition would facilitate the authentication of the acts by some semiofficial, nondiplomatic representative of the nonrecognizing state. In other words, it would be desirable to find an institution to relieve the "private" effects of nonrecognition. Many governments would gladly accept this.

The case of Mexico and Spain is sufficiently illustrative. Neither diplomatic nor consular relations were maintained by Mexico with the Franco government after 1939, although numerous Spaniards resided in Mexico, and there was a constant migratory flow.

There are, it is true, some agreements between these countries. For example, there are agreements on currency, aviation, and tourism; but these do not imply recognition. Mexico symbolically granted recognition to the representation of the Spanish Republic in exile. This authority, curiously, is one that can formalize and authenticate the acts and documents of (nonrecognized) Spanish authorities. Also, of course, third governments can effect that legalization, creating unnecessary complications because more steps are introduced in the chain of legalizations, such as the intervention of the ministry of foreign relations of the country of the consul granting the legalization.

Though there are no diplomatic relations with the German Democratic Republic nor with Hungary, for example, the priorities of those countries in patent applications are recognized without great difficulty.

I do not think that the courts should determine the legitimacy of a government or of a state. In my opinion, all questions that have to do with relations with a state or a nonrecognized government should be left to the executive, which should establish an ad hoc organ for handling questions that originate from nonrecognition. These questions include the treatment of the property of the nonrecognized entity, the capacity of the nonrecognized entity to appear in a judicial suit, its eligibility for immunities, and the status of its representatives.

The executive is much more capable of dealing with these matters. Such methods might be more flexible and expeditious with respect to countries whose international relations are not of great moment.

Finally, insofar as the substitution for recognition of some other more convenient attitude or institution is concerned, I have argued that the most consistent rule would be the automatic continuation of relations when a sudden change in government occurs. This would give continuity without expressing judgment of the conditions in which the new regime came to power. I have held elsewhere that this should be the correct interpretation of the Estrada doctrine.[53]

TREATIES AND THE INDIVIDUAL

In fact, there are few Mexican treaties in which the individual appears as beneficiary or from which effects may be indirectly derived for the individuals.

Insofar as Mexico is concerned, we may mention the Paris Union Convention for the International Protection of Industrial Property of 1873 (Revision of Lisbon, 1958);[54] the Universal Copyright Convention;[55] the Inter-American Copyright Convention;[56] the different treaties of extradition to which Mexico is a party;[57] and the Convention for the Recovery and Return of Stolen Automotive Vehicles, Airplanes, and their Component Parts, between Mexico and the United States.[58]

There have been serious problems in the application of these agreements in the Mexican internal order. The Mexican Law of

Industrial Property contains the principal dispositions that emanate from the revisions of the Convention of Paris, up to the London Revision of 1934.[59] The Lisbon Revision contains some improvements that are applied by the agency in charge of industrial property, since they are self-executing.

It is worth mentioning that by the principle of "minimum protection," any new rights recognized by the Paris Convention as belonging to foreigners are automatically extended to Mexicans; the same is true with respect to the copyright conventions.

Extradition agreements, as is natural, provoke problems of application, since there is conflict both with internal legislation and with the operation of the Law of Amparo, inasmuch as extradition agreements can intimately affect guarantees of individual rights.

The Treaty on Stolen Vehicles raised numerous incidents because in applying it the administrative authorities underestimated its effect on individual rights.[60] Nevertheless, the matters were resolved in favor of observance of the treaty.[61]

As has already been observed, the legal mechanism for obtaining the correct application of the treaties that refer to the individual, or for contesting an undue application of them, is the constitutional Writ of Amparo before the federal courts. Article 104 of the Constitution prescribes this.[62] We may add that in hierarchy treaties are comparable to the internal laws.

CONCLUSIONS

What has been expressed here naturally leads to the formulation of some conclusions on the topic of individual rights and the rights of the state in respect to the international legal order, as they operate in Mexico.

It can be observed that this country is strongly influenced by the European tradition and that its institutions and the behavior of its authorities is conducive to a reasonable protection of the enjoyment of individual rights, notwithstanding the pressures that tend to originate in developing nations such as ours that may restrict the interests of individuals. The Mexican legal regime is very liberal, and Mexicans abroad are generally not subject to restrictions.

The legal regime with respect to foreigners, domiciled or transitory, is also very liberal. Their admission is not difficult, and there is no discrimination whatsoever because of race or creed.

The determination of Mexico not to grant diplomatic protection to its nationals abroad is due, on the one hand, to the firm conviction that there should be juridical equality among states in the international order and, on the other hand, to its sad experience as passive subject of international claims, in which the gross frauds of Weil and of La Abra in the Commissions of 1872 were perpetrated. Another element may be its consistent adherence to the principle of self-determination of peoples, which brings about a natural reluctance to examine the acts of other states before the national courts, even in the case of seizure of the property of Mexicans by other governments.

One may also note a convenient operation of the international rules that benefit and protect the individual, notwithstanding the fact that domestic law has not advanced enough to provide mechanisms and techniques for application of the rules that emerge from customary international law, from treaties, and from the decisions of intergovernmental organizations. In this aspect municipal law has fallen behind with respect to international law. This is where jurists should direct their attention in order to devise the most effective and simple methods of avoiding conflict with the domestic law--conflict that is more apparent than real.

Because of its evident desire for universality, Mexico is more and more inclined toward the abandonment of recognition of de facto governments. Of course, it can be pointed out that Mexico has never used this institution as an instrument of national politics, which is obviously a desirable policy and which tends to bring about automatic relations with all countries. The cases in which reestablishment of relations has been delayed have been cases of external pressure or of very peculiar circumstances of Mexican political life, rather than exercises of diplomacy. Happily, care has been taken to minimize, in those cases, the effects of nonrecognition upon individuals. This is an encouraging sign. Also, the lack of diplomatic relations has not obstructed international relations.

NOTES

1. "Everyone has the right to enter and leave the Republic, to travel through its territory and to change his residence without the necessity of a letter of security, passport, safe-conduct or any other similar requirement." Constitution, Art. 11.

2. "Reglamento para la Expedicion y Visa de Pasaportes," Diario Oficial (Official Gazette) 12 April 1938.

3. Ibid., Art. 1.

4. Ibid., Art. 11.

5. "Ley del Servicio Militar Nacional of 19 August 1940," Diario Oficial, 11 September 1940.

6. "When in the case of extreme urgency in the opinion of the Secretariat of Foreign Relations, the interested parties cannot exhibit evidence, . . . a passport for only one trip may be granted."

7. "Ley del Servicio Militar Nacional," op. cit., Arts. 145, 146, 148.

8. Ibid., Art. 152.

9. Ibid., Art. 153.

10. Ibid., Art. 154.

11. During World War II, on 4 August 1942, an Agreement on Migratory Workers was signed by Mexico and the United States, and in 1943 it was extended until 1947. This agreement was concluded by the Mexican government when it possessed extraordinary powers because of the war (suspended in 1945). By informal agreements between the two governments, the 1942 agreement was extended until 1951. On 4 August 1951 a temporary agreement on agricultural laborers was signed by Mexico and the United States. This agreement enumerated the social and civil rights of the Mexican laborers who are employed exclusively in the harvest. This last agreement was extended year after year until it was finally terminated on 31 December 1964. As of this writing, a new treaty is in the process of being negotiated.

12. The Juicio dé Amparo (Writ of Amparo), which covers constitutional proceedings, legality and constitutionality of laws, and relief against arbitrary or illegal acts of authorities, is a vital institution in Mexican law because it controls or moderates excessive and arbitrary applications of any of the three powers, but mainly those of the executive. The Writ of Amparo bears much similarity to the writs of mandamus, certiorari, error, and habeas corpus and to some forms of injunctive relief in the law of the United States. It only differs basically from U.S. constitutional judicial procedure in the courts that apply it and in their proceedings. It protects the inhabitants of the republic in the enjoyment and preservation of the rights that the Constitution and constitutional laws grant against infringement by any of the three branches of government, as well as by the states of the federation. It creates a judicial review of constitutional matters. The Writ of Amparo is provided for in Articles 14 and 16 of the Constitution of the Republic and in the Law of Amparo. Regulatory Law of the Constitution, Arts. 103 and 107, 10 January 1936, revised in 1942, 1943, 1949, 1963, and 1967.

For literature in English on this writ, see R. D. Baker, Judicial Review in Mexico: A Study of the Amparo Suit (University of Texas Press, Austin, 1971); P. J. Eder, A Comparative Study in Anglo-American and Latin American Law (New York University Press, New York, 1950); P. J. Eder, "Judicial Review in Latin America," Ohio State Law Journal 570, 599-604 (1960).

13. Constitution, Art. 29.

14. Convention on Asylum, signed at Havana, 20 February 1928, at International Conference of American States, 6 Final Act 166 (Havana 1928); Convention on Political Asylum, signed at Montevideo, 28 December 1933, in International Conference of American States, 7 Final Act 162 (Montevideo 1933); Convention on Diplomatic Asylum, signed at Caracas, 28 March 1954; Panamerican Union, Convention on Diplomatic Asylum, signed at the Tenth Inter-American Conference, Caracas, 1-28 March 1954 (Washington 1954).

15. The case of attorney José Rojo Coronado should be mentioned. Defender of so-called "political prisoners," he sought asylum at the Chilean Embassy on 18 February 1970. Excelsior, 18 February 1970. He was extended a safe-conduct pass and departed from the country. Nevertheless, three weeks later he returned to Mexico. Excelsior, 12 March 1970. Hence his allegation that he was a victim of persecution appears to have been unfounded.

16. Law of Nationality and Naturalization, Art. 3, Diario Oficial, 20 January 1934. "Mexican nationality is lost: I.--By having acquired voluntarily a foreign nationality." It is understood that acquisition of foreign nationality is not voluntary when it has occurred by virtue of the law, by simple residence, or by being an indispensable condition for obtaining employment or keeping work previously obtained, in the judgment of the Secretariat of Foreign Relations.

17. Ibid., Art. 3, sect. 3.

18. Codigo Penal, 13 August 1931, Art. 4.

19. Address of President Diaz Ordaz in Guatemala City, 1 February 1965. Excelsior, 11 February 1965. In view of the strength of the executive branch within the governmental system, a declaration of this kind should be considered the general rule.

20. See Ley de Secretarias y Departamento de Estado, Art. 3, sect. 2; Organic Law of the Mexican Foreign Service, Art. 13, sect. 2; see also C. Molina, Practica Consular Mexicana (Editorial Porrúa, 1970).

21. For example, declaration of President Adolfo Lopez Mateos, Excelsior, 11 July 1961.

22. Feller pointed out in 1935 that the diplomatic history of Mexico could well be written in the terms of diplomatic claims, so intense has the pressure been on this country. A. Feller, The Mexican Claims Commission, 1923-1934 1-13 (Macmillan, New York, 1935). See also C. Sepúlveda, Dos Reclamaciones Fraudulentas contra México 20-41 (Archivo Histórico Diplomático, Secretaría de Relaciones Exteriores, Mexico 1965).

The effort of Mexico to obtain the incorporation of nonintervention as a conventional rule or its inclusion in decisions of international organizations is very well known. Its delegates have been instrumental in obtaining the Declaration of Havana of 1928, the Declaration of Montevideo of 1933, the Protocol of Nonintervention of Buenos Aires of 1936, and the inclusion of the principle in the charter of the Organization of American States in Bogotá in 1948. Mexico strongly supported the work that resulted in Resolution 2131 (XX) of the General Assembly of the United Nations in 1965. In addition, Mexico strongly supported Resolution 2625 (XXV) of the same body and Article 18 of the charter of the OAS. See, for example, C. Sepúlveda, "Derecho de los Débiles, Trayectoria de la No Intervención," Excelsior 13 July 1971.

The recognition of this intense international posture of Mexico is referred to, for example, in B. Wood, The Making of the Good Neighbor Policy especially 121-22 (Columbia University Press, New York 1961).

23. W. R. Manning, Early Diplomatic Relations between the United States and Mexico 775-76 (Johns Hopkins Press, Baltimore 1916).

24. See the Ley Relativa a Bienes y Negocios del Enemigo, 24 February 1944, Diario Oficial, 29 March 1944.

25. Convention of 19 November 1941 between Mexico and the United States. 4 UN Rep. Int'l. Arb. Awards 767, Diario Oficial, 30 May 1942.

26. Diario Oficial, 31 December 1941.

27. Matters relative to immigration are regulated by Ley General de Poblacion, 23 December 1947, Diario Oficial, 27 December 1947. See also, S. Dunn, Diplomatic Protection of Americans in Mexico 67 (Columbia University, New York 1933).

28. Ley General de Poblacion, Art. 50.

29. Ibid., Art. 58.

30. Ibid., Art. 48.

31. "The immigrant may leave the country or enter it freely; but if he should remain abroad for two consecutive years he will lose his migratory status, as he will if during a period of ten years he should be absent more than five."

32. Constitution, Art. 33.

33. The principle of public order is contained in Article 8 of the Civil Code, Diario Oficial, 26 May 1968, which states, "8.--The Acts fulfilled against the letter of prohibitive laws or of public interest shall be null."

34. "The Mexican laws, including those that relate to the State and the capacity of persons, are applied to all the inhabitants of the Republic, be they nationals or foreigners, be they domiciled in the country or in transit." Civil Code, Art. 12.

35. See notes of the Mexican government to the government of the United States, 3 August 1938 and 1 September 1938, State Department Press Releases, 25 August 1938 and 5 September 1938. See also G. H. Hackworth, 3 Digest of International Law 658-64 (1941).

36. See C. Sepúlveda, "La Situación de los Tratados en el Orden Legal Mexicano," Comunicaciones Mexicanas al VI Congreso Internacional de Derecho Comparado (1962).

37. Constitution, Art. 49.

38. "To conduct diplomatic negotiations and conclude treaties with foreign powers, submitting them to the ratification of the Federal Congress." Art. 89, sect. 10.

39. See "Tratado Interamericano de Asistencia Reciproca, Aplicaciones," 2 Pan American Union 66-67 (1964).

40. Ibid., at 69.

41. Ibid., at 71.

42. Ibid., at 187-88.

43. "Decisions which require the application of measures specified in Article 8 shall be binding upon all signatory states which have ratified this treaty with the sole exception that no State shall be required to use armed force without its consent." Art. 20.

44. "Tratado Interamericano de Asistencia Reciproca, Aplicaciones," 2 Pan American Union 119 (1964).

45. Constitution of the International Labor Organization, as amended 22 May 1963, Art. 19; Standing Orders of the Conference, Section E, Arts. 34-46.

46. Diario Oficial, 1 April 1970.

47. See International Labour Conference, 50th session, Record of Proceedings 582 (1966).

48. Charter of the Organization of American States, Art. 130.

49. Constitution of the World Health Organization, as amended 25 October 1960, Arts. 19, 21.

50. Treaty Establishing a Free-Trade Area and Instituting the Latin American Free-Trade Association, Montevideo, 18 February 1960.

51. Ibid., Art. 34.

52. Ley de Amparo, Art. 149.

53. C. Sepúlveda, La Teoría y Práctica del Reconocimiento de Gobiernos (Mexico 1954). See also C. Sepúlveda, "Reconocimiento de Gobiernos en América, Evolución y Estado Actual," 3 Anuario Hispano-Luso-Americano de Derecho Internacional 115 (Madrid 1967).

54. Diario Oficial, 11 July 1964.

55. Diario Oficial, 22 December 1955.

56. Diario Oficial, 13 February 1947.

57. Extradition Treaties with Belgium, Cuba, El Salvador, United States, Great Britain, etc., in 1 Tratados y Convenciones Vigentes entre México y otros países (hereafter Tratados) 61, 571, 177, 267 (Secretaría de Relaciones Exteriores, Mexico 1938).

58. In 6 Tratados 12.

59. Diario Oficial, 31 December 1942.

60. C. Sepúlveda, Curso de Derecho Internacional Público 76-79 (11th ed., Porrúa Hermanos, Mexico 1970).

61. Sepúlveda, "La Situación de los Trabados," op. cit., at 212.

62. "It is the function of the courts of the Federation to hear: I.--All controversies of civil or criminal nature that might arise from the compliance and application of Federal Laws, or a result of treaties concluded with foreign powers."

CHAPTER

14

POLAND AND SOME OTHER EASTERN EUROPEAN COUNTRIES

Krzysztof Skubiszewski

The first section of this chapter concentrates on the law and practice of the members of the Council for Mutual Economic Aid (Comecon),[1] though the coverage of the respective countries is not identical and the legislation of some has altogether been omitted. However, the material gives a bird's-eye view of the legal position in that part of Europe and should permit the reader to arrive at some generalizations.

Its discussion of the Act of State doctrine and of executive certificates are again linked to patterns that prevail in the Comecon countries, but the illustrative material is taken mainly from Polish law. On the other hand, implementation of international decisions is dealt with in the broader context of the Comecon. The paper ends by discussing some of the municipal aspects of recognition.

The chapter omits from its purview the problem of individual rights in relation to treaties. Treaties establishing investment guarantees of the free market type; the World Bank convention on the settlement of international investment disputes; and the agreements between parent states and newly-emerging independent countries, making provision for the protection of the continuing interests of nationals of the parent states, are examples of intergovernmental contractual transactions that concern neither the Comecon members nor individuals in those countries. Visa arrangements are referred to. The Comecon members have signed many agreements for the payment of compensation in respect to nationalization, but the individual interest appears only on the side of the West, and thus it belongs to other reports in this book. (See Chapter 1.) It would,

---

Reviewed and revised by the author in 1975 and 1976.

of course, be possible to discuss the general problem of the application of treaties to individuals in those countries, including the question of whether treaties equip individuals with enforceable rights in relation to the state. However, reasons of space preclude the inclusion of that subject. Since it encompasses the whole problem of the relationship between international and municipal law,[2] the treatment of it would necessarily result in a rather long chapter.

THE INDIVIDUAL

The Individual as National

Movement

Passports. The passport is an ancient form of document. It establishes the bearer's identity, and it attests to the bearer's right, under the law of the issuing authority, to travel. The passport also creates a presumption, though it is not irrefutable, that the bearer has the capacity, sometimes amounting to a right, to seek the protection of his own sovereign while traveling beyond the borders of the home country. When travel was more or less free, the role of the instrument was one of bestowing certain facilities and privileges on the bearer; examples of this were the *tractoria* of ancient Rome and the medieval *conductus nundinarum*, which differed from contemporary passports in that they constituted, in E. de Vattel's words, "a kind of privilege."[3] Today, in countries in which only some citizens qualify for a passport, it is also a privilege, but the word is then used in a different sense. Passports issued in time of war have fulfilled the role of safe-conducts.

As soon as restrictions were placed on the freedom of movement of certain categories of persons, the passport became primarily an instrument evidencing the consent of the authority that had issued it that the bearer might proceed to his destination. For example, passports were used by foreign travelers in France under Louis XIII who happened to go off the main postal routes or by craftsmen (*passeport des artisans*) when restrictions on their right to travel abroad had been imposed to guard their professional secrets and skills. However, changes were frequent, and where a passport was required at one time, it would be abolished at another. There was still no general obligation to have a passport while going abroad. Nevertheless, the number of cases in which a passport was required continued to grow. For instance, in eighteenth-century France prior to the Revolution a passport was required for those traveling to America or the Levant, and the fee was rather high. During the

French Revolution, as in some other revolutions, there were discrepancies between theoretical postulates and political reality. Although some denounced passports as a tyrannical invention,[4] the attempt in 1791 by Louis XVI to escape from France by using a passport written out in another name made the revolutionaries realize that passports might be useful after all. Following that incident the Constituent Assembly prohibited any egress, and soon thereafter it regulated the formalities governing the issuance of passports for trips abroad first to only a very limited group of persons (embassy personnel, merchants, and foreigners) and later to all those who, in the eyes of the Minister for Foreign Affairs, should benefit from the right to travel "for any purpose of obvious utility or indispensable necessity." In September 1791 the assembly reversed its position and, by a return to the letter and spirit of the Declaration of Human Rights of 1789, abolished passports and proclaimed the freedom to travel. This policy was rescinded after a few months, and passports were reintroduced.[5]

At almost the same time legislation was enacted in the United Kingdom providing for passports to be issued to aliens on their arrival by the local authorities[6] and on their departure by the central government.[7] At the beginning of the nineteenth century, British practice restricted the use of the word "passport" to permission given during a war to enemy subjects to travel in the United Kingdom or in occupied enemy territory.[8]

Passports as they were used by the French revolutionary government were rather close to what passports are nowadays. For some time, however, one basic difference remained, which was that passports were issued by the territorial rather than the personal sovereign. Thus foreigners traveled inside or outside the country under passports given to them by the territorial authority, and only such documents were valid.

It is possible that the contemporary passport is the descendant of the passports that were issued to ships.[9] These passports exclusively concerned a trip abroad and were issued by the flag sovereign. Such ship passports, which also comprised crew members and goods, were referred to in the Treaty of Peace and Commerce of 11 July, 1670 between Great Britain and Denmark,[10] but the practice of issuing passports to vessels prceded that particular treaty and was known to other countries as well.

During the nineteenth century governments continued to issue passports to both nationals and foreigners, though the requirement that aliens already be in possession of a passport rather diminished the number of instances in which non-nationals were given passports. Prior to 1914 several European states abolished passports, the most important exception being Imperial Russia.

The history of the passport during the French Revolution is illustrative of two conflicting trends, liberty of travel and a regulatory approach that limited that liberty to some degree by formalizing the right to cross national boundaries.[11] Wars and revolutions favored the second trend.

The liberal tendency to abolish passports and entry visas was brought to an end by World War I. The postwar efforts, especially under the auspices of the League of Nations, to facilitate travel between one country and another proved successful only a very limited degree. After World War II the division of Europe has also had its effects in the realm of travel. Across the dividing line, passports and visas are rigorously required, and the procurement of visas may prove quite difficult on both sides. The unconditional abolition of visas by Bulgaria for the year of 1967 was an exception that did not change the rule. On the other hand, within each of the divided parts of Europe there came about a facilitation of travel, to a large degree in Western Europe and on a different, yet progressing, scale in Eastern Europe.[12]

Passports and Inserts in the Comecon: Exceptions. To travel abroad, a national of any Comecon country must be in possession of a passport or a special insert to the national identity document. The latter is sufficient if the trip takes place in the Comecon countries or Yugoslavia; for all other trips a regular passport is required. Until 1972, inserts were valid for one trip only. Since 1973 Poland has issued inserts valid for five years and an unlimited number of trips to Bulgaria, Czechoslovakia, the GDR, Hungary, Rumania, and the USSR. Travelers to the USSR and Czechoslovakia are required to present an invitation or travel vouchers at the frontier.

The same regulations concern passports and inserts, though there are important simplifications of procedure with regard to inserts. This reflects the fact that trips within the Comecon countries are easier to arrange than travels to the outside world. Nonetheless, in principle, identical rules govern the issuance of passports and inserts. When passports are referred to in the rest of this chapter, the rule stated applies equally to inserts unless otherwise indicated.

In some cases inserts have been replaced by simpler documents. Thus the Conventions on the Regulation of Minor Frontier Traffic between Czechoslovakia and Poland (1959)[13] and between Czechoslovakia and Hungary (1962)[14] established frontier traffic zones comprising areas 15 kilometers wide along the frontier. Frontier traffic takes place on the basis of frontier passes, which are either permanent or valid for a single crossing. Of course, this type of simplified movement is not open to the public at large but only to residents of the areas covered by the conventions. By way of comparison, it may be added that a similar agreement in 1949 between Yugoslavia and Italy[15] provides for a somewhat narrower frontier zone formed by a strip extending 10 kilometers on either side of the frontier line. The 1950 convention between the United Kingdom, Belgium, France, Luxembourg, and the Netherlands concerning frontier workers also creates a zone in principle 10 kilometers in depth where a frontier worker's card authorizes crossing the border.[16]

An instance of simplified travel for all the nationals concerned is the 1955 agreement between Czechoslovakia and Poland on frontier tourist traffic, as revised in 1961.[17] It sets up a convention zone in either country to which nationals from the other state can travel, provided they secure a tourist card (under the text of 1955) or a tourist pass (under the present arrangement). The procedure for obtaining a pass is very short and simple.

Recently a beginning was made among the Comecon countries toward abolishing exit permits altogether. By the end of 1975 this had been achieved between the German Democratic Republic and Czechoslovakia and between the German Democratic Republic and Poland (Agreement of 25 November 1971). Citizens of the two parties may cross the frontier and travel in the other country when in possession of their national identity documents, bearing a special stamp by the local police. The stamp has permanent validity for an unlimited number of trips. As of 1 January 1977 this simple procedure (national identity card bearing a special stamp) has been extended to trips to Bulgaria, Czechoslovakia, Hungary, Romania, and the USSR. The requirement of an invitation or travel vouchers for the latter country and Czechoslovakia remains unchanged. Inserts continue to be required for trips to Albania and Yugoslavia.

<u>The Law of Poland and Hungary</u>. In Poland passports, and to some extent departures, are regulated by the Law on Passports of 17 June 1959, thereafter revised. The general principle of the law is that "every citizen has the right to be issued a passport, provided he submitted the required documents and paid the requisite fee."[18] In Hungary the law relating to passports and departures underwent several modifications.[19] The regulation discussed here dates from 1970 and finds expression in Decree Number 4 and Government Ordinance Number 4 of that year.[20] Paragraph 3 of the decree stipulates that "every Hungarian national has the right to obtain a passport and to go abroad insofar as he complies with the requirements imposed by law." However, that paragraph adds a substantial condition as part of the principle, which is that "the passport is to be

refused to any person whose trip or stay abroad violates or imperils national or economic interests or other important public interests of the Hungarian People's Republic." In fact, the difference between the two regulations, Polish and Hungarian, boils down to drafting and emphasis. Although the Polish formula is unqualified in tenor, it is nevertheless restricted by the detailed provisions of the law of 1959.

In contradistinction to officially sponsored trips or to those undertaken in organized groups, an individual who submits a passport application must, according to Polish regulations, join to it a formal invitation executed by a person or institution in the foreign country to which the applicant intends to travel. Such an invitation has to have been seen and stamped at the Polish consulate or by the local authority in the country of destination. However, in Poland the requirement of formal invitation is dispensed with in two cases. The first is trips to some of the Comecon countries, including Yugoslavia. The second is trips to the rest of the world, including the West, by persons who are holders of hard currency accounts with Polish banks or who have obtained permission to buy hard currency from Polish banks on an ad hoc basis. The second exception shows that one of the functions of the invitation is to create some guarantee that the person traveling abroad will not incur financial difficulties and thus cause problems for the host state and the Polish consular authorities.

Until 1973 the passport fee differed according to destination (Europe or other continents) and mode of covering the travel expenses (local or hard currency). Since then, this has been made uniform (2,000 złotys), and there is a 50 percent reduction for certain categories of persons, such as students, pensioners, and retired employees.[21]

Tickets to some destinations and/or by some means of transport, such as by an air carrier outside the Comecon area, can only be bought with convertible currency. The Comecon countries face problems of payments in that currency. States like Poland or Hungary, from which a considerable number of individual and private trips to the West take place, shift the burden of the cost involved onto the individual concerned. Probably this is an economic necessity, but the restricting effect of this regulation is obvious. Holders of hard currency apart, and they are not numerous, it is not always easy to obtain a transfer of money from abroad, and when this is done on the basis of a de facto loan, the prospective traveler may find it difficult to repay it. Such arrangements are, no doubt, easier among members of a family than among strangers.

Exchange problems, of course, limit the possibility of individual travel, but they are not a peculiarity of Eastern Europe.

Other countries know them as well, and there was a time when they also existed in Western Europe, both before and after the last war. The amount of money one can exchange or take with oneself to a Comecon country varies.

In principle the 1974 regulation in Poland provided that one person could exchange up to 8,100 złotys per year for the purpose of traveling to one or more of the Comecon countries; however, if the traveler bought convertible currencies, the amount would be correspondingly reduced. There were special rules affecting travel to Czechoslovakia, Hungary, and the German Democratic Republic. The regulations for 1975 reduced the exchangeable amount to 6,000 złotys for two years.

In contrast with 1972, when any Polish traveler could exchange an unlimited amount of money into GDR marks, limits, which became progressively smaller, have been imposed in each subsequent year. In 1975 the two-month limit was East DM 100. The liberal arrangements of 1972 had produced complications, since some travelers made large duty-free purchases. Money can be exchanged above the limit by those who are traveling for medical reasons and those who are visiting, or have prepaid for a stay in, the German Democratic Republic. For the past few years, Poland has allowed its citizens who are traveling to Yugoslavia and the West to buy hard currency every three years in an amount not exceeding $130 or its equivalent.

The procedure for convertible currencies is that each year prospective travelers submit applications. The nature and the purpose of the trip and the amount of foreign exchange at the disposal of the authorities concerned have an influence on whether the right to buy hard currency is granted, and to how many applicants.

The Hungarian ordinance also requires the submission of an invitation, which should guarantee the financial basis of the stay abroad.[22] No mention is made of foreign exchange, but there is a provision to the effect that tourist trips can be authorized more frequently if foreign exchange is available.[23]

Although the foregoing provisions undoubtedly create certain restrictions on the freedom of individual travel, it should be noted that in the Comecon countries much of the traveling abroad is done in organized groups set up by travel agencies, trade unions, professional associations, and various institutions, in which cases invitations and currency arrangements are redundant. The same applies to trips by individuals when the trips have official sponsorship but the individual concerned travels in his or her own capacity and not as an official delegate. This would include trips by scholars under the auspices of the Ministry of Higher Education or by artists sponsored by the Ministry of Culture.

Whatever the nature of the trip, any passport application in Poland must bear a notice from the applicant's employer (if he has one) that he will be granted a leave of absence for the purpose of the trip. This in fact amounts to the employer's consenting to the trip, though neither the law nor the application form explicitly gives his action consent or approval. What the employer does is simply indicate the duration of the leave. He does not express any opinion about the applicant or the departure itself. In this respect the law of Hungary goes further. There the employer, the school management, or the professional association (the latter with respect to private business or the nonemployed, such as writers and artists) expresses an opinion about the application. The Hungarian Ordinance adds that the passport authority must take such an opinion into account.

Although in individual cases the formal requirements governing a passport application can constitute a restriction on the freedom to travel abroad, the law lists specific reasons that may or do result in the refusal to grant a passport. There is some difference in the regulation of this matter between Polish and Hungarian laws. Article 4, Paragraph 2, of the Polish law of 1959 enumerates the causes of refusal as giving the deciding organ the right not to grant the passport. The decision, however, rests with the organ, and in spite of the existence of one of the causes it may still take positive action on the application. On the other hand, Paragraph 3 of the Hungarian ordinance simply states that "the passport is to be refused" if one of the circumstances therein stated is existent. No doubt, if the passport were issued in spite of an obstacle falling under that provision, the provision would remain an unenforced law. However, the regulations show a different degree of elasticity and a somewhat different approach to the general right of free travel. Also, Hungarian law knows of temporary impediments to the granting of passports that do not exist under Polish law, at least as a separate category.

In Poland, by Article 4, Paragraph 2(3) of the law of 1959, a passport can be refused to a person who while abroad "acted to the detriment of the interests of the Polish People's Republic or compromised Poland's good reputation by his conduct."[24] This obviously does not apply to an applicant who is soliciting a first trip abroad, who would have been physically unable to become guilty of the behavior in question. The rule is general enough to leave the authorities with a considerable latitude of interpretation, but the reason is specific and at least in part related to facts. Thus the applicant can argue his or her case on some objective grounds. The situation differs with respect to Article 4, Paragraph 2 (4), by which a passport can be refused when there are "important national considerations," other than those enumerated in the paragraph, against the issuance of the passport. In practice this provision equips the authorities with a wide power of decision. They are not obliged to explain in detail their actions by virtue of this rule.

The remaining motives for refusal are more specific. (1) Criminal proceedings have been instituted against the applicant. (2) The applicant has violated passport regulations. (3) The passport should not be delivered in view of the interests of a person who remains under the tutelage of the applicant or because of other important considerations of a social nature.[25] In addition, under Article 5 the issuance of a passport can be made dependent on prior performance of duties toward the state, such as payment of taxes or deliveries to the state economy.

At first sight the letter of the Hungarian legislation appears stricter than Polish law, though it is not necessarily so in practice. It has been already pointed out that Paragraph 3 of the law of 1970 contains a general rule on who does not qualify for a passport and why. The ordinance of the same date spells out the prohibition in more detail: the persons affected are those "whose stay abroad encroaches upon or imperils the internal or external security" of Hungary; "who intend to visit organizations or persons that act against any socialist state"; or "who lack the necessary material prerequisites to secure a stay abroad."[26] There are some further reasons that have an equally prohibitive effect, but the Minister of the Interior can "in justified cases" authorize the issuance of the passport. This clause concerns persons "against whom criminal proceedings have been instituted or who serve their sentence"; "who must report to the police or are subject to expulsion"; or "who intend to travel to a person that stays abroad unlawfully or whose parents, children, spouse, brother or sister stay abroad unlawfully." The latter reason for refusal remains valid even if the conduct of the persons involved is no longer punishable under Hungarian law, as may be the case as a result of an amnesty.[27]

Hungarian law also provides that certain other circumstances may deprive a person of the right to a passport, but for no longer than for five years, and the Minister of the Interior can make these limitations inoperative in individual instances.[28] These circumstances are (1) false statements relating to a passport; (2) "abuse of passport," which includes willful extension of a stay abroad, employment without permission, or a trip to an unauthorized country; (3) loss of the passport or its invalidity caused by the incumbent (obviously by its nonuse in the prescribed time); (4) harm to the interests of Hungary or behavior not becoming the citizen thereof during the previous trip; (5) encroachment upon the regulations on customs and foreign exchange; and (6) breaches of order punished by arrest.

In individual travel the rule under Article 8 of the Polish Law is that the passport allows for only one crossing of the national frontier. Thus every trip involves the initiation of the precedures as described. Polish passports granted for trips for private purposes have a validity of one year and sometimes of two years. In Hungary the validity is for five years,[29] but Paragraph 10 of the Hungarian regulations provides that private trips are authorized for "an average" of 30 days for Europe and 90 days for overseas. This rule should be read in conjunction with the provision on the effects of an unauthorized prolongation of the stay abroad. In Poland the duration of the intended stay and the countries to be visited are sometimes entered into the passport, but the consequences of such an entry are unclear. The entry is made in accordance with the holder's application for a passport. I am aware of cases in which a stay longer than indicated and visits to countries other than those specified did not involve any consequences whatever; nor were subsequent trips barred on account these actions.

If the passport is refused, the applicant may appeal. In Poland this appeal is made to the Minister of the Interior,[30] while in Hungary it is made to the superior organ in accordance with the general administrative procedure.[31] After the exhaustion of these remedies, the applicant can lodge a complaint with the organ of the last instance or with the higher authorities.[32]

On return to the home country, under Article 23 of the Polish Law the passport is to be rendered back to the issuing authority. This duty does not apply to private passports in Hungary.

A brief comparison between the law of Czechoslovakia and that of the German Democratic Republic illustrates the difference in the regulation of passports and departures that may obtain even among states that adhere to the same political system.

In 1965 a Czechoslovak law recognized, though with several limitations, the right of the citizen to travel abroad.[33] Under Article 4 of this law a passport can be refused to persons whose "trip abroad does not agree with the national interests." Trips are easier when the applicant can produce evidence that his or her transportation and stay abroad will be paid for in hard currency.

The Law of 1965 was amended and supplemented by a government ordinance in 1969.[34] A passport may be refused to a citizen "whose conduct permits the conclusion that he has the intention to remain abroad after the expiration of the authorized time of stay" or who intends to visit a Czechoslovak national "who stays abroad without the permission of Czechoslovak authorities." A passport may also be refused when foreign exchange is insufficient, with the exception, however, of trips to "linear descendants, brother or sister, and spouse," provided that their sojourn in the foreign country is lawful in the light of Czechoslovak regulations. The Law on Nationality of 1969[35] gives the Ministry of the Interior the power to deprive of nationality, among other causes, such Czechoslovak citizens who have unlawfully left the territory of the republic or who have not returned to Czechoslovakia within the authorized time limit.[36]

In the German Democratic Republic the Law on Passports of 1954[37] and the regulations for its execution[38] confer on the authorities the discretion to decide on individual passport applications. Until the stopping of the de facto free movement of persons from the eastern to the western sectors of Berlin in August 1961, the government of the German Democratic Republic faced special problems resulting from the division of the German nation into two separate state organisms. The law of the German Democratic Republic developed a system of severe penalties for unauthorized emigration to the Federal Republic of Germany[39] and unauthorized crossing of the frontier or attempts thereof.[40] Today the German Democratic Republic regards the Federal Republic of Germany as a foreign country. Although GDR law and practice formerly admitted the notion of "abandonment of the Republic," the Penal Code of 1968 makes "resistance to the order relating to the State frontier" punishable by imprisonment of not less than three years, and the "particularly serious cases" can be punished with life imprisonment or death.[41] A trip to a country other than that authorized is also a criminal act.

A certain relaxation of travel restrictions has been brought about within the framework of the improved relations and contractual arrangements between the two German states. In 1972 the German Democratic Republic agreed[42] to permit travel by citizens to the Federal Republic of Germany on account of "urgent family matters." Trips up to 30 days per year are allowed for the following reasons: birth of a child, wedding, silver or golden wedding anniversary, funeral, or critical illness. Those entitled are relatives in direct line and brothers and sisters.

Departure. Among the Comecon countries, the law of Hungary supplies a rare example of the possibility of leaving permanently for abroad. The departing person may ask for release from Hungarian nationality, but such a demand is not a condition of emigration; on the contrary, Hungarian law explicitly provides for retention of the citizenship as an alternative.

The general rule is to be found in Paragraph 12 (I) of the Law of 1970.[43] Though its subject is ostensibly procedural (it concerns the issuance of passports), the rule indicates who may ask for permission to leave the country permanently. The applicant must be more than 55 years old and must intend to live abroad in one household with his or her parents or spouse. The applicant must not be subject to an obligation to support someone in Hungary nor have any property or public obligations of a financial nature. The Minister of the Interior is empowered to dispense with any of these requirements.

The exceptional nature of the Hungarian regulation follows from the fact that the Comecon countries, as a matter of principle, do not favor the emigration of their nationals. Although emigration takes place in individual cases, for example, not unfrequently in Poland with regard to Polish women marrying foreigners, it does not exist as a matter of right for every citizen. The Polish government has recently intimated that it is against emigration of Polish nationals for employment purposes.[44] Parenthetically it may be observed that Polish policies differ diametrically from those of the pre-1939 government and, today, from the attitude of a country with a similar political system, Yugoslavia, that does not object to labor emigration. Nonetheless, large groups of individuals have emigrated from Poland since the early 1950s. Although this emigration has been comprised mostly of Polish nationals in the sense of citizenship, it has been limited to persons who were regarded as belonging to minorities, such as Germans and Jews.

By far the largest group has been the Germans. This chapter is not concerned with the more than 3 million Germans[45] who were compulsorily transferred from Poland, and especially from the former German territories that fell under the administration of Poland by virtue of the Potsdam Agreement on the Western Frontier of Poland.[46] These compulsory transfers took place on the basis of another Potsdam agreement,[47] the decision of the Control Council in Berlin,[48] and agreements executory to these acts signed by Poland with the British[49] and Soviet[50] military governments in Germany. The compulsory transfers came to an end in 1950, the bulk of the German population having been exeplled in the 1940s. The expellees were not Polish nationals, and this alone suffices to exclude the subject from the purview of this section. What is of interest is the fact that a number of persons who were ethnically German did stay in Poland. Most of them acquired Polish citizenship, but some resisted attempts to bestow it on them and thus remained aliens.[51] Since these Germans, whether technically Polish citizens or not, were willing to leave Poland, the Polish Red Cross, acting with the authorization of the government at Warsaw, entered in late 1955 into an arrangement with the West German Red Cross on voluntary emigration of the Germans to the Federal Republic of Germany. The scheme bore the name of a Family Reunion (Familienzusammenführung) because it involved persons with family links in Western Germany, though exceptions on humanitarian grounds in favor of persons with no such connections were admitted (widows, disabled, or lonely old persons). The family reunions came to an end in 1959 and comprised 250,000 or even more people.[52] However, the emigration of Germans from Poland continued, and between 1960 and 1969 about 150,000 left permanently for the Federal Republic of Germany.

Even after these additional departures, candidates for emigration still remained, and the matter was raised in the negotiations between Bonn and Warsaw in 1970; these negotiations led to the signing of the Treaty on the Foundations of Normalization of Mutual Relations of 7 December 1970.[53] The treaty passes over the problem in silence, but on the occasion of its initialing the Polish government inserted a Statement Relating to Humanitarian Questions as Note 36. The statement opened the door to emigration by "persons of indisputable ethnic German origin and persons from mixed families whose predominant feeling over the past years has been that they belong to that ethnic group." However, the emigration is not automatic and as of right. The Polish authorities emphasized that departure can take place only in accordance with "the laws and regulations applicable in Poland." This clearly implied a decision by the passport organs under the provisions explained in Subsection (a). Nonetheless, the government promised that "consideration will be given to the situation of mixed and separated families as well as to such cases of Polish nationals who, either because of their changed family situation or because they have changed their earlier decisions [to remain in Poland], express the wish to be reunited with near relatives" in one of the two German states. The Polish Red Cross was authorized to enter into contact with the Red Cross in the Federal Republic of Germany in the matter of departures.

It may be pointed out that the two governments have different views of certain aspects of the problem.[54] In 1970 the Polish side indicated that there were tens of thousands of people that might fall under the foregoing criteria, but the government in Bonn referred to a much higher figure. There was also a difficulty arising under the nationality laws. According to the national law in force in the Federal Republic of Germany,[55] many Polish citizens who are ethnically Poles and who have their domiciles in Poland are still regarded as German nationals. For instance, this would include ethnic Poles domiciled before the conclusion of the Potsdam Agreement, and their descendants born after that date, in that part of Upper Silesia that remained within the Reich frontiers under the settlement of 1921. Poland does not agree to a double nationality for these individuals. It treats them as exclusively Polish or, if they did not acquire Polish nationality, as German nationals and limits the eligibility for emigration to persons who are ethnic Germans or of mixed stock who consider themselves German. On the other hand, there is a tendency on the part of the Federal Republic of Germany to create immigration opportunities for all those inhabitants of Poland whom its law might regard as German nationals. To this the Polish government does not consent.

As for the Jewish community in Poland, after the proclamation of independence of Israel the government did not put obstacles in the way of individuals wishing to leave Poland permanently for Israel. Thus many families and single persons of Jewish extraction emigrated to the new state. In 1956 a new arrangement in Soviet-Polish relations resulted, among other things, in the repatriation to Poland of a number of people who, according to Soviet law and administrative practice, had been Polish nationals. Several of the repatriates were of Jewish extraction and after a more or less brief stay in Poland emigrated to Israel. The emigration of Jews from Poland took a new turn after the Israeli-Arab armed conflict of 1967 and internal developments in Poland in 1968.[56] The post-1967 emigration also included persons who did not settle in Israel but in other countries, mainly those of Western Europe or North America. Though the situation was known to the passport authorities, exit permits continued to be granted.

The departures of both the Germans and the Polish Jews are instances of expatriation. The exit permit is conditional upon a renunciation of Polish nationality by the applicant, who then travels abroad, not with a Polish passport, but with a special travel document of short validity. He or she is not a stateless person but a citizen under the law of the country of destination, either a German or an Israeli. If after the departure the person concerned has had second thoughts about the decision, the chances of a return through reintegration or resumption of the former Polish nationality are very slim, though the Polish Nationality Law[57] can be interpreted as not excluding such a possibility.

The Comecon countries do not follow an identical policy regarding emigration and expatriation. They share the general principle that there is no fundamental right of emigration for their citizens, but the practice of some countries, especially Poland, admits of various exceptions, especially in favor of minority groups. The divergence of approach is illustrated, on the one hand, by the Polish willingness to authorize the voluntary departure of several hundreds of thousands of Germans after 1950 and, on the other, by the Romanian unwillingness to agree to the departure of the German settlers in Transylvania.[58] Hungary went so far as to oppose the decision of the Great Powers on the forcible transfer of Germans.[59] Poland favored the emigration of Jews, though the reasons behind this differed widely before and after 1967. The Soviet Union was against it, as it was against expatriation of members of other ethnic groups or nationalities. However, the Soviet has begun to undergo a change with regard to the Jewish[60] and German[61] communities. The 1949 constitution of the German Democratic Republic provided that each citizen had the right to emigrate and that only the law of the republic could restrict that right.[62] In practice the restrictions excluded any emigration, and the Constitution of 1968[63] is silent on such a right.

On the signing of the Treaty on the Bases of Relations (Basic Treaty, Grundvertrag) with the Federal Republic of Germany on 21 December 19, the German Democratic Republic delcared that "in the course of normalization of relations after the entry of the Treaty into force" the government of the German Democratic Republic would take steps "to solve problems resulting from the separation of families." An explanatory instrument annexed to the treaty (Erläuterungen zum Briefwechsel) specifies that the family reunion will be comprised of husband and wife and parents or grandparents, with children or grandchildren when the former are in need of care and especially when only one parent or grandparent is alive. "In particular and exceptional cases" the organs of the German Democratic Republic will authorize the marriage of a GDR citizen with a person domiciled in the Federal Republic of Germany and allow the person to emigrate thereto.

It should also be noted that the Comecon countries did not formulate any reservations to Article 5 (d) (ii) of the Convention on the Elimination of All Forms of Racial Discrimination.[64] That convention stipulates that the parties "undertake . . . to guarantee the right of everyone . . . to equality before the law, notably in the enjoyment of the . . . right to leave any country, including one's own, and to return to one's country." Though the emphasis is on the prohibition of discrimination in the enjoyment of the right in question, and not on the material right itself, its nonexistence or denial would violate the convention whether or not there were discrimination.

Return. There are no limitations on return from abroad by the nationals of the Comecon countries. However, the status of the individual while abroad might undergo a modification, and in exceptional circumstances an individual may be deprived of his or her nationality. The laws of some Comecon members provide for such a denationalization.[65] Polish nationals who have remained abroad beyond the validity dates of their passports can usually obtain special passports making the return possible.[66]

Expulsion. In answer to a UN enquiry, three Comecon countries officially stated that expulsion was not known to their laws.[67]

Whether denationalization is a form of expulsion depends largely on how much legal content one attaches to the notion of expulsion. If expulsion is defined loosely and in political terms, various measures of public authorities that stand in connection with the individual's decision to leave for abroad would fall under this heading. In international law, however, expulsion has a primarily technical meaning.[68] The question of an individual who is deprived of the status of national of a Comecon country because of an unauthorized stay abroad is highly theoretical and in fact does not arise. Fugitives usually do not go back, and those who do would first regularize their positions regarding both entry and reintegration before seeking readmission.

The case of Bishop Kurt Scharf, President of the Evangelical Church in Germany, is hardly an exception to the principle stated. The GRD frontier authorities did not allow him to reenter East Berlin when he returned from a visit to the Western sector.[69] The fact that his GDR documents were taken away from him at the frontier control qualifies this case under expulsion rather than under prohibition of return, but either of the two headings is possible. Scharf's presence in the German Democratic Republic was regarded by the government of that state as undesirable. However, attempts to justify this exceptional measure by pointing to the purported doubts regarding Scharf's status as a citizen of the German Democratic Republic show the unwillingness, on the official side, to treat the incident as a clear case of expulsion or nonreturn of a national.

The Background of International Law. It can be said that contemporary international law does not bestow absolute power on the state to prohibit the egress of its nationals.[70] The territorial and personal supremacy of the state over the resident national does not seem to reach so far as to authorize the state to forbid temporary departure. Though there are states that do not comply with this standard, its denial runs counter to the practice of the majority of states and the almost universal consensus on freedom of movement as an internationally protected human right. That freedom is a necessary corollary of personal liberty.

The state, however, retains the competence to regulate the right to move freely. To a large extent the problem boils down to transposing the unfettered freedom of movement that exists inside most states onto the world plane, without necessarily linking it to a freedom of choosing one's residence. The right of emigration, even if accepted, must by its nature remain imperfect. It is difficult to imagine how most states could allow an uncontrolled influx of foreigners as permanent immigrants.[71] The state remains free[72] to allow or prohibit the emigration of its nationals, though it should agree to permanent departure if it is dictated by humanitarian purposes of compelling force, such as the uniting of displaced members of families. This basic difference regarding the extent of state powers does not seem unreasonable, depending on whether the departure is temporary or permanent.

The competence of the state to decide the issue of emigration does not, of course, imply the right to force any individual or group to emigrate. In this connection it may be recalled that by Article 5 of the treaty between the United States and China of 1868 (the Burlingame Treaty) the two parties joined "in reprobating any other than an entirely voluntary emigration."[73] This rule has been enunciated in connection with the prohibition, under the sanction of a penal offense, of taking the citizens from one country to another or to any other foreign country "without their free and voluntary consent."[74]

A reinforcement of the general duty of the state to permit temporary departure and the eventual creation of the duty to permit emigration may be achieved through the development of human rights under international law. International law has not been very promising in this respect. On the one hand, the standard enunciated in Article 13 of the Universal Declaration of Human Rights[75] is quite general and it goes rather far in giving definite preponderance to individual rights over state interests. On the other hand, the treaty instruments have not fully implemented the standard of the declaration. The treatment of the matter has been very cautious there. The European Convention on Human Rights[76] is silent on problems of movement, and only Protocol Number 4[77] filled the gap. Furthermore, for the foreseeable future the law of the Council of Europe will be limited to only one grouping of states, the Comecon countries remaining outside it. Whether Article 12, Paragraphs 2 and 3, of the International Covenant on Civil and Political Rights[78] will operate to change the law in the Comecon countries and, with respect to emigration, in the entire international community is still an open question.[79]

Protection

Extent of Freedom of Activity Abroad. In principle any activity abroad that becomes a source of income requires in Poland and in several other Comecon countries a prior authorization by the financial department, especially the branch supervising foreign exchange dealings. However, if the trip abroad is linked to employment or other money-earning activity, the authorization is usually implicit in the exit permit. Polish practice is rather indifferent to such an activity when engaged in by individuals who travel abroad in a private capacity; emphasis is put on compliance with foreign exchange regulations. Under Hungarian law one of the reasons for refusal of a passport is unauthorized employment abroad.

The Right to Diplomatic Protection. In Poland a national does not have a right to request that the government intervene on his or her behalf by way of diplomatic representation. However, the complaint procedure permits dissatisfied individuals to raise matters with the higher authorities if they feel that they should have been protected and were not. On the other hand, the constitution of the German Democratic Republic provides that every citizen who stays outside the republic "has a claim for legal protection by the organs" of the state.[80]

It may be added that in state-controlled economies problems of business activity abroad by private individuals and the resulting questions of diplomatic protection arise much less frequently and do not display so many facets as occur in relations involving free market economies.

The State and Compensation. The last observation applies also to distribution of compensation among injured nationals, the responsibility of the state for injury induced by its own conduct, and other problems of protection. In Eastern European practice the following situations should be noted.

In 1944 the Polish Committee of National Liberation signed agreements with three Soviet Republics (Byelorussia, Lithuania, and the Ukraine) on mutual repatriation of groups of population.[81] These agreements provided for voluntary transfer of Polish nationals of either Polish or Jewish ethnic origin from these republics (in their revised frontiers) to Poland and, a reciprocal transfer of Polish nationals of Byelorussian, Lithuanian, or Ukrainian ethnic origin from Poland to the republics concerned.[82] The latter undertook to allot individual plots between 7 and 15 hectares to transferred peasants, while other transferred persons were to obtain employment corresponding to their qualifications. The guarantee of individual plots embraced also agricultural laborers, that is, persons who had not owned any land before the transfer. The Polish side accepted similar obligations toward its nationals, but the ceiling for the privately owned land was set higher in accordance with the different agricultural system prevailing in Poland. The size of the farms to be assigned to the repatriates depended on the provisions of the Polish Agricultural Reform Act. Resettlers were to be reimbursed at their new domiciles for their current crops, which they had left at their former homes. The farms allotted to them were free for a certain period from taxes and insurance fees.

From the Polish end the agreements included a promise (toward a foreign party) to compensate hundreds of thousands of individuals who had lost their peasant holdings as a result of a fundamental modification of the frontier between Poland and the Soviet Union (the Curzon Line) in favor of the latter. This promise has been kept, though under Polish law the agreements have not been self-executing. The peculiar characteristic of this arrangement was that only some of the repatriates, though a considerable number, were to be compensated: the specific regulation concerned peasants and owners of farms of a certain maximum area. In practice the Polish authorities went further than the letter of the agreements. In their policy of populating the former German territories with Polish settlers, they took measures that resulted in the acquisition of various property rights by the transferred individuals, though they did not fall under the technical category of owners of peasant land.[83] As a result of the new territorial settlement, many Polish nationals suffered severe losses. Although not all have been compensated, an effort has been made to include many in the scheme; the actual compensation varied from region to region. No money was to change hands: instead there was an exchange of material objects, meaning land, or opportunities, such as commerce and crafts. The political and economic changes that were taking place in Poland explain why owners of more important property rights lost in the eastern provinces have not been included in the scheme.

The second matter that is of interest here is the reparation claims of the USSR and Poland with regard to Germany. The Potsdam Agreement on German Reparations of 2 August 1945[84] regulated the settlement of the reparations claims that the two governments had against Germany. The reparations claims of the USSR were to be met by removals from its zone of occupation, from appropriate German external assets, and from industrial capital equipment in the western zones of occupation. By virtue of Paragraph 2 of the agreement, the Soviet Union undertook "to settle the reparation claims of Poland from its own share of reparations." In Article I of the Protocol of 22 August 1953, signed with the German Democratic Republic, further reparations claims were waived, as follows:

> The Soviet Government, by agreement with the Government of the Polish People's Republic (in respect of its share in the reparations), shall, as from 1 January 1954, cease completely to require the payment of reparations by the German Democratic Republic, whether in the form of goods or in any other form.[85]

Accordingly the German Democratic Republic was released from the payment of the reparations that were still outstanding. On the next day (23 August 1953) the Polish government issued a statement that included the following:

> Considering that Germany has already complied to a considerable degree with her obligations relating to reparations and that an improvement in the economic situation of Germany lies in the interest of her peaceful development, the Government of the Polish People's Republic, in its desire to further contribute to the settlement of the German problem in a peaceful and democratic spirit and in accordance with the interests of the Polish nation and all the peace-loving nations, has taken the decision to relinquish the reparations due to Poland as of 1 January 1954.[86]

In spite of the general language of this renunciation, some claims by individuals have survived, though not on a state-to-state basis.

First, Polish victims of the medical and biological experiments that took place in Nazi concentration camps received compensation from the Federal Republic of Germany. The International Committee of the Red Cross in Geneva was instrumental in bringing about this arrangement. The government in Bonn took the position that the payments had been made at the discretion of the state and not out of a legal duty. Prior to the Normalization Treaty of 1970, the Federal Republic of Germany paid the sum of 40 million deutsche marks in settlement of some 1,300 individual claims. More than 5,400 applications for compensation were still outstanding, and these were settled by virtue of an agreement signed between the FRG Ministry of Economy and Finance and the Polish Ministry of Health and Social Care on 16 November 1972 in Geneva. The agreement provided for payment of a lump sum of 100 million deutsche marks, and it definitely liquidated all claims under this heading.

Second, there were claims by Polish nationals who had been inmates of concentration camps in the Third Reich. Another group of claimants were those who had been forcibly deported to Germany and employed there without any free choice of work and without adequate wages.

<u>The Background of International Law</u>. The state is free to regulate and control its nationals' activities abroad. Very few restrictions, if any, can be deduced from the treaties on establishment, human rights, or related subjects. However, the effectiveness of such

regulation and control depends on their extraterritorial application and also on the sanctioning procedures the national faces when he falls back under the territorial supremacy of his own state. However, an organ, in particular a court, of that state may be prevented, by its respect for the acts of another state, from defeating a transaction which, though unlawful in the light of the national's own legal system, takes place abroad under the umbrella of foreign legislation. Even if the organ is willing to frustrate the transaction, its efforts can still be futile. Without some measure of recognition on the part of the foreign state, the prohibitions of the personal sovereign will remain a dead letter. In international business the absence of any connection between the transaction and the legal order from which the prohibition emanates, in particular the absence of any effects resulting from the transaction on the territory of the prohibiting sovereign, militates against the applicability of the prohibitory legislation in the foreign state in which the transaction was made. Otherwise the restriction imposed on the jurisdiction of the foreign state, or the actual infringement thereon, would serve no reasonable or useful purpose.

The diplomatic protection of nationals is a right, not a duty, under international law. A trend toward change is not discernible. On the contrary, since the decision in the Nottebohm case,[87] formal, or noneffective, nationality is no longer sufficient to create the basis on which the state takes up a claim of its injured national against a foreign state. If the Nottebohm decision is followed, the result can easily be that some nationals will find themselves without protection, especially when the only way of obtaining satisfaction would be to persuade one's state to institute proceedings in the International Court of Justice.

The state is not only free not to espouse, on the international plane, the claim its national has against a foreign state, but it is empowered to dispose of it, that is, in one form or another it may renounce compensation due or agree to damages that are smaller than those to which the wronged individual is entitled. Whatever the position under the municipal law, international law permits disposal of the national's claim by the state. Lump-sum agreements are a convincing illustration of this point. Judge Moore put it as follows in his dissenting opinion in the Mavrommatis Palestine Concessions case:

> It is an elementary principle that, when a government officially intervenes on behalf of its citizen, it makes his claim its own, and may settle the claim on such terms as it may conceive to be proper. . . . The private citizen, in placing his

> claim in his government's hands, must be held to have accepted the necessary legal consequences of his action.[88]

Perhaps a change in such a state of the law might be created through the development of the protection accorded to property by the treaties on human rights. In their present form these treaties are extremely reticent about the protection of proprietory interests. The instruments that are meant for universal application, that is, the UN covenants, are silent on the subject, as was the European Convention. Only Protocol Number 1 set forth the rule that "no one shall be deprived of his possessions."[89] Probably this implies a right to compensation; but the same provision creates an exception "in the public interest," which is usually the motive behind a renunciation, and it refers to "the general principles of international law"; thus coming full circle, for does not that law permit the state to dispose of the nationals' foreign claims?[90]

However, the transformation, through government espousal, of a private claim into an assertion of the state's own right, has its limits. The right never becomes totally autonomous; that is it is never actually divorced from the individual's claim. The disappearance of the latter eliminates the former. The state's right is always of a derivative nature, since it cannot exist without the private claim. The main purpose of the exercise of diplomatic protection is to obtain satisfaction for the individual; a state that acts with other purposes in mind abuses its right.

Such a concept of diplomatic protection leads one to the conclusion that the proceeds of litigation must go to the individual, though the government may reimburse its own costs out of them. The practice of governments has been uniform: they have always turned the sums obtained over to the individuals that suffered the damage. True, payment of a sum by the foreign government vests the title to it in the recipient government. If the latter refuses to transfer the money so obtained to the private individual, he has no claim to it under international law and of course no international remedy to recover it. The persons who are entitled to compensation are easily identifiable under the treaties dealing with the matter. Some instruments specify claims person by person, naming the firm or enterprise entitled to compensation; an example of this is the 1953 Protocol on Danish Interests and Assets in Poland.[91] However, even an agreement of this kind does not give the individual concerned a claim against his or her national state. The treaties in question also contain the provision that the amount will be distributed in such a manner as the recipient government may determine. This rule, however, implies the duty of distribution; the government violates the treaty if it keeps the money for itself and does not proceed with distribution.

On the other hand, a remedy may exist in the municipal law, especially when that law treats the recipient government not as the owner of the sum, but as its administrator or trustee.[92] The payment of the sum is made for the benefit of the individual, not the state; were the latter to retain the money, it would unjustly enrich itself.

If the compensation received from the foreign state is insufficient in relation to the damage suffered, there is no international duty on the part of the national's own state to pay the difference; nor does the state bear any responsibility to its nationals for injury induced by its own international conduct. Compensation provided in such circumstances does not result from an international obligation unless the latter has been incurred by virtue of an express treaty arrangement.

The Individual as an Alien

Movement

Entry and Stay. The 29 March 1963 Polish Law on Aliens defines aliens as persons who do not have Polish nationality (citizenship).[93] This definition comprises two different categories: persons who are nationals of a foreign state and stateless persons. Though Polish law does not treat these two categories in an identical manner, and in several respects it gives stateless persons a status equal to nationals, including the exercise of certain public rights, in matters of entry and departure they form one group. This probably explains the rather simple definition of the Law of 1963: the law is concerned not with every and any facet of the legal status of aliens on Polish territory but only with their entry, stay, and departure.

The principle of the Law of 1963 is that the alien must obtain an entry visa.[94] International agreements have abolished visas in relations among the Comecon countries and with the Comecon countries and Yugoslavia. Bulgaria dispensed entirely with the requirement of an entry visa for the duration of 1967, maintaining the dispensation after 1967 on condition of reciprocity. Yugoslavia also abolished visas in 1967 and concluded agreements on their abolition with several countries. Czechoslovakia and Romania give visas at the frontier, and Romania recently abolished visas with regard to Zambia. Poland introduced certain facilities for obtaining visas by travelers from some countries, including France and the

Scandinavian states.[95] Poland has also abolished visas on the basis of reciprocity with Austria, Finland, and Sweden. Various facilities regarding trips, mainly of short duration, to, and transit across, the German Democratic Republic have been granted to German nationals from the Federal Republic of Germany and to the inhabitants of the Western sectors of Berlin under the Berlin agreements of 1971 and the intra-German treaties of 1972.

Under the Polish Law of 1963, certain other categories of persons are or can be exempted from the visa requirement: persons enjoying diplomatic, consular or analogous status, if the exemption has been arranged by the Minister for Foreign Affairs in agreement with the Minister of the Interior;[96] members of the crews of foreign vessels for the area of the port town; members of crews of foreign aircraft for the transit area of the airport, unless there is a bilateral arrangement with their country that provides for more favorable treatment; or persons employed in international railway, road, or inland waterway transport to the extent indicated by treaties binding on Poland.[97]

An alien who applies for an entry visa must be in possession of a valid passport or other travel or similar document. Where visas have been abolished, the alien enters the country with a passport, with a national identity card accompanied by a special insert (some Comecon countries and Yugoslavia), or with the identity card alone (German Democratic Republic with Czechoslovakia and Poland).

The Law of 1963 sets forth five reasons for the refusal or cancellation of an entry visa.[98] Two of them are broad categories that in fact leave the authorities with an unlimited freedom to decide whether to admit the alien or not. They reflect the customary rule of international law that the reception of aliens is a matter of discretion. Thus an alien may be refused an entry visa if "he has acted against the interests of the Polish People's Republic"[99] or if circumstances other than those enumerated in the law indicate that the admission of the alien is undesirable in view of the public interest.[100] More specific reasons for nonadmission are a criminal record in Poland or abroad; contravention of Polish regulations on the protection of state frontiers, on customs, or on foreign exchange; or deprivation of Polish nationality after 9 May 1945. An alien who has been refused a visa or whose visa has been canceled can submit a complaint to the superior of the deciding organ in accordance with the administrative procedure of 1960.

Once admitted, an alien must check in with the division for control of population movement of the local government in the place where he or she arrives (the hotel or landlord does it). Thus the alien is subject to the same duty as a local citizen who temporarily changes domicile within the country. Aliens who stay for a longer period, such as students or employees, must register with the police.[101]

Voluntary Departure. Unless the alien becomes involved in criminal proceedings, both judicial and administrative, as suspect or accused, there are no limits placed upon voluntary departure in Polish law. If the alien has been required to register with the police, and noncompliance with this duty is evidenced by the absence of an appropriate official stamp in the alien's passport, departure may be delayed until clarification of his or her position is obtained. Such delay does not involve any restriction on personal freedom within Poland.

Involuntary Departure: Expulsion and Deportation. The reasons for the expulsion of an alien are the same as those for the refusal or cancellation of an entry visa.[102] The expulsion order must indicate the deadline for departure, and it can also prescribe a certain route to be followed, as well as the crossing point at the frontier. Up to the moment of departure the alien may be ordered to remain in a specific locality and to report to the police.

An alien who has been ordered to leave the country and refuses to do so within the prescribed time limit is liable to be conducted to the frontier (deported). This is also possible when it is dictated by an "important public interest."[103]

There is no judicial remedy against expulsion or deportation. The alien may file a complaint with the superior of the organ that ordered the measure. The decision of the organ must indicate the legal grounds for the expulsion or deportation, but in some cases the organ is allowed to dispense with the duty to give reasons for the decision, which must otherwise figure in any administrative act, "if the interest of State security or public order so require."[104]

Aliens who have been granted asylum in Poland are not subject to any orders to leave the country. The constitutional laws of Comecon states specify which categories of persons are eligible for asylum.[105]

Under general international law the state continues to have the discretionary power to admit aliens and to demand that they depart.[106] The restriction that this power be not exercised arbitrarily is a rule which cannot be enforced. Retorsion appears to be the only means to compel the state not to abuse its power; however, not in every situation will there be room for, or the possibility of, retorsion. There is no absolute right of exclusion:[107] there must be a reason for it; but the territorial sovereign remains the judge of its own action. If a foreign state thinks otherwise and it does not succeed in making its opinion prevail, a stalemate is reached with the alien excluded, unless the parties are obliged to submit their dispute to a mode of settlement that results in a binding and definite solution. Whether the exclusion has been justified or arbitrary is a matter on which varying views are possible, since they stem from subjective judgments on values.

The post-1945 treaty law considerably relaxed the foregoing strict rules, but it did so in regional groupings only. Bilateral arrangements abolished visas, which resulted in the opening of several countries to free travel and temporary stays for nonemployment purposes by the nationals of the countries concerned, such as among the countries of Western Europe. More extensive rights are given to aliens by virtue of treaties of restricted participation such as the European Convention on Establishment (1955)[108] or the Treaty on the European Economic Community (1957).[109] At the present moment the chances for extending these standards to the level of world law are practically nil. This is reflected by those treaties on human rights that are meant for universal application. Articles 12 and 13 of the Covenant on Civil and Political Rights in no way improve the position of aliens with regard to their entry and expulsion under general law.[110] Article 1, Paragraph 2, of the Convention against Racial Discrimination adopted by the United Nations in Resolution 2106 (XX) expressly preserves the "distinctions, exclusions, restrictions, or preferences" made between citizens and noncitizens. The regulation contained in Protocol Number 4 to the European Convention is also not in any way significantly different; its prohibition of collective expulsion of aliens (Article 4) must be regarded as a formulation of a custom. On the other hand, Articles 13 and 14 of the Universal Declaration of Human Rights set forth standards that far surpass what follows from custom and treaties.[111] However, its standards relating to aliens have not yet become general law.

Protection

The diplomatic protection of aliens in the strict sense of the word, in contradistinction to inhabitants of UN trust territories; of the mandated territory of South West Africa, at any rate prior to General Assembly Resolution 2145 (XXI); or British Protected Persons, is exceptional. Today it results from arrangements that follow from the absence of diplomatic or consular relations. Such absence has different causes. It may result from nonrecognition. It is the usual consequence of an armed conflict, though there have been situations in contemporary history in which fighting did not put an end to diplomatic or consular relations, such as between China and India in 1962. Sometimes relations are broken off in peacetime, and "delegated protection"[112] is then resorted to by virtue of agreement involving the interested states. The functioning of Protecting Powers under the Geneva Convention of 1949[113] is still another example of protection of aliens.

Formerly, the relationship of dependence between states made protection of aliens a fairly frequent occurrence in international life. The disappearance of protected or vassal states and similar territorial units eliminated this type of diplomatic protection. An example in recent Central European history was the protection of citizens of the Free City of Danzig by Poland, which conducted the city's foreign affairs.[114] This arrangement did not survive World War II.

Today protection of aliens results from consent by the interested states. The consent concerns specific situations. One may wonder whether they in fact constitute "important exceptions," as the International Court described them,[115] to the rule of protection by the national state--that is a matter of evaluation. Nonetheless they are not exceptions under the general law. The latter permits the protection of aliens who are seamen or members of the armed forces;[116] but these are rare instances of dispensation with the link of nationality. Also, as Judge Badawi Pasha rightly pointed out, here "the condition of nationality is satisfied as regards the flag or the forces."[117] I am inclined therefore to agree with the view that the protection of aliens by the state is a problem of little significance.[118]

The instruments dealing with human rights are silent on the diplomatic protection of aliens; diplomatic protection is not a right guaranteed by these instruments. It may be concluded that the claim for diplomatic protection of an alien is valid and effective only if the other government has consented or consents to its presentation. The alien is then protected not by virtue of a right under general law but owing to a bilateral arrangement, which may also have an exclusively ad hoc nature. The doctrine of effective link as applied in the Notteböhm case does not operate in favor of the protection of aliens; it goes in the opposite direction, for it restricts the protection of certain categories of nationals.[119]

NATIONAL IMPLEMENTATION OF INTERNATIONAL RIGHTS AND DUTIES

The Act of State Doctrine

The Act of State doctrine in either the U.S. or the British meaning has never existed in the part of Europe that is now the Comecon countries. This does not amount to saying that the discrepancy between an act of a foreign state and international law is irrelevant for the courts when they decided on the application or effectiveness of the particular acts. The problem is approached in the Comecon countries not from the standpoint of a certain doctrine, but rather, in line with the continental tradition, in the framework of the relationship between international and municipal law and in the context of domestic law and order (ordre public).[120]

None of these, it is true, supplies a clear rule or directive. The laws of the Comecon members, with the exception of the Constitution of the German Democratic Republic, do not contain any guiding principles on the application of international customs and treaties in the domestic sphere, though there are provisions in specific statutory enactments that resolve this question for the purposes of some defined branches of law, such as air law, law of extradition, or law of international civil procedure. The problem is discussed below in the light of the law of Poland; similar solutions have been adopted in most of the Comecon countries.

The Polish law on conflict of laws prohibits the application of a foreign law when it "would produce effects contrary to the fundamental principles of the legal order" of Poland.[121] Though the enactment setting forth this rule is limited to situations regulated by private law, including labor law, the rule must be regarded as relevant whenever a Polish organ is confronted with an application of foreign law.

Foreign judicial decisions are enforced in Poland only if a treaty concluded by Poland provides that claimants could obtain an order from the foreign state requiring the appropriate officer to take action (exequatur).[122] They are then enforced by the competent organ; for instance, a debt is forcibly collected or chattels are taken and restituted. In defining the conditions of enforceability, treaties have priority over the Code of Civil Procedure.[123] If no enforcement comes into consideration but the question is only one of the effectiveness of the judgment in the Polish system, recognition of the foreign decision by a Polish court suffices unless a treaty provides otherwise.[124] The law enumerates the conditions of such recognition, one of which is the conformity of the decision with the fundamental principles of the social and political system of Poland.[125]

None of the provisions of the Law on Conflict of Laws has priority or preeminence over international law. On the contrary, Article 1, Paragraph 2, establishes the superiority of treaties.[126] The same rule applies to matters of international procedure governed by the Codes of Civil[127] and Criminal Procedure.[128] However, certain treaties, namely those on legal aid or legal relations concluded by the Comecon countries among themselves, do not contain the public policy clause. Thus a statute or a judicial decision by a contracting party is not subject to the controlling test of concordance with Polish public policy; the parties seem to surmise that the similarity of political systems excludes variations in public policy, which is a debatable proposition.

The relationships governed by those treaties apart, it may be submitted that noncompliance of a foreign act with international law makes it highly doubtful whether the act conforms to Polish public policy. In controversial issues the crucial question is the content of the international rule. One can assume that nonpayment of the "adequate, effective and prompt" compensation to the alien owner of nationalized property would not be regarded by Polish organs as contrary to Polish public order. Poland herself concluded treaties that provide for compensation that does not correspond to certain Western interpretations of the "adequate, effective and prompt" formula.[129] However, they definitely disposed of any claims arising out of nationalization.

When the prohibition of the application of foreign acts contrary to international law is founded on, and results exclusively from, the requirements of public policy, one inevitably confronts the whole issue of municipal application of international law. In part at least the place of that law in the domestic systems of the Comecon countries is not free from doubt, and Poland is a case in point.[130] Where specific statutes do not clearly guide the Polish courts on the relevance of international law, and usually such a statutory admonition is limited to treaties, passing over custom in silence, the testing of conformity to public order by establishing concordance with international law becomes highly problematical. The court, being uncertain about whether international law is applicable at all, may not be willing to explore the question of whether the foreign act conforms to that law.

With this weakness of concept in mind, one can conclude that foreign legislation and judgments that violate international law as binding on, and applied by, Poland are contrary to Polish public policy and for that reason should not be given effect or recognized by Polish courts. To a large extent this is a theoretical statement, because nowadays Polish courts do not often deal with problems that in free market economies engender litigation leaving room for resorting to the Act of State doctrine or analogous solutions. It is true that after the termination of hostilities in 1945 Polish courts often examined the conformity of the acts of the belligerent occupant of Polish territory with international law, that is, with the Hague Regulations of 1907.[131] The courts refused to respect the effects of those acts if they were found to be contrary to the regulations. There is no reason why this approach should not be followed in situations other than governed by the law of belligerent occupation. However, the significance of those cases remains limited. First, the courts put emphasis on the discrepancy between the act of the (foreign) occupant and the local law, which in the courts' view has to be applied, while the absence of such application violated the commands of the Hague Regulations. Thus the international aspect receded into the background. Second, the unlawful acts of a belligerent occupant seem to be a class in themselves, that is, not governed by the Act of State doctrine.[132]

Implementation of Decisions of International Organizations

Resolutions of the United Nations

In countries such as the Comecon members in which industry and commerce, including transport and other services, are controlled by the state, problems of domestic compliance with the resolutions of the United Nations are not complicated as far as implementing procedures is concerned. In contradistinction to those parts of the world in which the rules of a free market economy are in operation, the state-controlled systems reduce the matter to one level, namely to the decision by the government. If the government complies with the measures ordered or recommended by the United Nations, then implementation by state enterprises automatically follows and there is no chance for any defiance of the governmental decision, nor are there any loopholes in the substantive or procedural law that would allow for any deviations to take place. If, on the other hand, the government rejects the measures in the UN resolution, then trade continues unhampered under the official protection.[133] This is what happened when the USSR, Poland, and Czechoslovakia refused "to refrain from direct or indirect provision of arms or other materials of war to Albania and Bulgaria[134] or when all the Comecon members did not apply any embargo on shipment of certain goods to the People's Republic of China and to North Korea,[135] in defiance of the General Assembly recommendations. The policy decision by the government concerned resolved the issue, and commerce and other economic relations developed as if the countries involved had not become objects of the UN measures.

From the point of view of those governments, the fact that the measures in question were only recommended and not ordered was of a secondary importance. Noncompliance had a cause other than the recommendatory nature of the resolutions of the organization. The sanctions against Rhodesia, which were the subject of mandatory resolutions of the Security Council,[136] had the backing of the Comecon members and were put into operation, on instruction by each of the governments concerned, primarily by the agencies for foreign trade in these countries.[137]

Comecon Resolutions

At the present moment the resolutions by the Comecon that penetrate into the domestic domain are exclusively concerned with the relations among state enterprises for foreign trade. However, if and when unification of some portions of the municipal law of the Comecon countries develops through cooperation within that organization, the Comecon acts will start dealing with individual rights, and consequently the domestic implementation of such acts will become of interest to individuals.

The Comecon adopts two kinds of resolutions: decisions and recommendations. Article 4, Paragraph 2, of the Comecon charter provides as follows: "Decisions shall be adopted on organisational and procedural questions. Such decisions shall take effect, unless it is specified otherwise in them, from the date on which the record of the meeting of the Council organ concerned is signed." Thus in its legislative activities the organization cannot go beyond the sphere of its own internal affairs. Paragraph 1 of the same article deals as follows with the adoption of recommendations:

> Recommendations shall be adopted on questions of economic and scientific-technical co-operation. Such recommendations shall be communicated to the member countries of the Council for consideration.
>
> Recommendations adopted by member countries of the Council shall be implemented by them through decisions of the Governments or competent authorities of those countries, in conformity with their laws.

These nonobligatory acts can acquire binding force only through the subsequent consent of individual governments. The recommendations of the Comecon are recommendations in the strict sense and not law-making acts called recommendations like those of the European Coal and Steel Community or the North-East Atlantic Fisheries Commission.

In 1957 the Commission for Foreign Trade adopted an instrument called the General Conditions of Delivery.[138] It was thereafter amended. In 1962 the commission adopted the General Conditions of Mounting and Other Technical Services[139] and the General Conditions of Technical Operations.[140] From the point of view of the unification of the law on commerce among the member states, the General Conditions of Delivery play an important role. They deal in particular with the conclusion of the contract for delivery of goods, the rights and duties of buyer and seller ("basis of delivery"), place and time of delivery, quality and quantity of goods, packing, marking, technical documents, verification of the quality of goods, guarantees, shipping instructions and notifications of delivery, procedure for payment, circumstances relieving the parties from responsibility, claims arising from quantity or quality defects, fines, arbitration, and supplementary conditions.

The Comecon had no constitutional power to impose any of these texts on its members, but some or all of the members agreed to accept them and to abide by them. The next step was taken in the sphere of municipal law. In each of the accepting states, competent organs made enactments incorporating the provisions of the three sets of general conditions. Through these enactments, the General Conditions became binding on their addressees, that is, on state enterprises or corporations engaged in foreign trade. The source of law is domestic, since it is constituted by the municipal act.

This is not an instance of transformation of international legal rules into municipal law,[141] since such rules did not then exist on the international plane, a recommendation being unable to create them. Rather, it is an instance of literal incorporation of the international text into a municipal enactment, whereby this text acquired binding force. This device guarantees domestic compliance with the organizational instruments that were aimed at law making. The necessary basis, however, for its successful application is a prior agreement, no matter how informal, by the members that they will accept the Comecon recommendation and give effect to it in their municipal jurisdictions. The pattern followed with regard to the three sets of general conditions is a combination of action by the international organization, agreement by its member states, and domestic measures of a legislative nature.[142]

Procedures Related to the Issuance of Certificates and Suggestions by the Executive in Connection with Litigation in National Courts

Certification by the executive is known on the Continent,[143] but its forms and importance differ from the practice of the common law countries. This general observation applies to the members of Comecon, and Polish law can be taken as an example.

In civil matters the court that applies foreign law can ask the Minister of Justice to supply it with the text thereof and to explain foreign judicial practice.[144] Whether international law, or parts of it, have for Polish courts the status of foreign law[145] is a theoretical problem that involves the whole question of the place of that law in the domestic system; it need not be discussed here. Irrespective of the doctrinal position, the competence to demand guidance from the Minister of Justice can extend to international law and such specific problems involving a mixture of fact and law as recognition and the existence of a state of war. It is only the court, not the litigants, that has the power to approach the executive.

In criminal matters, if there is any doubt regarding immunity from jurisdiction, including arrest and duty to give evidence, the courts seek guidance from the Minister of Justice and public prosecutors from the Prosecutor General.[146] The accused is in no position to seek and obtain such guidance but is free to submit his or her views to the court.

The executive opinion is submitted in the course of, or made known during, the oral proceedings, and the parties have an opportunity to make comments thereon. The court is not bound by it, but it probably does not deviate from it when it itself has asked for the opinion. It is different, or may be so, when the prosecution presents a statement of the executive; the statement is then treated as the position of one party only.

In one instance the court will have to follow the opinion of the executive, and its contents will not be subject to any interpretation by the court. If the court applies a treaty on legal assistance and is informed by the executive that a point of interpretation has been settled by the contracting states, it cannot depart from the interpretation so agreed upon.[147]

The executive statement or opinion is not the only method by which the court can elucidate an international fact or foreign or international law. The court may hear experts and expert witnesses in both civil and criminal cases.[148] The court decides on the admission of expert evidence after hearing the views of the parties. The court is free to assess the value of expert evidence. It may appoint individuals to give expert opinions or it may ask an institute or research organization to deliver them.[149] Individual experts were heard, for instance, on points of international law in the Greiser[150] and Koch[151] cases.

The diplomatic or consular status of the defendant is usually established by the court before or during the oral proceedings. In some cases the sovereign immunity or otherwise of the foreign government was argued by the parties and the court decided the issue in the judgment. In the case of the British Treasury,[152] the Supreme Court by its own reasoning arrived at the conclusion that the United Kingdom enjoyed immunity from jurisdiction in Poland. The court attached considerable importance to the principle of reciprocity: "In case of doubt in this respect, one has to ask for the opinion of the Ministry of Justice, which gives it in agreement with the Ministry of Foreign Affairs."[153] It appears that in this case no doubt arose and the court did not ask for the guidance of the executive. In the case involving the French Consulate in Cracow,[154] the Supreme Court again considered the question of reciprocity in granting sovereign immunity. It referred to a letter by the Polish Consulate General in Paris, which stated the practice of French courts in this matter. The letter had been submitted to the court by the Minister of Justice; it thus had the formal approval of that department, though it had originated with the Ministry for Foreign Affairs. According to the letter (in the Supreme Court's words) French courts "always consider themselves incompetent to deal with cases concerning [pecuniary] claims if a foreign State is the debtor, while the Consulate does not know of any instance of deviation from that principle."[155] The court accepted this statement as conclusive and decided that France enjoyed immunity from jurisdiction.

Recognition and Nonrecognition

Recognition or nonrecognition does and will remain a tool of policy in interstate relations, but one may envisage the limitation of its effects to the sphere of politics and diplomacy. The resulting legal consequences would then concern the two governments involved, not other parties in the respective countries. On the internal plane, courts and administrative organs could apply foreign laws, regulations, or executive decisions irrespective of recognition.

The view is sometimes expressed that if the practice of domestic organs is divorced from recognition, the danger arises that the state will speak with more than one voice. In fact that danger does not exist. When the court treats an unrecognized state as a state or an unrecognized government as the organ of public authority in a territory, no recognition is brought about. There is no "recognition by courts," and general international law does not attach the consequences of implied recognition to any action by the courts or by executive organs other than those representing the state in foreign relations. Courts act on a different plane, and there is no inherent reason why they should apply foreign legislation and other acts by virtue of recognition alone.

Legal relationships among individuals and/or corporations do exist whether there is recognition or not. When courts decide points of law involving such relationships (in contradistinction to points of law arising between two states or governments), it is not clear why they should be guided by the criterion of recognition, which belongs to a different sphere from that of individual rights.

Other tests, such as reciprocity, seem more appropriate. If the court is assured that its own country enjoys or will enjoy sovereign immunity in the other jurisdiction, it can grant it to the defendant government or state without inquiring about recognition. Another test is public policy. If a foreign law or act does not contravene that policy, it can be applied, and considerations of recognition would play a secondary role, if any.

In matters involving private law, Polish courts apply foreign law irrespective of recognition. The test of recognition is absent from Article 1143 of the Code of Civil Procedure. That code is silent on nonrecognition as a reason for refusing legal assistance to foreign courts or other organs. The reasons given for refusing assistance are different: the act involved would be contrary to the fundamental principles of the Polish legal order; the act does not lie within the competence of Polish courts; or the state the organ of which seeks legal assistance refuses to render the same assistance to Polish courts.[156] The latter provision gives expression to the concept of reciprocity and may indirectly involve the problem of recognition. The hypothetical case is that the foreign state or government refuses legal assistance on account of its nonrecognition of the Polish state or government; but then nonrecognition enters the picture on the initiative of the other side.

The Code of Civil Procedure is equally silent on the role of recognition in assessing the value of foreign documents as evidence.[157] It is equal to that of Polish official documents. However, the existence of diplomatic or consular relations with the country in which the document originated may play a role. Thus foreign instruments concerning transfer of immovable property should be notarized by a Polish diplomatic mission or consulate before being submitted to a Polish court. The same rule applies to all foreign documents the authenticity of which is doubtful.

Similarly, in criminal proceedings legal assistance is not made dependent on recognition. It is refused when granting it would entail a violation of the principles of the Polish legal order or would encroach upon Polish sovereignty. Courts and public prosecutors can refuse legal assistance on some further grounds, but not on account of nonrecognition.[158] Lack of reciprocity may have a restricting effect on the granting of legal assistance[159] or on extradition,[160] but it is not a mandatory rule: the organ decides whether lack of reciprocity will have that effect. The Code of Criminal Procedure contains a general rule that provides that absence of reciprocity or absence of treaty are reasons for the nonapplication of the provisions of the code on international proceedings.[161] Nowhere is nonrecognition referred to as such a reason.

NOTES

1. 368 U.N.T.S. 253. The text published by the United Nations does not embody the amendments introduced into the Comecon charter (statute) at the organization's subsequent session.

2. See papers in Rapports polonais présentes au Congrès International de Droit Comparé (hereafter Rapports Polonais), volumes covering the sixth (1962) and seventh (1966) Congresses, at 109 and 150 respectively.

3. E. de Vattel, "Une espèce de Privilège," 3 Le Droit des gens, Chapter 17, Paragraph 265 (London 1758).

4. Le Moniteur, 29 July 1790 and 10 August 1790.

5. E. Reale, "Le probleme des passeports," 4 Recueil des Cours (Hague Academy) 89, at 93-104 (1934); M. d'Hartoy, "Histoire du passeport français," Depuis l'antiquité jusqu'à nos jours 31-71 (1937).

6. Act of 1793, Statutes at Large, 33 Geo. III, Chapter 4, at 292; K. Diplock, "Passports and Protection in International Law," 32 Transact. Grot. Soc'y. 42, at 46-47 (1946).

7. Act of 1793, Statutes at Large, 38 Geo. III, Chapter 50; Diplock, op. cit., at 47.

8. Ibid., at 48.

9. Ibid., at 45.

10. Consolidated Treaty Series 347 (C. Parry, ed.) 1969. The Treaty is cited by Diplock, op. cit., at 45.

11. P. Bonnafoux, Des passeports: étude historique et critique 116 (1927).

12. For a more recent discussion of the international legal aspects of passports, see F. Borella, "Le Passeport," 64 Revue Gén. Droit Int. Public 301 (1960) and D. C. Turack, The Passport in International Law (1972).

13. 363 U.N.T.S. 333.

14. 479 U.N.T.S. 301.

15. 33 U.N.T.S. 105.

16. 131 U.N.T.S. 99.

17. Unpublished.

18. 1967 Dziennik Ustaw (Polish Journal of Laws) No. 17, Item 81, Art. 4, Para. 1.

19. See E. Schweissguth, "Das neue ungarische Passrecht," 11 Jahrbuch für Ostrecht No. 1, 195, at 196-200 (1970).

20. 1970 Magyar Közlöny, No. 13. German translation of the two acts in 11 Jahrbuch für Ostrecht, No. 1, at 213, 215 (1970).

21. The official description is "passport fee," but in fact it is a fee the applicant has to pay for each exit permit. The average net salary per month in the nationalized sector in 1971 was 2,346 złotys. Maly rocznik statystyczny 312 (1972). In 1975 it was more than 1,000 zlotys higher.

22. 1970 Magyar Közlöny, No. 13, op. cit., 9 (I) b.

23. Ibid., § 9 (IV).

24. 1959 Dziennik Ustaw, Art. 4, § 2(3).

25. Ibid., §§ 2(1), 2(2), 2(5).

26. 1970 Magyar Közlöny, No. 13, op. cit., §§ 3 (I)a, 3 (I)b, 3 (I)f.

27. Ibid., §§ 3 (I)c-e, 3 (II), 4 (II).

28. Ibid., § 4.

29. Hungary, 1970 Government Ordinance No. 4, § 1 (II).

30. 1959 Dziennik Ustaw, Art. 4, § 5.

31. 1970 Magyar Közlöny, No. 13, op. cit., § 7. See Schweissguth, op. cit., at 209.

32. Regarding Poland, see W. Gellhorn, Ombudsmen and Others: Citizens' Protectors in Nine Countries 303-14 (1966).

33. 1965 Sbírka zákonů Československé Socialistické Republiky (hereafter Sbírka), No. 69.

34. 1969 Sbírka, No. 114.

35. Ibid., Nos. 35, 39.

36. J. Pokstefl, "Die Entwicklung der Rechtslage des Individuums in der CSSR seit dem Jahre 1968," 17 Osteuropa Recht 245, at 264-65 (1971).

37. [1954] Gesetzblatt der Deutschen Demokratischen Republik (hereafter GBl.) 786; [1957] GBl. I 650.

38. See, for example, regulations of 1963, [1963] GBl. II 691.

39. Originally within the concept of the Boykotthetze. See D. Müller-Römer, Die Grundrechte in Mitteldeutschland 122-23 (1965).

40. Amendment to the Passport Law, [1957] GBl. I 650.

41. 1968 GBl. I 1, § 101.

42. Letter by State Secretary M. Kohl of 26 May 1972, 27 Europa Archiv D 328 (1972), and exchange of letters between the German Democratic Republic and the Federal Republic of Germany of 21 December 1972, accompanying the signing of the Basic Treaty of the same day, 20 Bulletin 1842 (Presse- und Informations-amt der Bundesregierung, 1972).

43. Magyar Közlöny, No. 13, op. cit., § 12 (I), Note 21.

44. Statement ("Information") by the Polish Government of 18 November 1970, 17 Keesing's Contemporary Archives 24346, Col. 1 (1969-70).

45. The exact figure of the post-Potsdam transfers was 3,155,600, to which some would add 35,300 of repatriated German prisoners of war. Komunikaty Instytutu Bałtyckiego 6, at 64 (1967).

46. Chapter VIII B of the Potsdam Protocol and Chapter IX B of the Potsdam Communiqué, "The Conference of Berlin (The Potsdam Conference) 1945," 2 Foreign Relations of the United States, Diplomatic Papers 1491, 1509 (1960).

47. Ibid., at 1495, 1511.

48. The plan of transfers adopted by the council on 20 November 1945.

49. Memorandum of 5 January 1946, Zbiór Dokumentów 429 (1946); Agreement of 14 February 1946, 2 Europe Archiv 823 (1947); Agreement of 12 April 1947, unpublished.

50. Several agreements, unpublished. The basic agreement is of 5 April 1946. They are accessible in Polish archives; for indications see Banasiak, op. cit., and the principal monograph by Banasiak on the subject, Przesiedlenie Niemców z Polski w latach 1945-1960 (1968).

51. D. Rauschning, "Die deutschen Staatsangehörigen in den Gebieten jenseits der Oder-Neisse-Linie und die Regelung ihres Schicksals," 66 *Veroffentlichungen des Instituts für Internationales Recht an der Universität Kiel* (Ostverträge, Berlin-Status); M. Abkommen, *Beziehungen Zwischen der BRD und der DDR* 167, at 167-68 (1971).

52. The smaller figure is mentioned in the statement referred to above. The larger figure is 275,000-300,000, and it follows from assessments by statisticians, such as S. Waszak, "Liczba Niemców w Polsce w latach 1931-59," 15 *Przeglad Zachodni* Part 3, at 318. (1959).

53. London *Times*, 21 November 1970, p. 3, col. 1; The New York *Times*, 21 November 1970, p. 11, col. 1; 10 *International Legal Materials* 127 (1971).

54. These differences explain the slowing down of the departures. According to FRG sources, some 25,000 departed in 1971, while the figure for 1972 was about 13,500. In 1975 a new arrangement was reached between the Federal Republic of Germany and Poland providing for departures within the next few years.

55. Reichs- und Staatsangehörigkeitsgesetz of 13 July 1913, 1913 Reichsgesetzblatt 583. N. Nakarov, "Deutsches Staatsangehörigkeitsrecht," *Kommentar* 31 (1966). The West German position is based on Paragraph 25 of that law. Other relevant West German laws are the Gesetz zur Regelung von Fragen der Staatsangehörigkeit of 22 February 1955, 1955 Bundesgesetzblatt I 65, and to a lesser degree the Bundesvertriebegesetz of 19 May 1953, 1953 Bundesvertriebegesetz I 201.

56. The official policy of the government with regard to Jewish emigration from Poland found expression in the speeches by the first secretary of the central committee of the Polish United Workers Party on 19 March 1968 and by the premier on 10 April 1968, 15 *Keesing's Contemporary Archives* 22666, 22684 (1967-68).

57. *Dziennik Ustaw*, No. 4, Item 25. English translation in Yrbk. Hum. Rights 291 (1951). 1962 *Dziennik Ustaw*, No. 10, Item 49.

58. Apart from isolated cases involving reunion of families, 18 *Keesing's Contemporary Archives* 24708, col. 1 (1971-72).

59. J. B. Schechtman, *Postwar Population Transfers in Europe 1945-1955* 278-81 (1962). The then government of Hungary was composed of various political elements.

60. See the official statement reported in the London *Times*, 28 March 1972, p. 9, col. 1.

61. "The Volga Germans," *The Manchester Guardian*, 13 April 1972, p. 2, col. 7.

62. [1949] GBl. 4, Art. 10, § 3.

63. [1968] GBl. I 199.

64. The convention is annexed to Resolution 2106 (XX) of the UN General Assembly. For a Polish comment on it, see J. Balicki, "The Anti-racist Convention," 2 Polish Yb. Int'l. L. 24 (1968-69). In signing the convention, the Comecon countries made reservations regarding the jurisdiction of the International Court of Justice (Article 22) and declarations dis-

approving the restrictive effect of Articles 17 and 18, which excluded certain states from signing the convention or acceding to it. See 1969 Dziennik Ustaw, No. 25, Items 187 and 188.

65. See, for instance, 1951 Dziennik Ustaw, No. 4, Item 25; 1962 Dziennik Ustaw, No. 10, Item 49.

66. Such a passport is issued by a Polish consulate and is valid for the return trip only.

67. "Freedom from Arbitrary Arrest, Detention and Exile," U.N. Yrbk. Hum. Rights, New York, 1959. Or see "Study of the right of everyone to be free from arbitrary arrest, detention and exile," U.N. Economic and Social Council, B/CN.4/835, 2 January 1963.

68. Expulsion is a formal act of the state authorities. It is an order that directs the person to leave the country. See L. Oppenheim, 1 International Law 694 (8th ed., Lauterpacht, ed., 1955). Unfavorable conditions of life, deterioration in the position of individuals, or persecution on various grounds may all be conducive to emigration, but they are not expulsion in the legal sense as long as the persons are not ordered to leave.

69. London Times, 2 September 1961, p. 5, col. 2. For reports on the expulsion of peasants who opposed the setting up of collective farms, see Neues Deutschland, 5, 9, and 11 August 1961 and Müller-Römer, op. cit., at 126.

70. The classical rule on the movement of nationals is rigid. "Every State has, strictly speaking, a right of prohibiting their egress from their own country." Phillimore, 1 Commentaries upon International Law 444 (3d ed., 1879).

71. See the observations made by W. P. Danevski, 1 Posobiye k izucheniyu istorii i sistemy mezhdunarodnogo prava 10 ff. (1852).

72. The standard adopted by the Institute of International Law in 1897 that the freedom to emigrate "ne pourra être restreinte que par décision dûment publiée des gouvernements et dans les limites rigoureuses des nécessités d'ordre social et politique" was and remains a rule of law that ought to be. Draft Convention, Art. 1, 16 Annuaire 262 (1897).

73. J. B. Moore, 4 A Digest of International Law 187 (1906).

74. Ibid.

75. G.A. Res. 217 (III). According to Art. 13, "(1) Everyone has the right to freedom of movement and residence within the borders of each state. (2) Everyone has the right to leave any country, including his own, and to return to his country."

76. 213 U.N.T.S. 221.

77. European Treaty Series, No. 46, Basic Documents on Human Rights 361 (I. Brownlie, ed., 1971). According to Article 2, "2. Everyone shall be free to leave any country, including his own. 3. No restrictions shall be placed on the exercise of these rights other than such as are in accordance with law and are necessary in a democratic society in the interests of national security or public safety for the maintenance of 'ordre public', for the prevention of crime, for the protection of the rights and freedoms of others." According to Article 3, "1. No one shall be expelled, by means

either of an individual or of a collective measure, from the territory of the State of which he is a national. 2. No one shall be deprived of the right to enter the territory of the State of which he is a national."

78. G.A. Res. 2200 A (XXI). According to Article 12, "2. Everyone shall be free to leave any country, including his own. 3. The above-mentioned rights shall not be subject to any restrictions except those which are provided by law, are necessary to protect national security, public order (ordre public), public health or morals or the rights and freedoms of others, and are consistent with the other rights recognized in the present Covenant. 4. No one shall be arbitrarily deprived of the right to enter his own country."

79. For a recent discussion of the problems involved in the movement of persons, see K. Libera, Miedzynarodowy ruch osobowy (1969), and W. Riphagen, "National and International Regulation of International Movement and the Legal Position of the Private Individual," 131 Recueil des Cours (Hague Academy) 489, at 498-509 (1970, III).

80. [1968] GBl. I, Art. 33, § 1.

81. Unpublished. State Records Office (Archives) at Łódź. Documents of the P.U.R. (National Repatriation Office), Symb. 1, 3.

82. The critical date of nationality was 17 September 1939, that is, the date of entry of Soviet troops on Polish territory.

83. S. Banasiak, Działalność osadnicza Państwowego Urzedu Repatriacyjnego na Ziemiach Odzyskanych w latach 1945-1947 (1963).

84. Note "The Conference of Berlin," op. cit., 1485 and 1505. 9 International Legislation 583 (M. O. Hudson and L. B. Sohn, eds., 1942-45).

85. Protocol Concerning the Discontinuance of German Reparations Payments and Other Measures to Alleviate the Financial and Economic Obligations of the G.D.R., 221 U.N.T.S. 129.

86. 1953 Zbiór Dokumentów 1830, at 1831. During the negotiations with the Federal Republic of Germany in 1970 Poland confirmed its renunciation, "Zum Vertrag mit der Volksrepublik Polen," 1970 Presse- und Informationsamt der Bundesregierung Bulletin 1818, at 1819, Para. III 4.

87. Second Phase, [1955] I.C.J. Rep. 4.

88. P.C.I.J., Ser. A, No. 2, 54, at 63 (1924).

89. 213 U.N.T.S. 262; Basic Documents on Human Rights, op. cit., at 355, Art. 1.

90. It is, then, not surprising that a commentator of the protocol concludes: In sum, it is difficult to see what possible protection to property Article 1 offers." J. E. S. Fawcett, The Application of the European Convention on Human Rights 348 (1969). The same comment can be made with regard to Article 17, Paragraph 2, of the Universal Declaration of Human Rights: "No one shall be arbitrarily deprived of his property." The criterion of arbitrariness was rejected as imprecise during the drafting of the protocol.

91. 186 U.N.T.S. 301.

92. This point is illustrated by the case of American-Mexican Claims Bureau, Inc. v. Morgenthau, Secretary of the Treasury, et al., 26 F. Supp. 904; Ann. Dig. 336 (1938-40).

93. 1963 Dziennik Ustaw No. 15, Item 77. For a commentary, see E. Gralla, "Das polnische Ausländergesetz," 8 Jahrbuch für Ostrecht, No. 1, 233 (1967); T. Pusylewitsch, "Allgemeine Fragen des Ausländerrechts in Polen," 17 Osteuropa Recht 155, at 159-160 (1971).

94. 1963 Dziennik Ustaw No. 15, Item 77, Art. 3.

95. Libera, op. cit., 298-99. The Manchester Guardian, 27 March 1972, p. 2, col. 7.

96. Dziennik Ustaw No. 15, Item 77, Art. 23, § 3.

97. Ordinance of 20 March 1964, Relating to the Conditions of Frontier Crossing and Stay in the Territory of the Polish People's Republic by Persons Employed in International Transport, 1964 Monitor Polski, Item 187, and 1965 Monitor Polski, Item 97.

98. 1963 Dziennik Ustaw, No. 15, Item 77, Art. 5.

99. Ibid., Art. 5, § 1 (1).

100. Ibid., Art. 5, § 1 (5).

101. 1965 Monitor Polski, Item 162.

102. 1963 Dziennik Ustaw No. 15, Item 77, Art. 15, § 1.

103. Ibid., Art. 15, § 4.

104. Ibid., Art. 18, § 1.

105. See, for example, Constitution of Poland, 1952, Art. 75.

106. See Article 1 of the resolution of the institute, adopted at the session of Lausanne, 10 Annuaire 245 (1888).

107. It has been rightly stated by one authority from Eastern Europe that a state that refused to admit aliens as a matter of principle would exclude itself from the international community. L. Ehrlich, Prawo miedzynarodowe 601 (1958).

108. 529 U.N.T.S. 141.

109. 298 U.N.T.S. 11 (English translation).

110. For the text of Article 12, see above. According to Article 13, "An alien lawfully in the territory of a State Party to the present Covenant may be expelled therefrom only in pursuance of a decision reached in accordance with law and shall, except where compelling reasons of national security otherwise require, be allowed to submit the reasons against his expulsion and to have his case reviewed by, and be represented for the purpose before, the competent authority or a person or persons especially designated by the competent authority."

111. For the text of Article 13, see previous note on G.A. Res. 217 (III). According to Article 14, "(1) Everyone has the right to seek and to enjoy in other countries asylum from persecution. (2) This right may not be invoked in the case of prosecutions genuinely arising from non-political crimes or from acts contrary to the purposes and principles of the United Nations."

112. E. M. Borchard, The Diplomatic Protection of Citizens Abroad or the Law of International Claims 471 (1928).

113. 75 U.N.T.S. 2.

114. Article 104 (6) of the Treaty of Versailles, 112 British and Foreign State Papers, and Article 2 of the Polish-Danzig Convention of 1920, 6 L.N.T.S. 190.

115. Reparations for Injuries Suffered in the Service of the United Nations, I.C.J. Rep. 174, at 181 (1949).

116. Dissenting Opinion by Judge Hackworth, ibid., at 202.

117. Dissenting Opinion by Judge Badawi Pasha, ibid., at 207, footnote.

118. "The cases in which a State may protect those who are not its own nationals can . . . be dismissed as irrelevant," C. Parry, Nationality and Citizenship Laws of the Commonwealth and of the Republic of Ireland 12 (1957).

119. For a recent discussion of the position of aliens in the areas covered above, see F. G. Dawson and I. L. Head, International Law, National Tribunals and the Rights of Aliens (1971).

120. Constitution of 1968, Art. 8, Para. 1.

121. Private International Law of 1965, 1965 Dziennik Ustaw, No. 46, Item 290, Art. 6.

122. J. Jodlowski, "La reconnaissance et l'exécution des décisions judiciaires étrangères en Pologne," 93 Journal du Droit International 539 (1966).

123. 1964 Dziennik Ustaw, No. 43, Item 296, Art. 1150.

124. Ibid., Art. 1145, § 1.

125. Ibid., Art. 1146, § 1, subpara. 5.

126. C. Berezowski et W. Góralczyk, "La position respective du nouveau droit international privé et des engagements internationaux de la Pologne," Droit polonais contemporain, Nos. 7-8, 31, at 36 (1967).

127. 1964 Dziennik Ustaw, No. 43, Item 296.

128. 1969 Dziennik Ustaw, No. 13, Item 96, Art. 541.

129. Poland insisted, and in most cases succeeded in maintaining the position, that in ascertaining the value of nationalized property the general depreciation of the national wealth of Poland that had been caused by the war must be taken into account. This obviously did not meet with some concepts of adequate damages; nor were the payments prompt by any standard. In 1958 the view was expressed that under general international law there was no duty to compensate aliens for nationalized property. M. Lachs, "Nacjonalizacja i rozwój miodzynarodowych stosunków gospodarczych (zagadnienia prawne)," 13 Państwo i Prawo 513, at 521 (1958, Part II).

130. See Rapports Polonais, op. cit.

131. Examples are In re Will of Wincenty K., 24 I.L.R. 930 (1957); B. v. T., ibid., 962; In re Will of Józef K., ibid., 966; In re Will of Stefan J., ibid., 970; In re Will of Jan M., ibid., 971; Zbigniew G. v. Land and Building Company E. in Cracow, 26 ibid., 714; Józef B. v. Władysław B., ibid., 716; Municipality of Kielce v. Stefan D. and Others, ibid., 718; Wladyslaw F. and Others v. Państwowa Fabryka Mebli in Cracow, ibid., 719; Mikolaj G. v. Dominik S., ibid., 728; and Jan and Tekla S. v. Walenty and Katarzyna R., ibid., 729.

132. The cases to this effect are numerous. See the U.S. case of Aboitiz & Co. v. Price, 99 F. Supp. 602 (1951).

133. Unless the organization decides to initiate enforcement. An example is the incidents involving the Manuela and the Joanna V in application

of the S.C. Res. 221 (1966). The possibility of a Soviet veto makes such an action against a Comecon country highly improbable.

134. G.A. Res. 288 A (IV).

135. G.A. Res. 500 (V).

136. Res. 217 (1965), 232 (1966), and 253 (1968).

137. See replies by the following Comecon members: Bulgaria, U.N. Doc. S/7121, S/7706, and S/7800; Czechoslovakia, S/7167, S/7757, and S/7892; the German Democratic Republic, S/7794 and S/8504; Hungary, S/7156, S/7716, and S/7808; Mongolia, S/7159, S/7717, and S/7851; Poland, S/7087 and Add. 1, S/7715, S/7812, and S/8751; U.S.S.R., S/7068 and Add., S/7672, S/7888, S/8485, S/8736, and S/8920.

138. For an English translation of the 1957 version, see text appended to H. Berman, "Unification of Contract Clauses in Trade between Member-Countries of the Council for Mutual Economic Aid," Int'l. Comp. L.Q. 665 (1958). The full title of the instrument is General Conditions of Delivery of Goods between Foreign-Trade Enterprises of Member-Countries of the Council for Mutual Economic Assistance.

139. 1962 Dziennik Urzedowy Ministerstwa Handlu Zagranicznego (Official Journal of the Polish Ministry of Foreign Trade), No. 15, Item 140.

140. Ibid., No. 19, Item 170.

141. The transformation theory was upheld by J. Jakubowski, "Próby unifikacji prawa w ramach R.W.P.G., 18 Sprawy Miedzynarodowe, No. 9, at 52 (1965).

142. The place of the Comecon recommendations in the municipal law of the member countries is discussed by J. Sandorski, "Uchwały RWPG a prawo wewnetrzne PRL," 23 Nowe Prawo 1329 (1967). See also H. de Fiumel, Rada Wzajemnej Pomocy Gospodarczej: Studium prawnomiedzynarodowe (1967) and A. Wasilkowski, Zalecenia Rady Wzajemnej Pomocy Gospodarczej (1969).

143. A. B. Lyons, "Conclusiveness of the Statements of the Executive: Continental and Latin-American Practice," 25 Brit. Y. B. Int. Law 180 (1948).

144. 1964 Dziennik Ustaw, No. 43, Item 296, Art. 1143, § 1.

145. C. Berezowski, "Wzajemny stosunek prawa miedzynarodowego i prawa krajowego," 19 Państwo i Prawo 218 (1964, Part II), regards international law as constituting, in the domestic sphere, foreign law and not part of the municipal law.

146. 1969 Dziennik Ustaw, No. 13, Item 96, Art. 518.

147. For instance, Article 2 of the additional protocol to the treaty between Poland and the Soviet Union concerning legal assistance and relations in civil, family, and criminal cases, signed at Warsaw on 28 December 1957, 320 U.N.T.S. 3, at 100. This article provides that questions relating "to the interpretation of this Treaty, and particularly those arising as a result of changes in the legislation of the Contracting Parties shall be settled by consultation" between the Polish Ministry of Justice or the Office of the Prosecutor General and the Judicial Commission of the Soviet Government."

148. 1964 Dziennik Ustaw, No. 43, Item 296, Arts. 278, 1143, § 3; 1969 Dziennik Ustaw, No. 13, Item 96, Art. 176.

149. 1964 Dziennik Ustaw, No. 43, Item 296, Art. 290; 1969 Dziennik Ustaw, No. 13, Item 96, Art. 176.

150. Expert opinion by L. Ehrlich is not reported in the summary of the judgment in Ann. Dig. 357 (1946).

151. 30 I.L.R. 496, at 503.

152. 24 I.L.R. 223 (1957).

153. Ibid., at 225.

154. 26 I.L.R. 178.

155. Ibid., at 179-80.

156. 1964 Dziennik Ustaw, No. 43, Item 296, Art. 1131.

157. Ibid., Art. 1138.

158. 1969 Dziennik Ustaw, No. 13, Item 96, Art. 521.

159. Ibid., Art. 521, § 3.

160. Ibid., Art. 534, § 1 (5).

161. Ibid., Art. 541.

CHAPTER

15

SRI LANKA (CEYLON)

C. F. Amerasinghe

THE INDIVIDUAL

The Individual as a National

Movement

Before the 1948 Constitution there was no prohibition in Ceylon against legislation restricting a national's (citizen's) right of movement. On the other hand, before December 1971 there was no general legislation that pertained to this right of movement. There were, however, two sources of limitation on this right.

First, there was the common law deriving from the prerogative of the Crown, which was probably regarded to a large extent in the same way as it had been in England.

Passports. This meant that the executive had absolute discretion in regard to the issuance and renewal of passports. No citizen had a right to a passport. Problems might have been created in international relations, but under British law the individual would probably not have had rights against the state, and the position was probably the same in Ceylon.

Sri Lanka will, for convenience, be referred to as Ceylon in this paper. The views expressed in this chapter are those of the author and do not represent the views of the International Bank for Reconstruction and Development or the International Centre for Settlement of Investment Disputes.

Reviewed and revised by the author in 1975.

Departure. On the other hand, some cases had taken the view that once a citizen had been issued a passport the executive did not have the power to prevent that citizen from leaving the country or to make the citizen's departure conditional. In Aseerwatham v. Permanent Secretary, Ministry of Defense and External Affairs, it was held that a citizen who has a valid passport cannot be prevented by the executive from leaving the country for any reason, including refusal of permission to leave by the Exchange Controller.[1]

Return. As for the right to enter or return to Ceylon, the common law in England would probably have been followed in Ceylon, since the common law of Ceylon on matters of constitutional or public law was regarded as governed by British common law. It has been stated by the executive to the British parliament that it does not have the power in common law not to permit the entry into England of passport holders.[2] What this probably means is that the executive cannot prevent a citizen from returning to his or her country whether that citizen holds a passport or not, provided he or she is a genuine citizen. This position would therefore have been taken in Ceylon in the absence of specific legislation. There was no general legislation pertaining to the right of the citizen to enter or return to Ceylon, but a citizen could have been prevented from returning to Ceylon by being deprived of his citizenship by ministerial order, if he or she were a registered citizen. (See above.)

Expulsion. The general right of a citizen not to be expelled from the country must also have been based on British common law, since this area of public law must have been derived from British law, under which law the right of a citizen not to be expelled derives from the right of freedom from arrest, which is recognized in the absence of legislation to the contrary. The mere desire to expel a citizen is not a good reason, recognized by the statute law of Britain, for arrest. There are, however, specific laws that permit the arrest and deportation of anyone, including a citizen. In Ceylon the common law must have been similar. As for specific laws permitting expulsion, the Extradition Law is one that would have permitted the arrest and deportation of a citizen.

A second source of limitation on the right of movement was the fact that the executive could, under special emergency legislation,[3] declare an emergency and make regulations that would take precedence over common and statute law for the duration of the emergency. Under these statutory provisions, regulations were made after the 1971 insurrection making it necessary for passport holders to secure exit permits before leaving the country, the issuance of such permits being entirely at the discretion of the executive.

A third indirect limitation on the freedom of travel that may be mentioned is the general absence of freedom to convert Ceylon currency into foreign currency for purposes of travel abroad. The exchange restrictions are such that the permission of the Exchange Controller must be had before money can be taken out of the country. This permission is not normally given except for special and very limited purposes. There is no freedom of conversion of currency for ordinary travel or for investment abroad or emigration. However, it would appear that such restrictions as there are in Ceylon are of a kind that are general, especially in developing countries, and cannot strictly be regarded as an infringement of the right to travel.

In December 1971 a fourth limiting factor came into existence. Legislation was passed that seriously affected the general right of citizens to travel abroad. Act Number 53 of 1971 not only purported to deal with the powers of the executive to issue, withhold, and renew passports but also gave the executive wide powers in relation to exit permits. Under this legislation the following broad position prevails:

1. Passports are issued and renewed at the discretion of the executive, and no refusal to issue or renew a passport can be questioned in any court of law.

2. The executive has discretion to cancel or suspend passports at any time or to restrict at any time the validity of passports in terms of duration or countries of travel. There is no prohibition against contesting the exercise of this discretion in the courts, though it can probably be questioned only on vary narrow grounds, such as a breach of faith.

3. In addition to having a passport, any citizen, in order to leave Ceylon, must have an exit permit, unless that citizen resided in a foreign country for a period of not less than three months immediately prior to the date of the coming into operation of the act and has come to Ceylon after that date. The issuance of exit permits is at the discretion of the executive. The exercise of this discretion can probably also be questioned in a court of law within the limits mentioned above.

4. Where the executive is of the opinion that a person is leaving Ceylon for the purpose of engaging in employment in any foreign country, it can make it a condition precedent to the issue or renewal of a passport or to the issuance of an exit permit that that person enter into an agreement to remit in foreign exchange such an amount, up to 10 percent of his or her total monthly emoluments, as the executive may determine. The exercise of the discretion to issue an exit permit can probably be questioned in a court of law within narrow limits such as breach of faith or error of law, but the exercise of the discretion to issue or renew a passport cannot be questioned.

5. A similar provision applies to the issue or renewal of a passport to a person employed in a foreign country. The exercise of this discretion cannot be questioned in a court of law.

6. Any person who refuses to enter into such an agreement, defaults in the performance of its obligations, or fails to perform obligations under Compulsory Public Service Act Number 70 of 1961 cannot be denied the issue or renewal of a passport good for six months or less that is solely for the purpose of returning to Ceylon.

The powers given under this legislation did not derogate from and were in addition to the powers of the executive under the emergency law and other laws. The prerogative powers relating to return to Ceylon of citizens and expulsion from Ceylon of citizens presumably remained untouched.

Position under the New Constitution

Under the 1948 Constitution there has been some, though not much, change. Section 18(1) of the Constitution states that every citizen shall have the right to freedom of movement. It is not clear whether this right pertains only to movement within the country or to travel abroad as well. It is arguable that the latter is the case.[4] There are, however, two constitutional limitations on the protection of this right. First, the validity of existing laws that may be in violation of this right is preserved.[5] Second, the right is subject to such restrictions as the law may prescribe in the interests of national unity and integrity, national security, national economy, public safety, public order, the protection of public health or morals, the protection of the rights and freedoms of others, or the principles of state policy set out in the Constitution.[6] This limitation more or less erodes the right of movement, particularly since the principles of state policy are broadly expressed.

It may be said that to some extent future legislation interfering with the citizen's right to a passport, right to leave the country, and right to return to the country is controlled, but the exact extent of this control cannot be accurately described and is rather limited. Also it may be said that the executive has no power in the absence of constitutional legislation to interfere with these rights. On the other hand, it is equally clear that the existing legislation curtailing these rights remains valid.

As for the right not to be expelled from the country, constitutional protection is given only against arrest and detention that is not in accordance with law, so that it is only to the extent that there is no express law providing for arrest or detention with a view to expulsion that the citizen could object to it. The right not to be expelled from the country as such is not protected as a fundamental right at all. Hence, there is nothing to prevent legislation that would provide for the expulsion of citizens. On the other hand, in the absence of such legislation, the presumption that exists under the common law in favor of the existence of the right not to be arrested with a view to expulsion would protect the citizen.

It is clear that the constitutional protection given to the citizen in regard to the right to a passport, the right to leave the country, the right to return to the country, and the right not to be expelled is minimal. The position prevailing under the legislation already in existence and valid is the same as that which prevailed under the previous constitution. This position may be described as follows:

Passports. The citizen now has a right to a passport in the absence of legislation, but this right has been curtailed by the legislation of December 1971, by which the issuance and renewal of passports is at the discretion of the executive. Exercise of this discretion cannot be questioned in a court of law. The executive also has the discretion to cancel or suspend passports at any time or to restrict at any time the duration or countries of travel. The exercise of this discretion can probably be questioned in a court of law, but only on very narrow grounds such as breach of faith. It is specifically provided that where the executive is of the opinion that a person is leaving Ceylon for the purpose of employment abroad, upon the issuance or renewal of a passport it could impose the condition that that citizen enter into an agreement to remit in foreign exchange whatever amount, up to 10 percent of his or her total monthly emoluments, as the executive may determine. Also, where a person is already employed abroad, a similar condition could be imposed upon renewal or issuance of a passport. The exercise of the discretion to issue or renew passports in these circumstances could not be questioned in a court of law. There is a right to a passport enabling the citizen to return to Ceylon, as described above.

Departure. In regard to the right to leave Ceylon, the executive has the discretion to prevent departure to the extent that any citizen must have an exit permit in order to leave unless that citizen had been residing in a foreign country for three months or more prior to the date of the act and had come to Ceylon after that date. The executive can issue the permit or not, at its discretion. The same regulations (described above) which would limit the issuance of a passport, also apply to exit permits. Under the present emergency legislation, every citizen leaving Ceylon must have an exit permit, which means that the executive may prevent any citizen from leaving Ceylon. The freedom of leaving the country is further restricted by the exchange restrictions described above.

Return. There is no legislation governing the right to enter or return to Ceylon except the regulation that a citizen must be issued a passport for the sole purpose of returning if the circumstances arise that are described above. Further, under common law the citizen probably has the right to enter or return as described in the section on return at the beginning of this chapter. There is no legislation on the lines of the Commonwealth immigration legislation in England. A citizen, but only a registered citizen, may lose the right to return to Ceylon if he or she is deprived of citizenship by ministerial order, as will be described below.

Expulsion. There is no legislation governing the right not to be expelled. This right is protected by the general law preventing arrests, except where there is legislation permitting it. (See the section on expulsion at the beginning of this chapter.)

Compatibility with International Law

It cannot be asserted strictly with confidence that there is a customary international law that definitely ensures human rights as such. However, it may be argued that since the promulgation of the Universal Declaration of Human Rights and also in view of the subsequent drafting of the International Covenants on Civil and Political Rights and the International Covenant on Economic, Social, and Cultural Rights and the influence of the practice engendered under the European Convention of Human Rights, some customary practice and body of judicial opinion concerning at least some human rights is being created, and this is at least in the process of developing customary international law, if it has not been created already. These precedents exist irrespective of the issue of enforcement.

If there is a body of law relating to human rights, the content of that law is probably accurately represented by the Universal Declaration of Human Rights and possibly by the substantive sections of the International Covenant on Civil and Political Rights and the International Covenant on Economic, Social, and Cultural Rights. The Universal Declaration of Human Rights describes the right to travel in very general terms. Article 13(2) asserts a right of the individual to leave any country and to return to his or her own country. The International Covenant on Civil and Political Rights is somewhat more specific in Article 12, but not adequately so. The right to leave any country can only be subject to restrictions provided by law that are necessary to protect national security, public order, public health or morals, or the rights and freedoms of others, and it can only be consistent with other rights recognized in the convention. The right to return cannot be denied arbitrarily. Perhaps the more limited right recognized in the covenant is a more realistic measure of any right that might be recognized.

Measured against the standards set in the covenant, the position in Ceylon in regard to the right of movement would seem to fall short of what is desirable. The wide discretion to issue passports and exit permits and to withdraw and renew passports as it exists in Ceylon law cannot be reconciled with the formulation of the right to freedom of movement in the covenant. Similarly, the discretion granted to make the issue or renewal of a passport and the issue of an exit permit conditional upon the remittance of foreign exchange is not compatible with human rights as envisaged in the covenant. The right to return seems to be adequately safeguarded, however, especially by the express provisions of the legislation making the issuance of a passport mandatory for that purpose, but the ministerial power to deprive a registered citizen of citizenship is in conflict with such a right.

The right not to be expelled is not specifically protected by the instruments on human rights. It is indirectly protected by the provisions on arbitrary arrest in Article 9 of the Declaration and of the Covenant and by the provisions on the right to return to one's own country. The law in Ceylon on the right not to be expelled does not, as it stands, conflict with what is presumably meant to be the content of the right in the international instruments.

Protection

Extent of Freedom of Activity Abroad. Some of the limitations on the Ceylon citizen's right to leave the country and on the right to travel discussed above also have the effect of interfering with freedom of activity abroad. These are as follows:

1. Exchange control prevents free export of currency for investment or subsistence abroad.

2. A citizen who is employed abroad may have to remit up to 10 percent of his or her earnings from employment to Ceylon as a result of the 1971 legislation. If the citizen has had to enter into an agreement to do this in order to obtain or renew his or her passport or to secure an exit permit and does not observe the terms of that agreement, that citizen would be committing a punishable offense.

3. As described above, a citizen employed abroad may have to enter into an agreement to remit 10 percent of his or her earnings while abroad to Ceylon as a condition of passport renewal. Since the citizen may be refused a passport because of refusal to enter into such an agreement and thus be liable to deportation from the country in which he or she is employed, the freedom of activity abroad of that individual is limited.

The following restrictions imposed by the 1948 Citizenship Act,[7] as amended, could have an effect, direct or indirect, on the citizen's freedom of activity abroad.

1. Insofar as there are restrictions on dual nationality, it means that a citizen who may want to acquire another nationality in order to benefit from the laws of another state in respect to business or employment is unable to do this while still a citizen of Ceylon.

2. A citizen of Ceylon by registration rather than descent cannot reside abroad for five consecutive years without losing his or her citizenship.[8]

3. A citizen of Ceylon by registration rather than descent may be declared by the minister to have lost his or her citizenship who, since the date of becoming a citizen of Ceylon has for a period of not less than two years been ordinarily resident in the foreign country of which he or she was a national or citizen at any time prior to that date and has not maintained a substantial connection with Ceylon.

4. Similarly, a citizen of Ceylon by registration rather than descent may be declared by the minister to have lost that citizenship if the minister is satisfied that that individual has conducted himself or herself in such a way that allowing that person to continue as a citizen of Ceylon is detrimental to the interests of Ceylon. There are no guidelines for this type of decision. It is likely that the decision could only be questioned in court on very narrow grounds, such as breach of faith.

There are certain grave offenses for which citizens can be punished in Ceylon even if they are committed abroad, such as exchange law violations.

Comparison with International Law. International instruments do not refer specifically to the rights of the citizen relating to activity abroad. Certainly insofar as control of activity abroad impinges on the right of the citizen to leave or return to the country it would come under the same strictures as the power to control the right to leave or return to one's own country. In the case of Ceylon one questionable provision may be that which permits the minister to deprive a citizen by registration of citizenship in certain circumstances. Those circumstances are, however, limited enough to prevent the legislation from being an interference with human rights. The provision that a citizen by registration may lose citizenship by residing abroad continuously for five years also is not so unreasonable as to be a violation of human rights.

Right to Diplomatic Protection. In the nineteenth century the British Foreign Office frequently expressed the opinion that a national had the "right" to protection.[9] On the other hand, the British courts have held that a national does not have the right to physical protection abroad and that if such protection is afforded by the executive the national involved can be requested to pay for it.[10] In view of the fact that foreign affairs are within the prerogative of the executive, it is doubtful whether diplomatic protection in respect to claims and other than physical protection would be regarded in British law as a legal right of a national. The Foreign Office language may refer to a moral right. In any event there are apparently many limitations on the national's "right" to protection as recognized by the Foreign Office, such as that naturalized citizens do not have this right, nor do nationals who have enlisted in foreign armies. The whole matter is probably one of policy for the executive. The position is probably that it could not be said that under British law the national has the right to require the state to intervene on his or her behalf, either by way of diplomatic representation or by the commendement of international judicial proceedings.

It is an interesting fact that even the European Convention on Human Rights does not recognize as a right of the national that the state intervene on his or her behalf, either by way of diplomatic representation or by the commencement of international judicial proceedings. The Universal Declaration and the UN covenants are also silent on the matter.

In the case of Ceylon there is no constitutional provision that recognizes such a right. The question is whether there is any statute or provision of the common law that does. There is no statute on record that governs the matter, so far as is known. Since the common law applicable in this regard is probably Btitish law, it would appear that such a right would not be recognized in Ceylon law. An argument based on a possible view of U.S. law would not be sound because such a view of U.S. law would be based on the fifth amendment of the constitution of the United States, which has no parallel in Ceylon law.

<u>The State and Compensation</u>. It has sometimes been argued in U.S. cases that the claimant state has complete discretion in the disposition of the proceeds of a claim and is not even obliged to hand the proceed on to the individual whose claim it has pressed, whether they are obtained as a result of international litigation or not.[11] There was a Swiss case in which a similar view was taken.[12] On the other hand the view has been expressed by an international tribunal that at least in international law the claimant state is under an obligation to make payment to the individual on whose behalf it pressed the claim.[13] The discrepancy may be explained as follows. Clearly in international law there may be such an obligation, which means that the state against which the claim was made can complain

if due payment has not been made. Whether the individual concerned can claim payment from his or her government, on the other hand, will depend on the municipal law of that particular state, which may or may not reflect the consequences of the international rule.

Whether U.S. law recognizes the right of U.S. nationals to payment by the government as a result of the protection given by the Fifth Amendment is a debatable question on which no final pronouncement has been made. On the other hand, in British law it has been held that where an individual claim to payment of proceeds by his or her government must be based on a treaty, that individual does not have a right to such payment in the absence of incorporation of the treaty as part of the law of the land by legislation.[14] However, it has also been held that customary international law is "part" of the law of the land.[15] What this means is not entirely clear. Could it be argued, as a consequence, that in the absence of a treaty as the basis of a claim the English courts should recognize the right of the individual to the proceeds of a claim recovered by the state? If this were so, it would appear to be anomalous that a claimant could not rely on a treaty but could rely on general international law before English courts. The answer probably lies in the fact that in this case the prerogative of the Crown takes precedence over customary international law. It is within the prerogative of the Crown that the executive should have complete freedom in handling foreign affairs,[16] and since the claim of the individual against the executive arises from protection afforded in relation to a foreign state, it cannot be enforced in the courts.

In Ceylon law there is no constitutional provision from which a right to the payment of compensation recovered on behalf of an individual may be derived, nor is there any statutory provision on the matter. Although there is no Crown in Ceylon any more, the common law in Ceylon will probably be regarded as being similar to that in the United Kingdom, on the basis that the state has the same prerogatives as the Crown had earlier. Because of this position, there can be no doubt that the state is not obligated to "top up" the compensation received where it is less than the loss suffered by the citizen.

The position in Ceylon is not in conflict with international law as understood today nor with any provisions of international instruments, such as the Universal Declaration of Human Rights and the international covenants.

The Responsibility of the State for Injury Induced by Its Own Conduct. No constitutional or statutory provision in the law of Ceylon gives the citizen a right to damages or compensation in case of injury abroad as a result of the conduct of the state, such as that engendered by British intervention in Egypt in 1956.

In common law a claim along these lines would probably have to be based on delictual or tortious liability. Even if there is such a substantive basis for a claim, in Ceylon the state cannot be sued in tort or in delict.[17] Thus there would be no question that in law the citizen could not enforce any such claim against the state.

There is no case in which a Ceylonese citizen has suffered injury abroad as a result of the conduct of the state of Ceylon, particularly in regard to rights as an alien in another state, nor as a result is there any case in which supplementary compensation has been provided. In any event the payment of supplementary compensation in such cases would be entirely at the discretion of the state.

The position in Ceylon is not contrary to international law or the provisions of relevant international instruments.

Waiver. There is no provision of the constitution or statute law in Ceylon that governs the right of the state to waive the claim of its citizens in respect to injury caused by foreign states. The position in common law would probably be the same as in England, where the position taken would be that the question of waiver of such claims would be within the prerogative of the Crown (executive) relating to foreign affairs. Further, the view might be taken that in international law the claim of the citizen is no more than the claim that citizen's state has against the foreign state, so that it is entirely appropriate that the state should be able to waive that claim.

In this case, too, international law and the relevant international instruments do not take a position on the obligations of states with regard to their nationals, with the result that the position in Ceylon is unassailable.

Special Kinds of Protection. There are no examples of special kinds of protection, as far as Ceylon is concerned. In any event the question of whether such protection could be given or not would be entirely within the discretion of the executive and would not be a matter of law, since it would be regarded as within the foreign affairs prerogative of the executive. On the other hand, were the extension of special protection to involve state expense, this could require legislative authorization, if an allocation had not already been made by legislation to cover it. There is no constitutional or legislative provision on the matter at present.

International law and the relevant international instruments have nothing to say about this aspect of the individual's rights.

The Individual as an Alien

Movement

Entry and Stay. In addition to a valid passport or travel document, all aliens are normally required to have visas before they enter Ceylon, with the exception of definite categories such as diplomats, experts, and technical assistants. These visas are to be issued at the discretion of the executive. The legislation governs the exercise of this discretion, insofar as it specifies in what circumstances visas may be granted. Apparently no alien is entitled to a visa. The two main categories of visas are "residence visas" and "visit visas."

According to the Immigrants and Emigrants Act of 1948 (as amended), visas must not be issued to the following categories of persons: those unable to support themselves; the mentally deficient; those who for medical reasons it is undesirable to admit into Ceylon, such as people suffering from contagious diseases; those who have been sentenced in foreign countries for any serious offense; those who have been deported from Ceylon; those whose previous histories or antecedents give reasonable grounds for apprehension that their presence in Ceylon would be dangerous or prejudicial to the best interests of Ceylon; and those whose names are included in the Suspect Index.

Residence visas may only be issued to the following persons, and then only for two years (or five years, with the approval of the minister) at a time: (1) persons for whom places have been reserved in approved educational institutions; (2) apprentices or trainees in approved firms or business undertakings or persons serving periods of apprenticeship with a view to qualifying themselves for admission to professions; (3) persons who wish to spend holidays in Ceylon; (4) persons who wish to conduct approved trades or businesses, provided the Controller of Immigration is satisfied that they have the necessary aptitude and means to conduct such trades or businesses with reasonable prospects of success and that their conduct of such trades or businesses will not be prejudicial to the interests of the permanent inhabitants of Ceylon; (5) persons having definite prospects of securing remunerative employment in approved trades or businesses, provided the Controller of Immigration is satisfied that they have the necessary aptitude to be so employed and that their employment in such trades or businesses will not be prejudicial to the interests of the permanent inhabitants of Ceylon. These visas are renewable and are valid for several entries.

International law does not require that aliens be admitted to a country as a matter of course. It is true that if the right to leave the country is to be effectively protected, there must be a corresponding right to enter some country other than one's own. However, the relevant international instruments do not go this far. In these circumstances the law of Ceylon is in conformity with international law and the relevant international instruments.

Voluntary Departure. There are no special requirements for a foreigner to depart voluntarily from Ceylon, except that that foreigner must have a valid passport or travel document, according to Section 35 of the Immigrants and Emigrants Act.

Involuntary Departure: Expulsion and Deportation. Removal from Ceylon may take place if a foreigner commits certain offenses under Section 28(5) of the Immigrants and Emigrants Act and the minister makes a removal order. Such an order is declared to be final and cannot be contested in any court.

Deportation from Ceylon may take place on a deportation order made by the minister if the person being deported is shown, by evidence that the minister may deem sufficient, to be (1) a person incapable of supporting himself and his dependents; (2) a person of unsound mind or a mental defective; (3) a prostitute, procurer, or person living on the prostitution of others; or (4) a person who it is undesirable to allow to remain in Ceylon for medical reasons. Deportation from Ceylon may likewise take place on a deportation order from the minister (1) if the deportee has been convicted in Ceylon or in any other country of an offense for which a sentence of imprisonment has been passed and has not received a free pardon and, by reason of the circumstances connected therewith, is deemed by the minister to be an undesirable person who ought not to be allowed to remain in Ceylon; (2) if the deportee has been sentenced outside Ceylon for an extradition crime within the meaning of the Extradition Acts, 1870 to 1906, of the United Kingdom; or (3) if the minister deems it to be conducive to the public interest to make a deportation order against that person. Such an order may be contested in court by requesting and being granted the right to be heard or it may be prevented from being made or carried out by way of injunction because of failure to observe the rules of natural justice in making the order, or because the minister acted beyond the capacity of his office.

On the face of it the law as it stands does not conflict with international law, which lays down an international minimum standard for the treatment of aliens and therefore prescribes that the rules relating to the departure, whether voluntary or involuntary, of aliens must not fall below this standard. The rules in Ceylon do not fall below this standard. The only cause for concern is that an abuse of power by the minister in making a removal order cannot be rectified by the courts, thus making it easy for the minister to abuse this power. Further, it is understood that in the making of removal or deportation orders the minister must conform to the other requirements of international law relating to the treatment of aliens, such as those pertaining to the time allowed for departure. Where the courts can be resorted to, it is arguable that the legislation will be construed in the light of international law.

Protection

Since there are no specific circumstances in which the state must afford protection, obviously it does not have to protect any category of non-nationals. There is also nothing in law that prevents the state from protecting non-nationals, if need be. International law does not have any specific requirements in this regard.

NATIONAL IMPLEMENTATION OF INTERNATIONAL RIGHTS AND DUTIES

There have been no decisions of Ceylon courts nor any relevant Ceylon legislation in the field of national implementation of international rights and duties. The Constitution is also not very helpful in regard to the question. On the general relationship between international law and the law of Ceylon, it may be supposed that the position adopted in the United Kingdom or a variation of it would be followed. It is unlikely that the U.S. position would be adopted, since it sometimes differs from the English because of constitutional provisions. Furthermore, principles of English public law would therefore be more applicable in Ceylon. For similar reasons it would be difficult to argue that the position prevailing in one of the continental countries should be adopted.

Without embarking on a theoretical discussion of doctrine,[18] it may be stated that the general position would therefore be (1) that treaties are not part of Ceylon law unless they are incorporated by statute;[19] (2) that customary international law is given recognition as part of the common law,[20] provided it does not contradict statute law[21] or the established doctrines or rules of common law, such as the Act of State doctrine;[22] (3) that statutes are interpreted so as to conform to customary international law in the absence of express provision or necessary intention to the contrary;[23] and (4) that it is not certain what recognition would be given to general principles of law as part of international law where relevant, but it may be supposed that such principles would be assimilated into customary international law.

In regard to the three specific areas to be discussed, there is little authority in Ceylon law, but the approach likely to be taken may be outlined as in the following section.

The Act of State Doctrine

This is no reference to the constitutional "act of state" doctrine of the common law, which is related to the Crown prerogative, and describes the doctrine that may be used to exclude legislative and executive acts of foreign states and governments from challenge by citizens. The doctrine really comes into operation in applying rules of private international law. In British private international law it becomes involved with the exclusion of foreign laws on grounds of public policy. The general rule is that where a foreign law is applicable the courts will apply any act of the foreign state or government that is valid in the legal system of that state. This is obvious enough not to require the support of authority. In European systems of law it is generally the rule that any domestic rule designed to protect the public welfare must prevail over an inconsistent foreign rule by reference to the doctrine of public policy (ordre public). In English law there is probably not so broad a principle for excluding the application of an otherwise applicable foreign law. However, there are cases that support the view that, in the event that a taking of alien property by a foreign state under a valid law of its own legal system is contrary to international law, English courts will not recognize and give effect to such an act.[24] Whether this is part of a broader rule of exclusion[25] is not in point here, but the rule that was propounded in a case decided in Aden will probably be recognized by English courts, especially in view of the dicta of Upjohn J. in the Re Helbert Wagg case, which stated a broader principle. This means, for example, that where property that belongs to an alien and is in a foreign state at the time has been nationalized with no provision at all being made for the payment of compensation, the English courts, if such property has come within their jurisdiction, will probably not recognize such nationalization as having had the effect of transferring title to the property to the foreign state, since the nationalization was contrary to international law. Thus English courts have considerable power to protect aliens whose property has been nationalized contrary to international law. However, there obviously are limits to the operation of this doctrine of exclusion of the effect of foreign law. For example, it normally would not apply if the property concerned were not physically within the jurisdiction of the British courts. Also, the concept of international law that a court would adopt on the question of nationalization would be that which the court concerned chose, since the subject is open to great controversy.

There is no precedent in Ceylon law on the question at all. Since the doctrine of nonrecognition of the effects of foreign acts of state is tied to private international law, it is very probable that the Ceylon courts will follow the English practice in principle, at least. Technically Ceylon private international law is Roman-Dutch law, but on this aspect of the matter there seems to be no specific Roman-Dutch law. The alternative is for the courts to follow the English doctrine or adopt the wider continental European practice in civil law systems. Apparently the continental practice is not consistent.[26] It may very well be argued that the position taken by the Japanese court in the Nissyo Maru case[27] ought to be adopted. There the court took the view that it would not examine the compatibility of the legislation with international law. The French rule, which is based on the "justice" of the expropriation is also somewhat different, but it is dependent on an interpretation of specific provisions of the Civil Code,[28] and it may not be possible to import it easily into Ceylon law.

If the Ceylon courts were to follow the British practice, and the chances are that they might, it would be the Ceylon courts' conception of international law that would probably be applied to the situation. This may very well differ from that of the English courts.

There are no constitutional or statutory provisions that govern the matter in Ceylon.

It is not at all clear that international law in general requires the courts of one state not to give effect to certain acts of other states because they are in conflict with international law, although the courts of some states may follow this practice. On the other hand, international law does not prohibit the practice.

Implementation of Decisions of International Organizations

As far as English law is concerned, the decisions of international organizations do not form a special category. They have to be dealt with in the same way as treaties or customary international law. The question is which category they may be assimilated into. Since in Ceylon there are no constitutional or statutory provisions governing the implementation of decisions of international organizations in general, the governing theory would probably be the same as in England.

It is doubtful whether such decisions would be regarded as analogous to customary international law. In any event, much would depend on whether the decisions were binding or only hortatory (recommendations). Binding decisions stem from the original convention constituting the international organization and at the most would probably be regarded as norms flowing from that convention. Hence they would normally be regarded as more like treaties than like customary norms. In the event that they do give rise to customary norms as a result of state practice, they would be treated like customary norms and would probably be regarded as part of both English and Ceylon law, if they did not conflict with established decisions and doctrines. Where they are assimilated into treaties in the absence of the evolution of customary norms, they would have to be enacted as law by the usual procedures before they could be enforced by the courts.

All this applies very forcefully to the Security Council decision on Namibia. This decision cannot have effect in the internal law of Ceylon unless it gains passage into legislation. The legal consequences flowing from this decision are in the same position. They can have no relevance for the internal law of Ceylon unless they are in some way enacted as law. It makes no difference that these consequences have been determined in an advisory opinion of the International Court of Justice. Apart from the fact that the advisory opinion has no binding effect, its statement of the law, which may have some effect in the international legal system, will not as such have a direct effect on the internal law of Ceylon. It will be regarded as flowing from the Security Council decision, which is on the same footing as a treaty.

The same reasoning applies to other binding decisions of international organizations. In the case of the International Civil Aviation Organization (ICAO), for instance, binding decisions as to standards made under some conventions do not become part of Ceylon law automatically. There is legislation governing the ICAO conventions that enables the executive to embody any such binding decisions as part of legal regulations. The binding nature of the decisions for the internal law of Ceylon stems from the parent statute and the regulations made under it. There is no similar legislation in Ceylon law governing the decisions of organs of the United Nations.

Special mention may be made of the Bretton Woods Agreement Act of 1950, which has the effect of imposing the duty of carrying out certain decisions of the International Monetary Fund and the International Bank for Reconstruction and Development. Section 4(1) of that act reads as follows:

> There shall be paid out of the Consolidated Fund of Ceylon -
>
> (a) all sums payable to the International Monetary Fund under paragraph (b) of

section 8 of Article IV of the Fund Agreement (which relates to changes in the par or foreign exchange value of currencies of members);

(b) all sums required for implementing the guarantee required by section 3 of Article XIII of the Fund Agreement, that is to say, a guarantee of the assets of that Fund against loss resulting from failure or default of the depository designated by the Government of Ceylon under the said Article;

(c) all sums required for the redemption of any notes or obligations created and issued to that Fund under this Act; and

(d) any compensation required to be paid to that Fund or to any member thereof under Schedule D of the Fund Agreement (which relates to the withdrawal of members from the Fund) or under Schedule E thereof (which relates to the liquidation of the Fund).

Section 6 of the Act states as follows:

> There shall be paid out of the Consolidated Fund of Ceylon -
>
> (a) all sums payable to the International Bank for Reconstruction and Development under section 9 of Article II of the Bank Agreement (which relates to changes in the par or foreign exchange value of currencies of members); and
>
> (b) all sums required for the redemption of any notes or obligations created and issued to that Bank under this Act.

The effect of these sections is to make the decisions of the International Monetary Fund and the International Bank for Reconstruction and Development relating to the payment of the sums referred to in those sections part of the law of Ceylon so that they impose duties as such according to the law of Ceylon.

As regards hortatory resolutions by organs of international organizations, such as those of the General Assembly relating to Rhodesia, these are not binding as such even in international law.

They may give rise to customary international law as a result of becoming state practice in some form or other (this will be a question related to general theory), in which case they will be part of Ceylon law to the same extent that customary international law is part of Ceylon law. Many binding decisions or recommendations by international organizations may meet with the objection that since they are within the foreign affairs prerogative of the executive they are not enforceable by the courts as such, even if they become part of customary international law. If they do not result in customary international law, then they are enforced in the Ceylon courts only if they are made part of Ceylon law by legislation. There is no legislation as such relating to the resolutions on Rhodesia and Namibia.

It may be mentioned here that there is some legislation in Ceylon that gives the executive the power to implement these decisions by reference to Ceylon law to some extent. Thus the Export and Import Control legislation could very well be used by the executive to enforce trade sanctions, by means of regulatory procedures. On the other hand, the initiative lies with the executive, who may decide not to take action through regulatory procedures.

Procedures Related to the Issuance of Certificates or Suggestions by the Executive in Connection with Litigation in National Courts

The whole question of executive certificates is wide open in Ceylon law. There is no specific constitutional or statutory provision on it. Such certificates are largely of evidential value and hence would strictly be governed by the Evidence Ordinance of Ceylon. However, this ordinance is silent on the point. It is generally the case that where the ordinance requires interpretation, British law is applicable. The same is the case where there is a lacuna. Hence, in the case of the executive certificate, British law would probably be applied.

In British law, proof of such international facts, such as diplomatic status, date of territorial cession, and recognition by the executive of a foreign state or government or the public character of its property, is by executive certificate.[29] Often there are mixed questions of law and fact in these certifications, such as when the executive certifies that it recognizes a sovereign state. There is here a determination that the state is sovereign, which is a question of law to be argued on the facts and a statement relating to recognition, which is a question of fact. Where an executive certificate is admitted by the courts, it is probably conclusive,[30] although there has been some difference of opinion on the matter. This is so even if it is based on inconsistent information and even when the court would not on the information have arrived at the same result.[31] On the other hand, where the certificate is ambiguous the court may independently examine the issue left unclear.[32] Similarly, where the executive refuses to certify, the court may make its own investigations and arrive at its own conclusions.[33] Where a certificate is produced by either of the parties, it is evidential, but the court does not in the absence of presentation have to call for a certificate, though it may.[34] There are also some limits on the relevance of a certificate, especially when it is clearly a case in which the rights and duties of citizens will be altered without legislation.[35]

It is clear that either the court or the litigant may ask for a certificate. On the other hand, it is doubtful whether the executive is under an obligation to supply one. In any event, such an obligation would not be effective, since the executive still could temporize and therefore throw the burden of ascertaining the facts on the courts and the burden of proof upon the litigant. Also the court is not under an obligation to seek a certificate. Where the litigant requests a certificate, it would really have to be produced at that stage in the proceedings at which the litigant is entitled to prove its case. On the other hand, if the court decides to ask for the certificate, there is no limitation on its right to make the request and use the certificate at any stage of the proceedings. Apparently it is not decided whether the executive can supply a certificate in a case on its own initiative and, if so, when it should do so. However, since executive intervention as such is unknown in British law, it is unlikely that the executive would enjoy this privilege. Where it appears as a friend to the court (amicus curiae), it is possible that it may have the right to supply a certificate, and possibly this would have to be done during the stage when evidence is being adduced.

The content of a certificate is entirely within the discretion of the executive. The question of who may make representations about the content of a certificate and when these representations may be made is a matter for the executive. This is not controlled by the courts. As far as is known there are no administrative rules or regulations governing the matter. It is likely that the executive would closely guard its privileges in regard to the content of certificates and would neither be influenced by others nor allow others to influence it.

Recognition and Nonrecognition

Clearly the view taken by a municipal court on the relevance of recognition can have an influence on individual rights as determined by that court. For example, the fact of recognition may affect the cognizance of the acts of foreign legislatures or executives. It may also determine rights flowing from the existence of situations such as a state of war.

Unfortunately, in Ceylon there are no decided cases governing the question of recognition. However, it is likely that the Ceylon courts will follow British practice or, perhaps, U.S. practice on the subject, unless they decide to strike out on their own and propound some novel theories, which is very unlikely. Some modifications may, however, be adapted from the practice of some civil law systems.

It is not proposed here to deal in detail with all the possible alternatives. However, a brief discussion of the possibilities before the Ceylon courts will be presented. There is also a short discussion of the attitude of the executive toward the whole question of recognition as exemplified in the China case, which is the only case in which the issue really came to the fore.[36]

Recognition and the Executive

The government of Ceylon accorded legal recognition to the People's Republic of China on 5 January 1950, simultaneously terminating recognition of and relations with the Chinese nationalist government.[37] It would seem that Ceylon was merely following the policy of the United Kingdom in recognizing Communist China. The United Kingdom in fact recognized the new regime on the same day and withdrew recognition from the Nationalist government, also on the same day.

The British line of action in this regard was influenced by many factors, apparently, as far as its diplomatic policy went. Among these factors the position of the United Kingdom in Hong Kong was undoubtedly important. Also relevant were the large commercial interests the United Kingdom had in mainland China and the possible reactions of Chinese populations in the areas of Southeast Asia, which at that time were controlled by the United Kingdom.

However, British recognition of the communist regime in China came at the time it did for two special reasons. One was the fact that in late December 1949 the Indian government had decided to recognize the new regime,[38] and the other was the recommendation of a conference of British diplomats held in Singapore, which had suggested that the communist regime should be recognized before the end of 1949 in order to prevent disturbances among the Chinese groups in Southeast Asia. Apparently, consultations on the matter had been going on between the United Kingdom, the Commonwealth, the United States, and other states since August 1949. Also the question had been discussed at a meeting of the Commonwealth High Commissioners in London, and the British decision to recognize Communist China had been known to the representatives of the Commonwealth states.[39] Thus, the weight of evidence leads to the conclusion that as far as the mechanics of the recognition of Communist China were concerned, Ceylon merely followed the lead of the United Kingdom.

Recognition of Communist China was clearly regarded as a case of recognizing a revolutionary government, by both the United Kingdom and Ceylon. It was not a question of recognizing a new state. Insofar as recognition was withdrawn from the nationalist government by both of these states, it was clear that the act of recognizing the communist government amounted to a declaration that the United Kingdom and Ceylon regarded the communist government as being the sole authority capable of representing the state of China in its international relations. In this connection it was equally clearly indicated that the two states did not regard the nationalist government as having any international legal status in regard to the representation of the state of China, which merely continued its existence irrespective of the revolution. By its acts of recognition of the communist government and of withdrawal of recognition from the nationalist government, Ceylon unequivocally took the position that the communist government alone could represent what had been, was, and now is the state of China.

From a legal point of view it would have been of interest to know definitely whether the act of recognition on the part of Ceylon was regarded as being merely declaratory or as constituting a status and whether the act was performed in pursuance of a legal duty to recognize or as a matter of political expediency. The act of recognition itself did not contain any declaration on either score about what it was intended to be. It may be safe to assume that, following British practice,[40] Ceylon was acting on a constitutive view of recognition, but this can be no more than an assumption. It would also seem that the test regarded as relevant in this case of recognition was that of effectiveness. That is to say, recognition was accorded primarily because the communist government was in fact capable of securing the habitual obedience of the bulk of the population in China. It was not dependent on any added requirement, such as that the Chinese government was willing to fulfill its international obligations, which seems to be a requirement insisted on by the United States in the matter of recognition in general.

As to the legal duty to recognize, once the factual requirement of effectiveness was satisfied, it is not quite clear whether the Ceylon government considered such a duty in its actions or whether it acted purely from a sense of political expediency. It is unlikely that in 1950 the Ceylon government would have turned its attention to that question at all, but it would seem that Ceylon did in fact rather mechanically follow the British example, as pointed out earlier. The question then naturally arises of whether the British act of recognition was governed by any sense of duty. As indicated, there have been many policy factors that may have influenced the British decision to recognize China at the particular time it did. However, Elihu Lauterpacht has expressed the opinion[41] that British practice in regard to recognition had earlier been based on the belief that there was a legal duty to recognize when the factual conditions necessary for establishing that a government was effective were satisfied. It is therefore possible that in spite of the numerous policy reasons that the United Kingdom may have had for granting recognition at the time, the action was primarily motivated by a conviction that there was a legal duty to recognize the communist government because it was the effective government of China.

Judicial Effects of Nonrecognition

There follows below a brief account of the broad positions taken in British, U.S., and civil law courts that could provide guidelines for the Ceylon courts.[42]

Sovereign Immunity. On this point there is general agreement that an unrecognized state or government cannot claim sovereign immunity.[43] This position, which is to the advantage of the individual, would probably be followed in Ceylon.

Legislative and Executive Acts under British Law. British law refuses to acknowledge the validity of the legislative acts of unrecognized governments. Authority, however, is deficient on the attitude a British court would take toward perfunctory legal acts carried out in the normal process of administration under the jurisdiction of the unrecognized government. There is no good reason for refusing the validity of such acts when they are carried out pursuant to a law that has been unaffected by the change of government, and it can be taken that a British court would not do so. The situation is different, however, when the act in question is authorized by a law enacted by the unrecognized government. A distinction could well be drawn between such enactments as create completely new law and those that merely apply, adjust, or alter existing law. This may be illustrated by the distinction between nationalizing legislation and legislation altering personal status, on the one hand, and administrative amendments to legislation relating to registration of land titles, the contracting of marriage, or the winding up of estates, on the other. It cannot be said, however, that British law has explored this distinction, and there is judicial statement to the effect that a British court must disregard all legislative, executive, and judicial acts done by persons appointed by the nonrecognized government because their appointments must be regarded as invalid.[44]

The following particular rules have emerged in the cases that have come before British courts: (1) Contracts made by unrecognized governments will not be enforced in British courts.[45] (2) Changes of nationality will be acknowledged only after recognition.[46] (3) Legislation winding up companies or otherwise altering their legal status will not be given cognizance. This question is illustrated by the topical example of nationalization.[47]

Although the general rule is that the laws of governments not recognized as de facto governments by the Crown "cannot be recognized by the court,"[48] the court may be directed in some circumstances by executive certificate to give effect to such laws.

The British conflict-of-laws rules on the capacity to marry and the formal validity of the marriage might direct the court to the law of a country under a regime unrecognized by the British government. If the validity of the marriage depends upon whether the legislation of the recognized or the unrecognized government is to decide the matter, the question of recognition or nonrecognition is directly raised. Is a British court obliged to solve the question in the same way as it would a question of title to property confiscated by the unrecognized government? I submit that it is not. The court, it may be predicted, will do its utmost to save the validity of the marriage while at the same time refusing cognizance to the law of the unrecognized government.[49]

Legislative and Executive Acts under U.S. Law. Initially the courts of the United States took the same attitude toward unrecognized governments as did the courts of Great Britain. Chief Justice John Marshall laid down the doctrine in Rose v. Himeley,[50] which was to govern U.S. judicial practice for a long period. Until recognition, he said, courts must consider the former state of affairs as unchanged, and they are not free to take a different view from that of the executive.

After the Civil War the courts of the United States had to determine what value should be attributed to acts of the Confederacy. Clearly it was impractical to invalidate every action taken legislatively or administratively by the Southern authorities during the period of secession; logic could not be permitted to bring about economic and legal chaos. As it happened, most private matters were governed by the laws of the constituent states, whose internal sovereignty had not been affected by their secession from the union, and the U.S. courts needed to go no further than to assert the continued supremacy of the Constitution in relation to their enactments. Only in a few instances was it necessary to pass upon the validity of Confederate as distinct from state legislation. The Supreme Court in Thorington v. Smith[51] admitted that although the Confederacy had not been a government even tacitly acknowledged by the United States, it had been "of paramount force," the distinguishing characteristic being that the military power exacted compulsory obedience in civil matters by private citizens. Private contracts expressed in Confederate currency were therefore valid as "transactions in the ordinary course of civil society." The status of the Confederacy, however, was principally determined by the concession to it of belligerent rights by the United States, as the Supreme Court made clear in Williams v. Bruffy,[52] in which it refused validity to a Confederate law sequestrating a union resident's property. The ordinary administration allowed to a belligerent occupant was validly carried out by Confederate officials even though "there was no validity in any legislation of the Confederate States."[53]

The decisive shift in U.S. law occurred after the Civil War with the development of the doctrine that foreign acts of state are beyond question in U.S. courts. The perfunctory governmental functions of even unrecognized governments fell into the category of acts of state. The problem presented by the unrecognized Soviet government was, however, somewhat different, in that the acts of state in question were hardly perfunctory but in fact highly abnormal. Among these was the wholesale seizure and confiscation of bank assets and private property and the dissolution of corporations. One of the difficulties involved in the characterization of these activities as acts of state was that the purported authority of the actors, even under the Soviet decrees, and the intention of the decrees themselves, was questionable.

The nonrecognition of the Soviet Union by the United States was protracted until 1933, and during that period of nonrecognition, events forced themselves with increasing pressure on the attention of the courts. The courts could, of course, have ignored them, as the British courts tended to do, allowing no juristic issues to arise out of mere facts. To have done so, however, would have been to expose U.S. nationals, in some of the situations that arose, to the danger of double recovery. It became politic to give such effect to Soviet acts as would conform with "justice" and "common sense."[54]

In Sokoloff v. National City Bank in 1924, Judge Cardozo thought that the Soviet, as a group that had "vindicated by the course of events its pretensions to sovereign power but which has forfeited by its conduct the privileges or immunities of sovereignty, may gain for its acts and decrees a validity quasi-governmental, if violence to fundamental principles of justice or to our own public policy might otherwise be done." The proposition would seem to allow, if the occasion were suitable, that U.S. courts might give full effect to Soviet acts, though they might not admit them to have the force of law, as Judge Benjamin Nathan Cardozo said in the Petrogradsky Bank case six years later, when he described a Russian nationalization decree as no more than "an exhibition of power" in the absence of U.S. recognition.[55] He would take cognizance of actual facts, but only the juridical implications of those facts in the law of the recognized government were to be drawn.

For example, the courts might take cognizance of the physical seizure of bullion, but they could not allow the conclusion that this constituted a divesting of title unless such a conclusion were drawn in the law of the recognized government. "Surrender to overwhelming force," Judge Cardozo had already explained in the Sokoloff case, "would excuse the loss or destruction of the subject of a bailment whether the force that overwhelmed was legitimate or lawless."[56] The court might equally take cognizance of the physical impossibility that shareholders of a nationalized company could reelect directors and might in consequence apply the law of the still-recognized government to determine that the company's life had expired, but it could not make that deduction from the nationalizing decree of the unrecognized government, which did no more than create the impossibility concerned.[57] The result of this distinction between facts and their legal interpretation was to perpetuate moribund Russian companies and thus to permit "fugitive ghosts endowed with extraterritorial immortality," as Judge Pound put it in the Salimoff case, to haunt the corridors of U.S. courts.

The subtleties of the Cardozo doctrine were impatiently brushed aside in Salimoff & Co. v. Standard Oil Co. of New York in 1933.[58] In appearance this decision eliminated altogether the distinction between recognized and unrecognized governments, and it thus went much further than the Stoddard case, which was concerned only about protecting the U.S. investor and trustee from the danger of double recovery.[59] From Stoddard the proposition was drawn in 1941 in the Denny case by the Third Circuit Court of Appeals in a technical case of admiralty law that acts of the authority actually administering the government will be treated as valid in its own territory and binding on its own nationals to the extent to which the rights of U.S. citizens or residents are not involved.[60] At this point the interest of U.S. courts is directed to the nature of the act done and its locus rather than to the authority doing it, and the case is presented rather more as one of "recognition" of foreign laws than as one of political recognition.

The onset of the cold war may have suggested to U.S. courts, however, that they had been a little precipitate in presenting the question merely as one of cognizance of the acts of state of unrecognized as well as of recognized governments. In 1947 the Supreme Court of New York County returned to the proposition that "the public policy of the State determines when the foreign legislation will apply,"[61] at least so far as recognition of the effects of that legislation upon property in the forum is concerned. The implications of the Salimoff decision were narrowed in The Maret,[62] where, after a lengthy review of the 1930 cases and the literature, the Third Circuit Court of Appeals held that there was no distinction between nonrecognition of a sovereign and nonrecognition of its decrees and that an executive policy of nonrecognition bars the judicial examination of the effects of the decrees of unrecognized governments.

The difficulty with The Maret and the cases that have followed it is that the subject matter was situated extraterritorially at the time that the relevant decrees purported to affect it. Since comity regulates the recognition by U.S. courts of foreign legislation operating in respect to property situated beyond the sovereign's physical control, these courts are free to adopt their own policy toward the matter. They have in fact refused to recognize the effect within the jurisdiction of the forum of legislation that was confiscatory when the executive has not directed them to do so. Since the executive attitude toward the annexation of the Baltic republics was indicated to be hostile in the certificates from the State Department, the courts had no difficulty in deciding that there was a lack of comity necessary for judicial enforcement of the decrees.

It does not follow that the courts are bound, in the absence of executive direction, to refuse recognition to the effect of foreign legislation upon property situated within the jurisdiction of the sovereign. In other words, the post-1942 cases may be concerned only with extraterritorial as distinct from intraterritorial takings of property; if so, the question of political nonrecognition is restricted to the establishment or otherwise of the necessary comity upon which to base enforcement of extraterritorial decrees. It remains to be seen whether the formula adopted in these cases is sufficiently broad to also encompass the Salimoff situation, in which the point was judicial cognizance of the intraterritorial operation of laws.

There has been little authority on the question of the effect of nonrecognition upon personal status when this is dependent upon the law of the unrecognized government. Presumably the United States will not give effect to a nationality law of the latter.[63] There seems to be no good reason, however, why questions of fact may not be proved by reference to the official documents of unrecognized governments. For example, a birth certificate stamped by an official of such a government may be received without any implications of recognition or nonrecognition.[64] In The Denny, authentication of a power of attorney made before a public officer of the Soviet Republic of Lithuania was admitted as evidence of proof of agency. There has been no U.S. decision on the validity of marriage or divorce brought about by the law of an unrecognized government, but the reference to private rights being independent of recognition that was made in the Banque de France v. Equitable Trust Co. of New York[65] would lead one to expect that the courts of the United States would take cognizance of it.

If executive hostility toward judicial cognizance is manifested, the courts will not even acknowledge perfunctory acts such as notarial certification by officials of the unrecognized government.[66] If the executive is indifferent with respect to the point, the courts will probably acknowledge them.[67]

Civil Law Courts. Continental courts have swayed between the Luther v. Sagor principle and the Salimoff principle. The latter has prevailed in Swiss courts, but the former, making cognizance dependent upon recognition, has been generally adhered to elsewhere. A notable exception is Italy, whose courts apply the legal system indicated by their conflict-of-laws rules regardless of whether the state or government from which it emanates has been recognized by Italy. The rule is one of de facto territoriality.

On the whole, civil law courts have made change of nationality dependent on recognition. To be consistent with the theory that legislation by unrecognized governments has no validity in the eyes of foreign courts, most civil law jurisdictions applied the czarist and not the Soviet laws of marriage and divorce during the period of nonrecognition of the Soviet Union. One French decision proceeded on exactly the same pattern as Luther v. Sagor, reversing after recognition the refusal of a divorce petition founded on Soviet law.[68] In Switzerland, however, it was held that Soviet divorce law could not be taken cognizance of so long as it did not offend public policy.[69] This proposition was followed by the Tribunal Civil at Brussels in 1951, which decided that since international law does not forbid annexation the court could take cognizance of contingencies of fact, and it applied Soviet law in a divorce suit between two Latvians.[70] In doing so it reversed the tendency of Belgian courts during the 1920s.

Most of the civil law cases that dealt with the effects of legislation of the unrecognized Soviet government turned rather more on the noncognizance of confiscation, as offensive to public policy, than on executive nonrecognition. In a few instances, however, the issue of nonrecognition was raised. It could hardly be expected that a uniform approach would manifest itself in a diversity of jurisdictions, and it is therefore surprising to discover a good deal of unanimity favoring the rule of British law. Most courts that were required to apply Russian law applied czarist and not Soviet rules, especially in matters of succession to movables and in respect to the legal status of ships.

Distinctions, however, were introduced in certain instances. The Belgian courts held that, so far as the intraterritorial effects of Soviet law were concerned, the annulment of partnership created an impossibility of performance, which was as effective before a Belgian as before a Soviet court.[71] Acts by an unrecognized government that are purely administrative and conform with the old law can be taken into account when applying the contract law.[72] These decisions tended toward the Cardozo doctrine, but in some jurisdictions, notably Switzerland and Holland, a rule closer to that in the Salimoff case has been applied.[73]

TREATIES AND THE INDIVIDUAL

There are many treaties to which Ceylon is a party, both bilateral and multilateral, that protect individual interests. As pointed out in the outlining note, one difficulty is to determine which treaties particularly relate to individual interests, since almost all treaties ultimately benefit the individual. There is also the problem of deciding which features of such treaties should be highlighted as being of importance. A selection, necessarily arbitrary, has been made below of those treaties that the writer considers of special relevance to the protection of individual interests, and an attempt will be made to discuss only matters of special interest in them.

Multilateral Treaties

The following fall into the category of multilateral treaties:

1. The numerous ILO conventions relating to labor that Ceylon has accepted and that have been given effect in the internal law of Ceylon. These conventions relate to such subjects as the minimum age for labor, minimum-wage fixing machinery, the right of association in agriculture, workmen's compensation, and abolition of slavery, to mention only a few. The acceptance of these conventions has led to the recognition of numerous rights, some of which may be regarded as human rights in relation to the worker.

2. The Geneva conventions on the laws of war, which cover a large number of rights of the individual in time of war.

3. Many conventions for which the UN Secretariat serves as a depository, such as those relating to genocide, narcotic drugs, dangerous drugs, traffic in persons, customs matters, road traffic, slavery, and the recognition and enforcement of foreign arbitral awards, among others.

These treaties are of general interest and need no special discussion here, since they do not pertain particularly to Ceylon.

Bilateral Treaties

There are many areas in which bilateral treaties of particular relevance to individual interests have been entered into by Ceylon. An analysis of the treaties in the major areas is given below.

Extradition

There are a few extradition treaties between Ceylon and other countries. A typical example is the one applicable between Ceylon and the United States, in which provision is made for extradition of persons accused of certain enumerated crimes.[74] There are certain safeguards relating to double jeopardy,[75] statutes of limitation,[76] the principle of speciality,[77] the making of a prima facie case,[78] the limitation on the period for the production of evidence,[79] and nonextradition for political offenses.[80] It is of interest that the provision on nonextradition for political offenses states that "a fugitive criminal shall not be surrendered if the crime or offense in respect of which his surrender is demanded is one of a political character, or if he proves that the requisition for his surrender has, in fact, been made with a view to try or punish him for a crime or offense of a political character." It is interesting that a political offense is not defined. Indeed, most extradition treaties between states do not define the concept where nonextradition for political offenses is provided for. This raises the difficult but very important question of what a political offense for purposes of extradition is; this concerns in particular mixed offenses, that is, offenses of an ordinary nature with political elements.[81]

Permanent Residence and Visas

There are two agreements concerning permanent residence and visas. One is between Ceylon and Canada[82] and one between Ceylon and the United States.[83] In the former, dated 24 April 1951, Canada agreed to authorize the taking of 50 Ceylon citizens per year for permanent residence, provided they complied with the Canadian

Immigrants Act. Provision was also made for the admission to Canada for permanent residence of husbands, wives, or unmarried children of Ceylon citizens resident in Canada, provided the settlement arrangements were satisfactory. In the latter the Ceylon government agreed to a scale of charges for nonimmigrant visas and to the issuance on a reciprocal basis of these visas for any number of journeys during the period of the validity of the visa. The former agreement affects the interests of Ceylon nationals, while the latter affects those of U.S. nationals.

External Debt

Ceylon was a party to an agreement relating to the repayment of the external debt of Germany in 1953. It dealt extensively with such debt in regard to modalities of payment, exchange rates, gold clauses, and other matters and set up machinery for the arbitration of disputes in relation to such debt.[84]

Merchant Shipping

An agreement signed in 1964 between Finland and Ceylon makes provision for the mutual recognition of tonnage certificates of merchant ships.[85]

Double Taxation

In 1969 Ceylon had agreements relating to double taxation with India,[86] Sweden,[87] the United Kingdom,[88] Denmark,[89] Norway,[90] and some other countries. Each of these treaties gives specific relief to persons who may be taxed by Ceylon and also the other party.

Trade

Trade agreements give certain rights and impose certain obligations upon the parties that may have a direct effect on individual interests. Some of the rights and obligations are stated in general terms, such as the right to purchase from or export to the other party certain specified goods. On the other hand, there may be more specific covenants that can directly affect individuals. Many clauses of this nature incorporate the most-favored-nation standard of treatment. Thus, in a trade agreement signed between Ceylon and Germany in 1955, it was stated that the issuance of import licenses should be on this basis.[91] In the Ceylon-Pakistan treaty of 1955, the same standard of treatment was incorporated in relation to customs duties and charges and other import facilities.[92] In some treaties the most-favored-nation standard is subject to certain limitations, such as those contained in Article 2(2) of the agreement between Ceylon and Yugoslavia in 1953, which were that the standard would not apply where there was a grant of (1) advantages to contiguous countries to facilitate frontier traffic; (2) advantages resulting from any customs union or preference or free trade area to which either party is or may become entitled; and (3) advantages accorded by virtue of a multilateral economic agreement relating to international commerce.[93]

Such provisions, and others in trade agreements that involve individual interests, are implemented by provisions of the local law that either grant the privileges or enable them to be granted by the executive. However, it is doubtful whether the local law gives the individual a right that is enforceable in municipal law. On the other hand, it is clear that the affected individual's state can claim a violation of the treaty, if it is a party to it.

Investment Protection

There are two treaties, one with the Federal Republic of Germany[94] and the other with the United States,[95] whereby the property of nationals of the contracting parties is protected against nationalization or expropriation. Other forms of protection are also accorded by these treaties. The two agreements are significantly different. In the case of the U.S. treaty the concern is with protecting the interests of the United States as guarantor of investments. The individual benefits insofar as the existence of the treaty enables him or her to secure a guarantee for an investment from the U.S. government. For the rest, the treaty itself regulates relations between the two governments. In the case of the FRG treaty, the protection is afforded directly to the investor. Not only is there protection in the case of expropriation or nationalization, but also, for example, protection enabling the repatriation of capital.

The relevant provisions of the latter treaty are reproduced below in detail:

Article 1

> Each Contracting Party shall in its territory promote as far as possible investments by nationals or companies of the other Contracting Party and endeavour to admit such investments in accordance with its legislation and regulations framed thereunder. It shall in any case accord such investments fair and equitable treatment.

Article 2

Neither Contracting Party shall, in its territory, subject investments owned by, or under the control of, nationals or companies of the other Contracting Party or any activities carried on in connection with such investments to any discriminatory treatment on the ground that ownership or control of the investment concerned is vested in nationals or companies of the latter Contracting Party, unless specific stipulations are made in the document of admission as provided in paragraph (b) of Protocol Number 2.

Article 3

(1) Investments by nationals or companies of either Contracting Party shall enjoy full protection as well as security in the territory of the other Contracting Party.

(2) Investments by nationals or companies of either Contracting Party shall not be expropriated in the territory of the other Contracting Party except for a public purpose and against full compensation. It shall be actually realisable, freely transferable, and shall be made without delay. Provision shall have been made in an appropriate manner at or prior to the time of expropriation for the determination and the giving of such compensation. The legality of any such expropriation and the amount of compensation shall be subject to review by due process of law.

(3) Nationals or companies of either Contracting Party whose investments suffer losses in the territory of the other Contracting Party owing to war or other armed conflict, revolution, a state of national emergency, or revolt, shall be accorded treatment no less favourable by such other Contracting Party than that Party accords to nationals or companies of any third State, as regards restitution, indemnification, compensation or other valuable consideration. Such payments shall be freely transferable.

Article 4

Either Contracting Party shall in respect of investments guarantee to nationals or companies of the other Contracting Party the free transfer of the capital, of the returns from it and, in the event of liquidation, of the proceeds from such liquidation.

Article 5

If either Contracting Party makes payment to any of its nationals or companies under a guarantee it has assumed in respect of an investment in the territory of the other Contracting Party, the latter Contracting Party shall, without prejudice to the rights of the former Contracting Party under Article 10, recognise the assignment, whether under a law or pursuant to a legal transaction, of any right or claim from such national or company to the former Contracting Party as well as the subrogation of that Contracting Party to any such right or claim, which that Contracting Party shall be entitled to assert on the same conditions and to the same extent as its predecessor in title. As regards the transfer of payments to be made to the Contracting Party concerned by virtue of such assignment, paragraphs 2 and 3 of Article 3 as well as Article 4 shall apply mutatis mutandis.

Article 6

(1) To the extent that those concerned have not made another arrangement admitted by the appropriate agencies of the Contracting Party in whose territory the investment is situated, transfers under paragraphs 2 or 3 of Article 3, under Article 4 or Article 5 shall be made without undue delay and at the rate of exchange effective for current transactions on the day the transfer is made.

(2) The rate of exchange effective for current transactions shall be based on the par value agreed with the International Monetary Fund and shall lie within the margins above or below parity admitted under section 3 of Article IV of the Articles of Agreement on the International Monetary Fund.

(3) If at the date of transfer no rate of exchange within the meaning of paragraph 2 above exists in respect of either Contracting Party, the official rate fixed by such Contracting Party for

its currency in relation to the US Dollar or to another freely convertible currency or to gold shall be applied. If no such rate has been fixed, the appropriate agencies of the Contracting Party in whose territory the investment is situated shall admit a rate of exchange that is fair and equitable.

Article 7

(1) If the legislation of either Contracting Party or international obligations existing at present or established hereafter between the Contracting Parties in addition to the present Treaty, contain a regulation, whether general or specific, entitling investments by nationals or companies of the other Contracting Party to a treatment more favourable than is provided for by the present Treaty, such regulation shall to the extent that it is more favourable prevail over the present Treaty.

(2) Either Contracting Party shall observe any other obligation it may have entered into with regard to investments in its territory by nationals or companies of the other Contracting Party.

Article 8

(1) The term "investment" shall comprise all categories of assets including all categories of rights and interests.

(2) The term "returns" shall mean the amounts derived from investments as profits or interest for a specified period.

(3) The term "nationals" shall mean
- (a) in respect to the Federal Republic of Germany, Germans within the meaning of the Basic Law for the Federal Republic of Germany;
- (b) in respect to Ceylon, a person who is a citizen of Ceylon according to its laws.

(4) The term "companies" shall mean
- (a) in respect to the Federal Republic of Germany, any juristic person as well as any commercial or other company or association with or without legal personality, having its seat in the territory of the Federal Republic of

Germany and lawfully existing consistent with legal provisions, irrespective of whether the liability of its partners, associates or members is limited or unlimited and whether or not its activities are directed at profit;

(b) in respect to Ceylon, any juristic person or any company or association, incorporated in the territory of Ceylon and lawfully existing in accordance with its legislation.

NOTES

1. 6 Journal of the International Commission of Jurists 319 (1965). This case is also reported in the Ceylon New Law Reports. See also Gooneratne v. Permanent Secretary, Ministry of Defense and External Affairs, ibid., at 320.

2. 10 International Comparative Law Quarterly 547 (1961).

3. The Public Security Ordinance.

4. Apparently the constitutionality of laws cannot be questioned in a court of law. Instead there is a procedure by which unconstitutional bills can be questioned before a special Constitutional Court and be prevented from becoming law. Constitution, §§ 54, 55.

5. Ibid., § 18(3).

6. Ibid., § 18(2).

7. No. 15 of 1948. See Parry, Nationality and Citizenship Laws 810 ff.

8. Certain categories of periods during which the person is abroad are excluded from the calculation.

9. See Parry, 5 British Digest of International Law 303 ff.

10. China Navigation Co., Ltd. v. Attorney-General, (1932) K.B. 197.

11. See Frelinghuysen v. United States ex rel. Key, 110 U.S. 63 (1884), and The Great Western Insurance Co. v. United States, 19 Ct. Cl. 206 (1884).

12. Heirs of Oswald v. Swiss Government, Ann. Dig., No. 18 (1925-26).

13. Administrative Decision No. V (United States v. Germany), 7 UN Rep. Int'l. Arb. Awards 119, at 152 (1924).

14. Civilian War Claimants' Association v. R., (1932) A.C. 14.

15. See O'Connell, 1 International Law (hereafter O'Connell, vol. 1) 54 (2nd ed., 1970).

16. See West Rand Central Gold Mining Co. v. R. (1904) 2 K.B. 391.

17. Attorney General v. Nadarajah (1956) 59 New Law Reports (Ceylon) 136.

18. See O'Connell, vol. 1, op. cit., at 49, and works there cited.

19. Following War Claimants' Association v. The King, (1932) A.C. 14.

20. Following Triquet v. Bath, (1764) 3 Burr. 1478.

21. Following Mortensen v. Peters, (1906) 14 Scots L.T.R. 227.

22. Following Chung Chi Chuen v. The King, (1929) A.C. 160. West Rand Central Gold Mining Co. v. The King, (1905) 2 K.B. 391.

23. The Annapolis, per Lushington, (1861) Lushington 295, at 266.

24. See Anglo-Iranian Oil Co. v. Jaffrate, (1953) 1 W.L.R. 246.

25. See Re Helbert Wagg & Co., Ltd., (1956) Ch. 323.

26. See O'Connell, 2 International Law (hereafter O'Connell, vol. 2) 507 ff. (2nd ed., 1970).

27. I.L.R. 305 (1942).

28. Art. 545.

29. See O'Connell, vol. 1, op. cit., 114 (2nd ed., 1970).

30. See Duff Development Corp. v. Government of Kelantan, (1924) A.C. 797.

31. R. v. Bottrill ex p. Kuerchenmeister (1947) K.B. 41.

32. See the Gdynia-Ameryka Line v. Boguslawski Case (1953) A.C. 11.

33. Luigi Monta of Genoa v. Cechofracht Co. Ltd., (1956) 2 Q.B. 552.

34. De Jager v. Attorney-General of Natal, (1907) A.C. 326.

35. Bank voor Handel en Scheepvaart N.V. v. Slatford, (1942) 1 Q.B. 243.

36. See C. F. Amerasinghe, "Legal Relations between Ceylon and the People's Republic of China," 16 Malaya Law Review 83-96 (July 1974).

37. 10 H.C. Deb. Coll. 1713-14 (1951).

38. For the Indian attitude see Misra, 55 Am. J. Int'l. L. 398 (1961).

39. On the whole question of British policy see Kokikara, in 2 South Asian Studies 103, at 107 ff. (1967).

40. See P. Lauterpacht, Recognition in International Law 97, 55 (1947).

41. Ibid., at 158 ff.

42. This is based on O'Connell, vol. 1, op. cit., 168-83.

43. See The Annette 105 (1919).

44. Carl Zeiss Stiftung v. Rayner and Keeler Ltd. (1967) 1 A.C. 853, at 907.

45. Taylor v. Barclay, (1828) 2 Simmons 213, at 221.

46. Murray v. Parkes, (1942) 2 K.B. 123.

47. Luther v. Sagor, (1921) 1 K.B. 456. However, a British court may interpret "government" in a private contract to mean "unrecognized government," as in the Luigi Monta Case, (1956) 2 Q.B. 552.

48. The Carl Zeiss Stiftung Case, (1967) 1 A.C. 853.

49. See Fokas v. Fokas, (1952) S.A.S.R. 152 and Kochanski v. Kochanska, (1958) 147.

50. 4 Cranch 241 (1808).

51. 8 Wall. 1 (1869).

52. 96 U.S. 176 (1878).

53. Ibid., at 192.

54. 239 N.Y. 158, at 165 (1924).

55. 253 N.Y. 23 (1930).

56. 239 N.Y. 158, at 165 (1924).

57. Banque de France v. Equitable Trust Co. of New York, 33 F. 2d 202 (1929).

58. N.Y. 262 (1933).
59. N.Y. 149 (1925).
60. 40 F. Supp. 92 (1942).
61. A/S Marilaid & Co. Case, 71 N.Y.S. 2d 377 (1947).
62. 145 F. 2d 431 (1944).
63. The Kolemdjija Case, 155 Minn. 176 (1923).
64. The Werenjchik Case, 229 App. Div. 36 (1930).
65. 33 F. 2d 202 (1929).
66. See Re Luk's Estate, 256 N.Y.S. 2d 194 (1965).
67. See Upright's Case, 231 N.Y.S. 2d 417 (1961).
68. Chiger v. Chiger, Ann. Dig. No. 18 (1925-26).
69. The Tcherniak Case, Ann. Dig. No. 39 (1927-28).
70. The Pulenciks Case, I.L.R., No. 20 (1951).
71. The de Reademaker Case, Ann. Dig., No. 46 (1927-28).
72. The Paul Tchoureff Case, Ann. Dig., No. 34 (1924-27).
73. Switzerland: The Schinz Case, Ann. Dig., No. 23 (1924-26); Holland: Re Nix, I.L.R., No. 69 (1951).
74. 163 L.N.T.S. 59, Arts. 1, 3.
75. Ibid., Art. 4.
76. Ibid., Art. 5.
77. Ibid., Art. 7.
78. Ibid., Art. 9.
79. Ibid., Art. 11.
80. Ibid., Art. 12.
81. See the discussion of the problem in Amerasinghe, "Definition of Political Offences in the Law of Extradition," Studies in International Law (1969), Chapter 4, pp. 164-202.
82. 248 U.N.T.S. 101.
83. 280 U.N.T.S. 35.
84. 333 U.N.T.S. 3, Art. 28 ff.
85. 492 U.N.T.S. 287.
86. 315 U.N.T.S. 71.
87. 315 U.N.T.S. 85.
88. 337 U.N.T.S. 78.
89. 486 U.N.T.S. 299.
90. 559 U.N.T.S. 24.
91. 369 U.N.T.S. 58.
92. 286 U.N.T.S. 16.
93. 337 U.N.T.S. 104.
94. 1963. Not published in U.N.T.S.
95. 586 U.N.T.S. 91.

CHAPTER

16

SWITZERLAND

Lucius Caflisch

This chapter will briefly describe Swiss legislation and practice pertaining to individual rights and the state in foreign affairs, in accordance with the general scheme of this book. Some important topics, such as nationality, extradition, asylum, and admission and disabilities of aliens, are excluded from that scheme, but I shall take the liberty of dealing briefly with some aspects of these questions because they are of considerable interest to Switzerland.

This report is based on Swiss legislation and on the practice of the Swiss legislative, governmental, and judicial authorities. Particular attention has been paid to Swiss practice since 1967.[1]

The federal executive authority of Switzerland is vested in the Federal Council, a central government composed of seven members or Federal Councillors, that is ministers. Each of the seven members of the government heads a federal department or ministry; thus the federal ministry of justice is called the Federal Department of Justice and Police, while the federal foreign ministry is named the Federal Political Department. The Swiss Parliament consists of a lower chamber (National Council) and an upper chamber (Council of State); the two chambers make up the Federal Assembly. The Swiss judicial system is headed by the Federal Tribunal, hereafter referred to as the Swiss Supreme Court.

The word "decree" as used in this chapter corresponds to the French word arrêté, "regulations" is used for règlements, and "ordinance" for ordonnance. I made most of the translations of texts into English myself.[2]

Reviewed and revised by the author in 1975.

THE INDIVIDUAL

The Individual as a National

The Status of Swiss Nationals

There is a preliminary question that deserves some attention. What treatment is extended by Swiss law and practice to persons vested with Swiss as well as with one or several foreign nationalities?[3]

According to the Swiss Supreme Court, the individuals in question must be treated as Swiss citizens,[4] except in the following circumstances:

1. They will as a rule be denied diplomatic protection in dealing with their other national state(s), especially if they reside in the territory of the latter.[5]

2. They will be treated as aliens if conventional rules so provide. See, for instance, the treaties concluded by Switzerland with the United States, France, and Colombia pertaining to the military obligations of dual nationals.[6]

3. Their treatment will differ from that extended to persons who are vested exclusively with Swiss nationality if a rule of Swiss law specifically so provides. The Military Criminal Code, for instance, states that a Swiss national cannot be punished for having served in the army of a foreign country if that person is also a national of that country and resides on its territory.[7]

4. Further exceptions to the rule described above can be found in judicial decisions.[8]

In conclusion, it may thus be said that dual or multiple nationals possessing Swiss nationality are treated as Swiss nationals except in the exceptional circumstances listed above, where the "active" or "dominant" foreign nationality takes precedence.

Movement

Passports. In matters of freedom of movement, as well as in other fields, no distinction is made between ordinary citizens and persons who have acquired Swiss nationality through naturalization.[9]

The (federal) regulations relating to passports of 19 July 1959[10] contain two basic rules. Swiss passports are issued to Swiss citizens only, and in principle every Swiss citizen is entitled to obtain a Swiss passport or a prolongation thereof. This right flows from Article 45 of the Swiss Constitution, which grants freedom of establishment to Swiss citizens.[11] Contrary to the practice of certain states, the validity of Swiss passports appears to be unlimited ratione loci.[12] However, the basic rules outlined above do have some exceptions.

The issuance or prolongation of a Swiss passport can be refused in the following cases.

1. If the parents or guardian of a minor or any person under guardianship oppose the issuance of a passport or its prolongation.

2. If the issuance of a passport to a particular person is opposed by the local authority that is competent to decide on matters of residence. In cases in which the applicant resides abroad, such opposition must be validated by the Police Division of the Federal Ministry of Justice.

3. If proceedings are pending against the applicant under military criminal law or if the applicant has already been sentenced in absentia as a result of such proceedings. Decisions under this heading are within the competence of the Police Division of the Federal Ministry of Justice, which proceeds in consultation with the competent authorities of the Swiss army.

4. If the applicant has not been granted leave to go abroad by the competent authorities of the Swiss army or has failed to meet financial obligations toward the latter (nonpayment of the military exemption tax).

Under Article 10 of the federal regulations, valid passports can be withdrawn under the following circumstances:

1. If the bearer's parents or guardian have withdrawn their consent to his carrying a passport;

2. If criminal proceedings are pending against the bearer of the passport or if the bearer has already been sentenced and if extradition has not been, or cannot be, requested. If the bearer of the passport is abroad, the decision of withdrawal will be taken by the Police Division of the Federal Ministry of Justice after consultation with the authorities that are competent to try the case or to carry out the sentence.

Under Article 11, in certain circumstances valid passports must be withdrawn, especially if the bearer already holds another Swiss passport or has lost his or her Swiss nationality. The other grounds are the obtaining of a passport without right, illegal modification of a passport, the presence of unofficial inscriptions, and damage to the passport that makes it unusable.

If a passport is refused or withdrawn according to the regulations in Article 10, a short-term travel document may be issued according to the regulations in Article 6. This document will enable the bearer to return to Switzerland, or its validity ratione loci will be limited to the bearer's foreign country of residence. Such a short-term passport is also issued in the cases covered by Article 11 except if there is another passport or if nationality is terminated.

Under Articles 12 and 13, passports are issued by the applicant's canton of residence and by Swiss embassies, legations, and consultates. Under Article 17 (1), the decisions of these authorities may be challenged before the Police Division of the Federal Ministry of Justice, on condition that the cantonal remedies have been exhausted. The decision of the Police Division may, in turn be reviewed by the Swiss Supreme Court, acting as the country's highest administrative jurisdiction.[13]

Departure. As noted earlier, in principle every Swiss citizen is free to leave his or her country and is thus entitled to a passport.[14] These rights are derived from Article 45 of the Constitution, which grants freedom of establishment.[15]

The right to leave the country is not, of course, unlimited. First, the rules on passports summarized above must be borne in mind. Second, the right of departure is denied to persons who are under penal detention, who are being actively sought by the police for criminal offenses, or who have failed to obtain leave to go abroad from the competent authorities of the Swiss army. On the contary, nonpayment of taxes does not affect the citizen's right of departure.[16] However, as explained above, the granting of a passport may be refused for nonpayment of the military exemption tax. Such nonpayment also leads to refusal of a leave to go abroad by the military authorities, which renders any departure illegal.

Return. Because Article 45 of the Constitution grants freedom of establishment to Swiss citizens, the latter may return to their home country whenever they choose.[17] This rule is consonant with a norm of general international law under which states have to admit their own nationals to their territory, at least when they are no longer allowed to remain on the territory of other states.[18]

Expulsion. Despite an early precedent to the contrary,[19] Swiss citizens may not be expelled or banished from their own country. Articles 44(1) and 70 of the Swiss Constitution bear out this assertion,[20] which is, moreover, confirmed by writers.[21] Swiss nationals also cannot be extradited to foreign countries.[22]

One might ask, however, whether these rules also cover dual or multiple nationals. In the absence of evidence to the contrary, the general principle according to which dual or multiple nationals endowed with Swiss nationality are to be treated as Swiss citizens (see above) should apply. Thus the answer to this question would seem to be in the affirmative.

Protection

Extent of Freedom of Activity Abroad. Certain matters mentioned in the general scheme of this book can be disposed of summarily. I am not aware of any significant financial or economic control exercised by the Swiss state over the activities of its citizens abroad. To the best of my knowledge, there are no economic controls in relation to either export or repatriation of capital, nor does Swiss antitrust legislation appear to have raised any problems of a transnational character.[23]

Swiss law seems to attach no negative effects to the participation of Swiss citizens in foreign elections. The Federal Law on Acquisition and Loss of Swiss Nationality of 29 September 1953[24] nowhere states that participation in foreign elections may entail the loss of Swiss nationality. If it provided otherwise, a great number of Swiss citizens who are also vested with another nationality would be deprived of their Swiss citizenship.

There are, however, fields in which Swiss citizens abroad are subject to some control. Apart from the fact that certain acts committed against Switzerland by foreigners or Swiss nationals abroad may entail penal sanctions under Swiss criminal law,[25] behavior causing an important prejudice to the interests or the reputation of Switzerland--and this general formula may encompass more than the criminal conduct that has just been referred to--may deprive its author of Swiss nationality, provided he or she also possesses another nationality. Decisions in this matter, which is governed by Article 48 of the 1953 Federal Law on Acquisition and Loss of Swiss Nationality, are within the competence of the Federal Ministry of Justice. They may, however, be submitted for review to the Swiss Supreme Court, acting as the country's highest administrative jurisdiction.[26]

The Swiss state also exercises some control over its male citizens in army matters. Not taking into account the military status of dual nationals under bilateral treaties (see above), the situation can be described as follows. Persons who possess only Swiss nationality and who serve in a foreign army in peacetime are liable to imprisonment under Article 94 of the Military Criminal Code of 13 June 1927.[27] A Swiss national who serves in the armed forces of his or her second national state, on the contrary, is not punishable, provided he or she resides in that second state. The application of this provision has caused severe hardship to Swiss citizens residing in foreign countries that, unlike Switzerland, do not make service in the armed forces dependent upon citizenship.[28]

A further question is whether and to what extent Swiss citizens residing abroad are favored or discriminated against in their home countries.[29] This will be briefly considered because it has lately aroused some interest and discussion in Switzerland.

As a rule the rights of Swiss citizens residing abroad are identical with those enjoyed by Swiss nationals residing in their home countries.[30] Thus Swiss citizens abroad are granted the same individual rights and freedoms as Swiss citizens residing in Switzerland, except, of course, if these rights or freedoms presuppose the existence of a permanent residence in Switzerland.[31] They partake in particular of the freedom of establishment granted by Article 45 of the Swiss Constitution which implies the right to return to Switzerland at all times (see above), and they are in principle entitled to receive diplomatic protection.[32]

In some respects Swiss citizens abroad enjoy preferential treatment. In peacetime they are under no obligation to serve in the Swiss army.[33] They may of course do so voluntarily, at least if they fulfill certain conditions, in particular that of not also possessing the nationalities of their states of residence.[34] Unlike Swiss citizens who reside in their home country and who are exempted from duty on medical or other grounds, Swiss nationals abroad no longer have to pay an exemption tax, except under certain circumstances.[35]

In comparison with Swiss citizens residing in Switzerland, Swiss nationals abroad suffer, or have suffered, from discriminatory treatment affecting their exercise of political rights and acquisition of real estate in Switzerland.

In Switzerland political rights can be exercised only by Swiss nationals who reside permanently in their home country. This rule, which had hitherto been dictated by the text of Article 43 (1) of the Swiss Constitution,[36] was made amenable to change by the inclusion, on 25 March 1966, of a new Article 45 ff. into the Constitution. So far no change has occurred.[37]

Federal legislation enacted in 1961[38] has made the acquisition of real estate by persons having their permanent residence abroad --thus including Swiss nationals abroad--dependent upon a permit. This permit is to be issued by the authorities of the canton on whose territory the real estate to be acquired is located. The original objective of this legislation was to prevent the sale of real estate in Switzerland to foreign purchasers. Since Switzerland has concluded numerous treaties of establishment prescribing national treatment, it has proved impossible to make the new regulations applicable to foreigners only,[39] and hence the test of nationality had to be abandoned in favor of that of permanent residence. This solution resulted in the above-mentioned discrimination, not only against aliens residing outside Switzerland, but also against Swiss nationals residing abroad. In fact, however, the discrimination thus established against Swiss citizens residing abroad was circumvented by granting the required permit almost automatically.[40] The text enacted in 1961 was amended in 1965, and the requirement of a permit abolished for natural persons who are entitled to take up permanent residence in Switzerland.[41] This amendment was, of course, intended to mainly benefit Swiss nationals residing abroad.[42]

The Right to Diplomatic Protection. One does not have to be a dualist to concede that the question of the alleged right to diplomatic protection, in the broadest sense of the term,[43] has two facets, one pertaining to international, the other to domestic law.

That individuals have no right to diplomatic protection on the international level is beyond doubt.[44] The reason underlying this rule is simple. Only subjects of international law are capable of enjoying rights on the international level, and individuals (or companies) do not as a rule possess such a capacity. Or, to frame the same idea somewhat differently and more correctly, a person or entity is a subject of international law only if and inasmuch as that person or entity is endowed with rights and/or obligations that are directly enforceable on the international level. Clearly international law has not yet, generally speaking, endowed private persons with such rights and duties. Otherwise the institution of diplomatic protection would already have become superfluous and hence obsolete, which is obviously far from being the case.

These points are brought out clearly by the practice of Swiss governmental[45] and judicial[46] authorities as well as by Swiss writers.[47] In a note prepared by the Swiss Foreign Ministry on the question of whether Swiss citizens have a right to Swiss diplomatic protection, for instance, it was asserted that no such right exists under international law because the problem under consideration pertains to "the relationship between a State and its subject. By its very nature," continued the note, "such a relationship does not fall within the ambit of international law, which primarily governs intercourse between States." The note goes on to say that this would be true even if the state were bound to afford protection to its national under its own municipal law, "for as a rule, international law confers rights and duties upon States alone."[48]

Similar principles were proclaimed by the Swiss Supreme Court in the Oswald and Gschwind cases.[49] In the Oswald case, the following statement may be of interest:

> A State presenting a claim to another State on account of a boundary violation does so in its own right, which flows from the unlawful violation of its territorial sovereignty. This is in no way

> contradicted by the fact that the claim may also benefit private persons who have suffered an injury through the boundary violation, and the claimant State does not become an agent of the persons thus injured, even if its intercession was in fact due to their representations or complaints. The formulation of the claim against the foreign State as well as its continuation and its scope must remain within the discretion of the State. Political considerations, in particular the claimant State's relations with the foreign State in other fields, may justify the total or partial abandonment of a claim for damages based on the boundary violation without thereby creating a liability of the claimant State towards the persons attached to its territory.[50]

It could be argued, however, that the present instance is not one of genuine diplomatic protection because it pertains to a boundary violation and because in such cases the state is primarily injured in its own right rather than in the rights of its nationals. Although this argument may be perfectly valid in itself, the more recent judgment in the Gschwind case reveals that the Swiss Supreme Court also applies these principles in genuine cases of diplomatic protection. Indeed, in the Gschwind case the court observed as follows:

> If a Swiss subject alleges that he has suffered damage as the result of a breach of international law, and applies to the Federal Council for intercession with the foreign State and for steps to be taken with a view to obtaining compensation, such application can only have the object or drawing the attention of the federal authority to the case and of inducing it to examine the matter.[51]

Writers are in agreement with these principles.[52]

More debatable, and indeed more debated, is the question of whether there exists a right to diplomatic protection on the Swiss domestic level. So far the practice of Swiss administrative and judicial authorities has answered this question in the negative.[53] Writers share this view, at least insofar as the law is enforced. Thus Aubert expresses the opinion that Swiss citizens have no right to diplomatic protection. The competent authorities are free to choose the measures of protection they consider adequate or even to deny protection if such a course seems politically advisable.[54] This point of view appears to be correct, since present-day Swiss legislation affords no basis for individual claims to diplomatic protection.

It could be argued, however, that such claims could be based on Article 102 (8) of the Swiss Constitution, which provides that the Federal Council watches over the interests of the Confederation abroad and has general charge of foreign affairs.[55] This formula obviously includes matters of diplomatic protection, but it is equally obvious that in cases in which such protection would run counter to the general interest of the state, it cannot be granted. If, on the contrary, "the general interest is consonant with the interest of the individual, protection will be granted as a rule. This by no means implies, however, that the individual acquires a right to such protection."[56]

Further arguments in favor of an individual's right to diplomatic protection have been drawn from Article 6 of the Federal Law on Naturalization of Aliens and Renunciation of Swiss Nationality of 25 June 1903[57] and from Article 36 of the Consular Regulations of 26 October 1923.[58] These arguments have become obsolete as a result of the abrogation of both provisions.

The Federal Law on Acquisition and Loss of Swiss Nationality of 29 September 1953[59] contains no provision that is relevant to the context of diplomatic protection. The same cannot, however, be said of the Consular Regulations of 24 November 1967,[60] which are based on Articles 45 bis and 102 (8) of the Swiss Constitution.[61] (See above for the text of Article 102.) Article 16 of these new regulations sets forth the following rules:

1. If an individual cannot be reasonably expected to take care of his own interests, the Swiss diplomatic and consular offices will assist him and, if necessary, provide him with counsel before local courts.

2. The Swiss Foreign Ministry will issue instructions concerning the assistance to individuals and companies vested with dual nationality.

3. If Swiss diplomatic and consular offices are informed that Swiss interests are being threatened because their owners are incapable of looking after them they shall endeavor to do so in their place.

4. Swiss diplomatic and consular offices shall refuse to intervene or to limit their actions if such intervention might be prejudicial to the general interests of the Confederation, or if the person concerned has violated his elementary duties as a Swiss citizen, or if that person, being a Swiss national residing abroad, has failed to register with the competent Swiss diplomatic or consular office. These limitations do not, however, apply when the life of the individual is in danger or when he is threatened by bodily harm.[62]

This last provision could in itself be read to imply that, if the limitations mentioned do not apply and if the general interest of the state is parallel to that of the individual, the latter is entitled to protection.

The incorrectness of this interpretation is, however, shown by the fact the claim to diplomatic protection, if it existed, would not be enforceable under Swiss law. Under Article 100 (a) of the Law on the Judiciary,[63] matters of diplomatic protection can never be brought before the Supreme Court acting as the country's highest administrative jurisdiction.[64] A decision refusing diplomatic protection taken by the Federal Council, as any other decision of that authority, is subject to no review whatsoever. If the decision emanates from the Foreign Ministry, it can of course be reviewed by the Federal Council through the normal hierarchical procedure,[65] but not by the Supreme Court.

In 1959, Doehring drew attention to the change that might result from the enactment of the Federal Law on Liability of the Swiss Confederation, the Members of its Authorities and its Functionaries.[66] This law was adopted on 14 March 1958.[67] Unlike the old law on the same matter,[68] Article 3 (1) of the 1958 law makes the confederation civilly liable for the unlawful behavior of its agents. This liability would seem to extend to the conduct of foreign relations, including matters of diplomatic protection. It would seem further that under Article 10 of the new Law on Liability, read in conjunction with Article 116 of the Law on the Judiciary,[69] claims against the confederation founded on the unlawful behavior of its agents, including claims for damages caused by the refusal of diplomatic protection, could theoretically be addressed to the Supreme Court by means of a direct administrative claim (action de droit administratif). However, as pointed out by Grisel,[70] such a claim would be practically useless. Pursuant to Article 3 (1) of the 1958 law, liability on the part of the state can only arise if the conduct of its agents was "unlawful." Such unlawfulness will be difficult to establish in matters of diplomatic protection because the text (see above) is so elastic as to give the competent authorities of the confederation almost unlimited discretion in this field.

Recent efforts to insert a right to diplomatic protection into the Swiss Constitution after the manner of the Weimar Constitution[71] have so far been unsuccessful. Thus the rules summarized in the note of the Foreign Ministry mentioned earlier would appear to remain applicable. They read as follows:

> The decision on whether a person will be granted diplomatic and consular protection would be left to the discretion of the Federal Council or of the Swiss Foreign Ministry. For it must be examined in each case whether an intervention would be

> consonant with the general interest of the State and whether the claim is founded under the rules of international law. As it is impossible to identify in advance the situations in which these conditions are deemed to be met, such determination must be left in each case to the discretion of the authorities entrusted with the conduct of Swiss foreign relations.[72]

The State and Compensation. As explained above, the Swiss state is under no obligation to endorse the claims of its nationals on the international level. It follows that Switzerland may put forward only part of the claim of one of its nationals and accept any settlement it considers satisfactory. The accuracy of this statement is borne out by the numerous lump-sum agreements concluded by Switzerland[73] and by the internal legislation pertaining to the distribution of the lump sums obtained from foreign states.

The lump-sum agreements concluded by Switzerland are administered on the domestic level by a Nationalisation Claims Commission.[74] Article 18 of an ordinance relating to this commission[75] provides that the latter's initial awards, which are based on the full injury sustained by the individual claimant, may be proportionally reduced later on, in order to prevent the total of the sum attributed from exceeding the lump sum allocated to Switzerland under the applicable international agreement.[76] Appeals against awards of the Nationalisation Claims Commission are heard by a board of review.[77] Since 1 October 1969, decisions of the board of review have in turn been reviewable by the Supreme Court under Article 98 (e) of the Law on the Judiciary.[78] By way of conclusion, it may therefore be stated that the Swiss state is free to accept lump-sum settlements and that it is under no obligation to "top up" insufficient indemnities received under such settlements.

It remains to be seen whether the indemnity obtained by the state must be paid over to the injured individual. This question arose in the *Oswald* case,[79] the factual context of which was, however, somewhat peculiar. A boundary violation committed by Italy on the Italian-Swiss border resulted in the wounding and subsequent death of one Oswald, a Swiss soldier. Under Swiss law both Oswald and his survivors owned direct claims only against the Swiss Military Insurance, an official agency of the Swiss Confederation. Part of the indemnity obtained by the Swiss government from Italy on account of this incident was paid over by the former to the Swiss Military Insurance, and the remaining sum of the indemnity restituted to Italy. Oswald's survivors sued the Swiss Confederation for payment of the sum reimbursed to Italy, but their claim was rejected by the Swiss Supreme Court. The Oswald case is cited in support of the contention that under Swiss law the state is under no obligation to hand over the indemnity received from a foreign state to the individual claimant.[80] Nevertheless, one wonders whether this ruling would also obtain under different factual circumstances and whether a refusal to transfer the indemnity to the individual could not be qualified as "unlawful" in certain situations. If this were correct, the individual would be able to sue the confederation before the Supreme Court by a direct administrative claim,[81] or at least to seek administrative review before that court.[82]

Waiver. As noted earlier, the Swiss state is under no duty to endorse the claims of its nationals on the international level, since these claims are deemed to be vested in the Swiss Confederation. These points were brought out as follows in a message addressed by the Federal Council to the Federal Assembly relating to the lump-sum agreement concluded with Yugoslavia:

> In protecting the interests of its citizens abroad, Switzerland asserts its own right. . . . The Swiss Confederation puts forward its own claim. . . . If a State fails to treat a Swiss citizen in conformity with the principles of international law, it is the Swiss Confederation as such which acquires a right to reparation. This right is distinct from the claim of the individual. The latter, however, can only originate from Swiss domestic law. . . . The question of whether, in what manner, and to what extent it will present its claim falls within the entire discretion of the Swiss State. In deciding on these matters, the Swiss Confederation will weigh the general and individual interests in presence. Should the former be in contradiction with the latter, the former will prevail.[83]

Special Kinds of Protection. The special kinds of protection mentioned in the general scheme of this book are of little interest to Switzerland. The new Federal Law on Investment Guarantees of 20 March 1970 does, however, deserve mention.[84] One might also call attention to certain suggestions made in the parliamentary debates pertaining to the hijacking in 1970 of a Swissair aircraft by Arab guerrillas (The Zerka incident).[85] On that occasion, some members of Parliament urged the government to suspend its aid to the Arab states indirectly involved and block the latters' assets in Swiss banks. Had they been acted upon, these suggestions would have come under the heading of pacific reprisals. Therefore their connection with the subject matter discussed here would have been very remote. These suggestions were based on a precedent. The Swiss government had provisionally frozen Romania's assets in Switzerland as a consequence of the Romanian law of nationalization of 11 June 1948.[86]

The Individual as an Alien

Movement

The question of the legal status of aliens has been and still is an extremely sensitive area of Swiss constitutional and administrative law. On the one hand, by reason of its geographical position and its neutral status, Switzerland has attracted large numbers of aliens who have been objects of political and other persecutions abroad. On the other hand, Switzerland's highly developed technology is in need of foreign labor, both skilled and unskilled. In addition, the fact that the headquarters or offices of numerous intergovernmental and nongovernmental organizations are located on Swiss territory accounts for the presence of a considerable number of civil servants who are aliens. The combination of these three factors has resulted in an exceptionally large influx of foreigners.[87]

By and large this influx has been beneficial to the country; it is certain that without it Switzerland would never have attained its present level of prosperity and development. However, the presence of a large number of foreigners in Switzerland has engendered acute human, social, and legal problems, which in turn have led to some xenophobic reactions. These account for the relatively stringent provisions of Swiss law in respect to the admission and residence of aliens.

Entry and Stay. As a rule, the territory of Switzerland can be lawfully entered by anyone showing a valid passport.[88] This, of course, applies neither to cases in which a visa is still required nor to persons who have been previously expelled from Switzerland or declared "undesirable" by the Swiss authorities.

An alien who intends to take up employment in Switzerland must furthermore be in possession of an attestation delivered by the competent Swiss authorities that he or she will be granted temporary residence.[89] An alien who fails to meet this condition will be unable to obtain a temporary residence permit later.[90]

The special issues connected with the granting or refusal of asylum[91] will be touched upon only briefly. Switzerland considers it the prerogative of the state to grant or to refuse refuge, and not a right of the individual to obtain such refuge.[92] The granting of asylum, which cannot be considered an intervention into the domestic affairs of the foreign state with which the applicant has been hitherto connected,[93] depends on the fulfillment of certain conditions. These conditions have been laid down in instructions issued by the Federal Ministry of Justice on 10 October 1969. Under these instructions, asylum will be granted if the applicant shows that he would probably be persecuted in his or her country of origin or of last residence because of race, religion, nationality, political opinions, or social status. The applicant must furthermore prove that, on account of the above factors, the political regime of the country of origin or of last residence placed him or her under moral stress.[94] As already stated, individuals have no right to political asylum under Swiss law.[95] Accordingly, decisions on refusal or withdrawal of political asylum cannot be reviewed by the Supreme Court,[96] despite a contrary proposal submitted to the National Council by one of its members in 1969.[97] This proposal was rejected on the grounds that neither constitutional law nor conventional or general principles of international law confer a right to asylum upon individuals.[98]

Residence. Aliens who enter Switzerland[99] without any intention of taking up resident or doing business, since tourists and journalists are permitted to remain on Swiss territory for up to three months without any further formalities.[100]

All other persons admitted to Switzerland are required to apply to the competent cantonal authorities for a temporary residence permit.[101] For applicants seeking employment in Switzerland, the granting of such a permit depends on the limitations set by federal legislation for the employment of aliens.[102] Temporary residence permits are valid only within the territory of the cantons that issue them. Their granting may also be conditional and their duration limited, and their renewal or nonrenewal is within the full discretion of the competent cantonal authorities.[103] Temporary residence permits can be seasonal and do not necessarily extend to the holders' spouses and minor children.[104]

After having resided in Switzerland under a temporary residence permit for a certain length of time, which as a rule varies between five and ten years,[105] the alien may apply for a permanent residence permit. The latter will be granted if, in the opinion of the competent authorities of the canton, the applicant is sufficiently integrated into the local population. The permanent residence permit is unconditional and unlimited in time, and it also covers the family of the applicant.[106] It is granted by the canton, but the approval of the Federal Immigration Authority is necessary.[107]

Despite their somewhat misleading wording, the treaties of establishment concluded by Switzerland in no case exempt aliens from observing the rules on immigration described above; nor do they confer a right to establishment in Switzerland.[108] A foreigner who is protected by the clauses of a treaty of establishment nevertheless has one advantage over other aliens, provided he or she also holds a permanent residence permit. As in the case of Swiss citizens from other cantons, the validity of this permit will not be limited to one canton but will extend to the entire territory of the confederation.[109]

Articles 11 and 13 of an agreement concluded with Italy on 10 August 1964[110] deserve special mention. Although this agreement confers no right to immigration and is in this respect similar to the treaties of establishment, it gives nonseasonal Italian workers who have been continuously employed in Switzerland for five years the right to automatic renewal of their temporary residence permits. It furthermore allows Italians in Switzerland to change their employers and even their professions, and their permits extend to spouses and minor children. Similar rules would at first sight seem to apply to nationals of other Organization for Economic Cooperation and Development (OECD) countries by virtue of a decision taken by the Council of that Organization, then the Organization for European Economic Cooperation (OEEC) on 30 October 1953.[111] In a 1974 decision the Swiss Supreme Court has come to the conclusion, however, that the council decision lacks self-executing character and hence cannot be directly invoked by individuals on the domestic level.[112]

Foreigners who have been admitted to Switzerland and who cannot reasonably be expected to leave the country but who, by their conduct, do not "deserve" a temporary residence permit, are granted "tolerance." Such tolerance is limited in time; it may be conditional and is revocable. It requires the approval of the Federal Immigration Authority.[113] Very often, "tolerance" is only one step short of expulsion.[114]

Negative decisions by the cantons on matters of residence are in principle final[115] and can be reviewed by neither the Federal Council[116] nor the Swiss Supreme Court acting as the country's highest administrative jurisdiction.[117] Thus, the only remaining channel is that of review by the Swiss Supreme Court for denial of justice[118] under Article 4 of the Constitution.[119]

Status of Aliens. Aside from conventional rules, aliens in Switzerland are privileged in certain respects, while they enjoy national treatment in other respects. In some fields, however, their rights are less than those of Swiss nationals.

Aliens enjoy a privileged status in military and political matters and sometimes in the field of taxation. They are subject neither to duty in the Swiss armed forces nor to payment of the military exemption tax.[120] They have no political duties or rights, except possibly on the communal level. Although they generally pay the same taxes as Swiss citizens, they are sometimes granted preferential tax treatment.[121]

In many ways aliens enjoy national treatment, that is, the treatment to which Swiss citizens from other cantons are entitled. This is particularly true in respect to a great number of written and unwritten fundamental rights and freedoms, such as equality before the law;[122] freedom of conscience, belief, and worship,[123] the right of petition;[124] the right of solvent debtors to have personal claims brought before the judge of their permanent residence;[125] and the guarantees of personal freedom, of inviolability of abode and of private property.[126] Aliens also enjoy national treatment in other fields, such as civil law and procedure. They are endowed with civil capacity, the capacity to make contracts, to marry, to inherit, to own movable and immovable property, to sue and to be sued. They enjoy free access to courts and are not obliged to pay security for costs if they reside in Switzerland.[127] The principle of national treatment in these matters can naturally be set aside by treaty provisions and by the effects of Swiss rules on conflict of laws.

Certain individual rights granted by the Constitution to Swiss nationals are denied to foreigners. For instance, the freedom of establishment guaranteed by Article 45 of the Constitution only benefits Swiss citizens.[128] However, as pointed out above, aliens whose national states have concluded treaties of establishment with Switzerland and who reside permanently on Swiss territory enjoy a freedom similar to that granted to Swiss citizens by Article 45 of the Constitution. These two conditions must also be met by an alien who wishes to enjoy the freedom of trade and commerce guaranteed by Article 31 of the Constitution.[129] This freedom will not, however, encompass the exercise of certain professions that remain inaccessible to foreigners, particularly those of physician and of attorney-at-law.[130] Other exceptions to the principle of national treatment of aliens are to be found in the fields of administrative and commercial law. Thus only Swiss nationals may hold concessions for waterworks[131] and oil pipelines;[132] only nationals can be shareholders of the Swiss National Bank;[133] and only nationals can own vessels under Swiss registration.[134] The majority of the managing directors of corporations or cooperative societies with headquarters in Switzerland must be Swiss nationals domiciled in Switzerland.[135] Operating a foreign-controlled bank in Switzerland requires a special permit.[136]

Finally, attention must be drawn to some recent legislation bearing on foreign bank deposits in Switzerland. To curb inflation and to prevent the flooding of the country with foreign capital, in July 1972 the Federal Council enacted four ordinances, three of which are still in force. These were the ordinance of 4 July 1972 prohibiting the payment of interest on foreign funds deposited in Swiss banks;[137] the ordinance of 5 July 1972 making the obtaining of certain foreign funds by persons domiciled in Switzerland, with the exception of banks, dependent on the approval of the Swiss National Bank;[138] and an ordinance of 5 July 1972,[139] amended on 13 March 1975,[140] which provides that the holdings of Swiss banks in foreign currencies should not, in principle, be inferior to the total amount of the debts of these banks in foreign currencies. These ordinances, which are aimed at protecting the Swiss economy, evidently limit the freedom of aliens to deposit their assets in Switzerland, but it can hardly be argued that they are contrary to customary or conventional international law.

Voluntary Departure. Aliens are free to leave Switzerland unless they are currently serving penal sentences.[141]

Involuntary Departure: Expulsion and Deportation. The involuntary departure of aliens can be brought about in three ways: by an "order to leave the country," by expulsion, and by extradition.

An "order to leave the country" is the consequence of a revocation of "tolerance,"[142] of the nonrenewal, revocation, or annulment of a temporary residence permit,[143] or of the annulment of a permanent resident permit[144] because it was obtained by fraud. Until 1 October 1969 decisions of annulment and of revocation taken by the cantons could be reviewed by the Swiss Supreme Court only under Article 4 of the Constitution (denial of justice).[145] From that date, however, the correct procedure to follow has been that of review by the Supreme Court acting as the country's highest administrative jurisdiction.[146] There is nothing to prevent an alien who has previously been the object of an "order to leave" from later applying for a new temporary residence permit through the usual channels.[147]

Swiss law distinguishes between political, judicial, and administrative expulsion of aliens. Decisions on political expulsions are within the competence of the Federal Council. Under Article 70 of the Constitution, political expulsion measures may be taken against aliens who endanger the internal or external security of the confederation. They are subject to no review.[148] Judicial expulsion is an accessory punishment that may accompany a penal sentence pronounced by a criminal court for a violation of federal or cantonal penal law.[149] Decisions on judicial expulsion are accessory to ordinary penal judgments and may thus be reviewed through the usual judicial channels for criminal matters. Finally, administrative expulsion may be decided upon by the competent administrative authorities under the following circumstances:[150] (1) The person concerned has been sentenced to a prison term by a domestic or foreign[151] court of law and the sentence does not provide for expulsion from Switzerland; (2) the conduct of an alien shows that that person is unable or unwilling to adapt to the Swiss milieu; (3) a case of mental illness disrupts public order; (4) the alien is dependent upon public assistance. In cases of a prison sentence or public dependence, however, expulsion will take place only if the individual concerned is able to return to his or her home country and can reasonably be expected to do so. It would seem that decisions on administrative expulsion can be reviewed, first by the Federal Ministry of Justice[152] and then by the Swiss Supreme Court acting as the country's highest administrative jurisdiction.[153]

Extradition of aliens is granted or refused in accordance with the Federal Law on Extradition of 22 January 1891[154] and the extradition treaties concluded by Switzerland. Decisions on extradition are within the competence of the Federal Council, but they will automatically be brought before the Swiss Supreme Court if and as soon as the alien concerned objects to extradition.[155]

Protection

As pointed out earlier, aliens are not called upon to serve in the Swiss armed forces; hence the question of the protection of such foreigners does not arise. The question could present itself for aliens who serve in the Swiss merchant marine. I do not, however, know of any published case in which such protection has been contemplated or has in fact taken place. There remains the possibility that Switzerland "protects" aliens under the numerous mandates of protection entrusted to it by foreign states[156] on a temporary or permanent[157] basis. It seems, however, that interventions based on such mandates do not amount to genuine diplomatic protection of foreign nationals by Switzerland. The Swiss authorities merely act as agents of a foreign state by virtue of an international agreement,[158] but it is the foreign state that in reality continues to assert, through its agent, a right that has been violated in the person of its national. Thus the foreign state's claim as such is by no means transferred to the agent state, that is, to Switzerland. The duty of Switzerland is limited to presenting that claim on the international level according to instructions received by the state that owns the claim.

NATIONAL IMPLEMENTATION OF INTERNATIONAL RIGHTS AND DUTIES

The relationship between international law and Swiss domestic law has long been, and still is, an unsettled and complex question that deserves at least a brief analysis on the basis of recent Swiss practice. Three problems must be distinguished at the outset: the incorporation of international law into Swiss law; the hierarchical rank attributed to rules of international law within the Swiss legal order; and the validity and immediate applicability of norms of international law under Swiss law.

Norms of customary as well as of conventional international law are automatically incorporated into Swiss federal law. The rules of treaties become part of Swiss law at the moment they become binding on the international level.[159] Therefore no transformation is required,[160] unless of course parliamentary approval is also viewed as an act that brings about the transformation of the treaty into domestic law.[161]

As already pointed out, international law is automatically integrated into Swiss federal law; it thus partakes of the latter's nature and rank. Since the rules of international law form a part of federal law, there is no doubt that they take precedence over cantonal laws, whether the latter are enacted after the former or not.[162] Similarly, norms of international law are superior to federal enactments of a lesser nature, such as ordinances and regulations issued by the Federal Assembly or by the executive.[163] The real question is that of the relationship between rules of international law, especially treaty rules, on the one hand, and ordinary federal laws (statutes) and provisions of the Constitution, on the other.

Because the norms of international law are deemed to be on equal footing with federal laws or decrees, it would seem logical to assume that a treaty that is in open conflict[164] with an earlier federal law or decree takes precedence over the latter by virtue of the principle that a later statute overrules a previous statute in the same subject. The application of that same principle would lead to the further conclusion that a more recent federal law or decree abrogates an earlier treaty. Despite assertions to the contrary,[165] this still seems to be the practice of the Federal Council,[166] as well as of the Swiss Supreme Court.[167] Swiss authorities are well aware of the shortcomings of this solution, which in fact amounts to granting domestic law partial supremacy over international law and which, if applied strictly, could allow Switzerland to repudiate its international obligations by means of contrary internal legislation.[168] However, the Swiss state would incur international responsibility in such cases. In order to avoid this highly undesirable consequence as far as possible, Swiss authorities usually presume that in adopting a law or a decree the Swiss legislators had no intention of contradicting earlier treaties.[169] There is thus a presumption that the more recent domestic legislation conforms to earlier treaty law. Because this presumption is rebuttable, conflicts and problems are not entirely avoided.

Even more delicate is the question of precedence between the norms of international law and the substantive rules of the Swiss Constitution.[170] It is true that under Article 113 (3) of the Constitution the Swiss Supreme Court is prohibited from inquiring into the constitutionality of treaties approved by the Federal Assembly.[171] This does not mean, however, that the question of precedence is irrelevant, since it will arise whenever the executive and legislative powers contemplate the conclusion of a new treaty of doubtful compatibility with the Constitution. This question is very topical in view of the accession of Switzerland to the European Convention on Human Rights and Fundamental Freedoms of 4 November 1950 and to the United Nations. In order to forestall possible conflicts and controversies, it would seem wisest in such situations to amend the Constitution prior to accession to the treaty or to submit the latter to the procedure required for the amendment of the Constitution (obligatory referendum).[172] If no such precautions are taken, the ensuing legal situation will be very uncertain indeed. There are authors who contend that treaties prevail even over constitutional norms,[173] a view that seems somewhat unrealistic, since domestic judges have a natural tendency not to go against the rules of their own constitutions. Other authors assert that rules of constitutional law always take precedence over treaty norms.[174] A third view, which was expressed at one time by the Swiss Foreign Ministry[175] and also, on a later occasion, by the Federal Council,[176] is that treaty norms can never prevail over "fundamental," or "essential," norms of the Constitution. This view, reasonable though it may seem, leaves us with the difficult task of determining which rules of the Constitution are important and which are not. Fortunately this problem will in all probability remain academic, since the Federal Council is not likely to conclude treaties that run counter to important provisions of the Swiss Constitution.

It has already been shown that rules of international law, especially treaty provisions, acquire immediate validity in Switzerland as a result of their automatic incorporation into Swiss law. Once the validity and the rank of such rules on the domestic level have been duly ascertained, another quite distinct, question arises, which is whether the rules in question are immediately applicable in Switzerland.[177]

This is not necessarily the case. Although a convention may be perfectly valid on the internal level, for instance, it may explicitly or implicitly require the enactment of implementing legislation and thus lack "self-executing" character.[178] Hence, in order to be applicable as well as valid on the domestic level, a rule of international law must be sufficiently precise and specific to allow its application without the enactment of supplementary legislation. As far as individuals are concerned, this means that the rule must create specific rights and/or duties for such persons.[179]

The Act of State Doctrine

The Act of State doctrine pertains to the domestic applicability and enforcement of foreign public law.[180] It is mainly connected with the effects of foreign acts of confiscation. According to the Supreme Court of the United States, this doctrine means that for "considerations of comity, and of the highest expediency," the conduct of states "should not be called in question by the legal tribunals of another jurisdiction."[181] In the practice of U.S. courts the Act of State doctrine implies that judicial review of the conduct of a foreign state is possible only where the latter no longer exists at the time of suit and where the executive relieves the court of the doctrine's restraints (the so-called Bernstein exception),[182] where the issue raised is of minimal importance to the conduct of foreign relations, or where the foreign act violates highly codified principles of international law.[183] According to U.S. practice these problems should be properly dealt with by the executive. The Act of State doctrine may thus be viewed as a means of implementing the principle of separation of powers and of preserving the prerogative of the executive by allowing the latter to secure a solution through diplomatic rather than domestic judicial channels.[184] Accordingly domestic courts should not in principle sit in judgment over the action of a foreign state; on the judicial level these actions are therefore presumed to be valid.

Some civil law systems are more restrictive on this point. Foreign private law rules are widely held to be applicable by virtue of domestic rules on conflict of laws or of treaties, but the application of foreign public law is often rejected by holding that foreign public law can have no extraterritorial effects (principle of territoriality of foreign public law), by invoking domestic public policy (ordre public), or by resorting to a combination of both of these factors.

This last is the current practice of Swiss courts in particular. The attitude of the Swiss Supreme Court in this field can be summarized as follows:

1. Foreign private law rules apply if the domestic or conventional conflict rules of Switzerland so provide.[185]

2. Foreign public law is in principle inapplicable and unenforceable on Swiss territory, by virtue of the principle of territoriality, of that of public policy, or of both,[186] except if either its application and enforcement are required by treaty[187] or it comes to the aid of rules of Swiss or foreign private law that are deemed to be applicable, for instance by confirming private law rules protecting individual property.[188] It is evident that a foreign act of confiscation, for example, does not meet this requirement.

3. The question of whether a given foreign act is public or private in character is decided by Swiss courts in accordance with the law of the particular forum.[189]

4. The recognition or nonrecognition of the foreign state or government in question is irrelevant.[190]

This practice has elicited two principal criticisms, the first of which is that the principle of territoriality is of a doubtful validity, and in many cases it is difficult to distinguish between public and private law; the second is that the practice of Swiss judicial authorities confuses the principle of territoriality with that of public policy.

In formulating the first criticism, P. Lalive notes that no foreign law should be denied application ex sua natura.[191] The only reasons that may justify such an exclusion are those based on public policy.[192]

The second criticism is voiced by Niederer in an important essay that deals with questions of public policy in matters of foreign confiscations.[193] Niederer attempts to draw a line between the principle of territoriality and that of public policy and to determine, in the light of the practice of the Swiss Supreme Court, the extent to which these two rules warrant the nonapplication of foreign public law.

Following the Supreme Court, Niederer first draws a distinction between those rules of foreign public law that support private legal relationships and those that disturb such relationships, such as confiscation laws. While the applicability of the former must be readily conceded, the fate of the latter deserves closer scrutiny. If the confiscated assets are located outside the territory of the confiscating state, the taking is invalid under Swiss law by virtue of the principle of territoriality. In this context it is of no importance whether the foreign rules in question are directed against aliens or merely against the foreign state's own nationals; nor does it matter whether the takings are followed by compensation.[194] Since the nonapplicability of foreign public law results in this instance from the principle of territoriality, it is unnecessary to resort to motivations based on public policy.[195]

The principle of territoriality would, however, leave foreign states free to confiscate assets localized on their own territory, although Swiss courts would certainly refuse to apply such confiscatory legislation, at least if the victim were a Swiss national. Because the principle of territoriality would be inoperative, the only obstacles to the application and enforcement of the foreign confiscation law could be found in public policy. In the situation examined here, the confiscation law would be contrary to Swiss public policy, particularly because public international law forbids the taking of private property without compensation.[196] Niederer favors the same solution if the victim of the confiscation is a national of a third country or even of the confiscating state, although in these cases no violation of international law against Switzerland occurs because Swiss courts are adverse to any discrimination based on nationality in the field of public policy.[197]

In conclusion it may be said that the attitude of Swiss tribunals differs from that taken by U.S. courts in the following respects:

1. Swiss courts are entitled to assess the validity and applicability of acts of foreign states, especially in matters of confiscation; they are not bound by instructions from the executive.

2. Save for the exceptions mentioned earlier, Swiss courts refuse to apply and to enforce acts of foreign states by invoking the principle of territoriality, that of public policy, or possibly both.

3. The recognition or nonrecognition of the foreign state or government whose conduct is in issue is irrelevant.

The Implementation of Decisions of Intergovernmental Organizations

The pages that follow describe the ways and means by which general or particular rules created by intergovernmental organizations are incorporated into domestic law and made operative against individuals on the national level. If these rules have been enacted in conformity with the constitutive instrument of an organization of which Switzerland is a member, and if in addition they are sufficiently specific and precise to be self-executing, they would seem to be immediately applicable on the Swiss domestic level, for, as pointed out above, the constitutive instrument or treaty on which the rule is based would be automatically incorporated into Swiss law.

Apart from certain problems dealt with below, arising in connection with the World Bank Convention and the European Convention on Human Rights, the implementation of decisions by the following intergovernmental organizations requires brief consideration: the League of Nations (in the Italian-Ethiopian conflict); the

United Nations (sanctions against Rhodesia); and the European Free Trade Association.

League of Nations

As regards the conflict between Italy and Ethiopia and the sanctions proposed by the League of Nations, it may be recalled that the question of whether a state had resorted to war contrary to Articles 12, 13, and 15 of the League Covenant was to be answered individually by each state.[198] An affirmative answer given by a state, however, entailed a duty of that state to apply the sanctions mentioned in Article 16 of the covenant. In the Italian-Ethiopian conflict, the answer of 50 out of 54 member states was in the affirmative, and a committee was formed to coordinate the sanctions.[199] This coordination committee submitted five proposals to the member states, four of which are of interest here. Proposal 1 suggested an embargo on weapons, ammunition, and war supplies destined for Italy. Proposal 2 provided for certain financial sanctions. Proposal 3 contained a prohibition of imports from Italy. Proposal 4 called for an embargo on certain exports to Italy, especially raw materials.[200] None of these proposals was self-executing, and their implementation required additional legislation on the domestic level.

Switzerland accepted and carried out Proposals 2 and 4.[201] As for Proposal 3 (prohibition of imports from Italy), the Swiss government pointed out that it could not accept it fully, since Switzerland, being a neighbor of Italy, was dependent upon imports from that country. Because the proposal was aimed at preventing Italy from obtaining foreign currency, the Swiss authorities were of the opinion that the institution of a clearing procedure between the two states and the resulting reduction of imports from Italy to the level of Swiss exports to that country was sufficient to attain the objective of the proposal.[202] It was, however, the Swiss attitude toward Proposal 2 (embargo on weapons, ammunition, and war supplies) that caused the most dissatisfaction among the other members of the League of Nations. The Swiss government had decided to extend the embargo to both parties in the conflict.[203]

France, Great Britain, and the Soviet Union, as well as other powers, considered this attitude to be contrary to Article 16 of the League covenant and to the London Declaration made by the Council of the League of Nations on 13 February 1920,[204] by which Switzerland was authorized to maintain its military neutrality within the League system. The Swiss government replied that the fact of procuring weapons and war supplies to one party to a conflict while withholding them from the other ceased to be purely economic discrimination[205] and might be viewed as unequal treatment of the belligerents in military matters; thus the strict application of Proposal 1 might endanger Switzerland's military neutrality.[206]

This episode, in which Switzerland may seem to have violated its obligations under the League of Nations covenant,[207] serves here to demonstrate that some decisions by intergovernmental organizations can be made applicable to individuals only through complementary legislation enacted on the domestic level.

Rhodesia

Since the attitude of Switzerland in the Rhodesian question has been extensively dealt with by other writers,[208] some brief remarks will suffice.[209] It will be remembered that Switzerland, although not a member of the United Nations, was invited by the Secretary-General of the United Nations to join in the sanctions decreed by the Security Council against Rhodesia, pursuant to Article 2 (6) of the UN Charter. Invoking both the rule that treaties are not binding upon third states and the obligations flowing from its status of neutrality, Switzerland declined to do so as a matter of right but agreed to take measures to ensure "that Rhodesian commerce will be given no opportunity to circumvent United Nations sanctions on Swiss territory."[210] This promise resulted in the nonrecognition of Rhodesia as an independent state,[211] in a prohibition on the export of war supplies to Rhodesia, and in the adoption of internal legislation reducing imports from that territory to the normal flow of trade.[212] No restrictions on exports were deemed necessary besides those on war supplies because the goods placed under embargo by the Security Council--oil and oil products, motor vehicles and spare parts, aircraft and parts thereof--are not exported from Switzerland to Rhodesia either directly or indirectly.[213] This episode illustrates the fact that internal legislation may be needed to secure the compliance by individuals with a (nonbinding) decision by an intergovernmental organization.

Namibia

I am not aware of any demands made on Switzerland by the United Nations on account of the Namibian question, nor of course of any domestic legislation pertaining to that question.

European Free Trade Association

The application on the Swiss domestic level of the Stockholm Convention instituting the European Free Trade Association (EFTA), 4 January 1960,[214] does not appear to have caused major difficulties.

Clearly the provisions of the convention that are self-executing are valid and immediately applicable in the Swiss legal order.[215] The same would seem to obtain for decisions taken by the EFTA council under Article 32 of the convention.

Procedures Related to the Issuance of Certificates or Suggestions by the Executive in Connection with Litigation in the National Courts

Swiss law adheres quite strictly to the principle of separation of powers, and the executive exercises very little influence over litigation in Swiss courts. As regards the validity, interpretation, and application of rules of international law, particularly treaty rules, the courts are under no obligation either to solicit or to follow instructions and directives issued by the executive.[216] This is not to say that a court would be prevented from requesting a legal opinion from the Swiss Foreign Ministry, for example; such a request would in no way violate the principle of separation of powers.[217]

For a certain period a particular situation prevailed in the field of sovereign immunity.[218] During troubled periods the Federal Council, making use of its power to take measures to maintain Swiss security and neutrality, prohibited acts of sequestration[219] and other measures of enforcement against the movable assets of foreign states, provided the latter granted reciprocity in these matters. Under a first decree, issued in 1918 and abrogated in 1926,[220] measures of enforcement which had already been taken against foreign states were to be officially annulled by the Federal Council, whose decision of annulment was binding on other Swiss authorities.[221] A second decree, issued in 1939 and abolished in 1948,[222] again prohibited enforcement measures against assets of foreign states except when they were authorized by the Federal Council. Action taken in violation of the decree was considered void and had to be officially annulled by the competent authorities.[223] Since 1948, however, decisions on matters of sovereign immunity have been again within the realm of the judicial authorities. Although there are no precedents, it may be presumed that the recognition or nonrecognition of the government of the state claiming immunity is immaterial, provided the government in question does not lack effectiveness.[224]

TREATIES AND THE INDIVIDUAL

The conditions set by Swiss law for the validity of treaties and for their applicability to individuals have been described above. It may be added that treaties become binding on individuals only upon their publication in the Collection of Federal Statutes (Recueil officiel).[225]

Aliens or foreign legal persons,[226] but not foreign governments, may request the Federal Council to review legislative acts of the cantons and decisions taken by the highest cantonal authority that, in their opinion, violate applicable treaty provisions[227] on commercial relations, customs, trade marks, and the free movement and residence of persons.[228]

If the treaty provisions allegedly violated by cantonal authorities pertain to matters of civil law, bankruptcy, or criminal law, redress must be sought before the Supreme Court through the normal channels provided by federal procedure for these matters.[229]

If none of the above-mentioned channels are open, or if the decision from which relief is sought has been made by a federal agency, the case can be brought before the Swiss Supreme Court acting as the country's highest administrative jurisdiction (recours de droit administratif).[230] Review may include among other things, decisions, whether cantonal or federal,[231] taken "in violation of federal legislation [of which treaties form a part], including decisions based on excess and misuse of the power of appreciation,"[232] but not to decisions touching upon the internal or external security of Switzerland, its neutrality, diplomatic protection, and other matters connected with its external relations.[233] In any event, decisions of the government (Federal Council) are never amenable to review.[234]

Finally, if none of the means of redress described so far cover the alleged violation of a treaty right,[235] and if that violation is imputable to a cantonal authority,[236] the foreign claimant may apply to the Supreme Court for redress on constitutional grounds (recours de droit public).[237]

It may be inferred from the above that the judicial remedies available under Swiss law for the enforcement of the treaty rights of aliens are numerous. The judicial protection enjoyed by foreigners is thus extensive; the only decisions that are not reviewable are those of the Federal Council or decisions of lower agencies that pertain to high matters of state.

Among the treaties or types of treaties that are mentioned in the general scheme of this book, two are of particular interest because they grant individuals certain procedural as well as substantive rights on the international level. These are the World Bank Convention on the Settlement of International Investment Disputes, 18 March 1965 (hereafter referred to as the World Bank Convention),[238] and the European Convention on Human Rights and Fundamental Freedoms, 4 November 1950.[239] The other conventions or types of conventions relating to individuals and cited in the scheme have either been covered in the preceding pages or are of little interest to Switzerland.

In its message on the World Bank Convention addressed to the Federal Assembly on 15 December 1967,[240] the Swiss government describes at some length the salient features of the convention, emphasizing in particular the role to be played by individuals or companies in the fields of conciliation and arbitration. This role in principle excludes diplomatic protection[241] and thus the substitution of the individual or company by its national state,[242] but it leaves intact the latter's right to resort to state-to-state arbitration under bilateral agreements on the protection of foreign investments.[243] Furthermore the government draws the attention of the Federal Assembly to Article 54 of the convention, which declares that arbitral awards made under the convention are binding and that decisions that provide for the payment of a sum of money must be executed on the territory of the contracting parties as if they were final and binding judgments of their own national courts. According to the Swiss government, the implementation of this provision in Switzerland creates no problems.[244] As far as arbitral awards that do not allocate any sums of money are concerned, they will be recognized on Swiss territory according to cantonal procedure, which applies to Swiss and foreign awards alike.[245]

The accession of Switzerland to the European Convention on Human Rights has raised some interesting questions. In a report of December 1968,[246] the Federal Council suggested to the Federal Assembly that Switzerland accede to this convention despite the fact that certain provisions of Swiss law and, in particular, of the Swiss Constitution, were contrary to the convention and thus would have required the formulation of reservations.[247] At that time the Federal Assembly resolved to defer accession to the convention pending the elimination of these obstacles. Most of them have been removed.[248] In February 1972 the Federal Council submitted an additional report to the Assembly, and this report, in turn, was followed, in 1974 by a message in which the Federal Council proposed the ratification of the Convention by Switzerland.[249] On 28 November 1974 Switzerland ratified the convention and made the declarations provided for in Articles 25 (individual applications to the commission) and 46 (acceptance of the compulsory jurisdiction of the European Court of Human Rights). The 1968 and 1972 reports, in particular, analyze the relationship between the convention and Swiss domestic law in terms of the rights of individuals.

In its 1968 report the Federal Council observed that if Switzerland became a party to the European Convention on Human Rights, the latter will be automatically incorporated into federal law and thus acquire binding force on the national level.[250] Furthermore, and although this question has to be decided by the national courts in each concrete case, certain provisions of the convention and of its additional protocol relating to rights of individuals are self-executing and would thus be immediately applicable in Switzerland.[251] Most of the rights guaranteed by the convention and the protocol are already enjoyed by nationals and aliens under federal and cantonal law. Thus their automatic incorporation into Swiss law would raise no problem.[252] Some doubts were voiced about the conformity of present Swiss legislation with Article 13 of the convention, which requires the existence of an effective remedy on the national level against violations of the rights guaranteed by the convention. Prior to 1 October 1969 no genuine judicial remedy was available against federal decisions in general; however, this gap has now been filled by granting the Swiss Supreme Court the power to review most federal rulings, even on administrative matters.[253] Furthermore, Article 13 of the convention merely requires the existence of some effective remedy against violations of the rights guaranteed by the convention; it nowhere states that a remedy must be available at the level of the country's highest jurisdiction.[254]

A second issue, which is examined in the 1968 and 1972 reports, is whether the fact that procedure before the European Commission of Human Rights and the European Court of Human Rights would be open even to Swiss nationals would raise difficulties on the domestic level. The reports answer this question in the negative. As for the acceptance of the jurisdiction of the European Court, the Federal Council points out that Switzerland has already taken a more far-reaching decision by submitting to the compulsory jurisdiction of the International Court of Justice for state-to-state litigation.[255] As for the procedure before the European Commission of Human Rights, the Swiss government observes that that commission is not empowered to make binding decisions: the only possible sanctions against noncompliance with a report of the commission are those taken by the Committee of Ministers of the Council of Europe.[256] The reports add that the right of individuals to appear before the commission would be based on Switzerland's consent under Article 25 of the convention,[257] that the prior exhaustion of national remedies would be required under Article 26, and that the commission is entitled to reject anonymous or spurious applications at the beginning of litigation under Article 27.[258]

All these explanations do not, however, detract from the fact that the convention contains important and far-reaching innovations. Individuals are granted procedural as well as substantive rights on the international level,[259] and matters that have so far been within the ambit of domestic jurisdiction have been transferred to an international organ. Individuals may make international claims even against their own national states.[260] Finally, the convention in some cases allows for judicial review of Swiss federal legislation by an international organ, a power that the Swiss judicial authorities themselves do not possess.[261]

It must nevertheless be emphasized that under the convention the organs of the Council of Europe are not vested with "supranational" attributes.[262] The European Commission of Human Rights, unlike the European Court, has no decision-making power. The judgments of the court cannot annul rulings made by national authorities, because Article 50 of the convention leaves the implementation of these decisions to the contracting states.

CONCLUSION

Generally speaking, the treatment extended by Switzerland to its own nationals is very liberal. It must be pointed out, however, that Swiss citizens enjoy no enforceable right to diplomatic protection on the domestic level. It must further be remembered that Swiss nationals residing abroad are subject to discrimination in certain areas. This discrimination is compensated to some extent by the fact that very few restrictions are placed on the activities of Swiss nationals abroad.

In general the treatment granted by Switzerland to aliens conforms to the rules of international law. In a field that falls under the domestic jurisdiction of Switzerland, namely the admission of foreigners, present law and practice remain extremely restrictive owing to demographic and other considerations.

The relationship between international law and Swiss domestic law is and remains problematic, for theoretically at least, rules of international law can be superseded by more recent federal legislation. Most serious problems in this field have so far been successfully avoided, with the help of various devices, but there is no guarantee that this will always be possible in the future.[263]

Swiss courts refuse to give effect to foreign confiscatory legislation by invoking either the principle of territoriality of foreign public law, that of public policy, or both.

The implementation of decisions of the intergovernmental organizations of which Switzerland is or was a member has not created any difficulties except insofar as sanctions under Article 16 of the Covenant of the League of Nations were concerned (Italian-Ethiopian conflict).

Swiss law attaches great importance to the principle of separation of powers, and the executive has little if any influence over litigation in national courts.

At least since 1969, Swiss law has offered aliens an almost complete spectrum of procedures that ensures the enforcement of their treaty rights on the Swiss domestic level. Thus the procedural protection extended to individuals is on the whole satisfactory; it must be noted, in particular, that Switzerland has become a party to the European Convention on Human Rights and Fundamental Freedoms.

NOTES

Abbreviations Used in Citations

A.S.D.I.	Annuaire suisse de droit international
A.T.F.	Arrêts du Tribunal fédéral. Decisions of the Swiss Supreme Court and of the Swiss Supreme Court in Insurance Matters
c.	considérant (motivation, in a judicial decision)
F.F.	Feuille fédérale. Official journal of the Swiss Confederation
F.J.S.	Fiches juridiques suisses
J.A.A.C.	Jurisprudence des autorités administratives de la Confédération. Official collection of federal decisions and of opinions in administrative matters
Rapp. gest.	Rapport du Conseil fédéral sur sa gestion. Report of the Federal Council on its activities, presented annually to the Federal Assembly
R.O.	Recueil officiel des lois et ordonnances de la Confédération suisse. Collection of federal statutes, decrees, and ordinances, published yearly
R.S.	Recueil systématique des lois et ordonnances. Consolidated collection of federal statutes, decrees, and ordinances. If the volume and page are indicated, reference is made to the old collection published in 1947. If a decimal classification number is used, reference is made to the new collection, which is being published currently

1. Pratique suisse 1967-1972, 25-29 A.S.D.I. (1968-73), and the materials included in Pratique suisse 1973 and Pratique suisse 1974.

2. A few texts have been taken from Peaslee 3, Constitutions of Nations (3rd ed., 1968) and from the Annual Digest of Public International Law Cases.

3. On this problem, see Aubert, Traité de droit constitutionnel suisse, 2 vols. (1967, hereafter Aubert, Traité), No. 933.

4. Duchoud v. Banque Maurice Troillet, 22 February 1950, A.T.F. 76 I 34, Chapter 2, at 38.

5. Von der Weid case, Rapp. gest. 16-17 (1970), Pratique suisse 1970, 27 A.S.D.I. 177-78 (1971); see also 1 F.F. 1361, at 1363 (1973).

6. Treaty with the United States, 11 November 1937, Art. 1, 11 R.S. 549; Treaty with France, 1 August 1958, Art. 2, R.O. 223 (1959); Treaty with Colombia, 15 January 1959, Art. 2, R.O. 143 (1963).

7. Military Criminal Code of 13 June 1927, R.S. 321.0, Art. 94 (2). For another example of such legislation, see Federal Law on Maritime Navigation under the Swiss Flag, 23 September 1953, R.S. 747.30, Art. 20 (3), whereby dual nationals are considered to be Swiss only if their domiciles are in Switzerland.

8. Gromo di Ternengo v. Vormundschaftsbehörde Rubikon, 21 June 1928, A.T.F. 54 II 234, at 236-37; Baumberger v. Conseil d'Etat du Canton de Berne, 6 June 1963, A.T.F. 89 I 303, Chapter 3, 4, at 308-12. See also 34 (No. 21) Blätter für zürcherische Rechtsprechung 60 (1935).

9. See Aubert, Traité, No. 998. The freedom of movement of corporate entities, that is, the right to transfer company headquarters to establish subsidiaries abroad (or for other purposes) will not be considered here. On these questions, see, for example, R. L. Bindschedler, Der Nationalitätswechsel von Aktiengesellschaften (Aarau 1940).

10. R.S. 143.2.

11. Aubert, Traité, No. 1968.

12. See, however, the exception mentioned below. The following rules apply. Passports are delivered for a period ranging from one to five years. They can be extended for a period of equal length. They cannot be issued for more than a 15-year period. See Passport Regulations, Art. 5.

13. The claim is brought before the Supreme Court by a so-called administrative review (recours de droit administratif). See Federal Law on the Organization of the Judiciary, 16 December 1943, Art. 98 (c), as amended on 20 December 1968 (hereafter Law on the Judiciary), R.S. 173.110. The provisions relating to administrative review became effective on 1 October 1969. On this remedy, see also the section in the text of this chapter on treaties and the individual.

14. It is not always necessary to show a passport in order to cross the border. For some countries an identity card issued by the passport offices is sufficient.

15. Aubert, Traité, Nos. 1038, 1968, 1977; Manoloff v. Berne, 8 June 1910, A.T.F. 36 I 215, Chapter 4, at 222; Risch v. Regierungsrat Zürich, 4 December 1925, A.T.F. 51 I 388, Chapter 2, at 392-93; Schmid

v. Regierungsrat Zürich, 14 October 1927, A.T.F. 53 I 428, Chapter 2, at 433-34.

16. Aubert, Traité, Nos. 1038, 1977.

17. Ibid., Nos. 999, 1068.

18. Oppenheim, 1 International Law 645-46, 695 (8th ed., Lauterpacht, ed., London 1955).

19. The banishment from Switzerland, in 1873, of the Swiss bishop Mermillod. See Aubert, Traité, No. 999, Note 7, and No. 113.

20. "No Swiss national may be expelled from the territory of the Confederation or from his canton of origin." Art. 44 (1). "The Confederation has power to expel from its territory foreigners who compromise the internal or external security of Switzerland." Art. 70.

21. Aubert, Traité, No. 999, Note 7, and No. 1029.

22. See Federal Law on Extradition, 22 January 1891, R.S. 353.0, Art. 2 (1). The fact that the adoption of this rule was not necessarily based on a conviction that the rule in question corresponded to a duty under international law is shown by the case of Piguet, 6 March 1891, A.T.F. 17 85.

23. An exception must of course be made in cases such as that reported in Pratique suisse 1967, 25 A.S.D.I. 239 -48 (1968). This case pertains to the relationship between a treaty and the Federal Law on Cartels and Similar Organizations, 20 December 1962, R.S. 251.

24. R.S. 141.0.

25. Criminal Code, 21 December 1937, R.S. 311.0, Arts. 4-6; see also Military Criminal Code, op. cit., Art. 9.

26. This is done by applying for administrative review. See Law of 1953, Art. 50 (1) (b) and Law on the Judiciary, op. cit.

27. In time of war the sanction would be death or imprisonment. See Military Criminal Code, op. cit., Art. 90.

28. On this point, see Pratique suisse 1968-1969, 26 A.S.D.I. 148-49 (1969-70).

29. On this question, see generally Wiederkehr, Der Staat und seine Bürger im Ausland (Zürich 1963).

30. Aubert, Traité, No. 1039.

31. This is the case, for example, for the right guaranteed by the Constitution, Art. 59, according to which a suit for a personal claim against a solvent debtor whose permanent residence is in Switzerland must be brought before the judge of the debtor's place of residence.

32. The use of the word "entitled" does not imply the existence of an enforceable right.

33. Decree of the Federal Assembly on Service of Swiss Citizens Domiciled Abroad, in the Armed Forces, 8 December 1961 R.S. 519.3, Art. 1 ff.

34. Decree of the Federal Council on the Recruitment and Basic Training of Swiss Citizens Domiciled Abroad, 26 December 1961, R.S. 511.13.

35. See Federal Law on the Military Exemption Tax, 12 June 1959, R.S. 66, and Federal Law on the Military Exemption Tax as Applied to Swiss Citizens Abroad, 14 December 1973, R.S. 661.0.

36. "Every Citizen of the Canton is a Swiss Citizen. As such he may, after having duly proved his qualification as a voter, take part at his domicile in all federal elections and referenda" [emphasis added].

37. Message of the Federal Council to the Federal Assembly Relating to the Political Rights of Swiss Nationals Abroad, 3 March 1975, F.F. 1975 I 1305, proposes the adoption of a new law that would enable Swiss citizens domiciled abroad to exercise most of their political rights, at least if and when they are temporarily present in Switzerland.

38. Federal Decree Requiring a Permit for the Acquisition of Real Estate by Persons Domiciled Abroad, 23 March 1961 amended on 30 September 1965, 24 June 1970, and 21 March 1973, R.S. 211.412.41.

39. See Pratique suisse 1960, 18 A.S.D.I. 114-25 (1961), and Pratique suisse 1972, 29 A.S.D.I. 356-58 (1973). See, however, the decision of the Swiss Supreme Court in the case of Schubert, A.T.F. 99 Ib 39.

40. Pratique suisse 1964, 22 A.S.D.I. 160 (1965). Moreover, Art. 5 (a) of the initial text of the 1961 decree did not require a permit for persons who were born in Switzerland and had been domiciled there for at least 15 years.

41. Federal Decree, 30 September 1965, R.O. 1252 (1965). For the parliamentary debates leading to this change, see Pratique suisse 1964, 22 A.S.D.I. 158-74 (1965).

42. In fact, however, the amendment also benefits aliens who are entitled to permanent residence and who are temporarily absent. See Aubert, Traité, No. 1040.

43. For the meaning of this term, see Geck, "Diplomatischer Schutz," in 1 Wörterbuch des Völkerrechts 379-87, at 379 (Strupp, Schlochauer, eds., 1960).

44. Doehring, Die Pflicht des Staates zur Gewährung diplomatischen Schutzes 7-14 (1959).

45. See in particular the note of the Swiss Foreign Ministry on the question of whether Swiss citizens have a claim to diplomatic and consular protection against their home state, reprinted in 7 A.S.D.I. 184-92 (1950). See, furthermore, the opinion of the Federal Ministry of Justice, 27 May 1924 and the decision of the Federal Council of the same date, in 1 Salis, Burckhardt, Le droit federal suisse, No. 135/VII (1930); the instructions given on 20 February 1948 by the Swiss Foreign Ministry to Swiss legations and consulates on the protection of Liechtenstein interests, 7 A.S.D.I. 176-84, at 177 (1950); and the Message of the Federal Council to the Federal Assembly Concerning the Lump-sum Agreement concluded with Yugoslavia and Other Matters, 29 October 1948, F.F. 1948 III 672, at 683-84, 6 A.S.D.I. 129-30 (1949).

46. Heirs Oswald v. Swiss Confederation, 17 June 1926, A.T.F. 52 II 235, c. 4, at 259-61, Annual Digest No. 180 (1925-26); Gschwind v. Swiss Confederation, 14 October 1932, A.T.F. 58 II 463, c. 2, at 476, Annual Digest, No. 120 (1931-32); Schoenemann v. Swiss Confederation, 3 June 1955, A.T.F. 81 I 159, c. 3, at 170.

47. See in particular R. L. Bindschedler, Verstaatlichungsmassnahmen und Entschädigungspflicht nach Völkerrecht 103 (1950); Guggenheim, 1 Traité

de droit international public 310-11 (1st ed., 1953, hereafter referred to as Guggenheim, 1 Traité (1st ed.); Zellweger, "Der diplomatische Schutz als Rechtsinstitut," 28 Revue Suisse de jurisprudence 273-80 (1931-32).

48. Note of the Swiss Foreign Ministry, op. cit., at 185, 186.

49. Heirs Oswald v. Swiss Confederation, op. cit.; Gschwind v. Swiss Confederation, op. cit.

50. Heirs Oswald v. Swiss Confederation, op. cit., c. 4, at 259-60.

51. Gschwind v. Swiss Confederation, op. cit., Annual Digest, at 243.

52. See Bindschedler, op. cit.

53. See, in particular, Note of the Swiss Foreign Ministry, op. cit., and Gschwind v. Swiss Confederation, op. cit., and Schoenemann v. Swiss Confederation, op. cit.

54. Aubert, Traité, No. 999. In the same vein, see Bindschedler, op. cit., at 103-07, and Fleiner, Giacometti, Schweizerisches Bundesstaatsrecht 230-31 (Zürich 1949).

55. "It [the Federal Council] watches over the interests of the Confederation abroad, paying particular notice to its international relations, and has the general charge of foreign affairs."

56. Note of the Swiss Foreign Ministry, op. cit., at 188. See also the Message of the Federal Council, 29 October 1948, op. cit., at 683.

57. R.S. 1, 93. The provision in question reads, "Persons who, in addition to Swiss nationality, possess the nationality of a foreign State cannot claim the rights and the protection due to Swiss nationals, as long as they reside in that [foreign] State" [emphasis added].

58. R.S. 1, 325. According to this provision, all Swiss nationals "are entitled to consular protection."

59. R.S. 141.0.

60. R.S. 191.1.

61. See the preamble of the 1967 Regulations. Constitution, Art. 45 bis, deals with the status of Swiss citizens abroad.

62. Art. 16 (4).

63. See Law on the Judiciary, op. cit.

64. See Pratique suisse 1967, 25 A.S.D.I. 261 (1968).

65. Federal Law on Administrative Procedure, 20 December 1968, R.S. 172.021, Art. 72 (a). On this hierarchical channel of review, see Grisel, Droit administratif suisse 485 (1970).

66. Doehring, op. cit., at 77.

67. R.S. 170.32.

68. Federal Law of 9 December 1850, R.S. 1, 434.

69. See Law on the Judiciary, op. cit.

70. Grisel, op. cit., at 428.

71. German Constitution, 11 August 1919, Art. 112 (2).

72. Note of the Swiss Foreign Ministry, op. cit., at 191.

73. See the Message of the Federal Council, 29 October 1948, op. cit., at 683-84. In the case of the agreement concluded with Japan on 21 January 1955 (R.O. 1955, 357), the compensation eventually distributed amounted to 72.7 percent of the effective prejudice. See 14 A.S.D.I. at 212 (1957). An

up-to-date list of the lump-sum agreements concluded by Switzerland can be found in Caflisch, Propriété privée I: Les biens des étrangers en temps de paix, F.J.S. No. 826, at 24. To this list one must add the convention concluded with Hungary on 26 March 1973, F.F. 1973 I 1367.

74. The commission was created under a Federal Decree, 21 December 1950, R.S. 981. The decree was completed by an Ordinance of the Federal Council of 17 April 1951, R.S. 981.1. A special commission was instituted to distribute the global indemnity received by Switzerland under its arrangement with Japan of 21 January 1955, R.O. 1955, 357. It was set up pursuant to Federal Decree, 25 March 1955, R.O. 1955, 667, which was completed by Ordinance of the Federal Council, 5 July 1955, R.O. 1955, 669. The practice of the Japanese Indemnities Commission is described in 14 A.S.D.I. 201-14 (1957), while that of the Nationalisation Claims Commission has been analyzed by R. L. Bindschedler, "Recent Decisions in Switzerland --II," 3 Int'l. and Comp. L.Q. 512-20, at 513-20 (1954).

75. Ordinance of the Federal Council, 17 April 1951, R.S. 981.1.

76. A similar provision can be found in Article 14 of the Ordinance of the Federal Council, 5 July 1955, R.O. 1955, 669, concerning the Japanese Indemnities Commission.

77. This board was set up under Federal Decree, 21 December 1950, R.S. 981.

78. That is, under the court's administrative jurisdiction. On this point, see Pratique suisse 1967, 25 A.S.D.I. 261 (1968). Prior to 1 October 1969 the decisions of the Board of Review were considered to be final and binding. See Federal Decree, 21 December 1950, R.S. 981, Art. 4.

79. See Heirs Oswald v. Swiss Confederation, op. cit.

80. See Zellweger, op. cit., at 276-77.

81. This results from Law on Liability, R.S. 170.32, Art. 10, and Law on the Judiciary, op. cit., Art. 116.

82. Law on the Judiciary, op. cit., Art. 102 (a), states that administrative review is subsidiary to the direct administrative claim instituted by Art. 116 of that law. The right of administrative review would result from Art. 97 ff. of the Law on the Judiciary, op. cit. It could be argued that a refusal to hand over to the individual claimant compensation obtained from a foreign state is also a decision that pertains to diplomatic protection. Hence it could not, pursuant to Art. 100 (a) of the Law on the Judiciary, be the object of administrative review under Art. 97 ff. This does not, however, appear to be a sound argument, for the question considered here--the lawfulness of a refusal to hand over compensation received from a foreign State --arises only once the question of diplomatic protection has been given an affirmative solution.

83. F.F. 1948 III 672, at 683-84, Pratique suisse 1948, 6 A.S.D.I. 129 (1949).

84. F.F. 1970 I 507. The content of this law is summarized by Caflisch, op. cit., at 28-31. Under its Art. 4, the investment guarantee can be extended, not only to Swiss citizens domiciled in Switzerland or to companies with headquarters on Swiss territory and with a predominant

Swiss interest, but also to persons who fulfill only one of the above-mentioned conditions but are closely linked to the Swiss economy. Whether such other persons can also receive Swiss diplomatic protection remains an open question.

85. Pratique suisse 1970, 27 A.S.D.I. 185-97 (1971).

86. Rapp. gest. 1948, 98; Guggenheim, 1 Traité 343 (1st ed.).

87. In 1960 the total resident population of Switzerland numbered 5,429,061 persons, 584,739 of whom, or more than 10 percent, were aliens. Annuaire statistique de la Suisse 1970 14-15.

88. Decree of the Federal Council, 10 April 1946, R.S. 142.211. Sometimes a passport the validity of which has expired less than five years before is deemed sufficient. Furthermore, the nationals of certain countries may cross the Swiss border by simply showing official identity cards.

89. See the Decree of the Federal Council, 19 January 1965, R.S. 142.261.

90. Aubert, Traité, No. 1020.

91. See generally Guggenheim, 1 Traité 355-56, which has an extensive bibliography and is heavily documented.

92. Pratique suisse 1968-1969, 26 A.S.D.I. 152-56 (1969-70); Pratique suisse 1971, 28 A.S.D.I. 233 (1972).

93. Pratique suisse 1967, 25 A.S.D.I. 277-78 (1968); Pratique suisse 1971, 28 A.S.D.I. 233 (1972); statements made by Furgler, Minister of Justice, on 19 September 1973 and 21 March 1974; Bulletin officiel de l'Assemblee federale--Conseil National 1973 1075, and ibid., 1974, at 660; decision of the Federal Council, 2 July 1969, J.A.A.C., fasc. 34, No. 7 (1968-69).

94. Rapp. gest. 1969, 100, Pratique suisse 1968-1969, 26 A.S.D.I. 156 (1969-70); Rapp. gest. 1970, 16-17, Pratique suisse 1970, 27 A.S.D.I. 176-77 (1971).

95. The contrary is true, for example, in the Federal Republic of Germany. See the FRG constitution of 23 May 1949, Art. 16 (2).

96. See Art. 100 (b) (2) of the Law on the Judiciary, op. cit.

97. For the parliamentary debate on this proposal, see Pratique suisse 1968-1969, 26 A.S.D.I. 150-55 (1969-70). Art. 69 ter of the Swiss Constitution provides that: "The Confederation has . . . the right to give rulings in the last resort regarding: . . . refusals to grant asylum."

98. Pratique suisse 1968-1969, 27 A.S.D.I. 152-55 (1969-70).

99. On the residence of aliens in Switzerland, see Aubert, Traité, Nos. 1021-27, and Tzaut, Etrangers--séjour et établissement, F.J.S., No. 351. The subject matter is mainly governed by the Federal Law on Temporary and Permanent Residence of Aliens of 26 March 1931, as amended on 8 October 1948 (hereafter Law on Residence), R.S. 142.20, and by the regulations pertaining to that law of 1 March 1949 (hereafter Regulations on Residence), R.S. 142.201.

100. Law on Residence, Art. 2 (1), and Regulations on Residence, Art. 2 (1); Aubert, Traité, No. 1021.

101. Law on Residence, Art. 5; Aubert, Traité, No. 1022. For the categories of temporary residence permits that do not require the approval of the federal Immigration Authority, see Law on Residence, Art. 18 (2).

102. Decree of the Federal Council on the Limitation of the Foreign Working Population of Switzerland, 9 July 1974, R.S. 823.21. This legislation institutes quotas for the granting of temporary residence permits to aliens who wish to be gainfully employed or to do business in Switzerland. The Federal Council is, however, empowered to grant additional permits to aliens whose presence appears to be desirable for reasons of reciprocity. On this point, see a decision of the Federal Council of 31 October 1973, J.A.A.C., fasc. 38/II, No. 27 (1974).

103. Law on Residence, Arts. 5, 8, 9.

104. Aubert, Traité, Nos. 1022, 1024.

105. Law on Residence, Art. 17 (1).

106. Law on Residence, Arts. 6, 17; Regulations on Residence, Art. 11; Aubert, Traité, No. 1024.

107. Law on Residence, Art. 18 (3).

108. Aubert, Traité, No. 1035; Decisions of the Federal Council, 14 October 1953 and 3 January 1952, J.A.A.C., fasc. 22, Nos. 2 and 3 (1952); decision of the Federal Ministry of Justice, 20 March 1961, J.A.A.C., fasc. 30, No. 78 (1961). See further Pratique suisse 1967, 25 A.S.D.I. 250-51 (1968), and an unpublished decision of the Swiss Supreme Court, X v. Gouvernement du Canton des Grisons, 28 October 1974.

109. Aubert, Traité, No. 1035.

110. R.O. 1965, 406.

111. Krapf v. Regierungsrat Zürich, 13 July 1973, A.T.F. 99 Ib 197.

112. Wessely v. Regierungsrat Zürich, 12 July 1974, A.T.F. 100 Ib 226.

113. Law on Residence, Arts. 7, 8; Aubert, Traité, No. 1025.

114. Aubert, Traité, No. 1035.

115. Law on Residence, Art. 18 (1); Aubert, Traité, No. 1026.

116. It is true that under Federal Law on Administrative Procedure, 20 December 1968, R.S. 172.021, Art. 73 (b), the Federal Council may review cantonal decisions on matters that are connected with treaties granting free movement and with treaties of establishment, but, as pointed out earlier, this possibility is rather theoretical because the treaties of establishment concluded by Switzerland do not give aliens a right to admission to Swiss territory.

117. See Law on the Judiciary, op. cit., Art. 100 (b) (3). An exception must be made if the alien is entitled to have his permit renewed by virtue of treaty provisions: Piu-Azzaro v. Regierungsrat Zürich, 17 September 1971, A.T.F. 97 I 530, Chapter 1(b) and (c), at 533-34; Pratique suisse 1971, 28 A.S.D.I. 230-32 (1972); Banque de Credit International v. Conseil d'Etat du canton de Genève, 13 October 1972, A.T.F. 98 Ib 385, c. 2, at 387; Steiner v. Regierungsrat Zürich, 22 November 1972, A.T.F. 98 Ia 649, Chapter 1, at 650; Krapf v. Regierungsrat Zürich, op. cit., at 198-99; Reho v. Regierungsrat Zürich, 19 September 1973, Chapter 1 (unpublished

decision); Macheret, La recevabilité du recours de droit administratif au Tribunal fédéral 30-31 (1974); X v. Gourvernement du Canton des Grisons, op. cit., and Wessely v. Regierungsrat, op. cit., Note 123.

118. Law on the Judiciary, op. cit., Art. 84 ff.

119. This provision reads, "All Swiss are equal before the law. In Switzerland there are no subjects, or privileges of rank, birth, person, or family." Article 4 of the Constitution, despite its restrictive wording, applies to Swiss nationals and aliens alike, whether they are present in Switzerland or not. For the limits set to the possibility of invoking Article 4, see Steiner v. Regierungsrat Zürich, op. cit., and X v. Gouvernement du Canton des Grisons, op. cit.

120. Aliens may, however, be called upon to serve in civilian corps and police forces for the maintenance of public order. See Opinion of the Swiss Foreign Ministry, 21 April 1967, J.A.A.C., fasc. 34, No. 56 (1968-69).

121. Aubert, Traité, Nos. 995-97.

122. Constitution, Art. 4; Aubert, Traité, No. 1001. For recent confirmations of this statement, see Z. v. Conseil d'Etat du Canton du Tessin, 28 February 1968, A.T.F. 94 I 102, Chapter 1, at 105-06, Pratique suisse 1968-1969, 26 A.S.D.I. 147 (1969-70); X. v. Conseil d'Etat du Canton de Zürich, 15 March 1967, A.T.F. 93 I 1, Chapter 1, at 3-5, Pratique suisse 1967, 25 A.S.D.I. 251-54 (1968); Piazza v. Conseil d'Etat du Canton de Neuchâtel, 6 May 1970, A.T.F. 96 I 308, Chapter 1, at 310-11, Pratique suisse 1970 A.T.F. 96 I 308, Chapter 1, at 310-11, Pratique suisse 1970, 27 A.S.D.I. 175-76 (1971); Simon v. Conseil d'Etat du Canton de Genève, 23 September 1970, A.T.F. 96 I 624, Chapter 1, at 626, Pratique suisse 1970, 27 A.S.D.I. 176 (1971); Steiner v. Regierungsrat Zürich, op. cit.; Reho v. Regierungsrat Zürich, op. cit.; X. v. Gouvernement du Canton des Grisons, op. cit.

123. Constitution, Arts. 49, 50.

124. Ibid., Art. 57. See statement made by the Federal Council, 24 January 1973, Bulletin officiel de l'Assemblée fédérale--Conseil National 388 (1973).

125. Constitution, Art. 59.

126. Aubert, Traité, No. 1001 (with numerous references).

127. Ibid., No. 1008.

128. Ibid., No. 1004.

129. Pratique suisse 1968-1969, 26 A.S.D.I. 147 (1969/70); Aubert, Traité, No. 1005 (with references); M. B. Marti, Die Handels und Gewerbefreiheit der Ausländer in der Schweiz (Aarau, 1963).

130. Opinions of the Division of Justice of the Federal Ministry of Justice, 19 June 1933 and 22 January 1946, J.A.A.C., fasc. 7, No. 36 (1933) and fasc. 18, No. 27 (1946-47); decision of the Federal Council of 12 December 1958, J.A.A.C., fasc. 28, No. 29 (1958); Opinions of the Division of Justice of the Federal Ministry of Justice, 19 May 1959 and 4 April 1963, J.A.A.C., fasc. 29, No. 53 (1959-60) and fasc. 31, No. 51 (1962-63).

131. Federal Law on the Use of Hydroelectric Power, 22 December 1916, R.S. 721.40, Arts. 40 (2), 40 (3).

132. Federal Law on Pipelines, 4 October 1963, R.S. 746.1, Art. 4.

133. Federal Law on the Swiss National Bank, 23 December 1953, R.S. 951.11, Art. 7.

134. Federal Law on Maritime Navigation under the Swiss Flag, 23 September 1953, amended on 14 December 1965, R.S. 747.30, Arts. 19-24.

135. Federal Code of Obligations, 30 March 1911, R.S. 220, Arts. 711 and 895.

136. Federal Law on Banks and Savings Institutions, 8 November 1934, R.S. 952.0, Art. 3 bis.

137. R.S. 941.113.

138. R.S. 941.114.

139. R.S. 941.116.

140. R.O. 1975, 557.

141. Aubert, Traité, No. 1028.

142. According to Law on Residence, Art. 7, a "tolerance" is revocable at will. For the grounds of revocation, see Art. 9 (5) and (1).

143. A temporary residence permit can be revoked (1) if it was obtained under false pretenses; (2) if one of the conditions for its granting has not been met; (3) "if the alien's conduct gives cause for major complaints"; or (4) if the granting of the permit was revocable. Law on Residence, Art. 9 (2). For recent practice on the second point, see Steiner v. Regierungsrat Zürich, op. cit., and X v. Gouvernement du Canton des Grisons, op. cit.

144. Among the ways a permanent residence permit is nullified are (1) if another permit is obtained in another canton; (2) by reason of expulsion or deportation; and (3) if the alien announces his departure or has been abroad for at least six months (upon request this time limit can be extended to two years). The permit can be revoked, in particular, if it has been obtained under false pretenses. Law on Residence, Arts. 9 (3), and 9 (4).

145. Review for violation of constitutional rights (recours de droit public) under Law on the Judiciary, op. cit., Art. 84 ff.

146. See Law on the Judiciary, op. cit., Arts. 97-102; Steiner v. Regierungsrat Zürich, op. cit., Chapter 1, at 650; X. v. Gouvernement du Canton des Grisons, op. cit.

147. Aubert, Traité, No. 1028. (Quoted above.)

148. Law on the Judiciary, Art. 100 (a) (4). Review for violation of constitutional rights (recours de droit public) is not open either, since the decision in question emanates from a federal and not a cantonal authority. (See below.)

149. Swiss Criminal Code, op. cit., Arts. 55, 104 (2), 335.

150. Law on Residence, Art. 10.

151. Decision of the Federal Ministry of Justice, 5 May 1955, J.A.A.C., fasc. 25, No. 98 (1955).

152. This seems to result from Art. 20 (2) of the Regulations on Residence. See also Aubert, Traité, No. 1029 and Tzaut, op. cit., at 13, 14.

153. Law on the Judiciary, op. cit., Art. 97 ff.; Steiner v. Regierungsrat Zürich, op. cit., Chapter 1, at 650.

154. See above. For a recent example, see Losembe v. Ministère public fédéral, 11 July 1973, A.T.F. 99 Ia 547. On extradition in general, see Guggenheim, 1 Traité 360-67 (1st ed.).

155. Federal Law on Extradition, Arts. 22, 23.

156. According to a list published in Rapp. gest. 1974, 24, Switzerland assumed 22 such mandates on 31 December 1974. For statements by the Swiss government on these mandates and on the conflicts of interest they may entail, see Pratique suisse 1972, 29 A.S.D.I. 348-51 (1973).

157. The mandate conferred upon Switzerland by Liechtenstein is of a permanent nature. Thévanaz, La Suisse, Etat mandataire, 6 A.S.D.I. 9-36, at 15-18 (1949).

158. In addition, the consent of the receiving state must be secured.

159. See Aubert, Traité, No. 1325; Guggenheim, 1 Traité de droit international public 73-75 (2nd ed., 1967, hereafter Guggenheim, 1 Traité (2nd ed.); Fleiner, Giacometti, op. cit., at 829; Lardy, La force obligatoire du droit international en droit interne, 181-86, 197-203 (1966); Marck, Traites internationaux IV/V F.J.S. No. 385, 4-7; Wildhaber, Treaty-Making Power and Constitution 202-06 (1971). This view can be based on Constitution, Art. 113 (3), under which the Swiss Supreme Court "shall administer the laws passed by the Federal Assembly, and such ordinances of that Assembly as are of general application. It shall likewise act in accordance with treaties ratified by the Federal Assembly" [emphasis added].

160. Marck, op. cit., at 5-6; Wildhaber, op. cit., at 202-03. For some recent practice on this point, see Pratique suisse 1967, 25 A.S.D.I. 239-41 (1968), containing, among other things, an extract from the case of Librairie Hachette S.A. et consorts v. Société coopérative d'achât et de distribution des négociants en tabacs et journaux et consorts, 21 March 1967, A.T.F. 93 II 192, c. 1, 4, at 195, 197; Pratique suisse 1968-1969, 26 A.S.D.I. 91-133 (1969-70), which includes in particular an important declaration made on 10 December 1968, by Willy Spühler, Foreign Minister (at 92-101); decision of the Swiss Supreme Court in the case of Frigerio v. Département fédéral des transports et communications et de l'énergie, 22 November 1968, A.T.F. 94 I 669, Chapters 2-7, at 672-80 (at 119-33 of the Pratique suisse); Message of the Federal Council to the Federal Assembly Concerning the Hague Convention on the Law Applicable to International Sales of Movables, 20 October 1971, Pratique suisse 1971, 28 A.S.D.I. 224-27 (1972); Pratique suisse 1972, 29 A.S.D.I. 336-37 (1973); Banque de Crédit international v. Conseil d'Etat du canton de Genève, op. cit., c. 2 (a) at 387; Opinions of the Division of Justice of the Federal Ministry of Justice, 7 June 1967 and 4 March 1969, J.A.A.C., fasc. 33, No. 4 (1966-67), and fasc. 34, No. 4 (1968-69); Wessely v. Regierungsrat Zürich, op. cit.

161. This conception had been adopted by the Swiss Supreme Court in earlier cases. Lepeschkin v. Zürich Obergericht, 2 February 1923, A.T.F. 49 I 188, Chapter 3, at 195-96; Helvetia v. Kuch und Frauenberger, 15 April 1945, Pratique suisse 1946, 4 A.S.D.I. 143-44 (1947). For a refutation, see Wildhaber, op. cit., at 204-05.

162. Lardy, op. cit., at 203, 242; Marck, op. cit., at 7; Wildhaber, op. cit., at 280; X v. Administration fédérale des contributions, 23 December 1970, A.T.F. 96 I 237, Chapter 6(b), at 247-48, Pratique suisse 1971, 28 A.S.D.I. 242 (1972); Roussette v. Buchs, Canton of St. Gallen and Administrative Tribunal of St.-Gallen, 8 May 1974 (unpublished decision of the Swiss Supreme Court); Opinion of the Division of Justice of the Federal Ministry of Justice, 13 July 1973, J.A.A.C., fasc. 37/II, No. 32 (1973).

163. Lardy, op. cit.; Marck, op. cit.

164. For a recent case exemplifying the absence of an open and irreconcilable conflict between a (previous) law and a treaty by reason of the latter's being a lex specialis, see Hillmann v. Caisse suisse de compensation et Commission de recours de la Caisse suisse de compensation, decision of the Swiss Supreme Court in Insurance Matters of 13 October 1970, A.T.F. 96 V 140, at 140-41, Pratique suisse 1970, 27 A.S.D.I. 171-72 (1971).

165. Guggenheim, 1 Traité 75 (2nd ed.). For an opposing opinion see Lardy, op. cit., at 204 ff.

166. See Spühler's declaration in Hachette, op. cit., at 93-94, 97-99.

167. See Frigerio case, op. cit., Chapter 6 (a), at 678-79, 26 A.S.D.I. 125-26, 131-32 (1969-70), and the Schubert case, op. cit. See, however, Thareau v. Ministère public fédéral, 18 September 1974, A.T.F. 100 Ia 407, at 410.

168. See Spühler's declaration in Hachette, op. cit., at 92-93, 97 (1969-70).

169. See ibid., at 93-94, 97-99; Frigeris case, op. cit., Chapter 6 (a), at 678-79, 26 A.S.D.I. 125-26, 131-32; Schubert case, op. cit.; Thareau case, op. cit.; Lardy, op. cit. For an opposing opinion, see Schubert case, op. cit.

170. On this question in general, see Lardy, op. cit., at 225-42, 243-44; Marck, op. cit., at 11-15.

171. Wildhaber, op. cit., at 351. Article 113 (3) is quoted in a previous note.

172. Constitution, Art. 121. On this point, see also Wildhaber, op. cit., at 394-95, and the proposal of the Federal Council to institute an obligatory referendum for the accession to international organizations instituting a system of collective security or to "supranational" organizations. See Message of the Federal Council to the Federal Assembly Concerning New Provisions on the Referendum in Matters of Treaties, 23 October 1974, F.F. 1974 II 1133, at 1136-39.

173. Guggenheim, "Organisations économiques supranationales, indépendance et neutralité de la Suisse," 82 Revue de droit suisse 221-343, at 295 (1963, II).

174. Fleiner, Giacometti, op. cit., at 813.

175. Opinion of 15 August 1957, J.A.A.C., fasc. 29, No. 3 (1959-60).

176. Report of the Federal Council to the Federal Assembly on the Convention on Human Rights and Fundamental Freedoms, 9 December 1968, Pratique suisse 1968-1969, 26 A.S.D.I. 106-07 (1969-70). See further the statement made by Pierre Graber, Foreign Minister, on 30 September 1970,

Pratique suisse 1970, 27 A.S.D.I. 157-59 (1971) and the opinion of the Division of Justice, op. cit.

177. Lardy, op. cit., at 197-98; Marck, op. cit., at 3, 15. According to Wildhaber, op. cit., at 206, "Swiss practice has hardly exhibited any awareness of the distinction between self-executing and non-self-executing treaties." See, however, Rossier v. Cour de justice du Canton de Genève, 23 May 1962, A.T.F. 88 I 86, Chapters 4 (b), 4 (c), at 90-91; Message of the Federal Council, op. cit.; Opinion of the Federal Ministry of Justice, 20 March 1964, J.A.A.C., fasc. 32, No. 5 (1964-65), Opinions of the Division of Justice, op. cit.; Banque de Crédit international case, op. cit., Chapter 2 at 387 ff.

178. Report of the Federal Council to the Federal Assembly, on the 52nd Session of the International Labour Conference, 16 April 1969, Pratique suisse 1968-1969, 26 A.S.D.I. 101-02 (1969-70); Opinions of the Division of Justice, op. cit.; Opinion of the Division of Justice of the Federal Ministry of Justice, 4 March 1969, J.A.A.C., fasc. 34, No. 4 (1968-69); Wessely case, op. cit.; Marck, op. cit., 15 ff.

179. Report of the Federal Council, op. cit., at 111; Marck, op. cit., at 16. See also the Opinion of the Division of Justice, 4 March 1969, op. cit.; Wessely case, op. cit.; Marck, op. cit.

180. Sahovic, in Manual of Public International Law, ed. Max Sørensen (London, 1968), pp. 445-46.

181. Underhill v. Hernandez, 65 F. 577, at 579 (1895).

182. Delson, "The Act of State Doctrine--Judicial Deference or Abstention," 66 American Journal of International Law 82-93, at 90 (1972).

183. Banco Nacional de Cuba v. Sabbatino, 376 U.S. 398, at 428 (1964).

184. Delson, op. cit., at 93.

185. Hausner v. Banque internationale de Commerce de Petrograd, 10 December 1924, A.T.F. 50 II 507, at 512-13; Wilbuschewitsch v. Waisenamt Zürich, 13 July 1925, A.T.F. 51 II 259, Chapter 2, at 264; Schinz v. Obergericht Zürich, 4 June 1926, A.T.F. 52 I 218, at 219-20 (1925-26), Annual Digest, No. 23; Heirs Prochorow v. Zürich Obergericht, 26 October 1929, A.T.F. 55 I 289, Chapter 2, at 291-95; Zivnostenska Banka v. Wismeyer, 23 January 1953, A.T.F. 79 II 85, Chapter 1, at 89-93; VEB Carl Zeiss Jena v. Firma Carl Zeiss Heidenheim, 30 March 1965, A.T.F. 91 II 117, Chapter 4, at 126-27.

186. See, in addition to the cases cited in the preceding note, Compagnie fermière de la Grande Chartreuse et Pascalis v. Rey, 11 July 1918, A.T.F. 39 II 640, Chapter 8, at 652; Guigue, Dechandon, Auclair et Cie v. Stromeyer, 17 December 1914; A.T.F. 40 II 483, Chapter 3, at 486; La Nationale v. Biermann, 17 April 1916, A.T.F. 42 II 179, Chapter 3, at 183-84; In re Arnaboldi, 6 December 1917, A.T.F. 43 II 553, Chapter 1, at 555-56; Goldschmid v. Posteau, 19 April 1918, A.T.F. 44 II 163, Chapter 1, at 170; Weixler et consorts v Société des Transports internationaux, 1 April 1924, A.T.F. 50 II 51, Chapter 2, at 58; In re Bachert & Co., 3 May 1927, A.T.F. 53 III 54, Chapter 2, at 57-61; Nathan Institut A.G. v. Schweizerische Bank für Kapitalanlagen, 18 September 1934, A.T.F. 60 II

294, Chapter 5 (a), at 310-12; Rheinische Grundstucks-Handelsgesellschaft m.b.h. v. A.G. für Immobilienwerte, 8 October 1935, A.T.F. 61 II 242, Chapter 3, at 246; Allgemeine Elektrizitäts-Gesellschaft und Siemens & Halske A.G. v. Journaliag A-G. 1 February 1938, A.T.F. 64 II 88, Chapters 4, 5, at 96-100; Böhmische Unionbank v. Heynau, 22 December 1942, A.T.F. 68 II 377, Chapter 3, at 381-82; Wichert v. Wichert, 28 October 1948, A.T.F. 74 II 224; Chapter 4, at 228-29; London v. Schweiz. Bankverein, 13 May 1952, A.T.F. 78 II 242, Chapter 4 (b), at 248-49; Schweizerische Lebensversicherungs und Rentenanstalt v. Elkan, 26 March 1953, A.T.F. 79 II 193, Chapter 5, at 198-99; Ammon v. Royal Dutch Company, 2 February 1954, A.T.F. 80 II 53, Chapter 3 (a), at 61-63; Französicher Staat v. Legerlotz, 30 September 1954, A.T.F. 80 III 149, Chapter 5 at 160-61; Vereinigte Carborundum- und Elektrizitätswerkes Nationalunternehmen v. Eidgenossisches Amt für geistiges Eigentum, 25 September 1956, A.T.F. 82 I 196, Chapter 1, at 197-200; the Zeiss case op. cit., Chapter 7 (a), at 129-31, limiting the principle of territoriality to takings of assets located outside the territory of the confiscating state; Union de Banque Suisses v. Poljak, 4 February 1969, A.T.F. 95 II 109, Chapter 3, at 114; Pratique suisse 1968-1969, 26 A.S.D.I. 159-60 (1969-70). See further the opinion of the Division of Justice of the Federal Ministry of Justice, 30 July 1941, J.A.A.C., fasc. 15, No. 1 (1941), Pratique suisse 1948, 6 A.S.D.I. 125-27 (1949), and several decisions of lower courts reprinted in 39 Revue suisse de jurisprudence 302-03, 367-70 (1942-43), in Pratique suisse 1953, 11 A.S.D.I. 182-93 (1954), and in 69 Revue suisse de jurisprudence 224-25 (1973).

187. See in particular the Arnaboldi case, op. cit.; Nathan Institut, op. cit.; the Wichert case, op. cit., Carborundumwerke, op. cit.; Poliak case, op. cit.; Institut central des societes financières v. Union Nasic S.A., 27 February 1968, Chapter 4, Semaine judiciaire 1969, 433, at 440.

188. See Carborundumwerke, op. cit., and Union Nasic, op. cit., and the earlier case of Bayerische Bodenkreditanstalt v. Lecoultre, 26 February 1932, A.T.F. 58 II 124, Chapter 3, at 125-26.

189. See Carborundumwerke, op. cit.; Wismeyer, op. cit.

190. See Hausner case, op. cit.; Schinz case, op. cit.; Zeiss case, op. cit.; Billerbeck & Cie. v. Bergbau-Handel G.m.b.H. und Appellationsgericht des Kantons Basel-Stadt, 3 May 1967, A.T.F. 93 I 265, Chapter 1, at 269-70, Pratique suisse 1967, 25 A.S.D.I. 244-45 (1968).

191. Lalive, Sur l'application du droit public étranger, 27 A.S.D.I. 103-42, at 116-17 (1971).

192. Ibid., at 124-25.

193. Niederer, Einige Grenzfragen des ordre public in Fällen entschadigungsloser Konfiskation, 11 A.S.D.I. 91-104 (1954).

194. Ibid., at 94-96.

195. Ibid., at 96-97.

196. Ibid., at 97-99.

197. Ibid., at 99-101.

198. Schücking, Wehberg, Die Satzung des Völkerbundes, 618-19 (2nd ed., 1924).

199. League of Nations Assembly Resolution, 11 October 1935.

200. These proposals are reprinted in F.F. 1935 II 949-54.

201. Ibid., at 937, 945-46, 947.

202. Ibid., at 937, 946-47.

203. Ibid., at 937, 941-42, 944-45.

204. F.F. 1920 I 351-52.

205. F.F. 1935 II 945.

206. Ibid., at 937, 941-42, 944-45.

207. Objections were raised against the Swiss attitude, particularly by France, Great Britain, and the Soviet Union. See ibid., at 939. See also Zacklin, "Challenge of Rhodesia," International Conciliation, No. 575, at 56.

208. Bindschedler, "Das Problem der Beteiligung der Schweiz an Sanktionen der Vereinigten Nationen, besonders im Falle Rhodesiens," 28 Zeitschrift fur auslandisches öffentliches Recht und Völkerrecht 1-15 (1968); Zacklin, The United Nations and Rhodesia 85-87 (1974); Boczek, "Permanent Neutrality and Collective Security: The Case of Switzerland and the United Nations Sanctions against Southern Rhodesia," 1 Case Western Reserve Journal of International Law 75-104 (1969).

209. The principal statements made by the Swiss government are found in Pratique suisse 1966, 24 A.S.D.I. 196-97 (1967); Pratique suisse 1967, 25 A.S.D.I. 278 (1968); Pratique suisse 1968-1969, 26 A.S.D.I. 85-88, 179-80 (1969-70); Pratique suisse 1971, 28 A.S.D.I. 250-51 (1972); and Bulletin Officiel de l'Assemblée Fédérale--Conseil National 1973, 1062-63.

210. Rapp. gest. 1967, 37, 25 A.S.D.I. 278 (1968).

211. On 16 March 1970, the Swiss Consulate in Salisbury was closed down. See Pratique suisse 1970, 27 A.S.D.I. 174 (1971).

212. 26 A.S.D.I. 86-87 (1969-70). The prohibition of exporting arms was based on a Decree of the Federal Council on War Supplies, 28 March 1949, R.O. 1949, 315. The reduction of imports to the normal flow of trade was effected by a Decree of the Federal Council Concerning the Limitation of Imports, 17 December 1965, R.O. 1965, 1217. Imports from Rhodesia are made dependent upon an authorization; the latter is granted only as long as imports do not exceed the "normal flow." The "normal flow" was at first determined by reference to the average imports from Rhodesia in the years 1964-65. See Ordinance of the Federal Ministry of Public Economy, 17 December 1965, R.O. 1965, 1219. Later, it was determined by reference to the average of imports from Rhodesia in 1964-66. See Decree No. 2 of the Federal Council of 10 February 1967, R.O. 1967, 209, and Ordinance No. 2 of the Federal Ministry of Public Economy, 15 February 1967, R.O. 1967, 210.

213. See the declaration reprinted in R. L. Bindschedler, op. cit., at 14-15; see also ibid., at 12.

214. R.O. 1965, 635.

215. Pratique suisse 1967, 25 A.S.D.I. 240-41 (1968).

216. Report of the Swiss Foreign Ministry of 20 August 1934, J.A.A.C., fasc. 8, No. 7 (1934), asserting that courts of law are under no

duty to seek instructions from the Federal Council on the rules of international law governing diplomatic privileges and immunities. See also Guggenheim, 1 Traité 92 (2d ed.); Landis & Cie. A.-G. v. W. H. Joens & Co. und Justizkommission des Kantons Zug, 4 June 1952, A.T.F. 78 I 124, Chapter 3, at 130-31, commented on by Bindschedler, "Switzerland: Recent Trends in International Law," I. 3 Int'l. and Comp. L. Q. 93-100, at 100 (1954); Bertschinger v. Bertschinger, 14 July 1955, A.T.F. 81 II 319, Chapter 4, at 330-31; In re Pater, 13 October 1967, A.T.F. 93 II 354, Chapter 4, at 361-62, Pratique suisse 1967, 25 A.S.D.I. 238-39 (1968).

217. A contrary opinion was expressed in a decision of the Obergericht of Zürich, 28 September 1921, 20 Blätter für Zürcherische Rechtsprechung, No. 191 (1921).

218. On this question, see generally Gmür, "Zur Frage der gerichtlichen Immunität fremder Staaten und Staatsunternehmungen," 7 A.S.D.I. 9-76 (1950).

219. That is, the provisional freezing of the assets of certain categories of debtors. See Federal Law on Bankruptcy and Other Enforcement Measures, 11 April 1889, R.S. 281.1, Art. 271.

220. Decree of the Federal Council prohibiting Sequestration and Enforcement Measures against Movable Assets of Foreign States, 12 July 1918, R.O. 34, 791. The decree was abrogated on 8 July 1926.

221. Ibid., Art. 2.

222. Decree of the Federal Council Concerning Sequestration and Enforcement Measures against Debtors Residing Abroad, 24 October 1939, R.O. 55, 1340. This decree was abrogated on 3 September 1948.

223. Ibid., Art. 2.

224. In this sense Lémonon, Immunité de juridiction et d'exécution forcée, F.J.S., No. 934, 2.

225. Federal Law on the Binding Force of the R.S. 1848-1947 and of the New Series of the R.O., 12 March 1948, R.S. 170. 513.1, Art. 9; Pratique suisse 1968-1969, 26 A.S.D.I. 106 (1969-70); Marck, op. cit., at 6-7; Wildhaber, op. cit., at 205-06.

226. That treaties can be applicable to legal as well as to natural persons has been established by a consistent practice of the Swiss Supreme Court. For recent examples, see Hachetts, op. cit.; and Müller v. Transamet S.A., 27 February 1968, A.T.F. 94 II 62, Pratique suisse 1968-1969, 26 A.S.D.I. 148 (1969-70).

227. Declarations of reciprocity are assimilated to treaties. See Guggenheim, 1 Traité 90 (2nd ed.).

228. Federal Law on Administrative Procedure, op. cit., Art. 73 (1) (b). It results from Art. 79 (1) of that law that the decision of the Federal Council can in turn be reviewed by the Federal Assembly.

229. Law on the Judiciary, op. cit., Arts. 43 ff. (recours en réforme), 68 ff. (recours en nullite), 116 ff. (action de droit administratif), 128 ff. (recours or action de droit administratif in insurance matters) Federal Law on Bankruptcy and other Enforcement Measures, op. cit., Art. 19; Federal Law on Criminal Procedure, 15 June 1934, R.S. 312.0, Art. 268 ff.

230. Law on the Judiciary, op. cit., Art. 102.

231. Ibid., Art. 98.

232. Ibid., Art. 104 (a). If the decision to be reviewed emanates from a cantonal authority, cantonal remedies must have been exhausted previously. See Art. 98 (g).

233. Law on the Judiciary, Art. 100 (a). The exclusion, by this provision, of "other matters connected with external relations" does not mean that an alien is prevented from seeking enforcement of his treaty rights through the Supreme Court acting as the country's highest administrative jurisdiction. See Piu-Azzaro v. Regierungsrat Zürich, op. cit.

234. This flows from the contrary of the Law on the Judiciary, op. cit., Art. 98 (a), and Federal Law on Administrative Procedure, op. cit., Art. 79 (1).

235. Law on the Judiciary, op. cit., Art. 84 (2).

236. Ibid., Art. 84 (1). For alleged violations of treaty rights, exhaustion of cantonal remedies is permissible but not mandatory. See Law on the Judiciary, Arts. 86 (3) and 84 (1) (b); Engels v. Etablissement Sarina S.A., 5 March 1932, A.T.F. 58 I 96, Chapter 1, at 99; and Guggenheim, 1 Traité 90 (2d ed.).

237. Law on the Judiciary, op. cit., Arts. 84 ff.

238. R.O. 1968, 1022.

239. F.F. 1968 II 1160.

240. F.F. 1967 II 1460. Excerpts in Pratique suisse 1967, 25 A.S.D.I. 241-43, 245-50, 254-59, 271 (1968).

241. World Bank Convention on the Settlement of International Investment Disputes, Art. 27 Pratique suisse 1967, 25 A.S.D.I. 247-48 (1968).

242. Ibid., at 249-50.

243. Ibid., at 247.

244. Ibid., at 242.

245. Ibid., at 242-43.

246. Report of the Federal Council of 9 December 1968, on the Convention on the Protection of Human Rights and Fundamental Freedoms, F.F. 1968 II 1069. Parts of this report are reprinted in Pratique suisse 1968-1969, 26 A.S.D.I. 104-18, 135, 137-42, 149-50, 156-57, 172 (1969-70).

247. These reservations would have covered in particular Constitution, Arts. 51, 52 (prohibition of Jesuits' activities and prohibition of founding of new convents or religious orders or of reestablishing previously abolished convents and orders); political rights of women, which at that time were nonexistent on the federal level; and cantonal legislation permitting the so-called "administrative internment" of certain individuals.

248. Women are granted political rights on the federal level by Constitution, Arts. 74 (1), 74 (2), as amended on 7 February 1971. Articles 51 and 52 of the Constitution, relating to Jesuits, convents, and religious orders, were abrogated on 20 May 1973.

249. Additional Report of the Federal Council on the Convention on the Protection of Human Rights and Fundamental Freedoms, 23 February 1972, F.F. 1972 I 989; Message of the Federal Council to the Federal Assembly

Relating to the European Convention on Human Rights, 4 March 1974, F.F. 1974 I 1020.

250. 1968 Report, Pratique suisse 1968-1969, 26 A.S.D.I. 104 (1969-70). See also statement made on 4 December 1972 by Graber, Foreign Minister, Pratique suisse 1972, 29 A.S.D.I. 382 (1973).

251. 1968 Report, Pratique suisse 1968-1969, 26 A.S.D.I. 111 (1969-70).

252. Ibid., 112-13. See 4 December 1972 statement by Graber, op. cit.

253. See ibid., 110-11. Reference is of course being made to the possibility of having federal as well as cantonal decisions in administrative matters reviewed by the Swiss Supreme Court acting as the country's highest administrative jurisdiction.

254. 1968 Report, Pratique suisse 1968-1969, op. cit., at 110.

255. Ibid., at 114; 1972 Report, F.F. 1972 I 998-99. See also 4 March 1974 Message of the Federal Council, at 10.

256. 1968 Report, Pratique suisse 1968-1969, 26 A.S.D.I. 114, 135 (1969-70); statement made on 3 October 1972 by Graber, Foreign Minister, Pratique suisse 1972, 29 A.S.D.I. 380-81 (1973). See further the 4 March 1974 Message of the Federal Council, op. cit., at 1036.

257. 1968 Report, Pratique suisse 1968-1969, op. cit., at 139; 1972 Report, op. cit., at 998.

258. 1968 Report, Pratique suisse 1968-1969, op. cit., at 140.

259. Statement made on 7 October 1969 by Spühler, Foreign Minister, in ibid., at 142-45.

260. Ibid., at 114-15.

261. Ibid., at 143, 145.

262. Ibid., at 136; 3 October 1972 statement by Graber, op. cit.; 4 March 1974 Message of the Federal Council, op. cit., at 1037.

263. See Schubert case, op. cit.

CHAPTER

17

THAILAND

Sompong Sucharitkul

Few subjects in the progressive development of international law are more topical than individual rights and the state in foreign affairs. The individual is just as inextricably involved in the affairs of nations as in those of his or her own state. Relations between states and individuals in international affairs are therefore matters of common daily occurrence. It is accordingly desirable to explore the practice of states for indications of the direction in which the law of nations in regard to the rights and duties of the individual and of the state is likely to develop in the foreseeable future.

Individual human beings are gaining recognition and are acquiring their rightful place in the development of international law, especially in the fields of human rights and economic and social development, as well as in labor relations and manpower. To come to the aid and comfort of the individual against the authority of the state is indeed ideal, provided that the protection sought is simply designed to safeguard the fundamental rights of the individual, for which a certain minimum standard is sometimes said to exist, in theory if not everywhere in practice, under international law.

If the purpose of the general enquiry being undertaken in this book is therefore to ascertain state practice in the field under review, which may differ from country to country without attempting to lay down rules that subsequent generations could label as lopsided in favor of powerful individuals against the long-suffering states and their less-fortunate human elements, the conference convened to discuss such findings could make a useful contribution to the peace and happiness of mankind. In the search for truth, however, care

---

Reviewed by the author in 1975, but not revised.

should be taken lest the searchers, no matter how lofty their intentions, fail to discern the fine distinction between the state and the individual, or more precisely, lest they place too much emphasis on this fragile classification. After all, what is the state but an organism established by human beings? The state can have no actual physical existence that makes it separate and independent from its human components. It would be a false start to presuppose that there is an essential conflict of interest between the state and the individual and that as a result the rules of international law have evolved primarily to protect the one from suppression by the other. It is pointless, therefore, to proceed from the proposition that the individual necessarily requires adequate protection from encroachment by the state. An objective examination of history far from substantiates such an impression.

However, to state an objective view in this connection is to invite adverse comments and unpleasant reactions from certain quarters, in which international law may be believed to have been developed to preserve the economic and political interests of the European and Western powers and to perpetuate a state of affairs that leads to their exclusive advantage. It is not uncommon, nor unfashionable, in certain quarters, notably among the rich or among the more advanced nations, to entertain the impression that it is desirable under international law to devise at all costs effective protection for nationals who have accumulated wealth overseas, so that their riches can grow and accrue to their increasing benefit. According to this view, their investments in foreign lands should continue to be guaranteed, regardless of the vital and predominant interests of the developing local states.

The real dichotomy is not between the state and the individual as such. In international relations it is that which lies at the root of international conflicts, the dichotomy between the rich and the poor, between the haves and the have nots, both on the state and individual levels. In any conflict of interests between the rich and the poor or between a great power and a smaller, weaker, and poorer nation, it is the poor, the small, and the weak that invariably come out worse than before the conflict. Such have been the hard facts of international life.

Understanding this, an international lawyer in the true sense of the word is duty-bound to seek, perhaps not a far-fetched solution to the existing problems, but at least an improvement in the lot of the world populace. The lawyer should work to strengthen the position of the poorer nations against the continuing encroachment and exploitation of natural and human resources by the fortunate few. The powerful can persuade their also-powerful governments to put greater pressure on, and exert tighter control over, the poorer and less advanced nations. They can also afford rich lawyers and expensive counsel to represent their interests against the wretched and practically defenseless nations at international conferences, including governmental as well as private international conferences on the progressive development of international law.

A happy medium or an equitable balance could be maintained on the basis of peaceful coexistence between the individual and the state, as between the have and the have-not. Indeed, their mutual understanding and cooperation would be an advancement in international relations. The individual should coexist with the rich, the powerful, and the big. Humanity will be greatly served if the existing gap that divides the rich and the poor can be prevented from widening further. On the contrary, efforts should be made to seek to bridge, if not entirely close, the gap. More understanding should be shown by the fortunate nations of the needs of the poorer, smaller, and weaker nations. The necessity that the poor survive as decent human beings or respectable states must be recognized. Although rich individuals in the powerful states continue to live on the wealth of poorer countries, the poorer and less powerful states should be allowed to survive for the sake of peace and harmony. "Long live the individual and let live the states" is the thesis of this chapter. It will be seen that in the context of the general outline planned for the various chapters in this book, practically every topic appears to call for a reminder that, as a profession, lawyers have a responsibility to the community of nations to promote peace and progress for mankind in general and a particular duty to refrain from endeavors to suppress less-fortunate individuals or less-developed countries.

THE INDIVIDUAL

Individual rights in any free society are not unlimited. Their limitations are imposed and controlled by the state. For the purposes of this chapter, I shall treat individuals and their rights and duties in relation to the state either as national or as non-national. Other categorizations, such as slave or subhuman, will not be dealt with in this chapter, although in the past slavery under Roman law was an established institution, and slaves have been treated differently from citizens. They were neither nationals nor non-nationals in the modern sense of those terms.

The division of individuals into national and non-national categories immediately emphasizes the concept of nationality. It would, however, be beyond the scope of this book to go into the intricate details of the nationality legislation of each sovereign nation.

No attempt will therefore be made to explore the Nationality Acts of Thailand in detail. It will suffice to point out some of the salient features that may be of some relevance and interest.

The main nationality legislation of Thailand is the Nationality Act, B.E. 2495 (1952), as modified by B.E. 2508 (1965). Like other modern and uncomplicated laws on nationality, Thai law recognizes the dichotomy between nationals and non-nationals, or aliens. Thai nationality is acquired by birth, according to the location of birth as well as to the nationality of the family. It can also be acquired more or less automatically by marriage. For a long time a woman who married a Thai national acquired Thai nationality by virtue of the marriage alone, but now a declaration of intention is needed, and the discretion of the responsible authority has to be favorably exercised. On the other hand, a Thai woman does not lose her Thai nationality upon marriage unless she acquires the nationality of her husband and expressly declares to the marriage registrar her intention of giving up her Thai nationality. Thai nationality may also be acquired by naturalization. Once lost nationality can be resumed.

Thai law regards nationality as an artificial concept that is somewhat inferior to racial origin or parentage. Thus one of its distinct features has been the practice of the local or municipal administration to inquire further into the history of the person, as if to pierce the veil of nationality. In the census form, for instance, a person, whether Thai or foreign, is asked to state nationality as well as race, which could be deduced from parentage. Apparently this division would serve to distinguish cases of naturalization or subsequent changes of nationality. In fact, it is designed to satisfy certain requirements for a test of loyalty to the Kingdom of Thailand and could be explained by reference to the preoccupation of the kingdom with maintaining its sovereign and independent existence, rather than by nationalistic tendencies or any policy of racial discrimination. For all practical purposes the division has lost its significance, although it is still retained in certain areas, though without meaningful purpose.

The Individual as a National

Movement

People are born free, but they are not always born with passports. Freedom of movement in international fields is almost synonymous with an inherent right to a passport. Strange as it may seem, people used to enjoy far greater freedom of movement before the advent of the passport, which paradoxically has resulted in some curtailment of free movement in more ways than one.

Passports. The right to a passport is almost guaranteed as the birthright of a Thai national. Even a child still in the womb is considered to be a person under the Civil Code of Thailand and as such entitled to a passport, although at first it will have to share its mother's passport. Upon birth, if traveling separately or independently of its mother, a child is also entitled to apply for a travel document. However, to say that every person, as a matter of right, is given a passport as an indication of freedom to travel beyond the confines of his or her national boundaries is to state an ideal rather than a readily realizable condition of fact.

In Thailand a person can move freely within the kingdom. Whoever can demonstrate Thai nationality by a birth certificate or registration at birth is also free to move in and out of the realm. A convenient and readily acceptable proof of being a Thai national when crossing a frontier is a Thai passport. If a person happens to be in possession of a Thai passport, even if no longer valid because of lapse of time, the immigration authority of Thailand would in all probability allow that person into the country to enable the person to furnish further evidence of his or her Thai nationality.

Thus a passport, though not technically sufficient evidence of nationality in a court of law, goes a long way toward providing the necessary facilities in regard to movement in and out of the kingdom. Thailand being, as the name literally suggests, the land of the free, a Thai passport, which affords an undisputed right of entry into Thailand, is indeed a valuable possession.

In principle, every Thai national can have a valid Thai passport. However, in no way is this an absolute principle; nor is its application automatic. The rules that have evolved reflect the attitude of the state, which while imposing no restrictions on the movements of its nationals within the state boundaries, does not appear enthusiastic about encouraging its nationals to leave their homeland. They are free to come and go as they please, but the state shows no particular interest in promoting emigration because of either lack of employment opportunities or overpopulation. In fact, Thailand is a land of plenty, where unemployment is relatively unknown; and despite its population explosion, Thailand is still underpopulated. All things considered, the regulations concerning passports have been on the strict side, although in reality there have been comparatively few complaints of failure to obtain a passport because an application has not been approved.

Apart from the formal requirements, such as a recent photograph and payment of a nominal fee of about $10, there are also genuine substantive conditions.

Examination by the police department can operate as a deterrent to those whose good faith stands in doubt. The procedure can be protracted. Criminals or suspects will probably not be given police approval without further questioning. This requirement is dispensed with in the case of military personnel or civil servants traveling abroad in the course of their duties or with the authorization of their departments. For tourists in good standing, it appears that with the lapse of very little time a valid passport could be legally procured with endorsement by the police department, with some assistance from the tourist agencies. In actual practice, therefore, the requirement does not impede genuine applicants in good faith. Some such procedure appears to have developed in other countries, for there are a number of similar requirements, such as an application for permission to leave.

Evidence of financial means is also required. The state does not wish to see its nationals suffer abroad for lack of funds. Invariably a guarantor of some means is required, to promise to refund the state in the event that the cost of repatriation has been disbursed by the state through its embassy or consulate or other state agency. Unlike some other countries, which wish to see the last of their nationals, Thailand welcomes its nationals, and instead of refusing reentry to those who have left, welcomes their return to their fatherland. From the standpoint of the individual, fulfillment of this requirement also affords a comforting assurance of a safe-conduct back to the starting point. On balance this appears to be a satisfactory arrangement for the state as well as for its nationals. Both seem to know at least approximately where they stand. It does not give rise to much difficulty or hardship, but it necessarily involves a third party. The requirement is exempted in all cases in which the state itself is the ultimate guarantor, namely in cases of government employees traveling in the exercise of their functions or by order of the state. In such cases the state is directly responsible for the cost of repatriation.

Consent of a third party is needed in certain specified cases. In a sense, an application for a passport can be viewed as a contract between the national and the state. Here the law of the land governs capacity to contract. The question of capacity in civil law is peculiar to each particular legal system, which in turn is founded upon usage and customs. The law of persons and family relations generally reflects the prevailing traditions and culture of the society in which it operates. Thus a married woman in normal circumstances requires the consent of her husband to an application for a passport. The husband is to be made aware of, and must consent to, the proposed departure of the wife from her homeland. Here the state intervenes to protect the integrity of marriage and to allow the wife to travel only with the consent of the husband. However, this requirement has many exceptions. Apart from the dispensation by the state, as in other requirements, because of official duties, in which case consent is presumed to have been given, the issuing authority, namely the Ministry of Foreign Affairs, has a discretion to waive the requirement when the husband is absent abroad; when the couple is separated; or when the husband is not available to give consent, for instance when he is still in his monkhood or serving a prison sentence.

Similarly, parental consent is required for persons under age. Under the Civil Code of Thailand, a person comes of age at 20 or upon marriage, which is legally permissible at the age of 17 in the case of a male and 15 in the case of a female. The reason for this consensual requirement is to be found in the interest society has in the establishment and maintenance of order and respect within the family. In reality, the parents are often expected to answer for all acts of their children. This vicarious liability should therefore rightly be matched by a controlling authority, although exceptions do exist in some cases in which young persons may be granted passports even without the affirmative consent of their parents. Thus a person in public service, although not yet of age, could be instructed to travel abroad. Parental consent is presumed to have been given upon his or her entrance into public service. Orphans could also provide proof of quasi-parental consent in the absence of actual parental authority.

Departure. Once a valid passport has been obtained, a Thai national is at liberty to leave the country either temporarily or permanently. The attitude of the state in regard to the freedom of movement of its nationals is neither possessive nor indifferent. While the state does not wish to exclude its nationals from its territory and would invariably welcome their permanent stay in the country, it does not particularly seek to confine its own nationals within the kingdom. They are in theory free to leave the country and may do so in practice once the necessary travel document or a passport has been procured.

The difficulties in obtaining passports constitute a first series of obstacles to freedom of movement across international frontiers. They are by no means the only limitations. Other pressures or limitations also exist to encourage nationals not to remain too long abroad. A passport is normally valid for two years and renewable for another period of two years. Thus the life span of a passport is four years at the most. After its expiration, a new passport has to be applied for, at which point the entire process of application has to be repeated. In fact, this repetition has to take place every two years, since the procedures for renewal or extension of an existing passport are identical with those for obtaining a new passport.

In this way the state exercises a measure of control over its nationals in regard to their departure from the kingdom. Greater control is available in the cases of students, whose passports have to be renewed on a yearly basis. Students who fail to satisfy a certain minimum standard of performance or behavior can be recalled or sent home. Their passports can be cancelled or validity reduced. In any event, the state can refuse further renewals for several reasons.

In general, the arms of the state do not extend very far beyond the bounds of its territory. Nevertheless, the state can effectively exercise certain measures of control over its nationals abroad by refusing renewal of passports, canceling travel documents, or issuing passports with limited duration for the specific purpose of allowing individuals to regain their homeland. In addition, prior prohibitive measures are also available to prevent individuals from leaving the country. In the case of students, for instance, more rigid requirements have to be met to ensure that applications for passports with the object of studying abroad comply with very exacting regulations. Private students are more or less free to stay away from the country, subject to renewal of passports, but government scholars are required to return home upon completion of their courses of study. They are required to serve the government for a specified period of time in proportion to the lengths of their scholarships abroad.

The problem of the brain drain has become acute in some Asian countries, but Thailand has been more fortunate in this connection. Thai students, trainees, or experts invariably find greater comfort in their fatherland, though with perhaps considerably less, but sufficient, earnings and with far greater satisfaction. There tends to be longer absence abroad in the medical profession, since the program of specialization for practicing different branches of medicine in fact requires a longer time to complete, but eventually Thai doctors have returned home. In the very few exceptional cases in which doctors have chosen to stay away permanently, they have done so of their own accord and have also often opted for the nationality of their countries of residence. Thailand does not seek to compel its nationals to maintain their nationality in such or indeed in any other circumstances. A national of Thailand is always free to forsake his own nationality, but resumption of that nationality is not necessarily automatic.

Possession of a valid Thai passport will facilitate departure from the kingdom, but it does not guarantee an absolute freedom of departure. Anyone, including a Thai national, can be stopped at the frontier or at the airport or seaport by the immigration, police, or customs authorities for infringement of the law. A fugitive from justice can be arrested and thereby prevented from leaving the country. This is the rule rather than the exception, since individuals seeking to leave the country are screened. Thus a person serving a prison sentence or on parole could not expect to be allowed to leave the country for reasons of health or for other personal reasons.

Subject to the foregoing limitations, a Thai national is virtually free to depart from Thailand temporarily or permanently.

Return. The right to return to Thailand is clearer for persons who carry with them evidence of their Thai nationality. With a Thai passport a person seeking entry or reentry into Thailand does not need any visa. In point of fact, if proof of Thai nationality could be established a person could enter or reenter the kingdom and remain therein for as long as he or she pleased. In general this aspect of the right of return gives rise to no particular problem.

Related problems do exist, however, both in law and in fact. The first group of cases concerns persons who were born nationals of Thailand but who have subsequently left the kingdom and by process of naturalization, marriage, or otherwise have lost their nationality. Such former nationals are given very lenient and favorable consideration when they apply for entry visas into the kingdom, but they are not permitted to return to their former homeland or to resettle there as a matter of right.

The second group of cases involves persons with dual or multiple nationality including Thai. This could come about as the result of birth within one state to parents of another state. Thai laws encourage the exercise of choice of citizenship on attaining majority or at a certain time, but failure to exercise the option still entails problems. As a consequence, many foreigners carrying foreign passports on their departure from Thailand could return with valid Thai passports. This practice is not encouraged, but it nevertheless exists, to the undue advantage of those with a multiplicity of nationalities and passports.

A greater problem by far is the third group of cases involving true aliens who seek illegal entry into Thailand. For whatever motives, each year there are tens of thousands of reported cases of illegal entries into Thailand. Naturally there are probably an equal if not greater number of unreported illegal entries. Among the more usual cases may be counted foreigners of Chinese or Indian descent, who seem to find life more pleasant, or at any rate more tolerable and indeed sustainable in Thailand.

A specific type of case of illegal entry is entrance into Thailand with foreign travel documents. After entry, those who use this method appear before the Court of Law to have themselves declared by the court to be Thai, born in Thailand with proof of a birth certificate. In some cases the real persons to whom the birth certificates belonged have died some time ago, but their identity seems to fit loosely but enough to convince the court that the applicants were born Thai and therefore legally Thai nationals with an undisputed right to return to their fatherland.

A long line of judicial decisions have lent support to this practice. Thus in Pua v. Ministry of Interior, by a decision of 29 December 1953, the Supreme Dika Court of Thailand pronounced upon the nationality of the plaintiff and removed the expulsion order of the Immigration Office, under which the plaintiff was not permitted to remain in the kingdom after entry, treating her as an undesirable alien. The court pointed out, as part of its ruling, that the plaintiff had succeeded in furnishing satisfactory evidence of her birth in Thonburi, Thailand, on 6 December 1931, that her parents had been in Thailand for many decades, and that after her mother's death the father had taken her to China. Several years later she returned to Thailand with a Chinese passport indicating that she had been born in China. Nevertheless the court was not bound by the foreign passport but was free to search through other documents for evidence that would testify to the status of the individual in regard to Thai nationality. In this respect the court had acted correctly, since the possession or loss of Thai nationality is to be decided by Thai law, and a foreign public document cannot be held to provide primary, let alone conclusive, evidence of nationality, especially when it is the Thai nationality that the court is being asked to determine. Thai courts are known, therefore, to have rejected passports as proof of Thai nationality or the absence thereof. Thus an alien was held to be an alien although he carried a passport that indicated that his nationality was Thai, and conversely, a Thai was held to be a Thai national even though he carried a foreign passport indicating his foreign nationality.

For more than a decade after Pua's case, the situation remained clear. The door was wide open for persons born in Thailand who had left for mainland China, originally for good, but who, because of changes in the regime in China or personal reasons subsequently wished to return to Thailand. They could do so by seeking entry as aliens and making use of the above provisions of the law and relying on judicial precedents.

This state of affairs was drastically modified by the 1965 Nationality Act, B.E. 2508. Nationals of Thailand whose only tie with the kingdom was their birthplace, by accident or design, no longer had an absolute right to return to the kingdom as nationals. Since nationality is a purely artificial concept, the new legislation seeks to enquire more deeply into their patriotic attachments and genuine family ties with the country. Returnees such as Pua can no longer claim the privilege of a court's determination of their Thai nationality. Article 17 of the Nationality Act of 1965 provides for the withdrawal, cancellation, or loss of Thai nationality for persons who have acquired Thai nationality exclusively on territorial grounds or solely by virtue of their birth in Thai territory, in the following situations:

1. when the person left Thailand to reside in the country of which his or her father is or was a national for a continuous period of five years after attaining majority;

2. when there is proof that the person has made use of the nationality of his or her father or any other nationality or owes allegiance to his or her father's nationality or to any other nationality;

3. when a person has acted in any way affecting the security or against the interest of the state, or in any manner insulting the prestige of the state; or

4. when such a person has acted in a way inconsistent with public order or the moral good of the people.

In the first two situations the Minister of Interior has the power and discretion to withdraw or to restore Thai nationality, but in the last two situations the court must decide whether the persons in question have in fact acted in a manner provided in Article 17. Such persons also lose Thai nationality upon registration as aliens, under Article 21.

Without examining in greater detail other provisions of the Nationality Act of 1965 and more recent practice, suffice it to summarize at this point that a Thai national can generally return to Thailand very freely. There are no artificial bars against his or her return, except in cases in which a national's actions have raised doubts about his or her true nationality, loyalty, or allegiance, or indeed the genuine national character of the persons seeking to return or to continue to stay in Thailand.

Expulsion. What has been said regarding entry and return applies with equal force to expulsion. Here the rule is practically absolute. No Thai national can be excluded or expelled from Thailand. Deportation or expulsion orders are only possible in the cases of nonnationals.

A loophole could exist in borderline cases in which the Thai nationality is more artificial than real. Nevertheless, the Nationality Act of 1965 makes no provision for the state to expel its nationals or indeed to cancel or withdraw Thai nationality, once it has been acquired by birth.

There is no escape clause. Circumstances have called for a special provision in the 1965 act that authorizes withdrawal or in fact prescribes cases in which Thai nationality would be lost. Thus Article 18 of the act authorizes the Minister of Interior, where the circumstances require or where the national security or state interest necessitates, to withdraw or cancel the nationality of a Thai national whose father is an alien, or whose mother is an alien if there is no apparent legal father. The requirements of circumstances and necessities of national security are said to arise when (1) the father or mother has been given leave to enter the kingdom on a special ad hoc basis; (2) the father or mother has been given permission to remain in the kingdom for a limited duration and on a temporary basis; or (3) the father or mother has entered the kingdom without lawful permission as defined in the Immigration Act.

Like the persons mentioned in Article 17, those referred to in Article 18 are equally subject to the possibility of an expulsion order, having lost the artificial cloak of Thai nationality by its withdrawal by the Minister of Interior or by pronouncement of the court.

The conclusion to be drawn from the above analysis is that almost without exception, it is illegal to forcibly expel a Thai national from Thailand.

Remedies. As far as freedom of movement of the individual within or in and out of the state is concerned, the problem should be examined equitably, from the standpoint of the individual as well as of the state. The free movement of the individual is protected by the state in terms of the relative ease with which passports are granted and the maximum facilities afforded in connection with departure, entry, and return, and even with the existing relatively strict practice of control by the state, there is considerable room for abuse by the individual.

For instance, false or forged passports appear in the market. Thai passports bring a very high price in view of their intrinsic probative value. Each year there are reported cases of lost passports and stolen unendorsed passports, which show the extent to which misuse or abuse of the right to a passport is being committed. In reality there are considerably more persons with Thai passports who are not qualified to have them than there are Thai nationals whose right to a passport may for some reason or other have been curtailed.

Similarly, each year Thailand has seen many so-called Thai nationals leaving, entering, and remaining within the kingdom without legal authorization. It is not unnatural that with the land so rich and the people so generous, outsiders would wish to become nationals of Thailand in order to enjoy the fruits of the Thai heritage.

Against such a background and with the governmental stress on maintenance of Thailand's sovereign independence and on safeguarding law and public order, the state has a duty to guard against all possible abuses by the individual, whether by a true national or a pretended one. In this connection the power of the state is virtually unlimited, just as the ingenuity of the individual knows no bounds.

It is an undeniable fact that whatever remedy the state has or may have at its disposal, whether in the form of legislation, such as the Nationality Act of 1965; executive action, or enforcement measures, the individual who wishes to break the law is invariably ahead. It is a common phenomenon that in an orderly society the law has to correspond to the needs and requirements of its members. It is generally slow to catch up with developments within society. The state generally falls behind the individual when it comes to devising effective remedies to deal with abuses of certain fundamental individual rights guaranteed and protected by the state. Whatever legislative reform the state introduces to remedy certain defects, the individual invariably invents novel methods of evasion. Thus the circle continues.

Since the state represents the only authority within the territorial confines and therefore the only institution with power to control or restrict the freedom of movement of the individual, it follows as a matter of equilibrium that the individual also stands in need of adequate remedies in cases of abuse by the state or in cases of infringement of his or her rights by the authorities, whether competent or acting beyond the limits of their actual mandates.

For the individual, many remedies are readily available. In any case in which there is a possibility of abuse or excess of power, the individual can present an appeal or a petition to a higher authority, whether the subject is an application for a passport, an entry visa, or a permit to stay. There are, however, no administrative tribunals in Thailand to deal with such cases in particular. Ordinarily relief can only be sought within the framework of the branch of government concerned. Thus the Ministry of Foreign Affairs and the Police Department can entertain complaints about rejection of a passport application, while the Immigration Department can reexamine an expulsion order or an application for an entry visa. On the whole, government authorities have been more often lenient than strict about the letter of the law. The Minister of Foreign Affairs and the Minister of the Interior also have wide discretion to waive any otherwise rigid requirements concerning the freedom of movement of Thai nationals.

The absence of administrative tribunals under the legal system of Thailand is amply compensated for by the availability of regular judicial remedies against encroachments on individual rights. Under Thai law, while the state has a legal duty to protect the individual, the state itself cannot be reached or impeached before Thai courts. This anomaly does not stem from any theory of state or sovereign immunity; nor is it a result of the principle that the state is above the law and therefore above the court or the principle that the state can do no wrong or cannot be sued in its own court. Curiously enough, the state or indeed the government of Thailand, as a state or government cannot sue or be sued in a Thai court because under Thai law both the state and the government lack the necessary legal personality to sue and be sued before the courts of law. The most pertinent case is Phya Preeda Narubate v. H.M. Government. The court said in that case that "although the word 'Government' may refer to the central organ of the state or a group of persons, it is not a juristic person under the Civil Code or any other law, and is not, therefore, a proper party before the Court."[1]

No judicial remedies are available directly against the state or the government itself, but the individual may always proceed against the responsible departments of government or competent ministers or authorities concerned before the court of law. A recent case brought by Pridi Panomyong against the Thai ambassador to France and the Minister of Foreign Affairs of Thailand illustrates a number of points. The case related to a number of pending cases in which Pridi was involved, but his opponents challenged his physical existence, a technicality that barred his right to bring actions before a Thai court in absentia. In 1970 Dr. Pridi approached the Thai embassy in Paris for a certificate testifying that he was still alive, but the consular section of the embassy was reluctant to issue such a certificate. Thereupon Pridi brought action against the ambassador and the Minister of Foreign Affairs and demanded compensation on a personal basis for their failure to perform their duties of attestation. Although the case was ultimately withdrawn from the court some conciliatory attestation was accorded and a passport was issued. This was a controversial case full of political implications. The individual, with the help of the court of law, had been able to exercise his rights as a national, which essentially signify his freedom of movement.

Although judicial remedies are generally available in support of individual rights, the technical defect inherent in the lack of capacity of the government to sue or be sued before the courts of law may lead to further difficulties. Since by virtue of the Constitution the government can annul or amend contracts made by its ministers in spite of the legal responsibility of the latter according to the ordinary principles of private law, a litigant in such a case may be left without effective remedy. However, there has been no known case of such legislative intervention that has left the individual without any remedy.

It should be noted that although the state and the government as such have no legal personalities in Thai civil law, this does not necessarily imply lack of legal personality in international law.

Protection

Protection and control of individuals by the state may be conveniently discussed under the same heading, since the duty of protection is a corollary of the responsibility of the state resulting from the power, as well as the duty, to control its own nationals. The state has a certain responsibility toward the community of nations not to allow its nationals to commit irresponsible acts that jeopardize friendly relations among nations. Individuals also have a legal duty to refrain from acts that tend to impair the friendly relations of states or that constitute unfriendly interference or intervention in the internal affairs of other states.

Extent of Freedom of Activity Abroad. No one can seriously deny that the state has the power to control its nationals within its boundaries. Beyond that, the state is also under a legal duty to exercise a certain measure of control over its nationals outside its territory. Affairs of state, particularly interrelations among nations, should not be subject to the whims of individuals or the domestic politics of other states. How far the state should be held responsible for acts by its nationals that are injurious to the vital interests of other states, and especially those that adversely affect friendly intercourse among nations, is a matter that deserves the closest attention.

In this connection the laws of Thailand offer a noteworthy model. Chapter 4 of the Penal Code,[2] entitled "Offenses against friendly relations with foreign States," contains several interesting provisions, some of which are well worth quoting. Section 130 provides as follows:

> Whoever commits bodily harm, or commits any act of violence against the liberty of the Sovereign, the Queen or her Consort, Heir-apparent or head of a friendly foreign State shall be punished with imprisonment of one to fifteen years.
>
> Whoever attempts to commit such offence shall be liable to the same punishment.[3]

Section 131 contains a similar provision concerning offenses against the liberty of a foreign representative accredited to the Court of Thailand. Section 132 deals with the assassination or attempted assassination of persons specified in the preceding sections.

According to Section 133, "Whoever defames, insults or threatens the Sovereign, the Queen or her Consort, Heir-apparent or head of a foreign State shall be punished with imprisonment not exceeding three years or fine not exceeding six thousand baht, or both."[4] Section 134 contains a similar provision for offenses against a foreign representative accredited to the Court of Thailand.

Section 135 prescribes penalties for wrongful acts done to the flag or any other emblem symbolizing a friendly foreign state with intent to deride that state.

The above provisions of the Penal Code serve to illustrate the lengths to which the Thai government is prepared to go on treating foreign relations with respect. They also serve to show the extent to which Thai nationals, or foreigners in Thailand for that matter, are bound to refrain from certain acts that would tend to prejudice friendly relations among nations. Unnecessary tensions in world affairs would be reduced if all states adopted this kind of legislation. Such lines of action would help teach the public to leave to the state the conduct of foreign relations. The Thai model is consistent with the dictates of international courtesy.

In practice many irresponsible individuals in other lands, seeking to score domestic political gains, have gratuitously indulged in activities that in Thailand would have been contrary to the letter and spirit of the Penal Code and clearly punishable. For such harmful acts the otherwise responsible governments categorically disclaim their liability, often attributing such nefarious activities to individual whims and, among other things, to freedom of speech, even though in some cases the individuals hold very high legislative or executive positions. They are nevertheless allowed to hide behind the cloak of parliamentary privilege or under the guise of Western democracy, in the name of which many an international crime has been blatantly committed for which no one has been held responsible--neither the individual recalcitrants nor the irresponsible officials, nor even the respectable state they claim to represent.

The grave and urgent problem confronting the conference is therefore how to educate states and individuals alike to be more responsible for their actions, especially in the field of foreign affairs or international relations, in which a greater mutual understanding is required. Individuals should not be permitted to jeopardize friendly relations among nations; nor should states disclaim their responsibility toward the family of nations.

Thai penal laws also recognize Thai criminal jurisdiction over nationals of Thailand in respect to activities abroad regarding certain specified offenses, provided there is a request for punishment by the government of the country in which the offense has been committed or by the injured person.[5]

Control and awareness of a sense of responsibility are desirable on the part of the state as well as the individual in international relations. While the individual should refrain from interference with the internal affairs of other states, just as the state has a legal duty to restrain its nationals from taking part in such unfriendly activities, in normal circumstances the individual should be free to engage in business abroad. Apart from the duty of nonintervention and noninterference, how far should the state exercise control over the activities of its nationals?

On the whole the law and practice of Thailand has been very liberal in this respect. Apart from the sphere of foreign relations, Thai nationals are at liberty to engage in nonpolitical activities abroad on the understanding that they will obey Thai laws and owe allegiance to Thailand, as well as respect local laws and observe local customs. In case of conflict with Thai laws or allegiance to Thailand, Thai nationals are sometimes obliged to decide whether to remain Thai nationals or to lose Thai nationality. Thus, while the Thai government would not wish to see its nationals compulsorily drafted into foreign armed services, it would do little or nothing to prevent its nationals from voluntarily serving in a foreign armed force, either while maintaining or after having forsaken Thai nationality. On the other hand, Thai laws do not allow aliens to serve in the Thai armed forces even on condition of reciprocity or as a retaliatory measure against the foreign state that has conscripted Thai nationals; nor do Thai laws encourage Thai nationals to participate in internal political activities abroad.

In the field of economic activity there has been little guidance from the government. Thailand is a developing country with appreciable natural resources that await further exploitation by capital and skills, which preferably should come from within Thailand. Although the government welcomes foreign investment in Thailand and has created a number of incentives to attract private funds from abroad, it does not appear to be equally enthusiastic in promoting exports of capital or skills. The situation is quite clear. The country stands in need of capital investments as well as technology. The state, as such, accordingly does not extend its controlling arm over its nationals doing business abroad except in the form of monetary exchange and control on the transfer of capital. Since the baht, the Thai unit of currency, is one of the strongest in Asia and is generally convertible, and since Thailand is a member in good standing of the International Monetary Fund, such controls as there are, are minimal in practice. They do not in any way constitute a barrier to the free flow of capital across monetary frontiers and in fact are very little more than formalities.

The Thai government does not share the belief that it is the function of the state to protect the private trading interests of its nationals abroad. Thai nationals engaged in business abroad do so more or less at their own commercial and political risk. If Thai nationals are knowledgeable enough to do business abroad, they should be able to look after themselves and their own affairs. Only in exceptionally flagrant violations of international law is it likely that the Thai government will intervene in favor of its nationals.

The Right to Diplomatic Protection. The Thai government does not particularly favor business activity by its nationals in foreign lands. It is not surprising, therefore, that under the circumstances Thai nationals have no enforceable right to diplomatic protection; nor indeed is there a corresponding compelling duty on the part of the Thai government to protect its nationals abroad, the theory being that nationals engaging in commercial ventures abroad do so at their own risk. The law of nations concerning diplomatic protection has been based on the principle of self-help; weaker countries cannot be expected to enforce claims of right against stronger powers.

It is not difficult to explain the attitude of the Thai government. Thailand entertains no expansionist ambitions; nor does it seem inclined to overprotect the private commercial or trading interests of Thai nationals abroad. This attitude reflects deep feelings against the so-called doctrine of diplomatic protection of citizens abroad. As a first-hand witness, Thailand has seen many tragic instances of much-lauded success in the expansion of the European and Western colonial powers under the doctrine, invented in Western Europe, of protection of their so-called citizens abroad, which finds its application solely against the weaker nations in Asia, Africa, and Latin America. Some weaker European nations have also fallen victim to its application, but in most cases it has been the Asian states that have suffered at the hands of the private foreign individuals doing business abroad. These nationals of Western states naturally enjoyed the protection of their powerful governments, and in return for the generous hospitality of Asian states, ultimately took over property and land that had once belonged to the host countries. Private enterprises seeking ventures in unknown lands used to cling to the notion of protection, which was their almost unreserved right. Their states, on the other hand, preferred to regard the rights as belonging to the states, to grant or to refuse protection as they pleased. After all, in the ultimate analysis it was the state that had to initiate action by dispatching expeditionary forces or gunboats or by espousing claims to make them internationally justiciable. The right to protection is therefore more accurately termed the right to seek state protection or the right of the state to grant protection. In some cases this merely means the individual who runs the state, and therefore it is the individual or the influential trading enterprises that have a conclusive voice in the decision of the state in this particular connection. Thus the anachronism of traditional gunboat diplomacy continues to survive even in the contemporary era, in which the progressive development of international law no longer exclusively rests with the western powers.

The least abominable surviving form of diplomatic protection is diplomatic representation. It is least objectionable only by comparison to the outmoded gunboat diplomacy, the practice of naval blockade, or outright invasion; but great disparity still exists between the rich and the poor. Rich individuals, through their powerful states, continue to make threatening diplomatic representations, while the opposite cannot be done. The poor nationals of a weaker nation stand very little chance of recovering or redeeming any loss of natural wealth or resources through diplomatic representations or otherwise.

International judicial proceedings are costly, and therefore only within reasonable reach of the strong and the rich. The facts of international life are even more revealing. The superpowers or the powerful states are often reluctant to give up the pleasure of being irresponsible or the satisfaction of being untouchable. No poor citizen of a weak state can dream of asking that state to prosecute a claim against a powerful state or against its multimillionaire nationals who own and operate multinational corporations. Such big powers have never really condescended to agree to the compulsory jurisdiction of international tribunals or arbitration. It normally takes a war or a treaty of peace to settle private claims, and very often only in favor of the bigger nations at the expense of the poorer countries. Otherwise international law represents a partial settlement of disputes among richer states within the rich nations' club. Thus a Thai national will have to be highly persuasive to successfully induce the Thai government to espouse a private claim against a foreign government.

The State and Compensation. Thai nationals are generally protected by constitutional provisions against expropriation, requisition, and nationalization of private property by the state. However, the state has wide power to requisition or expropriate private property for the following three purposes: (1) for public utility, (2) for the defense of the realm in case of extreme necessity, and (3) for the acquisition and exploitation of natural resources. In addition the state may expropriate for "other interests of the State." Thus the state has an almost unlimited power of expropriation. There are, however, two significant limitations. First, expropriation is without exception subject to fair compensation. This is to be paid to the owner or to other persons who have the right to compensation. "Fair" compensation under Thai law is generally a matter of negotiation or arbitration. In actual practice it is difficult to obtain adequate compensation. Whatever the test that may be adopted, actual assessment tends to fall short of the minimum true value in most cases. A very few fortunate individuals are sometimes unjustly enriched by an overgenerous measure of compensation authorized or agreed upon by the state, but such cases are very rare.

The second limitation is one provided by the Expropriation Act, whereby the owner is enabled to recover the property expropriated if that property has not been used for the purpose for which it was expropriated within five years of expropriation.[6] This is a development that may have some interest in other countries, since the benefits of this constitutional protection also extend to aliens. The jurisprudence of the Supreme Court has been well established in favor of landowners whose property has been requisitioned. Thus in Chamnongburanapat v. Ministry of Defense (1952) the court allowed recovery of land expropriated for the defense of the country. Parcels of land that had not been used were returned to the owners, while the unused portions of other parcels were also restored. The Supreme Court gave judgment in favor of landowners in seven subsequent cases that were brought in 1953 against the Ministry of Defense and the Minister of Defense. In all these cases the court ordered restoration of expropriated land, although the delay beyond the statutory period of five years had been the result of failure on the part of the arbitrators to reach agreement on the amount of compensation. Thus lack of speedy procedure to ensure prompt compensation may sometimes be a blessing in disguise.

Such has been the attitude of the state in regard to compensation in domestic affairs. The state is not likely to adopt a more liberal view with respect to compensation acquired through an international claim. The state is not anxious to distribute the entire amount of compensation it might manage to secure from another state as the result of injury done to the latter by its nationals. In such a happy event the state might have to deduct the cost of international litigation as well as for the technical injury the state has theoretically suffered. "Topping up" of the compensation received is practically out of the question. The state is not obliged to top up so as to make the ultimate amount of compensation approximately equal to the loss suffered by its nationals.

The Responsibility of the State for Injury Induced by Its Own Conduct. In principle the state is responsible for whatever injury it may cause to its nationals. If state responsibility is established in a given case, compensation is forthcoming. Normally the individual can approach the state for such compensation, which as previously seen is subject to negotiation or arbitration. Judicial remedies are, in the last analysis, available against the state through the responsible ministries or departments.

There have been no reported cases in Thai practice comparable to the provision of supplementary compensation provided by the British government following the British action in Egypt in 1956. It would be difficult to imagine an action by the Thai government that would be so ambitious that it would induce injury to Thai nationals living in foreign countries. Even in such circumstances, it would still be difficult to conceive of procedures whereby practical remedies would be available to the injured nationals of Thailand. The Thai government might consider granting some form of aid or relief, but only as a matter of grace and not in fulfillment of a legal duty.

Waiver. Since the exercise of the right to take up or to espouse a private claim is purely discretionary on the part of the state, the decision of which is often influenced by political rather than economic considerations, the Thai government reserves the right to waive the claims of its nationals in respect to injury caused by foreign states. Such waiver by the state should not be so construed as in any way impairing whatever right Thai nationals have at their disposal before the municipal courts of the foreign states or within their own juridical system.

Questions arise about how far the state can waive in advance, by way of a treaty or international agreement, claims by its nationals in respect to injury caused by foreign states, and also to what extent limitations can be imposed on the amount of compensation in a given case. It is submitted that such treaty provisions constitute only international engagements binding upon the states as contracting powers, and not on the individuals or nationals of the contracting parties, although their chances of obtaining eventual compensation are thereby substantially reduced. Whatever the view regarding the legality or constitutionality of such a limitative clause, the individuals could be left with less effective remedies than were otherwise originally available.

The government of Thailand, wishing to avoid such futile controversy, has preferred not to enter into agreements with clauses that would limit its future course of action or restrict its options to the detriment of the rights of its nationals. When it chooses to waive a claim, it prefers to do so at the time the waiver is necessary.

Special Kinds of Protection. Thailand did not possess a powerful naval fleet during the time of gunboat diplomacy. Because of this, Thai nationals could not very well persuade their government to take up extrajudicial remedies for their protection or in support of their private claims. Even much later in the 1930s, when Siam was reputed to have the second-largest navy among the far eastern countries, the Siamese government preferred peaceful courses and kept its neutrality rather than exercise additional pressure to remedy unjust situations. It has never been the policy of the Thai government to seek further extralegal remedies to enforce the private claims of its nationals against foreign states. Quite the contrary, Thailand, as well as a host of other larger Asian countries, was on the receiving end of naval bombardments from the western powers, allegedly to protect Western citizens.

The special kinds of protection would have to be truly diplomatic, peaceful, and gentle in character, rather than such hostile postures as a threat to reduce or cut existing or future aid or other unsavory sanctions. Economic threats, such as the release of stockpiles of tin or rubber or the increase of subsidies on rice, would be considered as unfriendly gestures hampering the conduct of friendly relations among nations. Larger and more powerful states should be made to understand the deep feelings of the poorer and less fortunate nations, as well as the plight of their not-so-fortunate people. Instead of thinking up new and more effective methods of suppressing their livelihood, say by cutting off aid and other privileges where there is uncompensated taking of the property of their nationals, powerful states could show a more patient, tolerant, and humane attitude. Just as gunboats are no longer fashionable, states should also no longer feel compelled to blindly satisfy the greed of their rich and powerful citizens and help them deny other states and poorer individuals the right to live a decent life. States cannot deny legal and moral protection to their own nationals, but there is no compelling reason for them to overplay their obligation of protection. The age is long passed for colonial regimes or extraterritorial rights and jurisdictions. States are now equal, in law and before international tribunals, although they may have unequal economic or military might. Resort to measures such as the cutting off of aid or similar unethical devices should be abandoned once and for all.

The Individual as an Alien

It is now time to give some attention to the rights and duties of individuals as aliens. In the experience of Thailand, which is not unlike that of many other Asian and African countries, the expression "aliens" is one of the most formidable terms that has been invented to tax the patience and tolerance of the state. Aliens have been wont to claim, not only all imaginable rights, but also sometimes unthinkable privileges, while disclaiming any fundamental duties on their part, even the simple duty to respect and observe local laws or to refrain from acts affecting the national security or interfering with the internal affairs of the host state. In the nineteenth and early twentieth centuries, many sovereign states in Asia were subject to a regime of extraterritorial rights. Aliens were not only untouchable or unimpeachable, but they were also above the local law and outside otherwise perfectly valid local jurisdictions. They were subject only to the exterritorial jurisdiction of their respective consuls. Disputes among them, as well as between aliens and nationals, had to be decided by the exterritorial consular courts. Later, foreign judges also had to sit with the national judges in specially constituted courts of foreign matters having jurisdiction over disputes involving aliens.

"Aliens" were originally nationals of Western European powers who remained beyond the local laws and jurisdiction in spite of their physical presence in the local territory. Subsequently, by way of extension, the term also came to cover Asiatic subjects or nationals of the protected states of western powers. These second-class aliens also were above local laws and local jurisdictions. It is a challenge to any student of international law to attempt to define the kind of world order, or the concept of rule of law, that existed in such circumstances.

Movement

Against the background of superiority of aliens over law and jurisdiction, an understanding of their right of movement may be acquired.

Entry and Stay. The treatment of aliens in respect to entry is now of a lower standard than that accorded to nationals. Nationals enjoy an inherent right of entry, but the rights of aliens are subject to varying degrees of limitations in this regard.

National treatment is not accorded to aliens.

Border areas are given maximum facilities. Thus in the border areas between Thailand and Laos, between Thailand and Malaysia, and between Thailand and Burma, nationals of either side can cross the border with less difficulty than other aliens. In some cases only the presentation of a border pass secures entry, without the necessity of a passport or an international travel document.

Regional groupings, like The Association of Southeast Asian Nations (ASEAN), are also in operation. The nationals of participating partners enjoy special rights of entry into the other participating countries as part of efforts to achieve closer economic cooperation with a view to eventual partial integration.

Favored nations are still recognized; their nationals enjoy free entry without visas on a reciprocal basis. Thus nationals of the Federal Republic of Germany, Denmark, and the United States, for instance, can enter Thailand without prior visa. Likewise, the nationals enjoy reciprocal privileges of entry into the Federal Republic of Germany, Denmark, and the United States.

Standard treatment is accorded to nationals of friendly foreign states whether or not payment of visa fees is required. Entry without a visa is also granted for a limited time to tourists to promote tourism.

Special caution is taken in regard to certain groups of people, such as hippies, who are either not allowed in the country or are allowed subject to a deposit of caution money or other form of guarantee that they will depart. Such means are still in use to minimize the risk to which Thailand has been exposed to a high percentage of illegal entry and illegal residence, not to mention the influx of regugees from North Vietnam and of various political leaders from neighboring countries who have been accorded asylum.

In contrast to nationals, who can remain in Thailand for as long as they please, aliens may only stay for the duration of their permits subject to the conditions that may be prescribed in the permits. In practice visas are essentially distinguishable from permits to stay. While holders of visas acquire the right of entry, the length of their stay in Thailand is an entirely separate matter depending on the Immigration Department, although it is true that to some extent the duration of the permit to stay is governed by the type of visas accorded.

In some cases proof of intent to depart from Thailand, such as a plane reservation, now allows aliens with valid passports to stay in Thailand as tourists for seven days. When the week is up, there is no possibility of further extension.

Tourist visas enable their holders to remain in Thailand up to one month. Normally tourists may, upon entry, be given a more limited permit of stay that can be extended up to a period of one month, beyond which it is only extendable in case of emergency or sudden illness.

Nonimmigrant visas have to be authorized by the Immigration Authority in Bangkok. Holders are not given an indefinite permit to stay in Thailand. In fact, they are probably allowed a permit for one month at a time, which can be extended twice. Thus, after a total period of three months, nonimmigrant aliens have to leave the kingdom.

Immigrant visas are only granted with prior approval from the Immigration Department. They are valid for aliens residing permanently in Thailand. Resident aliens can also apply for reentry visas or nonquota immigrant visas for their return to Thailand.

Diplomats and staff members of international organizations with headquarters in Thailand are also given appropriate authorization to remain in the kingdom during their terms of office.

Students are given leave to stay in Thailand to complete their approved courses of study.

It should be observed that at present there is no other status between immigrant and nonimmigrant. Persons desiring to stay in Thailand for one, two, or four years have to apply for immigrant visas, which are subject to annual quota restrictions of 200 per nationality. Modern economic conditions have necessitated some modifications. As a consequence, since the 1950s a series of laws has been adopted to promote industrial investment. Such laws have authorized longer stays for foreigners, including skilled laborers and experts, who may remain for one, two, or three years, to be determined on the merits of each case by the Board of Investment. This practice is designed to attract private foreign investment, as well as to promote the types of industries that fit in with the overall national plans for economic development. Much has been done to alleviate the difficulties encountered by foreigners seeking to stay for a longer period of time than is otherwise permissible under current immigration laws, but much is still left to be desired.

If Thai laws are on the rigid side with regard to permit to stay, they have been very liberal with respect to the ability of aliens to work in Thailand. In principle the type of visa under which an alien enters Thailand should govern the conditions of his or her stay. For example, the alien may be forbidden to seek or take up employment while in the kingdom. In practice, however, state control has been very lenient. Many foreigners find employment as entertainers, singers, or dancers in the night clubs that abound in Thailand. They work without work or resident permits, earn a considerable amount of money, and pay no income tax. They do not remain longer than three months at a time, but can easily return after a few days in a border town just outside Thailand.

Foreigners are clearly not given the same treatment as Thai nationals in regard to their liberty to seek employment. Some occupations are reserved exclusively for Thai nationals. Only nationals may be hair dressers, welders of Buddha statues, or Thai crafts workers. These restrictions are becoming devoid of economic justification and are now awaiting either complete repeal or drastic amendment. The professions, such as medicine and law, are more or less open on the basis of reciprocal treatment, subject to the qualifying examinations for practicing members of the professions in question.

Within the Kingdom of Thailand, aliens are free to move about and to engage in any lawful pursuit or activity. Whatever their privileges in the past, aliens are today in no better position than Thai nationals in regard to the requirement to observe local laws and regulations, including the obligation to refrain from acts injurious to friendly relations between Thailand and foreign states. Aliens are also required to keep away from internal political entanglements.

They are not permitted to engage in local political activities or otherwise interfere with domestic affairs of state; nor should aliens do anything to affect the security interests of Thailand or contravene any part of the penal laws or fiscal regulations.

Aliens who are given asylum in Thailand for humanitarian considerations are obliged to discontinue political activities that might embarrass the host government as long as they remain in the kingdom. At present Thailand is the provisional home of a number of political refugees from neighboring countries, including Burma and Laos. They are required to refrain from political activities designed to overthrow their respective governments. Sometimes they are asked to remain some distance away from the sensitive frontiers between their fatherlands and Thailand. Thailand has undertaken the responsibility and the expense of seeing to it that they do stay away from sensitive areas. Such is the extent of the responsibility of Thailand as a host state. The aliens are also expected to conform to the wishes of the Thai government.

Refugees numbering tens of thousands came flocking across the Mekong River into Thailand after the battle of Dien Bien Phu in 1954. Again for humanitarian considerations, these fleeing Vietnamese from around Hanoi took refuge in Thailand by illegally entering the country. Technically, therefore, they are not treated as refugees. Some tens of thousands have been repatriated, but the remaining forty thousand or so still constitute a heavy burden on the host government, which has to bear the responsibility of controlling their activities. Vietnamese temporarily residing in Thailand as uninvited guests are obliged to refrain from political or subversive activities against Thailand or any of its friendly neighbors. To those neighboring states Thailand owes a duty to prevent persons residing in Thailand from engaging in activities that are detrimental to the national security of those states or harmful to the peace and harmony of the region.

Voluntary Departure. Subject to virtually the same conditions as Thai nationals, aliens are free to leave Thailand at any time. However, resident aliens should apply for reentry visas before leaving if they contemplate returning to Thailand in the future. If they fail to obtain reentry visas beforehand, they can still apply for nonquota immigrant visas, which are granted in due course with authorization from Bangkok. Controls are in operation in respect to customs, fiscal restrictions, and crimes. Fugitives from justice, criminal suspects, and international dealers in illicit drugs may not be free to leave the country before undergoing certain procedures, including confiscation of contraband or forbidden merchandise, or criminal prosecution that in turn may lead to fines and imprisonment. Otherwise, aliens are not required to present exit visas, as in some countries in Eastern Europe, or sailing permits, as in the United States. Foreigners are free to move out of the country with relatively little or no control, except customs and health regulations.

Involuntary Departure: Expulsion and Deportation. Aliens may be expelled from the country for a number of reasons. In the first place they are only allowed a limited stay, beyond which their presence becomes illegal and subject to expulsion procedures. Again, if aliens commit acts that make them "undesirable" or if they enter illegally, they may be expelled. Aliens whose activities threaten the national security, public order, or good morals of the Thai people are also liable to expulsion. Extradition proceedings can also be instituted, upon request by another state. Extradition proceedings pave the way for actual surrender once the court has decided that the offenses committed are extraditable and determined the nationality of the persons to be extradited.

Under Thai law, Thai nationals cannot be expelled, deported, or extradited. Thus the only assured remedy available against an expulsion, deportation, or extradition order is a challenge before the court of Thailand on the grounds that the individual is a national of Thailand and not an alien. Aliens have relatively little chance of reversing an order of expulsion or extradition. Nevertheless, an appeal against such an order is always possible on humanitarian or other admissible grounds. The order can then be reviewed by the Minister of Interior, who exercises wide discretion to defer or stay the order. A recommendation by a special commission dealing with immigration problems is generally determinative in this particular connection.

Protection

While they are in Thailand, the Thai government has a duty to protect and control aliens.

Since they cannot serve in Thai armed forces or own or operate Thai vessels (although they can serve as crew members), there is little point in discussing the possibility of extension of Thai diplomatic protection to aliens in foreign lands because of some connection with Thailand. International protection is possible but only indirectly, as in the case of alien shareholders of Thai corporations, in which case it is Thai corporate persons who are entitled to seek diplomatic protection, but foreign interests or foreign investors and shareholders are thereby afforded indirect protection. In other instances it is hardly conceivable for Thailand to protect the private interests of aliens in foreign lands, even though the aliens in question may be residents of Thailand. This does not preclude the state from subrogating the interests of resident aliens who have failed to pay their taxes.

NATIONAL IMPLEMENTATION OF INTERNATIONAL RIGHTS AND DUTIES

The international rights and duties of state as well as of individual, insofar as they are customarily recognized, are implemented in Thailand on a national basis. National implementation is the task of various competent organs of the state, notably the courts of law, the appropriate departments of government, and the legislature. Parliament is expected to pass laws giving effect to the treaties concluded by the state. Some treaties require prior parliamentary ratification, while others call for subsequent legislative enactment for effective implementation. International conventions are often given the force of law by mere promulgation once Thailand has decided to sign or ratify or otherwise accede to them.

The executive branch of the government, together with its departments, respects international rights and obligations that have been incorporated by legislative process or affirmative promulgation. The decisions of the government are generally based on respect for international rights and obligations.

Thai judges are presumed to have complete knowledge of the laws applicable in Thailand. Not only is Thai law within the competence of the judge, but all treaties and international conventions to which Thailand is a party and that have received legislative confirmation are also presumed to be known to the court. In principle there is no need to produce either the law or the treaties, since both are automatically known and applicable. Counsel often cites sections of the Penal or Civil Code or provisions of the applicable treaties; but in fact there is no need to adduce evidence of their contents. The court is presumed to know them all, insofar as they may be said to form part of the law of the land. Thus in Cussons' Sons & Co., Ltd., Phya Attakrom Manutti v. Riew Chiang, Director of Srimongkol Trading Corporation, the Supreme Dika Court of Thailand expressly preferred to base its recognition of the capacity of the plaintiff corporation to sue and be sued in Thai courts on the Anglo-Siamese Treaties of Commerce and Navigation of 1925 and 1937.[7] Like aliens, foreign corporations have guaranteed right of access to Thai courts on the basis of reciprocity. Such reciprocal obligations can be implemented in Thailand by national institutions.

The Act of State Doctrine

According to the practice of Thai courts, there are no cases in which the judges must abstain from deciding because there are no applicable laws. It is for the judges to search for appropriate rules to apply to the case at bar. In the absence of legislative enactments, the court will inquire into customs and usages and further into general principles of law that are broadly comparable to international law. Foreign laws may be admitted as facts or as evidence of local usages or prevailing customs. Thus some quaint notion of international law is not unfamiliar to Thai courts--quaint inasmuch as it resembles a conglomeration of rules that lie outside normal comprehension and hence application. Nevertheless, the courts are sometimes invited to pass judgments with casual reference to such rules. There is apparently a natural shyness on the part of Thai courts when confronted with typical questions of international law.

Thai courts are not inhibited by the Act of State doctrine, which often impedes their Anglo-American brethren. They know no such doctrine in the negative sense. They will not refuse to go beyond foreign legislation, and they will overrule that legislation if they find it to be incompatible with Thai law, public order, Thai notions of morality, or the rules of international law, of which Thai courts are beginning to have a vague idea.

That Thai judges should not feel encumbered by the Act of State doctrine is a clear and instinctive reaction against former recognition of foreign legislation with extraterritorial effect within Thailand. Since extraterritoriality was abolished, Thai courts have not regarded foreign laws as binding in Thai territory. The recovery of judicial independence by Thai courts leaves no room for admission of the Act of State doctrine, although it may have a familiar ring in the domestic context. In internal constitutional law, an act of state does not deprive the state or the individual of their respective rights and duties. It merely operates to exempt certain officials from certain kinds of personal liability.

Procedures Related to the Issuance of Certificates or Suggestions by the Executive in Connection with Litigation in National Courts

In the practice of Thailand there are no procedures for issuing of certificates or suggestions by the executive to the court as such. In litigation before national courts, the judges have the authority to summon officials of the Ministry of Foreign Affairs to give evidence about the nature and content of any rule of international law or to testify concerning the official status of an international organization or its staff members. Such evidence can be given in writing in the form of an affidavit or as letters from the Treaty and Legal Department or the Protocol Department. The court may do this on its own or upon the request of either party.

In theory judges can take no advice from the executive. Hence no suggestions are ever made about what the court should do or how a case should be decided. The question of the conclusiveness of Foreign Office certificates does not arise. However, as has been observed, the courts have displayed considerable shyness when dealing with international law or international organization and are apt to dismiss a case at the mention by the Ministry of Foreign Affairs or the Protocol Department that the accused or the defendant is on the official list of international staff of an international organization with headquarters in Bangkok. Sometimes the Treaty and Legal Department has to give a little more answer than was requested, to avoid misleading the court into granting immunity from jurisdiction where no such immunity exists. In this connection the executive has to brief the court in full.

Implementation of Decisions of International Organizations

The decisions of international organizations, especially those that are binding on Thailand or that the Thai government has expressly undertaken to respect, are faithfully implemented by Thailand. Sometimes implementation affects individual rights and obligations in a manner not contemplated by the original resolutions.

Rhodesia

Rhodesia affords an interesting illustration. Occasionally, acting on information from Western sources about the arrival of certain cargoes on board a ship from Rhodesia, the Thai customs authority has either confiscated or destroyed the cargo as part of the economic sanction against the regime. In effect it has been the innocent buyers in Thailand--whether Chinese, European, or Thai--who have suffered the losses, since payments were often already made in full. The Rhodesian regime remained literally untouched by such sanctions.

Namibia

The consequences of the termination of the mandate for Namibia are yet to be seen. Thailand will, as usual, observe international rulings, but care should also be taken concerning the ultimate outcome of such faithful observance, lest weaker and less developed nations again play into the hands of the high and mighty.

TREATIES AND THE INDIVIDUAL

Thailand has concluded several types of treaties that directly affect the rights and obligations of individuals in international affairs. Being a country where aliens once enjoyed a privileged position at the expense of nationals, Thailand cannot completely shut its eyes to the past, insofar as it might reflect the prospective situation. Without going into details, a brief review of the recent treaty practice of the Thai government and its progressive national policies in economic planning clearly indicates Thailand's rather liberal attitude toward foreigners. Individual rights and duties may be examined in the light of current treaty practice and local laws in some selected areas of special interest. Legislation in the 1960s aimed at promoting industrial investment and international tourism added an encouraging impetus to the favorable position held by aliens under current treaty provisions in the fields of commerce and navigation, as well as in respect to reciprocal protection and the guarantee of private investments. A few selected topics are worthy of special attention.

The treaty practice of Thailand in practically all general fields of trade and business ventures, including inland revenues, income taxes, import duties, and tariff and nontariff privileges, accords the same treatment to aliens or foreigners alike, regardless of nationality. This is the general principle of nondiscrimination in treatment of aliens at its best. The government of Thailand has viewed the most-favored-nation clause as an anachronistic legacy of colonialism, under which one Western power after another continued to seek further enhancement of its privileged position in Thailand through the application of the most-favored-nation clause. Ultimately all the foreign nations with which Thailand entertained bilateral treaty relations (which were mostly Western) obtained equally high and privileged positions. In effect the principle of nondiscrimination would have provided foreigners with equal status, but without additional privileges that would heighten their prestige beyond the dreams of avarice. The Thai government has sought to replace the most-favored-nation clause, with its damaging connotations, by the more democratic principle of nondiscrimination, which is better attuned to the modern doctrine of sovereign equality of states.

Under any conflict rule or by any rule of public international law, the law of the site must govern transfer of immovables. The land law of Thailand has followed a highly complex historical evolution. The government is liberal enough to allow foreigners to own land, which is an almost priceless possession in the kingdom; but foreigners can only become landowners if they are nationals of a country with which Thailand has concluded a treaty of friendship, commerce, and navigation or a treaty for economic cooperation with a clause recognizing and permitting the reciprocal rights of the nationals of the contracting parties to own land in each others' territory. In this connection a corporation is regarded as foreign if 49 percent of its shares are owned by foreigners, if foreigners have a controlling interest, or if the managing directors are of foreign nationality. Aliens and foreign corporations may only own land for specific purposes, as authorized by competent Thai authorities on the merits of each case, subject to periodic review of the implementation of the avowed objectives.[8]

It is now an internationally recognized principle that natural resources belong to the state and the nationals of that state on a permanent basis, without possibility of transfer to another state or a foreign corporation. The territorial state has the right to make binding concessions, covering such rights as the exploration and exploitation of oil and mineral resources, but the state has no power to deprive itself or its nationals of ownership forever. The territorial state continues to exercise permanent sovereignty over natural resources and to have an inherent right to expropriate or nationalize any property or enterprise within its territorial jurisdiction. This has been repeatedly recognized and protected under international law. Without such a principle, by now there would have been nothing left for the developing countries. This sovereignty is in conformity with the principle of the supremacy of the law of the site and consistent with the primacy of territorial sovereignty.

Though the right of the state to expropriate stands uncontested, it is likewise undisputed that expropriation should be accompanied by compensation. Constitutionally, Thai nationals are entitled to "fair compensation." (See above.) Foreigners whose rights are reciprocally protected in treaties or conventions are entitled to "just compensation." To what extent "fair" and "just" compensation may differ is a matter of pure conjecture. Fair compensation for Thai nationals is often a matter for negotiation and arbitration. Just compensation is the standard treatment incorporated in various bilateral treaties, with more or less intelligible explanatory notes. The idea is that compensation should be just and equitable for all concerned, not only for the rich foreign investors, whose original investments have already yielded more than double their inputs, but also for the territorial state, whose growing population largely depends on sustained national efforts to promote and accelerate economic growth and development. It is to be noted that investors continue to demand "prompt," and even "prior," "full compensation." In fact there is no limit to the amount of compensation sought, irrespective of the objective value of the property taken. However, reasonableness should prevail. In this as well as in other connections, regardless of the demands of the powerful companies and the application of pressures by the developed nations, justice must take its natural course and come to the aid of the victims of international social and economic suppressions, be they states or individuals.

NOTES

1. 724/2490 (1947).
2. Buddhist Era, B.E. 2499 (1956).
3. Ibid.
4. Ibid.
5. B.E. 2499 (1956), § 8a.
6. B.E. 2477 (1934).
7. 1490/2499 (1956).
8. See Land Code, B.E. 2497, A.D. 1953.

CHAPTER

18

UGANDA

P. J. Mugerwa

In 1972, Uganda had been independent for ten years. Before it achieved independence on 9 October 1962, Uganda was a British Protectorate. The rights of the inhabitants of Uganda were therefore enjoyed through British legislation and the common law, which were dispensed by British judges who were appointed by the British Crown. On its independence in 1962, Uganda was presented with a written Constitution that attempted to enshrine the fundamental rights of the individual in one document.[1] These fundamental rights were subject to a number of exceptions and reservations, which were set out at some length in the Constitution and which will be referred to in detail later in this chapter. The Statute Book retained the legislation enacted by the British administration, some of which has had an important bearing on matters discussed in this chapter. Since 9 October 1962, Uganda has undergone political evolution, some of which has been peaceful and some the result of coups d'etat. Because of this evolution, a third written Constitution was promulgated in September 1967,[2] and some parts of this Constitution were then suspended in 1971.[3]

The people of Uganda still look to the Constitution for the basic rules governing the rights of the individual, supplemented by legislation and a developing common law.

It should be made clear, however, that at this writing Uganda is at a crossroads. It has had a military government since January 1971. The 18-point statement made by the Armed Forces on 25 January 1971 reads as follows.

This chapter remains substantially as it was written in 1972.

It has been necessary to take action to save a bad situation from getting worse. We give here below examples of matters that have left the people angry, worried, and very unhappy:

(1) The unwarranted detention without trial and for long periods of a large number of people, many of whom are totally innocent of any charges.

(2) The continuation of a state of emergency over the whole country for an indefinite period, which is meaningless to everybody.

(3) The lack of freedom in the airing of different views on political and social matters.

(4) The frequent loss of life and property arising from almost daily cases of robbery with violence and kondoism without strong measures being taken to stop them. The people feel totally insecure and yet kondoism increases every day.

(5) The proposals for National Service which will take every able bodied person from his home to work in a camp for two years could only lead to more robbery and general crime when homes are abandoned.

(6) Widespread corruption in high places, especially among Ministers and top civil servants, has left the people with very little confidence, if any, in the Government. Most Ministers own fleets of cars or buses, many big houses, and sometimes even aeroplanes.

(7) The failure by the political authorities to organise any elections for the last eight years whereby the people's free will could be expressed. It should be noted that the last elections within the ruling party were dominated by big fellows with lots of money which they used to bribe their way into "winning" the elections. This bribery, together with threats against the people, entirely falsified the results of the so-called elections. Proposed new methods of election requiring a candidate to stand in four constituencies will only favour the rich and the well-known.

(8) Economic policies have left many people unemployed and even more insecure and lacking in the basic needs of life--like food, clothing, medicine and shelter.

(9) High taxes have left the common man of this country poorer than ever before. Here are some of the taxes which the common man has to bear:

Development Tax
Graduated Tax,
Sales Tax,
Social Security Fund Tax.

The big men can always escape these taxes or pass them on to the common man.

(10) The prices which the common man gets for his crops like cotton and coffee have not gone up and sometimes they have gone down, whereas the costs of food, education, etc., have always gone up.

(11) Tendency to isolate the country from East African unity, e.g., by sending away workers from Kenya and Tanzania, by preventing the use of Uganda money in Kenya and Tanzania, by discouraging imports from Kenya and Tanzania, by stopping the use in Uganda of Kenyan or Tanzanian money.

(12) The creation of a wealthy class of leaders who are always talking of socialism while they grow richer and the common man poorer.

(13) In addition, the Defence Council of which the President is Chairman, has not met since July, 1969, and this has made administration of the Armed Forces very difficult. As a result Armed Forces personnel lack accommodation, vehicles and equipment. Also general recruitment submitted to the Chairman of the Defence Council a long time ago has not been put into effect.

(14) The Cabinet Office, by training large numbers of people (largely from the Akokoro County in Lango District where Obote and Akena Adoko, the Chief General Service Officer, come from) in armed warfare, has been turned into a second army. Uganda therefore has had two armies, one in the Cabinet, the other Regular.

(15) The Lango development master plan written in 1967 decided that all key positions in Uganda's political, commercial, army, and industrial life have to be occupied and controlled by people from Akokoro County, Lango District.

> Also, the same master plan decided that nothing of importance must be done for other districts, especially Acholi District. Emphasis was put on development of Akokoro County in Lango District at the expense of other areas of Uganda.
>
> (16) Obote, on the advice of Akena Adoko, has sought to divide the Uganda Armed Forces and the rest of Uganda by picking out his own tribesmen and putting them in key positions in the Army and elsewhere. Examples: the Chief General Service Officer, the Export and Import Corporation Uganda Meat Packers, the Public Service Commission, Nyanza Textiles and a Russian textile factory to be situated in Lango.
>
> (17) From the time Obote took over power in 1962, his greatest and most loyal supporter has been the Army. The Army has always tried to be an example to the whole of Africa by not taking over the Government, and we have always followed that principle. It is therefore now a shock to us to see that Obote wants to divide and downgrade the Army by turning the Cabinet Office into another army. In doing this, Obote and Akena Adoko have bribed and used some senior officers who have turned against their fellow soldiers.
>
> (18) We all want only unity in Uganda and we do not want bloodshed. Everybody in Uganda knows that. The matters mentioned above appear to us to lead to bloodshed only.[4]

Even a cursory glance at the statement indicates that the present government was presented with an unenviable task requiring a thorough reorganization of the affairs of the country. The intention of the present government was to hand over power to a new civilian government as soon as humanly possible. Yet, decrees have been passed and other measures taken, some of which have encroached on the rights of citizens in general and of some citizens in particular. These measures were the result of a volatile situation and were not intended to be permanent.

THE INDIVIDUAL

The Individual as a National

Movement

Passports. The rights of departure and reentry are naturally related to the issue of passports. Immigration officials at border entry points must satisfy themselves of the identity and nationality of persons presenting themselves for exit or return. Usually a passport provides a means of identification, although a less formal document, such as the East African movement pass referred to below, may sometimes be sufficient.

Uganda has no statute providing for the issuance of passports to its nationals; the issuance of passports would appear to be a matter of grace. Indeed, passports, when issued, contain a statement to the effect that they are the property of the government of Uganda. Despite this, passports are issued to adult nationals as a matter of course and likewise to minors on the application of their lawful guardians. Passports have on occasion been confiscated by the police during the course of criminal investigations and have been retained by them for some time. They have, however, been returned.

Uganda has a Passports Act[5] empowering the Minister of Foreign Affairs to make rules requiring that persons entering Uganda shall be in possession of documents of identity. The rules made by the minister require non-Africans to hold passports.[6] Even this rule is not rigid, since the Principal Immigration Officer may permit any person to enter Uganda without documents. Since most Ugandans are of African extraction, it would appear that Ugandan Africans, in company with other Africans, are not required to submit passports on entry into Uganda. However, as stated earlier, it is customary for the immigration authorities to require some form of identification from persons requiring entry through border control points. Therefore, as a general rule, passports are required. The members of the East African Community--that is, Kenya, Tanzania, and Uganda--have evolved a system of interstate passes. These are simple passes that are not stamped by the immigration officials. They are issued for two years and are renewable for two-year periods, up to a total of ten years. These passes, which simplify entry formalities, are normally issued to officials of the community or officers of the respective governments. Passports are issued for five years, subject to renewal for a further five years, and reissued after ten years.

Departure. Clause (1) of Article 19 of the 1967 Constitution protects individual freedom of movement. The text of the clause is as follows: "No person shall be deprived of his freedom of movement, and for the purposes of this article the said freedom means the right to move freely throughout Uganda, the right to reside in any part of Uganda, the right to enter Uganda and immunity from expulsion from Uganda."

There are a number of reservations provided for in Article 19, most but not all of which would appear to relate to movement within Uganda. However, it is obvious that if a person's movement is, for example, restricted to an area of Uganda by the order of a court, that person will not be allowed to leave Uganda. A person may be ordered by a court to report to a probation officer[7] or to reside in a designated institution. While that person is under such an order, he or she may not move out of Uganda. This type of restriction is clearly justifiable in a democratic society, and it is not necessary to dwell on it.

The Constitution and the statute book of Uganda have other more unusual restrictions that are more worthy of note. Paragraph (j) of Clause (1) of Article 10 of the 1967 Constitution allows any law to impinge on the right to personal liberty if the law is

> for the purpose of making, varying, discharging or enforcing an order providing for the detention of any person or restriction of any person to any residence or area within Uganda or for prohibiting him from being within any such area or for restricting his possession of specified articles or his association and communication with other persons or for requiring him to notify his movements to any specified authority or imposing conditions reasonably necessary for the purpose of enforcing any such detention, restriction, prohibition or requirement.

Uganda has four enactments covered by this provision, namely the Deportation Act,[8] the Public Order and Security Act of 1967,[9] the Police Act (Section 62 only),[10] and the Suspension of Political Activities Decree of 1971.[11]

The Deportation Act has a misleading name. It provides for the restriction of persons to such areas as may be specified in the order of the Minister of Internal Affairs, but it makes no provision for deportation or exile of citizens. This act was passed in 1908 and was retained at independence. It was found unconstitutional in relation to the provisions of the 1962 Constitution,[12] and that part of Paragraph (j) relating to restriction of movement was introduced in the 1967 Constitution to validate the offending act. This act, like the Public Order and Security Act, was introduced to deal with political situations rather than criminal activities, which are well provided for in the criminal law.[13] As a matter of interest, the Deportation Act was not used after 1966, and the Public Order and Security Act has never been invoked. The former regime preferred to keep Uganda under a more or less perpetual state of emergency[14] and to detain political opponents in accordance with powers contained in the Constitution and the Emergency Powers Act,[15] which was replaced by the Emergency Powers Act of 1968.[16] Section 62 of the Police Act gives the Minister of Internal Affairs power to declare an area in which "an abnormal state of affairs exists," "a disturbed area." After this declaration the Commissioner of Police has wide powers, including the power to impose a curfew and the power to prohibit any persons or class of persons from entering or leaving the area or parts thereof. Such powers could interfere with the right of a national to leave Uganda. The power is not used frequently. It was last used in 1969.[17]

Although all the above laws are part of the statute book of Uganda, it is very doubtful that they could now be enforced, given the explicit philosophy contained in the 1971 18-point statement by the Armed Forces.

Such restriction on movement as would be consistent with the ideals of the military government are to be found in the Suspension of Political Activities Decree, Sections 8, 9, and 10. This decree provides for a straightforward restriction of the movement of a certain class of persons who, by reason of their former offices, may owe a political allegiance to the previous regime and might therefore be tempted to meet enemies of the present regime outside Uganda to generally engage in antigovernment activities. Although the requirements of the decree may cause inconvenience to the individuals concerned, I understand that persons who have good reason to travel abroad have obtained the required permission without difficulty. This is simply a precautionary measure and not intended to interfere with the free movement of citizens, except in a few cases.

Apart from the exceptional cases I have referred to, there is no other restriction on the departure of Uganda nationals.

Return. It will be seen from reference to Clause (1) of Article 19 of the 1967 Constitution, which has been quoted above, that a citizen's right of entry into Uganda is protected. This right has not been restricted in any way, and any national may return to Uganda at any time.

Expulsion. Clause (1) of Article 19 of the 1967 Constitution also safeguards a national's right to reside in any part of Uganda and provides immunity from expulsion. Whoever can show that he or she is a citizen cannot be expelled from the country. There are no laws providing for expulsion apart from the deportation and extradition laws applying to aliens, which are common to most countries. While on this subject, I should refer to naturalized citizens and temporary citizens. Under sections 9, 10, and 11 of the Citizenship Act,[18] the Minister of Internal Affairs may deprive persons who have become citizens by naturalization or registration of their citizenship in certain circumstances, mainly those revealing disaffection to Uganda or a criminal character. Once those persons have lost their citizenship, they may well be subject to deportation under Section 14 of the Immigration Act.[19]

Another type citizen that has at times been subject to expulsion is what I may term the "doubtful" temporary citizen. Under the Constitution of 1962,[20] certain classes of persons, all of whom were British subjects, were entitled to Uganda citizenship on registration. The majority of them were required under Section 12 to renounce any other citizenship they enjoyed by a specified date, which in the case of most adults was three months after acquiring Uganda citizenship. If they did not do this, they ceased to be Uganda citizens and consequently would be subject to expulsion if they were not in possession of valid entry documents under the Immigration (Control) Act.[21] The majority of the persons in Uganda who registered as Uganda citizens shortly after independence, who were mostly British citizens of Asian origin, failed to comply with the renunciation provisions. Many were required to leave but at the same time were required by the British authorities to obtain vouchers for entry to Britain under the immigration legislation relating to British subjects who were not born in Britain. This unfortunate situation has been one aspect of the so-called Asian problem of East Africa. At one time some of these unhappy people were shunted between Uganda and Britain without a home. Although the problem still exists, the phenomenon of the semistateless wanderers is virtually ended.

Remedies. I know of no case in which a Uganda national has found it necessary to resort to the courts to protect his or her right of movement out of Uganda and back or to obtain travel documents. Since the rights of movement, residence, and protection from expulsion are all guaranteed under Article 19 of the Constitution, it is likely that resort would be made to the High Court for their enforcement. Article 22 provides as follows:

> 22. (1) Subject to the provisions of clause (5) of this Article, if any person alleges that any of the provisions of articles 8 to 20 inclusive has been, is being or is likely to be contravened in relation to him, then, without prejudice to any other action with respect to the same matter that is lawfully available, that person may apply to the High Court for redress.
>
> (2) The High Court shall have original jurisdiction to hear and determine any application made by any person in pursuance of clause (1) of this article, and may make such orders, issue such writs and give such directions as it may consider appropriate for the purpose of enforcing, or securing the enforcement of, any of the provisions of the said articles 8 to 20 inclusive to the protection of which the person concerned is entitled:
>
> Provided that the High Court shall not exercise its powers under this clause if it is satisfied that adequate means of redress for the contravention alleged are or have been available to the person concerned under any other law.
>
> (3) Any person aggrieved by any determination of the High Court under this article may appeal therefrom to the Court of Appeal under article 89.
>
> (4) No appeal shall lie from any determination under this article that any application is merely frivolous or vexatious.
>
> (5) Parliament may make provision, or may authorize the making of provision, with respect to the practice and may confer upon the court such powers, or may authorize the conferment thereon of such powers, in addition to those conferred by this article as may appear to be necessary or desirable for the purpose of enabling that court more effectively to exercise the jurisdiction conferred upon it by this article.

If the matter referred to the court raises a substantial point of law in relation to interpretation of the Constitution, it may be referred to a constitutional court of not less than three judges, under Article 87 of the Constitution. Recourse has been made to the High Court on a number of occasions with regard to matters touching the Constitution and the rights protected thereunder, but as I have stated, not in relation to movement in and out of Uganda, expulsion, or for that matter the issuance of passports. A person requiring enforcement of an alleged right to a passport would probably apply for an order against the issuing authority demanding that the person do his or her lawful duty. This order, which if granted would require the issuance of a passport, would be given under the power provided under Section 34 of the Judicature Act.[22] It would appear that although the issuance of a passport is apparently a matter of grace, an application may well succeed, since failure to issue a passport or at least some document of identity might well impinge on the constitutional right to leave and enter Uganda freely.

Protection

Extent of Freedom of Activity Abroad. Uganda law provides no direct control over the activities of Uganda nationals abroad.

Nationals are required to obtain the consent of the Treasury to financial transactions involving the transfer of funds out of Uganda under the Exchange Control Act[23] and its subsidiary legislation. This certainly inhibits the establishment of businesses outside Uganda by Uganda nationals, except within the area of the East African Community. Under the Treaty for East African Co-operation of 1967,[24] in most cases the transfer of funds between the partner states of the community is allowed without restriction.

The law of treason provides serious penalties for some activities of Uganda nationals abroad. For example, aiding or abetting anyone to levy war against Uganda is an offense subject to the death penalty.[25] Whether or not the reader may agree with the penalty imposed, I am sure the need for this type of restriction will be seen as understandable.

Apart from financial restrictions and the control of criminal acts against the state, I am unaware of any other restrictions on Uganda nationals abroad, either in the field of commerce or otherwise.

The Right to Diplomatic Protection. Uganda nationals abroad are accorded assistance by Uganda missions or by foreign missions acting on their behalf abroad as a matter of course. However, as in the case of the issuance of passports, this assistance would appear to arise from a convention rather than from any formal law. There are no particular conditions attached to the provision of such protection and assistance, except that they are usually only accorded to Uganda nationals.

The State and Compensation. I know of no case in which Uganda received compensation from a foreign country on behalf of its nationals. If the case ever does arise, in my view the national for whom the compensation is obtained will have a right to receive the compensation as his or her property in the hands of the government. If the compensation is not handed over within a reasonable time, the individual will no doubt have recourse to Article 13 of the Constitution, which provides for protection from deprivation of property without adequate compensation. This article was successfully applied to nonpayment of the commission due to an agent by the Buganda government,[26] which was payable by the Uganda government after it took over the government of Buganda and its assets and liabilities. I see no reason why the principle should not be extended to the nonpayment of compensation due to an individual but held by the government.

The Responsibility of the State for Injury Induced by Its Own Conduct. Although Ugandans may have suffered losses because of international activities of the government, no provision has been made, either in the Constitution or elsewhere, for the granting of compensation. There have been occasions when the Uganda border with a neighboring territory has been closed, and there is no doubt that traders, transporters, and other businessmen have suffered losses as a result of this, but no claims have ever been made with respect to such losses. If they were it would be unlikely that they would be entertained by the government.

At the time of this writing the government has broken off relations with Israel and expelled its nationals. It remains to be seen what losses there will be, since the Israelis were, for example, engaged in a number of building contracts that will remain incomplete. Subcontractors, banks, and landlords will not be paid. This situation is not within the control of the persons who will suffer the losses, but as Uganda law stands, they will have no recourse to public funds to recoup their losses, although the government could decide that it is in the public interest to meet losses of this kind out of the public purse. It is, however, unlikely that the government will meet losses such as these, arising as they do out of an act of state.

Another circumstance in which losses have been incurred in the past is that in which Uganda, in accordance with international obligations, has ceased trading with certain countries. Examples are the cases of South Africa and Southern Rhodesia. The Uganda government has banned trade with both of these countries.[27] So far as I know, no reparations were sought by those who suffered losses, and none were offered. The question of when compensation should be paid and when it should not is not an easy one for governments to decide. A government acting in good faith may cause losses on a number of occasions. It would seem unwise to fetter the future actions of governments by a rigid provision for general compensation. There may be occasions when a government should offer compensation for losses occurring as a direct result of its international activities. I do not believe that a hard and fast rule about this can be extracted from current state practice.

Waiver. The law makes no provision for waiver of the claims of individuals against foreign states. Although it might well be possible to cancel the accrued rights of individuals without conflicting with Article 13 of the Constitution, it is difficult to see how rights that may be enforceable in a jurisdiction outside Uganda can be canceled under Uganda law. At the most Uganda law could deny access to the courts of Uganda in respect to such rights.

Again, the government could refuse to pursue claims of its nationals at the diplomatic level. I do not think the persons affected would have any right enforceable through Uganda courts to oblige the government to assist in the recovery of whatever may be due to them.

The Individual as an Alien

Aliens tend to be divided into classes under the law of Uganda. In line with international practice, diplomats and representatives of certain international organizations, such as the UN Secretariat, enjoy privileges and exemptions that are not accorded to other foreigners. Alien Africans from neighboring countries have privileges not enjoyed by others. Uganda is a member of the British Commonwealth, and in some respects citizens of other Commonwealth countries enjoy a status not accorded to the nationals of other states.

Movement

Entry and Stay. In common with most countries, Uganda requires foreign nationals to obtain an entry permit before they enter the country.[28] Only African citizens of Kenya and Tanzania, which are partners in the East African Community, are not required to obtain entry permits.[29] Uganda has narrowed the class of persons who may enter without a permit. Under Section 1 of the Immigration (Control) Act,[30] which was repealed by the Immigration Act of 1969, all Africans were exempted from the requirement to obtain entry permits.

Immigration policy is related to the integration of Ugandans into trade and industry. Entry permits for persons who intend to stay in Uganda for some time tend to be classified according to the occupations they wish to follow. Indeed, the decision whether or not an entry permit will be granted usually depends on the same criteria. In some cases there are financial conditions to be complied with. Sometimes this compliance takes the form of a deposit of money, while in others it involves proving that the applicant has not less than a given sum of money at his or her disposal for investment in a business or professional practice.

A person of means who wishes to settle in Uganda may obtain a certificate of residence or may be given a ministerial exemption from the necessity to have a permit. Persons residing in Uganda who are in possession of current permits are required to obtain re-entry permits if they leave the country and intend to return. If the individual concerned intends to return within the life of the entry permit, he or she is likely to be given a reentry permit. All permits, passes, and certificates are granted as a matter of discretion, and all of them can be canceled by the Minister of Internal Affairs without any reasons given. Apart from citizens of Kenya or Tanzania, no person who is not a citizen can claim to have a right to stay in Uganda.

There are a number of persons who are deemed by statute to be prohibited immigrants, such as persons against whom a deportation order is in force, persons who have entered Uganda unlawfully, persons without valid passports or other documents of identity, destitute persons, certain criminals, prostitutes, enemy aliens, and other persons deemed undesirable. Normally these individuals are not allowed to reside in Uganda, but the Immigration Regulations provide for the issuance of passes to such persons for limited periods.[31]

Voluntary Departure. As a general rule there is no restriction on the departure of aliens. Persons facing criminal charges are often required to surrender their passports to ensure their appearance in court. Aliens are required before departure to satisfy the tax authorities that they have no outstanding tax liabilities or to deposit a sum of money as security.[32] Otherwise, although the law is silent on movement out of Uganda, there is no restriction on the departure of aliens.

Involuntary Departure: Expulsion and Deportation. The Immigration Act provides for the deportation of aliens. Under Section 14 the Minister of Internal Affairs may in writing under his hand order any prohibited immigrant or "any person whose presence within Uganda is under the provisions of this Act unlawful to be deported from and remain out of Uganda." This means that any person considered to be an undesirable immigrant by the minister or the Principal Immigration Officer, on information they deem reliable, may be deported. A declaration by the Principal Immigration Officer is subject to confirmation by the minister, but the minister's decision is final.[33]

The law provides no right of appeal from the minister's decision. It is unlikely that a court will go further than ensuring that the minister has made the order under his hand. It will not go behind the decision. Uganda has had no case in which such an order has been challenged. In one case,[34] in which a detention order had been made under detention regulations,[35] the judge declined to go against the minister's order where the minister was entitled to exercise his power after being satisfied that "for the purpose of maintaining public order it is necessary to exercise control over any person." As a general rule this power is exercised only after careful consideration of the case concerned.

The Extradition Act provides for the surrender of fugitives from justice to those countries having reciprocal extradition arrangements with Uganda.[36] The surrender is confined to serious offenses, ranging from homicide to slave dealing. Surrender is specifically excluded for offenses of a political character. The full text of the reservation is as follows:

> 2(a) a fugitive criminal shall not be surrendered if the offence in respect to which his surrender is demanded is one of a political character, or if it appears to a court or the Minister that the requisition for his surrender has in fact been made with a view to try or punish him for an offence of a political character.[37]

Requisitions for surrender of fugitives have to be made to the Minister of Internal Affairs through the diplomatic mission concerned. It is for the minister to decide whether or not to make an order for the issue of a warrant, on political grounds. Apart from this, a fugitive must be committed to prison for 15 days before surrender and must be informed that he or she has a right to apply for an order of habeas corpus.

The law appears to provide reasonably adequate safeguards for the protection of political fugitives. However, the fugitive does not have the benefit of the safeguards contained in the Extradition Act, particularly if formal extradition procedures are not followed. A case in point is that of Rolf Steiner, who was arrested by the Uganda authorities on 4 October 1970. He was a German alleged to be a mercenary engaged in assisting the Southern Sudanese Anyanya in their war against the Sudanese government. It is unlikely that the

Sudanese government could have successfully applied for Steiner's extradition for an extraditable crime. Even if it could have done so, he would probably have been able to show that the extradition request was really an attempt to obtain his surrender to punish him for his alleged mercenary (political) activities. The Uganda authorities of the time ignored the extradition procedures and handed Steiner over to the Sudanese government. Steiner was subsequently tried for his mercenary activities by a military tribunal and sentenced to a term of imprisonment.

Apart from the Steiner case, which was of a political nature, there was a practice in the past of "criminal swapping" with a neighboring state. The police in both states, holding suspects wanted by both, would meet on the border and arrange an exchange. It is likely that the respective ministers were not aware of the practice. It is also likely that the persons who were handed over were criminals. However, the practice, if continued, might have led to serious abuse.

A recent case that may be of some interest is that of the ex-king of Burundi, Charles Ndizeye. He arrived in Uganda on 21 March 1972, without prior warning. It was made clear to him by the president of Uganda that the ex-king could not be permitted to carry out political activities in Uganda and that he should make every effort to return to his own country as a private citizen. As a result of correspondence between the president of Uganda and the president of Burundi, the ex-king voluntarily returned to Burundi. Assurances had been given to the president of Uganda by the president of Burundi that the ex-king would be assured of his life and safety if he returned. Shortly after he returned he was arrested for trying to invade the country with the help of mercenaries. This case was clearly outside the Extradition Act.

Special Kinds of Protection. I know of no case in which Uganda has afforded diplomatic protection to non-nationals, except possibly as an agent for a state not having diplomatic representation in a given country.

A small number of non-nationals go abroad on behalf of the Uganda government in connection with their duties as public officers. However, they invariably carry passports issued by their native countries; therefore the need for protection by the Uganda government is unlikely to arise.[38]

There are occasions when aliens may suffer injuries through no fault of their own while in Uganda. The injuries may not be inflicted by the Uganda government, but they may be such that, for the purposes of preserving international good relations and for humanitarian reasons, the Uganda government has undertaken responsibility for compensating the victims.

In 1966 a number of persons suffered damage in mob violence resulting from the situation arising from the takeover of power by the previous regime. In one particular case, two English surveyors were killed by a mob while working in the countryside on a government assignment. These men were not directly employed by the government but were members of a firm of surveyors it had engaged. The government paid compensation to their dependents and met certain expenses of the firm concerned in connection with the deaths. Legal liability was not, however, accepted by the government. In another case the government paid compensation for the damage caused during a shooting incident involving a minister's bodyguard, although again liability was not accepted. The persons compensated were non-nationals. More recently the government has compensated non-nationals for looting by unknown army personnel at Entebbe airport during the military takeover in January 1971.

Conversely, the government did not, except in one case, compensate non-nationals who suffered damage during a 1968 demonstration against the British policy in Rhodesia. In this case the damage was caused by Makerere University students, who were not under the control of the government but had government permission to hold a demonstration. The exception was the British government, which was compensated for damage to the High Commission in accordance with Article 22 of the Vienna Convention on Diplomatic Relations.

I am not claiming that there is any enforceable right to compensation vested in foreign nationals with regard to damage suffered during political disturbances. However, there would appear at present to be a convention that foreign nationals who suffer damage at the hands of government employees or while engaged on government contracts as a result of political unrest will be compensated, albeit on an ex gratia basis.

I have mentioned earlier that under Uganda extradition law persons may not be extradited for political offenses or punished for offenses of a political nature if extradited. For many years Uganda has been the recipient of thousands of refugees, principally from Rwanda, Zaire, and the Sudan. Uganda is not a party to the Convention on the Status of Refugees of 1951, but its law makes special provision for refugees.[39] Under the law, aliens declared to be refugees by the Minister of Internal Affairs are required to obtain a permit to remain in Uganda. Persons from other Commonwealth countries and the Republic of Ireland are not aliens for the purposes of the act. The minister has power to order refugees to remain in certain areas, which he in fact exercises as a general rule. Consequently a great number of the refugees in Uganda live in refugee settlements, where they cultivate their own crops, rear their own livestock, and are generally encouraged to support themselves.

The movement of refugees within Uganda and out of the country is controlled, and they are subject to deportation either under the order of the Director of Refugees or under the orders of courts that have convicted them of offenses. A deportation order must not be made if the refugee is likely to be punished for a political offense or subjected to physical attack in the territory he or she came from. Refugees are not deemed to be resident in Uganda for the purpose of acquiring citizenship. However, the minister may declare other provisions of the law relating to deportation and extradition not to be applicable to refugees.

Control over refugees is essential in a small country like Uganda, which at this writing is host to approximately 180,000 refugees. Those people have entered the country as a result of violent political upheavals in their own countries. Their entry was not sought by Uganda, but at the same time they cannot be turned away. The law therefore allows them a special temporary settlement status until such time as they may return to their own countries. Incidentally, they have the benefit of the educational system of Uganda which provides free education after a certain level.

NATIONAL IMPLEMENTATION OF INTERNATIONAL RIGHTS AND DUTIES

The Act of State Doctrine

In Uganda no legislation makes provision for, or limits consideration of, the validity of foreign legislation. The courts are likely to lean heavily on British precedents. The Rose Mary case would certainly have strong persuasive authority, coming as it does from the Supreme Court of Aden, which at the time the case was heard shared the same Court of Appeal as Uganda.

In other words, the likelihood is that the Uganda courts would tend to apply international law to foreign confiscatory legislation and only give judicial recognition to it if adequate and prompt compensation was provided for in the legislation.

Implementation of Decisions of International Organizations

Uganda law makes specific provision for the implementation of economic sanctions as a result of either compliance with decisions of international organizations, such as the United Nations and the Organization of African Unity, or of the government's own political decisions. Section 7 of the External Trade Act provided for the prohibition or limitation of the import or export of goods to or from any country, if in the opinion of the minister "such action is in the interests of Uganda or any other part of the Commonwealth."[40] This section has been replaced by Section 30 of the Export and Import Corporation Act.[41] Under the Import and Export Prohibition (Southern Rhodesia) Order,[42] all imports from and exports to Southern Rhodesia are prohibited. Persons who disobey the prohibition are liable to a fine or imprisonment or both.

This prohibition was made before the resolution by the Security Council of the United Nations imposing comprehensive mandatory sanctions, which was finally adopted on 29 May 1968. The act makes no provision for compensation of individuals affected by the prohibition. As Uganda law stands, individuals are not likely to recover compensation through the courts.

Apart from making use of the External Trade Act, the government has taken administrative measures to enforce embargos agreed upon at international meetings. For example, the Organization of African Unity resolved that its members should cut all contacts with South Africa. In compliance with this resolution, by administrative direction the government has prevented trade between Uganda and South Africa.

This implementation of international decisions has also been pursued through the Exchange Control laws. Travelers' checks issued in Uganda are not negotiable in Rhodesia or South Africa.

Again, nonofficial passports issued in Uganda are not valid for travel in Rhodesia or South Africa.

Procedures Related to the Issuance of Certificates or Suggestions by the Executive in Connection with Litigation in National Courts

No formal procedure is laid down under the law of Uganda for the issue of certificates by the executive in relation to matters of an international nature; nor, for that matter, is there any formalized right of any person or authority to information from the government concerning matters relating to foreign affairs.

However, government officers, like any other members of the public, are liable to be subpoenaed to give evidence before the courts. Their position is a little different with regard to the types of evidence they can be compelled to give. Under Section 121 of the Evidence Act,[43] a head of department has discretion to withhold evidence from unpublished official records relating to affairs of state if he thinks fit. Under Section 122 no public officer may be compelled to disclose communications made to him or her in the course of his duties if the officer considers that the public interest would suffer.

The sort of matters that would require a certificate from a responsible authority are hardly likely to be matters that would require the protection of the Evidence Act. For example, no difficulty has been experienced by the courts in obtaining either oral or written evidence from the Ministry of Foreign Affairs of the status of persons who claim to be diplomats.[44]

As far as I am aware, the occasion has not arisen for the courts to consider whether or not a particular government is recognized by Uganda, but I am sure an appropriate certificate would be forthcoming. I would say that either the litigant or the court could request a certificate. If the government were unwilling or dilatory in providing the required certificate, a litigant might well request a court to summon an officer of the government, probably the Permanent Secretary, to the Ministry of Foreign Affairs to give evidence. There is no particular rule concerning the stage at which this would be done. It would depend on when the evidence might be found necessary.

The content of certificates would depend entirely on the nature of the request. The extent of the information may be limited in accordance with the provisions of the sections of the Evidence Act to which I have referred. There is certainly no formal procedure for parties to make representations concerning certificates issued by the state, since the whole procedure is informal.

There is no provision under Uganda law for the executive to make formal suggestions or provide the courts with advisory opinions of any kind that may affect litigation. There are times when the Attorney General may be called in as an amicus curiae, but this is entirely within the discretion of the court; the representations the Attorney General may make are in no way binding on the court.[45]

The Attorney General does have a residual power as the guardian of justice to submit a case to the court for the issue of an order to quash or review a case in which there may have been irregularities. His right, unlike that of the ordinary individual, is unfettered by rules or a time limit.[46] This right cannot, however, affect the actual course of litigation except to the extent of remedying irregularities that have occurred.

TREATIES AND THE INDIVIDUAL

The treaty that undoubtedly has the most influence on the daily lives of individuals resident in Uganda is the Treaty for East African Cooperation, entered into by Uganda, Kenya, and Tanzania on 6 June 1967. This treaty established the East African Community, the aim of which, according to Article 2, is to strengthen and regulate industrial, commercial, and other relations of the partner states "to the end that there shall be accelerated, harmonious, and balanced development and sustained expansion of economic activities the benefits whereof shall be equitably shared."

The community states share the same postal services, rail services, and customs regulations. The East African Airways Corporation is also owned by the three partner states. Under Article 12 of the treaty, quantitative restrictions on the import of goods from other partner states are disallowed except in the case of some agricultural products. Article 25 of the treaty provides for almost unfettered transfer of currency among the partner states. Again, Article 11 forbids the imposition of duties in the nature of customs or import duties among the three states. It should therefore be possible for individuals to trade freely with persons in the other partner states. However, matters are not that simple. Article 20 of the treaty provides for a transfer tax. This is basically a tax that can be imposed by one partner on the goods of the others in order to protect new industries in the tax-imposing state. Individual states may impose internal taxes payable on goods whether imported or not. Again, in the case of Uganda and Tanzania, partner states may and have insisted that payments destined for the other states receive exchange control verification before being transmitted. It is therefore not as easy as perhaps it should be for individuals in the partner states to trade with their counterparts in the other two states.

The vast majority of Uganda's other treaties and international agreements, although generally entered into for the good of the community as a whole, are not concerned with the rights of individuals either of Uganda or other states. The agreements fall basically into three categories: loan agreements; cultural and technical cooperation or assistance agreements; and economic cooperation agreements.

The loan agreements, apart from containing matters relating purely to loans and terms of repayment, often tie the borrower either to specific projects or to using the proceeds of the loan for goods or services coming from the lending country.[47] Individuals and corporations in the lending countries may thus benefit considerably if they engage in the projects named.

Cultural and technical cooperation agreements again are usually intended for the general benefit of the two communities concerned. There often are clauses in them providing that technicians can be exempted from personal taxation and customs duties and technical equipment that can be imported duty free. Other clauses often guarantee free entry into Uganda of experts provided by the other party.

Economic cooperation agreements, which usually guarantee most-favored-nation treatment to each party by the other, often contain a provision for the protection of the property of nationals. For example, in the case of the Agreement on Economic Cooperation between Uganda and the Kingdom of the Netherlands, initialed in February 1969, provision is made that neither contracting party shall deprive nationals of the other party of their property unless the deprivation is in the national interest. This agreement is not discriminatory, and there is provision for adequate compensation. Similar provision is made in an Investment Protection Agreement between Uganda and Switzerland.

Apart from the main categories of agreement I have referred to, Uganda is party to a number of agreements on specific matters that affect the individual. For example, there are a number of double taxation treaties and conventions to which Uganda is a party.

One such agreement that affects a great many Uganda nationals is the International Coffee Agreement. Uganda is the largest producer of coffee in the Commonwealth, coffee earning about half of its foreign exchange. About 90 percent of Uganda nationals are engaged in agriculture, and a large proportion are coffee producers. The agreement that controls the quotas of coffee sold by each country to the so-called quota markets is considered essential, since in 1972 there has been world overproduction of coffee. Likewise Uganda is a party to the Commonwealth Sugar Agreement and is engaged in negotiations for a world tea agreement. These commodity agreements will benefit the country as a whole but are of specific interest to those persons producing the commodities to which they relate. Although the agreements, particularly the Coffee Agreement, are for their ultimate benefit, they control the prices they obtain for their produce and even the persons to whom they sell. Uganda's municipal legislation is to some extent tailored to the terms of the Coffee Agreement, because membership in this agreement imposes obligations on the government that have to be enforced by legislation. For example, the Coffee (Control of Exports) Rules[48] are intended to ensure as far as possible that Uganda does not exceed its annual quota exportable to quota markets, in accordance with the terms of the agreement.

A number of treaties and conventions to which Uganda is a party have been given the force of law by incorporation in a Uganda statute, including the Treaty on East African Cooperation,[49] the Vienna Convention on Diplomatic Relations,[50] and the Bretton Woods Agreements.[51] This has enabled persons who have wished to claim the benefit of the agreements a right under Uganda law that they would not otherwise have had, since individuals cannot be parties to these agreements themselves. The Diplomatic Privileges Act is particularly relevant since its provisions have been invoked before the courts.[52] Statutes are not usually enacted in respect to bilateral treaties.

There have been exceptions. For example, the Overseas Service Act[53] ratified the Overseas Service (Uganda) Agreement of 1961 between Uganda and Britain and provided for some matters connected therewith. The act charged certain payments, including pensions due to British nationals in the Uganda government service on the Consolidated Fund. This agreement would appear to be the only one that provided for the protection of the interests of British nationals remaining in Uganda after independence. The general protection of British nationals, and nationals of other countries for that matter, was left to the law of Uganda. Another useful statute related to international agreements is the Administration of Estates by Consular Officers Act.[54] Under this act a consul or vice-consul may administer the estate of a national of the country he or she represents if the need arises. The act applies to scheduled countries that have entered into treaties of commerce and navigation with Uganda. Since independence no country has been scheduled for the purposes of the act, and so at present it is inoperative.

NOTES

1. Constitution of Uganda, 1962, §§ 17-33.
2. Constitution of the Republic of Uganda, 8 September 1967 (hereafter 1967 Constitution).
3. Proclamation by Major-General Idi Amin Dada, dated 2 February 1971; Legal Notice No. 1, 1971.
4. Statement by the Armed Forces, 25 January 1971.
5. Caption 59, Laws of Uganda (1964).
6. Statutory Instrument 59; 1 Laws of Uganda (1964).
7. Probation Act, Caption 109, Laws of Uganda (1964).
8. Caption 308, Laws of Uganda (1964).
9. Act 20, 1967.
10. Caption 312, Laws of Uganda (1964).
11. Decree 14, 1971.
12. See Ibingira (Grace Stuart) v. Uganda (1966), East Africa 306.
13. See Penal Code Act, Caption 106, Laws of Uganda (1964).
14. Art. 21, 1967 Constitution Art. 8, Caption 307, Laws of Uganda (1964); Legal Notice No. 4, 1966. Legal Notice No. 4 was extended from time to time by resolution of parliament until it was replaced by Statutory Instrument No. 232 of 1969, which again was extended from time to time until revoked as of 20 February 1971. Constitution, State of Public Emergency Revocation Decree, Decree 9, 1971.
15. Caption 307, Laws of Uganda (1964).
16. Act 23, 1968.
17. Police (Declaration of Disturbed Area) Notice, 1969; Legal Notice No. 6, 1969.
18. Caption 58, Laws of Uganda (1964).
19. Act 19, 1969.

20. 1967 Constitution, at 35, Laws of Uganda, § 7.

21. Caption 60, Laws of Uganda (1964). Since repealed and replaced by the Immigration Act of 1969.

22. Act 11, 1967.

23. Caption 158, Laws of Uganda (1964).

24. See Schedule, East African Community Act (Act 28), 1967.

25. Penal Code Act (See reprint 1970), § 25.

26. See Shah v. Attorney General, E.A.L.R. 523 (1970).

27. The Southern African ban appears to be administrative. The ban on Rhodesian trade is contained in The Import & Export Prohibition (Southern Rhodesia) Order, statutory instrument No. 235, 1965.

28. Immigration Regulations, S.I. No. 165, 1969.

29. Immigration (Entry into Uganda) (Exemption) Order, S.I. No. 8, 1970.

30. Caption 60, Laws of Uganda (1964).

31. See Regulation 7, S.I. 165, 1969.

32. East African Income Tax Management Act, Caption 24, Laws of the Community (1958), § 116.

33. See Immigration Act, § 14.

34. In the Matter of Habeas Corpus, Application by Diagne Ibrahim and Others, Miscellaneous Cause No. 26, 1969.

35. Emergency Powers (Detention) Regulations, S.I. No. 65, 1966.

36. Caption 114, Laws of Uganda (1964).

37. Ibid.

38. Diplomatic Privileges Act, Act 2, 1965, § 1.

39. Control of Alien Refugees Act, Caption 64, Laws of Uganda (1964).

40. Caption 103, Laws of Uganda (1964).

41. Act 4, 1970. The section now omits reference to the Commonwealth.

42. S.I. 235, 1965.

43. Caption 43, Laws of Uganda (1964).

44. See Campagnola v. Stepanov, Civil Suit 119, 1969. In this case a certificate concerning the status of an employee of a diplomatic mission was given by the Chief of Protocol at the request of a litigant.

45. West Nile Administration v. Dritoo, E.A. 324 (1969).

46. See In the Matter of an Application by the Attorney General for an Order of Certiorari, Miscellaneous Cause No. 23, 1967.

47. See, for example, the Agreement between Uganda and Denmark, 1 April 1968, specifically related to four projects, and in addition "such other machinery and equipment for the implementation of Uganda's development projects as may be agreed upon between the parties."

48. S.I. 230, 11 Laws of Uganda (1964).

49. East African Community Act, Act 28, 1967.

50. Diplomatic Privileges Act, Act 2, 1965.

51. Bretton Woods Agreements Act, Caption 161, Laws of Uganda (1964).

52. Campagnola v. Stepanov, Civil Suit 119, 1969.

53. Caption 280, Laws of Uganda (1964).

54. Caption 145, Laws of Uganda (1964).

CHAPTER

19

THE UNITED KINGDOM

John G. Collier

THE INDIVIDUAL

The Individual as a National

Movement

Passports. From the earlier statements in the Magna Carta and in learned writings, it might be supposed that every national has a right to be issued a passport. Indeed, the Indian courts have relied upon the Magna Carta in deciding that nationals are so entitled.[1]

However, it seems clear that in contradistinction to the law of India and of the United States[2] there is no such right, the issuance of passports being a matter of the exercise of the prerogative of the Crown, which thus may act at its discretion.[3]

There appears to be no formal means of securing the review of a decision by the Passport Office, a department of the Foreign Office, not to grant a passport. An attempt might be made to compel the passport officer to issue one by the specific order of a court (writ of mandamus), but such an order does not lie against the Crown itself, nor against one of its officers, unless it is intended to compel that officer to perform a duty that is owed to the individual. Such an action would raise the question of whether the officer is acting in the question of issuing passports solely in line with his or her duties toward the Crown, and this in turn would raise the original question of whether the issuing of passports does lie entirely within the Crown prerogative.

Reviewed and revised by the author in 1975.

Support for the view that it does may be derived from the terms in which it is issued. It is expressly stated that the passport remains the property of the government. In a case in 1928 it was held that a passport did not belong to a bankrupt person in the sense that it would pass with that person's property to his or her trustee in bankruptcy.[4] Furthermore, the holder of a passport is expressly informed in that passport that it is liable to be revoked or impounded at any time. It has been held in South Africa that the holder may compel the renewal of a passport on the ground that he or she has paid for it and thus has a contractual right to have it renewed,[5] but this seems to be incorrect, at any rate so far as the United Kingdom is concerned, since payment is made as a fee rather than as contractual consideration.

The grounds upon which passports have been denied, revoked, or impounded were stated in Parliament in 1968.[6] About 2,500 passports are seized each year. Sometimes this is in order to prevent persons accused of crimes from departing. The largest group is that of holidaymakers, stranded and destitute whilst abroad, who are repatriated on government loan. Between 1945 and 1968 only 20 passports, or nearly one a year on average, were denied on political grounds.

The cause of the parliamentary statement in 1968 was the withdrawal of the passport of Sir Frederick Crawford because of his activities in connection with the Smith regime in Rhodesia. Crawford was sufficiently influential to have the matter debated in Parliament, but to no effect. One M.P. thought the Parliamentary Commissioner (Ombudsman) would be entitled to review the Secretary of State's action under the provisions of the Parliamentary Commissioner Act of 1967. The Secretary of State promptly certified that the withdrawal of a passport affected relations between governments and thus fell within an area of governmental activity that is excluded from the purview of the commissioner. After protests, the Secretary of State appointed a committee to advise him upon such cases.

Departure. The subject is almost certainly free to leave the country even without a passport. In 1968 a journalist, Colvin, tried to leave Heathrow Airport for Portugal without one. The Chief Immigration Officer prevented him from doing so. The Home Office admitted in Parliament that a citizen cannot be refused permission to leave simply because he or she has no passport, but sought to justify the action of the officer on the ground that Article 7(1) of the Aliens Order of 1953 stated that "every person . . . who lands or embarks in the United Kingdom shall, if so required by the immigration officer, produce either a valid passport . . . or some other document satisfactorily establishing his identity and nationality or citizenship."

However, the order did not say "if the immigration officer is satisfied." If proceedings were brought by the subject, it would seem to be for a court to say whether the evidence was satisfactory. Colvin unfortunately did not bring such proceedings, though he was carrying documents evidencing his nationality and identity. Under the Immigration Act of 1971, which replaces the Aliens Order, the immigration officer may detain a person pending his decision, but if he were to make a wrong decision, there appears to be no protection for him against an action for wrongful refusal.[7]

In fact, for other reasons it may be impossible for a person to leave the country without a passport because (1) it is virtually impossible to enter another country lawfully without one and (2) as a consequence the carrier may, and probably will, make it a condition of the contract of carriage that the customer should possess one, since the carrier might otherwise have the trouble and expense of transporting the passenger whence he or she came.

Although the prime legal purpose of British passports is to certify the willingness of the government to protect the holder while abroad, the passport is secondarily important as an identity card and certificate of nationality. Its desirability also arises because its possession obviates possible inconveniences that may occur upon entry into the United Kingdom without one. It is high time that at least the granting and withdrawal of passports was made the subject of review by the courts.

According to Article 42 of Magna Carta, 1215, "it shall be lawful for any man to leave and return to our kingdom unharmed and without fear, by land or water, preserving his allegiance to us except in time of war for some short period, for the common benefit of the realm." Though this provision was not repeated in subsequent revisions of the Great Charter, Blackstone, writing in the eighteenth century, stated that the right of a free man to leave the realm is a common law right, and that the only possible restriction upon it is the possible issuing against him of the prerogative writ ne exeat regno, which forbids him to leave the kingdom.

This prerogative writ evolved in medieval times and was originally used by the Crown to prevent persons from leaving the realm in order to evade their legal duties, in particular the duty of military service. Later it became useful to private creditors, who could use it to prevent certain classes of their debtors from leaving the country in cases in which common law and statute law did not provide a sufficient remedy. Its use by private suitors was discussed in 1968 in the Felton v. Callis case, in which an application was unsuccessful.[8] Apparently it was last issued for such a purpose in 1893.

The extent to which the writ may still be used by the Crown for its original political purpose is a matter of controversy. In theory it still exists, although it has not been employed in this way for a couple of centuries, since the prerogative is not lost by mere disuse. It is sometimes suggested that its use would be limited to times of war or national emergency, but it is difficult to see why. Indeed, the Crown has other powers that it may use to the same ends in time of war, for it is usually empowered to act by virtue of statute. In truth, the use of prohibition to leave the kingdom is but little discussed by modern writers.

However, in 1971 there was an application for the writ in New Zealand, but in circumstances that did not really provide a definitive statement of the relevant law. In Parsons v. Burk[9] a private individual sought the writ for political purposes. He was attempting to prevent the departure of the New Zealand International Rugby Union Team to play in South Africa and Rhodesia, since, he alleged, this would bring New Zealand hatred, ridicule, and contempt in the United Nations. He failed; the court held that the claim did not disclose anything prejudicial to New Zealand in the sense of being prejudicial to its safety and benefit.

Two other factors may also explain the decision: the application was not by the Crown but by a private individual, and it was not sought in order to prevent the departure of a particular person, but of a group. Nevertheless the court appears to have thought that in a proper case an application by the Crown might have been successful, though the situation was not one of war or national emergency.

In fact, the writ prohibiting exit from the kingdom appears to survive, but only as an historic relic. In time of peace the Crown hardly needs to resort to it, since persons may effectively be prevented from departing by virtue of passport controls. (See above.)

In passing it may be noted that the fourth protocol to the European Convention on Human Rights would be of little assistance to an individual who is prevented from leaving, since the United Kingdom has not ratified the protocol; in Article 2(3) the right is recognized to be subject to severe restrictions; and even if the United Kingdom were a party, it would be necessary to translate the provisions of the Protocol into English law by legislation, which has not so far been done with any of the provisions of the convention to which the United Kingdom is a party, in order to defeat an application for a writ prohibiting exit from the kingdom.

Return. Until the 1960s it was the law that any British subject had the right of entry into the United Kingdom with or without a passport, but recent legislation has qualified this right. This is hardly the place for a disquisition upon British nationality law, which is exceedingly complex. It is necessary, however, to state the different categories of persons who exist for the purpose of determination of national status. They are (1) British subjects, citizens of the United Kingdom and its colonies; (2) British subjects, citizens of states that are members of the Commonwealth (alternatively and more conveniently entitled "Commonwealth citizens," including Canadians, Indians, and Tanzanians; (3) British Protected Persons, that is, inhabitants of Protectorates or Trust Territories; (4) aliens, meaning citizens of all other countries except the Republic of Ireland; and (5) citizens of the Republic of Ireland, who have an odd status, being neither British subjects nor aliens but just Irish, with rights of free entry into the United Kingdom. Until 1962 all except aliens had automatic right of entry; aliens were subject to immigration control and had to have permission to enter.

The Commonwealth Immigrants Acts of 1962 and 1968 subjected Commonwealth citizens and British Protected Persons under a separate system from aliens. These acts also produced a distinction between, broadly speaking, (1) Citizens of the United Kingdom and its Colonies having passports issued by U.K. authorities and (2) those having passports issued by colonial authorities, who were grouped by these acts with Commonwealth citizens for the purpose of immigration. (The 1968 act restricted this second category further than had the 1962 act.)

The Immigration Act of 1971, which entered into force on 1 January 1973, has taken the process a step further, and now it is necessary to distinguish between only two classes of persons: (1) "patrials" who have what is called the "right of abode" and (2) all other inhabitants of the world. The former are not subject to immigration control but the latter are, whether they come from the Bahamas (a colony), India (a Commonwealth country), or Peru (a foreign country), and even in some cases from the United Kingdom itself. With some small distinctions between Commonwealth citizens and others, all are treated alike. These distinctions will be dealt with below. It is clear that nationality as such, in this context and in the context of expulsion or deportation, has no particular significance. What is vital is whether the individual is a "patrial."

According to Section 2(1) of the Immigration Act, a patrial is a person who is (1) a citizen of the United Kingdom or its colonies by birth, adoption, naturalization, or registration (available to persons in the Crown service, wives of U.K. citizens, and British Protected Persons) in the United Kingdom or the Islands (Isle of Man, Channel Islands); (2) a citizen of the United Kingdom or its colonies by descent from, or adoption by, such a citizen, who had such status by birth or adoption in the United Kingdom or whose own parent had that status; (3) a citizen of the United Kingdom or its colonies who has been settled in the United Kingdom and has been ordinarily resident for five years or more; or (4) a Commonwealth citizen born to, or legally adopted by, a citizen of the United Kingdom or its colonies, by birth in the United Kingdom. Section 2(2) of the act deals with the wives of such persons.

All patrials have the "right of abode," which is to say that, according to Section 1(2), they are free to live in, and to come and go into and from, the United Kingdom without let or hindrance, except for the formalities they are required to undergo in order to establish their rights.

Thus a patrial has the right to enter freely, upon proof of identity, if required, by a passport or by any other document establishing such identity. Possession of a passport, though not an exclusive requirement, is obviously the best way of avoiding difficulty, there being no legal need for a British subject to carry any identity certificate.

Expulsion. There appears to be no right, common law or statutory, by which the Crown may expel a British subject who is a patrial. For those who are not patrials see below. There is, however, nothing in principle or in British extradition law to exclude extradition of British subjects; basically this depends upon the relevant treaty.

Protection

Extent of Freedom of Activity Abroad. Mainly for historical reasons, British law generally does not seek to govern the activities of British subjects who are abroad; nor does British criminal law apply to offenses committed abroad so as to make acts subject to punishment in Britain that would be offenses if committed in the United Kingdom. The need is not particularly pressing, at any rate, where the act in question does not primarily affect the interests of the United Kingdom, since there is no general prohibition of law against the extradition of British subjects who have committed offenses upon the territory of another party to an extradition treaty.

By statute, however, certain offenses committed abroad by British subjects, and exceptionally by aliens, may be tried if the offender is later found in England. Among these crimes are treason,[10] treasonous felony, murder,[11] manslaughter, and bigamy,[12] as well as offenses against the Official Secrets Act of 1911, the Merchant Shipping Act of 1906, the Representation of the People Act of 1949,[13] and the Exchange Control Act of 1947. Under the Foreign Enlistment Act of 1870 it is an offense for a British subject to enlist in the military or naval service of any foreign state at war with a state in friendly relations with Her Majesty (that means, not actually at war), or to quit H.M. Dominions for that purpose.[14]

One important piece of legislation concerns the reaction of the U.K. government to the requirements of the demands by the U.S. authorities to foreign shipping companies to produce documents relating to liner conferences. By the Shipping Contracts and Commercial Documents Act of 1964, where measures have been taken under the law of a foreign country for regulating or controlling the terms or conditions of carriage by sea, and those measures, insofar as they apply to things done or to be done outside the territorial jurisdiction of that country by United Kingdom business, constitute an infringement of the jurisdiction that belongs to the United Kingdom under international law, the minister may direct that business to notify the minister of any requirement or prohibition, including the requirement to produce documents not within the jurisdiction of the foreign country, and may prohibit compliance therewith.[15]

By a special provision of the British Nationality Act of 1948,[16] a British subject who is not a citizen of the United Kingdom or its colonies cannot be guilty of an offense against its laws for an act done in a Commonwealth country, in the Republic of Ireland, or in a foreign country unless it would be an offense if the act were done in a foreign country and that individual were an alien. Thus the United Kingdom disclaims a large measure of extraterritorial jurisdiction over offenses committed by such persons. The only cases in which they would be liable to be tried in Great Britain are those in which such offenses as are mentioned in the last two paragraphs are offenses when committed by an alien.

Thus it is necessary to determine which of those statutes affect aliens as well as British subjects. Not all do, and in fact an alien can never be tried for an offense committed on land abroad, save under the rule in D.P.P. v. Joyce,[17] that is, where the offense charged is treason and the offender is fraudulently in possession of a British passport or where the offender is otherwise constructively a British subject, such as a "British officer" under the Official Secrets Act of 1911. Also, by Section 70 of the Army Act of 1955 and the Air Force Act of 1955, an alien subject to military or air force law can be tried by court martial for any act or omission wherever it occurred, if it would be punishable if committed in England. A person of whatever nationality who is accused of committing, aiding, abetting, or procuring a grave breach of the Geneva Red Cross Conventions of 1949, whether in or outside the United Kingdom, may likewise be convicted in proceedings in England.[18]

Another of the statutory offenses listed above does not appear to be limited to British subjects. That is the offense under Section 1(5) of the Perjury Act of 1911 of making false statements abroad for the purposes of judicial proceedings in England. It may be noted in this connection that under Clause 11 of the European Communities Act of 1972, "a person who, in sworn evidence before the European Court [of Justice] makes any statement which he knows to be false or does not believe to be true shall, whether he is a British subject or not, be guilty to an offence and may be proceeded against and punished" for perjury under the principal act.

Other offenses committed outside the United Kingdom may, if committed by British subjects or aliens, be tried in the United Kingdom if done on board aircraft[19] or upon British ships,[20] notably the offense of hijacking as defined in the Hague Convention of 1970.

One incident is perhaps worth mentioning at this point. It foreshadows the Shipping Contracts and Commercial Documents Act of 1964. In the course of the 1952 investigation by the U.S. courts into possible violations of the Sherman and Clayton Anti-Trust Acts by U.S. and foreign oil companies, a letter was sent by the British Minister of Fuel and Power to, among others, the Anglo-Iranian Oil Company, requiring it not to produce to the U.S. court, in answer to a subpoena, any documents not relating to business in the United States without the authority of the British government, on the grounds that "the disclosure of some of these documents or of information relating to business outside the United States may well, in the opinion of Her Majesty's Government, prejudice or endanger the economic, strategic, or political interests of Her Majesty's Government and of the Western Powers."

Later, by a letter delivered to the court through the State Department, the Secretary of State for Foreign Affairs stated that the above letter "embraced a claim of sovereignty in that it was addressed to British subjects and organisations by Her Majesty's Government in the exercise of their Governmental authority and in the British public interest, including the economic strategic and political interests of Her Majesty's Government."

On the basis of these observations the court held that the government was making a claim of sovereignty and asserting its immunity and accordingly "sovereign immunity is extended to Anglo-Iranian."[21]

This possibly surprising conclusion was no doubt gratifying to the U.K. government, but what is puzzling is to try to discover the legal grounds for the assertion by the government of a right to prevent a British subject from doing the act in question in a foreign state. No doubt it may demand that documents that belong to the Crown be not produced, and their production might in any case give rise to prosecution under the Official Secrets Acts; but the claim is not so limited and extends to any documents, which may not belong to the Crown or even have been seen by the British government. If the Crown really has the legal authority that it seems to be asserting, it is difficult to understand why it was necessary to pass the 1964 act.

The power of the Crown to deprive persons of their nationality for such acts as entering into the service of a foreign state, voting in elections abroad, or committing offenses there is very restricted. By such activities the individuals may lose the protection of the Crown against the state in which they are carried on,[22] but a natural-born British subject cannot be deprived of national status. Under the British Nationality Act, a citizen of the United Kingdom or its colonies can be deprived of national status by an order of the Secretary of State only if he or she is a citizen by registration or naturalization. Apart from the case of a person who obtains this registration or naturalization by fraud, a naturalized person may be deprived of citizenship on grounds of (1) disloyalty, (2) trading or communication with the enemy, or (3) imprisonment for not less than 12 months in any country. Further, the Secretary of State may deprive a naturalized person of citizenship if satisfied that the latter has been ordinarily resident in foreign countries for seven years without being in the service of the Crown or an international organization and without annually registering at a British consulate his or her intention of retaining citizenship. The Secretary of State must in any case be satisfied that it is not conducive to the public good that the person should continue to be a citizen.[23]

The power is discretionary in the Secretary of State, but before the order is made, the person in question must be informed of the grounds on which the secretary proposes to make it. If the ground is that citizenship has been obtained by fraud or one of the grounds mentioned above, if the person requests it (and he or she must be informed of this right) the Secretary of State must hold an inquiry before a committee whose chairman has judicial experience. An inquiry may be held in any case if the Secretary of State thinks fit.

The Right to Diplomatic Protection. Although the possession of a British passport is often said to entitle a person to the protection of the Crown, in the eyes of the law it is clear that as of legal right there is no duty, or at any rate no duty that is enforceable. Throughout the nineteenth century the law officers of the Crown, in advising upon cases in which British subjects were injured in foreign states, spoke almost invariably of a "right" to protection, but it is clear that they were using the term somewhat loosely.[24]

The question was really answered beyond further doubt by the Court of Appeal in 1932, in what has been described as the "encyclopaedic" case of China Navigation Company v. Attorney-General, although the case concerned protection by military rather than by diplomatic means. In fact, the Crown was willing to assign rather more armed men to the petitioning company upon its vessels in the China Seas than the Crown itself deemed necessary for their protection against pirates, but it insisted that the extra men whose services were desired should be paid for by the company. In part the case was concerned with the Crown's right to tax and its right to contract with individuals for its services, but the court fully discussed the question at issue here. Lord Justice Scrutton said, "In my opinion there is no legally enforceable duty [of the Crown] to protect British property from danger in foreign parts."[25] It was pointed out that the subject's remedy, "if any, is pressure brought by Parliament on Ministers to take steps either by diplomatic action or otherwise to protect British subjects."[26]

By saying that the remedy was pressure upon ministers through Parliament, it is clear that the court intended to exclude the possibility of compelling the government through the courts to take steps by diplomatic action.

There is one well-known case that appears at first sight to lend some support to the view that there is a legal duty upon the Crown to protect not merely its own subjects, but even foreigners who owe allegiance to the Crown. This was the decision of the House of Lords in Joyce v. Director of Public Prosecutions.[27] William Joyce was a U.S. citizen who lived in England during most of the 1930s and indulged in various fascist activities. At the outbreak of war in 1939 he, having acquired a British passport by falsely representing himself to be British, went to Germany and threw in his lot with that state and carried out anti-British activities, mainly by broadcasting propaganda directed at Britain, where he became known as "Lord Haw Haw." He was arrested at the end of the war, tried, convicted, and hanged for treason.

Treason consists essentially of acts that amount to a breach of the individual's duty of allegiance. Whence did Joyce derive this duty? It is clear that a friendly alien when resident within the realm owes a measure of local allegiance, and had Joyce adhered to the king's enemies while resident in England he would have been guilty of treason.[28] It was held that this allegiance continued after his departure to Germany because he departed with a British passport, since his allegiance was correlative with the Crown's duty of protection, as evidenced by his passport.

As a learned writer pointed out at the time,[29] there is no such correlation. The court confused two sorts of protection. The cases relied upon in the judgments as establishing the duty in Joyce's case, especially the decision of the House of Lords in Johnstone v. Pedlar,[30] were concerned with the Crown's duty to protect a friendly alien within the realm. Such a duty does exist, and can be correlated with the duty of local allegiance. All it means, however, is that the Crown must abstain from committing illegal acts upon that alien, which may be called a negative protection. This has nothing to do with positive protection, that is, with protection by the Crown against foreign states in the case of an individual outside the realm. Indeed, the House of Lords itself, referring to Oppenheim's International Law,[31] made the following statement:

> By a universally recognised customary rule of the law of nations every state holds the right of protection over its citizens abroad. The rule thus recognised may be asserted by the holder of a passport which is for him the outward title of his rights. It is true that the measure in which the state will exercise its right lies in its discretion.[32]

It is thus clear that although the court talked of the duty of the Crown to protect and the right of the individual to "demand" protection, these are not legally enforceable duties and rights; if they were, there could be no discretion about the matter.

The constitutional freedom of the Crown in this regard enables it to comply with such suggested rules of international law as those concerning continuous and dual nationality and the "genuine link" principle. It also enables it to decline to present a claim when to do so might imply recognition of a regime or acquisition of territory when it would be impolitic to do so, or where the individual in question or the claim itself is regarded as unmeritorious.

The State and Compensation. If the government secures compensation from a foreign country for an injury done by the latter to a British subject, the agreement by which this is effected is regarded as an act of state and is thereby beyond the jurisdiction of the courts. It is clearly the rule that an individual cannot base any right of action upon such an act of state. There is therefore no legal means by which the individual can compel the Crown to pay over such compensation.[33] In theory, if the individual can show that in entering into such an agreement the Crown was intending to contract on his behalf, or if having received the monies the Crown were to constitute itself trustee of them for the individual, then there might be a right of action. The courts will not imply such intention or trust out of the mere fact of the making of the agreement; this is true of any individual claim, as has been stated in many cases, the latest being Oyekan v. Adele.[34]

As a matter of fact, there is usually little difficulty about the matter. The normal practice is to pay to the claimant whatever is obtained from the foreign government, subject to deductions for expenses. Apparently expenses incurred by the government in the conduct of the case are not usually deducted, though the claimant may be charged with special costs incurred for the purpose of pursuing the claim, such as a valuation of property, and an undertaking by the claimant to meet such costs is obtained before they are incurred.[35]

However, under statute the individual may be able to obtain the compensation, or a portion of it. If this is so, that individual may only proceed under the provisions of the statute.[36] Nowadays such statutory provisions do exist, for where compensation has been obtained from foreign states by compensation agreements, in the form of global agreements, its distribution is carried out through the Foreign Compensation Commission (F.C.C.) under the Foreign Compensation Acts of 1950-69. The operations of this commission have been examined by Lillich.[37]

Since 1950, when general settlements of British claims have been made it has been normal to make distribution through the commission, though there is no obligation upon the government to do so. For example, £.5 million received from the government of Japan on account of the peace treaty and prewar claims was distributed administratively through the Foreign Office. Another example is the case of the monies obtained under the Anglo-German Agreement of 1964 for compensation for victims of the Nazis. This was also distributed through the Foreign Office. Mistaken views of its own powers by that department, which led to the refusal of compensation to former inmates of Sachsenhausen concentration camp, led to an inquiry and criticism by the newly created Parliamentary Commission for Administration (Ombudsman), whose views were acted upon and who thus succeeded in obtaining compensation for the individuals concerned.[38]

The terms upon which distribution is made by the commission are within the discretion of the government but are in fact laid down in Orders in Council giving effect to the wishes of the government in the matter, which may or may not reflect the provisions of the relevant compensation agreement with the foreign state.

The Foreign Compensation Act of 1950 established the commission and authorized the Crown by Order in Council to provide for the distribution of funds received under the agreement with Yugoslavia of 1948[39] and the agreement with Czechoslovakia of 1949[40] and to permit the commission to register and determine claims should the United Kingdom contemplate or enter into agreements with any foreign country. Examples of such agreements have been those with Poland in 1954[41] and Egypt in 1959.[42]

The commission is a quasi-judicial body consisting of a chairman and such other members as may be necessary. There is no requirement that the members be legally trained, but in practice they have been. The Lord Chancellor appoints them on such terms as he thinks fit. The composition of the commission has, since 1961, been one chairman and about eight commissioners. Its procedure is governed by rules composed by itself, subject to the Lord Chancellor's approval. Claims must be filed, whereupon they are screened and examined by the legal officers. The latter may recommend that the commission admit the claim, and if it does not do so, it must file an answer to it containing those matters that it believes require consideration. The decisions on individual claims are not published, and the answer, which is also sent to the claimant, provides reasons for the commission's action. The claimant has 21 days in which to reply and may make a written demand for an oral hearing of the claim. Broadly speaking, the procedure at an oral hearing is of a judicial kind. As has been stated, the decision is not published, and though obviously it is communicated to the claimant, the reasons are not.

The Foreign Compensation Act of 1950 provided that "the determination by the Commission of any application made to them under this Act shall not be called in question in any court of law." The Tribunals and Inquiries Act of 1958, which provided that statutes making decisions of similar bodies final should no longer preclude the review of a decision by the courts, expressly excluded the F.C.C.[43] This was partly because the award is discretionary and partly because it was thought that if substantial claims were taken before the High Court, the money would not be distributed within a reasonable time.[44] Nevertheless, in 1968 the House of Lords, in a very important case, declared a decision of the F.C.C. to be beyond its authority and void.[45] Section 4(4) of the act, it was held, would bar any challenge to such a decision on the grounds of error but could not preclude any challenge on the grounds that it had exceeded its jurisdiction. The F.C.C. had rejected a mining company's claim in respect to the payments made by the Egyptian government after 1956. The F.C.C., construing the relevant regulations, had required the claimants to show that their successors in title were of British nationality, whereas in a true construction this was irrelevant. The error amounted to imposing a condition that the commission had no power to impose.

One result of this case was that, after considerable controversy, Parliament took advantage of the opportunity to insert in the Foreign Compensation Act of 1969 a section that provides for appeal from the F.C.C. on questions of construction and its jurisdiction to the Court of Appeal only, but not at all restricting proceedings based on the grounds that the rules of natural justice, such as the right of the claimant to be heard in his or her own cause, had not been observed by the F.C.C.[46]

There is no obligation upon the government to "top up" the compensation received from a foreign state to make it equal to the actual financial loss suffered by the national; nor can it do so unless Parliament appropriates the funds for such a purpose. (See below.)

The Responsibility of the State for Injury Induced by Its Own Conduct. Two types of situations may be distinguished here. The first is that the U.K. government or its agents directly injure a British subject by their own acts. In this case there is nothing to prevent the individual from pursuing whatever legal remedies he or she may possess in the English courts. Even if the Crown were able to plead that its acts constituted an act of state, it appears from the leading case, decided in 1970,[47] that this will be no defense against a British subject. Thus, at least in the view of one judge of the House of Lords (Lord Reid), if the house of a British subject in Egypt had been damaged by British troops when they were seizing the Suez Canal, its owner would have been able to recover damages in an English court. The whole of this topic is in an unsatisfactory state, for it is far from clear exactly what are or are not acts of state in this sense, or indeed who are British subjects for this purpose. Indeed, the decision of the House of Lords raised more questions than it answered.

The second type of situation is that as a result of an action by the U.K. government, a foreign government commits an injury upon a British subject. There are only two known examples of the government making good such losses by "topping up" the funds available for satisfying claims. After the lump-sum settlements between the United States and Great Britain in 1802, and after a British national commission had adjudicated the claims, Parliament appropriated supplemental funds to compensate one class of claimants further.[48]

After the Suez Affair of 1956 an agreement with Egypt secured £27,500,000 in settlement of British claims, as against £80,000,000 outstanding. The government admitted that it was its own initiative that had led to the plight of the claimants, and in 1962 Parliament provided funds for additional compensation.[49]

Waiver. Since the Crown has a discretion whether or not to espouse individual claims, it follows that it may waive them, in whole or in part. Indeed, the global settlements achieved with other states since World War II, by which lump sums have been obtained, all amount in effect to a waiver of individual claims to a greater or smaller extent.[50] An obvious example is the Suez affair referred to above.

The Individual as an Alien

Movement

Entry and Stay. The common law governing the admission, control, and expulsion of aliens was not entirely clear. As to their admission, it seems that they had no legal redress in case of its refusal.[51] That case actually concerned an act of the legislature of the Australian State of Victoria, but the Privy Council expressly stated that no common law right of admission existed, though a refusal to admit might be such a breach of international "comity" as would give rise to diplomatic remonstrance on the part of the government of the affected individual. Whether this was because the power of regulation depended upon the royal prerogative is uncertain.

The first statutory regulation of entry was in 1793. By a series of statutes of 1905, 1914, and 1919, powers were given to exclude and deport certain classes of aliens, and these powers conferred very wide discretion upon the executive. The detailed executive powers that were contained in the Orders in Council made under the 1919 act, the principal order being that of 1953, must be exercised by immigration officers. Their prerogative included an overriding discretionary power to refuse permission to any alien to land. Instructions to immigration officers, which were unpublished until 1968, were given by the Secretary of State. Furthermore, conditions might be imposed upon aliens granted leave to land, the most onerous being that an alien admitted for a fixed period of more than three months should be registered with the police and report changes of address, occupation, and status.

In theory, these powers being statutory powers, their exercise could be controlled by the courts. Nevertheless, their breadth makes this impossible in practice. In particular, the latest decisions show that the alien is entitled to no hearing in the case of refusal of admission or nonrenewal of a limited entry permit, upon the grounds that in such cases there is "no legitimate expectation" that permission will be given.[52]

Until 1962 there was no power to refuse entry to any British subject, but this was altered by the Commonwealth Immigrants Act as amended and supplemented in 1968. The discretion of immigration officers under these acts was not absolute as in the case of aliens. In determining questions of fact, they were obliged to give the entrant an opportunity to explain himself or herself and they were not to take into account legally irrelevant considerations.[53] There was a general power to refuse admission or to admit subject to conditions regarding the duration of stay, but returning residents and others, such as holders of employment vouchers, were not exposed to the full rigor of this power. Further, the instructions to immigration officers were published.

After 1969 there was statutory regulation of appeals against refusals to land and/or conditions placed on permission to land, refusals to vary or revoke, and deportation orders for breach of conditions placed on permission to land. This statute, the Immigration Appeals Act, which was repealed but reproduced, with amendments, in the Immigration Act of 1971, was also concerned with appeals in deportation cases and will be dealt with later in this chapter, after consideration of the power to deport.

Voluntary Departure. There appears to have been no rule of the common law that in time of peace could justify refusal to allow the voluntary departure of an alien. The writ prohibiting exit from the kingdom was limited to subjects of the Crown. The Immigration Act of 1971 gives such a power as a weapon of retaliation, since it states that the Crown, by Order in Council, may "make provision for prohibiting persons who are citizens or nations of [a country that imposes restrictions upon the departure from that country of citizens of the United Kingdom or its colonies] from embarking in the United Kingdom or from doing so elsewhere than at a part of exit."[54]

Involuntary Departure: Expulsion and Deportation. The position at common law was also somewhat obscure regarding involuntary departure. It was not clear whether the Crown had power (1) to order an expulsion and/or (2) actually to deport an alien, and if so, whether this was by virtue of the prerogative. However, the same series of statutes that dealt with immigration also dealt with deportation.

An Aliens Act of 1848 authorized the removal of aliens from the realm, but except for Irish aliens, it expired after one year. Under the Aliens Order of 1953, an alien could be deported (1) to effectuate a refusal to give the alien permission to land, (2) on the recommendation of a court or on conviction for an offense punishable with imprisonment, (3) for breach of landing conditions, or (4) whenever the Home Secretary "deems it to be conducive to the public good." The decision must be made by the Home Secretary in person.

As for judicial remedies in case of deportation orders, although these orders might be attacked on the ground that the proper formal procedure had not been complied with,[55] the courts have held that the Home Secretary is exercising an executive discretionary power, that he is under no duty to afford the deportee any hearing in his own case, and that the validity of the order cannot be impugned on the ground that it is unreasonable.[56] The only recourse has appeared to be for the deportee to show that he or she was not an alien.

The case of R. v. Brixton Prison Governor, exp. Soblen,[57] a cause célèbre at the time, affirmed the Venicoff case and demonstrated the essential nonjusticiability of the executive power. It did suggest, however, one slight possibility of upsetting a deportation order, that is, if the deportee could show that the power was being used not for the real purpose of ridding the country of an unwanted alien, but in order to extradite him to a country that was not entitled to require his extradition, he having not committed or been accused of an extraditable offense. Soblen had been convicted in the United States of espionage, but jumped bail and fled to Israel, whence he was deported by air. On arrival in London he had to be detained in hospital, since he had inflicted wounds upon himself. Eventually a deportation order was made, which Soblen challenged mainly upon the grounds that it was a form of disguised extradition. The Court of Appeal held that although this was the practical effect of the order, it was valid because the applicant had failed to prove that it was a sham. He would have had to show that the Home Secretary was motivated by an ulterior purpose and did not genuinely believe that it would be conducive to the public good to deport him. The evidence for this was lacking, since Crown privilege was successfully claimed for the correspondence between the two governments on the matter, and the court would not draw adverse inferences from the material before it.

Under Part II of the Commonwealth Immigrants Act of 1962, courts were empowered to recommend a Commonwealth citizen, a citizen of the Republic of Ireland, or a British Protected Person for deportation who had committed any offense punishable with imprisonment, unless that individual had close connection with the United Kingdom itself or had been continuously resident there for five years. Appeal could be made to a higher court and must be accepted by the Home Secretary. The grounds for deportation were thus much narrower than in the case of an alien, and in particular there was no power to deport a Commonwealth citizen in "public good" cases.

Remedies in Cases of Nonadmission and Deportation. In either case the possibility of obtaining any remedy through the courts was therefore very slim indeed. However, improvements have been made in providing extrajudicial machinery for the hearing of appeals. In 1956 a form of purely administrative proceeding was provided for some classes of deportation cases that made a court's recommendation unnecessary. The deportee could ask for any representation to be heard by a metropolitan magistrate at Bow Street. The magistrate would then make an advisory recommendation to the Home Secretary about whether the order should be put into effect.

This administrative concession, which was made in order to provide some semblance of compliance with the European Convention on Human Rights, suffered from severe defects. For example, the alien was not told the reasons for deportation nor what the recommendation was. The concession did not apply at all where the order was made on grounds of public security or on the grounds that the alien had landed without permission or that, having been in the country for less than two years, the alien had failed to observe the conditions attaching to his or her stay.

The Immigration Act of 1971. In 1967 the Wilson Committee on Immigration Appeals made certain recommendations about appeals in cases of refusal of admission, refusal to extend a stay, and deportation. These were given effect in the Immigration Appeals Act of 1969 and the Rules of 1970. With one important exclusion, and other amendments, these have now been reenacted in the Immigration Act of 1971.

This act is extremely long and technical, and only a broad account of its provisions can be given here. The general provisions for regulation and control apply to all persons who are not patrial. These provisions are contained in Section 3. The Secretary of State is empowered to make rules to be followed in the administration of the act for regulating the entry into and stay in the United Kingdom.

Section 3(1) provides that a nonpatrial is required to have leave to enter, which may be given, as may leave to remain, for a limited or indefinite period, subject to employment or occupation in the United Kingdom or registration with the police.

There are special cases, which are dealt with in the Immigration rules.[58] These include provision for persons coming for the purpose of taking employment or study, as visitors, or as dependents of persons lawfully in or entering the United Kingdom.[59]

There are also cases of recognition of, as it were, an acquired right to enter in the case of Commonwealth citizens settled in the United Kingdom at the coming into force of the act (and their spouses and children). The rules are to be framed in such a way that such persons are not less free to enter and leave the United Kingdom than if the act had not been passed.[60]

Any nonpatrial who was settled in this country at the time of enactment is in a better position than one who was not, since he or she will be treated as having received indefinite leave to enter and remain, subject to a continuing liability to deportation.[61]

The grounds upon which deportation may be effected are given as follows in Section 3(5):

> (a) if, having only a limited leave to enter or remain, he does not observe a condition attached to the leave or remains beyond the time limited by the leave; or
> (b) if the Secretary of State deems his deportation to be conducive to the public good;
> (c) if another person to whose family he belongs is or has been convicted of an offence punishable by imprisonment and on conviction is recommended for deportation by a competent court.

Of these, Section 3(5)(b) is a repetition of the previous grounds for deportation under the Aliens Order of 1953 and is clearly of the very widest import, since it gives an almost unfettered discretion. There is no need for the secretary to show, for example, that there are reasonable grounds for deeming the deportation to be for the public good. Indeed, it is so wide a power that it is not easy to see why other grounds for deportation are necessary.

One mildly embarrassing fact concerns the definition of "United Kingdom nationals" for the purpose of reciprocal treatment among member states as regards free movement of labor under the EEC regulations. The following definition has been accepted:

> citizens of the United Kingdom and Colonies or British subjects not possessing that citizenship or the citizenship of any other Commonwealth country or territory, who in either case, have the right of abode in the United Kingdom and are therefore exempt from United Kingdom immigration control.

Since the entry of the United Kingdom into the EEC in January 1973, nationals of other member states of that organization possess rights to work and to settle that are greater than those enjoyed by other aliens or nonpatrial citizens. The immigration rules, which are designed to implement EEC obligations, provide that when an EEC national (other than an Irish citizen, for whom special rules exist) is given leave to enter, no condition may be imposed restricting his or her employment of occupation in the United Kingdom. Prospective workers, businessmen, or self-employed persons must be admitted without a work permit or other prior consent. The rules about the families of such persons are more liberal than those affecting other persons seeking entry.

Thus we have the paradox of an immigration scheme one of the primary objects of which was to disentitle Commonwealth immigrants coming for long-term settlement, which was immediately followed by another move having as its object the granting of the same right for the first time to certain classes of aliens.

One may add, of course, that the massive expulsion of Asians from Uganda in 1972 did in fact partly frustrate the objectives of the Immigration Act, since the United Kingdom admitted them.

The System of Appeals. The system of appeals is dealt with in Part II of the act.[62] There are two appeal bodies, each of which may hear appeals in different kinds of cases in the first instance. These are, as under the 1969 act, (1) adjudicators, appointed by the Secretary of State, and (2) the Immigration Appeal Tribunal, appointed by the Lord Chancellor.

Normally a decision not to refuse entry, to vary the conditions of admission, to uphold the conditions of admission, to uphold a deportation order, or to fix a particular place of destination of deportation must be made within time limits--14 to 28 days, depending on the circumstances. The appellant may be represented (appellants who are abroad are not allowed to attend in person). Written evidence may be submitted, and witnesses are called. Any statement by the Home Office is usually in writing. Adjudicators sit in all major ports of entry and are either lawyers or former civil servants.

Further appeal can be made to the Immigration Appeal Tribunal, the members of which must be lawyers of at least seven years' standing. The appeal may be made by either the applicant or the Home Office.

In the following cases there is no right of appeal at all:

1. A decision to exclude a nonpatrial if the Secretary of State certifies that he or she personally gave directions not to admit the appellant on the ground that the exclusion was conducive to the public good.[63]

2. A decision to reduce, to terminate, or not to extend a period of entry or to deport the person on the ground that the deportation is conducive to the public good "as being in the interests of national security or of the relations between the United Kingdom and any other country or for other reasons of a political nature."[64]

3. Deportation ordered on a court's recommendation, since appeal lies to a higher court.

If deportation is on "public good" grounds, but not in the interests mentioned, in the first instance appeal will be to the Immigration Appeal Tribunal, as it will be in cases in which deportation has been ordered for members of the family of a person ordered to be deported.

The decision to make "public good" determinations taken on security grounds unappealable is a variation from the 1969 act, under which appeals in such cases were heard by a specially constituted panel of the Tribunal, before which relevant evidence could be withheld from the appellant and his or her advisers on security grounds. This procedure has now been abandoned as a result of the controversy aroused by the appeal of Rudi Dutschke against the refusal of the Home Secretary to vary his landing conditions, thereby compelling him to leave the country. The special panel of the tribunal heard the case but took evidence on security matters in secret and dismissed the appeal. Had Dutschke's appeal been allowed, the Home Secretary would not have been bound to give effect to the decision, but the Home Secretary appeared to think that in such a situation he would have been in an intolerable political position. Indeed, as a result of an administrative concession[65] the aggrieved person may have his or her case referred on a nonstatutory basis to three advisers who at present deal with appeals by civil servants against security dismissals and transfers. Their advice will not be disclosed, nor will it be binding upon the Home Secretary.

It should be noted that these provisions do not necessarily imply that the ordinary courts cannot question the decisions of these tribunals. In theory such decisions can be reviewed on various grounds, such as excess of jurisdiction, abuse of discretion, patent error in the law, contravention of the rules of national justice, or a refusal to give the applicant a proper hearing. In view of the attitudes that the courts have adopted in the past in such cases, such as in Soblen's and Schmidt's cases, which dealt with the exercise of discretionary executive powers in relation to immigration and deportation, little must be expected in the way of judicial interference in the future.

Special provisions are contained in the act with respect to the acquisition of nationality by, and the deportation of, Commonwealth citizens, but not aliens, who were resident in the United Kingdom at the end of July 1971.

1. They may acquire U.K. citizenship automatically by registration after five years' ordinary residence, provided that there have been no conditions imposed upon their leave to stay during that period.

2. They cannot be deported on the grounds that it would be conducive to the public good if at the time a decision is taken to deport them, they have been ordinarily resident since July 1971.

3. They cannot be deported on any other grounds once they have been ordinarily resident for five years and have continued to live in the United Kingdom.

4. They cannot be recommended for deportation by a court once they have been ordinarily resident for five years.

Section 33(5) of the act provides that it "shall not be taken to supersede or impair any power exercisable by Her Majesty in relation to aliens by virtue of her prerogative." This saving clause is intended to preclude the rule of law that were action in a field in which the prerogative has been exercisable is regulated by the statute, the prerogative is henceforth either in abeyance (the better view) or is abolished. However, as has been mentioned above, it is not clear whether the Crown did have a prerogative power to refuse admission to or to deport aliens. If it did, it seems that, somewhat oddly, Section 33(5) would enable the government to bypass this elaborate structure of regulation and appeals entirely. Perhaps this is unlikely to happen, but the provision in question serves to illustrate the confusion that bedevils the whole matter.

Protection

In the past, British protection has been afforded to certain classes of people who did not possess British nationality.[66] The British Digest of International Law contains accounts of practice in the period before 1914 in relation to the protection of persons in the countries under Crown jurisdiction by virtue of the Capitulations. These are, of course, no longer of practical interest. There remains the much diminished category of British Protected Persons, that is, inhabitants of protectorates, protected states, mandates, and trust territories for the international relations of which the United Kingdom is responsible.[67]

In view of the very wide category of persons who are British subjects by municipal law, it is probable that the really important question is not so much whether protection should be extended to non-British subjects, but whether the government should have an unrestricted right to afford international protection to persons who have that status.

As regards those who are British subjects by virtue of being nationals of states that are independent member states of the Commonwealth, there is one example of an international arbitration to which the United Kingdom was a party and the individual concerned was a national of such a state. That was the Pugh claim against Panama in 1934.[68] The case is of somewhat limited value at the present time, since Pugh was a citizen of the Irish Free State before it became a republic. At that time the right of that state to conduct its own international relations free from interference by the British Empire was not clearly established, and the case antedates the separation of members of the Commonwealth from allegiance to the Crown. A leading author has clearly expressed doubts about the standing of the government of the United Kingdom in such circumstances since that time.[69]

There probably is no real basis of entitlement in municipal or international law for the United Kingdom generally to interfere diplomatically on behalf of Commonwealth nationals who owe no allegiance to the Crown. The same is probably the case with respect to those states that do owe such allegiance, such as Canada. Some modern examples of British protection of such persons can be found, including the protection of Maltese subjects in Tunisia and Kenyans in Yugoslavia in 1966.[70]

With respect to other classes of persons, the practice of the United Kingdom seems clear. In relation to aliens who may be, for instance, members of diplomatic missions, the written observation of the U.K. government made to the International Court in the Reparation for Injuries case recognizes that states do make such claims when injuries are committed upon persons who are in their service, though it was expressly stated that the basis of these claims is the international wrong done to these states by reason of loss of services.[71]

The right to exercise protection of alien seamen on board nationally owned ships who are injured by a direct injury to the ship, which has been asserted by some states, including the United States of America, is apparently not supported by the British government.[72] Indeed, O'Connell asserts that "the United Kingdom has no basis in municipal law for making such a claim."[73] It may be noted, however, that in 1841-42 the Law Offices of the Crown reported in the case of a Russian member of the crew of a British merchant vessel at Havana that a foreigner serving on a British vessel is entitled to the same protection as a British subject.[74]

One question that may in the future be raised is suggested by the Immigration Act of 1971 in connection with those who are British subjects because they are citizens of the United Kingdom or its colonies and who have no other nationality, but who are not patrials by virtue of the new legislation. There may be difficulties in their protection, for it may be possible for a third state to argue that they have no "genuine link" with the United Kingdom. How much of an objection in law this would be depends to some extent, of course, on the proper ambit to be placed upon the decision in the Nottebohm case.[75]

Nevertheless, embarrassment might be caused to the U.K. government if when it presented a claim on behalf of, say, a Kenyan Asian against "Utopia," the government of Utopia were to answer that the United Kingdom, having decided for its own purposes to treat the individual as an alien, could not now claim that individual as one of its own against another state.

NATIONAL IMPLEMENTATION OF INTERNATIONAL RIGHTS AND DUTIES

The Act of State Doctrine

Though the term "act of state" used with reference to foreign sovereign acts and usually to foreign legislation has not attained the status of a legal term of art, as it has in the United States, neither it nor the questions it raises are entirely unknown in English law.[76] The question of whether there is such a doctrine has been recently discussed by the Court of Appeal, though rather inconclusively, in Buttes Gas & Oil Co. v. Hammer.[77] From this decision, concerning whether to strike out portions of the pleadings on interlocutory proceedings upon the ground that they did to some extent question acts of state of the United Kingdom, Sharjah, and Iran (the application to strike out was unsuccessful), it appears that such a doctrine does exist and that it is not the same as the U.S. doctrine. However, it remains quite unclear to what extent there does exist a separate category of acts of foreign states that cannot be questioned in an English court, as distinct from foreign laws whose application would, in accordance with the normal rules of the conflict of laws, render an act that would be actionable as a tort in English law not actionable by reason of nonactionability by the law of the place where the act was committed,[78] or whose application would have the consequence under the rules of conflict of laws of effecting a change in the ownership of property in accordance with the law of the site.

Indeed, the relevant judicial decisions are almost entirely connected with foreign governmental seizures of property. The principle upon which English courts proceed when deciding whether to recognize foreign governmental decrees purporting to seize private property is simple to state. The decree is recognized as having deprived the owner of his or her property if the property was within the territory of the foreign state at the time of the decree, but not otherwise.[79] In a particular case, the applicability of the principle depends upon the answer to three questions. (1) Where was the property legally situated? (2) Did the decree purport to affect property there? (3) Is the decree a part of the law of the place that the English courts will recognize?

It should be said in passing that the government in question is assumed to have been recognized (for unrecognized governments see below). Should the foreign government have a just claim to the property, of course, these questions will not be answered or even considered if the foreign government raises the plea of sovereign immunity.[80]

It is only the third question that requires discussion here. It is assumed that the property whose ownership is at issue was within the foreign state at the time of the decree. The courts have, with one exception, consistently held that the owner's right to the property is destroyed or otherwise affected and that it will be irrecoverable, as in the cases in the 1920s concerning expropriations by the Soviet regime.[81]

The exception is the well-known case of The Rose Mary, decided by the Supreme Court of Aden.[82] Justice Campbell distinguished this from the other cases on the ground that the Russian decrees in those cases purported to affect the property of Russian nationals and hence were not a breach of international law, whereas in the instant case the Iranian decree was directed against the property of an alien and was in breach of international law, so it could be disregarded.

The grounds for the decision, which were that the English courts may refuse to give effect to the legislation of a foreign state if that legislation itself amounts to a breach of international law and therefore excludes the operation of the principle that the ownership of property is governed by the law of the site, has been criticized by many writers. This ruling is perhaps not compatible with the U.S. case of Banco Nacional de Cuba v. Sabbatino.[83] It was not laid down by a court in England itself. These grounds were the basis of the sole case that is any authority on the point, and they were rejected by one English judge, Justice Upjohn.[84]

Justice Upjohn's rejection of this reasoning was made in a case that concerned Nazi German legislation in respect to debts in Germany "owned" by British subjects. The legislation was not regarded as being contrary to international law, but Upjohn went out of his way to say that in his view Luther v. Sagor was of general application and not intended to be limited to cases of seizure of property belonging to subjects of the expropriating government.

The decision in the Rose Mary case could be thought to be justified on the ground that the Iranian decree was penal, since it discriminated against a single company. Since a decree could be contrary to international law without being discriminatory, this basis for nonrecognition is narrower, in one sense, than the rationale of the decision in the Rose Mary case. Of course, it is wider in another sense, since it could afford grounds for nonrecognition of a foreign decree directed against its own nationals. For example, it might be directed against the members of one family, as in the case of the decree confiscating the property of the House of Romanoff mentioned in Princess Paley Olga v. Weisz (the princess's property was not caught by this decree since her marriage to the Grand Duke Paul was morganatic). It may be that a decree could be treated as penal if no or inadequate compensation is payable under it. This is somewhat dubious, since in two cases Nazi decrees confiscating German Jewish businesses were treated as penal because no compensation was payable, but only in respect to property outside Germany. It was held that as regards property in Germany the decrees would be recognized as valid and effective.[85]

The most that can be said is that the status of the decision in the Rose Mary case is open to doubt.

With respect to legislation in any other field by a recognized government, there appears to be no authority.

Implementation of the Decisions of International Organizations

The decisions of international organizations that affect individual rights and obligations may only be made law in the United Kingdom by legislation. This may be of a general kind, empowering the Crown to make subordinate legislation on an ad hoc basis, or by making provision for the future by which such decisions would operate automatically within the United Kingdom. See, for example, the European Communities Act of 1972, enacted in part to enable decisions taken by the relevant body of that organization to become part of British law.

As regards decisions of the United Nations, there is a general provision in the United Nations Act of 1946 enabling the U.K. government to make by Order in Council such provision as appears necessary or expedient to enable it to apply measures that the Security Council may under Article 41 of the UN Charter call upon the U.K. government to carry out and to make provision for the apprehension, trial, and punishment of persons offending.

In the case of Rhodesia and sanctions against it, measures have been resorted to, but not altogether under that provision. Rhodesia, of course, is a special case. The Southern Rhodesia Act of 1965, passed upon the Smith regime's Unilateral Declaration of Independence on 11 November, recited the sovereignty of the Crown over Rhodesia and by Section 2(2)(c) enabled the Crown by Order in Council to impose "prohibitions restrictions or obligations in respect of transactions relating to Southern Rhodesia." It was under this provision that the Sanctions Order in Council of 1968 was enacted.

The act was not extended to overseas territories. With regard to them the sanctions were carried out under the United Nations Act.

The Exchange Control legislation has also been resorted to for the purpose. By the Exchange Control Act (Scheduled Territories) Order of 1965, that territory was removed from the list of scheduled territories, so causing the Exchange Control Act of 1947 to apply to it.

The Export to Southern Rhodesia Direction of 1965, applying Section 23(1) of the act, had the effect of prohibiting the exportation of goods from the United Kingdom to a destination, including an ultimate destination, in Southern Rhodesia unless payment for the goods is made prior to exportation.[86]

The provisions of the United Nations Act would clearly enable the government to take any measures ordained by the Security Council short of force in respect to Namibia were it minded to do so. The Crown could simply comply with any enforcement action under Article 42 by virtue of the prerogative right of the Crown to command the disposition of its armed forces.

Procedure Related to the Issuance of Certificates or Suggestions by the Executive in Connection with Litigation in National Courts

The usual method by which the views of the executive are communicated to the courts in respect to matters of international importance is known as the Foreign Office Certificate. Though this is a convenient generic description, it is something of a misnomer, for the statement of the attitude of the executive may in appropriate cases be given by other departments, and by means other than a certificate in the strict sense.

In the decided cases, the certificate has emanated from the Colonial Office,[87] the India Office,[88] the Commonwealth Office,[89] and the War Office.[90] In The Fagernes[91] the views of the Crown were communicated by the Home Office through the medium of the Attorney General.

In some cases, information was given orally. In The Parlement Belge[92] and The Constitution,[93] the Attorney General filed an information and protest against the arrest of a vessel and the Solicitor General and Admiralty Advocate, as well as junior counsel, appeared and argued the point at issue. In The Fagernes the Attorney General made an oral communication, and in The Gagara[94] he did so in support of a written statement. If the communication is in writing, it may be a formal document;[95] a letter, as in many of the cases cited below; or a sworn affidavit.[96]

Apart from the right of the Crown to intervene of its own motion, either the parties or their representatives may wish to be furnished with the information,[97] or the court itself may address a letter to the relevant department of state.[98]

In Carl Zeiss Stifftung v. Rayner and Keeler[99] the questions that the parties wished to be put to the Foreign Office were first placed before the court, which selected from them those that seemed proper to be asked and communicated them by letter.

It is to be noted that Vallat, a former Foreign Office legal adviser, wrote that although there is no objection to the parties or their solicitors writing to the Foreign Office where litigation is contemplated, for example, against someone who may be entitled to diplomatic status, where proceedings have commenced, the proper way in which to approach that department is by a request from the court, for the court is always entitled to insist upon submitting its own question and receiving a certificate (if one is given) from the Secretary of State.[100] However, Lord Sumner in Duff Development v. Government of Kelanton[101] stated that the court's intervention was not indispensable.

The issuance of a certificate is at common law best regarded as being of the nature of a prerogative act or act of state connected with the Crown's functions in the sphere of foreign relations. However, there are several statutes that make provision for the giving of certificates and for their effect. If the position at common law is as stated, the Crown must follow the statutory procedure strictly, by virtue of the rule that when a statute covers the same field as a prerogative power, the prerogative power is either superseded or in abeyance until the statute is repealed.[102]

An example of a statutory provision of this kind is to be found in Section 4 of the Diplomatic Privileges Act of 1964, which provides that if in any proceedings a question arises of whether or not a person is entitled to a particular privilege or immunity under the act, a certificate issued by or under the authority of the Secretary of State attesting to any fact relating to that question shall be conclusive evidence of that fact.[103]

The certificate may be asked for or given at any stage of the proceedings, whether litigation is only contemplated or whether it has commenced. In the Carl Zeiss case the point of nonrecognition was not raised in the court below, and the certificate was only requested when it was required for the purposes of a hearing in the Court of Appeal.

The executive cannot be compelled by any rule of law either to answer any question at all or to answer it fully or in any particular way. In White Child & Beney v. Eagle Star, etc.,[104] the Foreign Office felt unable to reply to the question "where and in what persons or body the sovereign executive and legislative power in Russia resided at [material] dates." Further, it has been observed that the principle of the conclusiveness of the certificate does not relieve the courts of the substantial duty of both interpreting the statement of the executive and drawing from it the appropriate legal consequences.[105] This was done, for example, in The Gagara, The Annette, Luther v. Sagor, and Arantzazu Mendi.

The executive will in fact decline to state the law. Moreover, in one type of case, namely one in which what has been involved is the construction of a commercial document or an Act of Parliament employing some such term as "war" and "government," the Foreign Office has on one occasion suggested that its attitude may not necessarily be conclusive.[106] This suggestion has been acted upon by the court in this kind of case.[107]

Cases in which a certificate has been refused or appears ambiguous, or where it has not been considered to be conclusive, upon analysis may generally be found to be cases in which the question put has related to something other than an act of the Crown itself and not peculiarly within its cognizance. The court itself may refuse to put a question of this kind, as in Bank voor Handel v. Slatford, in which the court said that it would be wrong to ask the executive a question about the effect of foreign confiscatory legislation, since it "would put it in the power of the Crown to legislate in a way which might affect the rights of British subjects, for example, creditors of a foreign national, without the authority of Parliament."[108]

The court will not allow questions that amount to examination of the executive.[109]

What is not entirely clear is whether, if the question is one that is appropriate for proof by an executive certificate, it is nevertheless open to the court to seek evidence other than that before the court. Clearly, where the question is not of that type, other evidence may be procured, as it must be if the executive declines to give the information. On the other hand, where a statute requires certification it would seem to exclude other evidence.[110] Further, it would seem that if a certificate is given, for example, that a monarch is not recognized by the Crown as a sovereign, it would be improper to search for other evidence. The conduct of Sir R. Phillimore in The Charkieh case in conducting his own historical research to determine the status of the Khedive of Egypt was condemned by Lord Esher, Master of the Rolls, in Mighell v. Sultan of Johore (although in the circumstances perhaps unfairly).

The types of information upon which certificates have been given all seem to depend upon some kind of recognition by the executive. They are (1) whether a foreign state or government has been recognized de jure or de facto;[111] (2) whether a particular territory is under the sovereignty of one state or another;[112] (3) the sovereign status of a foreign state or government;[113] (4) the status of property that is the subject of claims by foreign states to immunity;[114] (5) whether the Crown is at war with a foreign state[115] or whether two foreign states are at war;[116] (6) whether a person is or has ceased to be entitled to diplomatic immunity;[117] (7) the extent of British jurisdiction in any foreign place;[118] (8) the extent of British territory;[119] and (9) the status of the British and Allied armed forces.[120]

Recognition and Nonrecognition

As English law seems to stand at present, recognition or nonrecognition by the government may have considerable consequences in English litigation. Since an unrecognized government or state cannot be a proper plaintiff in an English court, it cannot recover property in England to which it has a claim.[121] It is also not entitled to plead sovereign immunity in actions in which its rights may be impleaded. The same is also true of a government recognized as having de facto authority over certain territory where there still exists a de jure government and where the property involved in the action is situated outside that territory.[122] Once the de facto authority is recognized as being the government, these disabilities disappear, and it does not matter whether recognition is as a de jure or only as a de facto government.[123]

Perhaps the greatest inconvenience involved in the question of recognition is in connection with the recognition of legislation of foreign governments concerning matters within their own territory. With regard to governmental decrees affecting title to property, the matter is illustrated by the decisions of Justice Roche and the Court of Appeal in Luther v. Sagor,[124] a well-known case that scarcely requires rehearsing, save to say that when the case was heard at first instance the Soviet government had not been accorded recognition and its decree was regarded as ineffectual to pass title, but when it was heard on appeal that that government had secured de facto recognition that operated retrospectively to validate the decree in the eyes of English law. Thus the victory of either part in private litigation depended entirely upon the presence or absence of recognition.

The decision at first instance in Luther v. Sagor was upheld in effect by the Court of Appeal, and later by the same court in the case of Carl Zeiss Stifftung v. Rayner & Keeler,[125] which concerned another type of legislation by an unrecognized government, that of the German Democratic Republic. The House of Lords reversed that court upon the ground that there was a recognized government in East Germany--that of the USSR, whose agent was the government of the German Democratic Republic. By this curious route the highest tribunal in the land was able to avoid giving a direct answer to the question posed by Luther v. Sagor in the only case of its kind to reach it (although Lord Wilberforce was dubious about the correctness of the earlier case).

It is not clear, however, whether this refusal to give effect to the legislation of unrecognized regimes when it affects property extends to a general refusal to recognize any legislation or act of such a regime. A decree of divorce given by a Rhodesian judge appointed after Unilateral Declaration of Independence was refused recognition in Adams v. Adams[126] on the ground that the decree was not given by a competent court. That decision may turn upon the peculiar situation of Rhodesia in relation to the British Crown, and it has been reversed in any case by legislation of 1971 governing the recognition of foreign divorces generally. No case has been before the courts involving such questions as whether, supposing an unrecognized government alters the local marriage formalities, persons going through the newly prescribed ceremony would be regarded as validly married or their children as legitimate in the eyes of English law. Such consequences would appear absurd.

So far as it goes, the law seems quite rigid in the matter; nor does there seem to be any escape through "suggestions" of the executive about the actual existence of a nonrecognized regime as have enabled the U.S. courts in such cases as Salimoff v. Standard Oil Co.[127] to circumvent the situation in which the English courts found themselves in Luther v. Sagor.

However, the matter is not quite settled. The decision in the Carl Zeiss case does not preclude the House of Lords from reviewing the law and distinguishing between "recognition" as a political fact and "cognition" of actual facts. It may be, and has been argued that it would be, improper and embarrassing for the executive and judiciary to speak with contradictory voices; but this probably would not be the case were the English courts to proceed to recognize acts of nonrecognized governments. For the government to deny recognition to a regime is one thing; for a court to refuse to apply its laws when they are relevant is another. As U.S. courts have shown, they are not the same and there is no logical or necessary connection between them. For a court to act in this way would not entail recognition of the government itself.

It has been suggested that a reason for the present rule is that a government may not be recognized because among other reasons it has taken private property. Nonrecognition of such a taking provides a sanction in support of such a governmental policy. This seems somewhat farfetched and would seem to have little relevance in a situation such as Luther v. Sagor.

As the law stands at present, it may be said that it puts private rights and their vindication and enforcement at the mercy of purely political considerations. That the ownership of property should depend upon this seems somewhat regrettable.

TREATIES AND THE INDIVIDUAL

There are relatively few examples of recent treaties of direct concern to individuals other than those concerning extradition; conventions and so forth of the International Labor Organization; and the European Convention on Human Rights, being entered into by the United Kingdom. Of course, in the past Great Britain has entered into many treaties of commerce and navigation,[128] but since the end of World War II the only one that has been concluded was with Japan in 1962.[129] This covers traditional matters such as free entry and travel, exemption from official service, freedom of religion, and most-favored-nation treatment for companies and in respect to customs duties. It also provides for acquisition and protection of property and access to the courts, and for access to ports and liberty to take part in the carrying trade.

Compensation agreements have been entered into with several states since 1945.[130]

The United Kingdom is a party to the International Investment Disputes Convention of 18 March 1955.[131] Consequent legislation has provided for the recognition and enforcement of arbitral awards made under the convention in the United Kingdom.[132]

Arrangements for the reciprocal abolition of visas have been concluded, invariably by exchange of notes, with over 40 states, including all the European states outside the Eastern bloc and with most Latin American countries.

Agreements entitled Public Officers' Agreements have been made with several newly independent states.[133] These agreements deal with the conditions of service of officers who continue in the public service of the new state and for payment of their pensions if they have retired upon independence.

NOTES

1. Sawnhay v. Assistant Passport Officer, London Times, 15 April 1967.

2. Kent v. Dulles, 357 U.S. 116 (1958).

3. This was clearly stated to be the case by the Immigration Appeals Tribunal in Secretary of State v. Lakdawalla (1972) Immigration Appeals Reports 26. A Committee of Justice, the British section of the International Commission of Jurists, has recently examined the question of passports and has made several recommendations, the most important being that a British subject should be accorded an absolute statutory right to a passport. Going Abroad, a Report on Passports, Her Majesty's Stationary Office (1974). For comment, see 38 Modern L. Rev. 314 (1975). See also 23 International and Comparative Law Quarterly 642 (1974).

4. In re Suwally (1928), B. & C.R. 142.

5. Sachs v. Donges (1950), I.L.R. 23.

6. 289 H.L. Deb. column 1860, 16 June 1968; 764 H.C. Deb., written answer 183 and column 110, 13 May 1968.

7. Street, Freedom, the Individual and the Law 280-81 (3rd ed., 1972).

8. (1968) 1 Q.B. 200.

9. (1971) N.Z.L.R. 244. In a Scottish case in the House of Lords, Lord Simon commented upon the New Zealand decision and suggested that use of the unit prohibiting exit had gone into a "cataleptic trance." McKendrick v. Sinclair, (1972) Scots Law Times Reports 110, at 117.

10. Treason Act, 1381.

11. Re Azzopardi, (1843) 1 Carrington & Kirwan's Reports 203.

12. Offenses against the Person Act, 1861, § 57; R. v. Earl Russell, (1901) A.C. 446.

13. Section 80 makes it a criminal offense to use a wireless transmitter abroad with intent to influence a parliamentary election in the United Kingdom.

14. See generally on this complicated topic Glanville Williams in 81 L.O. Rev. 276, 395, 578 (1965).

15. By U.S. law, a party required to produce documents may resist such a demand if by compliance that party would act illegally under his or her own law. Ings. v. Ferguson, 282 F. 2d. 149 (1960).

16. § 3 (1).

17. (1946) A.C. 347.

18. Geneva Conventions Act, 1957, § 1.

19. Tokyo Conventions Act, 1967; Hijacking Act, 1971.

20. Merchant Shipping Act, 1894, esp. §§43, 681; R. v. Lopez, (1858) Dears & Bell 1105; R. v. Anderson, 161 Law Journal Reports, Cases Reserved (1868). For this purpose a British ship is not one registered in the United Kingdom but one owned by a British subject. R. v. Bjornssen (1865) Leigh and C. 545.

21. In re Investigation of World Arrangements with relation to Production etc. of Petroleum, 13 Federal Rules Decisions 280; Whiteman, 6 A Digest of International Law 172-73 (1968).

22. 5 British Digest of International Law 309-34 (1924).

23. § 20; see also §§ 21, 22.

24. 5 British Digest of International Law 303 ff (1924).

25. (1932) 2 K.B. 197.

26. Ibid.

27. (1946) A.C. 347.

28. De Jager v. Attorney General for Natal, (1907) A.C. 326.

29. Williams, 10 Camb. L.J. 54 (1948).

30. Johnstone v. Pedlar, (1921) 2 A.C. 293.

31. Lissa Francis Lawrence Oppenheim, International Law: A Treatise (8th ed. edited by Hirsch Lauterpacht (London: Longman Green, 1955).

32. (1946) A.C. 347 at 371 per Lord Jowitt, L.C.

33. Rustomjee v. The Queen, (1876) L.R., 2 Q.B.D. 69; Civilian War Claimants Association v. The King, (1932) A.C. 14.

34. (1957) 1 Q.L.R. 878 as to Act of State in this sense. See Collier, 26 Camb. L.J. 102 (1968).

35. F. A. Vallat, International Law and the Practitioner (Manchester: Manchester University Press, 1966) 41 (n).

36. Baron de Bode's Case, (1851) 3 H.L.C. 449.

37. Lillich, International Claims: Post-War British Practice (1967).

38. Third Report of the Parliamentary Commissioner (1967-68).
39. Cmd. 7600, Treaty Series No. 2 (1949).
40. Cmd. 7797, Treaty Series No. 60 (1949).
41. Cmd. 9343, Treaty Series No. 77 (1954).
42. Cmd. 723, Treaty Series No. 35 (1959).
43. § 11 (3).
44. House of Commons Standing Committee B, 15 July 1958.
45. Anisminic Ltd. v. F.C.C., (1969) 2 A.C. 147.
46. § 3.
47. Nissan v. Attorney General, (1970) A.C. 179, see Collier, op. cit.
48. Moore, 3 International Adjudications (Modern Series) 357.
49. 11 Eliz. 2, Chapter 4.
50. In addition to the agreements cited in the Command Papers cited above, see the agreements with Bulgaria, Hungary, Romania, and the Soviet Union. Cmd. 9625, Treaty Series No. 82 (1960); Cmd. 3517, Treaty Series No. 12 (1968).
51. Musgrove v. Chun Teeong Toy, (1891) A.C. 727. To the same effect is the Scots case of Poll v. Lord Advocate, (1899) F. 823. The Court of Appeal has recently held that the same is true in respect to a British Protected Person. Thakrar v. Home Secretary, (1974) 2 A 11 E.R. 257-320. The Immigration Act of 1971 is a comprehensive code of immigration law.
52. Schmidt v. Home Secretary, (1969) 2 Ch. 149.
53. Re H.K. (an Infant), (1967) 2 Q.B. 617; R. v. Chief Immigration Officer, Lympne, (1969) 1 Q.B. 333.
54. § 3(7).
55. Musson v. Rodrigues, (1953) A.C. 530.
56. Ex parte Venicoff, (1920) 3 K.B. 72.
57. (1963) 2 Q.B. 243.
58. There are four sets of rules, two for Commonwealth citizens, Hof C. Papers 1972-73, Nos. 79 (Control on Entry) and 80 (Control after Entry), as amended in 1974 by Cmnd. 5715-16, and two for EEC nationals, ibid., Nos. 81 (Control on Entry) and 82 (Control after Entry), as amended in 1974 by Cmnd. 5715-13. With respect to the right of the United Kingdom to exclude individual nationals of the EEC for personal reasons connected with the public good, see also Van Duyn v. Home Office (1972), 1 W.L.R. 1107 (High Court, reference to the European Court of Justice); (1975) W.L.R. 760 (E.C.J.).
59. § 1 (4).
60. § 1 (5).
61. §§ 1 (2), 2 (3)(c), 33, 34. They may become exempt from deportation if they have been resident for five years if they are Commonwealth or Irish citizens. § 7.
62. §§ 12-23.
63. § 13 (5).
64. §§ 14/3 15/3.
65. 819 H.C. Debates, cols. 375-77, 15 June 1971.
66. 5 British Digest of International Law, § 3, at 385-436.

67. British Nationality Act, 1948, § 32(1).

68. 3 U.N. Rep. Int. Arb. Awards, 1439.

69. Nationality and Citizenship Laws of the United Kingdom and Republic of Ireland 121-22 (1957).

70. E. Lauterpacht, British Practice in International Law 105-106 (1966).

71. (1950) I.C.J. Rep., Pleadings, etc., at 36. See also statement of G. G. Fitzmaurice, at 121.

72. Watts, 7 Int'l & Comp. L.Q., ser. 2, 1050.

73. Daniel Patrick O'Connell, 2 International Law 1050 (2nd ed., 1970).

74. F.O. 83; 2369; 82 Law Officers' Reports Reprint (1970).

75. (1970) I.C.J. Rep. 4.

76. Indeed, the U.S. doctrine appears to have its origin in the decision of the House of Lords in Duke of Brunswick v. King of Hanover (1848), 2 H.L.C. 1. See generally Mann, Studies in International Law 420 (1973).

77. (1973) 2 W.L.R. 524. Parallel proceedings in the United States were dismissed in 1971 on the grounds of Act of State by the U.S. District Court in California. The decision was later confirmed by the Court of Appeals, and the subsequent prayer for relief to the Supreme Court was denied.

78. A leading example is Carr v. Fracis Times, (1902) A.C. 176.

79. Luther v. Sagor, (1921) 3 K.B. 532; Lecouturier v. Rey, (1910) A.C. 262; The Jupiter (No. 3) (1927) 122, 256.

80. The Cristina, (1938) A.C. 485.

81. Luther v. Sagor, (1923) 3 K.B. 532; Princess Paley Olga v. Weisz, (1929) 1 K.B. 718.

82. Anglo-Iranian Oil Co. v. Jaffrate, (1953) 1 W.L.R. 246.

83. 376 U.S. 398.

84. Helbert Wagg & Co's Claim, (1956) Ch. 323, esp. at 344-49.

85. Frankfurther v. W. L. Exner Ltd., (1947) Ch. 629; Novello v. Hinrichsen Edition Ltd., (1951) Ch. 595. To the like effect are statements in re Helbert Wagg's Claim and in Bank voor Handel een Scheepvaart v. Slatford, (1953) 1 Q.B. 248, at 260-63. In Oppenheimer v. Caitermoles, (1974) 3 W.L.R. 406, three members of the House of Lords stated (though it was not relevant to the case) that, had it been necessary to deal with the point, they would have been inclined to regard a Nazi decree of 1941 purporting to deprive German Jews of German nationality as so inhumane and repugnant to civilization as to be of such a nature that English courts should not regard it as law at all and hence might not apply it. It was also suggested that that decree was contrary to international law but that this should be examined further. The other two members of the House disagreed expressly, however.

86. See Superheater Ltd. v. Commissioners of Customs, (1969) 2 A 11 E.R. 469.

87. Mighell v. Sultan of Johore, (1894) 1 Q.B. 149; Duff Development v. Government of Kelantan, (1924) A.C. 797.

88. Statham v. Statham and the Gackwar of Baroda, Law Reports, (1912) 92.

89. Kahan v. Federation of Pakistan, (1951) 2 K.B. 1003.

90. Preston v. Preston, Law Reports (1963) 114; 2 All England Reports (1963) 405.

91. (1927) 311.

92. (1880) 5 P.D. 197.

93. (1879) 4 P.D. 39.

94. (1919) 95.

95. Engelke v. Mussmann, (1928) A.C. 433.

96. Ex parte Mwenya, (1960) 1 K.B. 24.

97. Examples are Re Suarez, (1918) 1 Ch. 176; Luther v. Sagor, (1921) 1 K.B. 456; The Jupiter, (1924) 236.

98. See Taylor v. Barclay, (1828) 2 Sim. 213; The Charkieh, (1873) L.R., 4 A. & E. 59; Mighell v. Sultan of Johore, op. cit.; Civil Air Transport v. Central Air Transport, (1952) 2 A 11 E.R. 733. The Foreign Office communicated with the Admiralty Marshall in The Gagara, 1 Annual Digest of International Law Cases 45 (1919) L.R. 105 (1919); The Annette, 1 A.D.I.L.C. 43, L.R. (1919) 95; The Arantzazu Mendi, 9 A.D.I.L. 60 (1938), L.R. Probate Division (1938) 233.

99. (1965) Ch. 596 (C.A.); (1967) A.C. 853 (H.L.).

100. Vallat, op. cit., at 63.

101. (1924) A.C. 797.

102. Attorney General v. De Keyser's Royal Hotel, (1920) A.C. 508.

103. See ex parte Teja, (1971) 2 Q.B. 274.

104. (1922) 38 T.L.R. 337.

105. H. Lauterpacht, 3 Modern L.R. 1, at 5 (1939).

106. K.K.K.K. of Kobe v. Bantham S.S. Co., (1939) 2 K.B. 544.

107. Luigi Monta of Genoa v. Cechofracht Co., Ltd., (1956) 2 Q.B. 552, re Al-Fin Corporation's Patent, (1970) Ch. 160.

108. (1953) 1 Q.B. 248.

109. Carl Zeiss v. Rayner & Keeler, (1955) Ch. 596; (1967) A.C. 853.

110. For example, Diplomatic Privileges Act, § 4. See Vallat, op. cit., at 58.

111. Examples are Luther v. Sagor, op. cit.; Carl Zeiss v. Rayner & Keeler, op. cit.

112. Foster v. Globe Venture Syndicate, (1900) 1 Ch. 811.

113. Examples are Mighell v. Sultan of Johore, op. cit., and Duff Development v. Kelantan, op. cit.

114. As in the Parlement Belge, (1880) 5 P.D. 197.

115. R. v. Bottrill ex parte Kuechenmeister, (1947) K.B. 41.

116. K.K.K.K. of Kobe v. Bantham S.S. Co., op. cit.

117. Diplomatic Privileges Act, 1964, § 4.

118. Foreign Jurisdiction Act, 1890, § 4.

119. The Fagernes, (1927) 311.

120. Preston v. Preston, op. cit.

121. City of Berne v. Bank of England, (1804) 9 Vesey Junior 283.

122. Haile Selassie v. Cable and Wireless Ltd., (1938) 1 Ch. 545, 839; (1939) 1 Ch. 182.

123. The Arantzazu Mendi, op. cit., at 233.

124. (1921) 3 K.B. 532.

125. (1964) 3 A 11 E.R. 326.

126. (1971) 188.

127. 262 N.Y. 220 (1933).

128. The Index of British Treaties 1101-1968 lists approximately 130 treaties entered into since the first with France in 1606.

129. Cmd. 2085, Treaty Series No. 53 (1963), Commerce, Establishment and Navigation.

130. These include Yugoslavia, Czechoslovakia, Poland, Egypt, Bulgaria, Hungary, Romania, and the Soviet Union. Cmd. 7600, Treaty Series No. 2 (1949); Cmd. 7797, Treaty Series No. 60 (1949); Cmd. 9343, Treaty Series No. 77 (1954); Cmd. 723, Treaty Series No. 35 (1959); Cmd. 9625, Treaty Series No. 82 (1960); Cmd. 3517, Treaty Series No. 12 (1968).

131. 575 U.N.T.S. 159.

132. Arbitration (International Investment Disputes) Act, 1966. The convention is contained in the schedule thereto.

133. Arrangements have been made with Uganda, Tanganyika, Sierra Leone, Gambia, Jamaica, Kenya, Malaysia, Trinidad and Tobago, Guyana, and Ceylon, among others. That with Jamaica, as an example, can be found in 478 U.N.T.S. 9.

CHAPTER

20

UNITED STATES OF AMERICA

Monroe Leigh

THE INDIVIDUAL

The Individual as a National

Movement

Passports. As has frequently been pointed out, until 1952 U.S. law did not require the use of a passport by a national of the United States as a prerequisite either for departure from the United States or for entry into the United States except in wartime.[1] During the greater part of the national history of the United States a passport has been a convenience for purposes of foreign travel but not a necessity. Parenthetically it should be added that a passport has never been necessary for travel by a national of the United States within U.S. territory. There is no specific reference to the issuance of passports in the U.S. Constitution.

Because of this historical background, relatively little litigation on the subject of passports, constitutional or otherwise, arose in U.S. courts prior to World War II. Since World War II a combination of circumstances has generated a considerable volume of litigation on this matter. Among other things, this litigation has dealt with the effect of dual nationality on entitlement to a passport; the requirement for a due process hearing prior to the withholding of a passport; the constitutionality of requiring the passport as a prerequisite for reentry into the United States; and the authority of the Secretary of State to impose territorial limitations on the use of the passport. A review of the cases demonstrates in the most incontrovertible fashion that the tendency of the courts is progressively to restrain and circumscribe the discretion the State Department originally claimed as within the secretary's inherent authority.

In 1939 the Supreme Court indicated that the discretionary authority claimed by the Secretary of State in the matter of the issuance of passports was subject to judicial review. In the case of Perkins v. Elg,[2] the Supreme Court upheld an order enjoining the Secretary of State from refusing to issue a passport to Marie Elg "solely on the ground that she had lost her native-born American citizenship." The department had decided that she had lost her native-born U.S. citizenship when her parents moved to Sweden while she was a minor.

In 1952, in Bauer v. Acheson,[3] the District Court for the District of Columbia ruled that the Secretary of State could not, consistent with the due process clause of the Fifth Amendment, revoke or withdraw a passport without first affording the holder of the passport a hearing concerning the basis for revocation. As a consequence of the Bauer decision, the State Department passport regulations were significantly revised and a Board of Passport Appeals was created.

In 1955 the Court of Appeals overturned a decision of the Secretary of State in the case of Shachtman v. Dulles, in which a passport had been refused to Shachtman solely because he was chairman of the Independent Socialist League, an organization included on the Attorney General's list of subversive organizations. The court took into consideration the fact that the Independent Socialist League had been attempting to obtain a hearing from the Attorney General to challenge its inclusion on the list of subversive organizations, an administrative act that had been taken without notice or hearing. The basis of the court's decision was that the State Department must show reasonable grounds for its decision denying a citizen a passport and further that these grounds must be established in an administrative proceeding consistent with due process of law. This decision was not appealed by the executive branch, and Shachtman was granted a passport.[4]

In 1958 the Supreme Court decided the cases of Rockwell Kent v. Dulles[5] and Walter Briehl v. Dulles.[6] In the Kent case the painter, Rockwell Kent, who wanted to go abroad to attend a meeting of the World Council of Peace in Helsinki, was denied a passport because he was a Communist. In the Briehl case Walter Briehl, a psychiatrist, was denied a passport because he refused to provide an affidavit concerning membership in the Communist Party. The Court ruled that the statute authorizing the Secretary of State to grant and issue passports did not authorize the withholding of passports because of the ideological beliefs of the citizen applicants. It thus avoided the ultimate constitutional question of whether a statute limiting the right to a passport to those who are not Communist would be consistent with the Bill of Rights. The Court stated as follows:

> We deal with beliefs, with associations, with ideological matters. We must remember that we are dealing here with citizens who have neither been accused of crimes nor found guilty. They are being denied their freedom of movement solely because of their refusal to be subjected to inquiry into their beliefs and associations. They do not seek to escape the law nor to violate it. They may or may not be Communists. But assuming they are, the only law the Congress has passed expressly curtailing the movement of Communists across our borders has not yet become effective [Section 6 of the Internal Security Act of 1950]. It would therefore be strange to infer that pending the effectiveness of that law, the Secretary had been silently granted by Congress the larger, the more pervasive power to curtail in his discretion the free movement of citizens in order to satisfy himself about their beliefs or associations.[7]

In its opinion the Court referred to "the right to travel" as "a part of the 'liberty' of which the citizen cannot be deprived without due process of law under the Fifth Amendment."[8]

Following the Supreme Court decision in Kent v. Dulles, the State Department urgently applied to Congress for legislation granting the authority that the Supreme Court had found wanting. In applying for this statutory authority the Secretary of State stated as follows: "The Supreme Court specifically said that the Secretary has no authority, in the absence of statute, to deny passports to persons who are members of the Communist Party or affiliated with that Party."[9] As of 1975 the Congress had not acted to supply the statutory authority requested by the Department of State.

In 1961 the Supreme Court in Communist Party of the United States v. Subversive Activities Control Board[10] upheld the validity of the board's ruling that the Communist Party of the United States was required to register under Section 7 of the Subversive Activities Control Act. Thereafter it was merely a question of time before the Supreme Court reached the ultimate constitutional issue, since administrative application of Section 7 brought into effect Section 6(a) of the same act, purporting to make it unlawful for a member of a listed organization to apply for, use, or be issued a passport.

In 1964, in Aptheker v. Secretary of State,[11] the Court held unconstitutional Section 6 of the Subversive Activities Control Act of 1950, insofar as it made unlawful the issuance of a passport to a member of a listed organization such as the Communist Party. The gist of the Court's opinion is the following:

> In our view the foregoing considerations compel the conclusion that Section 6 of the Control Act is unconstitutional on its face. The section, judged by its plain import and by the substantive evil which Congress sought to control, sweeps too widely and too indiscriminately across the liberty guaranteed in the Fifth Amendment.[12]

Thus at the end of a long period of litigation the rule stands that the citizen may not be denied a passport solely because he or she is a Communist or solely because of his or her political beliefs.

Geographical Limitations. Special attention must be devoted to the question of whether the Secretary of State may limit the geographical areas in which the U.S. passport may be used.

In 1959, in a case involving the newspaperman William Worthy, the Court of Appeals for the District of Columbia upheld, in Worthy v. Herter, the authority of the Secretary of State to restrict the travel of U.S. citizens to specified geographical areas for foreign policy reasons and to deny passports to individuals whom the secretary believed would not abide by the restrictions. Worthy had declined to undertake not to travel to China, a state not recognized by the United States. The Court concluded as follows:

> If, then, the designation of a foreign area as a potential trouble spot is a "foreign affair" and the extraction of a citizen from trouble in a foreign country is a "foreign affair," is the refusal of the Executive to accord Government approval for a citizen to travel in such a designated area also a "foreign affair"? We think it is.[13]

The Supreme Court declined to review the case.

Worthy, however, was more successful in another confrontation with the Secretary of State. Section 215 of the Immigration and Nationality Act of 1952[14] makes it unlawful after presidential proclamation in time of war or national emergency for a citizen of the United States either to leave or to enter or attempt to leave or to enter the United States without a valid passport. In 1961 Worthy left the United States and returned to the United States without a passport. He was subsequently indicted for reentering the United States without a passport. This restraint on the citizen's freedom of movement was declared unconstitutional by the Court of Appeals for the Fifth Circuit in 1964, insofar as it was sought to be used to abridge Worthy's right of return to his land of allegiance. The court stated as follows: "We think it is inherent in the concept of citizenship that the citizen when absent from the country to which he owes allegiance, has a right to return, again to set foot on its soil."[15]

The issue of geographical limitations arose again in the case of Congressman Charles O. Porter, who applied for a passport to travel to Communist China and was refused. The Court of Appeals upheld the secretary's action. In 1965, in Zemel v. Rusk,[16] Chief Justice Warren found that the Secretary of State was "statutorily authorized to refuse to validate the passports of United States citizens for travel to Cuba." Despite the fact that the Court has upheld the lawfulness of area restrictions, it has nevertheless ruled that such area restrictions upon the use of an otherwise valid passport are not criminally enforceable under Section 215(b) of the Immigration and Nationality Act of 1952.[17] Thus the result is that at present the secretary has legal authority under the earlier nonpenal statutes to refuse to validate passports to certain areas, but no penal sanctions are available to punish those who disregard area restrictions.

Remedies. As the foregoing discussion of the cases illustrates, a wide variety of judicial remedies is available to the citizen to challenge the Secretary of State's actions with respect to passports. The citizen may seek injunctive relief as in the Elg case, declaratory relief as in the Bauer case, or by way of appeal from a criminal conviction as in Travis v. United States.[18]

Departure. Section 215 of the Immigration and Nationality Act of 1952, previously referred to, makes it unlawful to leave the United States without a passport in time of war or national emergency. The national emergency declared in 1950 during the Korean War is still in force. However, the grounds on which the passport may be denied to a citizen are severely restricted by decisions of the courts. The grounds presently considered applicable are listed in regulations issued by the Department of State and published in the Code of Federal Regulations.[19] Under these regulations a passport may not be issued to fugitives from justice[20] or to applicants who are subject to court orders forbidding departure or who are subject to extradition. Passports may be refused to minors and mental incompetents. In addition the regulations state that the passport may be refused if the applicant's activities are likely to cause "serious damage to the national security or the foreign policy of the United States." All denials are subject, however, to judicial review.

Return. As previously stated, the courts have held that a citizen has a constitutionally protected right to return to the United States. This was decided in the case of Worthy v. United States.[21]

Expulsion. No authority for expulsion of a citizen has been found in the Constitution or in the laws. If an attempt were made to expel, there is no doubt that the writ of habeas corpus would be available to challenge the attempt.[22]

Internment. Special attention should be given to the restrictions imposed during World War II on U.S. citizens of Japanese ancestry. In 1943 in Hirabayashi v. United States,[23] the Supreme Court unanimously upheld the constitutionality of a military curfew order imposed on all persons of Japanese ancestry in certain areas on the West Coast. In 1944 in Korematsu v. United States,[24] the Court, with three justices dissenting, upheld the constitutionality of a military order under which U.S. citizens of Japanese ancestry were completely evacuated from certain areas on the West Coast. However, in Ex parte Endo,[25] a habeas corpus case, the Court decided unanimously that the War Relocation Authority had no legal power to keep evacuated citizens of Japanese descent in detention in relocation centers. The majority achieved this result by making a narrow interpretation of the statute under which detention was attempted, thus avoiding the constitutional question. Two justices concurring separately insisted that detention of citizens in relocation camps because of Japanese ancestry, even in time of war, would violate the Constitution.

It seems doubtful if any of the foregoing military measures taken against Japanese Americans in World War II would survive constitutional challenge today in comparable circumstances. Conceivably such measures could be taken against citizens on a nondiscriminatory basis under authority of martial law. However, the U.S. Constitution provides that "the privilege of the Writ of Habeas Corpus shall not be suspended, unless when in Cases of Rebellion or Invasion the public Safety may require it."[26] In the post-Civil War case of Ex parte Milligan,[27] the Supreme Court overturned the conviction of Milligan by a military commission sitting in the State of Indiana in 1864, pointing out that the civilian courts were open and functioning in that area and holding that under such circumstances neither congressional, executive, nor judicial action could deprive a citizen in civil life of the constitutional right to trial by jury. In that case the president, acting pursuant to the Habeas Corpus Act of 1863, had suspended the writ in certain areas.

<u>Protection: Extent of Freedom of Activity Abroad</u>

<u>Criminal Acts</u>. It is not easy to generalize regarding the extent to which U.S. nationals are subject to U.S. criminal sanctions, federal or state, for acts committed outside the territory of the United States. There is no provision making it a crime for U.S. nationals to do abroad what would be a crime if done within the United States. More often than not the federal laws have confined the definition of crimes to include acts done within the territorial jurisdiction of the United States or within the territorial and admiralty jurisdiction of the United States, a term that includes the high seas. Indeed, the position adopted by the American Law Institute in the Foreign Relations Law of the United States is as follows: "Rules of United States statutory law, whether prescribed by federal or state authority, apply only to conduct occurring within, or having effect within, the territory of the United States, unless the contrary is clearly indicated by statute."[28]

Nevertheless, certain offenses, such as treason,[29] espionage,[30] and perjury before a U.S. consul[31] are punishable irrespective of the situs of the crime. Piracy on the high seas is, of course, punishable as a crime.[32] On the other hand, enlistment in the military service of a foreign state appears to be punishable as a crime only if the act of enlistment takes place within the United States.[33] Such common law offenses as rape[34] and robbery[35] are punishable only if committed within the maritime and territorial jurisdiction.

<u>Expatriation</u>. It has long been the policy of the Congress of the United States to encourage immigration to the United States. Inevitably conflicts have arisen between the United States and foreign states of origin regarding the allegiance of immigrants to the United States. Partly as a consequence of these conflicts, Congress in 1868 proclaimed by statute that "expatriation is a natural and inherent right of all people, indispensable to the enjoyment of the rights of life, liberty, and the pursuit of happiness."[36] The courts of the United States have made similar statements.[37] Presumably, therefore, a U.S. national is free to expatriate himself or herself.

A somewhat different question arises where Congress by statute has declared that the citizen shall be deemed to have renounced his or her citizenship if certain acts, such as voting in a foreign election and enlisting in the armed forces of a foreign power, occur.[38] In 1958, in <u>Perez v. Brownell</u>,[39] the Supreme Court by a vote of 5 to 4 upheld the constitutionality of such a provision. However, in 1967, in <u>Afroyim v. Rusk</u>,[40] the Supreme Court by a 5 to 4 vote reached the opposite conclusion, holding that the Congress has no power to "rob" a citizen of citizenship because there is no specific grant of such authority in the Constitution and also because of the nationality clause of the Fourteenth Amendment, which provides that "all persons born or naturalized in the United States and subject to the jurisdiction thereof are citizens of the United States." For this reason, in 1967 the Supreme Court held unconstitutional Section 401(e) of the Nationality Act of 1940, which provided for loss of nationality when a citizen votes "in a political election in a foreign state."

In 1971, however, in Rogers v. Bellei,[41] the Supreme Court upheld against constitutional attack a provision of the Immigration and Nationality Act of 1952[42] that provides that a U.S. citizen born abroad shall lose citizenship unless he or she resides in the United States continuously for five years between the ages of 14 and 28. The vote was 5 to 4. Justice Hugo Black, who had dissented in 1958 in the Perez case and who had written the majority opinion in Afroyim v. Rusk in 1967, wrote a bitter dissent. From the foregoing it can be seen that the question of congressional power to legislate concerning acts of expatriation cannot yet be regarded as finally settled.

Antitrust Laws. It is a painfully advertised fact that the U.S. antitrust laws apply to acts of citizens abroad if those acts have a substantial anticompetitive effect on U.S. interstate and foreign commerce.[43]

Internal Revenue Laws. A U.S. national traveling or residing abroad remains subject to the Internal Revenue Code.

Economic Controls: Export of Capital and Repatriation of Profits. Since January 1968 the Department of Commerce has maintained comprehensive mandatory controls on foreign direct investment and has enforced repatriation of some earnings. A complementary program administered by the Federal Reserve Board imposes similar control on capital outflows arising from banking transactions. Since 1963 there has been an interest equalization tax designed to discourage individual and portfolio investors from using dollars to purchase foreign securities. All of these measures are based on balance of payments considerations and are intended to improve the balance of payments accounts.

Economic Controls: Export Control Program, Munitions Control Program, Foreign Assets Control Program, Foreign Transactions Control Program. The United States maintains a bewildering variety of programs aimed at the control of U.S. trade considered to be of strategic significance. Traditionally U.S. policy has been more rigorous than that followed by other nations in the Coordinating Committee of the Trade Control System.

The Department of Commerce controls nonmilitary exports from the United States under the authority of the Export Administration Act of 1969.[44] This includes control over the export of "technical data," an increasingly important item of trade.

The Department of State maintains controls over the movements of munitions under the authority of Section 414 of the Mutual Security Act of 1954, as amended.[45]

The Department of the Treasury, under the authority of Section 5(b) of the Trading with the Enemy Act of 1917,[46] controls dealings between overseas subsidiaries of U.S. companies and certain embargoed countries or restricted destinations. These regulations, in particular, have produced a number of spectacular judicial and diplomatic confrontations between the United States and its allies, as in the Fruehauf case in France,[47] and in the British sale of Viscount aircraft to the People's Republic of China.

These regulations, especially in their application to China, were drastically modified and liberalized during the Nixon Administration. It should not be overlooked, however, that as of this writing they continue to apply with full force to Cuba. For example, it would be illegal for a U.S. citizen to carry on business transactions with Cuba, to establish a plant there, or to make an investment there.

The Right of Diplomatic Protection. U.S. nationals do not have the right to require intervention by the State Department on their behalf, either by way of diplomatic representation or by initiation of proceedings before an international tribunal.[48] Thus under U.S. law it is incorrect to speak of a "right" to diplomatic intervention. The State Department firmly maintains that espousal is a matter within its discretion, although in recent years the department has been more responsive than heretofore to the views of private claimants.

Although no legal decisions have been found in support of the proposition, it is probably correct to say that as a practical matter the State Department is less free to withhold diplomatic support in a case involving arrest or detention of a U.S. citizen abroad than it is with respect to claims for property loss. Prior to espousal, the claim of the citizen is subject to control by that citizen and he or she is entitled to any reparation paid to him or her by the foreign state.[49] It should be noted that the Logan Act, which makes it a criminal offense for a U.S. citizen to hold intercourse with a foreign government with intent to influence that government in relation to any dispute or controversy with the United States, is subject to an exception. This exception provides that the right of the citizen to apply to the foreign government for redress of injury shall not be abridged.[50]

The State and Compensation. Traditionally it has been the practice of the United States to negotiate compensation agreements for injuries done to its nationals abroad. In small individual cases the claimant presents the facts of his case to the Department of State. The Department of State then undertakes to obtain compensation. In theory the amount of compensation sought in the first instance and the amount accepted in satisfaction of the claim fall within the discretion of the Department of State. Although in theory the State Department has the right to compromise such claims, it is doubtful whether this right is exercised over the objection of the claimant in minor cases involving single claims.

In recent years, however, the bulk of the work of the State Department in the espousal of claims has been in cases in which wholesale expropriations have occurred and hundreds or thousands of individual claims are involved. In such cases the practice has been for the State Department to invite the private claimants to "register" their claims with the State Department. This practice has been followed with respect to most of the claims handled since World War II. During the early part of this period it was the practice of the State Department to undertake the negotiation of "lump sum" settlement agreements. Under these agreements the expropriating foreign government undertakes to pay a specific sum to the United States either immediately or over a period of years in satisfaction of all claims by U.S. nationals falling within the categories described in the agreement. In return the United States agrees to discharge the foreign government from any further obligation toward U.S. nationals for claims within those categories.

Almost invariably the amount accepted as a lump sum has been far short of the total amount of the claims "registered" originally with the State Department. Thus the judgment of the State Department in deciding how much the original claims should be discounted in order to reach agreement on a lump-sum payment was an extremely important factor affecting the ultimate recovery of the claimant. During much of the postwar period the State Department had no systematic method for evaluating either the validity or the amount of the individual claims that were registered, and the number of lawyers assigned to the claims section of the Legal Adviser's Office was inadequate to remedy this defect.

Once the agreement has been reached with the foreign country for the lump-sum payment, the usual practice has been for the State Department to seek legislation from the Congress providing for the adjudication of such claims by a commission. At present this function is carried out by the Foreign Claims Settlement Commission. Under varying statutory provisions, this commission and its predecessors have determined the validity and the amounts of thousands of claims since World War II. It has been the principal adjudicatory agency for deciding how compensation payments from foreign governments shall be distributed among individual claimants. Seldom if ever is the amount of money available adequate to meet the adjudicated value of the individual claims. Under this system the State Department bargained for a lump-sum settlement without having the results of a careful adjudication of the claims.

In recent years, however, a system for the "preadjudication" of claims has come into use. Under the preadjudication system the Foreign Claims Settlement Commission undertakes to adjudicate the validity and amount of individual claims under statutory guidelines established by Congress, irrespective of whether there is a fund from which such claims can be met. The most important of these measures are the Cuban claims legislation of 1964 and the China Claims Act of 1965.[51]

The preadjudication technique, which has been strongly supported by private claimant groups, has not been enthusiastically accepted by the Department of State. The reasons are not hard to discover. Under the old system the State Department's discretion in reckoning the value of particular claims was not subject to any official scrutiny. This meant that the department had great flexibility in narrowing the gap between the total of registered claims and the amount that it was politically feasible to demand from the foreign government. Under the new preadjudication system, the department will have to justify in a general public relations sense any difference between the total value found by the Foreign Claims Settlement Commission and the lump-sum settlement that the department negotiates.

If and when funds are available to pay holders of awards under the Cuban and Chinese programs, presumably Congress will be asked to decide how these funds shall be distributed, including the vexatious question of whether certain claimants shall be preferred above others.

There is no legal requirement that the government "top off" the compensation received to make it more nearly equal to the claimant's loss. Also, Congress has not indicated that such a step is likely to be achieved by legislative enactment.

The Responsibility of the State for Injury Induced by Its Own Conduct. As indicated above, there is no example in U.S. practice in which the government has accepted a responsibility to "top off" the amounts that otherwise would be received by citizen claimants. However, the notion that the government is chargeable in some way for improvident settlements has been much debated and apparently is destined for continued debate. This is assured by the very fact that the expropriations in Cuba, which are the largest ever suffered by U.S.

investors abroad (about $1,758 million) were beyond doubt triggered by the action of the Eisenhower Administration in terminating the sugar quota, under which Cuban sugar had enjoyed a lion's share of the U.S. quota as well as the subsidized sugar prices that resulted from it. Indeed, the Cuban expropriation decrees are gounded on the alleged "aggression" of the United States in reducing Cuban participation in the U.S. sugar market. However, neither the executive nor the legislative branch of the government has shown any disposition to recognize on this account a special "topping off" obligation toward private claimants. On the contrary, in 1962, not long after the Cuban expropriations, the Congress inserted a provision in the Foreign Assistance Act of 1961, as amended,[52] expressly providing that no monetary assistance shall be made available under the foreign aid legislation to any foreign government that would use that assistance for the compensation of expropriated U.S. owners.

The position of the private claimant in dealing with the State Department is further aggravated by the fact that the State Department customarily enters into lump-sum settlement agreements by means of an executive agreement rather than by means of a treaty. If a treaty were involved it would have to be submitted to the Senate for advice and consent prior to ratification by the president. If, however, an executive agreement is utilized, it becomes effective on the date specified therein, irrespective of legislative approval. Although the Congress can thereafter pass legislation invalidating the agreement or making it impossible for the president to carry it out, this act can have effect only in the domestic sense and does not relieve the United States of the international obligation already assumed under the agreement, one of the provisions of which stipulates that upon payment of the agreed upon sum all claims on behalf of private U.S. owners are satisfied.

Representatives of private claimants have argued that when the executive branch makes an improvident settlement of U.S. claims against a foreign country, that action amounts to a taking of private property, for which compensation is due under the Fifth Amendment. The counterargument is that the value of the claim is not measured by what the claimant lost but rather by what can be collected internationally from the expropriating power. These conflicting arguments generally cannot be resolved. On the other hand, there have been cases in which the courts have gone some distance toward accepting the theory that a less than full value settlement constitutes a taking of private property for a public purpose in those cases in which the executive can be shown to have derived something of political value in return for discounting the claims of its nationals. The origins of this theory are found in the case of Gray v. United States,[53] one of the most fascinating cases in U.S. judicial history. The claims involved in that case originated in 1800, when U.S. negotiators surrendered the so-called French spoliation claims resulting from French depredations on U.S. commerce, in exchange for release from a 1778 treaty obligation under which the United States had agreed with the French that the United States would protect French West Indian possessions against attack by Great Britain.

The French spoliation claims were advanced in Congress on various occasions between 1800 and 1886, at which time the Court of Claims gave an advisory opinion to the Congress to the effect that the Fifth Amendment required the United States to compensate the holders of the French spoliation claims.

In 1970 the same issue arose before the Court of Claims in the case of Aris Gloves v. United States.[54] In that case the Court of Claims refused to accept the theory that a compromise of private claims constituted a taking of private property for which compensation must be paid under the Fifth Amendment. The Supreme Court refused to review the case, but if Justice Frankfurter was right, no conclusions one way or the other can be drawn from this fact. Undoubtedly the theory of the Gray case will be reargued on other occasions and before other tribunals, and the matter will not be settled until the Supreme Court has spoken.

Waiver. The rule in the United States is that the government, once it has espoused the claim of a national, can waive that claim without that national's consent.[55]

Special Kinds of Protection. The list of special protections for the interests of U.S. nationals abroad is much too long to give in full. The following are examples of measures taken by Congress in the belief that they would afford some additional degree of protection; many have not proven effective.

1. The Fisherman's Protective Act. Originally enacted in 1954, the Fisherman's Protective Act was extensively revised and broadened in 1968. As amended, the principal features of the legislation are as follows:

If a vessel of the United States is seized by a foreign country claiming a wider territorial sea than that recognized by the United States, the owners are entitled to collect from the United States an amount equal to any fines paid plus any other actual costs resulting from damage to the vessel or confiscation thereof, loss of cargo, and one-half of gross profits. The Secretary of State is directed to collect from the taking state or, failing in that effort, to withhold from the current year's aid programmed for that country an amount equal to the unpaid claim.[56] It is reported that the Secretary of State has never made any collections and has never withheld programmed aid. On the other hand, the secretary has certified hundreds of thousands of dollars to the treasury for payment to the owners of fishing vessels seized by such countries as Mexico, Ecuador, Peru, Colombia, Panama, and Honduras. As of 1968 the total paid out of the treasury amounted to $333,000. In 1968 it was estimated that the continuing program would cost the government about $150,000 per year as a minimum.

It is rumored that Ecuador uses a U.S. ship on loan from the United States to that government as the boarding vessel for the arrest of U.S.-flag vessels fishing within the 200-mile zone claimed by Ecuador. Early in 1972 Congress added a rider to the Foreign Assistance Appropriation bill that prohibits aid to Ecuador by name unless the president executes a special waiver.[57]

2. The Gonzalez Amendments. These amendments, adopted in 1972, require the U.S. representatives to the Asian Development Bank, to the Inter-American Development Bank, and to the International Development Association to vote against loans to a nation that has expropriated U.S. property if the president finds that such a nation has failed to provide for compensation or has failed either to arbitrate pursuant to the Convention for Settlement of Investment Disputes or to negotiate in good faith.[58] A somewhat similar amendment proposed by Senator Wayne Morse has been on the books since 1965 but applies only to a portion of the loan program of the Inter-American Development Bank.[59]

3. The Hickenlooper-Adair Amendment. This amendment, adopted in 1962 as a congressional reaction against the expropriation of an ITT subsidiary in Brazil, requires termination of aid in the event of expropriation unless "appropriate steps" are taken to pay compensation.[60] Brazil agreed to pay compensation early in 1963. The amendment was applied against Ceylon, and Ceylon thereafter paid compensation.

4. The Dirksen Amendment. This amendment, adopted in 1962, prohibits assistance to any nation that is indebted to any U.S. citizen for goods or services furnished, provided the citizen has exhausted local remedies, the debt is not denied, or the debt arises from an unconditional guarantee given by the government in question.[61]

5. The Cuban Amendment. This amendment, adopted in 1963, prohibits aid to Cuba until the president determines that Cuba has taken appropriate steps to make restitution of properties taken or to provide "equitable compensation" to U.S. citizens.[62]

6. The Sabbatino Amendment. This amendment, adopted in 1964 and modified in 1965, removes the Act of State doctrine as a bar to suit by a U.S. national in a U.S. court to recover property taken from that national in violation of international law if that property comes within the territorial jurisdiction of a U.S. court.[63] It

was applied in the Sabbatino case itself on remand, as will be explained below.

7. The Sugar Act Amendment of 1965. This amendment requires the president to suspend the sugar quota of any country that has expropriated and failed to pay compensation or to submit to binding arbitration.[64]

8. The Sugar Act Amendments of 1971. These amendments added an additional provision to that just discussed. Under the additional provision the president is authorized to impose and collect an impost of $20 per ton on sugar imported from any expropriating country and to place such collections in a "special trust fund" from which the claims of the U.S. owners are to be paid.[65] Apparently no steps have been taken to impose and collect such a levy.

The Individual as an Alien

Movement

Entry and Stay. The traditional doctrine under U.S. law with respect to the admission of aliens into the United States is that aliens have no right to enter the United States; it is purely a matter of privilege. The courts defer to the Congress in its determination of whatever standards of admission it chooses to enact and to the president and his delegates in the executive branch both for the provision of further standards and in the application of all such standards. This doctrine is based upon the notion that exclusion of aliens is an inherent sovereign right, as follows: "The exclusion of aliens is a fundamental act of sovereignty. The right to do so stems not alone from legislative power but is inherent in the executive power to control the foreign affairs of the nation."[66]

The power of the executive in its determination whether to refuse entry is considered to be final and conclusive. The determination is considered to be political in character, arising out of the conduct of foreign affairs, and not subject to judicial review. In fact, it has been stated by the Supreme Court, in total deference to executive discretion in this area, that the executive right to exercise the power of exclusion "cannot be granted away or restrained by anyone."[67]

The power to exclude includes the power to exclude aliens who have been long-time residents of the United States. For example, in Lem Moon Sing v. United States[68] an alien resident in the United States for over two years took his first trip abroad and was refused reentry. The most notorious case of refusal to allow reentry of long-time resident aliens is the Mezei case,[69] where an alien who had been resident in the United States for 25 years was refused reentry.

In 1952 Congress enacted legislation that might confer upon certain aliens the right of reentry to the United States. This right has been conferred upon persons who qualify as "permanent residents" and who have been granted that status by, and at the sole discretion of, the Attorney General.[70] Aliens with permanent-resident status clearly enjoy substantial advantages over other aliens within the United States, in that they are entitled to many procedural protections against unlawful expulsion. They can remain within the United States indefinitely; they can engage in lawful employment; and they may apply for naturalization.[71]

Theoretically, aliens with permanent-resident status may also travel freely to and from the United States, but this right appears to be more theoretical than real, from a 1953 decision in the Supreme Court, Shaughnessy v. United States ex rel. Mezei.[72] Mezei had been admitted to the United States as a permanent resident and had remained in the United States with his family for 25 years. He left the United States intending to go to his native Romania to visit his mother who was ill. Romania refused to admit him, and he remained instead in Hungary for 19 months. Arriving in New York, he was ordered temporarily excluded on the basis of confidential information and without hearing. Despite his 25 years in the United States, his former status as a permanent resident, and the fact that he had no country to which to return, the Supreme Court held that it would not review his exclusion.

> It is true that aliens who have once passed through our gates, even illegally, may be expelled only after proceedings conforming to traditional standards of fairness encompassed in due process of law. . . . But an alien on the threshhold of initial entry stands on a different footing: "Whatever the procedure authorized by Congress is, it is due process as far as an alien denied entry is concerned." Knauff v. Shaughnessy. . . . And because the action of the executive officer under such authority is final and conclusive, the Attorney General cannot be compelled to disclose the evidence underlying his determination in an exclusion case. . . . In a case such as this, courts cannot retry the determination of the Attorney General.[73]

The Mezei court distinguished a case decided in the same year, Kwong Hai Chew v. Colding,[74] which held that a permanent resident could be excluded only if he had been afforded proper due process protection. The ground for the distinction was that Chew had obtained from the Immigration and Naturalization Service a security clearance and papers that apparently authorized reentry; the court noted, however, that even such papers would not automatically entitle a permanent resident alien to reenter if excludable on any other statutory grounds--a qualification so broad as to give the executive almost unlimited discretionary authority to exclude.

In a 1971 case a novel basis was suggested for limiting executive discretion to exclude. In Mandel v. Mitchell[75] a three-judge federal court held unconstitutional two sections of the Immigration and Nationality Act that had been used by the Attorney General to exclude a nonresident alien. Mandel, a Belgian economist and marxist, was invited to participate as a speaker at a conference at Stanford University. He was denied a visa under two sections of the Act, one excluding aliens "who advocate the economic, international, and governmental doctrine, of world communism,"[76] and the other excluding aliens "who write or publish . . . or who knowingly circulate . . . any written or printed matter, advocating or teaching . . . the economic, international and governmental doctrines of world communism."[77] The Attorney General has authority to waive these provisions and admit an alien (he had done so twice before for Mandel), but he refused to do so on this occasion. The plaintiffs, who were the U.S. citizens who had invited Mandel to speak, sued for a declaratory judgment that these sections of the act were unconstitutional and for an order enjoining the Attorney General from their enforcement.

The lower court found them unconstitutional as a violation of the First Amendment (free speech) rights of U.S. citizens to hear the views of others. It should be noted that the court expressly refrained from holding that Mandel, as an alien, had any substantive or procedural rights when attempting to enter the United States or even that he had standing to sue. The executive, it was conceded, has virtually absolute discretion to exclude, and it was only rights of U.S. citizens that gave rise to the constitutional challenge.

> Mandel's status as a party does not rest on any individual right to enter (for he has none) but exists only as against the effort to exclude him on a ground that denies to citizens of this country their primary right to hear Mandel and debate with him.[78]

However, this ingenious but narrow exception to the executive's power to exclude aliens was nipped in the bud when the decision was overruled by the Supreme Court.

Voluntary Departure. Aside from certain isolated circumstances in which, because of the nature of an arrest or certain pending judicial proceedings, a court has ordered a person not to leave its jurisdiction, applicable not because of a person's status as an alien, the only peacetime limitations placed upon the departure of aliens from the United States appear to be those related to tax laws.

The Internal Revenue Code and Regulations provide that, with the exception of industrial trainees or students who have received no gross income in the United States before departure, certain persons on temporary visas, employees of foreign embassies or international organizations, and persons in a few other detailed categories, no alien may depart from the United States without filing a certificate indicating that he has complied with all U.S. tax laws and paid all income taxes due. He may be further required to appear before an officer of the Internal Revenue Service and submit proof of compliance.[79]

Involuntary Departure: Expulsion and Deportation. While an alien is within the United States he is entitled, almost without exception, to all rights of due process and equal protection to which U.S. citizens are entitled.[80] In addition, the following has been stated by the Supreme Court: "Aliens who have passed through our gates, even illegally, may be expelled only after proceedings conforming to traditional standards of fairness encompassed in due process of law."[81] Notwithstanding this and other judicial statements of principle, due process standards do not in practice appear to be readily available to aliens confronted with the threat of involuntary expulsion from the United States.[82]

The basic rules under which the Immigration and Naturalization Service can deport aliens are contained, among other things, in Sections 241-44 of the Immigration and Nationality Act.[83] The powers and rules under these sections are directly applicable to the Attorney General; he, however, has delegated his authority under the act to the Immigration and Naturalization Service.[84]

These sections of the act list the classes of deportable aliens and establish procedures for their arrest and for determination of whether they should be deported. Arising out of these sections are elaborate and extensive regulations governing procedures for hearings, decisions by special hearing officers, and the method and right of appeal.[85]

Generally the act and its implementation have probably led to fair proceedings for most aliens. Both the act and the quasi-constitutional doctrine surrounding deportation of aliens, however, contain so many areas of executive discretion--judicially unreviewed or unreviewable--that there is a substantial potential for abuse. Many categories of aliens, for example, are entitled to remain within the United States only upon findings that are made at the discretion of the Attorney General. The Attorney General can "withhold" deportation, under one section of the act, of any alien to any country where the Attorney General believes that individual would be subject to religious, racial, or political persecution.[86] Under another section, the Attorney General can "suspend" the deportation of an alien who has continuously resided in the United States for seven years, who possesses good moral character, and whose deportation would result in extreme hardship to the alien or certain of his relatives.[87] Aliens remaining in the United States under these two provisions do so, however, entirely at the unfettered discretion of the Attorney General.

Furthermore, many aspects of the procedure under which an alien can be arrested, heard, and deported lack traditional due-process safeguards. For example, the act empowers officers of the Immigration and Naturalization Service (INS) to interrogate without warrant any alien or person believed to be an alien about his or her right to be or to remain in the United States and, further, to arrest without warrant any alien whom the officer has reason to believe is within the United States in violation of any law or regulation and likely to escape before an arrest warrant can be obtained.[88] The hearing provisions and safeguards of the Administrative Procedure Act do not apply to hearings before the INS, and aliens are not protected in deportation proceedings by the constitutional prohibition against the retroactive imposition of laws.[89] Additionally, in some INS proceedings decisions can be made on the basis of confidential information not placed on the record,[90] and that information need not be disclosed to the alien.[91]

Although some courts have challenged what they consider to be blatant abuses of discretion by the INS,[92] it is quite unlikely that these challenges indicate a substantial judicial movement to limit INS discretion in deportation determinations. In many instances hearings are considered to be granted as a matter of privilege rather than right. Consequently, all that is probably required is procedural rather than substantive due process, and an alien could even be deprived of a right to that procedural due process by being deprived statutorily of the privilege of a hearing.[93]

Protection. There are a number of ways in which the United States asserts the right to protect by diplomatic representation persons who are not U.S. nationals. The primary categories of persons afforded such protection are (1) aliens employed by U.S. embassies, (2) aliens who are members or dependents of members of the U.S. armed forces, and (3) the property rights of aliens to the extent that they own or possess equity interests in companies that are owned substantially by U.S. nationals.

Diplomats. The 1963 Vienna Consular Convention provides for protections and immunities of consular officers and their families and dependents.[94] The 1961 Vienna Convention on Diplomatic Relations provides protections and immunities for diplomatic agents and their families and dependents, as well as other members of the staffs of missions in the performance of the functions of the missions.[95] The United States is a party to the Consular Convention,[96] and although not a party to the Diplomatic Convention, it subscribes substantially to the doctrines established in that diplomatic convention.[97] Consequently, U.S. practice in this area of the law is no different from that of other nations.

It is in fact not necessary for the United States to assert the immunity of aliens as diplomatic agents because the problem does not arise; U.S. policy is not to hire diplomatic or consular officers who are not U.S. nationals. As for dependents and other employees of missions who are non-U.S. nationals, the United States generally asserts its right to represent them diplomatically and to protect their immunities to the same extent provided in the two conventions.[98]

Status of Forces Agreements. U.S. status of forces agreements contemplate exercise of jurisdiction over certain persons who may not be U.S. nationals. To the extent that U.S. jurisdiction can be waived in such agreements,[99] the United States is effectively in a position to represent these persons diplomatically in negotiations with the host country government.

Under the North Atlantic Treaty Organization (NATO) Status of Forces Agreement,[100] the United States has certain jurisdictional rights over persons who are part of the U.S. "force" or the U.S. "civilian component" or who are "dependents" of members of U.S. forces or civilian components. "Force" is defined as follows: "the personnel belonging to the land, sea or air armed forces of one Contracting Party in the North Atlantic Treaty area in connection with their official duties."[101] "Civilian component" is defined as follows: "the civilian personnel accompanying a force of a Contracting Party who are in the employ of an armed service of that Contracting Party, and who are not stateless persons, nor nationals of any State which is not a Party to the North Atlantic Treaty, nor nationals of, nor ordinarily resident in, the State in which the force is located."[102] "Dependent" is defined as follows: "the spouse of a member of a force or of a civilian component, or a child of such member depending on him or her for support."[103]

The definition in the treaty of "force" gives the United States the right in proper circumstances to assert jurisdiction and, consequently, to represent diplomatically all persons (and qualified dependents) who are part of that force, despite the fact that these persons are nationals of a state other than the United States, or are stateless, or are nationals of the host state. The definition of "civilian component" is not so broad, and assertion of jurisdiction and diplomatic protection is consequently limited to persons who are U.S. nationals or persons who are nationals of another NATO state other than the host state.

Diplomatic representation of such persons--both U.S. nationals and non-nationals--where the United States asserts military jurisdiction, under the NATO Status of Forces Agreement or otherwise, is not always optional. In some instances it may be required to the extent that the State Department feels bound to act in conformity with Senate resolutions. In ratifying the agreement, the Senate added the following declaration of the sense of the Senate:

> 2. Where a person subject to the military jurisdiction of the United States is to be tried by the authorities of a receiving State, under the treaty the Commanding Officer of the Armed forces of the United States in such state shall examine the laws of such state with particular reference to the procedural safeguards contained in the Constitution of the United States;
> 3. If, in the opinion of such commanding officer, under all the circumstances of the case, there is danger that the accused will not be protected because of the absence or denial of constitutional rights he would enjoy in the United States, the commanding officer shall request the authorities of the receiving state to waive jurisdiction in accordance with the provisions of paragraph 3(c) of Article VII (which requires the receiving state to give "sympathetic consideration" to such request) and if such authorities refuse to waive jurisdiction, the commanding officer shall request the Department of State to press such request through diplomatic channels and notification shall be given by the Executive Branch to the Armed Services Committees of the Senate and House of Representatives.[104]

Property Substantially Owned by U.S. Nationals. Many statutory protections are afforded to properties or corporations situated abroad that may not be U.S. nationals, that may be owned in part by non-U.S. nationals, and that may even be nationals of the host country. For example, the Hickenlooper Amendment to the Foreign Assistance Act provides as follows:

> The President shall suspend assistance to the government of any country . . . when . . . [that] government . . . (A) has nationalized or expropriated or seized ownership or control of property owned by any corporation, partnership, or association not less than 50 per centum beneficially owned by U.S. citizens, or (B) has taken steps to repudiate or nullify existing contracts or agreements, . . . or (C) has imposed or enforced discriminatory taxes or other exactions, or restrictive maintenance or operational conditions, or has taken other actions, which have the effect of nationalizing, expropriating, or otherwise seizing ownership or control of property so owned, and such country fails within a reasonable time . . . to take appropriate steps . . . to discharge its obligations under international law toward such citizen or entity.[105]

The effect of this statute is to assert the right of the United States, among other things, to represent diplomatically, and to assert the applicability of the standards of international law not only to its own nationals, but also to the property and entities constituted as nationals of another country or owned (up to 50 percent) by nationals of another country, so long as at least 50 percent of the property or entity is beneficially owned by U.S. citizens. Other legislation contemplating diplomatic negotiation and settlement is based upon a similar standard of ownership. For example, the 1971 amendment to the Sugar Act[106] protects the same categories of properties as those protected by the Hickenlooper Amendment.

There have been many assertions by the United States of its right to represent corporations or property that do not possess U.S. nationality. One such example is the conduct of U.S. negotiations with the government of Peru concerning the expropriation by Peru of the properties of the International Petroleum Company, a wholly owned subsidiary of a U.S. national (Standard Oil Company of New Jersey) but, itself, a Canadian corporation.

Such assertions of diplomatic interest are not consistent with the judgment of the International Court of Justice in the Barcelona Traction case.[107] Apparently, however, this contrary judgment has not led the United States to modify its traditional position.

NATIONAL IMPLEMENTATION OF INTERNATIONAL RIGHTS AND DUTIES

The Act of State Doctrine

The Act of State doctrine has had an interesting and in recent years a controversial development in U.S. jurisprudence. The present position of U.S. law on the subject of the Act of State doctrine is best understood if its judicial development is taken up on a chronological basis.

The classic statement of the Act of State doctrine is found in the Supreme Court decision of 1897 in the case of Underhill v. Hernandez.[108] In that case Chief Justice Fuller, speaking for a unanimous Court, stated as follows:

> Every sovereign State is bound to respect the independence of every other sovereign State, and the courts of one country will not sit in judgment on the acts of the government of another done within its own territory. Redress of grievances by reason of such acts must be obtained through the means open to be availed of by sovereign powers as between themselves.[109]

Application of this broad doctrine led to the dismissal of a suit by Underhill, a U.S. citizen, against Hernandez, a revolutionary military commander, for unlawful assault, coercion and detention in Venezuela by the Hernandez government, which was later recognized by the United States.

The decision in the Supreme Court in Underhill v. Hernandez does not specify whether the broad principle previously quoted is based on the law of conflicts, comity, international law, or mere political expediency.[110] There is no indication whether the application of the doctrine was required by the U.S. Constitution.

In Oetjen v. Central Leather Company in 1918,[111] the Supreme Court appeared to adopt the view that the Act of State doctrine was based upon principles of comity. This was a suit by a U.S. citizen to recover a quantity of hides that he claimed by virtue of an assignment from a Mexican citizen. The hides had allegedly been unlawfully taken from the Mexican assignor as a military levy by General Villa, acting for the forces of General Carranza, whose government was recognized by the United States subsequent to the trial but prior to the decision of the Supreme Court. After the hides were seized by General Villa, they were sold to a Texas corporation, which shipped them to the United States and assigned them to the defendant, Central Leather Company. The plaintiff claimed in this litigation, which took place initially in a court of first instance in the State of New Jersey, that the hides had been seized from their original Mexican owner in violation of the Hague Conventions.

The Court brushed aside this contention, finding that the conventions did not apply to a civil war and that even if they did, the seizure, which had taken place in Mexico, did not violate those conventions. The Court instead pointed out that recognition under U.S. constitutional law is a political question confided by the Constitution to the legislative and executive departments of the government, and the Court then applied the well-known rule that recognition operates to validate past acts. Finally, it reaffirmed the Act of State doctrine in the following terms:

> The principle that the conduct of one independent government cannot be successfully questioned in the courts of another is as applicable to a case involving the title to property brought within the custody of a court, such as we have here, as it was held to be in the cases cited, in which claims for damages were based upon acts done in a foreign country, for it rests at last upon the highest considerations of international comity and expediency. To permit the validity of the acts of one sovereign State to be reexamined and perhaps condemned by the courts of another would very certainly "imperil the amicable relations between governments and vex the peace of nations."[112]

On the same day that the Central Leather case was handed down, the Supreme Court decided Ricaud v. American Metal Company,[113] a case in which the facts were quite similar except for the fact that this time the owner of the goods confiscated in Mexico was a U.S. national rather than a Mexican national.

Another general of the Carranza forces seized lead bullion as a military levy. The lead was owned by a U.S. national who was not in Mexico at the time though a resident of Mexico at the time of seizure. The Court reaffirmed earlier cases and stated as follows:

> The fact that the title to the property in controversy may have been in an American citizen, who was not in or a resident of Mexico at the time it was seized for military purposes by the legitimate Government of Mexico, does not affect the rule of

> law that the act within its own boundaries of one sovereign State cannot become the subject of re-examination and modification in the courts of another. Such action, when shown to have been taken, becomes, as we have said, a rule of decision for the courts of this country. Whatever rights such an American citizen may have can be asserted only through the courts of Mexico or through the political departments of our Government.[114]

It is worth noting that in each of these cases the moving party was a U.S. national seeking to recover losses sustained in a foreign country. Moreover, in each case the question of recognition was one of the important factual issues to be resolved. Under U.S. constitutional doctrine, recognition is one of the few constitutional powers that rests exclusively within the competence of the president.[115]

The next case which needs to be considered is the Bernstein case, in which the plaintiff Bernstein attempted to attach and recover the proceeds of property formerly owned by him in Germany but allegedly confiscated by the Nazi German government. In the first Bernstein case, in 1947,[116] Judge Learned Hand held that the Act of State doctrine applied and prevented the court from examining the legality of the confiscation of the plaintiff's property by the Nazi government, of which the plaintiff had been a national at the time of seizure. However, the opinion broadly suggested that the result might be different if the executive branch gave an indication that the Act of State doctrine need not apply in view of the fact that hostilities with Germany had come to an end and that the Nazi government no longer existed.

In the second Bernstein case, in 1954,[117] counsel for Bernstein produced a resounding letter from the State Department declaring that it was the

> policy of the Executive, with respect to claims asserted in the United States for the restitution of identifiable property (or compensation in lieu thereof) lost through force, coercion or duress as a result of Nazi persecution in Germany, . . . to relieve American courts from any restraint upon the exercise of their jurisdiction to pass upon the validity of the acts of Nazi officials.[118]

In the second Bernstein case the Court of Appeals held that the letter from the State Department referred to above effectively removed the

Act of State doctrine and permitted judicial consideration of the validity of the Nazi confiscations. In U.S. law this has become known as the Bernstein exception to the Act of State doctrine.

The Act of State doctrine has received increased attention and a degree of notoriety in the United States in the celebrated Sabbatino litigation, which arose out of the wholesale confiscations of U.S.-owned property by the Castro government of Cuba. What gave the Sabbatino litigation particular importance was the fact that it brought into focus two conflicting lines of judicial authority in U.S. law. For the first time the act of state that was under consideration was an act that was an obvious violation of international law. Indeed, the State Department had publicly so characterized the confiscation. The question was whether the courts should give effect to the Act of State doctrine even if the act in question violated international law.

At this point it should be noted that it is a well-established proposition in U.S. law that the municipal courts in the United States apply international law as a part of the domestic law of the United States.[119] A frequently quoted summary of the U.S. law on this proposition reads as follows:

> International law is part of our law, and must be ascertained and administered by the courts of justice of appropriate jurisdiction, as often as questions of right depending upon it are duly presented for their determination. For this purpose, where there is no treaty, and no controlling executive or legislative act or judicial decision, resort must be had to the customs and usages of civilized nations.[120]

The Sabbatino litigation began with a proceeding in a New York State court in which the proceeds from the sale of sugar expropriated in Cuba from U.S. owners were directed to be transferred to a receiver (Peter L. F. Sabbatino), appointed to represent such owners. Thereafter, the government of Cuba instituted an action in the federal District Court in New York to recover the proceeds. The federal district judge was called upon to decide between application of the Act of State doctrine, in which case he would have found that the proceeds of the sugar sale should be awarded to the government of Cuba, or the principle referred to above, that international law is to be applied as a part of the law of the United States, in which case the proceeds would be awarded to the former U.S. owners. Confronted with this conflict, the judge decided that the Act of State doctrine should not be applied if the expropriations in Cuba constituted a violation of international law. Upon analysis he concluded that the

Cuban expropriations did in fact violate international law, not only because they were retaliatory in purpose and discriminatory against U.S. nationals, but also because inadequate provision was made for compensation.

The decision was promptly appealed to the Court of Appeals for the Second Circuit, which affirmed the lower court decision, although on somewhat different grounds. Upon application the Supreme Court of the United States granted certiorari and agreed to review the judgments below. Between the time the Supreme Court agreed to hear the case and the time of argument, the United States for the first time imposed a freeze order on Cuban government assets in the United States. The Department of State, through the Justice Department's brief, strongly argued for reversal. On 23 March 1964 the Supreme Court decided by a vote of 8 to 1 to reverse the lower courts, holding that the Act of State doctrine should be applied. The Supreme Court stated as follows:

> If the Act of State doctrine is a principle of decision binding on federal and state courts alike, but compelled by neither international law nor the Constitution, its continuing vitality depends on its capacity to reflect the proper distribution of functions between the judicial and political branches of the government on matters bearing upon foreign affairs. . . . We decide only that the judicial branch will not examine the validity of a taking of property within its own territory by a foreign sovereign government, extant and recognized by this country at the time of suit, in the absence of a treaty or other unambiguous agreement regarding controlling legal principles, even if the complaint alleges that the taking violates customary international law.[121]

The majority opinion declined to approve or disapprove the so-called Bernstein exception to the Act of State doctrine.

Justice Byron R. White's dissent argued strongly that the Court had an obligation to dispense justice to litigants properly invoking its jurisdiction and expressed dismay that the Court had

> with one broad stroke, declared the ascertainment and application of international law beyond the competence of the courts of the United States in a large and important category of cases. . . . No other civilized country has found such a rigid

> rule necessary for the survival of the executive branch of its government; the executive of no other government seems to require such insulation from international law adjudications in its courts; and no other judiciary is apparently so incompetent to ascertain and apply international law.
>
> I do not believe that the Act of State doctrine, as judicially fashioned in this country, and the reasons underlying it, require American courts to decide cases in disregard of international law and of the rights of litigants to a full determination on the merits.[122]

It is not too much to say that the Supreme Court opinion in the Sabbatino case created consternation among international lawyers, business executives, and banking interests throughout the country. Recourse was had to Congress, with the result that Senator Hickenlooper proposed an amendment to the Foreign Assistance Act designed to modify the ruling of the Court. The status of the law following the Court's decision was that no court in the United States could challenge the validity of a foreign act of state, unless perhaps in rare cases, such as the Bernstein case. Unless the State Department affirmatively stated otherwise, the presumption was that any adjudication on the merits by the Court would embarrass the conduct of U.S. foreign policy. The declared purpose of the amendment was to reverse this presumption and create instead the presumption that the courts might proceed to make a determination on the merits in each and every case in which their jurisdiction was properly invoked, except in those cases in which the president or his designee specified that adjudication might be embarrassing to the conduct of foreign policy.

Over the objection of the State Department and of the Attorney General, this amendment was adopted and took its place in the statutes as Section 620(e)(2) of the Foreign Assistance Act of 1961, as amended.[123] It is referred to sometimes as the Sabbatino Amendment, sometimes as the Hickenlooper Amendment, and less frequently as the Rule of Law Amendment, the latter being the term used by its proponents before Congress.

During its legislative course the amendment was extensively revised in order to take into account difficulties foreseen by banking and insurance interests. As ultimately enacted it reads as follows:

> (2) Notwithstanding any other provision of law, no court in the United States shall decline on the ground

> of the federal act of state doctrine to make a determination on the merits giving effect to the principles of international law in a case in which a claim of title or other right to property is asserted by any party including a foreign state (or a party claiming through such state) based upon (or traced through) a confiscation or other taking after January 1, 1959, by an act of that state in violation of the principles of international law, including the principles of compensation and the other standards set out in this subsection: Provided, That this subparagraph shall not be applicable (1) in any case in which an act of a foreign state is not contrary to international law or with respect to a claim of title or other right to property acquired pursuant to an irrevocable letter of credit of not more than 180 days duration issued in good faith prior to the time of the confiscation or other taking, or (2) in any case with respect to which the President determines that application of the Act of State doctrine is required in that particular case by the foreign policy interests of the United States and a suggestion to this effect is filed on his behalf in that case with the court.[124]

The first application of the Sabbatino Amendment occurred in the Sabbatino case itself on remand in the lower courts. In the District Court it was held that the amendment applied, and when after invitation by the presiding judge the executive branch of the government declined to invoke the proviso of the amendment, the court proceeded to find that the Act of State doctrine did not apply, that the confiscations had indeed been in violation of international law, and that the property in dispute should be awarded to the former owners.[125] On review by the Court of Appeals for the Second Circuit, this judgment was upheld, and the Supreme Court declined to hear the case.[126]

During the District Court proceedings, counsel for the government of Cuba contended that the statute was unconstitutional. However, attorneys for the Department of Justice stated that they found no constitutional objection in the enactment.

While it may be said that the Sabbatino Amendment achieved its main purpose of assuring that foreign acts of expropriation in violation of international law are not given effect in the U.S. courts, it is also true that in two cases at least, courts in the United States have shown a disposition to construe the Sabbatino Amendment and its application as narrowly as possible. For example, in French v. Banco Nacional de Cuba,[127] the Court of Appeals in New York went to some lengths to find that the 15 July 1959 Cuban currency regulation preventing foreigners from converting Cuban pesos into foreign exchange did not amount to a taking of "property" within the meaning of the amendment.

A similar disposition is reflected by the Court of Appeals for the Second Circuit in Banco Nacional de Cuba v. First National City Bank.[128] In the latter case the government of Cuba brought an action in the federal courts in New York to recover certain funds that the bank claimed as a set-off for the expropriation of its bank properties in Cuba. The facts are interesting. Prior to the controversy the bank had loaned the government of Cuba a sum of money that was secured by collateral. When Cuba defaulted on the loan, the bank sold the collateral. It happened that the proceeds from the sale of collateral were greater than the amount of the loan. The bank applied this excess toward its claim for uncompensated expropriation of its bank properties in Cuba. This contention was allowed by the District Court but was twice disallowed by the Court of Appeals for the Second Circuit.

It is interesting to observe that the State Department twice intervened to request that the Supreme Court review this case, each time with the obvious purpose of securing a reversal of the Court of Appeals decision. In the first Court of Appeals decision, that court decided that the Sabbatino Amendment did not apply because of the textual formulation of the statute. When the Supreme Court first agreed to review the case, it remanded the case to the lower court with the injunction that it should take into account the statement prepared by the State Department, which indicated that the foreign policy interests of the United States would be best served if the Act of State doctrine were not applied. The Court of Appeals in its second consideration refused to give effect to the State Department position and substantially undermined the authority of the so-called Bernstein exception, previously referred to.

On 7 June 1972 the Supreme Court handed down its decision. Unfortunately the Court was so badly divided that the law has been left in a very uncertain state. Three judges voted for reversal on the basis of the Bernstein doctrine, which is based on the view that the courts should defer to the executive in cases involving the Act of State doctrine. One judge voted for reversal on the basis of the Republic of China doctrine,[129] which holds that when a foreign government seeks justice in a U.S. court it may not defeat a counterclaim by setting up a defense of sovereign immunity, by analogy an Act of State defense. A fifth judge voted for reversal on the more general ground that the Sabbatino case had been wrongly decided. Four judges dissented and favored award of the disputed collateral to Cuba. None of the four opinions mustered a majority in its support. Thus the naked result was a reversal of the Court of Appeals, a disallowance of the Act of State doctrine as a defense, and an allowance of First National City Bank's set-off claim to the excess collateral in dispute. However, clarification of the doctrinal basis of the Act of State principle will have to await some future ruling by the Supreme Court.

Implementation of Decisions of International Organizations

The U.S. practice in implementing the decisions of international organizations presents little that is distinctive. Theoretically the United States may have conceded some of its sovereignty in its adherence to the United Nations Charter, and perhaps even some of its sovereignty in its (conditional) acceptance of Article 36 of the International Court of Justice. Theoretically also, U.S. sovereignty is limited to the extent that its courts administer both U.S. and international law, the latter being considered a part of U.S. law. In practice, however, international treaty and customary law is as determined by the United States and its courts; and in reality the decisions of international organizations are implemented only to the extent that they are considered desirable and consistent with U.S. law and policy.

The termination of the mandate for Namibia has had no consequences in U.S. law. Neither the executive nor the legislative branches of the government have determined, by positive action or by default, that it is desirable to incorporate any consequences of cessation of the mandate into U.S. law. The courts have not seen fit to take a different course.

On 4 October 1971 Secretary of State William Rogers issued a statement affirming U.S. acceptance of the advisory opinion of the International Court of Justice. The United States further supported the 20 October 1971 Security Council resolution, which agreed with the conclusions of the advisory opinion, affirmed the direct responsibility of the United Nations for Namibia, called on South Africa to withdraw from Namibia, and urged states to discharge their responsibilities toward Namibia. In explaining its vote, however, the United States pointed out that its acceptance of the advisory opinion does not mean that it accepts all of the reasons that led to the court's opinion. Particularly, the United States disputed certain of the court's interpretations regarding the binding effect of Security Council decisions not taken under the UN Charter provisions for mandatory action.[130]

Notwithstanding this external support, the only action taken internally by the U.S. government was to advise U.S. investors of this policy in an attempt to discourage investment and to continue U.S. implementation of the 1963 United Nations arms embargo against South Africa. Although it is claimed that investment in Namibia actually was discouraged, it has not been prohibited or made more difficult or more expensive by law. Further, the arms embargo on South Africa was an old policy aimed at avoidance of support of internal repression or military advancement of apartheid by South Africa. It was not related to the Namibia opinion.[131] In short, individual rights and obligations with regard to activities related to Namibia and the Union of South Africa continue as before, unaffected, except for an arms embargo, by any determination of the International Court.

Rhodesia has presented a different situation. The United States has continued to regard the United Kingdom as the de jure sovereign government of the territory and has consistently refused to recognize Rhodesia's claim to independence.[132]

Pursuant to the Security Council resolutions on Rhodesia adopted in 1966 and 1968,[133] which called on all member states to apply sanctions against Rhodesia, the United States has prohibited any trade or commerce between that country and any U.S. nationals or persons within the territory of the United States. These U.S. sanctions were imposed by executive orders issued by the president.[134] Executive orders do not require specific congressional approval. These particular orders were issued by authority of section 5 of the United Nations Participation Act of 1945,[135] as well as generally "by virtue of the authority vested in . . . [the President] by the Constitution and laws of the United States."[136] Section 5 of the United Nations Participation Act is quite significant in that it constitutes express and broad congressional authorization for the president to take steps, including the creation of new categories of prohibitions subject to penalty, to apply and implement measures that the United States has been called upon to carry out by the Security Council under Article 41 of the UN Charter.

These executive-imposed sanctions remain in full force with one exception. In November 1971 the Armed Forces Procurement Appropriations Act of 1972 became law.[137] An amendment was inserted into that law called the Byrd Amendment to the Strategic and Critical Materials Stockpiling Act,[138] which prevents the president from prohibiting the importation of Rhodesian chrome ore into the United States despite the mandatory provisions of the Security Council sanctions resolutions and the otherwise full authority of the president to issue orders under the United Nations Participation Act. With this one exception, however, the prior congressional authorization contained in the United Nations Participation Act has been used only in the Rhodesian situation to its fullest extent to implement Article 41 Security Council resolutions.

On 12 April 1972, in United States v. Hamilton et al., the United States secured an indictment against certain individuals for violations of the executive order imposing sanctions against Rhodesia. At the time of writing, the case is not yet reported but according to press reports, the defendants have pleaded guilty.

Procedures Related to the Issuance of Certificates or Suggestions by the Executive in Connection with Litigation in the National Courts

Sovereign Immunity

The current law and practice relating to State Department suggestions of sovereign immunity to state and federal courts is of recent vintage. The U.S. courts rather consistently maintained, at least until World War II, the doctrine of absolute immunity of sovereigns to civil suit in U.S. courts. Guidance away from this doctrine to a more flexible approach to sovereign immunity came not from within the courts but instead from the State Department. Perhaps as a consequence, this new flexibility is exercised, not by the courts, but instead by the State Department; it is effectively exercised by the courts only in the absence of a clear State Department position.

When the State Department suggests to the courts that it recognizes the sovereign immunity of a state or its instrumentality in a particular case, that suggestion of immunity is unquestioningly followed by the courts and the suit is dismissed. Conversely, almost without exception, where the State Department clearly expresses the view that sovereign immunity should not be granted in a particular case, the defense of sovereign immunity is overruled.

Historically a claim of sovereign immunity by a state or its instrumentality was always recognized by the courts. This doctrine of absolute sovereign immunity was founded upon, and developed out of the opinion of, Chief Justice John Marshall in The Schooner Exchange v. McFaddon.[139] In that case the plaintiffs who were U.S. nationals sought to reclaim a vessel that they alleged had belonged to them but had been seized on the high seas by agents of Napoleon. Later, sailing under French flag as a French warship, it put into Philadelphia for repairs, where plaintiffs sought attachment and execution against the vessel in a U.S. court. The State Department filed with the court a suggestion that the ship was a public vessel of the Emperor of France and requested that the vessel be released from attachment on the ground that this property of the Emperor was immune from the court's jurisdiction. The court released the vessel, and the action was affirmed by the Supreme Court.

The executive suggestion in the Schooner Exchange case was taken into account by the Chief Justice in his opinion, but does not appear to have been given conclusive weight or authority. The decision, instead, was based upon the Court's view of the general principles of international law and upon the potentially dangerous repercussions upon U.S.-French relations if the ship were awarded to the plaintiffs. Reliance by Chief Justice Marshall upon the executive suggestion seems to have been directed more toward its conveyance of the information that the ship was in fact a French warship and that the government of France was recognized by the United States as a friendly power.

The Schooner Exchange holding, although in fact applied only to a warship of the French Navy, was adopted subsequently by U.S. courts for the proposition that unless there is an express waiver, a state and all of its property and instrumentalities are immune from the civil jurisdiction of the courts. Although the State Department continued the practice of issuing suggestions of immunity, these suggestions were afforded conclusive weight and were, in fact, relevant, not to the precise question of whether immunity should be granted, but instead to whether the defendant was or was not owned or possessed by a recognized friendly foreign sovereign.[140] If sovereign, then immunity followed automatically.

The doctrine of absolute immunity persisted well into the twentieth century. In the Pesaro case,[141] absolute sovereign immunity was expressed by the Supreme Court to be a doctrine of international law, independent of, and in this case implicitly contrary to, the views of the State Department.

After the Pesaro case, the courts gradually began to move away from the doctrine of absolute immunity. In Ex parte Peru,[142] a Cuban sugar company sought recovery against a vessel owned and operated by the Peruvian government and anchored in a U.S. port. The dispute arose out of the alleged breach by that Peruvian vessel of a haulage contract. At the request of the Peruvian government, the State Department filed a suggestion with the district court that it "recognize and allow" Peru's claim of immunity. That court, however, rejected this suggestion and made a determination on the merits, on the ground that by prior acts Peru had waived its sovereign immunity.

The Supreme Court, at Peru's request, granted a writ of prohibition and directed the lower court to dismiss the suit. It held that U.S. courts were bound by law not to "embarrass" the executive, as follows: "Courts may not so exercise their jurisdiction, by the seizure and detention of the property of a friendly sovereign, as to embarrass the executive arm of the Government in conducting foreign relations."[143]

By thus holding in this case and in the previous case of The Navemar,[144] the Court found effectively that the law applicable to sovereign immunity was no longer a substantive principle of international law for U.S. courts to interpret, but rather a policy that the U.S. courts should not reject a claim of sovereign immunity in circumstances in which that rejection is contrary to U.S. policy as articulated by the Department of State.

The converse of that rule was soon after adopted by the Court. In Republic of Mexico v. Hoffman,[145] the Supreme Court denied a claim of sovereign immunity to a merchant vessel owned by the Mexican government but operated by and in the possession of a private company under contract with the Mexican government. Although the State Department submitted to the court a "suggestion" to the effect that it "accepted as true" the Mexican government's claim to ownership of the ship, it declined, in these circumstances, to submit any suggestion or express any opinion about whether immunity should be granted. The Supreme Court took the position that the courts should not grant sovereign immunity when the State Department indicates, positively or by default, that conference of such immunity is unnecessary to the conduct of U.S. foreign relations.[146]

The Tate Letter[147] is often viewed as a landmark in the development of the U.S. law on sovereign immunity. It consolidates the evolution of that law and formulates for the United States the "restrictive theory" of sovereign immunity--that immunity should generally only be recognized and granted to a state for sovereign or public acts (jure imperii), but not for private acts of a commercial nature (jure gestionis). It should be noted, however, that the United States accepts the restrictive theory only insofar as it involves attachment of the property of sovereigns; the property of sovereigns continues to be absolutely immune from execution.[148] The Tate Letter, issued in 1952, adopts this restrictive theory as the policy of the State Department, as follows: 'It will hereafter be the Department's policy to follow the restrictive theory of sovereign immunity in the consideration of requests of foreign governments for a grant of sovereign immunity."[149]

The restrictive theory adopted by the State Department in the Tate Letter has been followed by the courts as the rule of law to be applied by the courts in circumstances in which immunity is claimed and the State Department has not clearly stated to the courts its preference about whether that claim of immunity should or should not be recognized.[150] The rule of practice of all U.S. courts appears to be, however, that except for rare statutory exceptions,[151] when State Department policy can be ascertained either by clear suggestion or by announced rules, it is the duty of the courts to follow that policy.

This policy of deferring to the State Department's suggestions of sovereign immunity is followed by the courts even when a foreign sovereign is found to have previously waived its right to immunity. For example, when the Republic of China brought suit in U.S. courts against a U.S. national, it was held to have waived its right to sovereign immunity with respect to a counterclaim raised by defendant. In that case the State Department did not issue a suggestion of immunity.[152] When, on the other hand, waiver of immunity is found but the State Department subsequently submits to the court a suggestion of immunity, that immunity will be recognized by the courts.[153]

The deference of the judiciary to the suggestions of the State Department is seen most vividly in those cases in which the court has deferred to a State Department suggestion of immunity in circumstances in which that suggestion is clearly contrary to even those principles of law expressed in the Tate Letter, which the State Department purports to adopt for its own. In Rich v. Naviera Vacuba,[154] a Cuban vessel that had come into Hampton Roads, Virginia, after barratry on the high seas by its crew was immediately libeled by several claimants. The State Department was contemporaneously negotiating with the Cuban government for the release of highjacked U.S. airplanes then held in Cuba. The Cuban government had not requested that the vessel be granted sovereign immunity. Nevertheless, in a most unusual move, the State Department sent a message to the Cuban government through the Swiss embassy, asking whether that government "asserts ship and cargo are entitled to sovereign immunity and if so basis therefor." The Cubans cabled back that the vessel and cargo were the property of the Cuban government and requested recognition of sovereign immunity. Thereupon the State Department wrote a suggestion of immunity through the Attorney General to the court by stating that "the prompt release of the vessel is necessary to secure the observance of the rights and obligations of the United States."[155] Even though it found this statement "infelicitously expressed," the Court of Appeals found that the statement "sufficiently set forth the requisites of a valid suggestion for the allowance of sovereign immunity."[156] The court went on to hold that "the certificate and grant of immunity issued by the Department of State should be accepted by the Court without further inquiry."[157]

The absolute duty of U.S. courts to accept and adopt a State Department suggestion of immunity was further solidified in Chemical Natural Resources, Inc. v. Republic of Venezuela,[158] a case in which the majority grounded its decision upon sovereign immunity although the dissent considered the issue to be whether there was a proper act of state defense. In this case the State Department filed a suggestion of immunity as applicable to a commercially operated merchant ship owned by the Republic of Venezuela. The court drew the following conclusion from the department's suggestion: "It appears that the State Department has silently abandoned the 'revised and restricted policy" set forth in the Tate letter and has substituted a case by case foreign sovereign immunity policy."[159] The court held as follows:

> If and when the State Department concludes that a foreign nation is entitled to Sovereign Immunity that determination, we repeat, is conclusive no matter how unwise or, in a particular case, how unfair or unjust the Department's determination appears to be (a) to injured American citizens and (b) to vast numbers of the American people and (c) to our Courts.[160]

With this perspective that a State Department suggestion of sovereign immunity is most valuable because it effectively constitutes an absolute immunity from civil jurisdiction, we now turn briefly to the procedure a sovereign would normally undertake to secure such a suggestion from the department. This discussion of procedure can be brief, not because the courts and State Department have not established at least the broad outlines of such a procedure, but because, as can be seen from the discussion of cases such as Rich v. Naviera Vacuba,[161] the procedures need not be followed and department suggestions can be secured on an ad hoc basis.

To raise the defense of sovereign immunity, it is necessary to conform to certain court-developed procedures. In past practice the defense could be raised merely by having the embassy's counsel appear as amicus curiae and raise the objection of immunity to suit.[162] That practice ended in Ex parte Muir,[163] however, when Justice Van Devanter enumerated the only permissible methods of raising the sovereign immunity defense to jurisdiction. The first method is by special appearance of the foreign government before the court; the second is a suggestion from the Attorney General or his representative stating that the executive recognizes the claim of sovereign immunity.[164] Only the second method is of concern in this paper.

Seeking from the State Department a suggestion of immunity is quite unlike seeking relief in a court or quasi-judicial tribunal, in that the request is for action regarded by the department as entirely within the discretion of an executive department and review of the decision of that department is unavailable. Nevertheless, in most cases the following practice is followed in approaching the department with a request:

> The first step towards obtaining a "suggestion of immunity" is usually the submission of a note from the embassy of the foreign state to the State Department in which the foreign state requests that its immunity be recognized. The note is normally referred to the Office of the Legal Adviser. That office notifies the attorney for the plaintiff that a request for recognition of immunity has been made and that he has the opportunity of presenting his views in the matter to the Office of the Legal Adviser. An opportunity for expressing the views of the foreign state is also given to its attorney or to officers of the embassy. Thereafter, the Department, acting through the Office of the Legal Adviser, answers the note of the embassy by informing it as to whether or not it "recognizes and allows" the claim of immunity.
>
> If the Department recognizes and allows the claim of immunity, it so informs the Attorney General and requests that the court be so notified, through the appropriate United States Attorney.
>
> If the Department does not recognize and allow the claim of immunity, it takes no official action beyond informing the embassy, although the Department of Justice is normally given informal notice of the decision.[165]

Normally the court will not request a determination from the State Department. Such a request is left to the defendant.[166]

Generally, when a foreign embassy requests a suggestion of immunity from the State Department, the department will arrange for a hearing of sorts, in which both parties to the litigation may be heard before the staff of the State Department Legal Adviser. Such a hearing is not mandatory. In this hearing the "presiding officers," that is, State Department lawyers, seek to ascertain facts relevant to legal issues (as framed in the Tate Letter), such as the ownership or possession of the property, whether the property sought to be attached is of a commercial or a public nature, whether or not the claim is based upon an act of the state acting in the sovereign capacity, and whether the foreign state has acted in a manner that might constitute waiver of its immunity. The adviser's conclusions on these legal issues, combined with, and perhaps dominated by, policy considerations, will lead to a decision by the department about whether to issue a suggestion of immunity. The department's decision is made known only by the issuance or nonissuance of a suggestion; it never issues an opinion of law or fact.[167]

Because of the confusion resulting from the State Department's inconsistent application of the Tate Letter, a number of commentators have suggested that the whole subject should be clarified by statutory enactment.[168]

Act of State

When the State Department issues to a court a suggestion of sovereign immunity, that suggestion is followed almost without exception. The State Department also occasionally issues a suggestion to a court relating to other defenses or issues of law--primarily acts of state, recognition of foreign governments, and interpretation of treaties. The courts do not always defer to the State Department's suggestions on these other matters, as has been seen in the discussion of the Act of State doctrine earlier in this chapter.[169]

State Department suggestions relating to recognition by the United States are almost universally accepted on their face; there is no consensus, however, about the legal effect to be accorded to the recognition. Attempts by the State Department to suggest to courts its view of the proper interpretation of treaties have similarly met with such differing judicial reaction that no particular rule or even vaguely uniform practice can be ascertained.[170] Although treatment of State Department suggestions concerning acts of state is also somewhat uncertain and in a state of flux, it has become a pressing, vital issue in the United States and will thus be more closely examined.

The general rule followed by the U.S. courts was, as expressed in Underhill v. Hernandez[171] and Banco Nacional de Cuba v. Sabbatino,[172] that the courts should abstain from any determination on the merits of the legality of a confiscation or other act of state by a foreign government, because that determination might embarrass the executive branch in the conduct of foreign relations.[173]

In the Sabbatino case,[174] the Supreme Court refused to inquire into the validity of a Cuban nationalization decree, holding that the Act of State doctrine precludes examination of acts carried out by the government of Cuba within its territory. As previously explained, this refusal led to the enactment of a statutory modification of the Act of State doctrine. The Sabbatino, or Hickenlooper, Amendment provides as follows:

> No court . . . shall decline on the ground of the federal act of state doctrine to make a determination on the merits giving effect to the principles of international law in a case in which a claim . . . is asserted . . . based upon . . . an act of state in violation of the principles of international law.[175]

The mandate to ignore the Act of State doctrine is not, however, made absolute by the statute. It goes on to provide that the prohibition of the Act of State doctrine as a defense is inapplicable

> in any case with respect to which the President determines that application of the act of state doctrine is required in that particular case by the foreign policy interests of the United States and a suggestion to this effect is filed on his behalf in that case with the court.[176]

Thus, under the Sabbatino Amendment, a defendant in a suit arising out of an alleged illegal act of a foreign government cannot unilaterally invoke the defense of Act of State. If, however, the defendant secures a suggestion from the State Department to the court that it is contrary to the foreign policy interests of the United States for that court to examine the legality of the disputed act of the foreign government, then that suggestion constitutes an absolute defense to prevent a judgment on the merits.[177]

Recognition and Nonrecognition

No consistent doctrine of U.S. law has developed concerning the effect to be given to a determination by the government to recognize or not to recognize a foreign state or government. To a large extent cases appear to be determined on an ad hoc basis.

Four reasons can be suggested for this. First, the failure of the U.S. government to recognize an established government that objectively controls a defined territory, and the lives and relationships of the people within that territory, cannot be followed unquestioningly by U.S. courts in their determination of the validity of all acts taken under the laws of that government without producing some unrealistic, if not ridiculous, results.

Second, the documents that the executive forwards to the courts are often not merely simple statements that the United States does or does not recognize a foreign government; rather, the statements are often lengthy, may be filled with qualifications, and are frequently confusing.

Third, with respect to any particular government or state not recognized by the United States, there are other countries friendly to the United States whose courts accord validity to many or all acts taken under the laws of that particular state or government.

Fourth, with respect to almost every state whose government the United States does not accord de jure recognition, there are many activities and relations conducted between the nationals (and governments) of the United States and that state, including trade. These activities are not disapproved and in many cases are positively encouraged by the U.S. government. Failure of a U.S. court to treat these activities as valid would undermine these executive-approved or encouraged relations.

A Foreign State as a Litigant

In the era when U.S. courts granted to foreign governments sovereign immunity from suit, recognition or nonrecognition of a government by the United States was irrelevant to the status of a de facto government in the courts. Proof of de facto control of a territory was sufficient for it to invoke its claim to sovereign immunity.

In Wulfsohn v. Russian Socialist Federated Soviet Republic,[178] the plaintiff brought a quasi in rem action against the then unrecognized Soviet Russian government. That government claimed immunity. The plaintiff admitted that the defendant was the de facto government in Russia but argued that only recognized governments were entitled to sovereign immunity. The New York Court of Appeals held that no government, recognized or unrecognized, could be sued without that government's consent.

Although entitled to immunity from suit, unrecognized sovereigns were not recognized by the courts as persons entitled to bring suit. In Russian Socialist Federated Soviet Republic v. Cibrario,[179] it was held that an unrecognized government is barred from suing in the courts of the United States.

The Wulfsohn doctrine, affording sovereign immunity to unrecognized governments, was based upon the view that recognition is a political decision to be made by the executive branch of the government and that to deny immunity and permit suit would constitute an interference with this political function and might embarrass the government. The Cibrario doctrine was based upon the view that it would be contrary to the public policy of the United States, as established by the executive branch, for the courts to allow an unrecognized government the privilege to sue in U.S. courts.

Although neither view leads inevitably to the corresponding doctrine invoked, each is still considered to be the law today in the sense that neither has been repudiated by successor courts or in successor cases.[180] The problem is, however, that as other doctrines change and as each successive set of facts presents a slightly novel situation, the precise doctrine that a sovereign unrecognized state is entitled to immunity, and that the same state cannot bring suit in U.S. courts, is of little utility for the courts in determining or for litigants in predicting the outcome.

For example, when Wulfsohn was decided, immunity was considered an absolute right of a sovereign government. Today it is granted theoretically only to a government with regard to its acts in its sovereign capacity and in practice virtually only when the State Department suggests that immunity be granted. (See above.) It is unlikely that the State Department will often suggest that the property of a government whose de jure sovereignty it has refused to recognize is entitled to sovereign immunity from a suit in U.S. courts. Thus, although the Wulfsohn doctrine remains untouched, the complementary doctrine of soverign immunity has changed, leading to results contrary to Wulfsohn.

Variations in the facts tend to undermine Cibrario. In Bank of China v. Wells Fargo Bank & Union Trust Co.,[181] the appointees of the unrecognized CPR government were denied the right to sue to recover in a federal court the U.S. deposits in the Bank of China, the majority of the stock of which was state controlled. On the other hand, in Upright v. Mercury Business Machines Co.,[182] the U.S. assignee of a corporation totally operated and controlled by the unrecognized GDR government--in fact, considered by the court to be an instrumentality of that government--was allowed to sue in the New York courts on an obligation to pay for goods sold and delivered to the defendant. Both Upright and Bank of China cite Cibrario with approval.

If a government or its instrumentality are refused the right to sue in court, its claim could be lost forever, since nonrecognition does not toll the applicable statute of limitations.[183] In Union of Soviet Socialist Republics v. National City Bank, the court stated as follows:

> One of the results of nonrecognition of a foreign government is its incapacity to bring suit in our courts. Were it decided that during that period of nonrecognition the statute of limitations was merely tolled and did not run, one of the most effective sanctions of nonrecognition would lose most of its value.[184]

Apparently this result can be avoided by the unrecognized foreign sovereign, at least for claims of a colorably commercial nature and whenever a state structures and directs its activities through separate corporations or assignees who can claim an existence at least formally identifiable and separable from the government.[185]

The Legal Effect of Acts of Unrecognized Governments

The general rule is that lawful acts of a recognized government of a state will be given effect outside of the territory of that state. In fact, such acts will be given effect not from the date when recognition was accorded, but retroactively to the time that the government began to exist in fact.[186]

There is no converse of the rule for unrecognized governments. Generally the acts of unrecognized governments, to the extent that they affect people or territories not under their de facto control, will not be given legal effect by U.S. courts. This general rule is subject, however, to a general exception that commercial or other acts untinged by political issues will usually be given effect. Also, generally, despite failure of the U.S. government to recognize the de jure existence of a de facto government, courts will give legal effect to all acts taken by the de facto government that relate to its own people and that take place within its own territory, unless these acts are clearly abhorrent to U.S. policy as articulated by the State Department or interpreted by the courts. The exceptions to the general rules are so broad that they themselves constitute general rules. These rules are complicated by confusing representations by the State Department on the subject of whether, and the extent to which, the United States recognizes a government or the legitimacy of its acts. This package of considerations is still further complicated by the sometimes virtually inseparable questions of immunity and Act of State and by the general desire of the courts to avoid a manifestly unjust or unrealistic decision.

Historically the U.S. courts have never felt entirely bound to equate U.S. government recognition of a foreign government with the legitimacy of that government's acts. A series of post-Civil War decisions formed the basis of this quasi-independence of the judiciary from the political arm of the government, although the political arm is charged with responsibility for recognition.

The Confederacy was never recognized by the United States, either as possessing a legitimate government or as constituting a separate entity. Nevertheless, in a series of U.S. Supreme Court cases, laws enacted or acts taken by the Confederacy relating to the functioning of its society and economy and not directly related to the war or attempted separation were held to be legally valid and enforceable, after the war, in U.S. courts. For example, in United States v. Insurance Cos.,[187] the Court held that the rebel state and government of Georgia could create corporations that could sue in U.S. courts after the war.[188] On the other hand, U.S. courts would not, in Texas v. White,[189] recognize the validity of the transfer of title to bonds used to finance military purchases by the Confederacy.

Decrees by an unrecognized foreign government within its own borders and affecting its own citizens are usually accepted as valid under U.S. law. The more ordinary, commonplace, or apolitical the act, the more likely a court will be to give it legal effect. In Petrogradsky Mejdunarodny Kommerchesky Bank v. National City Bank, Judge Benjamin Cardozo stated as follows: "Every-day transactions of business or domestic life are not subject to impeachment, though the form may have been regulated by the command of the usurping government."[190]

The everyday transactions that usually fall into this category include authentication of a birth certificate by officials of an unrecognized government for purposes of proof of birth;[191] marriages under the laws of an unrecognized government;[192] and powers of attorney executed and acknowledged before a notary of an unrecognized government.[193]

The issues become more difficult when the laws or acts of a state's de facto government, though directed only toward nationals of that state and only within the territory of that state, contravene the court's view of U.S. policy, or even the judge's own personal policy views. The foremost example is that of nationalizations of private property rights.

In Sokoloff v. National City Bank,[194] the plaintiff sued for restitution of monies he had deposited in New York in exchange for a promise by the defendant to pay rubles in its Russia branch. The defendant raised the defense that its Russian assets had been confiscated by the unrecognized Soviet government. Judge Cardozo held that this was not a valid defense because the Soviet Government was not, in U.S. law, the de jure government and because the defendant, a U.S. corporation, did not cease to exist because of these decrees. Although the court refused to grant legal validity to the confiscation at least in part because of the refusal of the United States to recognize the confiscating government, the court did state that there could be circumstances in which the validity of such acts would be accorded, as follows:

> A body or group which has vindicated by the course of events its pretensions to sovereign

> power, but which has forfeited by its conduct the privileges or immunities of sovereignty, may gain for its acts and decrees a validity quasi-governmental, if violence to fundamental principles of justice or to our own public policy might otherwise be done.[195]

In M. Salimoff & Co. v. Standard Oil Co.,[196] it was held by Judge Roscoe Pound that the law of the de facto Soviet government would be applied to determine the validity of the seizure by that government, within its territory, of oil from a Russian national. The Salimoff decision was made easier for the court by the fact that the State Department sent to the court a note stating somewhat vaguely that it was "cognizant of the fact that the Soviet regime is exercising control and power in territory of the former Russian Empire."[197]

Subsequent cases, including The Maret[198] and Latvian State Cargo & Passenger S.S. Line v. Clark,[199] refused to confer validity upon seizures of the property of nationals of the then recently seized Baltic countries by the Soviet government, unrecognized by the U.S. government as the lawful government in these countries. These decisions appear to be the result of strong statements by the State Department to the courts not only that it did not recognize the Soviet government as the de jure government of the Baltic republics, but also that it was contrary to the policy of the United States to recognize confiscatory decrees. It should also be noted that the challenged decrees in both of these cases nationalized ships that were not then within Soviet or Baltic-country waters, and as such might be considered extraterritorial expropriations, contrary to U.S. policy.[200]

Reverting back to a more ad hoc, goal-oriented approach, the U.S. district court in the Carl Zeiss[201] case noted the Baltic ships cases and noted also that "our Government's policy of nonrecognition has been taken into consideration in denying extraterritorial effects to confiscatory expropriation decrees of an unrecognized foreign state," but stated that "this Court has not considered itself bound by our nonrecognition policy to disregard German law as construed by courts of [unrecognized] East Germany."[202]

The effect of nonrecognition upon the validity of decrees of foreign governments in U.S. courts thus appears to be somewhat unpredictable, depending on a mixture of perceived (or represented) U.S. policy, the particular interests of U.S. nationals or the nationals of countries friendly to the United States who are directly involved, the judicial inclination not to disrupt ongoing ordinary private or commercial transactions, and some notion that attention must be paid to the U.S. government's policy of nonrecognition.

TREATIES AND THE INDIVIDUAL

This section does not purport to be a comprehensive discussion of all U.S. treaties benefiting the individual. Instead the purpose of this section is to identify some of the more striking examples in which treaties and executive agreements have been used by the United States to secure the "advancement or protection of the individual interest."

Bilateral Treaties Affecting the United States and Canada

Article III of the Jay Treaty, which definitely settled relations between the United States and Great Britain following the War of the Revolution, provides that citizens of the two countries shall be free to navigate all the waters on the continent of America and also specifically guarantees freedom of navigation on the Mississippi River.[203] There also exists a provision guaranteeing free movement of American Indians across the international boundary and duty-free treatment of their belongings. This freedom of movement for American Indians is recognized in Article II of the Immigration and Nationality Act of 1952. Article III of the Webster-Ashburton Treaty of 1842 secures freedom of navigation on the St. John River to citizens of the United States and Canada.[204] Article I of the Treaty of 1846, which defined the international boundary west of the Rocky Mountains, provides for freedom of navigation on either side of the international boundary in the Straits of Juan de Fuca.[205] Similarly, Article XXVI of the Treaty of Washington of 1871 secured for U.S. citizens freedom of navigation on the St. Lawrence River,[206] and confirmed and replaced many of the rights secured by the Jay Treaty and other prior treaties.

Article XI of the Jay Treaty also provided that private debts between citizens of the two countries should not be sequestered or confiscated in time of war or national differences.

Of special significance is the Boundary Waters Treaty of 1909, which defined boundary waters between Canada and the United States and established a permanent International Joint Commission to regulate the use of "boundary waters." Article II expressly provides that interference or diversion of such waters resulting in injury on the other side of the boundary would "give rise to the same rights and entitle the injured parties to the same legal remedies as if such injury took place in the country where such diversion or interference occurs."[207]

This means that a U.S. citizen suffering injury on the U.S. side of the boundary can sue in the Canadian courts for redress, and vice versa.[208] More often, however, under Article IX such claims have been referred by one government or the other to the International Joint Commission. Air pollution complaints have been referred to the commission on an ad hoc basis. The most celebrated example is the Trail Smelter arbitration.[209]

It is significant to note that private parties frequently file applications directly with the International Joint Commission.[210]

Treaties of Friendship, Commerce, and Navigation

Throughout its history the United States has been active in negotiating treaties of friendship, commerce, and navigation (FCN). The Jay Treaty of 1794 was an early example of the type. Immediately after World War II the State Department made a major effort to update and modernize the FCN treaty system. The effort has had only limited success. The treaties negotiated with Germany and Japan are quite similar and may be taken as models for what the State Department sought to obtain. The more important provisions of the U.S.-German treaty are the following:

> 1. Nationals of each party shall be entitled to "fair and equitable treatment" for their persons, property, enterprises, and other interests as well as "freedom of commerce and navigation." They are entitled to entry and sojourn for commerce and development of investment. Freedom of conscience and religion is guaranteed. The foregoing are subject to necessary measures to protect public order, health, morals, and safety.
>
> 2. Aliens are guaranteed constant protection and security which shall not be less favorable than that accorded nationals of third countries or that required by international law.
>
> 3. Property of nationals and companies of either party are to "receive the most constant protection and security." Nor shall such property be taken except for a public purpose and in accordance with due process of law. Nor shall it be taken without "just compensation" and such compensation must be equivalent to the property taken and must be in "an effectively realizable form," which means convertible currency.
>
> 4. Nationals of either party are entitled to "national" treatment with respect to access to courts and administrative tribunals. Provisions

are included to facilitate enforcement of arbitral awards. Aliens are assured the right to control and manage their enterprises. Nationals of either party are to be accorded "national treatment" as to leasing land, buildings and other real property.

5. Nationals of either party shall not be subjected to taxes more burdensome than those borne in like cases by natives or by nationals of third nations.

6. Products of either party are to be accorded "most favored treatment" in all matters affecting internal taxation, sale, etc.

7. Freedom of transit for persons and baggage is assured.[211]

Economic Cooperation Agreements

When the Marshall Plan was inaugurated, the United States entered into a number of bilateral executive agreements with European countries. The 1948 agreement with France is typical. Among other things it provided in Article X that, after exhaustion of local remedies, claims of U.S. nationals against France will be submitted to the International Court of Justice or to arbitration.[212]

Investment Guaranty Agreements

At one time high hopes were held that agreements between the United States and foreign aid recipient countries could be used as a vehicle for protecting investments. These hopes have not been realized. The current provision of the Foreign Assistance Act of 1961, as amended, requires only that there must be an agreement between the United States and the host government "to institute a program for insurance or guaranties."[213] In practice the agreements only bind the host government to recognize the rights of the United States when it is subrogated to the insured private investor as a result of its payment of the insurance claim of such an investor. The United States agrees not to guarantee any project not approved by the host government.[214]

International Convention on Settlement of Investment Disputes

The United States is a member of the International Center for the Settlement of Investment Disputes (ICSID) but has not been a party to any arbitration or conciliation proceedings submitted to the center. This is not surprising, considering that comparatively few of the less developed countries have joined ICSID and that none of those countries in which the United States has an investment dispute has joined. Indeed, most of the nations of Latin America have been opposed to ICSID, even though under its terms no party is bound to submit investment disputes to ICSID for arbitration or conciliation.

It remains to be seen whether the ICSID will develop into a useful international institution. More than 60 nations are members.

Lump-Sum Settlement Agreements

As indicated earlier, the United States has made numerous lump-sum settlement agreements securing compensation for the claims of its nationals abroad for expropriation or war damage losses. The sums agreed upon, though almost always inadequate to cover such claims, have been accepted by the United States as full and final settlements of such claims. Almost all of these agreements have been executive agreements rather than treaties.

Status of Forces Agreements

The United States is party to numerous international agreements, such as the NATO Status of Forces Treaty[215] and the Administrative Agreement with Japan,[216] which govern the exercise of criminal jurisdiction over its military forces abroad. These agreements have specific clauses assuring a variety of procedural and substantive safeguards that must be observed when a member of the U.S. armed forces is subjected to trial for criminal offenses by the receiving state in which he or she is stationed abroad. Among these are the right to prompt trial; confrontation of adverse witnesses; legal counsel of the defendant's own choosing; the services of an interpreter; and specification of the charges against the defendant.[217]

Other provisions deal with civil obligations arising from claims, and so on.

The provisions of these agreements, which contemplate exercise of jurisdiction in certain cases by the United States over civilians and dependents accompanying the forces abroad, have been rendered obsolete by action of the U.S. Supreme Court holding unconstitutional those provisions of the Courts Martial Code that purport to apply to civilians abroad.[218]

Double Taxation Treaties

The United States is party to a large number of treaties intended to relieve its citizens living abroad or engaged abroad from the burden of double taxation. Typically the treaties relieve the alien taxpayer from double taxation of income and of estate and gift taxes. Usually the income tax treaty is a separate treaty from the estate or inheritance tax treaty. The U.S.-Japanese treaties were signed in 1954.[219] There is a new income tax treaty with Japan, which was signed in 1971.[220]

The Supremacy Clause of the Constitution

No discussion of U.S. treaties in relation to the individual would be complete without some treatment of the domestic or municipal law effect in the United States of a treaty. In contrast with the practice in the United Kingdom, for example, a treaty under U.S. law may be self-executing and take effect under the supremacy clause without the necessity for separate legislative enactment by Congress. Under the supremacy clause of the Constitution (Article VI Clause 2), a treaty becomes the supreme law of the land when proclaimed by the president. A treaty may therefore supersede prior statutory enactments by the federal or state legislatures, if they are plainly inconsistent with the treaty.[221]

The decision about whether Congress should be asked to pass separate legislation to implement the terms of a treaty is made in the first instance by the executive branch when it presents the treaty to the Senate for advice and consent. In certain cases implementation by specific legislation is necessary with respect to portions of a treaty. If, for example, appropriations are needed to carry out parts of the treaty, Congress must act separately to appropriate the necessary funds.

RESTRICTIONS UPON EMPLOYMENT OF ALIENS AND OF NATIONALS WHO HAVE CLOSE RELATIVES WHO ARE ALIENS

Contrary to the assumed situation in most countries, non-U.S. nationals are eligible for employment by many federal, state, and local government agencies and contractors. A short discussion of the relatively unique U.S. practice in this area is therefore of some interest and is combined with the discussion of the few employment restrictions on nationals with close relatives who are aliens.

In many circumstances aliens are protected from discrimination based upon their alien status by provisions of the Constitution or by statute or regulation. In the courts, for example, the trend of decisions in recent years has been directed toward invalidating state legislation that discriminates against employment of aliens by state and local governments or by private employers performing quasi-governmental or public utility functions. Many such statutes have been generally invalidated, either on the basis that they violate the Equal Protection Clause of the Fourteenth Amendment (note that the Equal Protection Clause requires that states give equal treatment to all "persons," not only to citizens),[222] or that they interfere with the statutory scheme of Congress for admitting aliens into the United States.[223]

The federal government itself is not covered by the Fourteenth Amendment, which specifically governs only state activity. There is some federal case law that "incorporates" into the Fifth Amendment, which forbids the federal government to deprive a person of life, liberty, or property without due process of law, many of the "equal protection" safeguards of the Fourteenth Amendment.[224] Past restrictions on federal employment of aliens or on nationals with aliens who are close relatives have not been tested under the Fifth Amendment in the courts. There is a reasonable likelihood, however, that the Fifth Amendment may be held, some time in the future, to encompass the Fourteenth Amendment insofar as nondiscrimination against aliens is concerned.

Judicial extension to aliens of the Equal Protection Clause may, however, be of mere historical interest because of the enactment of the Equal Employment Opportunity Act of 1972, amending the Civil Rights Act of 1964, and the regulations that have been issued pursuant to those acts. Although to date no court cases based on the Civil Rights Act have invalidated either state or federal legislation discriminating against aliens in public employment, the Civil Rights Act, as amended, clearly seems to cover this area.

The Civil Rights Act of 1964, as originally passed, did not cover discrimination in employment practices by state governments themselves. The 1972 amendments to the Civil Rights Act, however, prohibit an employer from discriminating on the basis of race, color, religion, sex, or national origin in hiring or discharging or in pay practices. These amendments specifically include as an "employer" governments and governmental agencies (but not the United States itself) that act as employers of 15 or more workers in "an industry affecting commerce."[225] This could cover much governmental activity, especially government-operated enterprises or utilities.

Furthermore, in implementing the Civil Rights Act, the Equal Employment Opportunity Commission (EEOC), an agency created by the Civil Rights Act of 1964, has issued regulations interpreting that act. While these regulations might not bind courts in their decisions under federal law, they are usually a good indication of the way in which courts will interpret the law, since U.S. courts usually accord great weight to the administrative practice of the agency charged with enforcement of the statute. In one regulation the EEOC has specifically dealt with the problem of discrimination in employment based on national origin, as follows:

> (d) Because discrimination on the basis of citizenship has the effect of discriminating on the basis of national origin, a lawfully immigrated alien who is domiciled or residing in this country may not be discriminated against on the basis of his citizenship, except that it is not an unlawful employment practice for an employer, pursuant to section 703(g), to refuse to employ any person who does not fulfill the requirements imposed in the interests of national security pursuant to any statute of the United States or any Executive order of the President respecting the particular position of the particular premises in question.
>
> (e) In addition, some States have enacted laws prohibiting the employment of noncitizens. For the reasons stated above such laws are in conflict with and are, therefore, superseded by Title VII of the Civil Rights Act of 1964.[226]

Based on the statute as amended and the regulations issued by the EEOC, it would appear that discrimination against aliens in public employment by state government will no longer have to be adjudicated on the basis of the Fourteenth Amendment, but instead is a practice expressly forbidden by federal legislation.

This policy against discrimination based upon nationality or national origin seems to have been incorporated into federal government employment practice. Title VII of the Civil Rights Act, as amended by the 1972 Equal Employment Opportunity Act, banning all forms of discrimination based on race, color, religion, sex, or national origin, specifically protects all employees of the executive, legislative, and judicial branches of the federal government whose jobs are subject to competitive service. Executive orders have announced a policy of equal employment opportunity without regard to race, color, sex, religion, or national origin.[227] All executive agencies have issued regulations implementing these executive orders.[228] In general the Secretary of Labor is responsible for establishing federal guidelines for the other executive agencies. The EEOC is a part of the Department of Labor, and it seems likely that EEOC regulations, including the regulation quoted above, apply in their entirety to the federal government.

One notable exception to this emerging overall policy against discrimination based solely upon the alien status of the employee or the employee's relatives is the State Department, where certain job categories are prohibited to all aliens and to those U.S. nationals who are married to aliens. Appointment as a foreign service officer is conditioned upon the candidate's having been a U.S. citizen for at least ten years, and if the candidate is married, on his or her spouse's possession of U.S. citizenship.[229] A different policy exists in the Defense Department, where resident aliens may serve and in many circumstances be drafted into the U.S. armed forces and must serve, subject to security clearance restrictions, in the same capacity as citizens.[230]

The major exception to the general policy against discrimination in government (and government contract) employment of aliens or of U.S. nationals with close relatives who are aliens relates to those positions involving access to material or information restricted for purposes of national defense.[231] All agencies that are required to limit access to information based on national defense considerations have established regulations for the issuance of security clearance to their employees and to the employees of private industry who have access to classified information. Typical of this regulatory scheme is the Industrial Security Program of the Defense Department, which establishes criteria for granting security clearances both to its own employees and to employees of private contractors who do business with the department. Among the factors considered in granting a security clearance are the following:

> Any facts or circumstances which furnish reason to believe that the individual may be subjected to coercion, influence, or pressure which may be

> likely to cause action contrary to the national interest. Such facts may include: the presence of a close relative of the applicant or the applicant's spouse in a nation whose interests may be inimical to the interests of the United States, or in satellites or occupied areas of such a nation, under circumstances permitting coercion or pressure to be brought on the individual through such relatives which may be likely to cause action contrary to the national interest. The term close relative includes parents, brothers, sisters, offspring, and spouse.[232]

Because a large number of jobs in government, as well as in industries that do business with the government, require that the employees have access to classified information, obviously an employee who cannot obtain a security clearance because of alienage or because the employee or the employee's spouse has relatives in a nation whose interests are judged to be potentially inimical to the United States, is substantially limited in the kinds of jobs he or she can hold. It should be noted, however, that these security regulations do not prohibit employment because of the alien status of the prospective employee or his or her relatives, as such, but rather only upon those aliens, or nationals with close relatives who are aliens, whose alienage is of such a nature as to warrant a denial of a security clearance, such as nationality of an unfriendly power.

In one further area of employment, aliens may encounter certain difficulties not experienced by most citizens. In occupations that traditionally require oaths of allegiance to the United States because of their position of public trust, such as lawyer, school teacher, or police officer, some resident aliens may not be able to take the required oath. Although loyalty oaths have been severely proscribed by the courts because of the possibility that they may infringe on an individual's right under the First Amendment to say or not say what he or she wants to say and to associate with or not associate with whomever he or she wishes, in 1972 the Supreme Court upheld, in Cole v. Richardson,[233] the validity of a loyalty oath that was required of all state employees in Massachusetts. To the extent that states may seek to refuse employment to aliens who, it might be argued, cannot swear "to uphold and defend the Constitution of the United States of America," Cole v. Richardson indicates that loyalty oaths may be a valid excuse for denying employment by state agencies to aliens who are not seeking to become citizens.

Notwithstanding Cole v. Richardson, if such oaths are upheld in future court decisions, it will perhaps be only with regard to employment positions having a uniquely public character, with regard to which it can be demonstrated that allegiance to the U.S. government and Constitution has a rational relationship to the job. This is the teaching of cases such as Dougal v. Sugarman,[234] in which the court found that no legitimate state interest can be shown in a broad requirement that state employees be citizens, that the New York statute at issue conflicted with the federal immigration laws, and further, it would follow that a loyalty oath cannot be used as a test for all state employment if it acts to discriminate against aliens and there is no showing "that the loyalty requirement bears a relationship to a compelling interest of the city and state."[235]

On balance, in the United States aliens enjoy a remarkable amount of access to government and government-related employment. As for U.S. nationals with alien spouses, the only restriction against their public employment appears to be with respect to positions in the foreign service or with respect to positions that require security clearance.

NOTES

1. Whiteman, 8 Digest of International Law, 195 ff. (1967).
2. 307 U.S. 325 (1939).
3. 106 F.Supp. 445 (D.D.C. 1952).
4. 225 F.2d 938 (D.C. Cir. 1955).
5. 357 U.S. 116 (1958).
6. 357 U.S. 116.
7. 357 U.S. 116, 130 (1958).
8. Ibid.
9. Whiteman, op. cit., at 237.
10. 367 U.S. 1 (1961).
11. 378 U.S. 500 (1964).
12. Ibid., at 514.
13. 270 F.2d 905, 910 (D.C. Cir. 1959); cert. denied, 361 U.S. 918 (1959).
14. 66 Stat. 190, 8 U.S.C. Section 1185.
15. Worthy v. United States, 328 F.2d 386, 394 (5th Cir. 1964).
16. Zemel v. Rusk, 381 U.S. 1 (1965).
17. United States v. Laub, 385 U.S. 475 (1967).
18. 385 U.S. 491 (1967).
19. 22 C.F.R. § 51.70.
20. In such cases departure is also directly prohibited by the Criminal Code. 18 U.S.C. §§ 1073-74.
21. 328 F.2d 386 (1964).
22. For the purposes of this section we have not considered "extradition" as included within the term "expulsion."
23. 320 U.S. 81 (1943).

24. 323 U.S. 214 (1944).

25. 323 U.S. 283 (1944).

26. U.S. Const., Art. I § 9, Clause 2.

27. 71 U.S. (4 Wall.) 2 (1866).

28. Restatement, Second, Foreign Relations Law of the United States § 38 (1965); Foley Bros., Inc. v. Filardo, 336 U.S. 281 (1949).

29. 18 U.S.C. § 2381; Tomoya Kawakita v. U.S., 343 U.S. 717 (1952).

30. 18 U.S.C. § 794. Prior to the 1961 amendment the espionage chapter applied only to offenses within the territorial and maritime jurisdiction of the United States.

31. 18 U.S.C. § 1621.

32. 18 U.S.C. § 1651.

33. 18 U.S.C. § 959.

34. 18 U.S.C. § 2031.

35. 18 U.S.C. § 2111.

36. 15 Stat. 223; R.S. 1999 (1868).

37. See Lapides v. Clark, 176 F.2d 619 (D.C. Cir. 1949), cert. denied, 338 U.S. 860 (1949).

38. 8 U.S.C. § 801(e).

39. 356 U.S. 44 (1958).

40. 387 U.S. 253 (1967).

41. 401 U.S. 815 (1971).

42. 8 U.S.C. § 1401(a).

43. United States v. Aluminum Company of America, 148 F.2d 416 (2d Cir. 1945).

44. 50 U.S.C. App. § 2401.

45. 22 U.S.C. § 1934.

46. 50 U.S.C. App. § 5(b).

47. Fruehauf Corp. v. Massardy, 5 International Legal Materials 476 (1966).

48. Restatement, Second, Foreign Relations Law of the United States § 212; Whiteman, 8 Digest of International Law 1216 (1967).

49. Restatement, Second, Foreign Relations Law of the United States, § 211 (1965).

50. 18 U.S.C. § 953.

51. 22 U.S.C. § 1643.

52. 22 U.S.C. § 2370.

53. 21 Ct. Cl. 340 (1886).

54. Aris Gloves v. United States, 420 F.2d 1386, U.S. Ct. Cl., 1970.

55. Restatement, Second, Foreign Relations Law of the United States § 213 (1965).

56. 22 U.S.C. §§ 1971-77.

57. P.L. 92-242 § 113.

58. P.L. 92-245 § 18; P.L. 92-246 § 21; P.L. 92-247 § 12.

59. 22 U.S.C. § 283(1).

60. 22 U.S.C. § 2370(e)(1).

61. 22 U.S.C. § 2370(c).

62. 22 U.S.C. § 2370(a)(2).

63. 22 U.S.C. § 2370(e)(2).

64. 7 U.S.C. § 1158.

65. P.L. 92-138 § 17.

66. United States ex rel. Knauff v. Shaughnessy, 338 U.S. 537, 542 (1950). See also Fong Yue Ting v. United States, 149 U.S. 698 (1893).

67. Chae Chan Ping v. United States, 130 U.S. 581, 609 (1889).

68. 158 U.S. 538 (1895). Sing was born in China, and although he did not become a naturalized citizen of the United States, maintained a residence and engaged in trade in the United States for a continuous and uninterrupted period of over two years. He departed from the United States for a temporary visit to China. During his absence, an Act of Congress was passed authorizing immigration officers of the United States to prevent illegal entry by persons of Chinese extraction. Lem Moon Sing was denied entry, and on appeal, the Supreme Court held that it was without power to review either the Act of Congress or the exercise of executive discretion.

69. 345 U.S. 206 (1953).

70. 8 U.S.C. § 1255(a) extends the permanent resident qualification to aliens already within the United States who were not originally admitted as permanent residents, so long as they are not nationals of countries in the Western Hemisphere or certain other countries, with the exception of Cuba, pursuant to a 1966 amendment to the Immigration and Nationality Act of 1952. That amendment is 80 Stat. 1161 (1966), amending 8 U.S.C. § 1255(c).

71. See C. Gordon & H. Rosenfield, Immigration Law and Procedure, § 1.32 (1966).

72. 345 U.S. 206 (1953).

73. Ibid., at 212.

74. 344 U.S. 590 (1953).

75. 325 F.Supp. 620 (E.D.N.Y. 1971), appeal docketed, 40 U.S.L.W. 3035 (U.S., 13 July 1971).

76. Act of 27 June 1952 (Immigration and Nationality Act), § 212(a)(28)(D), 8 U.S.C. § 1182 (a)(28)(D).

77. Ibid., § 212(a)(28)(G)(v), 8 U.S.C. § 1182 (a)(28)(G)(v).

78. 325 F.Supp. at 631-32; reversed sub nom. Kleindienst v. Mandel, 408 U.S. 753 (1972).

79. Section 6851 of Internal Revenue Code of 1954, Treas. Reg. § 1.6851.

80. Yick Wo v. Hopkins, 118 U.S. 356 (1886).

81. United States ex rel. Knauff v. Shaughnessy, 338 U.S. 537 (1950).

82. Compare Yick Wo v. Hopkins, 118 U.S. 356 (1886), and Wong Wing v. United States, 163 U.S. 228 (1896).

83. Immigration and Nationality Act of 1952, 8 U.S.C. §§ 1251-54.

84. 8 C.F.R. § 103.1 (1971).

85. 8 C.F.R. § 242.

86. 8 U.S.C. § 1253(h).

87. 8 U.S.C. § 1254(a).

88. 8 U.S.C. § 1357(a)(1) and (a)(2). See also Fernandez v. United States, 321 F.2d 283, at 285 (9th Cir. 1963), upholding the constitutionality of this section as "congressional recognition of the right of the United States to protect its own boundaries against the illegal entry of aliens."

89. Marcello v. Bonds, 349 U.S. 302 (1955).

90. Sovich v. Esperdy, 319 F.2d 21 (2d Cir. 1963).

91. Chao-Ling Wong v. Pilliod, 285 F.2d 517 (7th Cir. 1960).

92. See Berdo v. Immigration and Naturalization Service, 432 F.2d 824 (6th Cir. 1970); Kovac v. Immigration and Naturalization Service, 407 F.2d 102 (9th Cir. 1969).

93. See Jay v. Boyd, 351 U.S. 345 (1956); Galvan v. Press, 347 U.S. 522 (1954); Vardjan v. Esperdy, 197 F.Supp. 931 (S.D.N.Y. 1961).

94. See, for example, Arts. 26, 40, 53.

95. See, for example, Arts. 31, 37, 38.

96. Whiteman, 7 Digest of International Law, Chapter 18 §§ 12-13 (1970).

97. Ibid., Chapter 17 §§ 25-26.

98. Ibid., 31-32.

99. See, for example, North Atlantic Treaty Organization, Status of Forces Agreement, Treaties and Other International Acts series 2846, Art. 7 par. 3(c).

100. Ibid.

101. Ibid., at Art. I par. 1(a).

102. Ibid., at Art. I par. 1(b).

103. Ibid.

104. Ibid., at 36.

105. Foreign Assistance Act of 1961, as amended, § 620(e)(1), 22 U.S.C. § 2370(e)(1).

106. Sugar Act of 1948, § 408(c), as amended, 7 U.S.C. § 1158(c).

107. I.C.J. Rep. 227 (1970).

108. 168 U.S. 250 (1897).

109. Ibid., at 252.

110. Delson, "Act of State Doctrine--Judicial Deference or Abstention," 66 Am. J. Int'l. L. 82, 87 (1972).

111. 246 U.S. 297 (1918).

112. Ibid., at 303.

113. 246 U.S. 304 (1918).

114. Ibid., at 310.

115. U.S. Const., Art. II, § 3.

116. Bernstein v. Van Heyghen Freres, 163 F.2d 246 (2d Cir. 1947), cert. denied 332 U.S. 772 (1947).

117. Bernstein v. N. V. Nederlandsche-Amerikaansche, 210 F.2d 375 (2nd Cir. 1954).

118. Ibid., 20 Dep't. State Bull. 592, 8 May 1949.

119. The Nereide, 13 U.S. (9 Cranch) 388, 423 (1815), Opinion of Marshall, C.J.; The Paquete Habana, 175 U.S. 677, 700 (1900); Restatement, Second, Foreign Relations Law of the United States, Section 3 (reporter's note).

120. The Paquete Habana, 175 U.S. 677, 700 (1900).
121. Banco Nacional de Cuba v. Sabbatino, 376 U.S. 398, 427 (1964).
122. Ibid., at 439.
123. 22 U.S.C.A. § 2370(e)(2).
124. 79 Stat. 659, 22 U.S.C.A. § 2370(e)(2) (Supp. 1965).
125. Banco Nacional de Cuba v. Farr, 243 F.Supp. 957 (S.D.N.Y. 1965).
126. Banco Nacional de Cuba v. Farr, 383 F.2d 166 (2d Cir. 1967); cert. denied, 390 U.S. 956 (1968).
127. 23 N.Y.2d 46, 242 N.E.2d 704, 295 N.Y.2d 433 (1968).
128. Banco Nacional de Cuba v. First National City Bank, 442 F.2d 530 (1971), cert. granted 92 S. Ct. 79 (1971).
129. National City Bank v. Republic of China, 348 U.S. 356 (1955).
130. Report of the Secretary of State, United States Foreign Policy 1971, State Department Publication No. 8634 (March 1972), at 186, 282-83.
131. Ibid., at 186-87.
132. Ibid., at 187.
133. Rhodesia Resolutions, U.N. doc. S/RES: 232 (1966), U.N. doc. S/RES 253 (1968).
134. Executive Order 11322, January 5, 1967. Executive Order 11419, July 29, 1968.
135. This act reads as follows:

> Sec. 5. (a) Notwithstanding the provisions of any other law, whenever the United States is called upon by the Security Council to apply measures which said Council has decided, pursuant to article 41 of said Charter, are to be employed to give effect to its decisions under said Charter, the President may, to the extent necessary to apply such measures, through any agency which he may designate, and under such orders, rules, and regulations as may be prescribed by him, investigate, regulate, or prohibit, in whole or in part, economic relations or rail, sea, air, postal, telegraphic, radio, and other means of communication between any foreign country or any national thereof of any person therein and the United States or any person subject to the jurisdiction thereof, or involving any property subject to the jurisdiction of the United States.
>
> (b) Any person who willfully violates or evades or attempts to violate or evade any order, rule, or regulation issued by the President pursuant to subsection (a) of this section shall, upon conviction, be fined not more than $10,000 or, if a natural person, be imprisoned for not more than ten years, or both; and the officer, director, or agent of any corporation who knowingly participates in such violation or

> evasion shall be punished by a like fine, imprisonment, or both, and any property, funds, securities, papers, or other articles or documents, or any vessel, together with her tackle, apparel, furniture, and equipment, or vehicle, or aircraft, concerned in such violation shall be forfeited to the United States. 50 Stat. 620, 22 U.S.C. § 287c.

136. Executive Order 11419, 29 July 1968.

137. P.L. 92-156, 17 November 1971.

138. 60 Stat. 596, 50 U.S.C. § 98.

139. 11 U.S. (7 Cranch) 116 (1812).

140. Communications from the State Department to the courts about whether a particular state or government is viewed by the United States as a recognized friendly power are still important with respect to the assertion of rights other than that of sovereign immunity. See the discussion of Carl Zeiss Stiftung v. V.E.B. Carl Zeiss, Jena, 293 F.Supp. 892 (S.D.N.Y. 1968) in the section of this chapter on recognition and nonrecognition.

141. Berizzi Brothers Co. v. S.S. Pesaro, 271 U.S. 562 (1926). The claim involved in the Pesaro case was a commercial claim alleging the failure of a merchant ship to deliver a cargo from Italy to New York. The Supreme Court held that the doctrine of sovereign immunity in the Schooner Exchange case conferred sovereign immunity to all property and vessels owned, possessed, or operated by a government irrespective of their nature or use. It thus dismissed the action on the sole ground that the ship was owned by the Italian government. The State Department disagreed with this view and with the court's decision in the Pesaro case. It contended that as a matter of law sovereign immunity should not be granted to a commercial property in a claim arising out of a commercial transaction. Although this State Department view was brought to the court's attention, it was never formally transmitted by the Department of Justice, which had declined in that instance to submit the State Department's letter to the court. See Lowenfeld, "Claims Against Foreign States--A Proposal for Reform of United States Law," 44 N.Y. Univ. L. Rev. 901, 904 (1969).

142. 318 U.S. 578 (1943).

143. Ibid., at 588.

144. Compania Espanola De Navegacion Maritima v. The Navemar, 303 U.S. 68 (1938).

145. 324 U.S. 30 (1945).

146. This decision reads, in part, as follows:

> It is . . . not for the courts to deny an immunity which our government has seen fit to allow, or to allow an immunity on new grounds which the government has not seen fit to recognize. The judicial seizure of property of a friendly state may . . . be regarded as such an affront to its dignity and so may affect our relations with

> it, that it is an accepted rule of substantive law governing the exercise of the jurisdiction of the courts that they accept and follow the executive determination that the vessel shall be treated as immune. But recognition by the courts of an immunity upon principles which the political department of government has not sanctioned may be equally embarrassing to it in securing the protection of our national interests and for their recognition by other nations. Ibid., at 35-36.
>
> More important, and we think controlling in the present circumstances, is the fact that, despite numerous opportunities like the present to recognize immunity from suit of a vessel owned and not possessed by a foreign government, this government has failed to do so. We can only conclude that it is the national policy not to extend the immunity in the manner now suggested, and that it is the duty of the courts, in a matter so intimately associated with our foreign policy and which may profoundly affect it, not to enlarge an immunity to an extent which the government, although often asked, has not seen fit to recognize. Ibid., at 38.

147. Letter to Acting Attorney General Perlman from Acting Legal Adviser of the Department of State Tate, 19 May 1952 (hereafter the Tate Letter), 26 Dep't. State Bull. 984 (1952).

148. See New York and Cuba MSS Co. v. Republic of Korea, 132 F.Supp. 684 (S.D.N.Y. 1955); Weilamann v. Chase Manhattan Bank, 192 N.Y. Supp. 2d 469 (S. Ct., 1959).

149. The Tate Letter, op. cit.

150. This failure of the State Department to express a preference clearly has confronted the courts in circumstances either where there is no communication whatever from the department or where a litigant has requested that the State Department communicate with the court and the department has complied with the request, but in a manner so vague and equivocal that the court cannot determine its preference. This was the case in Republic of Mexico v. Hoffman, 324 U.S. 30, 35 (1945), in which the Court chose to treat the suggestion only that it had "accepted as true" the assertion by the Mexican government of ownership (not its assertion of immunity), as an expression of a suggestion that immunity should not be granted. Vague or equivocal State Department suggestions are not at all uncommon, in fact. See, for example, Ocean Transport Co. v. Republic of the Ivory Coast, 269 F.Supp. 703 (E.D. La. 1967); Sullivan v. State of Sao Paulo, 36 F.Supp. 503 (E.D. N.Y. 1941); Stephen v. Zivnostenska Banka, National Corp., 23 Misc. 2d 855, 199 N.Y.S. 2d 797 (S. Ct. 1960).

151. For example, the Civil Aeronautics Board permits that are issued to foreign air carriers require the foreign holder to "waive any right

it may possess to assert any defense of sovereign immunity from suit in any action or proceeding in any court or other tribunal in the United States based on claims arising out of its operations under the permit." 14 C.F.R. § 399.13(b) (1970).

152. National City Bank v. Republic of China, 348 U.S. 356 (1955).

153. Isbrantsen Tankers v. President of India, 446 F.2d 1198 (2d Cir. 1971), Rich v. Naviera Vacuba, 295 F.2d 24 (4th Cir. 1961).

154. 295 F.2d 24 (4th Cir. 1961), affirming 197 F.Supp. 710 (E.D. Va. 1961).

155. 197 F.Supp. 715.

156. 295 F.2d 25.

157. Ibid., at 26.

158. 420 Pa. 134 (1966), 215 A.2d 864, cert. denied 385 U.S. 822 (1966).

159. Ibid., at 876.

160. Ibid., at 870.

161. 295 F.2d 24 (4th Cir. 1961).

162. See, for example, The Roseric, 254 F. 154 (D.N.J. 1918); The Adriatic, 253 F. 489 (E.D. Pa. 1918); "Restrictive Sovereign Immunity, the State Department, and the Courts," 62 Northwestern L. Rev. 397, 408 (1967).

163. 254 U.S. 522 (1921).

164. Ibid., at 532-33.

165. Restatement, Second, Foreign Relations Law of the United States, § 71, Reporter's Note 1 (1965).

166. Pan American Tankers Corp. v. Republic of Vietnam, 291 F.Supp. 49 (S.D.N.Y. 1968), 196 F.Supp. 361 (S.D.N.Y. 1969).

167. See Lowenfeld, op. cit., at 901, 912-13.

168. Proceedings, 1969, 63 Am. J. Int'l. L. 182.

169. Restatement, Second, Foreign Relations Law of the United States § 72 (1965):

> Under the law of the United States an objection based on the rule of immunity, . . . if made on behalf of a foreign state by means of a suggestion from the executive branch of the government of the United States, . . . is conclusive as to issues determined by executive action within the exclusive constitutional competence of the executive branch of government and as to other issues directly affecting the conduct of foreign relations. As to all other issues, such a suggestion will be given great weight.

170. See generally, "The Relationship between Executive and Judiciary: The State Department as the Supreme Court of International Law," 53 Minn. L. Rev. 389 (1968).

171. 168 U.S. 250 (1897).

172. 376 U.S. 398 (1964).

173. Banco Nacional de Cuba v. Farr, 243 F.Supp. 957, 975 (S.D.N.Y. 1965). A very narrow court-designed exception to this doctrine had evolved out of the Bernstein cases. Bernstein v. Van Heyghen Freres, S.A., 163 F.2d 246 (2d Cir. 1947), cert. denied 332 U.S. 772 (1947); Bernstein v. N.V. Nederlandsche-Amerikaansche, S.M., 210 F.2d 375 (2d Cir. 1954). Plaintiff in these cases was, at the time of injury, a German national in pre-World War II Germany. His property, including a ship, the subject of the litigation, had been seized by agents of the Nazi government according to its policy of depriving Germans of Jewish ancestry of their rights and property. He sought recovery of that property, which was found at the end of the war in a U.S. port. Judge Learned Hand, in the first Bernstein case, 163 F.2d 246, declined to grant relief on the ground that the acts complained of were acts of state and their legality should not be determined by a U.S. court. The State Department declined to give any indication of its position.

Several years later the plaintiff brought a second action against the property, and this time he succeeded. 210 F.2d 375. Two factors had changed since the first and second decisions. First, the plaintiff's claim for compensation from reparations from Germany had been denied, precluding any avenue for relief other than in the courts. Second, the State Department communicated to the court the following statement:

> The policy of the Executive, with respect to claims asserted in the United States for the restitution of identifiable property (or compensation in lieu thereof) lost through force, coercion, or duress as a result of Nazi persecution in Germany, is to relieve American courts from any restraint upon the exercise of their jurisdiction to pass upon the validity of acts of Nazi officials. Ibid., at 376.

With this indication of executive branch policy, the court created an exception to the judicially self-imposed act of state doctrine of abstention, and ruled that the State Department letter enabled the court to decide the case on the merits. This exception, known as the Bernstein exception, has subsequently been so narrowly applied that there appear to be no reported cases in which it has again been invoked. Its continued vitality is at best quite doubtful.

174. Banco Nacional de Cuba v. Sabbatino, 376 U.S. 398 (1964).

175. Foreign Assistance Act of 1961, as amended, § 620(e)(2), 22 U.S.C. § 2370(e)(2).

176. Ibid.

177. Despite this seeming certainty, various U.S. courts have stumbled on collateral issues such as the scope of the Sabbatino Amendment prohibition against invocation of acts of state as a defense (First National City Bank v. Banco Nacional de Cuba, which in 1971 came before the U.S. Supreme Court a second time. Supreme Court Docket No. 70-295, October Term, 1971; 442 F.2d 530 (2d Cir. 1971), case remanded for

reconsideration in light of State Department suggestion, 400 U S. 1019 (1971); 431 F.2d 394 (2d Cir. 1970); 270 F.Supp. 1004 (S.D.N.Y. 1967); whether the courts should defer to the State Department's view of the legality of an act of state (Banco Nacional de Cuba v. Farr, 243 F.Supp. 957 [S.D.N.Y. 1965]); confusion about the locus of a particular act of state (Carl Zeiss Stiftung v. V.E.B. Carl Zeiss, Jena, 293 F.Supp. 892 [S.D.N.Y. 1968]); confusion about whether the appropriate claim submitted by the defense should be characterized as a claim of Act of State rather than one of sovereign immunity (South African Airways v. New York State Division of Human Rights, 64 Misc. 2d 707, 315 N.Y.S. 2d 651 [1970]); and the inability to make a clear distinction among the issues of not only Act of State and sovereign immunity, but also U.S. recognition of foreign governments (Carl Zeiss Stiftung v. V.E.B. Carl Zeiss, Jena, 293 F.Supp. 892 [S.D.N.Y. 1968]).

Added to this confusion is the failure of the State Department, to date, either to take a clear position on the definition of act of state generally or on the Sabbatino Amendment, or fully to accept the direction and implications of that amendment. The Sabbatino Amendment was enacted by the Congress over the vehement opposition of the State Department. See Whiteman, op. cit., vol. 6, at 1 ff. (1968). Of special interest is the 1971 letter written by John Stevenson (Stevenson Letter, 10 International Legal Materials 89 [1971]), Legal Adviser to the State Department, to the Supreme Court (via the Solicitor General), stating his department's view that the Act of State doctrine should not be applied to prevent recovery on a counterclaim against an instrumentality of the Cuban government in First National City Bank v. Banco Nacional de Cuba, now pending in the Supreme Court. The Stevenson letter suggested to the court that "the act of state doctrine should not be applied to bar consideration of a defendant's counterclaim or set-off against the Government of Cuba in this or like cases." It made no attempt, however, to present a definition of an act of state or of the scope of the Sabbatino Amendment. It relied instead on the facts that "(a) . . . the foreign state's claim arises from a relationship between the parties existing when the act of state occurred; (b) the amount of relief to be granted is limited to the amount of the foreign state's claim; and (c) the foreign policy interests of the United States do not require application of the doctrine." In its letter the department placed no reliance upon either the Sabbatino case or the Sabbatino Amendment, but relied instead entirely upon the isolated Bernstein exception.

Although it is conceivable that the First National City Bank decision will clarify some of the issues relating to Act of State, it is unlikely to resolve all the issues.

178. 234 N.Y. 372; 138 N.E. 24 (1923).

179. 235 N.Y. 255; 139 N.E. 259 (1923).

180. See, for example, Bank of China v. Wells Fargo Bank & Union Trust Co., 92 F.Supp. 920 (N.D. Cal. 1950), appeal dismissed, 190 F.2d 1010 (9th Cir. 1951), judgment, 104 F.Supp. 59 (N.D. Cal. 1952), modified, 209 F.2d 467 (9th Cir. 1953); Upright v. Mercury Business Machines Co.,

13 App. Div. 2d 36, 213 N.Y.S. 2d 417 (1st Dept. 1961); reversing 26 Misc. 2d 1069, 207 N.Y.S. 2d 85 (S. Ct. 1960).

181. Ibid.

182. Ibid.

183. United States v. Guaranty Trust Co., 304 U.S. 126 (1938).

184. 41 F.Supp. 353, 355 (S.D.N.Y. 1941).

185. Russian Volunteer Fleet v. United States, 282 U.S. 481 (1931); Amtorg Trading Corp. v. United States, 71 F.2d 524 (3rd Cir. 1934); Upright v. Mercury Business Machines, Inc., op. cit.

186. United States v. Pink, 315 U.S. 203 (1942); United States v. Belmont, 301 U.S. 324 (1937); Carl Zeiss Stiftung v. V.E.B. Carl Zeiss, Jena, 293 F.Supp. 892 (S.D.N.Y. 1968).

187. 89 U.S. 99 (1875).

188. See also dicta in Upright v. Mercury Business Machines, Inc., op. cit.

189. 74 U.S. 700 (1868).

190. 253 N.Y. 23, 28, 170 N.E. 479, 481 (1930). See also Vladikawkazsky Ry. Co. v. New York Trust Co., 263 N.Y. 369, 370, 189 N.E. 456, 460 (1934), where it was stated that "we recognized and enforced 'mere ordinary legislation' relating to 'everyday transactions of business or domestic life.'"

191. Werenjchik v. Ulen Contracting Corp., 229 App. Div. 36, 240 N.Y.S. 619.

192. Banque de France v. Equitable Trust Co., 33 F.2d 202, 205 (S.D.N.Y. 1929).

193. The Denny, 127 F.2d 404 (3rd Cir. 1942); In re Estate of Bielinis, 55 Misc. 2d 191, 284 N.Y.S. 2d 819 (S. Ct. 1967).

194. 239 N.Y. 158, 145 N.E. 917 (1924).

195. Ibid., at 166, 145 N.E., at 919.

196. 262 N.Y. 220, 186 N.E. 679 (1933).

197. Ibid., at 224, 186 N.E., at 681.

198. 145 F.2d 431 (3rd Cir. 1944).

199. 80 F.Supp. 683 (D.D.C. 1948), affirmed Latvian State Cargo & Passenger S.S. Line v. McGrath, 188 F.2d 1000 (D.C. Cir. 1951), cert. denied, 342 U.S. 816 (1951).

200. See Lubman, "The Unrecognized Government in American Courts: Upright v. Mercury Business Machines," 62 Colum. L. Rev. 275, 288-90 (1962).

201. Carl Zeiss Stiftung v. V.E.B. Carl Zeiss, Jena, 293 F.Supp. 892 (S.D.N.Y. 1968).

202. Ibid., at 915. The result of this case, however, might have made the assertion of judicial independence easier, since the trademarks in dispute were awarded by the court to the FRG corporation.

203. 1 Malloy 592. As for the Mississippi, a similar provision was included in the Treaty of 1782. Ibid., at 580.

204. Ibid., at 650.

205. Ibid., at 656.

206. Ibid., at 700.

207. 2 Malloy 2607-08.

208. Whiteman, op. cit., vol. 3, at 768.

209. Ibid., at 789, 840.

210. Ibid., at 826 ff.

211. 7 U.S.T. 1839 (1954).

212. Bevans, 7 Treaties 1266.

213. 22 U.S.C. § 2197.

214. See, for example, the agreement with Chile, 12 U.S.T. 254 (1961).

215. 4 U.S.T. 1793.

216. 4 U.S.T. 1846.

217. NATO Status of Forces Agreement, 4 U.S.T. 1802, Art. VII 9.

218. Kinsella v. United States, 361 U.S. 234 (1960); McElroy v. United States, 361 U.S. 281 (1960).

219. 6 U.S.T. 149 (Income Tax); 6 U.S.T. 113 (Estate, Gift and Inheritance Tax).

220. Prentice-Hall, Federal Tax Treaties, paragraph 54,002.

221. Restatement, Second, Foreign Relations Law of the United States § 141 (1965).

222. Graham v. Richardson, 403 U.S. 365 (1971); Takahshi v. Fish and Game Commission, 334 U.S. 410 (1948); Purdy & Fitzpatrick v. State of California, 71 Cal. 2d 566, 456 P.2d 645 (1969).

223. Immigration and Nationality Act of 1952, as amended, 8 U.S.C. §§ 1101 ff.; Purdy & Fitzpatrick v. State of California, op. cit.

224. See, for example, Bolling v. Sharpe, 347 U.S. 497 (1954).

225. See Title VII, Section 703, Civil Rights Act of 1964, as amended, 42 U.S.C. 2000e-3 ff. (1970), as amended by P.L. 92-261 (92nd Congress, 2nd Session, 1972).

226. 29 C.F.R. § 1606.1 (1971).

227. See, for example, E.O. 11246, E.O. 11478, 3 C.F.R., Ch. IV.

228. See, for example, 32 C.F.R. §§ 191, 300 (Defense Department); 17 C.F.R. § 200.90 ff. (Securities and Exchange Commission); 39 C.F.R., Part 747 (Postal Service).

229. 22 C.F.R. § 11.1(a).

230. 50 U.S.C. Appendix § 454(a) (1970).

231. See, for example, E.O. 10501, 3 C.F.R. Ch. IV.

232. 32 C.F.R. § 155.5(s). See also, for example, 10 C.F.R. §§ 10.10, 10.11 (Atomic Energy Commission); 32 C.F.R. § 505 (Department of the Army); 32 C.F.R. § 891 (Department of the Air Force).

233. Cole v. Richardson, 40 U.S.L.W. 4381 (No. 70-14, decided 18 April 1972). The text of the oath under consideration by the court was as follows: "I do solemnly swear (or affirm) that I will uphold and defend the Constitution of the United States of America and the Constitution of the Commonwealth of Massachusetts and that I will oppose the overthrow of the government of the United States of America or of this commonwealth by force, violence or by any illegal or unconstitutional method."

234. 40 U.S. Law Week 2304 (S.D.N.Y., decided 9 November 1971).

235. Ibid.

INDEX

ABOUT THE EDITORS AND CONTRIBUTORS

ELIHU LAUTERPACHT, Q.C., is Legal Adviser of the Australian Department of Foreign Affairs.

JOHN G. COLLIER is Fellow and Tutor, Trinity Hall, and University Lecturer in Law, University of Cambridge, England.

C. F. AMERASINGHE is Senior Counsel, International Bank for Reconstruction and Development.

GAETANO ARANGIO-RUIZ is Professor of International Law at the University of Bologna, Italy.

JOSEPH-MARIE BIPOUN-WOUM was, at the time of the conference, a member of the faculty of the Université Federalé de Cameroon in Yaounde, Cameroon.

YEHUDA Z. BLUM is Associate Professor in International Law at the Hebrew University, Jerusalem.

LUCIUS CAFLISCH is a member of the faculty of the Graduate Institute of International Studies of the University of Geneva.

ISI FOIGHEL is a member of the faculty of the Institute for International Law of the University of Copenhagen.

MONROE LEIGH was formerly Legal Adviser of the U.S. Department of State. He is presently in the private practice of law.

JACQUES-YVAN MORIN is a member of the Faculty of Law of the University of Montreal.

P. G. MUGERWA was formerly the Attorney General of Uganda.

FRANCISCO ORREGO VICUÑA is Director of Studies of the Institute of International Studies of the University of Chile.

IGNAZ SEIDL-HOHENVELDERN is a member of the Faculty of Law of the University of Cologne.

CÉSAR SEPÚLVEDA is Director of the Instituto Mexicano, "Matias Romero" of Diplomatic Studies.

IBRAHIM F. I. SHIHATA is Senior Legal Advisor to the Kuwait Fund for Arab Economic Development.

KRZYSZTOF SKUBISZEWSKI is Dozént, University of Poznań.

SOMPONG SUCHARITKUL is a member of the Thai diplomatic corps; at the time of the conference he was attached to the Embassy of Thailand to Japan.

MICHEL WAELBROECK, formerly of the faculty of the Université Libre de Bruxelles, is now practicing law in Belgium.

PROSPER WEIL is a member of the faculty of Law, Economics, and Social Sciences of the University of Paris.

RELATED TITLES
Published by
Praeger Special Studies

CRIMES AGAINST INTERNATIONALLY PROTECTED PERSONS--PREVENTION AND PUNISHMENT: An Analysis of the UN Convention
Louis M. Bloomfield and Gerald FitzGerald

THE STATUS OF ALIENS IN EAST AFRICA: Asians and Europeans in Tanzania, Uganda, and Kenya
D. C. C. Don Nanjira

THREE NON-ASSIMILATING MINORITIES: Jews in Tunisia and Morocco and Arabs in Israel
Mark A. Tessler

Published under the auspices of the American Society of International Law

*THE CONSTITUTION AND THE CONDUCT OF FOREIGN POLICY
edited by Francis O. Wilcox and Richard A. Frank

*Also available in paperback as a PSS Student Edition.